has received
Sir Charles and Lady Johnston
to a Dance at Windsor Castle
be given by The Queen and The Duke of Edin—
on Wednesday, the 18th June, 1980, at 10.30 p.m.
to celebrate the 80th Anniversaries of
Queen Elizabeth The Queen Mother
Princess Alice, Duchess of Gloucester
and The D—

...er Jacket should be addressed to
...er of the Household, Buckingham...
...at the Castle...

The Lord Chamberlain is commanded by
Their Majesties

to invite
The Duke & Duchess of Marlborough
to the Ceremony of the Marriage of
His Royal Highness The Duke of York K.G.
with
The Lady Elizabeth Bowes-Lyon,
daughter of the Earl and Countess of Strathmore and Kinghorne
in Westminster Abbey
...1923, at 11.30 o'clock a.m.

E R

OF
...ES &
...H

Earl Marshal

This ticket is issued on the condition that it is not resold.
Resale of the ticket will render it invalid.

THE CORONATION of THEIR MAJESTIES
KING GEORGE VI & QUEEN ELIZABETH
WEDNESDAY 12 MAY 1937
THE MALL STANDS

STAND   BLOCK   ROW   SEAT No.   PRICE
49   E   D   12   15/-

ADMIT ONE

Issued under the authority of the First Commissioner of Works etc.

E R
The Lord Chamberlain
is commanded by The Queen to

Mr. Hugo Vickers
to a Thanksgiving Service
in Commemoration of the 100th B—
Queen Elizabeth The Queen M—
in St. Paul's Cathedral
...1th July 2000, at 11

...ERNOON PARTY
...M PALACE
...th July, 1948
...cess of Marlborough
...be replaced, must be given up at the entrance
...only by
...mbridge Gate

WINDSOR CASTLE

Funeral of
MAJESTY KING GEORGE VI
...riday, 15th February, 1952
...RER to the Home Park Private

ATHLONE
Governor of Windsor Castle
...Constable of the Royal T—

No. 55
CORONATION
OF THEIR MAJESTIES
King George VI and Queen E—
Wednesday   12th Ma—

PASS THE BEARER TO TH—
PRESS GALLERY DINING ROO—
HOUSE OF COMMONS
In accordance with the Police Regul—

Charles A—
Serjea—

THIS PORTION TO BE RETAINED BY BEARER

State
...STER HALL

C. H. Johnston Esq
Royal Chapel of St. George,
Windsor

The Order
the Burial

ELIZABETH
THE QUEEN MOTHER

Also by Hugo Vickers

GLADYS, DUCHESS OF MARLBOROUGH
COCKTAILS AND LAUGHTER (Editor)
CECIL BEATON
VIVIEN LEIGH
LOVING GARBO
ROYAL ORDERS
THE PRIVATE WORLD OF THE DUKE AND DUCHESS OF WINDSOR
THE KISS
ALICE, PRINCESS ANDREW OF GREECE
THE UNEXPURGATED BEATON (Editor)
BEATON IN THE SIXTIES (Editor)
ALEXIS – THE MEMOIRS OF THE BARON DE REDÉ (Editor)

ELIZABETH
THE QUEEN MOTHER

Hugo Vickers

HUTCHINSON
LONDON

First published by Hutchinson in 2005

1 3 5 7 9 10 8 6 4 2

Endpaper design by Elizabeth Vickers

Hutchinson
The Random House Group Limited
20 Vauxhall Bridge Road, London SW1V 2SA

Random House Australia (Pty) Limited
20 Alfred Street, Milsons Point, Sydney
New South Wales 2061, Australia

Random House New Zealand Limited
18 Poland Road, Glenfield
Auckland 10, New Zealand

Random House South Africa (Pty) Limited
Isle of Houghton, Corner Boundary Road & Carse O'Gowrie,
Houghton, 2198, South Africa

The Random House Group Limited Reg. No. 954009

www.randomhouse.co.uk

A CIP catalogue record for this book is available
from the British Library

ISBN 0 09 180010 2

Papers used by Random House are natural, recyclable products made from
wood grown in sustainable forests. The manufacturing processes conform to
the environmental regulations of the country of origin

Typeset in Erhardt by Palimpsest Book Production Limited, Polmont, Stirlingshire

Printed and bound in Great Britain by Clays Ltd, St Ives plc

FOR

HUGH MONTGOMERY-MASSINGBERD

Friend and Counsellor

Contents

Illustrations

The Queen Mother at the State Dinner at Government House, Ottawa, 1954 (*Tim O'Donovan Collection*)
The Queen Mother and Prince Charles at Royal Lodge, Windsor
The Queen Mother at the Faculty of Agriculture of Makerere College, University College of East Africa, 1959 (*The Times/Tim O'Donovan Collection*)
The Duke of Windsor, 1953
Princess Margaret and the Queen Mother at the Royal Opera House, 1959
Princess Margaret with Antony Armstrong-Jones, 1960 (*The Times*)
The Queen Mother and Sir Arthur Penn, 1956
The Royal Family at Princess Margaret's wedding, 1960 (*The Times*)
The Queen Mother's 60th birthday, 1960
Fishing in New Zealand, 1966 (*Getty Images*)
The Queen Mother with Sunyboy, 1976 (*Corbis*)
The Queen Mother with Peter Cazalet, 1955 (*Tim O'Donovan Collection*)
The Queen Mother with Princess Anne
The Queen Mother at the Epsom Derby with Princess Marina, Duchess of Kent, The Queen and The Princess Royal (*©EMPICS/Tim O'Donovan Collection*)
Dancing at London University Senate House, 1958 (*©EMPICS*)
The Queen Mother alighting from a helicopter, 1965
The Queen Mother and Diana, Princess of Wales (*Tim O'Donovan Collection*)
The Queen Mother with Paul Getty

Section Five

The Queen Mother photographed by Cecil Beaton, 1948 (*Camera Press, London*)
Walking on the beach in Norfolk, 1982 (*Getty Images*)
The Queen Mother with the Princess of Wales at Royal Ascot, 1987 (*Corbis*)
The Queen Mother with the Prince and Princess of Wales, 1986 (*Getty Images*)
The Queen Mother at her 90th Birthday Tribute, 1990
The Queen Mother in a gondola, Venice, 1984 (*Tim O'Donovan Collection*)
The Queen Mother wearing three strands of Mrs Greville's necklace, 1994

The Queen Mother with Sir Richard Branson

The Queen Mother with Sir Alec Guinness

The Queen Mother with Lady Dufferin

The Princess Royal and the Queen Mother returning from the Garter ceremony, 1998 (*Elizabeth Vickers*)

The Queen Mother at Studio Cottage, Windsor Great Park, 1994 (*Elizabeth Johnston/Courtesy of Miss Joanna Johnston*)

The Queen Mother at Diamond Day, Ascot, 2000

The Queen Mother with the Prince of Wales, St Paul's Cathedral, 2000 (*Getty Images*)

The Queen Mother on her 101st birthday, 2001 (*Joe Little*)

The Queen Mother after Princess Margaret's funeral at St George's Chapel, 2002 (*Evening Standard*)

Lying-in-State, Westminster Hall, April 2002 (*Getty Images*)

Unless otherwise attributed, all photographs are from the author's collection.

The author wishes to thank Melanie Blake, Colin Menzies and J. M. Wood.

Every effort has been made to contact all copyright holders. The publishers will be glad to make good in future editions any errors or omissions brought to their attention.

Acknowledgements

When writing a biography, I like to do as much of the work myself as is humanly possible. I do my own research, at home and overseas – all the interviews, as well as the visits to libraries and private papers. I select the photographs (a few of which I even took myself), suggest the layout for these, create my own family trees, and for all the faults that a professional indexer might detect, I have always done my own indexes. In this case, I also laid out the endpapers, my wife photographing these – one of her photographs of Queen Elizabeth also appearing in the book. Therefore any errors and failings can be laid squarely at my door.

Having said that, it would not have been possible to undertake such a book without considerable help.

I am grateful to Her Majesty Queen Elizabeth II for permission to quote extracts from certain letters written by Queen Elizabeth The Queen Mother in this book, and to Sir Robin Janvrin (Private Secretary) and Edward Young (Assistant Private Secretary) in this connection. I am grateful to HRH The Duke of Kent for permission to quote extracts from letters written by his father, Prince George, Duke of Kent, to Prince Paul of Yugoslavia. I am grateful to HRH Prince Michael of Kent for allowing me to quote his account of a visit to Queen Elizabeth at Sandringham in 2002. I am also grateful to TRH Prince and Princess Alexander of Yugoslavia for their advice about Prince Alexander's father, Prince Paul.

I am especially grateful to the Hon. Lady Murray for allowing me access to the papers, diaries and letters of her parents, Lord and Lady Hardinge of Penshurst, and to the present Lord Hardinge of Penshurst for permission to quote from these. I am also grateful to the late Hon. Lady Johnston for considerable help in the 1990s, and to Lt-Col. Sir John Johnston for his help and for access to letters, and to Joanna Johnston for permission to reproduce the photograph taken by her mother. The collective kindness of many members of the Hardinge family over many years has greatly enriched this book.

Ashe Windham, former Equerry to the Queen Mother, and now Chairman of the Queen Elizabeth Castle of Mey Trust, has helped me immeasurably, and has been a consistent source of advice. I am grateful to Dame Frances Campbell-Preston, lady-in-waiting to the Queen Mother since 1965, for two interviews and for showing me parts of her unpublished memoirs, and also to the Hon. Nicholas Assheton, Treasurer to the Queen Mother, and to Mrs Assheton. Sir Michael Oswald, Her Majesty's Racing Manager, guided me over the racing, and I am very grateful to him and to his wife, Lady Angela Oswald. The Dowager Countess of Strathmore helped with certain specific questions in relation to Glamis Castle, and I am also grateful to the help of Jane Anderson, the archivist at Glamis Castle. For advice over many years I am grateful to Sir Edward Ford and Sir Edmund Grove, and to Dr Alastair Niven concerning Cumberland Lodge.

I first went to the office at Clarence House in 1972. Over a period of many years, I was lucky to know and talk to several members of the Queen Mother's Household, no longer alive, including Sir Martin Gilliat, Sir Ralph Anstruther, Lord Adam Gordon, the Dowager Duchess of Abercorn, Patricia, Viscountess Hambleden, Ruth, Lady Fermoy, Lady Elizabeth Basset and Lady Jean Rankin.

William Tallon, who first entered the King's service in 1951 and was Page to the Queen Mother throughout her widowhood, has been exceptionally kind and helpful.

Sarah Bradford, biographer of George VI and the present Queen, was most generous in giving me access to notes and interviews undertaken for her biography of the Queen, and in leading me to many letters written by the Queen Mother.

Richard Jay Hutto was able to produce vital material relating to the various Americans who appear in this book, and to trace dates for an enormous number of elusive characters. Dr Will Swift was immensely helpful over all matters concerning the Roosevelts.

Tim O'Donovan kindly allowed me access to his considerable collection of meticulously organised photographs, and also to invitation cards, and other material collected over many years.

Ian Shapiro gave me access to many sources, including official programmes and papers, and photographs. He is unfailingly generous to biographers working in this field.

Oliver Everett, former Librarian at Windsor Castle, showed me considerable kindness over many years, and oversaw the compilation of a selection of the Queen Mother's letters, which was published in the *Sunday Telegraph* on 31 March 2002. James Fergusson commissioned an obituary of Her Majesty for the *Independent* as long ago as 1986. It was completely re-written in 1990, and updated many times until 2002. Jamie was staying with us when the Queen Mother died, and the last changes were tackled before the official announcement was made over the airwaves.

During the last decade of the Queen Mother's life, I worked closely with ITN. This was an absorbing experience, involving rehearsals and interviews, all leading to the inevitable end, and coverage of the Lying-in-State and funeral. Chris Holker was my staunch ally during all that time. I particularly enjoyed working with John Suchet on several broadcast commentaries, and being interviewed by Katie Derham, Mary Nightingale and Nicholas Owen. Dame Sue Tinson oversaw the early days. It was a happy decade.

For special help with this book, I thank Karen Anson, the Countess of Avon, Anne Bawtree, Joyce Bellamy, Hon. Sir Clive Bossom, Gyles Brandreth, Hugh Cecil, Lisa Cohen, Fleur Cowles, Conrad Dehn, Sandra de László, Andrew Dent, Charles Duff, Maureen Emerson, Colin Farley-Sutton, Rev. David Farrant, Grania Forbes, Donald Gillies, Adrian Goodman, Philip Goodman, Robert Golden, Geordie Greig, Hon. Desmond Guinness, Basia Hamilton, Nigel Harris, Coryne Hall, Tim Heald, Bevis Hillier, Philip Hoare, Margaret Holmes, Nigel Jaques, Fraser Jansen, Sir Ludovic Kennedy, Robert Lacey, John and Celia Lee, Joe Little, Mark McGinness, Barrie McIntyre, Robin Martin, Suzy Menkes, Hugh Montgomery-Massingberd, Charlotte Mosley, Geoffrey Munn, David Murphy (The Royal Scots Regimental Museum), Robert Nedelkoff, Jonathan Petropoulos, Christopher Phillips, Joanna Pitman, Marquis de Ravenel, Elizabeth Roche, Michael Romain, Kenneth Rose, Lady Rumbold, Meryle Secrest, Hon. Jeremy Stopford, Hon. James Stourton, Georges-Charles Tomaszewski, Mrs T. E. Utley, Bertrand du Vignaud, Michael Wade, Nicholas White, Rupert Willoughby, and Julian Winston.

I visited Polesden Lacey, and am grateful to Christine Lunch, Jane Goodfellow and Paul Dearn, who then invited me to lecture to their guides when the house was closed to the public.

There were many who helped me understand the Queen Mother to varying degrees, sometimes long before I decided to write about her. Amongst these, alas now all dead, were HRH The Princess Margaret, Countess of Snowdon, HRH Princess Alice, Duchess of Gloucester, HRH Princess Paul of Yugoslavia, HRH Princess George of Hanover, Theo Aronson, Iris Banham-Lee, Sir Cecil Beaton, Lord Charteris of Amisfield, Lady Diana Cooper, Mrs Peter Cazalet, Maureen, Marchioness of Dufferin & Ava, Prince Jean-Louis de Faucigny-Lucinge, Dickie Fellowes-Gordon, Alastair Forbes, Lady Fry, Sir Michael Hawkins (Private Secretary to HRH The Duke of Gloucester), Hon. David Herbert, Lt-Col. C. L. Hodgson, Sir Charles Johnston, Anita Leslie, the Countess of Longford, Lady Caroline Lowell, Laura, Duchess of Marlborough, Dermot Morrah, Sir Anthony Nutting, Hon. Sir Steven Runciman, Audrey Russell, Mrs John Barry Ryan, Mark Simpson, 2nd Viscount Stuart of Findhorn, Hon. Stephen Tennant, Sister Anne Thomson, Group Captain Peter Townsend, John Utter (Private Secretary to HRH The Duke of Windsor), Commandant Paul Louis Weiller, and Captain Andrew Yates.

Rebecca Sieff (now the Hon. Mrs Simon Howard) helped me with the research for my biography of Princess Andrew of Greece. At that time she also delved into the Public Records Office (now the National Archives) and found many wonderful files, particularly relating to the Queen Mother's official visits overseas in the 1950s. In the long years during which this book came to life, I would also like to thank Louise Corrigan for her help in the 1980s, and Brenda de Lange (now Mrs Justin Sykes) for her help in 2001–2.

Over the years I have been into many archives and seen many papers, which have been of considerable help for this book.

I made much use of the papers of Harold Albert, Theo Aronson, Sir Charles & Lady Johnston, Gladys, Duchess of Marlborough and Stephen Tennant, all of which, along with my own papers and records (including the notes for my biography of Sir Cecil Beaton) are in my archives.

Recently I worked in the following archives with help from librarians: Bahkmeteff Archives, Rare Books & Manuscript Library, Columbia University, NY (Prince Paul of Yugoslavia) – Tanya Chebotarev; British Library (Lady Ottoline Morrell) – Dr Christopher Wright; Churchill Archives Centre, Cambridge (Sir Winston Churchill, Lord Lloyd). I am grateful to the Master, Fellows and Scholars of Churchill College, Cambridge and the Sir Winston Churchill Archive Trust for access to these, and also to Allen Packwood and staff of the Archives Centre; Firestone Library, Princeton University (Bruce and Beatrice Blackmar Gould) – Margaret Sherry Rich; House of Lords Record Office (Viscount Davidson) – Robert S. Harrison; Humanities Research Center, University of Austin at Texas (John Masefield, Lady Ottoline Morrell, John Pudney, Dame Edith Sitwell, Sir Osbert Sitwell, Sir Sacheverell Sitwell); Lambeth Palace Library (Alan Don, Bishop & Mrs Bell, Geoffrey Fisher, Cosmo Gordon Lang) – Dr Richard Palmer and the library staff; Maidstone County Record Office (Lord & Lady Hardinge of Penshurst) – Michael Carter (Centre for Kentish Studies, Maidstone); Reading University (Nancy, Viscountess Astor) – Verity C. Andrews; Victoria & Albert Museum & Registry (Oliver Ford) – Lynn Young.

Anne Clarke, at Special Collections, the University of Birmingham, kindly sent me extracts from the papers of Neville Chamberlain, and Oliver Lodge, and the Harriet Irving Library, University of New Brunswick, Canada kindly sent me copies of the letters of Sir Martin Gilliat to David Walker.

I also worked in the Family Division of the High Court of Justice, London, the Family Records Centre, the London Library, the National Archives, Kew, and the General Register Office for Scotland, New Register House, Edinburgh.

I am grateful to the following for permission to quote from private papers (other than those already mentioned above): Reading University Library – Nancy, Viscountess Astor; The Countess of Avon – her 1963 letter to Cecil Beaton; The Literary Executors – Sir Cecil Beaton; The writings of Sir Winston Churchill are reproduced with permission of Curtis Brown Ltd, London, on behalf of The Estate of Sir Winston Churchill, copyright © Winston S. Churchill; Mr G. Bruce Smith (Executor) – Marion Crawford Buthlay; Mr Charles Duff – Sir Michael Duff and Lady Juliet Duff; Sir Edward Ford – his note on Grigg; Mr Antony Beevor – the private letters of his uncle, Sir Martin Gilliat to David Walker; The Manuscripts Division, Department of Rare Books and Special Collections, Princeton University – Bruce and Beatrice Blackmar Gould Papers (The material obtained there has been published with permission of the Princeton University Library. The Library assumes no responsibility for copyright or any other matter pertaining to literary rights, extending permission as owner of the physical property only.); Lord Gladwyn – extracts from the diaries of his mother, Lady Gladwyn; Lord Hardinge of Penshurst – the letters and papers of his grandparents, Lord & Lady Hardinge of Penshurst; Mrs Ted Hughes – for the poem by Ted Hughes, copyright © The Ted Hughes Estate; The Literary Executor – Sir Charles Johnston; The Trustees of the Lambeth Palace Library – Rt Revd Cosmo Gordon Lang, Bishop and Mrs Bell, Rev. Alan Don, Rt Revd Geoffrey Fisher; Mrs T. E. Utley – her father, Dermot Morrah; The British Library Board – Lady Ottoline Morrell. The author wishes to apologise to any copyright holder that he has been unable to trace, and will be glad to rectify this in any future edition.

The Internet is a relatively recent source for authors. How did we live without it? I would particularly like to credit what I feel the Queen Mother would have called 'dear' Google.com.

*   *   *

Many editors have shown forbearance in the long years since this book was first commissioned by Christopher Sinclair-Stevenson in 1989. Most recently I could not have been luckier than to have Sue Freestone as my editor. She has mastered the art of how to keep an author content in his work. Never once did I experience feelings of panic, as is sometimes the experience of the harassed writer. Andrew Rosenheim guided this book over several hurdles, and I am grateful to James Nightingale for putting up with my endless demands and requests. Richard Collins was a sympathetic copy-editor, who rescued me from many inconsistencies. I am especially grateful to Robert Harris for steering me to Hutchinson. I feel quite exceptionally lucky.

As always, and with this book more than ever, I am grateful to Gillon Aitken, my agent and protector since 1977. More than once, he rescued this book and me from potential danger. I am also grateful to Ayesha Karim.

I am acutely aware that a great many people have helped, advised and encouraged me over a considerable number of years. Some I have omitted because I feel they would prefer not to be mentioned in print, but I am haunted by the fear of having inadvertently failed to mention others. If so, I hope they will not feel that my gratitude is any the less. Exceptional kindness has been shown to me during the creation of this book.

Finally, there is the home team. Abigail Naude has worked alongside me on every aspect of this book, including research at Lambeth Palace Library and Reading University. She has helped me find elusive papers and documents in my own archives, run my office, saved me from many administrative chores, and watched the development of this book from its first page to its page proofs. Not least did she succeed in preventing the media from finding me in February 2005 – no mean achievement. To her I am very grateful.

During the writing of this book, I have spent longer at my desk than any family should have to endure, absenting myself from too many aspects of family life. Finally I thank Mouse, Arthur, Alice and Georgie for their understanding during this time.

As always, it seems, the last days of a book are rather frenetic. One in particular I will always remember. I was checking page-proofs under some pressure. Thus I read them before a meeting in the Crypt of Lambeth Palace, and thought of Cosmo Gordon Lang's retreat there during an air raid. I checked them sitting on a seat on the Queen's Walk (part of the Jubilee Walkway), opposite the Houses of Parliament, with the distant sounds of police sirens in quest of suicide bombers. I checked them further at a lone supper in the Savoy, and again between acts of a Kirov

Ballet performance of *La Bayadère* at the Royal Opera House, Covent Garden. Earlier in the day I had been to Buckingham Palace to see Queen Elizabeth's 1938 white wardrobe on display. On reflection, that seemed rather a Queen Mother sort of day, as is the day on which I lay down my pen.

Hugo Vickers
Wyeford, 4 August 2005

CARDINAL WOLSEY: O! how wretched
Is that poor man that hangs on princes' favours.

Shakespeare, *Henry VIII*, Act III, Scene 2

Aspiration, vision, truth,
The noble aims of resilient youth,
The musing beauty of old age,
To doubt these must be sacrilege.

From an unpublished poem by Stephen Tennant
dedicated to the Queen Mother

Introduction

This book on the Queen Mother is the result of forty years of study in one form or another, a brazen claim, but true.

In the summer of 2004 my example was used in a sermon in Eton College Chapel. The thrust of this was that a boy had come to the school in the 1960s and that his housemaster had tried, without much success, to establish which of the more traditional interests would engage him. The Field Game, the School of Mechanics, the piano? Despairing of me, he apparently then asked:

'Well, what are you interested in?'

'Windsor Castle, sir.'

'Very well, go and find out everything you can about Windsor Castle.'

The message to the listening boys was that they should follow their interests and that it might lead somewhere, in this case to commenting or doing commentaries on state occasions. It led to this book.

In fact, I was fascinated by the Royal Family virtually since emerging from the pram.* Then in the Easter term of 1964, my prep school headmaster took some of us to the St John Passion at St George's Chapel. While we waited in the queue, he talked of the history of the chapel, of the Garter Knights, of the Royal Vault, and I determined that on arriving at Eton I would make my way to St George's Chapel at Windsor to explore it properly for myself.

This I did on the first Saturday of the Autumn 'half', in September 1964, and presently I took to going there every Saturday, then every Sunday as well, in due course (aged fourteen) being appointed a school guide and showing tourists around on Sunday afternoons – among whom was Peter Cazalet, the Queen Mother's trainer, whose son was my direct contemporary at school.

While still at school, I was allowed to sit in the Organ Loft during Sunday services. From there I witnessed several Garter services, and

---

* Sir John Peel (b. 1904), the Queen's gynaecologist, brought me into the world, and my mother's maternity nurse, Sister Thomson, later went to Clarence House to look after Princess Margaret when Lord Linley was born. She was the first person with direct knowledge to talk to me about the Queen Mother.

the funeral of Princess Marina, the only time I ever saw the Duke of Windsor.

There came a Sunday in November 1968 when I was positioned beside the wooden door of a structure in the North Quire Aisle that would become the King George VI Memorial Chapel, and to which, presently, the King's coffin would be moved. Royal visitors were expected. First to come round the corner was the Queen in a blue coat and no hat, with Prince Edward, then aged four, held by the hand. There followed a long silence, broken eventually by the Queen enquiring, 'Are you one of the guides in the chapel?' I replied, 'Yes, Ma'am', both nervous and excited by this first encounter with my Sovereign.

Then around the corner came the Queen Mother, followed by Princess Anne. The Queen Mother advanced with hand outstretched and asked, 'And who are you?' 'Hugo Vickers, Ma'am,' I replied with growing confidence. 'Oh yes,' she said, and I flattered myself that someone (perhaps the Dean of Windsor, who then hove into view) had told her I might be there. Nonsense, of course; it was just her way of putting me at my ease and making me feel special.

I thought of that scene more than twenty-three years later, when in the same North Quire Aisle I had my last glimpse of the Queen Mother, on her last outing, aged 101, at the funeral of Princess Margaret. For me there was a strange symmetry, those two occasions separated by so many years and with so much else in between.

In the course of those long years, I moved from being a figure in the crowd to what might be called the inside track. In November 1976, the Queen Mother came to an exhibition in the Guildhall, Windsor, of which I was the Chairman, and presently I was invited to public functions at which she was present, and later to a great many private ones. But I was also an outsider, an observer.

In the late 1980s there were two further developments. In 1989 I was first commissioned to write this book, and at about the same time I was contracted to TV-AM to do commentaries, and provide information and interviews, particularly in the event of the Queen Mother's death. Happily she outlived TV-AM by a great number of years, while eventually I settled with ITN, being interviewed on occasions good and bad, occasionally issued with a bleeper or put into a hotel near their studio while the Queen Mother was in hospital. In August 2001 I was summoned to the King Edward VII Hospital in London to witness her emergence down the steps, in powder blue, with pearl necklace and diamond brooch, a couple of days before her last birthday, dressed, it seemed, in her Ascot finery.

While there were these dual commitments, the interest and involvement ran much deeper. It is no exaggeration to say that a day could not have passed in the previous ten years or more when I had not thought of her. I had been acutely aware of her since childhood. I had seen her often in the newspapers and on television, and, if not before, I first saw her live walking with the late Duke of Gloucester in her Garter robes in June 1965. Thereafter there follows a kaleidoscope of memories: the Queen Mother leaving church, at the Birthday Parade, at great state occasions, on smaller public engagements, and then those lunches and dinners, the small social gatherings where she talked differently, and became vividly alive.

The Queen Mother survived so many falls, operations, illnesses and other scares that her immortality seemed assured. I was not alone in being surprised when the end finally came. On the afternoon of Saturday 30 March 2002 I was at home in Hampshire, in that strange period between Good Friday and Easter Sunday. Unusually the house was full of visitors. The telephone rang.

I do not answer the telephone when there are guests, so I ignored the first ring. But then it rang again immediately. The double ring instantly alarmed me. I had been half-alert for bad news – in particular concerning the Queen Mother – for some years. As the years went by, the fear obviously grew.

A voice introduced himself from the *Sunday Mirror* and told me that they had been given advance warning of an official announcement that the Queen Mother had died. Many more calls followed as I made my way to London and ITN.

I was on duty as a Lay Steward at St George's Chapel at the Easter service the following morning.* Already the Queen Mother's Garter banner, which had hung over a series of different stalls since her appointment to the Order in December 1936, had been taken down, as is traditional when a member of the Order dies. The Royal Family elected to go to church at the chapel at Royal Lodge, and thus avoided the media scrum. Nevertheless, the congregation was swelled by the more enterprising reporters who, by attending the service, could report on it later.

The days that followed were extraordinary – the crowds that came out to see the procession to Westminster and queued for long hours to see the lying-in-state.

I knew what to expect in Westminster Hall, but I was deeply moved by the intense feeling of emotion that accompanied the stillness, with the

* A member of the public evidently called St George's Chapel to enquire if Easter would be cancelled due to the Queen Mother's death. He was respectfully informed that God took precedence.

bright lights bearing down on the coffin through the shadows of night, picking up the sparkle of the Koh-i-Noor diamond in the crown, as the Gentlemen-at-Arms stood at attention at each corner.

For me it was a strange moment in time. First, it was as though the clock reeled back to January 1965, when I had been taken out of school to see the lying-in-state of Sir Winston Churchill. My aunt was an MP and she brought me in with my parents through a side door. They were all dead now.

A whole host of these memories has come to me since then, particularly during the long weeks that followed while writing this book.

On a cold night in November 1976, I was asked to deliver some programmes to Royal Lodge for the exhibition the Queen Mother was opening the following day. Although not expected, I was allowed past the gates and drove up to what appeared to be the front of the house:

> There were lights on in the house and as I approached, the front door was wide open. The Corgis were running around and the unmistakable figure of Queen Elizabeth The Queen Mother was standing silhouetted against the doorway. She had a sort of felt hat on and a coat. She went in.
>
> As I got out of the car, the Corgis scampered up to me. I went over and, though the door was open, I rang the bell. A lot of barking suddenly took place and simultaneously a uniformed sergeant, very smart, appeared from the background, and the Queen Mother came out of her bedroom. I handed over the envelope to the sergeant, speaking clearly so that the Queen Mother could hear. She said 'Thank you so much' in a charming voice and I departed into the night.*[1]

So much for royal security. Within three years, Lord Mountbatten was murdered and everything changed.

The Queen Mother was an enigmatic figure. I am glad that I was always an outsider, an observer, watching her whether on public or private occasions. Did she really sit in her car on the way to church, smiling to the crowds, while mouthing: 'It's all because the lady is a tramp!' I feel sure she did, just as she told an Ambassadress, while pulling on her gloves before entering a drawing room: 'Right, let the show commence!'[2]

One evening in 1987 I sat next to the Queen Mother during a charity performance at St James's Palace, for which I was again Chairman. A few

---

* Typically, the Queen Mother thanked me for delivering the catalogues when she saw me at the exhibition the next day, though I apologised for having intruded.

days later, after a dinner in London, I sat with her once more and we spoke of the charity evening:

> I said that it had a warm and euphoric atmosphere about it 'which is not always the case with charity evenings'. She said: 'I know what you mean', then paused. 'It was very intimate . . . so few people.'
>
> We spoke of Vivien Leigh, whose life I was writing. The Queen Mother said: 'She was so beautiful. I'm glad *you're* doing that. Such horrid things come out about people after they die.'[3]

From 1994 onwards I took part in many rehearsals for ITN, in which Chris Holker devised a succession of ingenious deaths in different locations to test the television team. I found these all too realistic and in consequence disturbing, as if the Queen Mother had really died. After one such rehearsal, I was happy to accept an invitation from her chaplain in the Great Park to attend morning service at the chapel by Royal Lodge. It was a relief to hear the click of the latch to the royal pew and presently to see the reassuring brim of a feathery hat by the column and the Queen Mother's gloved hand reaching for her hymnal. And reassuring too to have a talk with the Queen Mother after the service and to find her in the peak of health. She was then ninety-three.

An equally surreal experience occurred after the Queen Mother died. On Monday 8 April 2002 I was seated in the front row of the sanctuary of Westminster Abbey. The Abbey was alive with television lights, crenallating cables, monitors, men with headphones, the Dean and Canons and visiting clergy were in their appointed places. The Lord Chamberlain's Office had taken over the abbey church, as they do on royal occasions.

Nigel Harris, the Senior Verger at St Margaret's Church, Westminster Abbey, approached me, silver verge in hand, and mouthed: 'Follow me.' I walked slowly down the aisle behind him, through the serried ranks of the Yeomen of the Guard, pikes in hand, with the great Collegiate procession behind me. We moved to the West Door.

This gave me a good impression of taking part in the long-planned funeral of the Queen Mother at the same time the next day. For this was the rehearsal, and the verger had asked me to stand in for the Dean of Windsor, while John Suchet, the voice of ITN next day, represented the Moderator of the General Church of Scotland.

It was also the best preparation possible for the marathon television commentary that John Suchet would conduct from an underground studio in Gray's Inn Road, and with which I would assist him. It was the end of a long week, a time long dreaded, long prepared for, and now eventually come to pass.

The Queen Mother could be surprising. In Old Windsor, she came to drinks with a neighbour, Captain Andrew Yates. Sutton Place was being done up by an eccentric millionaire. 'I hear rumours of cascades,' she said disapprovingly. With me she talked of aesthetes such as Cecil Beaton and Stephen Tennant. 'They had such fun those boys, I think. And they were so individual.' She threw a disapproving glance at my conventional grey suit. 'It's so *easy*!'[4]

Some anecdotes about royalty do not lead anywhere. Sir Alec Guinness told me of his experience sitting next to her at a dinner at which we were both guests. She told him she had been depressed during the day.* Then she wrestled with a potato that was in danger of flying off the table. Suddenly she had a long fit of giggles about this and told Guinness that this had ended her depression. At the end of a very long evening, she leaned over to him and said: 'Potato!'[5]

At another of these dinners in 1990, the Queen Mother's ninetieth year, she talked of the opera:

> John Nutting was very good with her. He had seen her at a gala at Covent Garden for *L'Elisire d'Amore*. She said: 'You were a very good audience – lots of clapping and applause. Sometimes, you know it's just . . .' – and she clapped very gently. She said: 'The doctor was very good, and his wife . . .' She continued: 'The opera house is so wonderful and the flowers! I thought – the poor old Benevolent Fund . . .'
> 'They were donated, Ma'am.'
> 'Oh, yes, but think of all those noughts!'

Later, we spoke about biographies and she asked me: 'Do you think it's a help to know the subject?' I replied that I thought it was a help to have met them, but perhaps not to come from the same world.[6] It is in that spirit that I have approached this book.

Writing about the Queen Mother has been a fascinating and absorbing experience. Odd scenes from as far back as the 1960s and 1970s have found their way from the recesses of my memory – and sometimes from my diary – into the pages of this book. I was lucky to be able to observe

* What caused the depression? Penelope Mortimer's hostile book, *Queen Elizabeth*, had just been published. Prince Andrew was about to announce his engagement to Sarah Ferguson. It may have been neither of these things.

her – at first from afar – and gradually from closer and closer. I was lucky to have known a great number of people who knew her well, some of them her contemporaries, ladies-in-waiting and friends, all of them long since dead. Fortunately I made notes of what they told me.

Of all the books that I have written, never before have so many impressions and experiences been gleaned over so many decades, and been united in one volume. I have loved every minute of writing it.

I

Early Days

'Oh the delight of brotherhood', the best relationship in the world
– the Queen Mother

For eighty years it was assumed that Elizabeth Bowes-Lyon, ninth child of Lord Glamis, was born on 4 August 1900 at St Paul's Walden Bury, Hertfordshire. A number of plaques and many commemorative items supported that date and place. 4 August 1900 was a Saturday, so it might well have been that Lady Glamis was resting at the country home, rather than in London at the end of the season.

However, Lord Glamis was lax in recording the birth and did not fulfil his legal obligations until Friday 21 September. On that day he went to the Hitchin registry office because he needed a birth certificate so that the vicar at St Paul's Walden Bury could christen his daughter the following Sunday. He had been in Scotland when his daughter was born. By this time he could neither remember the exact location, nor, it is said, even the date.[1] Unaware of the destiny of his child, he recorded St Paul's Walden Bury and 4 August.[2]

The discrepancy came to light in July 1980 when preparations were well advanced to mark the Queen Mother's eightieth birthday. An eagle-eyed parishioner at St Paul's noticed that the place of birth was being omitted. Clarence House was consulted and the official line then changed. The Queen Mother had been born in London. 'It really doesn't matter where she was born, or if there were inaccuracies,' said a spokesman. 'Strathmore did the evil deed, and he is dead. If he did wrong, it didn't show.'*[3]

It was evidently Sir David Bowes-Lyon, the Queen Mother's brother, who told the author Dorothy Laird that she had not been born at St Paul's. In her 1966 biography, Dorothy Laird refrained from mentioning any place of birth,[4] though she gave 4 August as the date.

---

* It was going too far to suggest that Lord Strathmore might have been tried under the Forgery Act of 1861, for giving false information, and that had he been convicted as a felon, he might have been sentenced to penal servitude for life.

The exact place of birth has not been established and the Queen Mother claimed not to know. 'I might have been born in the back of a taxi,' she told her lady-in-waiting, while her page, William Tallon, stated categorically: 'I know she was born in the back of a horse-drawn ambulance. That's why she was always on the move.'[5]

Many aristocratic children were born in London as the gynaecologists were better there. Had the child been born in a hospital, the details would almost certainly have come to light by now. In 1900 the Glamises had no London home, though the Strathmores had a flat in Belgrave Mansions, Grosvenor Gardens.[6] That might have been the place; Lady Glamis stayed with her mother at Forbes House, Ham Common; or they may have rented a house for the season.

It would be interesting if evidence were to come to light to suggest that the Queen Mother was born earlier than 4 August. Had Lord Glamis been late in recording the birth, he might have settled for a date that fell closer to the legal deadline rather than one earlier. This theory has been advanced in court circles. It has also been dismissed.

The Queen Mother's reluctance to specify where she was born may be more easily explained if it turns out that she wished to veil a different date of birth, so as not to cause havoc among those who manufacture birthday souvenirs.*

Lord Glamis was the heir to the 13th Earl of Strathmore and Kinghorne, head of an ancient, aristocratic Scottish family. Elizabeth was born while Queen Victoria's court was in mourning for King Umberto I of Italy, who, to the Queen's 'utmost horror and grief',[7] had been assassinated at Monza on 29 July. Then the Queen's second son, Alfred, Duke of Edinburgh and Duke of Coburg since 1893, died in Coburg, and court mourning was extended until 13 September.

Court mourning forced the ladies of the court into black dresses with white gloves, and the gentlemen into black court dress, with black swords and buckles. The hour of Elizabeth's own death more than 101 years later would itself inspire a modified form of court mourning appropriate to the twenty-first century. None of the royal ladies wore black crepe veils at the Queen Mother's funeral.

Lady Glamis had no idea that she had given birth to a girl whom she would later describe as 'my little queen'.[8] The child was named Elizabeth

---

* It is a pity that she was not born in Scotland, for it fell to the Factor at Glamis to register births and deaths in the family in the registry office at Forfar, and each Factor in turn was invariably down there the same day, thus ensuring accurate records, which can be found at West Register House in Edinburgh.

Angela Marguerite. She was not born Lady Elizabeth: she was Hon. Elizabeth until her grandfather died in 1904 and her father became the 14th Earl.

Elizabeth's ancestry was distinguished on both her father's and her mother's side.* Through the Lyons she descended twice over from Robert The Bruce, King of Scotland. The Lyons were landed in Forfar as long ago as 1372, becoming Earls of Kinghorne in 1606 and of Strathmore in 1677. A judicious marriage with the Bowes family in 1767 brought them wealth and both Streatlam Castle, Co. Durham, and Gibside Castle, near Newcastle. In 1887 the 13th Earl of Strathmore, a peer of Scotland, was given an English peerage as one of eight Golden 'Jubilee' Barons, styled Baron Bowes of Streatlam Castle. He was Elizabeth's grandfather.

Her mother was a Cavendish-Bentinck, a descendant of the Tudor King Henry VII, the Kings of Ireland, and of the Dukes of Portland, Devonshire, Somerset, Ormonde, Suffolk and Newcastle. The Queen Mother's friend, the Duke of Grafton, cited Bentinck blood as the cause for her longevity. One of her Bentinck cousins, Lady Victoria Wemyss, lived to be 104.

The Strathmores had various homes when Elizabeth was young. She was mainly raised at St Paul's Walden Bury, Hertfordshire. From 1906 until 1920 there was the large London house at 20 St James's Square, between the Cleveland Club and the Board of Trade. In the square their neighbours were the Duke of Norfolk, the Duchess of Buckingham, the Bishop of London and the Earl of Derby.

The family paid occasional visits to Streatlam Castle, the Durham estate which, to the Queen Mother's chagrin, was sold by her father, gutted in 1927 and demolished as part of a Territorial Army exercise in 1959. They occupied these various houses with strict adherence to the shooting seasons. 'We follow the birds', as the Queen Mother put it.

Above all, they spent long summers and autumns at Glamis Castle, the romantic, magnificent and mysterious red-stone castle in Scotland, near Forfar. It is with Glamis that Elizabeth is most usually associated, a castle hung about with haunting tales and mysteries, and even if it was not Shakespeare's setting for Duncan's murder in *Macbeth*, it is always associated with *Macbeth* in the popular mind.†

Parts of Glamis – the crypt and lower part of the central tower – were built in the early years of the fifteenth century. It was last remodelled in

---

* See Appendix I: The Ancestry of Queen Elizabeth (p. 504).
† Harry Gordon Slade considers it more likely that Malcolm, Duncan's eighty-year-old grandfather, may have died at Glamis from wounds acquired in a nearby ambush.

1891, when a baronial-style wing was added at the east end. Then it lost its outer fortifications, and, like Windsor Castle, it stands amid acres of beautiful lawns, an ancient fortress surrounded by the symbolic landscape of a more peaceful age.

When Elizabeth was born, the castle was presided over by her grandfather, the 13th Earl, and his wife Frances Smith, whose father, Oswald Smith, had been born in 1794. In 1865 the tenants of Glamis had presented the Earl with a silver ship 'in appreciation of his liberal conduct as a landlord'.

On 28 September 1903 six hundred guests gathered to celebrate their Golden Wedding. Mr Neill of Forfar (who later taught Elizabeth to dance) led a string orchestra. There was a garden party, with Frances in silver-grey satin, black lace trimmed with black velvet ribbons and a grey bonnet. Sitting on her grandfather's knee was one of the Queen Mother's earliest memories.

The next day the menu at dinner was consommé Lyonnais, côtelettes de saumon, medaillons de gibier, selle d'agneau, salade, grouse, pommes à la Claude, gelée de fruits à la St Michael and croûtes au dragon. One of the many grandsons ran round dressed, as was traditional, as a little girl.

Soon afterwards Lord Strathmore recognised that his indifferent health might profit from a warmer climate and restore his 'wonted vigour'.[9] He retreated with his wife to Bordighera in Italy, where he died in the evening of 16 February 1904. He was brought home for burial at Glamis eight days later, mourned by five surviving sons and daughters, and thirty grandchildren.

He was succeeded by Elizabeth's father, Claude. He was a kind figure, very much in the tradition of a Scottish peer, and he sported a flowing moustache, which he parted courteously before kissing his offspring. Having served in the 2nd Life Guards from 1862 to 1876, he went on to succeed his father not only in the title and estates but also as Lord-Lieutenant of Forfar. At Petersham in 1881 he married Nina Cecilia Cavendish-Bentinck, daughter of Revd Charles Cavendish-Bentinck (who had died in 1865), and of his wife Caroline Burnaby, by then Mrs Scott, and living at the magnificent Forbes House, in Ham.

Lord Strathmore took a keen interest in his estates and was unusually kind to his tenants and staff. He had a great number of smallholdings and was a keen and knowledgeable forester; he rode out on his pony every day to inspect his property. He developed many plantations and was one of the first to rear larch, which he brought from Norway. The Queen Mother liked to tell the story of people enquiring at St Paul's whether

Lord Strathmore was there, to be told: 'His Lordship only comes when the sap rises.' His favourite recreation was cricket. He once got a hat trick against the Dundee Drapers. His team rewarded him with a Panama hat.

He was a man of inflexible habit. He made his own cocoa for breakfast and ate plum pudding for lunch every day. Beside his place was a jug of water with which he diluted his wine. He smoked endless cigarettes, and used to bowl Christmas puddings down the table towards his wife.

Lord Strathmore moved from one of his houses to the next, often without a moment's notice, causing his wife some stress in the process. When they went north, they travelled in the *Flying Scotsman*. When in London, he frequented Tattersalls, but he preferred the outdoor life.

Sporting he may have been; well-informed he was not. Lord Crawford called on him a year after he succeeded to Glamis and observed:

> I am amazed at the phenomenal ignorance of the castle and its contents, displayed by Lord and Lady Strathmore, and the two eldest sons. The second son asked his mother about the identity of a portrait which turned out to be a portrait of his own grandmother. They are nice boys, and Strathmore is a delightful man: by the way he put two pellets into my wrist while we were driving some grouse this afternoon.[10]

As he grew older, Lord Strathmore became extremely deaf, but was deemed charming, if hard work to sit next to at dinner. He also looked older than his years. He was eccentric, though not exceptionally so. When he died in 1944, Elizabeth wrote of the mutual love between her father and his children, how she loved to go home and to bask in his love for her. She was grateful to have had him so long.[11]

For all its estates and its 65,000 acres, life at Glamis was never luxurious. The Strathmores did not have a lot of money compared to other aristocratic landowners in Scotland.* Queen Mary's bachelor equerry,

---

*When Lord Strathmore died in 1944 he left personal estate valued at £75,955 6s, and, when all had been taken into account, his estate was worth £432,663 17s 1d, with estate duty of £26,899 12s to be paid. In 1908 he made a settlement which granted him a life interest, with others such as his son Patrick, the new Lord Strathmore, his mother, his son, John (Jock), devolving on to trustees following his death. This was to protect the various estates in Scotland and Durham for the benefit of future Earls of Strathmore. Lord Strathmore's personal effects included income from the sale of timber, Royal Bank of Scotland capital stock and fees as an Extraordinary Director, income from the Bowes estates, British Assets Trust, New Zealand and Australia Land Company, Strathmore estates, and £20,000 being the sum apportioned to him under Clause 40 of a settlement he made on 12 November 1908.

Sir Richard Molyneux, who plied his way from one such castle to another, described it as 'an average picknicky place – parlourmaids and that sort of stuff'.[12]

But it was at Glamis that the young Bowes-Lyons spent their holidays, and where Elizabeth lived during the Great War. They played with other Scottish children of whatever state or background. Elizabeth had a tiny leather-upholstered carriage, which was pulled by a pony, and she rode a donkey; when it stopped to eat grass, she slipped down its neck. She grew up inside those thick walls, later eating in the new Victorian dining room, which seated forty, with family portraits of her ancestors gazing down.

All about there were portraits of the Kings and Queens of England, many of them wearing the robes of the Garter, Charles II and James VII by Sir Peter Lely, Elizabeth I by Sir Martin Bower. This meant that such figures were not as distant as they would have seemed to King Edward VII's other subjects.

There was much to delight a young family: the body-stocking armour of the 3rd Earl, St Simon wearing spectacles in the same Earl's chapel, Our Lord wearing a hat. Elsewhere, English Minton tiles proclaimed gentle home truths: 'East or west – home is best' and 'Where friends meet, hearts warm'. There stood (indeed, still stands) a European brown bear, apparently killed by Highland cattle in the middle of the 19th century.

Elizabeth's mother enjoyed formidable qualities and these she passed on to her youngest daughter in full measure. When she died, Elizabeth described her as 'so much the pivot of the family, so vital and so loving and so marvellously loyal to those she loved, or the things she thought right – an Angel of goodness and fun'.[13] She also wrote:

> She was a true 'Rock of Defence' for us, her children, and thank God, her influence & wonderful example will remain with us all our lives.
>
> She had such a good perspective of life – everything was given its *true* importance. She had a young spirit, great courage & unending sympathy whenever or wherever it was needed, & such a heavenly sense of humour. We all used to laugh together and have such fun![14]

Lady Strathmore was strong in mind and body. She loved to play the piano, she loved gardens, starting to create a formal Dutch garden in

1907, though running out of money, and also creating an Italian garden at Glamis, inspired by visits to her mother at her villa at Bordighera. She enjoyed reading and poetry. She was a keen needlewoman and personally repaired the bedspread which covered the bed where Prince Charles Edward once slept. She wore fine silks which could be heard rustling as she approached.

She was intelligent and could be sharp. In 1937 she wrote to her cousin, Lady Ottoline Morrell, enquiring about a certain Mrs Wellesley – '*but, is she any close relation to a most tiresome Maud Frizell, who teases both Elizabeth & me at every public meeting we happen to attend?*[15] Under a veneer of gentle if rather grand domesticity, there beat a heart of steel.

Lady Strathmore would lose four of her ten children in her lifetime, which created wounds that never healed but which gave her a particular sympathy and rare understanding of other people. In 1931, after the death of her son Jock, she wrote to Ottoline Morrell, 'I have had so many great sorrows myself . . .'[16]

She was full of feeling and set a high example in the way she approached her roles as daughter, wife and mother. She enjoyed life and had an enchanting laugh. Since she rarely asked questions, people were inclined to volunteer information to her. She possessed courage and wisdom. In later life, she was rather eccentrically attired in voluminous black dresses with white lace collars.

A lifelong friend wrote: 'Life in those days still held a sense of security and permanence. The age of privilege survived, and time and space had not been obliterated by science . . . She seemed to sail through life, like a swan on a mirrored lake . . . She was the directing force of the family . . .' Her smile, he wrote, held 'the serenity that comes from religious faith, the dignity derived from true nobility in its highest sense, the kindliness which belongs only to greatness of soul'.[17]

Elizabeth was the ninth of ten children born. By the time of her birth, there was already a host of older brothers and sisters, the eldest of whom, Violet, born in 1882, had died on 17 October 1893. It is surely rare among siblings that one sister should die in 1893, and another in 2002, a span of nearly 110 years.

Lord Glamis called his first daughter Violet Hyacinth after the flowers he loved. She died of heart problems resulting from diphtheria and was laid to rest in the churchyard of St Paul's Walden. The family was then almost complete. Three weeks later, on 1 October, Michael was born. There were already six children: Mary, born in 1883; Patrick, the next heir and eventually 15th Earl, born in 1884; John in 1886; Alexander in

1887; Fergus in 1889; and Rose in 1890. The younger two would arrive some years later, Elizabeth in 1900 and David in 1902.

Seven years after Violet's funeral, Elizabeth was christened in the same church. St Paul's, parts of which date to the twelfth century, lies in the old hamlet of St Paul's Walden. The Bury, as the manor was known, another house inherited from the Bowes family, stands on a high hill, and was founded as a direct result of the troubled times in the latter half of the fourteenth century. Most of Elizabeth's first fourteen years were spent there. The house was not a grand one. According to a contemporary account, it possessed: 'no extravagance or luxury: there was no attempt to be modern or up-to-date'.[18]

The world of childhood was punctuated by lessons with governesses, and the tedium alleviated by a miscellany of horses, dogs and field sports. Elizabeth grew up playing country games beside walls covered with magnolias and honeysuckle. In the evenings Lady Strathmore played the piano, while the older children played charades. When Elizabeth was six weeks old, she was placed in the care of the nanny who went on to look after many nephews and nieces and even the present Queen; this was Clara Cooper Knight, always known as 'Alah', the daughter of a tenant farmer at Glamis. Fond though she was of Alah, the Queen Mother later observed that a holiday in Sandwich in 1932 was the first time she ever displayed any enthusiasm.[19]

With her favourite brother David, she roamed the grounds and woods at the Bury, accompanied by dogs, cats and tortoises. Solemnly they buried birds that died and fed the hens. There was a Shetland pony which followed her into the house, and even upstairs. The young pair were educated simply but sensibly, under the creative influence of her mother.

Here, according to one now long-dead villager, the young Elizabeth would ride her pony down the long avenue from her father's house to the church. 'Lord bless you, I can see her now galloping across with the groom behind all out of breath, and her laughing,'[20] said the old character. One governess, Laurel Grey, thought her charge adorable, recalling how she loved to dress up and how pretty she looked in a Van Dyck dress.

Of her childhood Elizabeth wrote: 'I have nothing but wonderfully happy memories of childhood days at home, fun, kindness, & a marvellous sense of security.'[21] And perhaps significantly, she mused on her relationship with her brothers:

'Oh the delight of brotherhood', the best relationship in the world. I was lucky enough to be surrounded by brothers, mostly older, but one younger, and grew up in the marvellous atmosphere of gaiety, loyalty to each other & absolute confidence that I suppose one took for granted as a child.[22]

From an early age Lady Elizabeth impressed the grown-ups. The Duchess of Atholl noted her charm and dignity at the age of about three: 'I felt as if she was a little princess who had stepped out of an eighteenth-century picture.'[23] She was described as 'the most astonishing child for knowing the right thing to say. Had she been consciously rehearsing for her future she could scarcely have practised her manners more assiduously.'[24] Even as a child Elizabeth strove hard to put others at their ease, while employing charm to get her way, which included obtaining delicious food from the kitchen.

At Glamis Elizabeth played with a dolls' house made in 1868. Her first piano lesson was 'The Musical Pathway'. With David, she once poured 'boiling oil' from the ramparts – effectively cold water – and tried to frighten their older siblings with impressions of the 'Grey Lady'. David would dress up as a jester, and she, perhaps with prescience, as a princess. One day she was caught by the Factor in some danger on the ramparts and punished.

2

Childhood

'I'm never wrong, as you know'
– Elizabeth Bowes-Lyon at thirteen

Royalty have to endure the recollections of their childhood friends finding their way into newspapers. Even the Queen Mother had to endure such a figure, despite her longevity. But she was fortunate in Joan Ackland,* from whose writings we learn something of school days.

In 1908 Elizabeth and David went to a Froebel kindergarten school called Miss Goff's at 25 Marylebone High Street in London, run by Constance Goff, then aged twenty-eight. Joan Ackland recalled that it was 'a very good school and Elizabeth would have learned as easily as we all did'.[1]

Pupils wore tussore smocks. The children performed plays in French and German; the boys boxed and the girls fenced. At the age of eight, Elizabeth wrote an essay entitled 'The Sea'. She began it with two Greek words from *The Anabasis* of Xenophon, gleaned from an older brother, and was roundly ticked off for being a show-off. She had not meant to show off, she said later.[2] She was protective of her younger brother.

One child on whom she made a great impression was Lord David Cecil, son of 4th Marquess of Salisbury. He met her at a dancing class at Lansdowne House and recalled in 1980: 'great sweetness and sense of fun; and a certain roguish quality. The personality which I see now was there already.'[3] He claimed her as the first love of his life, and they remained life-long friends. When she became Queen, she told him, the qualities needed were 'patience and anger'.[4]

She may have made a similar impression on another small boy met at a party given by the Duchess of Buccleuch for her grandchildren at Montagu House, Whitehall, in 1905.† Here she met the young Prince Albert for the first time.

---

* Joan Ackland (1900–82), daughter of Robert Ackland, CBE (1865–1923), Senior Dental Surgeon of St Bartholomew's Hospital, who lived at 54 Brook Street, London, and in Norfolk, and who helped to found Miss Goff's school. In 1923, she married Edgar Woollcombe (1891–1935), a former intelligence officer, and later a stockbroker. She was appointed OBE. In later life she was a journalist and lived in Devonshire Close, London.
† Some sources say the Countess of Leicester gave this party, but this is incorrect.

One afternoon when Elizabeth was about nine, Lady Strathmore invited Miss Goff to tea at St James's Square. Lady Strathmore was late and Miss Goff was surprised at how well Elizabeth deputised, presiding over tea and making conversation in her mother's absence.

All Elizabeth's brothers were at Eton, a school much loved by the Queen Mother in later life, despite the brothers living in 'dangerous wooden houses' and being so cold that they suffered from chilblains.[5]

On 21 November 1908 Elizabeth's eldest brother, Patrick (or 'Pat'), then serving in the Scots Guards, married Lady Dorothy Osborne, third daughter of the 10th Duke of Leeds. The wedding took place at Wellington Barracks with Elizabeth as bridesmaid and David as page. Patrick was 'of extremely handsome Nordic appearance, fair and blue-eyed'.[6] His sister-in-law, Lady Guendolen Osborne, considered he had a perfect nose. Later he sported a moustache to match his father's. After his marriage he settled at Streatlam Castle and was somewhat separated from his siblings, though he appeared for part of the London season. He and Dorothy had four children.

In 1909 Elizabeth attended the school for pianoforte opened by Miss Mathilde Verne,* a concert pianist who had studied with Franklin Taylor and Clara Schumann, and worked with the talented and later tragic child-prodigy pianist Solomon. She recalled the youthful Elizabeth as a lively girl who liked sliding down the banisters.

In the same year Elizabeth paid a visit to her maternal grandmother, Mrs Harry Warren Scott, at her villa in Bordighera. On this visit, Elizabeth bargained for and purchased a pair of exquisite antique angels, which she kept all her life and later placed on the corner of her bed head at Clarence House. She paid three lire for them.

On 4 July 1910, Elizabeth was a bridesmaid to her eldest surviving sister, Mary or May, then twenty-seven, when she married the thirty-eight-year-old 16th Lord Elphinstone, whose family had been Barons since 1510. Elphinstone spent half the year wandering about Central Asia, India or America and the other half being entertained in Britain. He kept kangaroos at Carberry Tower, Musselburgh, his Scottish seat just south-east of Edinburgh, famous as the last place where Mary, Queen of Scots, enjoyed a breath of freedom in 1567 before her long incarceration.

---

* Mathilde Verne (1865–1936). She died dramatically during an evening to celebrate the publication of her memoirs, *Chords of Remembrance*, on 4 June 1936. She played a duet with her sister, Adela, and then Mme Mignon Nevada sang. The singer asked for a glass of water, and Mathilde rose to see if it was on its way. She sank to the floor and was taken to Charing Cross Hospital, where she was pronounced dead.

In December 1905 he invited the American divorcée Nancy Lang-
horne Shaw to Carberry to hunt. He proposed to her, promising not to
tie her down to a dull life; to his horror, the following March she rejected
him. 'I had built up such a happy future, which at half a dozen words
from you yesterday crumbled to dust,' he wrote her.[7] She married Waldorf
Astor instead. In 1909 Nancy Astor earmarked him for her sister, Nora,*
but she married Paul Phipps. After these entanglements, his wedding to
May Bowes-Lyon took place at St Margaret's, Westminster, with
Elizabeth in attendance wearing a white Romney gown with blue sash
and a large picture hat.

In June 1911 Elizabeth enjoyed the Coronation of George V, staying
in lodgings at Westminster with her mother, Patrick and Rose. Her parents
and her brother-in-law, Lord Elphinstone, attended the ceremony,† while
the others watched the procession and she was struck by the Grenadier
Guards and pleased to recognise Field Marshals Lord Roberts, VC, and
Lord Kitchener. She was impressed by the Indian troops and the Life
Guards. As to the central characters, in an essay she wrote on this she
misidentified her future parents-in-law as King Edward and Queen
Alexandra.[8]

Soon afterwards, their spinster aunt, Violet Bentinck, took Elizabeth
and David by train to stay with Mrs Scott again, this time to the Villa Capponi
in Fiesole. Mrs Scott's villa was set in a lovely garden among cypress trees.
They were taken sightseeing in Florence, her aunt showing her the pictures
in the Uffizi and the Pitti Palace, one at a time. Afterwards they drank a
thimble of Vermouth at Doney's. It was a rare trip abroad, for no foreign
travel would be possible during her adolescence due to the war.

Later in the same year Elizabeth lost the first of her brothers. Alexander
had been destined for a commercial career in London, and was employed
at the time in an insurance firm. He was a good shot, a keen angler and
altogether an affable fellow. He played in the Glamis cricket XI, where
he was considered 'a steady reliable batsman, and could always be relied
upon to get runs'.[9] Cricket was to bring about his untimely death. In the
summer of 1910 he was taken seriously ill in London, suffering from a
brain tumour, having been hit on the head by a cricket ball. His fellow
clerks at work covered for him, hoping that he might recover, and he was
well enough to spend the summer of 1911 at Glamis. He was even seen
out and about in Forfar, making purchases with his sister Rose. But then,
on the afternoon of 18 October 1911, he did not feel well enough to

* She was the mother of Joyce Grenfell.
† Her sister, May Elphinstone, was too pregnant to attend. She produced her first daughter,
Elizabeth, on 2 July.

accompany the guns out shooting, and stayed in bed. At 3.30 a.m. the following morning he died in his sleep. He was twenty-four, and the cause of death was a tumour at the base of the cerebrum, from which he had suffered for eighteen months.[10]

In the autumn of 1912 David left home for prep school in Kent. Elizabeth missed him 'horribly' while David said later: 'We were never separated if we could avoid it . . . Everything we did together was fun, and we did everything possible together.'[11]

That October Elizabeth went to the only real school she ever attended. Lady Strathmore sent her to Misses Irene and Dorothy Birtwhistle at 30 Sloane Street in London, who had 'very select classes for girls of preparatory school age'.[12] The younger sister, Dorothy, who had studied Froebel at the Bedford Training College, recalled: 'When the Queen Mother came to us we held our classes at 30 Sloane St. The number of pupils was about 30.'[13]

A teacher described the Misses Birtwhistles as 'modest, quiet, very unassuming people but with a real love of children, and a skill to know and meet their needs . . . Miss Dorothy Birtwhistle was so straight and honest that she never over-praised work. "Good" was indeed the highest, well-earned word of commendation.'[14]

School reports confirm that Elizabeth did well, though she did not excel at mathematics. She won the literature prize and did well at scripture. She also made friends with a girl at the school called Betty Cator, who remained a friend, came home to meet her family and later married her brother Michael. At the end of the Easter term in 1913, Lady Strathmore took Elizabeth away from school and consigned her education to a German governess.

Here we have the fullest report of Elizabeth, the child, as she entered her adolescent years, for Fraulein Kaethe Kübler wrote her memoirs some years later, and a rare copy of this has survived.*

Fraulein Kübler was the twenty-one-year-old daughter of a Prussian official, and was engaged as a holiday governess for the Easter holidays of 1913. She loved her new charge. 'Lady Elizabeth was charming to look at. She had a small, delicate figure, a small, sensitive, somewhat pale little face, dark hair, and very beautiful, violet-blue eyes,'[15] she wrote.

Fraulein Kübler arrived at St Paul's Walden Bury for her interview in April 1913:

---

* This memoir seems to have eluded most of the Queen Mother's biographers.

I arrived in the afternoon at five o'clock, when everyone was having tea in the garden-room, whose large French windows, extending to the floor, enabled one to view the lovely park beyond. I was asked to join the group, and we were soon enjoying the liveliest conversation. I sensed so much warmth and friendliness, that I had no chance to feel strange or ill at ease.

After tea, my new pupil, led me to the stables, and showed me the horses, and her favourite dog, Juno, and her five puppies, and, when she noticed that I loved animals, I had won her heart. A warm companionship soon became established between us, friendship and affection followed, and, after only a fortnight, Lady Strathmore asked me whether I wished to stay for a longer period, in fact, for years to come.[16]

Kaethe Kübler soon concluded that Elizabeth's education so far had been dismal. The French governesses had failed to teach her much, while school had been little more than adequate. Now Elizabeth would enter a Germanic routine, with science lessons, technical subjects and piano lessons. She proved an eager pupil, though the new schedule was exacting.

Elizabeth's day began with her running early into her mother's bedroom, where they read together a passage from the scriptures. Then Fraulein Kübler gave her a piano lesson before breakfast, Elizabeth proving keenly musical.

At 9.30 proper lessons began, including German and French, history, geography, mathematics, nature study, drawing, needlework and gymnastics. The governess spoke English during the lessons, but otherwise only German. Ironically, in later life Elizabeth spoke better German than French. With her 'discerning heart' she often directed their talks to Erlangen, Fraulein Kübler's home.

After only a year Elizabeth was entered for the Oxford Local Examination. The governess drove her hard and Elizabeth became pale and thin, causing Lady Strathmore to comment: 'Good health is more important than examinations.' She passed with distinction.

The schoolroom routine was tempered with walks through the green meadows near the Bury and games of tennis and golf. At Glamis the strawberries in the kitchen garden were covered with closely woven nets to protect them from the birds, but Elizabeth was dexterous at dipping under these and would lie on her stomach, helping herself.

At 4 p.m. when they finished formal lessons, they often went for a picnic, harnessing the pony to a lightweight carriage. The butler brought out a basket of cakes, fruit and sandwiches and they set off to a clearing in the woods, tied the pony to a tree and lit a fire with brushwood to boil the kettle.

One Sunday morning in the summer of 1911, Elizabeth and David were sent to church alone, arriving late as the first hymn was being sung. Afraid to go in, they stayed outside the church, sitting behind a hedge with their prayer books. The children plodded through the entire service at such a slow pace that before they had finished people were already streaming out of church. 'This did not prevent them, however, from carrying out their service to the end, and then returning home, content and carefree'.[17]

In May Lord Strathmore opened his London house, 20, St James's Square, for the season, which continued until July, and the whole family and all the servants moved there. Neither Elizabeth nor her governess enjoyed this phase, two of which they shared – in 1913 and 1914 – as much as life in the country. Their lessons continued as before, and now included dancing and ballet, and their breaks were taken walking in Hyde Park. Here Elizabeth enjoyed seeing the cowman selling glasses of milk at the park gates, his cow at his side. Sometimes they went to the cinema, and once to Earl's Court to the pleasure gardens where Elizabeth rode on roundabouts and the scenic railway 'and screamed loudly as the railway rushed through a tunnel'.[18]

One afternoon they attended a conjurer's show. He conjured dark, red roses into an empty glass, and then bowed solemnly and presented governess and charge with two of the beautiful roses. Lord Strathmore appreciated this when told it at breakfast the next morning: 'That is a man who knows how to behave,' he said approvingly.

Dances were given for the children while Elizabeth's sister Rose, a 'fine, deeply shy being', offered them glimpses of the life to be with her stories of attending three or four balls a night, and specifically a magnificent ball given by the Curzons for the coming out of their daughter, Irene, in May 1914.

Elizabeth and her governess loved to look over the banisters from the third floor when beautifully dressed guests were entertained by the Strathmores. Her parents received them on the first floor at the top of the stairs outside the reception rooms.

The London season fulfilled one of its particular functions in exposing the young of such families to the great men of the age. Thus, just entering her teenage years, Elizabeth sat at the table with Lord Rosebery, who had served Queen Victoria as Prime Minister, and with several former and future Viceroys of India, the great Lord Curzon, Lord Lansdowne and Lord Goschen. So too did the governess, and when these great men told her they had studied in Germany, Elizabeth secretly pressed her hand under the table.

The family invariably drove out to St Paul's Walden Bury at the weekends to spend Sunday in the country, to attend church there and to enjoy village cricket matches, in which Lord Strathmore, his older sons, the butler and the valet took part. Elizabeth's father was happiest on these occasions, and would be full of dry-humoured jokes at tea afterwards.

As usual the family retreated to Glamis in August, travelling, as ever, in the *Flying Scotsman*. When they arrived at Forfar a car met them and conveyed them to the castle. There, with an ever-changing set of guests, they would enjoy the different shooting seasons, grouse from 12 August, partridges from 1 September and pheasants from 1 October. Most of the thirty guest rooms were filled and the linen room piled high with snow-white tablecloths, sheets, towels and napkins ready for the constant stream of visitors. Six washerwomen worked in the laundry, and a French chef presided over the kitchen. Uniformed footmen waited at table, and a variety of cars, coaches and riding horses were at the disposal of the guests.

'In Glamis, the Past overshadows the Present . . . The whole atmosphere seems to breathe so unmistakably of the Past . . . the Kirk, the Castle, even the distant line of hills, so suggestive of the Everlasting, all speak of an order of things long since established, and apart from that of the Present, with which it would seem to have little sympathy.'[19] So wrote Revd John Stirton, Senior Minister of Crathie, in his authorised history of the castle, dedicated to Queen Elizabeth in 1938.

Like so many Scottish castles, there were rumours of ghosts, though their neighbour, Lord Crawford, observed that the Bowes-Lyons amused themselves by inventing ghost stories 'to suit the idiosyncrasies of each guest'. He worked out the mystery of the castle's alleged secret. 'There is a secret: the secret is that there is *no* secret.'[20]

There was no shortage of terror from which to weave these tales. Sir Walter Scott had described his visit in the late 1700s and how he became increasingly uneasy as he was conducted to his rooms in a distant part of the castle: 'I must own that when I heard door after door shut, after my conductor had retired, I began to consider myself as far too far from the living, and somewhat too near the dead.'[21]

Hanging over the history of Glamis, never mentioned by today's guides, and a story that only the stout of heart would have dared raise in the presence of the Queen Mother, was the legend of the monster, or at any rate the secret chamber. 'A matter of common knowledge',[22] its location was, however, known to but three people at any given time – the Earl of

Strathmore of the day, the eldest son, to whom the secret was imparted when he came of age, and a third party, very often the Factor.

One legend had it that many centuries ago the then Lord Glamis was entertaining the then Earl of Crawford (known variously as 'Earl Beardie' or 'The Tiger Earl') in the secret room. They were playing cards on a Saturday night and did not realise that the hour was late and that Sunday was approaching. When alerted to the time, they swore an oath that they would play till the game was finished even until 'the crack of doom'. Midnight struck and a stranger appeared. He informed them that he would hold them to their word, as a result of which the ghostly pair meet once a year on the anniversary of that night and play cards – as they will until the dreadful day of judgement.

The 13th Earl of Strathmore took the secret room more lightly. He used to relate that a church dignitary – a man noted for his relentless pursuit of funds for the construction of churches – once stayed at the castle. He retired to bed when all at once a ghost appeared – a long-dead Strathmore from an earlier age. The cleric addressed the ghost, asking him for money. Would the ghostly Earl kindly give him a subscription and write the details in his collecting book? The erstwhile Scottish peer vanished at once, never to be seen again.

Augusta Maclagan, wife of the Archbishop of York, recorded that the cleric in question was Dr Nicholson, Dean of Brechin, sleeping in Earl Patrick's room, off the central staircase, who saw a 'tall figure in a cloak, fastened with a clasp, standing by his bed'.[23] In her version, Bishop Forbes offered to exorcise the ghost, but the 13th Earl was afraid to agree to this.

If there was a monster, he was said to have been a deformed heir, incarcerated generations before, and living on way beyond his natural span.*

Raymond Asquith, son of H. H. Asquith, attended a ball at Glamis in September 1905. 'The place is an enormous 10th century dungeon,' he wrote. 'It was full of torches and wild men in kilts and pretty women pattering on the stone stairs with satin slippers . . . I was glad to find I had enough illusibility left to fancy myself in a distant century. It gives one a certain thrill to sit out in the room where the King was murdered in *Macbeth*.'[24]

The young aesthete-to-be Stephen Tennant visited Glamis with his parents, Lord and Lady Glenconner, between 16 and 19 October 1913, when he was nine. His memories of the castle were colourful. He remembered 'rotting tapestries, hideous Danish furniture', and that his room

---

* There was a child born in 1821, said to be the origin of the monster.

contained 'spinachy green and sour yellow tapestries'. Lady Strathmore told him that one wing of the castle was never used, yet as they came down to dinner one evening he observed a footman cross the hall, dip under a rope and head up a staircase, bearing 'an enormous tray of steaming food'. This was presumed to be for the famous monster, who was, according to Stephen, 'a huge sheepdog' or 'half-man, half-baboon'.[25] Stephen confirmed that the Queen Mother would never refer to it, though her mother was said to have kept a scrapbook with all the monster stories in it.

More plausible ghosts included the wretched Lady Glamis, who was 'horribly' burned as a witch in Edinburgh in 1537, but makes friendly visits to the chapel in the guise of the 'Grey Lady'. To this day a chair is left free for her to the left of the altar, where there was once a door. There is also the sad tale of a disobedient page, who was told to sit immobile on a stone seat outside the room which became the Duchess of York's sitting room. He sat there all night and froze to death. Evidently he makes his presence known by sticking out a ghostly leg and sending the occasional tourist flying headlong into the room, giving a new definition to the word 'tripper'.

Elizabeth's sister Rose (later Countess Granville) related how children used to wake up screaming and how no one was ever put into Earl Patrick's room, or in the Hangman's Chamber, so-called because the family employed their own private hangman in days past. More recently, a butler had chosen that room in which to hang himself. Rose recalled:

> Some years ago, Arthur Lowther, son of Mr Speaker Lowther, later Lord Ullswater, asked my father if he could sleep in the Hangman's Room. He got up in the night and walked about. The floor gave way. His legs went through the ceiling of the room below. Colum Stuart* was sleeping there. He woke up with a shower of plaster on his face and saw two legs waving through the ceiling at him – far worse than a ghost!'[26]

In the early 1920s Helen Cecil was a regular guest. She recalled that visiting maids were terrified of the legendary monster and even the guests trembled somewhat before the eerie climb to bed. The castle having no electricity until 1929, Helen remembered 'the gleam of candlelight' at the foot of the dark staircase, 'before we all climbed to our rooms'.[27]

Elizabeth was brought up with the friends of her older brothers and sisters and thus matured quickly, even precociously. One of her sister

---

* Lord Colum Crichton-Stuart (1886–1957), third son of 3rd Marquess of Bute, Lord-Lieutenant of Buteshire from 1953.

May's friends, Lady Cynthia Colville,* daughter of the Marquess of Crewe, was fascinated by the younger children, Elizabeth and David, recalling: 'Full of conversation and yet unspoilt and non-aggressive, they were among the most attractive children I have ever come across.' She was amused to find 'that the Queen Mother at a very youthful age kept up a correspondence with more than one young man who found her childish but intelligent exuberance quite irresistible'.[28]

One such young man was Eddie Campbell,† the third son of Sir Guy Campbell, Bt, of the 60th Rifles. He was born in 1893 and would presently serve in the war in his father's regiment, to be wounded and mentioned in despatches. He was a contemporary of Elizabeth's brother Michael (born within a week of him) and they were at Eton together.

Eddie Campbell stayed at Glamis in the summer of 1913, and forged a rapport with his friend's sister. On 1 September she wrote to him from Glamis, addressing him as Fizy to thank him for a hair-ribbon which could now replace the bootlace she was using. It was the first letter she had received in four weeks:

The idea of Ian‡ saying I was wrong! I'm *never* wrong, as you know . . .

Thank you muchly for hoping I'm having a gay time. Its rather dull. Rosie, Jock, Mick & Fergie go away tomorrow for some time. My German governess comes back next week. So I shall have somebody to rag. I hope your walking is getting verrrrrry fast. I also hope you are enjoying yourself. It was topping weather last week, but it's terrible cold just now. If you draw a particularily (?) good head of yourself, do send it to me. I have not overeaton [sic] myself lately, but David did badly yesterday. I *hope* I shall see you sometime soon. Yours affec Eliza.[29]

With the letter she enclosed a poem, which began: 'Won't you come, come, up with me darling, Up into the sky . . .'. It talked of mooning and spooning, and making love and hugging every time.§[30]

Fraulein Kübler appeared a few days later, as expected, after four weeks'

* Lady Cynthia was appointed Woman of the Bedchamber to Queen Mary in 1923.
† Lt-Col. Edward FitzGerald Campbell, DSO (1893–1958). The second son of the family, Rt Hon. Sir Ronald Ian Campbell (1890–1983) was Envoy Extraordinary and Minister Plenipotentiary in Paris 1938–9, where, ironically, a later Ambassador was Sir Ronald Hugh Campbell.
‡ Possibly his brother.
§ Two versions of this poem were sent. Lady Elizabeth Basset, the Queen Mother's lady-in-waiting, believed it was a well-known song of the period [Lady Elizabeth Basset to Nicholas White, Clarence House, 2 February 1993].

leave in Germany. Elizabeth showed her round the whole castle, other than the guest rooms occupied by hunting guests. She opened trap doors and secret staircases and explored the haunted rooms. On Sundays there was a service in the castle's chapel, which Elizabeth and her governess never missed, wearing medieval-looking lace hoods.

The way of life at Glamis, which had continued for so many centuries, emphasised the structure of aristocratic society at that time. Following the three-month London season, the aristocrats retired to their estates, where they remained from August to November. They invited other aristocrats to join them in their sport, be it shooting or hunting. While Parliament was in recess from July until October, or even November, the political business of the day was continued over the dining-room tables of men like Lord Strathmore. Between the daily outings to the hillsides in quest of the bird then in season, policies were formed and business quietly conducted. After the First World War, crippling taxation severely curtailed that way of life.

And thus did Elizabeth enjoy life in her formative years. A maid arrived in her room with early morning tea, biscuits, hot water and fresh towels. She may therefore have been unique in the twentieth century in never ever having had to draw her own bedroom curtains. She undertook her piano lesson at eight, took breakfast with the house party, and then worked until one. She listened to the exploits of the hunt at luncheon for thirty. In the afternoons she watched the shooting with her father, or the more skilled work in fly fishing at the Glamis burn. In the evening, Lord Strathmore and his sons put on their kilts and dinner was served, while two men played the haunting bagpipes in the hall. At Glamis they remained, protected from the outside world, until they went south for Christmas.

It was a withdrawn life, punctuated by simple excursions, perhaps to the village where all the villagers knew and loved Elizabeth. The local vicar invited Fraulein Kübler to come to meetings of the German Club in Forfar, and Elizabeth went along eagerly in the hope that it might be amusing. There were about ten or fifteen members, all Scots who had visited Germany, and they liked to converse in German.

In November, when the sporting season was over, the guests left and there were only five at meals in the castle dining room – Lord and Lady Strathmore, Rose, Elizabeth and the governess, David having returned to boarding school at Broadstairs.

Christmas was celebrated at St Paul's Walden Bury, with the full ritual of turkey, plum pudding, mince pies and holly. Then they returned to Glamis to see the New Year in. By now it was bitterly cold, and the youngsters enjoyed tobogganing in the snow. Then they went south again for an early season in London in February and March.

The spring of 1914 was especially beautiful, everything green and in luxuriant bloom. Lady Strathmore was delighted with Elizabeth's progress and hoped that her governess would stay until she was eighteen, helping her to cultivate her gift for languages, music and history of art, and planning journeys to Germany, Italy and Austria.

Then, on the morning of 29 June, Fraulein Kübler came into the breakfast room at St James's Square to find Lord Strathmore ashen faced, reading the *Morning Post*. The headlines spoke of the murder the day before of Archduke Franz Ferdinand and his wife at Sarajevo. He handed the paper to the governess, and told her: 'Here, read it, this means war.'[31]

On 12 July Fraulein Kübler left for Germany. Lady Strathmore embraced her and made her promise to return. She gave the same promise to Elizabeth. It was to be a dream forever unrealised.

On the evening of 4 August, her fourteenth birthday, Elizabeth went to the London Coliseum, where she saw a vaudeville performance with Charles Hawtrey and G. P. Huntley. On the way to the theatre she saw the billboards announcing that Britain was at war with Germany, and the whole structure of life immediately changed.

In that hot summer, it was hoped, and believed that the outcome would be favourably resolved by Christmas. That it would continue for more than four long years, killing the flower of English youth and leaving many families bereaved was something only considered by those prescient enough to realise that wars are invariably easier to get into than to get out of.

Without hesitation Elizabeth's four older brothers set off to France, Patrick and Jock in the 5th Battalion of the Black Watch and Fergus in the 8th, while Michael served in the 3rd Battalion, Royal Scots. Likewise the pompous family butler and Lord Strathmore's valet volunteered for service.

Elizabeth's two elder unmarried brothers immediately married within days of each other. On 17 September, Fergus married Lady Christian Dawson-Damer, daughter of the 15th Earl of Portarlington in Sussex. On 29 September Jock married the Hon. Fenella Hepburn-Stuart-Forbes-Trefusis, younger daughter of the 21st Lord Clinton, at Fasque, Kincardineshire. At both weddings, Elizabeth was a bridesmaid.

Fraulein Kübler never returned to Britain. She found herself in white cap and apron as a nurse in the Reserve Hospital of Erlangen. Elizabeth was able to correspond with her for a time in 'short, inadequate letters',[32] which were forwarded by the English Consulate in Holland, but when Fraulein Kübler was sent to the Western Front the correspondence ceased for many years. For Elizabeth it was a deeply personal blow.

Only Rose and Elizabeth remained at Glamis with their parents. Rose was now twenty-four. She went south to train to be a nurse in London, but returned to Glamis before the first arrivals from Dundee Royal Infirmary in December 1914. Elizabeth's lessons were neglected as she crumpled up tissue paper to be used as lining for sleeping bags. She was also busy knitting for the Black Watch, in which three of her brothers were serving.

Glamis was transformed into a Red Cross convalescent home for wounded servicemen. Beds were moved into the dining room and billiard room, and all too soon shell-shocked men started to arrive from the trenches, broken in mind and body. Elizabeth was too young to nurse the injured, but she wrote letters for them, played cards with them and bought them cigarettes and chocolates. That quality of consideration for others which was already such a hallmark of her character found an outlet in comforting these sad and wounded men. One sergeant said that his three weeks at Glamis were the happiest he had ever known.

The war brought anguish to the Strathmore family as to so many others. The pre-war days of cricket matches and house parties were over-shadowed by the fear of bad news and the onset of decline in some of Elizabeth's brothers. Every morning Elizabeth intercepted the postman in fear of a telegram from the War Office.

After nearly a year away, first at Aldershot and later in France, Fergus, small and dark with brown eyes, was able to come home to celebrate his first wedding anniversary on 17 September and to see his new daughter, Rosemary, born on 18 July. Then he departed for France again and was killed at the Battle of Loos on 27 September, the day after his return.

Fergus's death was typical of so many First World War tragedies. The advancing British never stood a chance at Loos. They started in old German trenches which the German artillery knew well. After sustaining many casualties, the 8th Black Watch returned to the Brigade at about 4 a.m. As they prepared breakfast, Fergus approached and apologised. He said they had to go back to the Hohenzollern to 'take out some Germans'. He seemed apprehensive but knew where his duty lay. As the group set off in single file, with Fergus in the lead, German bombs began to fall. One of his legs was blown off and he fell back into the arms of his sergeant. Then he was hit by bullets in the chest and shoulder. Two sergeants sat with him as he died. He was taken away on a stretcher to be buried. The dreaded telegram duly arrived at Glamis.

Elizabeth's surviving brothers were all shattered by the experience of war. Patrick, the eldest, was wounded and badly shell-shocked. He resigned his commission as a major in the Black Watch due to ill health and never fully recovered from his experiences. After the war, Rose went to nurse him. He lived at Streatlam for a time and began to develop a parliamentary career, but his wife, Dorothy, hated living there and made him move south to East Grinstead, where he lived at Shovelstrode Manor. He became chairman of John Bowes and Partners, a firm in Durham with considerable mining interests in the Durham–Northumberland area, but in the 1930s this was badly hit by the Depression. Later business interests were even more unsuccessful.

There were also problems within Patrick's family, since Dorothy developed a considerable dislike for her son, John, Master of Glamis, the eventual heir. When the children came down to play, the daughters were kept by the fire while he was sent 'to the cold end of the room to play with telephone directories'.[33] Before long, Lady Strathmore rescued John from this ménage and took him to Glamis where she raised him as an adjunct to her own family. Patrick's family died out in the male line.

Jock, the next brother, who had the Nordic looks of his handsome elder brother, lost a finger early in the war. He was so badly wounded on the Western Front that he was sent out to serve in the British Embassy in Washington, where, in 1917, his first child, Patricia, died before her first birthday from acidosis, in those days still an incurable disease.

Worse was to follow. His wife, Fenella, 'a very vague person',[34] passed on a strain of mental deficiency inherited from the Clintons. They had four more daughters, two of whom, Nerissa, born in 1919, and Katherine, born in 1926, were unable to develop mentally or to speak.*

Michael was another brother of whom Elizabeth was particularly fond. Mike, or Mickie, was dark, like Fergus. Before the war he was at Oxford, from which he went straight to war. He kept a diary of his wartime

---

* Gentle, sensitive creatures, Nerissa and Katherine were first sent to a special school in Hemel Hempstead, Hertfordshire, and then, in 1941, some years after Jock's death, were admitted to Royal Earlswood Mental Hospital, a purpose-built home for the mentally handicapped, built in 1860, where they remained for the rest of their lives. Nerissa died on 22 January 1986 of pneumonia, 'severe mental deficiency' being mentioned on the death certificate, and a few months later the existence of these sisters, long declared dead in *Burke's Peerage*, was discovered and their story related in the tabloid press, much being made of the fact that the Royal Family took no interest in them. The Queen Mother's patronage of Mencap, which campaigns against families placing their mentally challenged relations in state care, was also mentioned. The surviving sister, Katherine, was photographed menacing the cameraman from the *Sun*, a not unreasonable reaction to the invasion of her fragile privacy.

experiences from April to July 1917 with tales of arriving at trenches only two feet deep at three in the morning. On 28 April he was leading a company through Roeux wood and village, near Arras, where they faced a heavy counterattack. At one point Michael was observed firing a revolver in his left hand and pulling out the pins of a hand grenade with his teeth and throwing it as far away as possible with his right hand. Eventually, in the face of 'hundreds of Germans about 20 or 30 yards off coming on in a counter attack',[35] the company surrendered and was taken captive.

On 3 May a War Office telegram reached Lord Strathmore in London with the news that Michael was missing. The family went into mourning, though David refused to join in, convinced that he had had visions of Michael alive, though very ill, his head bound with a bandage. Michael's diary of 10 June 1917 recorded 'a letter to Buffy'*[36] which may or may not have arrived, but after thirty-five agonising days a postcard written to his father from the Karlsrühe Hotel on 4 May did reach home. He reported that, after his capture, he had been given tea by a German officer: 'He tried to get a lot out of me but when he found he could not, sent me off to join the others.'[37]

Elizabeth was able to correspond with Michael, her first letter reaching him on 23 June. Twelve tins of milk and some shaving soap arrived from his parents, and eventually they were told he was at an officers' camp at Strochen in good health. Michael gave up his place as an exchange hostage to a man more gravely wounded than himself, and remained in captivity, only returning home as the year ended.

Rose fared better than her brothers. In May 1916 she married the seventeen-stone William ('Wisp') Leveson-Gower at St James's, Piccadilly, with Elizabeth again a bridesmaid. Though a second son, he succeeded his childless brother as 4th Earl Granville. He went on to enjoy a good career in the Royal Navy, rising to vice-admiral, and served as Governor of Northern Ireland from 1945 until his health deteriorated in 1952.

On Saturday 30 August 1916 a fire broke out at Glamis between 5 and 6 p.m. Two wounded soldiers discovered the blaze in Laight Tower, the fire having started in rooms below the servants' quarters. By 9 p.m. the fire was under control, and two days later the *Dundee Courier* proclaimed that Lady Elizabeth 'was a veritable heroine in the salvage work she performed even within the fire zone'.[38]

The cause of the fire was never established, but either an overheated

---

* 'Buffy' was a family nickname for Elizabeth.

flue set fire to an adjoining timber or burning soot fell on to the boards of a roof. The Forfar Fire Brigade was unable to cope, but the Dundee Fire Brigade pumped water from the Dean and controlled it. Over the years stories of the fire became exaggerated. One of the more sober reports confirms: 'Had it not been for the untiring efforts of the Lady Elizabeth Bowes-Lyon in organising a body of willing workers with brooms to speed the torrent down the great stair, the damage would have been immense and the seventeenth-century plaster ceilings would almost certainly have been lost.'[39] Fortunately there was no wind that evening. A temporary roof was placed over the damage, and the final repairs were undertaken between 1924 and 1926.[40]

In November 1916 Elizabeth was confirmed at St John's Episcopal Church, in Forfar, having chosen to share this experience with other local girls, all of them in white with veils.

The war ended in November 1918 by which time some 1500 wounded soldiers had passed through Glamis. The castle remained a hospital through 1919. Armistice Day was a moment for rejoicing and for counting the cost. The Kaiser had been defeated, but many families were depleted. Lord Strathmore was growing old and deaf; Lady Strathmore had suffered, as only a mother could, the loss of two sons, one to illness, another to war. Towards the end of the war, on 6 July 1918, her mother, Mrs Scott, had died in Dawlish, Devonshire.

The men of the Strathmore family were damaged for life. A strain of alcoholism ran in the family, and when Bowes-Lyons are spoken of, they are referred to as heavy drinkers. They were destined for sad ends, and even in the next generation there were suicides and early deaths.*

The only member of the family to emerge strengthened from the war was Elizabeth. She began it as a fourteen-year-old girl and ended it an eighteen-year-old woman. She should have had a carefree adolescence. Instead she was a star, having borne grief on her own behalf and her mother's, and having proved her ability by helping the many soldiers who passed through Glamis. Her experiences set her in good stead for life. She had been called upon to put tired and broken men at their ease, to give them hope and optimism where little was forthcoming. She had grown up fast. For years afterwards patients would write in with fond memories of the young Elizabeth. Later still their descendants continued to write. She made a genuine and lasting impression on them.

Elizabeth had been the only daughter at home and the constant

* See Appendix II: The Descendants of the Earl of Strathmore (p. 508).

companion of her mother. There are two descriptions of her at this time. The first, written for publication, was by her mother's friend, Lady Airlie:

> Lady Elizabeth was very unlike the cocktail-drinking, chain-smoking girls who came to be regarded as typical of the nineteen-twenties. Her radiant vitality and a blending of gaiety, kindness and sincerity made her irresistible to men. One knew instinctively that she was a girl who would find real happiness only in marriage and motherhood. A born home-maker.[41]

The second account was by Stephen Tennant, whose brother, Christopher, 2nd Lord Glenconner, would presently be one of Elizabeth's suitors:

> She looked everything that she was not: gentle, gullible, tenderness mingled with dispassionate serenity, cool, well-bred, remote. Behind this veil she schemed and vacillated, hard as nails; she picked her men with the skill of a chess player, snobbish, poised – with a rather charming vagueness. She schooled her intentions like a detective, totting up her chances. I sensed her air of puzzled disdain, noted her skill and tact.[42]

The two descriptions need not be seen as wholly contradictory.

In the summer of 1918 Elizabeth emerged in society. She attended a ball given by the Countess of Powis at 45 Berkeley Square, for her daughter, Hermione,* a direct contemporary. 'I remember dancing with a nice young American . . .' she wrote later, 'and the amazement and thrill when the next day a huge bunch of red roses arrived! In those days flowers were very rare!'[43] At a time when young girls were excited by lunches at the Ritz, and young men coming to tea, she added: 'one was thrilled by that sort of thing!'[44]

Sometimes, at the end of a ball, Elizabeth would be collected in a brougham with a coachman and one tired old horse. There would be stops and Elizabeth would put her head through the window and ask the coachman what the problem was. 'It's quite all right, Milady, but the horse has stopped for a little sleep.'[45]

Elizabeth was in London for the Armistice celebrations in November 1918 and she watched President and Mrs Woodrow Wilson drive through

---

* Lady Hermione Herbert (1900–95), married 1924, 11th Duca della Grazia. In later life she lived in the Hôtel Beaurivage in Lausanne, Switzerland.

the streets of London on their visit to King George V and Queen Mary on Boxing Day. There was a limited social season in London in 1919 with some dances in the early summer. The King and Queen went to the Derby and to Royal Ascot (the latter attended by Elizabeth). Garden parties were resumed at Buckingham Palace, and the British upper classes tried to re-establish the life that had been denied them for four and a half years.

She was also in London during the week, spending her weekends at the Bury, as in earlier times, and visiting David at Eton when this was allowed. During the war years she had kept in touch with the girlfriends that made up her immediate set. While the war had made it difficult for them to meet, they exchanged news and letters. In that first summer after the Armistice they emerged into society.

Of these friends many would accompany Elizabeth into later life. They were a close-knit, almost impenetrable group, born into aristocratic families in different parts of England, Scotland and Ireland. They called themselves privately the 'Mad Hatters', or the 'Chorus', exchanged silly jokes and rhymes, confided their exploits to each other and said nothing to the outside world. Elizabeth's girlfriends were kind and self-contained, though there were one or two fast members of the set, Mollie Lascelles in particular.

Elizabeth spent the late summer of 1919 at Glamis, where for the first time her heart was stirred. Having older brothers meant that she was exposed to young men older than herself and these men had been matured by war. In late September Michael invited James Stuart to join the house party. Elizabeth had met him at a musical entertainment she attended with Michael at Tivoli Gardens.

Born in 1897, James Stuart was the younger son of the 17th Earl of Moray. He had served with Michael in the Royal Scots and won a Military Cross and bar. He survived many gruelling wartime experiences on the Somme, at Arras and at Ypres. This gave him confidence. He considered himself lucky to have survived, alive and unwounded. Throughout the war he turned to a girl called Elfie Finlayson, whose father lived at Coldoch, not far from the Morays at Doune Lodge, Perthshire. His father and his elder brother were equally fond of Elfie, the father and she maintaining a slightly risqué correspondence, and the elder brother at one time proposing to her. When the war ended, Stuart and Elfie became closer still. For a time in 1919 they were engaged.

Stuart was then studying law at Edinburgh University. In July he was happy to visit Elfie at Coldoch and equally happy to go alone to Glamis in September for a ten-day visit. In October he was appointed equerry to the King's second son, Prince Albert. Thus he spent the autumn of

1919 and the spring of 1920 at Trinity College, Cambridge, looking after the Prince and his younger brother, Prince Henry. The appointment was to be more significant than any of them realised.

3

The 'Dear Duke'

*'Elizabeth and Prince A. were allowed to go on miles ahead which
agitated the former rather . . .' –* Helen Cecil

There was no reason to suppose that 1920 would be an unusual year for
Elizabeth. The normal events of the season followed in succession, gossip
was passed between the various girlfriends, suitors were discussed with
the avidity of youth, there were dances and weekend parties.

Elizabeth was carefully chaperoned by her parents. She was only
allowed to go to the most respectable of houses. Nor did she wish to go
elsewhere. Stephen Tennant recalled that at parties she was 'afraid of
meeting the wrong people'.[1] It is therefore ironic that it was the house
of a scoundrel, Lord Farquhar, that Elizabeth met Prince Albert, and
where he was first attracted to her.

Horace, 1st Earl Farquhar, was considered a most distinguished figure
by all except those with privileged knowledge of his misdemeanours. He
was one of George V's few genuinely close friends. He had been Treasurer of the Conservative Party and served as Lord Steward of the
Household under Edward VII and George V. He was a Privy Counsellor,
had the GCVO and in 1922 would be given the GCB.

His origins lay in the Highlands of Scotland, at Farquharson Castle,
Braemar, where Mar first raised his standard in 1715, in the vast woods
and purple moors of Aboyne. As a young man, Farquhar had befriended
the 5th Earl of Fife, whose uncle's trustees leased the Balmoral estate
to Queen Victoria in 1847. Farquhar persuaded the young Earl to
'exchange the barren honours of a Highland landlord for the more remun-
erative career of a private banker',[2] in which he made a considerable
fortune. Young Fife married Princess Louise, later the Princess Royal,
eldest daughter of King Edward VII, and became a Duke and a Knight
of the Garter.

Farquhar was Director of Parrs, bankers to the Duveen brothers, and
had advised Edward VII on his complicated financial affairs. He had been
the conduit for obtaining honours for families such as the Monds,
Sassoons and Cassels, and certain Rothschilds who provided Edward VII

with money. The Astors had paid him a million dollars for a viscountcy.*
He had taken a large sum from the Conservative Party and he went on
to embezzle many thousands of pounds from the estate of his friend, the
Duke of Fife. He had pushed shares in a Siberian gold mining company
to great personal gain.

Farquhar had risen through the ranks from knight to Earl. He lived
at 7 Grosvenor Square, in London, and rented White Lodge in Richmond Park, and Castle Rising, near Sandringham, Norfolk, for shooting.
Duveen Brothers furnished all three, never sending him a bill. In
exchange he had alerted them to people who were financially embarrassed, sometimes through losing heavily at cards to Edward VII.

Farquhar had persuaded Edward VII to commission Duveen Brothers
to de-Victorianise the royal residences when the King succeeded Queen
Victoria in 1901. They also smartened up Westminster Abbey for the
1902 Coronation, adorning it with oriental carpets and French and
Flemish tapestries.

In the spring of 1920, as always, Lord and Lady Farquhar were to the
fore in the splendid entertainments they gave at their huge house in
Grosvenor Square. In January they held a large dinner for seventy-two
guests to celebrate their Silver Wedding, with Prince and Princess Arthur
of Connaught as guests of honour. On 17 February, Queen Alexandra was
observed to be 'in great spirits' at the reception at 7 Grosvenor Square for
Lord Blandford, heir to the 9th Duke of Marlborough, after his wedding
to Mary Cadogan. Farquhar was one of those present when the Prince of
Wales was introduced into the Privy Council in March, before the Prince
sailed to Australia. In the same month he gave a 'very exclusive dinner'[3]
for the King and Queen at 7 Grosvenor Square and soon afterwards was
in the King's party for the Grand Military Meeting at Sandown.

In Lord Farquhar, two of the Royal Family's great loves were conveniently linked – Scotland and money. Though there would be a sharp
posthumous fall from grace, at this time he was gliding through calm
waters, all sails unfurled, a magnificent, seemingly untouchable galleon.

On 2 June 1920 Lord Farquhar gave the party that would unwittingly
find Britain a new Queen Consort. That day the King and Queen had
gone to the Derby, to be received by the splendid Lord Lonsdale. That
night the King gave his once-traditional, all-male Derby night dinner
for members of the Jockey Club at Buckingham Palace, entertaining the
Dukes of Richmond, Montrose and Portland, the Marquesses of

---

* Farquhar obtained this by saying $200,000 would go to a private charity in which the King took
a great personal interest and the balance would be divided between the Conservative Party and
Lloyd George.

Londonderry, Zetland and Crewe, the Earls of Derby, Carnarvon, Lonsdale, Harewood and others.

On the same night Lord Farquhar gave a dinner at 7 Grosvenor Square, 'the chief social event of the week'.[4] That morning, Prince Albert and Prince Henry had come down from Trinity College, Cambridge, for a short visit, with James Stuart in attendance. Queen Mary put on a blue and silver brocade dress with a train and a diamond tiara, and took them and Princess Mary to dinner at 7 Grosvenor Square.

Farquhar had arranged three tables of twenty, set with priceless old china and decorated with sweet peas. Among those present were the Duke and Duchess of Northumberland, the Duchess of Roxburghe, the Marchioness of Londonderry, the Countess of Derby and the American Ambassador and Mrs Davis. Lady Beattie was more than striking in a 'vivid tomato frock'.[5]

Afterwards there was a ball, to which the Strathmores brought Elizabeth. Presently James Stuart was dancing with her, which caught the eye of Prince Albert, who asked his equerry: 'Who was that lovely girl you were talking to? Introduce me to her.'[6] They danced together and the seeds of romance were sown in his heart, if not in hers.

Prince Albert, or 'Bertie' as he was known in the family, was undergoing an important transformation. On the following day, the King's fifty-fifth birthday, the King created him Duke of York. In bestowing on him the title he had himself held for more than nine years at the end of Queen Victoria's reign, George V commended his second son for having 'behaved very well, in a difficult situation for a young man' and having 'done what I asked you to do'.[7] This cryptic line has long been in the public domain, but only recently has it become clear what the King had asked his son to do. In May 1920, the Prince of Wales, away at sea, received three 'long, sad' letters from Bertie in which he said he had been 'getting it in the neck [from his father] about his friendship with poor little Sheilie'.[8]

The King disapproved of Bertie's tepid romance with Lady Loughborough,* a beautiful Australian girl, then uncomfortably married to the

---

* Sheila Chisholm (1895–1969), daughter of Harry Chisholm, an Australian bloodstock agent. She met 'Luffy' when she was nursing soldiers and he was convalescing from wounds received at Gallipoli. They married in 1915 and had two sons. His gambling soon landed them in financial trouble. They divorced in 1926. She then married Sir John 'Buffles' Milbanke, who died in 1947, and then, in 1954, Prince Dimitri, a grandson of Tsar Nicholas I of Russia. She inspired Evelyn Waugh to write *The Loved One*. She died in London on 31 October 1969.

There was a persistent rumour in Sydney, Australia, that her brother Roy's wife, the former Mollee Little, had had an affair with the Prince of Wales during his 1920 visit, and that their son, Tony, was his. Tony's mother explained the resemblance as the result of having often looked at a photograph of the Prince during her pregnancy. The Prince of Wales was Tony's godfather. Tony died in June 1987.

heir to the 5th Earl of Rosslyn, a man heavily addicted to gambling and the bottle. Bertie had been forlornly in love with her, while she was in love, not with him, but with the good-looking Russian émigré Prince Serge Obolensky.

Perhaps it was not so tepid. Sheila Milbanke used to relate that after the Second World War, George VI reminisced with her about old times, and how she realised, rather uncomfortably, that Queen Elizabeth was listening. She thought it prudent to damp it down and said: 'And when you think, Sir, how innocent it all was . . .'. The King went red with fury: 'Innocent? I don't know what the devil you mean!'⁹

Prince Bertie's renunciation of Sheila – or, more correctly, of his infatuation with her – marked his escape from the raffish set in which his brother dwelt, and into which, more than understandably, he had himself been lured. But Bertie was a more serious character than the Prince of Wales and never particularly comfortable in his set.

Prince Albert was the second son of King George V and Queen Mary. He had the misfortune to have been born on the anniversary of the death of both the Prince Consort and Princess Alice, Grand Duchess of Hesse, on 14 December 1895, prompting mixed reactions in his great-grandmother, Queen Victoria, who became his godmother and presented him with a bust of the Prince Consort as a christening present. He was born at York Cottage, Sandringham, and christened Albert Frederick Arthur George.

In his youth he was overshadowed by his elder brother, and, like all his siblings, he was terrified of his father. Already shy and retiring by nature, he developed a stammer when he was six or seven, which was later attributed to his fear of the future George V. He was rather poorly tutored at home by Henry Hansell, but persevered to the best of his ability, passing into the Royal Naval College, Osborne, with good oral French and more than acceptable mathematics. Many hurdles did this young man face, and time after time he proved himself by application. Not overly cerebral, it was his determination that won him through.

He undertook a training cruise in HMS *Cumberland*, visiting the West Indies and Canada, and was posted as a midshipman to HMS *Collingwood* in the Home Fleet. As a sublieutenant, he saw active service at the Battle of Jutland, but during many of the war years he suffered from gastric trouble, only partly alleviated by an operation for appendicitis in 1914 and further relieved by an operation for a duodenal ulcer in 1917.

His health caused him to leave the Navy, and in 1918 he was gazetted a flight lieutenant in the newly formed Royal Air Force. He became dedicated to physical fitness and proved himself a keen tennis player. (In 1920, he would win the Air Force tennis doubles, playing with his Comptroller, Wing Commander Louis Greig.) In 1919 he left the Royal Air Force as a qualified pilot.

Prince Albert's inherent shyness had not helped him form relationships. Through Louis Greig he met Phyllis Monkman, the glamorous singer. Evidently he 'showed no sign of the usual interest in the opposite sex, so perhaps some delightful, trustworthy young woman could be chosen to initiate the young prince into the rites of sex. It was agreed by all who knew her that the well-known dancer-actress Phyl Monkman would be a suitable person . . . The young prince responded as expected.'[10]

There was then a brief attraction to Lady Maureen Vane-Tempest-Stuart, eldest daughter of 7th Marquess of Londonderry, but in November 1920 she married Oliver Stanley, disregarding her father's warning of the consequences when 'Park Lane stoops to Bayswater'.[11]

In October 1919, the Prince of Wales wrote intriguingly to his so-called mistress, Freda Dudley Ward: 'And so his [Bertie's] friend, Miss Fuller was there. I long to see her merely out of curiosity!!'[12] This might have been the actress Rosalinde Fuller, who was popular at that time.*

That she was a few years older than Prince Albert, that she was carving her name and had entertained the American troops in France does not identify her conclusively with the 'Miss Fuller' the Prince of Wales claimed he would rather like to meet. But the fact that the Prince mentions the ragtime dancer Mrs Vernon Castle in almost the same line does draw the field closer.

When Prince Albert accepted the Dukedom of York, his elder brother was furious. He was particularly irritated since he was aware that any friendship between Bertie and Sheila Loughborough had been over since the previous January:

---

* Rosalinde Fuller (1892–1982), actress. She claimed to have been born in Portsmouth in 1901, though in fact she was born in 1892. Raised in Dorset, she was known as a singer of folk songs from the age of twelve. She was discovered by Cecil Sharp, who advised her to go to America in 1914, where for four seasons she sang folk songs. During 1918 she appeared in the chorus of a revue at the Folies Bergère in Paris, and entertained American troops in France in 1919. She made her first stage appearance in Maxine Elliott's Theatre in New York, becoming an instant success in a Murray Anderson revue, *What's in a Name* on 19 March 1920. She played Ophelia opposite John Barrymore in *Hamlet* in 1922. She was in the United States until 1927, when she returned to England, and scored an instant success as Nubi in *The Squall* at the Globe in November that year.

James Agate thought her best remembered in *The Unknown Warrior* and *Martine*, but commented that in *Fritzi* (1935), while she did 'her bright vivacious best', he protested against 'an assumed accent which says: "Forgeeve you? Ach, no! Thees cannot bee!" That the character is French is no excuse for making her talk Viennese' (James Agate, *More First Nights* (Victor Gollancz, 1937), p. 225).

Bertie may be a Duke now for all I know as I think that his rather pompous nature makes him want to be one. Of course if he really loved Sheilie he wouldn't care a d— about dukes or anything else; but the point is that he doesn't really love her & she loves him less so that I would strongly advise him to quit the top of the Loughborough volcano as fast as he can if it's as hot as he says it is!![13]

The Prince of Wales would never renounce that set. Between his arduous travels, he continued to wallow in it, and thus he descended, sometimes enjoyably and selfishly, late-night cocktail in hand, intoxicating and intoxicated grin on face, into a pitiful state. He rode roughshod over the affections of many on the way, and caused his family and courtiers increasing and deepening concern. There were times when he endured periods of despair and depression, wondering if the monarchy would survive, and seeking a means of escape. And finally, he sank into an exhausted state of self-abasement and boredom. In this weakened condition, his fate would be sealed by his encounter with the twice-married American Mrs Wallis Simpson. The result would be disastrous for him, though not for his country.

For Prince Albert it was different. He was not a carouser by nature. He was dutiful and his dukedom gave him a new perception of his role. He would behave better and would take life more seriously. Whether he realised it that night, there could not have been a better time for him to meet Elizabeth Bowes-Lyon.

But it was not a *coup de foudre* because he was still moping over Sheila, though later he told his mother's lady-in-waiting, Lady Airlie, who took a benign interest in him, that 'he had fallen in love that evening, although he did not realize it until later'.[14]

Meanwhile, Elizabeth was blissfully unaware of the interest being directed towards her. She was content in her own world, enjoying a fabulous London season in which she was sensationally popular.

While the Duke of York returned to Cambridge with Captain Stuart still in attendance, Elizabeth remained in London, surrounded by her host of admirers. Within the week she was dancing a sixteensome at the Royal Caledonian Ball in the Connaught Rooms, dressed in white with the tartan of her clan over her shoulder. Among the sixteen accompanying Elizabeth was another debutante, a somewhat reluctant one, who, a few days later, was taken to the first court held by the King and Queen since 1914 and presented by her mother – Lady Alice Montagu-Douglas-Scott, daughter of the 7th Duke of Buccleuch, who was destined to become Elizabeth's sister-in-law, as Duchess of Gloucester.*

For a rather wet Royal Ascot in June Elizabeth stayed with her mother's friend, the loquacious Lady Nina Balfour,† a 'dynamic, extrovert character'.[15] Lady Nina was normally to be found at Newton Don, a spacious Regency house on rising ground north of Kelso, with a fine view over the Tweed. But every summer until her husband's death in 1921 she took Bisham Abbey, a beautiful house on the Thames at Marlow. Like Glamis it was said to be haunted, and Alan Lascelles, later to play his part as George VI's irascible Private Secretary, recalled that he always woke with a jump at two in the morning when he stayed there and had to read a book until the birds began to sing.[16]

Lady Nina was a noted hostess who liked to mix the young and the old, and to entertain the great figures of the day. Princess Alice, Duchess of Gloucester, thought her 'a great character and an incorrigible matchmaker, which was rather off-putting, but there was no hostess in Scotland who could equal the deliciousness of her food, her impeccable taste and flair for a party'.[17] Among her protégés from Oxford were the friends of her sons Jock (later an ambassador) and Archie, Prince Paul of Yugoslavia,‡ Viscount Gage and Henry 'Chips' Channon. Elizabeth and her friend Lady Doris Gordon-Lennox, daughter of the 8th Duke of Richmond, were there together in the summer of 1920, attracting interest in varying degrees from among the Oxford group.

It was at Bisham Abbey during Ascot week that the Duke of York began his courtship. Helen Cecil, one of Elizabeth's 'chorus' of friends, reported in September: 'Apparently when they were all at Lady Nina's he held Elizabeth's hands under Nina's very nose in the famous electric launch. Elizabeth says it was quite worth it just to see Nina's face.'[18] Thus it is clear that though the 'Dear Duke', as Elizabeth began to call him to her friends, was making his feelings gently known, Elizabeth was still treating him as a suitor about whom funny stories could be told.

By July Elizabeth was in Scotland, and she came to Edinburgh with her parents for the King and Queen's visit. Lady Strathmore attended the royal garden party and on the next afternoon, 6 July, she formally presented her daughter to the King and Queen at an afternoon recep-

---

* For those who like such details, the Duke and political Duchess of Atholl were in the set, and in reel five danced Captain Lord Carnegie, who would marry Princess Maud of Fife in November 1923.
† Lady Helena (Nina) McDonnell (1865–1948), youngest daughter of the ten children of the 5th Earl of Antrim, married 1888, Captain Charles Barrington Balfour (1862–1921), Lord-Lieutenant of Berwickshire. The discovery of coal on his land at Balgonie had made him a very rich man.
‡ In those days he was invariably described as Prince Paul of Serbia.

tion at Holyroodhouse. In the normal scheme of things Elizabeth would have been presented the year before, but presentation courts had not been revived at that time. She was but one of a long string of aristocratic Scottish girls and made no impression on George V that day. He did not focus on her until the following year.

Both the Duke of York and Elizabeth were out and about in London society enough that summer for the Duke to receive an invitation to come to Glamis for a weekend in September. For him it would be a welcome escape from the confines of Balmoral life as conducted by George V and Queen Mary. For her it had more worrying implications.

We now have witnesses in both camps who can give an inside picture of life at Glamis as well as Balmoral. Helen Cecil and Captain Alexander Hardinge, the man to whom Helen was secretly engaged and would marry the following February, exchanged regular letters giving daily bulletins of developments in both castles. Helen was the daughter of the late Lord Edward Cecil and his wife, by then Viscountess Milner. Alec was the heir to Lord Hardinge of Penshurst, the former Viceroy of India, and brother of Diamond Hardinge, another close friend of Elizabeth's. He had recently become equerry and Assistant Private Secretary to the King. This was his first summer at Balmoral.

Throughout the late summer there had been the usual house parties at Glamis. At the end of the first week, on 8 September, Elizabeth attended the Forfar County Ball, at which she danced with Victor Cochrane-Baillie, son of Lord Lamington, Prince Paul of Yugoslavia, George Gage, Lord Doune (the eldest brother of James Stuart) and John McEwen, from Marchmont, in Berwickshire, the brother of her great friend Katharine (later Countess of Scarbrough). And she also danced with James Stuart – a foxtrot, followed by a reel.

But soon afterwards news reached Glamis that Stuart had embarked on an affair with the very pretty but flighty Mollie Lascelles, described as a 'fresh affair', implying that there had been an earlier one. News of this entanglement received wider circulation than it should have done and, though Mollie was not staying at Glamis, she got into trouble with her girlfriends there, some of whom were disagreeable to her. Mollie then accused Helen Cecil of having broadcast it. Helen rebuked her for this.

Every social set contained at least one 'kind girl', as the 10th Duke of Marlborough described fast girls, who went further than their more cautious contemporaries. Mollie Lascelles was a fair-haired beauty, brave, outspoken, precocious. Cecil Beaton said her only imperfection was 'a nose like a Red Indian tomahawk'.[19] She was invariably in some scrape or other when young, and not only when young. In later life she was known as 'Midnight Mollie' on account of her adventurous private life, which included affairs with James Stuart (again), the foxhunter and well-known stud Tommy McDougal,* and even the Duke of Kent. She enjoyed a curious later-life romance with the aesthetic Alan Pryce-Jones, who eventually moved to Newport, Rhode Island, some said to escape her.† She was only half amused when Sir Frederick Ponsonby, the King's Treasurer, described her as 'rackety' after overhearing her account of a 'harmless ball' near Windsor, in which she said how lovely it had been 'in the down, over the Thames'.[20]

Some say that Elizabeth never spoke to her again. Yet she was one of the Duchesses who carried the canopy at her Coronation in 1937. In widowhood Mollie would proudly announce that she had been the Queen Mother's rival in love for James Stuart.[21] This rivalry caused warning bells to sound. Lady Cynthia Colville, one of Queen Mary's ladies-in-waiting, and a contemporary of May Elphinstone, wrote of Elizabeth's admirers:

> It was commonly believed . . . that she found it difficult to decide upon which of them to bestow her ultimate favour; not because she was by nature flirtatious, but on the contrary, because she felt that marriage was desperately important and irrevocable. Indecision on her part was countered by similar changes of front among many of the young men of her acquaintance.[22]

This was a coded reference to Stuart.

The vacillating Stuart arrived at Balmoral on 12 September to go in waiting on the Duke of York. Hardinge reported: 'He was v. much upset at having got Mollie Lascelles into trouble. I assured him that it was of no consequence, and that it was quite a matter of routine with her! What a nice thing to say, but he took it very well!'[23] Hardinge was aware that women were irresistibly drawn to Stuart. 'You won't let James cut me out, will you, Helen? He is so attractive that there would be every justification for it. If you were like Mollie Lascelles life would not be worth living for me, and I should come to an untimely end in the Dee.'[24]

The house party at Glamis consisted of Elizabeth's brother Mike, Lord Doune ('nice but too odd'),[25] Prince Paul, George Gage and Tom Bevan

---

* Major T. McDougal, MC (1895–1950), MFH of the Berkshire Hounds. He counted Lady Diana Cooper and Loelia, Duchess of Westminster, among his conquests.
† The present author recalls seeing them dining à deux in the Travellers' Club in the 1980s, more Pryce-Jones's venue than hers.

('rather a friend of Elizabeth's'),[26] and various girls, including Lady Katharine (Katie) Hamilton, daughter of the 3rd Duke of Abercorn, Lady Doris Gordon-Lennox, Diamond Hardinge, Hilda Blackburn, Bettine Malcolm,* Grisell Cochrane-Baillie and Adele Biddulph,† who, with Helen Cecil, made up the 'Chorus'. Helen set the scene:

Elizabeth is playing 'Oh Hell' on the piano on purpose for me & Diamond is singing it which is most distracting! Now they've switched off into another tune which is better! We are sitting in Elizabeth's sitting room. It is such a nice & friendly place even in this overwhelming house. The men, of whom there are only 4 have been safely disposed of for the day with the exception of Lord Gage who is to be seen off by the chorus (*us*, you'll be surprised to hear) later on . . .

Last night I was terribly sleepy & had to sit next to Lord Strathmore who is charming, but *very* deaf which meant rather hard work & a silence always fell just as one was shouting any platitude that came into one's head! It was awful & half way through dinner he seized me by the arm to ask me to pass something, thinking that I was Elizabeth & I nearly got the giggles.

After dinner Elizabeth, D [Doris], & Adele Biddulph all came to my room to talk but we did not stay up late because everyone was so sleepy.

It is very nice being here & Elizabeth is the *greatest* darling. She has been so nice tho' I have hardly seen her alone at all yet. She asked if you couldn't come to stay but I told her that was not possible & she quite understands about my coming over on Thursday. In fact she understands everything & I love her!

Diamond has had a huge success here & enjoyed it wildly. She's in glorious form & keeps us all in fits of laughter . . . You should see her with Lord Strathmore whom, even you, could not accuse of being a 'young ass'. She's *so* good with him, in fact she is with everyone.

There are some odd tales of last week's party, going about . . .[27]

Elizabeth arranged a car to convey Helen to Braemar for the day later in the week and insisted that she stay on for the Duke of York's visit.

---

* Bettine Malcolm (1900–73), married 1922, Captain Robert Somerset. She was the mother of the 11th Duke of Beaufort.
† Hon. Adelaide Biddulph (1901–85), known as 'Dig', married 1929, Henry Vincent Yorke (1905–73), the novelist Henry Green. The Queen Mother was godmother to her son, Sebastian Yorke, a role she shared with Maurice Bowra. They later lost touch.

There was an excursion to Airlie Castle, and 'violent' mealtime banter about the merits of Eton versus Harrow, Elizabeth and Helen supporting the former, while Diamond opted for Harrow – 'I don't think this comes at all well from you, Helen,' said Diamond to shrieks of laughter. They then pitted the Grenadiers versus the Coldstream Guards.[28]

On 16 September Elizabeth's godmother, Mrs Arthur James,* descended on Glamis, producing 'an uncomfortable atmosphere of unrest tho' she is very amusing with it all. She & Lord Strathmore played a game of bo-peep round & round the big screen this morning after breakfast which was very comic!'[29]

The 'Dear Duke' was due to arrive on 18 September. Plans for his visit began to preoccupy Elizabeth and were further complicated by the news that his sister, Princess Mary, was planning to come over from Airlie Castle on Saturday. Elizabeth suggested that they should all dance in order to entertain Princess Mary, but then the princess decided to come for the day on Sunday instead.

On Friday 17 September Elizabeth took Helen with her when they collected her brother David from where he was staying about twenty-five miles away. Elizabeth was aware that Helen was enduring a long separation from her fiancé, but said to her: 'You don't look very unhappy, Helen. I've never seen anyone so beaming with happiness, you're full of beams!'[30] Helen then described their day:

It was very nice & David was so pleased to get away that he began shouting for joy almost before we'd left the front door, while Elizabeth with her usual tact waved to the host & hostess who were watching our departure. We played the fool all the way back. Elizabeth & David L. are so nice together. On arrival we rang the bell & asked if Lady Strathmore was at home.

David L. told the chauffeur that he was the most dangerous driver he'd ever seen & then accused the footmen of dropping his gun case on to his, David's, foot after which he insisted on their carrying him into the house as he was too injured to walk. Elizabeth & I laughed so much we could hardly get upstairs.

I quite like Mike Lyon after all & he is so funny! They played tennis yesterday evening & Mrs James played too. Everyone lost

*Venetia Cavendish-Bentinck (1863–1948), daughter of Rt Hon. George Cavendish-Bentinck, Judge Advocate-General, married Arthur James, MVO (1853–1917), of Coton House, Rugby. She was a second cousin of Lady Strathmore. An unashamed snob, she once dismissed a house party as 'mangy – only one viscount and one baronet'. Mrs Ronnie Greville surprised a group by declaring that she did not like her, 'because she was such a snob!'.

their tempers over the score until they looked at Mrs J. & then they were so consumed with laughter that they could not go on quarrelling!

Elizabeth & Mr [Michael] Lyon dined at Airlie last night. He had to be dragged there by main force! . . .

Mrs J. was being very patronising to Lady S. yesterday about D. Lyon's looks & saying what a 'pretty boy' he was etc etc! Lady S. said quite quietly 'yes & he's a very nice one too, which is better!' I love Lady S.

There is a *fearful* fuss over tonight & the weekend in general. We are to have reels & all sorts of strange wild things tonight which will be awful.[31]

Meanwhile, the Duke of York had left Balmoral to stay with The Mackintosh* at Moy Hall, Inverness, where he attended the Inverness Gathering, presented some colours and distributed various decorations. Lord Gage, Diamond Hardinge and Adele Biddulph left Glamis, but Elizabeth's sister, Rose Leveson-Gower, arrived as did Lord Carnegie, the tall Scots Guards officer from Kinnaird Castle, and heir to the Earldom of Southesk, who would presently join the Royal Family in unusual circumstances.

As the hour of the Duke's arrival approached, the house party became on edge, and any sudden noise made them think it was the approach of his car. The 'Dear Duke' duly arrived with James Stuart in attendance, an ironic situation.

On the first night they danced 'strange wild things' – reels and ordinary dances. Lady Airlie and Mrs James performed sliding races up and down the slippery floor, which caused great amusement, while Doris and Katie Hamilton were caught in the middle of an adept dual impersonation of their 'eminent visitors'. They were 'in full swing when P.A. came round the screen & nobody could warn them that they were rushing to their fate!'[32]

The house party was given strict instructions to be punctual for breakfast, which introduced further strain. Helen was the only one who coped, and made herself useful by singing hymn choruses to the Duke of York, which made him laugh.

The party went 'with a roar'. On Sunday they played tennis during the day, went to chapel in the afternoon, had tea and then Princess Mary arrived from Airlie Castle with Lady Joan Mulholland, a war widow, in attendance.

---

* The Mackintosh (1851–1938), Alfred Donald Mackintosh, Chief of the Clan Chattan, Lord-Lieutenant of Inverness. He owned 124,000 acres.

Before dinner they played 'every kind of wild & exhausting game both indoors & out'. After dinner Helen reported that they sang 'the most appalling songs at the *very* top of our voices & nearly brought Glamis Castle down altogether! They sang "Oh Hell" & everybody sang it at me especially Prince A. who did it with more gusto than any of them. It really was rather alarming!!'[33]

In the evening Helen tried to slip away 'but several people disappeared & Elizabeth's signals of distress were so obvious that it would have been beastly to go away'.

James Stuart was the quiet star of the party as usual, Helen finding him 'quite delightful . . . I wonder he isn't spoilt with all the women making such fools of themselves over his good looks'. Late in the evening, Elizabeth, Doris, Katie and Helen dropped him a deep curtsey on the stairs in a chorus row, and went upstairs by candlelight, where, terrified of being discovered, they made apple-pie beds for him and for young David.[34]

The Duke was thoroughly amiable throughout his visit. At breakfast on the Monday morning everyone was hoarse from the singing the night before. Helen took up the story once more:

> We all went out for a walk this morning after breakfast in the bitter cold. Elizabeth & Prince A. were allowed to go on miles ahead which agitated the former rather but *we* thought ourselves rather tactful!
>
> The humbler members of the party ran races & played the fool. I was included in that happy lot. Doris, Katie & I hid most successfully from Lord D, Captain Stuart, Mr Lyon & David L. & then stalked them. They retaliated in the meanest possible way afterwards by waiting on our path & throwing mud at us. They were terribly good shots too, tho' I pointed out how bad they were at the time, & we got badly defeated I'm afraid. Doris was awfully courageous, but I'm ashamed to say we did not support her very well. Captain Stuart was trying to revenge his apple-pie bed which seemed to rankle with him rather! Everybody emerged from the contest quite filthy & was then hurried into the house to say goodbye to P.A. who was looking *too* immaculate for words.[35]

The Duke returned to Balmoral, bearing a letter from Helen to Alec Hardinge, which he promised to deliver without telling anyone. He intercepted Alec on the way to his bath and handed it over. 'I discovered that he thoroughly and genuinely enjoyed himself,'[36] wrote the young Private Secretary. At Glamis everyone relaxed and there were no further incidents other than Lady Strathmore plying the guests with port before they left. At least this kept them warm on their journeys.

It is clear from the veiled references to Elizabeth's anxious signals on the Sunday evening, and her agitation when left to walk alone with the Duke, that she was not keen to encourage his interest. The reasons for this have been clarified over the years.

Helen Cecil knew the story intimately. In a later book she defined the reasons as follows: first, Elizabeth came from a large, unusually happy and 'extremely tight-knit' family; she was reluctant to leave the 'almost idyllic' life she had led between her family's three homes; she was further reluctant because it meant exchanging the informal country atmosphere in which she had been raised for the 'relentless duties of a member of the Royal Family'. And it meant that, as the wife of a royal Prince, she would be plunged into public life, and she was uncomfortable at having to enter a situation where 'privacy would have to take second place to her husband's work for the nation'.[37]

Perhaps significantly, Helen wrote: 'Lady Elizabeth had had nothing against the Duke himself',[38] which hints at a lack of positive enthusiasm. This was a confusing time for Elizabeth since she had a host of admirers to choose from.

What Elizabeth did not yet appreciate was that the Duke of York had set himself on a determined course. From this he never wavered.

For the Duke the house party at Glamis stood out as a highlight of his summer. His life at Balmoral that summer had been deadly dull. The King and Queen had their traditionally elderly house party, the content of which never varied from one year to another. Figures such as Lord Esher, Harry Stonor, Lady Joan Verney and Princess Mary's spinster lady-in-waiting, Dorothy Yorke, were civil but uninspiring company for young princes.

At one lunch Prince George ignored and virtually turned his back on his asthmatic cousin, Princess Maud, who was deemed the occupational hazard of life at Balmoral, since she and her dull mother, the Princess Royal, were forever descending on the castle from nearby Mar Lodge. Any encounter with the Fife family was dreaded by the Household. ·

Desperate evening entertainments involved Queen Mary, Princess Mary, the Duke of York and Lord Stamfordham, the King's Private Secretary, entertaining the house party with songs, 'an event quite without precedent'.[39]

Other features of that Balmoral summer were the Braemar Games – 'from all accounts the worst among the numerous deadly functions of the year!'[40] – visits by the Archbishop of York and Sir Walter Lawrence,* and the arrival of the King's elderly uncle, the Duke of Connaught, who gamely went out stalking though he could not 'hit a haystack at 50 yds!'.†[41]

No significance was placed on the Duke of York's visit to Glamis. Alec Hardinge, longing to see Helen, wrote: 'Oh the lucky brute – and it means *so* little to him, and all the world to me, and I cannot go.'[42] To outsiders the Duke's visit was nothing more than a welcome escape from the confines of Balmoral. On 28 September he went south to shoot with Lord Pembroke at Wilton.

Hardly had he left than James Stuart returned to Glamis, ostensibly to shoot.

---

* Sir Walter Lawrence (1857–1940), Indian civil servant, Private Secretary to Lord Curzon, Viceroy of India. Chief of Staff to the then Prince and Princess of Wales on their tour of India in 1905–6.
† One day Alec Hardinge heard 'some shooting like a machine-gun, so I expect the D. of Connaught is blazing away. He never hits anything [save] by chance!' (Hardinge to Helen Cecil, 27 September 1920).

4

The Proposals

'That bitch Queen Mary, that cow, she ruined my life!'
– James Stuart

The Duke of York made two unsuccessful bids for Elizabeth's hand, the first in the spring of 1921, and the second soon after Princess Mary's wedding in 1922. The final proposal in January 1923 was accepted.

We know from Helen Hardinge that it took the Duke 'years of persistent courtship and repeated proposals' before Elizabeth 'finally accepted him'.[1] Nor have the official biographers contradicted this. Sir John Wheeler-Bennett wrote: 'There were uncertainties and delays and, although the Duke pressed his suit with dogged pertinacity, he had to be a patient suitor for over two years.'[2]

The first time that George V became aware of Elizabeth was at the wedding of Helen Cecil to Alec Hardinge at St Paul's, Knightsbridge, on 8 February 1921. The King and Queen were there as friends of old Lord Hardinge of Penshurst, and Elizabeth was one of the bridesmaids, dressed in love-in-the-mist blue tulle, with Diamond Hardinge, Doris Gordon-Lennox, Mollie Lascelles and one other. Arthur Penn, another of Elizabeth's admirers, was best man, and the Duke of York and Princess Mary were guests.

The King and Queen had every reason to examine that particular bridesmaid with interest. After the war the Prime Minister (at that time David Lloyd George) had told the King that he would not tolerate any foreign alliances for sons of the Royal House. In the post-war world, an alliance with a German princely house was unthinkable, and England was going through a somewhat xenophobic phase. Queen Mary told Lady Airlie: 'I don't think Bertie will be sorry to hear that. I have discovered that he is very much attracted to Lady Elizabeth Bowes-Lyon. He's always talking about her. She seems a charming girl but I don't know her very well.'[3]

Having been born into a morganatic branch of the Württemberg Royal Family, Queen Mary was deeply conscious of royal alliances, but she was aware that although Elizabeth was only a Scottish aristocrat, she did at least descend twice over from the Kings of Scotland, not to mention Henry VII. That made a difference.

It is interesting that it was to a relatively small area of Scotland that the Royal Family looked in quest of royal consorts – Elizabeth for the Duke of York, Lord Carnegie for Princess Maud and Lady Alice Scott for the Duke of Gloucester. All were friends and contemporaries, and lived to be 101, 98 and 102 respectively.

Lady Airlie was a confidante of the shy, young Duke of York, and, according to her memoirs, both he and Elizabeth took to dropping in on her at her flat, 56 Ashley Gardens, to touch on the matter. Lady Airlie found Elizabeth 'frankly doubtful, uncertain of her feelings, and afraid of the public life which would be ahead of her', while the Duke was 'deeply in love but so humble'.

Lady Airlie stated categorically that the first proposal came in the spring of 1921. Elizabeth turned the Duke down, leaving him disconsolate. Lady Strathmore wrote to Lady Airlie: 'I do hope he will find a nice wife who will make him happy. I like him so much and he is a man who will be made or marred by his wife.'⁴ Lord Strathmore disapproved of royalty. He thought Edward VII was too stout and told Robert Sencourt: 'If there is one thing I have determined for my children, it is that they shall never have any sort of post about the Court.'⁵

Mothers like Lady Strathmore operate by stealth. She was determined that Elizabeth would remain single until she accepted her royal suitor. In those days parents still controlled the fate of their daughters. Rival suitors would be rebuffed.

In April 1921 Elizabeth went over to Paris to stay with Diamond Hardinge, whose widowed father was British Ambassador in Paris. Diamond was 'a madcap, a tomboy, clumsy in her movements'. She once ordered that the bread rolls for an important lunch be baked in the shape of frogs. She had perfected the art of cracking her jaw with a loud report, and frequently did so in public places like the theatre.⁶ What better friend and place to escape to had Elizabeth just turned down the Duke's proposal?

Elizabeth was intrigued to discover that old Lord Hardinge had a mistress, who gave her husband the slip and came to stay at the Embassy. Elizabeth endured the diplomatic functions, but she and Diamond prevailed upon Anastasia Cheetham, the Russian wife of the minister Sir Milne Cheetham, to arrange more amusing expeditions in the company of the young secretaries. They went to the Foire de Neuilly where they descended the chute in a barrel, and Elizabeth expressed the wish to visit the Acacia, a short-lived nightclub lately opened by Elsa Maxwell in partnership with the couturier Captain Edward Molyneux. This club should have been a huge success, because all the plans were well devised. A rented room at 7 rue des Acacias could accommodate fifty people, though sometimes took in three hundred. Elsa and the captain sat at tables flanking the entrance, personally vetting all those who were admitted. Word was spread that this was the most exclusive club in Paris. As Elsa put it: 'Soon the social élite were clamouring to get into the place.'⁷ Clifton Webb, an excellent dancer long before he was taken up by Hollywood, danced there, and a Hungarian girl called Jenny Dole made a spectacular entrance each night, bedecked in a cape of gardenias.

Friends of Elizabeth asked 'Dickie' Fellowes-Gordon, Elsa's girlfriend, if she could arrange the visit. Dickie sent a message back saying that all Elizabeth had to do was to ask for Elsa's table. Dickie recalled: 'And she arrived with a young American millionaire* from Chicago, who obviously adored her and gazed at her throughout the evening. And she was her usual charming self and charmed everybody.'⁸

A visit to a nightclub was a rare treat for Elizabeth, easier to accomplish in Paris than in London. She returned home for the London season, though, perhaps significantly, not in time for the wedding of Mollie Lascelles to the Earl of Dalkeith, heir to the Duke of Buccleuch, on 21 April. She stayed for a last Ascot season with Lady Nina Balfour at Bisham, since Lady Nina was widowed on 31 August and never took the place again. Towards the end of July, Elizabeth danced at the Caledonian Ball in a group that included Lady Mida Scott and her younger sister Alice.

At the beginning of September, the Duke of York was joined by James Stuart when he stayed with the Ancasters at Drummond Castle, Crieff. They went on to Balmoral on 3 September.

Soon after this the royal party split up, Queen Mary going over to stay with Lady Airlie at Airlie Castle for a spirited tour of the local sights, while the King went to Moy Hall for a rather ponderous shooting party with The Mackintosh, where there was the habitual slaughter of grouse, seven hundred brace in one day. Then Queen Mary made an important manoeuvre.

On 9 September she descended on Glamis for the day, accompanied by Lady Airlie, with Derek Keppel in attendance. The visit came at a time when Lady Strathmore was developing cancer. The Queen found Elizabeth not only running the castle and acting as hostess, but also nursing her mother, at both of which tasks she was adept.

The visit enabled Queen Mary to inspect the set-up at Glamis and to examine the girl who was preoccupying her son's thoughts, and

---

* The American was one of the Armour family (possibly a grandson of Philip Danforth Armour, who had founded the largest pork-packing firm in the United States).

furthermore to emphasise that the Duke of York was to be taken seriously. 'I always felt that the visit to Glamis was inspired by her desire to help him,' wrote Lady Airlie, with supreme understatement, 'although she was much too tactful to let it be apparent.'[9]

Queen Mary came away convinced that Elizabeth was the right girl for Bertie, but she informed Lady Airlie: 'I shall say nothing to either of them. Mothers should never meddle in their children's love affairs.'[10]

But how much did she meddle in the business? Queen Mary's hand can be found in two matters which came to fruition in 1922: the departure of James Stuart and the selection of Elizabeth as a bridesmaid to Princess Mary at Westminster Abbey.

Stuart was a serious threat to any advancement of the Duke of York's cause. 'He was the love of her life'[11] is a comment attributed to a former courtier and a member of the Queen Mother's family,* and supported by Mabel Stringer, the Queen Mother's dresser, when she was interviewed in her nineties†: 'He was an absolute heart-throb and they fell for each other in a big way. It was obvious when you saw them together that they were madly in love.'[12]

Stuart ceased to be the Duke of York's equerry in 1921. In his rambling memoirs‡ he recalled that Sir Sidney Greville offered him a job with Lord Cowdray. The family company, Pearson, had vast commercial interests worldwide. Stuart was invited 'to go into the oil business as a learner at the production end in America, with a view to promotion to higher things after I was trained'.[13]

Greville had been a courtier to Edward VII, Queen Alexandra, George V and the Prince of Wales. His sister, Lady Eva Dugdale, was a lady-in-waiting to Queen Mary. He was well placed to do the Queen's bidding.

In January 1922 Stuart spent a few days at Glamis; he was the only visitor. Then he sailed to America, not quite knowing what to expect. He found himself employed in the oilfields of Oklahoma. He did not come home until 1923, by which time Elizabeth was engaged to the Duke.

Years later, in 1951, Stuart confirmed to Sir Anthony Nutting that it was Queen Mary who caused him to be sent away: 'That bitch Queen Mary, that cow, she ruined my life! I was in love with the Queen Mother and she with me, but Queen Mary wanted her for the Duke of York.'[14]

Stuart's son did not disagree: 'Certainly Lady Strathmore wanted my

---

* Lord Charteris and Lady Mary Clayton.
† Yet Mabel Stringer's story about Princess Mary and Lord Dalkeith being caught red-handed by an impromptu arrival of Queen Mary at Glamis is surely ludicrously far-fetched (see Grania Forbes, *My Darling Buffy*, pp. 157–9).
‡ Stuart's memoirs were ghosted by a professional ghost, Stephen Watts, at the behest of the publisher, Alexander Frere.

father out of the way. I think she was a friend of my Scottish grand-mother, the then Countess of Moray, and also of my English grandmother, the Duchess of Devonshire, who was then Queen Mary's Mistress of the Robes, and the mother of Rachel [Cavendish].'[15]

So Stuart's days were numbered when, on 24 September, with Queen Mary safely back at Balmoral, the Duke of York arrived for a week's stay at Glamis. This time the party consisted of Lord Strathmore, Michael, David, Rose and her husband, Wisp Leveson-Gower, Doris, Katie, Lady Mida Scott, the Hardinges, Godfrey Thomas and Arthur Penn. Lady Rachel Cavendish, who was later to marry Stuart, was also there.

From Glamis the Duke wrote to Queen Mary: 'It is delightful here & Elizabeth is very kind to me. The more I see of her the more I like her.'[16] His letters to Queen Mary after that time contained frequent references to her.

Then, in October 1921, Lady Strathmore had to undergo a hyster-ectomy from which she made a slow but good recovery. Elizabeth stayed on in Scotland to nurse her mother during her prolonged convalescence. Meanwhile, the Duke accompanied the Prince of Wales deer stalking at Dunrobin, and came south in October. By the end of 1921, he was no nearer his goal, but at least James Stuart was soon to be out of the way.

In the New Year Elizabeth was chosen as a bridesmaid to Princess Mary. The wedding came only three weeks after her paternal grand-mother, the Dowager Countess of Strathmore, died aged eighty-nine, on 5 February 1922.*

Princess Mary married Viscount Lascelles, heir to the 5th Earl of Hare-wood, at Westminster Abbey on 28 February. There is no doubt that Elizabeth was a friend of Princess Mary's, though not a close one, since King George V had not been aware of her until a year before. The selec-tion of bridesmaids was a way for the court to promote certain suitable young ladies as potential brides for the Duke of York. The candidates chosen were Elizabeth, Lady Doris Gordon-Lennox, Lady Rachel Cavendish and Lady Mary Thynne, daughter of the 5th Marquess of Bath.† The first three were all possible royal brides at one time or another.‡

---

* The Countess lived at 19 Hans Place with her unmarried daughter, Lady Maud Lyon. She was buried at Glamis on 10 February. In her later years she had survived a motor accident in which both her arms were broken. It was said that 'she retained her mind and strength of body in a remarkable manner to the end of her long life' (*The Lady*, 16 February 1922).
† The others were Princess Maud and Lady Mary Cambridge (later Duchess of Beaufort), who were first cousins, with younger trainbearers, Lady May Cambridge (later Abel Smith), another first cousin, and Lady Diana Bridgeman (later Abdy), daughter of the 5th Earl of Bradford.
‡ Lady Katharine (Katie) Hamilton, another obvious choice, was wintering in South Africa with her father, the Duke of Abercorn.

It could be argued that it was the Prince of Wales who was most in need of a bride, being still unmarried at the age of nearly twenty-six. However, he was away on a prolonged tour of India and Japan from which he did not return until 20 June. Thus he missed his sister's wedding. The Duke of York was in the Abbey, with his parents and his aged grandmother, Queen Alexandra, who needed a solicitous hand, readily given by the King.

The wedding took place on one of those bright, sunlit, early spring days. It was witnessed by an impressive crowd, many of whom had slept on the pavements overnight, and some of whom fainted or collapsed. The Archbishop of Canterbury's car got stuck in the wedding traffic, and a disobliging policeman attempted to divert it along the Embankment until the Archbishop told him he would take his number, at which point the PC mounted the vehicle and rode with it past the police cordon. There was further upset when the Archbishop arrived to be robed in the Jerusalem Chamber to discover a speck of blood on his collar from a shaving cut.

The bridal procession arrived. The Archbishop's chaplain described Princess Mary:

> The Princess looking straight and true and determined, with a real strength in her face, and beautifully dressed in white and silver, with a necklace of pearls and the whole shimmering, and a long train shining behind, borne by two bridesmaids, with the other six following behind.
>
> When [the ceremony] was over, the Archbishop, (bidding them follow) went back to his chair with me (who had stood immediately behind him all the while of the marriage); and the Bride and Groom came up towards the Altar, where they were to kneel. The two train-bearers in attendance, but the bridesmaids stood by the Altar still . . .[17]

Inspired by Elizabeth's performance at the Abbey, the Duke then made his second unsuccessful proposal. Again he was turned down. Stuart may have been out of the way, but he had been replaced by a new suitor.

In April, not long after Princess Mary's wedding, Elizabeth retreated to Glamis, not something she normally did at that time of the year.

There are two reasons for her retreat. First, her mother still needed her. Secondly, she wished to avoid the aftermath of the second proposal. This is confirmed by a cryptic message in a letter she wrote to James Stuart, then in New York, on 12 March, telling him that she was returning to Glamis, adding that the most extraordinary things had been happening to her in the past three weeks. She thought it probably a good thing to be away.[18]

This message disturbed Stuart, who was then languishing in a cheap hotel on East 55th Street, called Allerton House, where he occupied a cell-like room and shared a shower and WC with a friend. Her mention of 'extraordinary things' made him jealous, and he assumed that this was because 'you and Glenconner are seldom apart', as a friend had written to him, 'so I suppose it's that – or is it Michael? Not that it's any of my business but you know what a fool I am. I hope he's very nice.'[19]

The new suitor was Christopher, 2nd Lord Glenconner, a neighbour at Glen, in Scotland. That he was a serious contender is without doubt. He was named as one of six disappointed suitors by his brother Stephen, reclining in his bed as a corpulent recluse in 1980. And in 1981, before a luncheon with Lady Diana Cooper, the Queen Mother herself said: 'Oh! Stephen. I'd love to see him again. It brings back so many memories of when I was young . . . Christopher . . .'[20]

Christopher's niece, Pauline Rumbold, recalled that Christopher was very good-looking before he lost his hair, and was convinced that Elizabeth wanted to marry him. That she did not do so was because her parents disapproved. Their overriding reason was that they knew the Duke of York was in love with her. Their further reservation was that Lord Glenconner came from a family only lately ennobled. His father, Edward Tennant, had only been created a peer in 1911 and was the most junior Baron present at George V's Coronation.[21]

Christopher Glenconner was the most straightforward and sensible member of a wildly eccentric family. They lived in Queen Anne's Gate in London, at Glen, an enormous mock-baronial house in Peebleshire, and at the romantic Wilsford Manor in the winding Avon Valley, just south of Amesbury. The house was presided over by Christopher's mother, Lady Glenconner, the former Pamela Wyndham,* a 'Soul' with all the whimsical ideas of that set, a poetess, a writer, a mystic, the devoted friend and neighbour of the spiritualist Sir Oliver Lodge.

Elizabeth entirely understood Pamela as she herself was in the Pamela mould, both literary and poetic, while governed by an iron will. Cecil Beaton described Pamela as 'gracious and queenly as a fairy godmother', and recorded that she would speak of a woman who wanted to have diamonds studded in her teeth so that she could even say 'Good morning' brilliantly.[22]

---

* On 4 June 1922, Pamela quietly married Viscount Grey of Fallodon, the former Foreign Secretary.

Elizabeth relished her visits to Wilsford, which offered the best of Wiltshire life – village gardens filled with roses and Sweet William, the air scented with hay, the distant sound of sheep-bells, and within that house of chequer flint and stone, with its mullioned windows, the conversation rapid and inspired, sometimes electric, sometimes so lyrical as to defy belief. The Queen Mother remembered that Christopher's brother Stephen 'used to ride over the downs in a carriage, thinking lovely thoughts or whatever one did in those days',[23] while the young Tennants liked to sleep out in the garden but would come in around midnight 'shrugging with cold'.[24]

It was hardly a real world, more a world of dreams and mystery. Pamela wrote: 'There is a super-sensible world as well as a physical world, just as there is a spiritual body as well as a physical body.'[25] She dabbled in spiritualism with her bearded neighbour, Sir Oliver Lodge, who called her his 'sympathetic friend and kindly neighbour'.[26] Together they searched for contact with her son, Bim, killed in the war. Elizabeth found Wilsford 'most entrancing' and retained 'such *vivid* memories' of visiting Lodge at Normanton House, at nearby Lake.[27]

The actress Hermione Baddeley who later married David Tennant, the brother between Christopher and Stephen in age, and the mother of Pauline, recalled meeting Elizabeth with Christopher and David and how the two brothers were amused that both girls were small in stature. They made them stand back-to-back and then argued as to which was the taller. 'Eventually they decided there wasn't a whisker of difference.'[28]

The same evening David Tennant told Hermione how keen Christopher was on Elizabeth. She had seen it too and predicted wedding bells. Sir Steven Runciman confirmed: 'He was rather hoping to be engaged to her.'[29] Hermione Baddeley's version of the end of the relationship was that Christopher was intent on proposing and even armed himself with a wedding ring, but when the moment came he said nothing. She put this down to Christopher having been unexpectedly called to do a tour of duty in the Navy. Whether Queen Mary had been dabbling in naval matters on this occasion is not clear.

Pauline Rumbold recalled that at Colin Tennant's wedding in 1956 a room at Holkham was set aside for the Queen Mother to sit and have a private chat with Christopher. Into this room Pauline strayed inadvertently and there they were happily reminiscing about olden times.

Periods of indecision do not make for happiness and while Elizabeth continued to move about in society, she knew that the state could not last indefinitely. Her mother was set on her marrying into royalty, then considered the highest marital victory.

Elizabeth continued to hunt, riding well to hounds, and she cut a notable figure at the Berwickshire Hunt Ball. Most of her tastes were outdoor ones. She was a keen lawn tennis player, and she enjoyed reading and music. Contemporary observers noted that she was said to be 'an exceptionally beautiful dancer, even in these days, when good dancers abound'.[30]

She remained conventional, in no sense modern, but with a hint of the picturesque in her clothes, and her own slightly individual style. She was considered unaffected and generally liked. She had a particularly fine complexion, wore her dark hair parted in the middle and sported a fringe. Her radiant smile was her best feature, and was used to good advantage. Her voice was low-toned, and her inner intelligence, even determination, was expressed in her deep-blue eyes, which were thickly fringed with dark lashes and gave her what Cecil Beaton later called a thrush-like beauty.

There were other suitors. Doris's brother, the heir to the Duke of Richmond, was an admirer. He drove her to a pub near Goodwood and once took her out for a drive, but, cars being what they were, they only reached Croydon before having to turn back. The stream of admirers, serious or otherwise, included Freddie Dalrymple-Hamilton, who dropped in regularly for lunch at St James's Square, confident that an extra place was always laid for such an outcome, Arthur Penn, to whom she confided her doubts and fears about marrying the Duke of York, and Bruce Ogilvy, son of Lady Airlie.

A further phalanx of admirers included the Oxford ménage of Lord Gage and Prince Paul of Yugoslavia, to which 'Chips' Channon was appended. They met Elizabeth through her brother, Michael, who was at Oxford with them, and with Lady Nina Balfour, whose son, Archie, was there. Gage, Channon and Prince Paul shared a house in Mount Street in London, after coming down from Christ Church, causing jokes about 'Mr and Mrs Chips, or Lord and Lady Gage'.*[31]

George ('Grubby') Gage was in love with her. He lived at Firle Place, a lovely Elizabethan house in Sussex. Elizabeth went there often, and Chips Channon commented: 'Poor Gage is desperately fond of her – in vain, for he is far too heavy, too Tudor and squirearchical for so rare and patrician a creature as Elizabeth.'[32]

---

* When Neil Balfour was researching his biography of Prince Paul, the Queen Mother invited him to lunch at Clarence House. He advanced the opinion that all Prince Paul's friends seemed to have been queers. 'They may have been,' she retorted, 'but they were decent people.' He was not asked again.

Gage's father loved the fresh air, while his mother, an asthmatic, did not, so windows were forever being opened and closed at Firle. The family had nineteen servants and twelve gardeners, and the hall contained two stuffed crocodiles, a tiger skin and a mantrap. Heads, horns, swords and spears adorned the walls, and when the young George first attended daily prayers he sat in a seat, the back of which sported entwined antelope horns. The family did not entertain much, other than shooting parties, but every now and then the blind Landgraf of Hesse came for a visit.

Gage succeeded his father in 1912, and his mother died in 1915, by which time he was serving in the war. He had transferred from the 5th Sussex Territorials to the Coldstream Guards, just before most of the former were wiped out, and, like Fergus Bowes-Lyon, he took part in the Battle of Loos. Of his wartime experiences he wrote: 'I did not feel at all Homeric in that ocean of mud.'[33] Seriously wounded in 1917, he was nevertheless strong enough to carry a Colour in victory marches both in Paris and London. He left the Army in 1919. By the time he was one of Elizabeth's suitors, he was Master of Firle, 'somewhat battered about, sadder, but perhaps not wiser than I might have been if I had not been through all this, . . . facing my share of post-war Britain'.[34] In old age, Gage recalled: 'I loved her *madly* but really madly. You've no idea what a *wag* she was, so full of witty teasing and captivating jokes.'[35]

His close friend Chips Channon also promoted himself as having been 'a little in love with her'.[36] He stayed at Glamis in the summer of 1922, when the Duke of York was there, and on a rainy afternoon pretended that he could read cards. He predicted 'a great and glamorous royal future'. Elizabeth laughed, 'for it was obvious that the Duke of York was much in love with her'.[37]

Channon was no suitor. Years later the Queen Mother said: 'I was too much the Quaker girl for him. Not smart enough.' She also recalled that the King could not stand him. 'Once Chips's house had been lent for a wedding reception that we were invited to. He quite firmly dropped me on the pavement – wouldn't come in.'[38]

Prince Paul was another matter. Elizabeth had visited him at Christ Church, taken there with four other young beauties by Lady Nina Balfour. Prince Paul thought Elizabeth the prettiest girl in England. He also contemplated her friend Doris Gordon-Lennox, but, after a fight with her at Glamis, had to renounce that idea.

As early as 1921 he invited Elizabeth to call him by his Christian name. When she was in Paris in April 1921 he wrote to say how much he missed her and hoped she would still be there by the time he arrived from

Belgrade on 24 May, 'as I am simply longing to see you again & also we might have some of our fast parties in the gay French metropolis'.[39]

Then there was the enigmatic figure of Archibald ('Archie') Clark Kerr, a somewhat older figure, born in 1882. He was in the Foreign Office. As third secretary in Berlin in September 1908, he had fallen for Crown Princess Sophie of Greece. Dancing with her, he was 'almost persuaded to think that the pleasure was shared by her – so completely did she resign herself to my grasp'.[40] He went to her bedroom later, but was frustrated to find her sister with her.

Clark Kerr spotted Elizabeth at a dance given by Lady Islington, when he was on leave from Cairo in the summer of 1922. Meeting her two days later, he described her as 'wonderful, so beautiful, and so, so gentle – of the stuff of dreams, the voice and the spirit of the thing I had been hoping and waiting for for years'.[41]

Some years later Clark Kerr said: 'All my life I have been beset, or perhaps I should say tormented, by a very lively imagination. It has carried me eagle-like into very exalted and unexpected places, where it has a habit of dumping me and allowing me to roll quietly down to the sort of level to which I naturally belong.'[42] He came to believe he might be a successful suitor, though he was forty and Elizabeth twenty-two.

They met several times and found much in common, notably a love for Scotland. While he was staying in Angus, Elizabeth invited him for lunch at Glamis on 31 August, assuring him that he would be met by 'a large but rather uncertain motor car which was once green', and alerting him to the fact that the only other guests would be two cousins who never spoke above a whisper.[43]

More letters were exchanged, but after Glamis his chances with her were slim. Had she married him, she would have become Ambassadress in Sweden, Iraq, China, Russia and the United States. She would also have been the wife of a man who was an expert on classical and modern erotica, and who shocked Harold Nicolson by painting nude models.

The Duke and Elizabeth saw each other from time to time during the summer season of 1922. Doris Gordon-Lennox reported that on the evening of 26 June the Duke had dined with 'all the gang' at Claridge's:

> They all danced afterwards & when he was going away 4 or 5 of them came to see him off. He said a ceremonious goodnight to them & then, signing to Elizabeth, said 'Get in' pointing to his car which was waiting. Elizabeth tripped in the royal-auto & they departed together about 1 o'clock in the morning!![44]

Though this was a clear sign that the Duke could be assertive when necessary, it was not enough.

Elizabeth and the Duke were among the fifty guests at the Duchess of Northumberland's dinner at Syon, which was followed by a dance. Both were at Lady Curzon's dinner dance for four hundred for the coming out of Lord Curzon's youngest daughter, Alexandra ('Baba'). Parties, meetings, punctuated by royal engagements, all added to the uncertainty of the situation.

The matter was made worse by 'the failure of the Stamfordham mission to Glamis'.[45] In an ill-conceived move, the King had sent his Private Secretary over to ascertain the Duke of York's chances, in effect to propose on his behalf. That kind of testing of the water is entirely consistent with court manoeuvring. The Duke of York was 'overwhelmed'[46] at the outcome of this – a stern rebuff. The Duke descended into a state of increasing despair, as he was inclined to do. His stalwart Comptroller, Louis Greig, came to the rescue.

On 25 July the Duke carried out an engagement in France, which was to prove significant. He crossed the Channel in the destroyer *Versatile* to lay the foundation stone of the War Memorial at Dunkirk. Lord Athlone and various admirals were with him.

The Duke was only on French soil for two hours, and, after drives and speeches and many a toast drunk in sweet champagne, he returned to *Versatile*. As the guns thundered their farewell, the Duke repaired to the wardroom, where Greig steered John Davidson, the young MP who was accompanying the party, to the Duke's side. The two men spent three hours in deep conversation. Greig knew that Davidson had been turned down by his wife several times before successfully persuading her to marry him.*

Davidson found a deeply unhappy man, with a huge worry assailing him. The Duke spoke to him of the difficulties of being a King's son and various abstract problems of life, before coming to the point. Davidson's account, written after the King died in 1952, explained:

> He declared that he was desperately in love, but that he was in despair for it seemed quite certain that he had lost the only woman he would ever marry. I told him that however black the situation looked he must not give up hope; that my wife had refused me consistently before she finally said yes, and that like him, if she

---

* Thus Davidson let loose on the world Hon. Frances Dickinson, a lady who herself became an MP, and later the formidable Baroness Northchurch, DBE, in her own right. They were married in 1919.

had persisted in her refusal, I would never have married anyone else.

To this he replied that his case was different from mine. The King's son cannot propose to the girl he loves, since custom requires that he must not place himself in the position of being refused, and to that ancient custom, the King, his father, firmly adhered. Worse still, I gathered that an emissary had already been sent to ascertain whether the girl was prepared to marry him, and that it had failed. The question was, what was he to do? He could not live without her, and certainly he would never marry anyone else.

The advice which I ventured to give him was simple. I suggested that in the Year of Grace 1922 no high-spirited girl of character was likely to accept a proposal made at second-hand; if she was fond of him as he thought she was, he must propose to her himself . . . His mood when we parted was much brighter and more buoyant than at the beginning of our talk.[47]

This is a very odd and by no means convincing account. History does not support the theory that royal princes do not propose in person. Harold Nicolson, the official biographer, wrote that George V (then Duke of York) proposed in person to Princess May of Teck in the garden of his sister, the Duchess of Fife, at East Sheen, on 3 May 1893. However, he was expecting a positive response, both parties having been well prepared. We know too that Queen Victoria proposed to Prince Albert. There are enough contemporary accounts of the Duke of York having made more than one unsuccessful proposal to Elizabeth. But, whatever the exact circumstances, the Davidson nudge was clearly beneficial.

When King George VI died in 1952, Davidson wrote to the Queen Mother to tell her of the conversation aboard *Versatile*, explaining that at that moment 'the fences seemed unjumpable, if he rode at it with determination and confidence and threw his heart over it, he would land safely and win his bride'. Furthermore he remembered saying: 'If she accepts, go straight to your mother, and if your mother is like mine, she will square the King.'[48]

The Queen Mother replied to Davidson:

I wanted to send you my heartfelt thanks for your thoughtfulness in writing so charmingly of such a personal and poignant episode . . . I must tell you that we were ideally happy, due to the King's wonderful kindness & goodness and thought for others. I never wanted to be with anyone but him, & during the last ten terrible years, he was a rock of strength and wisdom & courage. So that in thanking you for your letter, I thank you also for the advice you gave the King in 1922.[49]

In the late summer Elizabeth stayed a few days with her sister May Elphinstone at Carberry, and witnessed Princess Mary open the Memorial Club in Edinburgh to the Royal Scots (the regiment of her brother Michael and of James Stuart) as their Colonel-in-Chief. The Duke of York also headed north to Balmoral, eventually joining his parents at Balmoral.

Then came the Glamis house party at which the Duke was a guest, as was Prince Paul. Lady Airlie invited them over to a dance at the Masonic Hall, to which Elizabeth came, her dress 'fashioned in fuchsia taffetas on Early Victorian lines'. The first dance was an old-fashioned eightsome reel in which they all joined with zest, though Elizabeth 'had at times to prompt her partner, the Duke not being too intimately acquainted with all the intricate steps of this Highland dance'.[50]

There has long been the notion that one of the reasons Elizabeth was reluctant to accept the Duke of York was that if she was to submit to a royal marriage then it would be with the Prince of Wales, a more glamorous prospect than his shy younger brother.

There is some evidence to support this. Even late into 1922, Elizabeth was still resisting the Duke, while in October there came an opportunity for her to test her chances with the Prince of Wales. The Prince had taken a hunting box at Easton Grey, near Malmesbury, in Wiltshire and was hunting in that neighbourhood for some weeks.

On 27 October Elizabeth attended the coming-out ball of Lady Patricia Herbert at Wilton. Patricia had been reluctant to have such a ball and only agreed to it if her forty-nine-year-old friend Mildred Olivier,* sister of the novelist Edith Olivier, would share the ball with her. Elizabeth stayed with the Pembrokes for this small dance in a house party that included the Duke and Duchess of Sutherland, Lady Cranborne, Lady Rachel Cavendish, Lady Alexandra Curzon, Lady Mary Hope, Prince Serge Obolensky, Lord David Cecil and Lord Anglesey. Forty-six guests sat at round tables for dinner. The gold plate was used and 'lilies-of-the-valley, with their pale green leaves were set in the golden vases and epergnes'.

---

* Mildred Olivier (1875–1924), daughter of Revd Canon Dacres Olivier, Rector of Wilton and Canon of Salisbury Cathedral.

At the ball which followed the Prince of Wales danced two or three times with Patricia Herbert. He also spent time sitting out with Elizabeth. Mildred Olivier's niece, Rosemary, recalled seeing Elizabeth with the Prince, the two of them laughing their heads off together, the picture of happiness. Such was the scene that there was every reason to suppose that romance might be in the air.[51]

But had Elizabeth been contemplating the Prince of Wales as a husband, she would soon have realised there was to be no luck in that quarter. After a few hours' sleep he went back to his hunting at Biddestone and made no attempt to see her again. Elizabeth retreated to London.

On 13 December the relentless society hostess Mrs Ronald Greville gave a dinner and dance at which the Duke of York was present, as was Elizabeth, in a frock of silver tissue. Christmas dispersed the families as usual.

The dawn of 1923 found the King at York Cottage, Queen Alexandra in the Big House, with her sister, the Dowager Empress of Russia, and other assorted royalty in the vicinity. The King's sons spent their time hunting with the West Norfolk and attending parties. Presently the Duke of York returned to London.

On 5 January Elizabeth was staying with George Gage at Firle, when the *Daily Star* announced the imminent engagement of the Prince of Wales to 'the daughter of a well-known Scottish peer, who is the owner of castles both north and south of the Tweed'[52] – clearly Elizabeth. Gage, Channon and the others in the house party thought it great fun: 'We all bowed and bobbed and teased her, calling her "Ma'am"',[53] which upset her. That evening she looked distracted and unhappy. Buckingham Palace issued a denial of the rumour.

Elizabeth did not like her name (or the implication of her name) being bandied about in the popular press. She did not want it tarnished. Her appearances in print had been restricted to occasional references in the social magazines and to accounts of Princess Mary's wedding.

This clearly affected her thinking in the next days. Could she have felt that appearing to fail with one brother, she might now lose the other? What would her mother's reaction have been? We can but speculate, but she was only twenty-two and there was much at stake. Lady Airlie recorded a visit from her to Ashley Gardens:

When she came to tea at my flat one afternoon at the beginning of January 1923 I meant to make a final effort. But instead I found myself talking of my own marriage – of how much I had hated the Army life at first, and only tolerated it for David's sake, but how I had grown to love it. After she had gone I feared I might have bored her by bringing up a chapter of my past which had closed before she had been born, and wished that I had talked more of the Duke.[54]

On 10 January Elizabeth returned to Wiltshire for a ball given in the drawing room of Longleat by the Marchioness of Bath for her daughter Lady Mary Thynne, a close friend and another of Princess Mary's bridesmaids. Once again she was a lone figure, playing her own path. The Duke had not escorted her to either of the recent balls in Wiltshire.

And yet a few days later he came to see her at St Paul's Walden Bury. On Sunday 13 January they did not go to church. Instead he took her for a walk in the woods, proposed again and this time she accepted him. Had she panicked? Was it Lady Airlie or the *Daily Star* that provoked her to relent? Had she always accepted her eventual fate, and was the time now right? The Duke telegraphed his mother at once: 'All Right, Bertie.' The engagement was formally announced on 15 January after which Elizabeth wrote to a friend: 'The cat is firmly out of the bag and there is no chance of stuffing him back in again.'[55] Channon was convinced that the swift announcement was to prevent the bride from changing her mind,[56] while Elizabeth told her brother David: 'I could hear the door clanging behind me – never to open again.'[57]

In his letter of thanks to Lady Airlie, the Duke wrote of 'the dream which has at last been realized', how happy they both were, and added 'I owe so much to you and can only bless you for what you did'.[58]

Elizabeth was quick to inform her family. One reaction was intriguing. Lady Jean Rankin, many years later a lady-in-waiting to the Queen Mother, was staying with the Elphinstones on the day the letter about the engagement arrived from Elizabeth. 'Lady Elphinstone read the letter in silence and passed it across the table to her husband. He did the same.'[59] Can it be that they thought she was letting the side down? It does not sound an enthusiastic response. Lady Jean did not elaborate. It does not matter.

By his persistence, the Duke of York had made the best decision of his life.

5

The Wedding

'I am so happy – it's all wonderful, except the publicity which I hate, but that will soon be over' – Elizabeth Bowes-Lyon

News of the betrothal was greeted with the delight that is customary on such occasions. When the Duke visited the London Electric Wire Company in Leyton on 18 January, some five hundred women and girls surrounded his car, cheering and crying out 'The Prince wants to get back to his sweetheart.'[1] Those who knew the Duke with his shy character and his earnest approach to life welcomed the idea that he had found a bride who was 'bright-eyed, full of fun and laughter, yet with a very serious and practical side to her character'.[2] That it was the Duke who was taking a wife and not his elder brother, the Prince of Wales, was likewise no great surprise. The Duke was taking that first vital step towards his dynastic obligations. He was thrilled. Thanking the Archbishop of York, he wrote of his new happiness. He thought the prelate would find Elizabeth even more charming than her sister Rose, at whose wedding he knew he had officiated.[3] The bride was also busy thanking well-wishers. She thanked Nancy Astor for her 'delicious letter', declaring herself immensely happy, despite the publicity.[4]

Chips Channon, who had lately been teasing her about the Prince of Wales, noted: 'We have all hoped, waited, so long for this romance to prosper, that we had begun to despair that she would ever accept him.'[5] Inevitably there were those to whom the engagement was a shock, especially among the rejected suitors. Prince Paul was taken by surprise: 'What do you think of Elizabeth's engagement? I didn't expect it especially after my visit to Glamis in September when I was there with Bertie York.'[6] In February he commissioned John Singer Sargent to sketch Elizabeth as his wedding present.

Jasper Ridley* told Duff Cooper that he had 'long been in love' with Elizabeth despite being married since 1911, and that he never 'believed she would do it and it had been a very sudden *volte face* on her part' as she had refused the Duke several times.[7]

---

* Hon. Sir Jasper Ridley (1887–1951), son of 1st Viscount Ridley. He was given a KCVO in 1946 for his services as Chairman of Coutts, the royal bankers.

Archie Clark Kerr was distraught. He wrote to his mother that he thought he had never really had a chance, 'nevertheless I had clung to it and tried to tell myself that all things were possible. And now that it has become impossible I feel tired and battered and dismal and whenever I think of it, and I think of it even in moments of greatest crisis, my head buzzes.' He prised a letter from Elizabeth in which she asked him not to feel sad, hoping that 'surely we can remain friends as before'.*[8]

James Stuart returned too late from Oklahoma. He then announced his engagement to Lady Rachel Cavendish, the day before the York wedding, and they were quietly married that August.

It is always suggested that the Queen Mother only gave one interview in her entire life, and this was just after the engagement.† This did not prevent her, on 24 April, from allowing the special Royal Wedding supplement of the *Dundee Advertiser* to publish a letter from her in facsimile handwriting, containing the paragraph: 'My engagement has only occasioned an even warmer manifestation of that kindness which has always been shown to me during the whole of our association.'[9]

The King and Queen were quick to invite the Strathmores and their daughter to York Cottage. They arrived with the Duke of York the next weekend. This was Elizabeth's first introduction into the life to which she had lately committed herself. She was late for dinner, an unpardonable crime in the eyes of George V, and yet that crusty old monarch responded benignly, to the astonishment of his family: 'You are not late, my dear. I think we must have sat down two minutes too early.'[10]

Elizabeth was taken over to the Big House to be presented to Queen Alexandra. This proved an uncomfortable occasion, for although the aged Queen was eager to take the young bride under her wing, she was so deaf that it was almost impossible to get through to her. In private she tried to follow conversations with the use of an elaborate ear trumpet.

If York House was small and easily overcrowded, the Big House was grand and empty of life, save for faint echoes of its glamorous Edwardian past. It was nearly sixty years since Queen Alexandra had arrived in England, the Princess from across the sea in Denmark. She was still elegant, but she too had faded, her face so heavily enamelled that she could no longer smile. She made vague gesticulations with her hands, almost balletic in movement. These indicated a friendly disposition but did not make conversation easy.

---

* In 1925 Clark Kerr married an eighteen-year-old Chilean millionairess called Maria Theresa Diaz Salas, reputedly the most beautiful girl in Santiago. He became Lord Inverchapel in 1946.

† Of course she was interviewed in various television programmes such as *Royal Heritage*, in a documentary about her racing, *Royal Champion*, and in informal chats while walking about her garden at Royal Lodge, with Alastair Burnet and Martin Charteris. She appeared in the 1969 film *Royal Family*, and other similar programmes.

With her was her sister, the Dowager Empress of Russia, who often stayed in England, still refusing to believe that her son, the Tsar, and his family had perished in the Russian Revolution. She was accompanied by one of two enormous Cossack servants, who took it in turns to sleep outside her bedroom at night. Then, in perpetual attendance on Queen Alexandra were her redoubtable old courtiers, Charlotte Knollys, her maid of honour, and Sir Dighton Probyn, VC, her Comptroller.

Sir Dighton could often be seen on the Sandringham estate, being driven around the grounds in a horse-drawn basket, led by his groom. Through Probyn's Horse, he had become an honorary Sikh and never cut his long white beard, which modestly covered his Victoria Cross when he was in uniform. For an eightieth birthday treat Queen Alexandra took Sir Dighton to the Hendon Air Show, but he was so rigid that they had to lie him on the ground so that he could see the aeroplanes flying overhead. T. E. Lawrence wrote of Sir Dighton's 'gaping mouth' which 'wagged almost unseen and unheard in the thicket of beard which overgrew the waistcoat'. He described Charlotte Knollys as 'incredibly old, wasted and sallow', and wrote of Queen Alexandra's 'red-rimmed eyes, the enamelled face, which the famous smile scissored across all angular and heart-rending'.[11]

At church on Sunday, the royal party was further augmented by Queen Maud of Norway, Queen Olga of Greece, Prince George of Greece, the Princess Royal and Princess Maud, who were all staying with Queen Alexandra.

The Duke spent the days after the engagement calling in on his fiancée at Bruton Street, and occasionally seizing a day in the hunting field with Captain George Drummond at Pitsford Hall. He was invariably back in London each evening to dine with Elizabeth and her mother.

The young couple dined at Claridge's as guests of Lady Marian Keith Cameron, Elizabeth wearing ivory laces, the low waist of one side finished with a shower posy of roses. The society pages commended her as 'decidedly petite, with small feet'[12] and noted that she danced well.

In early February, the young couple were again at Sandringham, inspecting the King's horses at Egerton House racing stables; the bride was presented with a sapphire engagement ring (Princess Mary's had been emerald), and they went to inspect White Lodge, Richmond, which the ever-generous Lord Farquhar* was vacating so that they could make it their first married home.

It was announced that the marriage would be celebrated at Westminster

---

* Lady Farquhar had died while dressing for dinner in the Prince's Hotel in Hove on 6 April 1922. In a rare break with tradition, Queen Alexandra attended her funeral at the Chapel Royal, St James's. She was accompanied by Princess Victoria, the Princess Royal and Princess Maud.

Abbey, following the recent precedents set by Princess Patricia of Connaught in 1919 and Princess Mary in 1922. There were some who demurred at the alteration from the previous tradition that royal weddings were solemnised quietly either at the Chapel Royal, in St James's Palace, St George's Chapel, Windsor, or the private chapel at Buckingham Palace.

The bride-to-be made a favourable impression as she received formal addresses from a succession of worthy bodies. She was spotted 'looking very happy as she drove by with the Duke of York in a closed car'.[13] She made a speech to the Pattenmakers and spent a few days at Windsor Castle, alive with daffodils, pink and blue and very pale yellow hyacinths, and primroses. On 10 April, the Duke accompanied her to Lady Doris Gordon-Lennox's wedding to Clare Vyner at Chichester Cathedral, Elizabeth in 'a happy shade of brown, a long fur-trimmed coat (for it was a very cold day) and a small cloche hat with a cluster of roses at the side.'[14]

She veered between feeling happy and daunted. At a pre-wedding ball, the former Prime Minister H. H. Asquith observed the 'poor little bride' standing in with the King and Queen – 'completely overshadowed'.[15]

The wedding took place at Westminster Abbey on 26 April. The bride wore an all-English trousseau, Queen Mary lending her some real old dentelle for her train. Her dress was designed by Madame Handley Seymour, her favourite designer for the next twelve years. Since the Duke of York disliked veils, she wore flowers in her hair. As bridesmaids she chose mostly personal friends rather than royal relations. They wore frocks of billowing ivory-lined chiffon, and a feature was made of the thistle and the white rose of York. The overall effect compared badly to Princess Mary's dress and looks decidedly dated to the modern eye.

The bridesmaids included two nieces of Queen Mary's, Lady Mary Cambridge, who would presently marry the Marquess of Worcester, later 10th Duke of Beaufort, and Lady May Cambridge (later Abel Smith), Diamond Hardinge (already in indifferent health), who would soon marry Captain Robert Abercromby, Katie Hamilton, Cecilia Bowes-Lyon, daughter of her brother Patrick, Elizabeth Elphinstone, daughter of her sister May, Lady Mary Thynne, whose party at Longleat she had lately attended, and her old school friend Betty Cator, who would eventually marry her brother Michael in 1928. The Queen Mother outlived them all.

Elizabeth was married from 17 Bruton Street, in Mayfair, the home of the Strathmores since 1920. As she left the house she hid her hands under the folds of her dress, as her gloves had been forgotten. They were whisked to the Abbey just in time.

It is invariably said that the Queen Mother caused the weather to be fair on important days in her long life. Her wedding day was an exception, the morning being dull and grey:

> It was almost a relief when, with the first chords on the organ, about half an hour before the commencement of the actual service, all the electric lights in the Abbey were switched on. That, however, was nothing compared with what was to come. The bride, supported by her father, had passed right up the whole length of the great building. There at the head of the steps leading up to the Sacrarium stood her royal bridegroom waiting to greet her. And then, just at that very moment, the Abbey was flooded with a glorious burst of sunshine. It was wonderful and dramatic and unforgettable.
>
> It was just the same, too, at the end of the service . . . She came away, leaning upon her husband's arm, in a blaze of sunshine which flooded the old building from end to end, and seemed almost completely to destroy the effect of the artificial lights.[16]

The King and Queen were there, Queen Mary in blue and silver brocade and a toque of gleaming silver tissue. Queen Alexandra wore her traditional black, enriched with large golden embroideries, an ermine stole and a small hat in dark purple. She came with her sister, the Dowager Empress, in a Parma violet cape.

The Duke of York arrived in the Abbey in his Royal Air Force uniform, accompanied by his Supporters,* Prince Henry and Prince George, and made his way to the front. When Queen Alexandra saw him, she stepped forward to greet him. He bowed and kissed her hand and she kissed him on both cheeks.

Lady Strathmore wore black with blue feathers on her hat and a collar of blue roses, giving a somewhat eccentric and theatrical impression.

The bride herself looked beautiful, but pale, as she entered the Abbey in her simple medieval dress, leaning on the arm of her father. She paused to place her flowers on the tomb of the Unknown Warrior, establishing a tradition that has been followed by later royal brides, and then glided up the aisle, a journey that she was destined to undertake many times in the next seventy years.

There were six tables for the wedding breakfast in the State Dining Room of Buckingham Palace, Elizabeth sitting between the Duke of York and the King. Also at that table were Queen Mary, Queen Alexandra, the

* Members of the Royal Family have two Supporters instead of a best man.

Dowager Empress, the Prince of Wales, the Duke of Connaught (last surviving son of Queen Victoria) and her parents. All the other guests were either members of the Royal Family, Bowes-Lyons or bridesmaids. Included were various foreign royalties such as Prince Paul of Yugoslavia.

Jewels were given her in profusion by her new family: a set of diamonds and turquoise, tiaras, a necklace of pearls and amethysts and a pendant of diamonds and sapphires.

The new Duke and Duchess of York honeymooned at Polesden Lacey, the lavishly Edwardian (though in fact 1820s) Dorking home of Mrs Greville, lately returned from South Africa. Various staged pictures showed them in the conservatory, walking on the sweeping lawns or playing a tame game of golf.

They returned to London and were then seen off on the night train to Scotland by the Prince of Wales. They stayed at Glamis between 8 and 17 May, arriving there on a fine summer morning to be welcomed by the tenantry, villagers and local schoolchildren, and the new Duchess called all those she knew by name. Later they settled at Frogmore, awaiting the completion of the changes to White Lodge, Richmond. Here the Duchess developed whooping cough, perhaps a reaction to her new life.

That summer Elizabeth had a foretaste of the restrictions of royal life. On 9 June Princess Christian, one of Queen Victoria's surviving daughters, died at Schomberg House. As a result, Elizabeth was prevented by court mourning from attending Diamond Hardinge's wedding on 12 June.*

Elizabeth had married into a large family, most of whom, including Princess Christian, had attended her wedding. At the head of it was George V. A man of inflexible habit and bounden duty, he could be brash and off-hand. Alec Hardinge noted that many were scared of him, because he was violent in speech, though not in action. Anyone who worked for him needed to learn that he meant little by his manner.

Primarily a country man, he had enjoyed his early life in the Navy, and, given his way, would have remained in the country, shooting whatever bird was in season at the time, stalking and enjoying other country pursuits. When detained indoors by inclement weather, he rearranged his stamp collection. Conversation with him was not always easy, though Lieutenant Colin Buist, presently the Duke of York's equerry, found he

---

* On 11 January 1927, a few days after the Yorks set off to New Zealand, Diamond died. After enduring bouts of ill health, she was taken seriously ill in May 1926. 'Unfortunately a cruel malady, which baffled the highest medical skill to stay its progress, after months of brave, patient endurance, borne by her without a murmur, sapped her strength and she passed away peacefully,' said Revd Charles Giles, a few days after burying her within the policies of Forglen House, Banffshire.

'only had to mention the word, *Britannia*, & then sit back with his arms folded for the rest of the evening while H. M. roared on'.[17]

The King loved his ferocious parrot, Charlotte, invariably to be found in his study or his bedroom and inclined to make messes which he concealed furtively. He could be endearing. He had a terrier called Bob. When the Bishop of Durham was summoned to talk to him in his bedroom, the little dog barked. 'That was meant for Wigram,* not for you,'[18] said the King. When a guest at Balmoral inadvertently dropped a hairpin into her soup at Balmoral, he enquired: 'Were you expecting to eat winkles?'

His game book makes terrifying reading. According to the place and the season, a succession of grouse, pheasants, partridges, hares, rabbits, woodcock, wild duck and teal fell to his gun – 416 pheasants at Sandringham on 24 November 1920, 602 the next day, 975 grouse at Moy Hall on 6 September 1921, 454 the next day, 1330 the day after, and 506 the day after that. On 25 August 1922 a party of seven got 1300 grouse at Ruthven (staying with The Mackintosh). On that day the King broke his previous record, with 102 in the big drive, 189 in three drives from the same butt and about 180 brace in the day.[19]

At Sandringham he lived a life of contented tedium, which most found deadly dull. At Christmas, he went to watch meat being given to the tenants, a custom initiated by Queen Victoria. There were ritual bonfires and visits to the Big House, where sometimes the guests danced to the gramophone. There were inspections of the Stud, and guests and courtiers knew that offence would be caused if they wriggled out of attending.

Queen Mary was in awe of her husband, even afraid of him, and subjugated her particular interests in art and antiques to remaining in his shadow. She only emerged as a character in her own right in widowhood, liberated from his yoke. Unlike the King, she loathed the country, much preferring London. After the King's death she never returned to Balmoral, though she took summer holidays at Sandringham. She was obsessed by royal connections, having suffered from the stigma of being born a Teck, a morganatic branch of the Württemberg family. She only spoke freely when travelling in a car. She liked to be read aloud to, and was a hard taskmaster, obliging her ladies-in-waiting to read for long hours without a break.

She looked rather austere with her matronly figure and toques. She wore a wig, which was silver by day and gold in the evening. She wore an enormous quantity of magnificent jewellery.

---

* Clive, Lord Wigram, the King's Private Secretary.

Royalty tended to be unsentimental. Meeting so many people limited the extent to which they could care for individuals. Queen Mary only liked people for the information they imparted to her. She would listen avidly, absorbing all she could, interested in most subjects. Once they ceased to interest or inform her, they ceased to exist. As her new daughter-in-law was soon to discover, there would be many expeditions to places that Queen Mary wanted to see, particularly when they all stayed at Balmoral.

The Duke of York had three surviving brothers. There was the Prince of Wales, Prince Henry and Prince George, who had lately had his two little toes chopped off, and Princess Mary, the shy sister, who was now married to Viscount Lascelles* and living largely away from court.

The Prince of Wales was not at ease when under his father's roof, as Elizabeth soon spotted. She wrote to him: 'I know now your feelings of relief and freedom when you get away from England on your own – away from the petty little annoyances and restrictions that drive one crazy.' She told him that she too hated 'being always under the eye of a narrow-minded autocrat',[20] an unflattering reference to George V. Elizabeth forged a supportive friendship with him during the remaining years of George V's reign.

Prince Henry was more of a professional soldier, who enjoyed his hunting and sometimes got into trouble with his father for failing to leave word as to the time of his return. His great joy in life was to laugh and he found humour in many unlikely situations. When told of Bertie's engagement, he had been 'a little slow . . . to appreciate his brother's discernment, maturity and good fortune'.[21]

Prince George, a man with a certain lazy charm and an amused outlook on life, would visit his father with high expectations which were invariably dashed. One summer he arrived at Balmoral, 'looking forward to a chance of intimacy with his father . . . and only got a blackguarding for his pains'.[22] He alleviated the tedium by keeping a four-month-old Alsatian wolfhound under his bed, unbeknown to the King. Fritz Ponsonby found that Prince George said 'such witty things and is most outspoken in his criticisms of his father and of the deadly dullness of his visit to his parents'.[23]

Living mainly at Sandringham, Queen Alexandra paid occasional visits to Marlborough House. With her at most times was her unmarried

---

* On 7 February 1923, Princess Mary gave birth to a son, the present Earl of Harewood, his birth hailed by the King as 'this great occasion in our family life'. He was born Hon. George Lascelles, which some felt was not good enough for a grandson of the monarch, but the King did not wish to raise Viscount Lascelles to a title senior to that of his father, the Earl of Harewood, who would live until 1929.

daughter, Princess Victoria, a frustrated spinster who never missed the chance to report the misdeeds of her nephews to the King. Every July, on her birthday, Queen Alexandra gave a children's party for her at Marlborough House, which must have served as a sharp reminder of her protracted spinsterhood. When the King and Queen made a rare excursion in the Royal Yacht from Genoa, Princess Victoria ruined it for Queen Mary, who longed to see Pompeii, by making philistine jokes with the King.

There was then a veritable gerontocracy of aunts, uncles and cousins. The one they all liked was the old Duke of Connaught, who combined a life of duty and service to his country with an enjoyable private life, enriched by some glamorous ladies whom he pursued with differing degrees of success. He lived at Clarence House in London, Bagshot Park in Surrey and had a villa on Cap Ferrat in the South of France. His son, Prince Arthur of Connaught, was then serving as Governor-General of South Africa. His statuesque daughter, Lady Patricia Ramsay, was a painter, considered by some of the cousins to be rather too contemporary. Princess Marie Louise wrote: 'Her paintings are rather modern – in fact, very modern – and sometimes I realise that I am not sufficiently "up" in the expression of modern art to appreciate all her pictures, though I know they are brilliantly clever.'[24]

The Duke of Connaught's two remaining sisters lived in apartments at Kensington Palace. One was Princess Louise, Duchess of Argyll, a sculptress, who of all of them had led the most Bohemian life and whose past was hung about with all manner of rumour and innuendo. She had been married to the Duke of Argyll, a man whose tastes were not wholly heterosexual. The marriage produced no children.

The youngest sister, Princess Beatrice, had been enslaved by her mother, Queen Victoria, and had been forbidden to leave home even when she married Prince Henry of Battenberg. Converted from being a minor German princeling into a Royal Highness, a Knight of the Garter, Prince Henry had never felt at home in the land of his adoption. In 1895 he sailed off to the Ashanti Expedition, but died of malaria before seeing so much as a shot fired. Princess Beatrice had therefore been a widow since 1896. She spent her twilight years transcribing parts of Queen Victoria's diaries and destroying the originals.

Rather more amusing than they looked were Princess Helena Victoria and Princess Marie Louise, the more or less spinster daughters of Princess Christian, who had lately died. They lived together and were never far from the royal scene. Princess Marie Louise wrote a good volume of memoirs, entitled *My Memories of Six Reigns*.

And then there was that most energetic of survivors, Princess Alice of Albany, who was married to Queen Mary's brother, the Earl of Athlone. Rigid in her appreciation of her own royal status, she kept herself so busy that she invariably knitted while on long walks. In later life she was often to be seen travelling by bus in Kensington. A tiny, bird-like figure, she had a great sense of humour and was a stalwart character, who lived on until 1981, dying at the age of nearly ninety-eight.

Queen Alexandra had two other daughters, Louise, Duchess of Fife (the Princess Royal), and Queen Maud of Norway. The latter was the youngest daughter, and she divided her time between Norway and Appleton House near Sandringham. Her husband, a Danish prince, had been chosen to be King of Norway in 1905, and changed his name to King Haakon. They had one young son, Olav,* who became King of Norway in 1957, and reigned until his death in 1991.

The elder sister, the Princess Royal, was desperately insecure and dull. She married the 5th Earl of Fife in 1889, created Duke of Fife in 1899, who became a rich man thanks to his association with Lord Farquhar. The whole Fife family nearly drowned in December 1911 when the ship in which they were travelling ran aground off Cap Spartel on the south Moroccan coast. The Duke died in Aswan, Egypt, on 29 January 1912.

Louise had two daughters. The elder was Alexandra, who succeeded her father as Duchess of Fife in her own right and married her cousin Prince Arthur, son of the Duke of Connaught. She was a professional nurse by training, who loved talking about gruesome operations in which she had played a part, and later succumbed to severe rheumatoid arthritis. The younger daughter was Princess Maud, then the permanent companion to her mother, a somewhat dismal role.

It seemed that Princess Maud might be rescued from this by the munificence by Lord Farquhar, ever to the fore. But the saga came to an unexpected conclusion. In August 1923 it was clear that this supposed benefactor of royalty was dying. Because her sister, the Dowager Empress of Russia, had fallen ill after the York wedding and was confined to Marlborough House that summer, Queen Alexandra had stayed in London throughout August. She visited Farquhar in his room (to which he was confined for the last two weeks of his life) on 21 August. His old friends the King and Queen had been to see him a week before. Lord Farquhar died on 30 August.

There was a hint of trouble to come in his *Times* obituary: 'It will be

---

* A recent biography by Tor Bomann-Larsen suggests that he was born by artificial insemination and may therefore have been the son of the royal doctor, Sir Frances Laking. Queen Maud's clothes were exhibited at the Victoria and Albert Museum in 2005.

remembered that when the Coalition fell and Mr Bonar Law became Prime Minister, Lord Farquhar felt some hesitation about handing over certain funds to Lord Younger, on a ground that a portion of them had been subscribed for Coalition purposes. The difficulty was however, ultimately, adjusted, and he was succeeded by Lord Younger as trustee.'[25]

Lord Farquhar's last will was signed on 8 June 1922, not long after his wife's death. In it he left the King his two Louis XVI commodes bought from Duveen and any contents he wished from Castle Rising. To Queen Alexandra he left his oriental Sang de Boeuf vase and to the Princess Royal the silver basket of flowers given him by Edward VII. Everything at White Lodge (save what should have been in the Grosvenor Square house) was left to Queen Mary. Princess Arthur of Connaught would receive the lease of the Grosvenor Square house and all the remaining contents. She and her young son Lord Macduff would split the rest of the estate between them.

Princess Maud was left £50,000, a fantastic sum in those days. On 23 April 1923, Farquhar created a third codicil to the will, in view of the contemplated marriage between Princess Maud and Lord Carnegie, who had been staying at Glamis during the Duke of York's first visit in 1920. If the marriage 'be solemnized' then Lord Carnegie would get the £50,000 instead. The lure of the £50,000 was a way of rescuing poor Princess Maud from her mother's side and tempting a suitor.

The contents of Farquhar's will were made public on 12 September, and the good fortune of Lord Carnegie and his bride made known in the press. In full expectation of his dowry of £50,000, Lord Carnegie married Princess Maud on 12 November that year, despite the fact that he would have preferred to marry Anne Thesiger, daughter of Viscount Chelmsford, under whom he had served in India, when Chelmsford was Viceroy.*

Then matters took a sinister turn. It was discovered that Farquhar had enormous debts and was in fact penniless. As Lord Crawford put it: 'He left handsome bequests to sundry minor figures of the Royal Family (he was always a perfect snob) and when the estates were valued, it transpired that there was nothing to divide.'[26]

For the Princess Royal the effects were graver. Far from profiting from his bequest, she discovered that, due to his partnership with her late husband, the Duke of Fife, she was liable for the debts. So, on 18 July 1924, she sold 139 pictures, including important Old Masters, at Christie's in order to raise £13,577.

Though Farquhar failed to enrich the Royal Family financially, he

---

* In 1921 she had married Lord Inchiquin.

deserves posthumous credit for the one legacy he brought the family and nation, albeit unwittingly. He was the man who brought Elizabeth and the Duke of York together in the first place, at a dance at his house in the summer of 1920.

6

The Delicious Duchess

'Elizabeth's charm of manner invariably controls her desire to be funny' – Lady Katharine Hamilton

In the summer of 1923 the Yorks settled into White Lodge, in Richmond Park, a royal residence into which the King and Queen had moved in June 1894, shortly before the birth of the Prince of Wales. The young couple were presently spotted at the Richmond Show. Later in the month they went to the Hendon Air Show with the King and Queen and Queen Alexandra, and the King and Queen lunched with the Yorks when they went to the lawn tennis.

They joined the King and Queen when they moved into Holyroodhouse in Edinburgh on 9 July, the Duchess arriving in mist-grey, though hovering rather in the shadow of Queen Mary. At the palace the royal party had their meals together, before visiting disabled soldiers on a very wet day, a garden party attended by little-known Scottish peers (some disguised as members of the Royal Company of Archers), the traditional tedium enlivened by a lunch with a heavily pregnant Mollie Dalkeith.

Elizabeth's first lady-in-waiting was appointed in the form of fifty-two-year-old Lady Katharine Meade, who had been with the recently deceased Duchess of Albany since 1910 and was considered by Elizabeth's friends to be no great asset – 'that well meaning old cup of tea',[1] as she was described.*

On her public engagements 'the little Duchess' (as she was so often called) looked shy and mousy, dressing sweetly in pale colours, as when they joined an outing of East End children in Epping Forest. Already she was beginning to make her mark. It was noted: 'The young Duchess has a particularly pleasing manner and address, and that happy knack of being interested in all she does.'[2] On a day of engagements in Liverpool on 24 July it was said: 'The Duchess, who won all hearts by her charming graciousness, wore a soft broche gown of palest biscuit colour and a toque of the same shade with drooping feather.'[3] At the Palace garden party

---

* Lady Katharine Meade (1871–1954), daughter of 4th Earl Clanwilliam. She 'resigned' in 1926.

the Duchess wore 'a champagne-coloured lace dress and a wide hat with black velvet streamers'.[4]

Social life was also lived on a grand scale. The Yorks attended the Duchess of Sutherland's masked ball at Hampden House, at which there was much changing of costumes in order to avoid recognition, the Prince of Wales one moment Bonnie Prince Charlie, the next a Chinese coolie, and the Duchess in a white picture dress with flowing skirts. They were at a dinner with their honeymoon hostess, Mrs Ronald Greville, at her home in Charles Street, and at the Air League Ball at Albert Hall. Then Elizabeth's godmother, Mrs Arthur James, gave a dinner-dance at which both Yorks were present, while Princess Mary, Lord Lascelles and Prince George came in later. At the end of the season, they went to stay at Molecomb for the races at Goodwood, as guests of Lady March, the mother of Doris, now married to Clare Vyner. This time Elizabeth wore 'a becoming coat and skirt of dark blue, with bright embroideries on the collar, and a blue feathered hat'.[5]

It has been suggested that the Yorks were not part of the smart set. It is true that they did not frequent the Embassy Club, nor did they attract the perpetual attention of the social diarists such as Chips Channon, but it is wrong to assume that they were not often and very grandly entertained. There were regular invitations to the great London houses that survived, to balls given by the Duchess of Sutherland, the Marchioness of Londonderry, the Countesses of Derby and Pembroke and others. They were more conventional and aristocratic in their choice of hosts, and less raffish than the Prince of Wales and his set.

Their most persistent hostess, and one whose company they relished, was the Hon. Mrs Ronald Greville, or Hon. Dame Margaret Greville as she should more properly be styled. She entertained them to dinners and dances given at her London house, 16 Charles Street, and also for weekends at Polesden Lacey, where they had spent the first days of their honeymoon, on account of Mrs Greville's friendship with the Duke and the Royal Family.

Polesden Lacey was a large house near Great Bookham in Surrey, converted into a house where royalty could be entertained. The style varied from room to room, and each was filled with genuine pieces of furniture. The final result was opulent. Mrs Greville served delicious food, and, unlike many such houses, the kitchen was close to the dining room.

Maggie Greville herself was a larger-than-life figure who loved nothing more than entertaining royalty. She was the illegitimate daughter of

William McEwan, the Edinburgh brewer who had acquired many lucrative securities in America, and in consequence she was very rich. Her marriage to Hon. Ronald Greville in 1891 gave her an entrée into society, and she was soon entertaining King Edward VII and the Keppels. Captain Greville died in 1908, two years before Polesden Lacey was ready.

Many descriptions survive of her, not least that of Queen Elizabeth, written to Osbert Sitwell after her death, and one which also mirrors her own character: 'She was so shrewd, so kind and so amusingly unkind, so sharp, such fun, so naughty . . . altogether a real person, a character, utterly Mrs Ronald Greville and no tinge of anything alien.'[6]

The obituarists wrote that she deployed her great wealth 'for the purposes of a wide but discriminating hospitality'[7], while Harold Nicolson wondered that 'this plump but virulent little bitch should hold such social power?'.[8] Some of Mrs Greville's guests were dour, none more so than Sir John Simon, whose smile, it was said 'could illuminate his countenance as a name-plate does a coffin'.[9]

The house party was assembled with particular care when the Yorks stayed, which they did often in the summers before 1936. One guest who proved a success and thus established a firm friendship with the Duchess, further fostered at Trent Park, home of Sir Philip Sassoon, was Captain Osbert Sitwell. He had been sceptical about the assurances of Sonia Cubitt that he would find the Duchess of York charming, intelligent and well read, so was doubly surprised.

The Yorks enjoyed their visits even if one night was 'like jazz night at the Palladium. All the butlers were drunk – since Maggie was ill – bobbing up every minute during dinner to offer the Duchess of York whisky.'[10] On another visit, Beverley Nichols was a guest. Once a prodigy, this now forgotten writer was no stranger to hyperbole. It is perhaps forgivable to quote one description of the Duchess which achieves an excess of zeal:

From the moment when, before dinner, she appeared at the top of the staircase, in a shimmering dress of white satin, with the soft lights gleaming on a treble rope of perfect pearls, I found myself captivated. The keynote to her personality is 'radiance', and it comes from within. There is a light *behind* her eyes, as well as upon them, and one knows too that there is a light in her heart. There are some women of exceptional purity and sweetness of whom I have always had the fancy that they would shine in the dark, as though they were phosphorescent. [The Duchess of York] is one of those women.[11]

On the Sunday morning, Nichols rose earlier than the house party and found his way to the drawing room, which, in the early morning light, he thought looked 'more like the entrance to a bordel than ever'. He removed several ornately framed photographs of Grand Duchesses from the grand piano and began to improvise some variations on the National Anthem, playing it in the style of Debussy's *Jardins sous la Pluie*, a funeral march and as a Chopin mazurka. He was just embarking on a version as a Bach fugue when the door opened and the Duchess of York slipped in. Nichols leapt to his feet:

'But please do not stop. What was it you were playing?'
'It was . . . It was just something of my own, Ma'am.'
'I see. Somehow it sounded . . . faintly familiar. Can you play it again?'
'I would rather play some Chopin, Ma'am.'
'Yes, perhaps it would be better.'[12]

The Duchess sat down. Not without relief, Nichols threw himself into the Scherzo in B flat minor, which he felt matched the occasion.

Mrs Greville also entertained the Yorks in London, on which occasions the house was frequently awash with minor British royalty such as the Ramsays, Carisbrookes, Mountbattens, or foreign royalty, the King of Egypt, the King of Italy or the occasional Maharajah. She once gave what she called 'a *wee, wee* party for Queen of Spain'.[13]

One of the problems faced by the new Duchess of York was to establish who her real friends were. She was twenty-two years old in the season of 1923 and had to find her way in this shark-infested social world. Cautious as ever, she trod the path with care. There was wisdom in this, for in that post-war era of cocktails, jazz and nightclubs, there was trouble afoot for anyone who cared to seek it. Infidelities abounded, and marriage did not always signal the end to courting and flirting.

The fastest of the group was Mollie Dalkeith, who, despite her marriage in 1921, was still pursued on all sides. In the summer of 1924 she had some trouble shaking off the unwanted attentions of Prince George of Russia. At another party at which Elizabeth was not present, James Stuart, one of Mollie's steady admirers, was observed being almost 'torn asunder' by Audrey Coats (Edward James's sister, and the first fiancée of Lord Louis Mountbatten) and Poppy Baring, girlfriend of Prince George – in sharp competition with each other. Raymond de Trafford, known as the 'Borstal Boy', was another louche figure on the London scene, later to ply his way in the 'Happy Valley' set in Kenya. There he fell for Alice de Janzé, described as 'a young American man-eater who played with lion cubs and was said to look like a "wicked Madonna"'*.[14] All these men shared one ambition – to seduce the women they met at parties.

In the midst of them was the Prince of Wales, still unmarried and dancing as many nights away as his energy permitted. Nor was he the ideal guest. He was given a thirtieth birthday party by Mrs Cornelius Vanderbilt at Spencer House, but rudely left early, horrified by the entertainment prepared for him.

As a commoner married into the Royal Family, Elizabeth had problems coming to terms with her position. She resented those who treated her differently now that she had become 'a blooming Duchess', as she put it. She was surprised when some of her 'chorus' held back out of fear of overstepping the mark. Queen Mary's older ladies-in-waiting had warned her old friends about being too familiar and Elizabeth was confused by the decorous formality with which some of them now treated her.

Elizabeth found herself pursued by socially ambitious people, but as she told Helen Hardinge: 'I find I don't make friends with them you know, Helen. Isn't it a pity?'[15]

It was only natural that her friends should examine how the new Duchess was adapting to her royal role. A year later, in the summer of 1924, Helen Hardinge had this chance as they gossiped together late at night:

> Elizabeth was quite perfect as she never fails to be. Her ideas of home life, friends, fun & happiness are all delicious. She is her own calm, enclosed, truthful yet charming personality always. She said the people who never left them in peace she found she could not make friends with: i.e. Lady Ancaster, Lady Massereene, Nortons, Victoria & Malcolm [Bullock] (whom she spoke of as having made unkind mischief over Prince George), Portia [Stanley], whom she says hates her (cries of 'impossible') & hurts the Prince [of Wales], Cynthia de T., Philip Sassoon, the old crowd. She is too simple & perfect for them tho' being a Princess they take her friendship as a right.

* In 1927 de Trafford went to Paris to inform Alice that, as a strict Catholic, he could not marry her. She came to his railway compartment at the Gare du Nord, shot first him and then herself. Neither died. They married in 1932, but were divorced in 1938. While in Kenya, de Trafford made an attempt to seduce Lady Alice Scott, but she sidestepped him.

This was a daunting group to confront. Lady Ancaster was formerly Eloise Breese from New York state, the American wife of 2nd Earl of Ancaster, Joint Lord Great Chamberlain in the reign of George VI. The Ancasters offered plenty of good sport at Drummond Castle in Perthshire, and the Duke of York was a regular visitor. Lady Ancaster now began to invite the Yorks to dinners at Claridge's.

Eloise's fortune came from her stepfather, Harry V. Higgins, impresario of the Royal Opera House, Covent Garden, while her real father and uncle had been present at the notorious 1895 'Pie Girl' dinner given by the architect Stanford White. A huge pastry was brought in, the waiters chanted 'Sing a Song of Sixpence', and at the punch line the pie opened, a flock of canaries flew out, followed by a sixteen-year-old girl, swathed in black veiling. The press castigated the evening as a bacchanalian revel.

This story received further publicity, when, in 1906, White was shot dead by Harry K. Thaw, a millionaire from Pittsburgh, because he had seduced his sixteen-year-old showgirl wife, Evelyn Nesbit. Though the Duchess of York was probably more interested in who was dancing which reel at the Forfar County Ball, some of the nuances of trials, brawls, affairs, lawsuits and insanity hung about Eloise's reputation if only in the occasional well-timed frown of a dowager.

Eloise Ancaster and Jean Ainsworth, the Scottish wife of 12th Viscount Massereene & Ferrard, were both more the generation of Elizabeth's mother. Lady Massereene invited the Yorks to dances at 108 Lancaster Gate. In the war she had been Commandant of Women's League Canteens, but was dressed so inappropriately that on a day visit to a canteen, some soldiers asked her if she had had any luck at the Piccadilly the night before. She once commented of Colin Buist, the Duke of York's equerry: 'Oh yes, he's very good-looking and attractive, but not quite the clean potato.' As Helen Hardinge put it: 'It comes well from her.'[16]

Richard Norton (later 6th Lord Grantley) was a wit and a kind man. Nicholas Phipps wrote that he combined these qualities 'in a degree we have scarcely known since Charles James Fox. Like Fox, also, he had a high contempt for his personal prosperity.'[17] Immaculately dressed and invariably sporting a monocle, Norton was one of the more dashing members of White's. He had 'a roving eye for a pretty face and a poor sense of marital loyalty'.[18]

His wife, Jean Kinloch, whom he married in 1919 as a tousled-haired Scottish girl, with Mollie Lascelles as a bridesmaid, developed into one of the chicest beauties of her day. They were in the Prince of Wales's set. Michael Arlen used Jean in a scene set in the Embassy Club in his novel *The Green Hat*: 'One of them stared with wide blue eyes right into people's faces, and blinked vaguely.' Dancing with a prince, 'she stared thoughtfully at the glass dome of the ceiling. She looked bored with boredom.'[19] The Nortons were too fast for the Yorks.

The others were inter-related. Captain Malcolm Bullock, MP, later a baronet, was married to Lady Victoria Primrose, the widow of Rt Hon. Neil Primrose, and the adored daughter of 17th Earl of Derby. When she was killed in the hunting field in 1927, her father wrote: 'I loved her, as no man has ever loved his daughter, and with her has gone all joy from my life.'[20]

'Portia' (Sybil) Cadogan was married to Ed Stanley (Rt Hon. Lord Stanley), son of 17th Earl of Derby, who suffered indifferent health and would die in his father's lifetime. Her sister, Cynthia Cadogan, was married to Sir Humphrey de Trafford, 4th Bt,* brother of Raymond. They were two of the four daughters of Viscount Chelsea, himself the son of Earl Cadogan, the daughters collectively nicknamed the 'Cadogan Square'. Of the others, Edith was married to Lord Hillingdon, and Mary had married the Marquess of Blandford, heir to the Duke of Marlborough.

The sisters had success, despite being large, handsome, rather powerful girls. Lady Letty Benson, Diana Cooper's sister, thought them patronising and that they condescended to evil: 'Well they look like death's heads – that's our consolation.'[21]

Of these sisters, Portia Stanley had been spoken of as a possible bride for the Prince of Wales, who later wrote of having been in her 'clutches',[22] but had fallen out with her in 1919. Yet in the summer of 1924 Mollie Dalkeith observed her 'making great running with [the Prince] at recent dances'.[23]

There was a fifth Cadogan girl, Victoria, known as 'Tor-Tor', born in 1901. She was rather different from her four sisters, as the youngest of such families sometimes are. She was the favourite and – among the Cadogan girls – the sole beneficiary of her mother's second husband, Admiral of the Fleet Sir Hedworth Lambton (later Meux).† This bequest and the fact that the admiral had been enamoured of Lady Chelsea for some years before she was conveniently widowed in 1908, makes it likely that she inherited Lambton genes, setting her apart from the 'Cadogan

---

* They were the grandparents of Andrew Parker Bowles.
† Sir Hedworth commanded the naval brigade at Ladysmith. He became a millionaire when the brewer's widow, Lady Meux, took a shine to him and on the strength of that bequeathed him Theobald's Park, near Walthamstow (in which stood Temple Bar until its return to the City of London in 2004), Sheen House, at East Sheen, a house in Park Lane, another house in Brighton, a château in Paris and a legacy of £5000. When he died in 1929, his fortune was assessed at £958,801.

Square'. Indeed, in a biography of the Lambtons by Sir John Colville there are some strong hints that this was the case.

Unlike the others, Tor-Tor was a life-long friend of Elizabeth's, and was chosen to be her lady-in-waiting on the 1927 New Zealand and Australia tour.

In 1920 Tor-Tor had married 'Jack' Gilmour, and was the mother of a son, Ian, who later became a minister in the Thatcher Government.* They were already divorced by the time Sir Hedworth died in 1929.

A little later on, Ed Stanley and his brother, Oliver, fell out, while Portia had a row with Tor-Tor Gilmour, and Audrey Coats went out two nights running with the Prince. Lady Maureen Stanley, Oliver's wife, asked: 'Is she prepared to go all the lengths with that?' And Jock Gilmour said: 'I should guess so. She looks it anyway.'

The last in the group was Sir Philip Sassoon, a rich, eligible bachelor, one of the great hosts of the age, and the brother of the Marchioness of Cholmondeley. He lived splendidly in Park Lane, and at Trent Park, later building Port Lympne, near Hythe. He entertained the Yorks a fair amount, the Duke enjoying tennis there with the famous French player Jean Borotra,† in July 1924. The Yorks flew in Sassoon's private plane around Trent Park, which might have alarmed the Air Ministry. When Sassoon died in 1939, the Queen Mother wrote to his sister, of whom she was fond, about his good taste and capacity for friendship,[24] so evidently she came round to him.

Elizabeth was also a friend of Sassoon's cousin, Hannah Gubbay, who inherited Trent Park, though in 1978 she told Sacheverell Sitwell, then in quest of her letters from his brother Osbert, that she feared her letters were filled with 'extremely bad form' jokes about 'dear' Hannah Gubbay.[25]

Another of this set, briefly mentioned earlier and one much liked by the Yorks, was Lady Maureen Stanley, the outspoken eldest daughter of the Marquess of Londonderry. The Duke of York had loved her briefly towards the end of the Great War. Oswald Mosley had proposed to her six times, but she turned him down in favour of Oliver Stanley. Katie Hamilton summed up the similarities and differences between the Duchess of York and Maureen, observing how kind Maureen was to her friends, yet how witty at the expense of outsiders:

---

* Of Sir Ian Gilmour, John Colville wrote: 'As Ian became an MP and at one time a Cabinet minister, the Lambton influence was indirectly maintained in political circles' (John Colville, *Those Lambtons*, p. 96).

† Borotra won the Singles Championship at Wimbledon in 1924. Along with Lacoste, Cochet and Brugnon, he was known as one of the 'Four Musketeers' of French lawn tennis.

It is the same attitude as Elizabeth's, viewing the world as an inner group of intimates otherwise populated by dolts – (Maureen's outsiders are dolts) (Elizabeth's are queer – undesirable people) but Elizabeth's charm of manner invariably controls her desire to be funny whereas with Maureen she cannot leave a witty thought still-born.[26]

In that first summer of her marriage Elizabeth assumed her first new role, as President of the Royal School of Needlework. In August the Duke took his bride to his Boys' Camp at New Romney, before they headed to Glamis. Lady Strathmore, dressed in a black marocain gown, cloak and black hat, gave a garden party for the newly-weds, the Duchess 'so dainty and petite . . . in palest fawn georgette and a white crinoline hat, under the brow of which nestled a single pink rose'.[27] The Prince of Wales stayed at Glamis, giving his verdict on his brother's bride: 'I'm so fond of Elizabeth, she is too sweet for words and she was the life and soul of the party.'[28]

Then they began a routine of Scottish visits which would scarcely alter in the next decade: visits to the Elphinstones at Carberry, going from Glamis to the Ancasters at Drummond Castle, back to Glamis, on to the predictable routine of Balmoral, the Braemar Games, lunches with the Princess Royal at Mar Lodge, and occasional excursions such as a visit to see the work of wounded soldiers and sailors at Ballater. Under the wing of Queen Mary, Elizabeth was swept off on a ceaseless round of expeditions, some of which held little appeal. Occasionally they escaped to Holwick Hall, on Upper Teeside, one of Lord Strathmore's shooting boxes, where Elizabeth's brother Lord Glamis and his wife Dorothy were staying.

While in Scotland, they learned that they were to undertake their first official trip overseas together as soon as October. Informed at short notice, the Duke cursed Lord Curzon for insisting on it. They left London by train, the Duchess smiling at the window, wearing 'a neat grey travelling dress, over which she wore a short coat of moleskin fur',[29] for the christening of the Crown Prince of Serbia at the Royal Palace in Belgrade.

The Duke of York was chief sponsor to the infant Crown Prince as he embarked on his chequered path through life. The Duke held the child throughout the service, while the Patriarch, who dropped him in the font (from which the Duke rescued him), named him Peter, and his grandmother, Queen Marie of Romania, placed a cross around his neck.

On this occasion the Duchess met a great number of exotic members of foreign royal houses. The only one she knew well was Prince Paul, who, the following day, married Princess Olga of Greece. Prince Paul had first spied his bride at a ball given by Lady Zia Wernher earlier that summer, a few months after she broke her engagement to the hard-drinking Crown Prince Frederik of Denmark, allegedly having disliked his habit of picking his teeth with a communal toothpick. The Duke of York was Prince Paul's best man.

Elizabeth now met Olga's sister, Princess Marina, with their autocratic mother, Princess Nicholas of Greece, the Kings of Romania and Yugoslavia, Queen Elisabeth of Greece, and Queen Sophie of Greece. She was given her first foreign order, the Grand Cross of the Order of St Sava, which rather swamped her due to the width of the ribbon. Queen Marie later wrote of Elizabeth: 'She has an inborn sweetness and is in reality much more attractive than in the pictures taken of her . . . She is not imposing, but she is sweet and loveable.'[30]

This visit prompted the departure from the Duke's household of his Comptroller, Wing Commander Louis Greig, who had been with his household since 1918. Greig had been the staunchest of his bachelor friends since Osborne days. George V had appointed him a CVO at the time of the Duke's wedding. The Duke confided in him and trusted him completely. He even wrote to him from Polesden Lacey on his honeymoon to report that all had gone well.[31] Young wives do not always wish to retain those who enjoy such intimate confidences.

Greig had been such a mentor to the Duke of York that it was inevitable that he should now be in danger of proving superfluous. A row developed over him not accompanying the Yorks on their Romanian trip, it being decided that Ronald Waterhouse, who had been there with the Duke the previous year, would be more suitable. Greig took offence, especially since Waterhouse was no longer part of the Duke's household.

Even when the King suggested that the Duke might take both men, the Duke did not want Greig. This may have been to suit Elizabeth. The result was that Greig resigned. The King and Queen were angry when the Duke explained that he felt that, being married, it was 'better to have a change as things have not been working too smoothly and we both feel the time has come'.[32] The rumour in London was that it was the Duchess who was responsible for the rift, preferring to have her own team in place. Elizabeth wrote to Greig on 14 November distancing herself from the fracas, thanking him and expressing her regret about his departure. But had she wanted him to stay on, she would have been more than capable of having intervened. This, conspicuously, she did not do.

During this phase the Yorks were able to escape to Guilsborough Hall for their hunting. The early months of 1924 were spent between White Lodge and hunting in Northamptonshire. When in Richmond, the Duke liked to play golf at Sudbrook, where he was elected captain. The Duchess was the Club's only lady member and she played mid-week.

At royal engagements she was popular, introducing as light a touch as she dared. When at Kingston District Hospital, a small boy of ten missed his chance to take a snap of the Duke and Duchess, they went back to him, posing until he had got the frame.

Occasions involving the King were more fraught, since he held strong views on ladies' fashions, and he fulminated against modern hairstyles. Flesh-coloured stockings were one of his dislikes. Lady Godfrey-Faussett, wife of the King's equerry, went through agonies when her husband insisted she wore black stockings. She had no old ones and black ones were no longer made. Helen Hardinge favoured shingled hair, but always put on a false bun in the presence of the Royal Family. George V did not like the Duchess of York's fringe and told her so. She apologised but retained the fringe nonetheless.

During the first state visit since her marriage, that of King Ferdinand of Romania, a state banquet was held, the Duchess wearing 'turquoise-blue, with beautiful jewels of delicate design'.[33] These were fraught occasions, Lord Milner summoning his tailor to help him dress, which took an hour and a half, and Lady Milner's false hair falling into the pudding. Ramsay MacDonald, the first ever Labour Prime Minister (elected that January), entered with the Duchess of Buccleuch on his arm, to the fury of the Scott family, while Daisy Bigge* announced that Lord Spencer had danced with MacDonald's spinster daughter, Ishbel, which was cited as 'an example of our democratic world'.[34]

That summer the Yorks were loaned Chesterfield House in Mayfair, the London home of the Duke's sister, Princess Mary, and her husband, Lord Lascelles, which they found more convenient than Richmond.

Elizabeth had certain engagements connected with charities. Younger members of the Royal Family did not work nearly as hard as in the latter part of the twentieth century. In those days ladies of the manor and mayoresses were asked to undertake duties in the shires and provinces. Later, as a result of television, either film stars or royalty were wanted. One engagement involved manning a stall for the Art Needlework Sale in Exhibition Road, at the end of May. Of this Helen Hardinge left a grim account:

> Elizabeth arrived to the strains of 'God Save the King' and was charming all through a most toilsome afternoon. Her lady-in-waiting

---

* Hon. Margaret (Daisy) Bigge (1885–1977), daughter of Lord Stamfordham, the King's Private Secretary.

[Lady Katharine Meade] is useless. Everything fell on Kat [Lady Katharine Hamilton] and [me]. The Principal, Miss Bradshaw, was charming, but rushed to [me] on every occasion. 'Do you think you could get those awful people away from the Duchess?' 'Do come and talk to her.' 'That lady over there with the red face and the feather boa will buy. She is very rich, could you get her?' etc. etc.

Solid, staring, goofish phalanxes of freaks surrounded Elizabeth. Their bad manners were beyond words. I said to Katie 'We can't stand this, we must get a little air to breathe.' So Kat and I charged the freaks tirelessly all the afternoon through with information about prices. Before this they melted like the snow. Lady Glentanar, Lady Northcote, Lady Wemyss, Lady Lansdowne were retrieved by me from the awful crowd and all bought.

I finally induced the Principal to take Elizabeth down to tea where Miss Bradshaw kindly insisted on K. & I coming too to join them. Princess H.V. [Helena Victoria] also had to be rescued several times during the course of the afternoon![35]

Another occasion, scarcely less grim, was the Trebovir Road annual meeting at which the young Duchess presided:

It was very interesting and a splendid crusade feeling about it. [Elizabeth] talked to all the gallant people who are making it the success it is and listened to their exalted but practical plans.

She was asked to propose something and mumbled sadly as it was burst upon her without one second's warning.[36]

On 19 July the Yorks sailed to Larne, to pay an official visit to Northern Ireland to be made Doctors of Letters at Queen's University, attend a dinner at Stormont Castle, lay the foundations of the new City Art Gallery in Belfast and for the Duke to receive the Freedom of the City.

According to the Duke of York, a rope that stretched from their destroyer to a tug caught the top hats of the welcoming committee, sweeping these into the sea. This story he elaborated for the benefit of his house party, adding that a man was sent up to remove the rope, but, while descending in sitting position, impaled himself on a bayonet held up by one of the Guard of Honour. The press had apparently reported that the Duchess had nearly been swept into the sea herself, which was strenuously denied by the Governor of Northern Ireland's Private Secretary, Commander Oscar Henderson, dubbed 'Dear Oscar' by the Duchess of York.

When the Yorks were at Clandeboye for the weekend they overheard an angry conversation instigated by Henderson, which boomed out through an open window to the lawn outside.

> Henderson: 'HRH nearly pushed off the pier this morning.'
> Duchess of York (*sotto voce*): 'Liar.'
> Henderson: 'It is a bit too much, you know, but if you promise it won't happen again . . .'
> Duke of York: 'No, because she is not going anywhere near a pier again.'

The Duke of Abercorn had been Governor of Northern Ireland since 1922. In order to entertain the Yorks for the weekend he had taken over Clandeboye, the 1820s house near Bangor in County Down of the Marquess of Dufferin and Ava, which was filled with souvenirs of the 1st Marquess's exotic travels, including tusks, hieroglyphs and a large, stuffed grizzly bear. His hostess was his daughter, Katie Hamilton, the Duchess of Abercorn being unwell.

Helen Hardinge was in the party. She and Katie were gossiping happily when the stamping of feet and blowing of trumpets announced that the Yorks had arrived. The house was soon filled with clanking swords and general bustle. Elizabeth changed into a thin frock, but realised she had no petticoat so one had to be smuggled to her past a barrage of staff officers, who had overrun the house. Helen had the chance to observe the young married couple together:

> Elizabeth was so sweet this afternoon trying to show P. B. his sitting room. He became absorbed in some jungle prints along the passage and would not come. The corners of her mouth went down after the third attempt & putting both hands on his shoulders she said angelically: 'Bertie do listen to me.' He kissed her and came at once. The wisdom of the serpent![37]

While the Duke was changing, Elizabeth, Katie and the Duke of Abercorn sat in the garden and observed that there was a naval officer looking out of practically every window. Then a phalanx of six guards marched round the corner bearing a huge dining-room table which was hoisted in through the window. There was no sign of the Duke, so Elizabeth went in to see 'if he had died quietly in his room', as she put it. The delay was explained by his valet having packed the right shoe in one suitcase, the left shoe in another. Helen continued:

Elizabeth, Katie, Prince Bertie and I sallied forth arm in arm
through the woods to the great Lord Dufferin's grave. This Dufferin
had a humble wish – that his sons should be buried with him. One
was killed in S. Africa, where his body lies, one in France where
his body was never found, the wife of a third wished another burial
place, and only one now survives.[38]

Official engagements lay ahead, but this weekend the Yorks were
delighted to be 'away from all the pushers'. They talked of their forthcoming visit to Africa, the peace of being away from London, how much
they looked forward to their annual holiday in Scotland and how nice it
was that there were no anxious hostesses threatening them with a game
of bridge or Mahjong. In the peace of the garden, Elizabeth asked Helen
to sing 'The bells of Hell'. That evening they had so much fun playing
poker that the Duke of Abercorn had to press the Duke of York to go up
to bed since the official guests were pining to go home.

On Sunday the house party went to Clandeboye's chapel. The clergyman addressed them on sins that none of them had committed. Helen
observed the Yorks listening with 'the poker expression of people trained
not to laugh when they want to', which was hard when the clergyman
intoned: 'Even if man is descended from a gibbering ape in an African
forest . . .' which nearly set them off. That evening Helen sat with the
Duchess after dinner telling improper stories. The evening ended with
the Yorks, Helen and Katie ragging about:

P. B. [Prince Bertie] possesses a ticklish hand. This discovery made
by his wife came in most useful in controlling HRH's ragging form
which otherwise might have become a bit too compelling.[39]

On Monday 21 July the official tour began and there was a procession into Belfast with the inevitable Guard of Honour, and an 'awful
walk round a most depressing hospital', at the end of which the party
was extremely hungry. Eighty-four addresses were presented by 'some
of the best comic turns in Ulster', and most of the curtseys were achieved
by the ladies sticking out their posteriors. In the evening there was a
dinner followed by a supper, long before the dinner had been digested,
and one guest was overheard to say: 'The Duchess is so lovely and so
h-animated.'

The Duchess was nothing if not professional. Her main regret was
that the supper had gone on so long with so much time wasted that she
had not been able to shake hands with enough of the assembled Northern

Ireland gentry. 'When I do a thing I do like to do it well and feel people are satisfied,' she said. All her life she hated to disappoint.[40]

They ended that day staying with the Duke of Abercorn at his own home, Baronscourt, County Tyrone, visiting scouts and guides and flax mills, where the managers showed them mens' underwear in the making, of which they were proud. This was 'productive . . . of a great deal of Royal wit' from the Duke later that evening.[41] The tour continued with visits to Dungannon and Londonderry, where they stayed at Mount Stewart. In the evenings Katie and Helen escaped to Elizabeth's room to gossip about the day and the Duke joined them. Elizabeth told them that the Lord Mayor, next to whom she had sat at lunch, 'burst into flames'. He told her 'it had gone right through to his pants.'[42] They sailed home on 27 July.

Life was not pressed with official engagements, particularly not in the late summer. The contrast of the Yorks' life in Scotland was very marked depending on whether they were at Balmoral with the King or at Glamis with Elizabeth's family.

Elizabeth and her friends feared Balmoral every bit as much as the later generation, in particular Diana, Princess of Wales. But, unlike Diana, she made the best of such situations.

One evening Elizabeth sat next to the King during an 'entertainment' and later made her friends laugh by telling them she was black and blue from his 'friendly elbowings' as he 'accompanied every raucous chuckle with an elbow thrust in her direction'. She teased the Duke of York: 'I'm sure when we're old, Bertie, you & I will be sitting at the play together & you will be doing that to me.'[43]

An interlude at Glamis was a happy contrast. Helen Hardinge arrived with her husband on 24 August:

> E greeted us in the dark of Duncan's Hall and took us to have tea. She has a lovely large golden Labrador called Glen, which she spoils deliciously.
>
> After shaking hands & listening to Lady Nina [Balfour]'s cease-less outpourings for half an hour, E. & I went for a turn in the garden. We walked along between the yew hedges and looked back on the picturesque turrets of the castle which were somewhat marred by the repairs which are being done on the roof where the fire [of 1916] destroyed it. E & I gossiped peacefully. She talked of their trip to Africa and how Portia [Stanley] had arranged everything for their trip with the King and with the Queen – which of them, Portia

or E, should take a maid. Firmness and tact have extracted the Yorks from the awkward position of 4 months trips with the Stanleys.

She spoke highly of Tor-Tor [Gilmour] and indignantly of the patronising airs of her sisters: 'Who are they – to be so frightfully pleased with themselves – why should anybody think as much of themselves as all that?' Glen, the dog, was so good.[44]

Elizabeth fed her dog and gave her mother a cocktail before dinner. The Duke was in humorous mood, full of what he considered risqué stories: 'One peeress to another in the gallery of the House of Lords. "Do you believe in a *second chamber?*" Answer: "Oh yes, my husband is a very *Liberal* peer".'

After dinner Lady Strathmore played the piano 'and looked so charming, just the two candles showing up her really angelic face. E. spoke of the set expression her mother always gets when occupied and said she was exactly similar. The set expression is such a pleasant one that its setness doesn't matter.'

Lady Strathmore had bought some bright lamps, the castle still being without electricity. Elizabeth did not like these, so she embraced her mother warmly and then asked her where she had got those 'frightful lamps'. She insisted on turning them off and Glamis reverted to candle-light, which showed the room in a gentler, if slightly haunting light.

The men of the party came up from the dining room and 'clustered round the piano making vulgar suggestions which they expected her to render tuneful. However she continued her own attractive tunes with great placidity.' The evening ended with the lamps being lit again for games, laughter and general chaos, Lady Nina Balfour still chattering away ceaselessly, and the rest of the party playing bridge and rummy.

Lady Nina was in full voice at breakfast next morning, prompting David Bowes-Lyon to speculate that she must have read aloud to herself all night to keep her facial muscles in good working order. In the evening the girls of the party sat with Elizabeth in her room. As she flicked through the social columns, with pictures of people on the Lido or at Deauville, she observed 'in a voice tinged with thought': 'Fancy going on a long journey with the Mountbattens.' When pressed as to whether the Prince of Wales had chosen the Mountbattens or vice versa, she said: 'Oh they chose him.'[45]

Then it was Balmoral again, where a redeeming feature of church attendance at Crathie was to sit behind the King, his baldness gleaming in the morning light, and to observe the embarrassed faces of those in the congregation, obliged to worship directly under the royal eye.

Life at the castle was no lighter than usual. In a desperate attempt to lighten the mood at dinner Elizabeth suggested that Diamond Hardinge's clothes were all held by pins and might fall to the floor at any moment. The King and the Duke of York seized the mood of the moment and 'expatiated on this joke beyond the bounds of the vulgar'.[46]

On the rare occasion when guests were invited, the King made a point of entering from the dining room at about two minutes to ten, and announcing: 'I'm sure it must be long past your bedtime' to provoke the guests to leave. Elizabeth was taken to a lunch party at Dunnecht, after which she felt sick. There had been ten courses.

The King did not hesitate to declare that 'all people who wore their hair piled on their heads & hats perched on this edifice were "monstrous & disgusting".'[47] He thought all the young girls looked exactly alike, choosing the unfortunate examples of Maureen Stanley, Dorothé Plunket and Portia Stanley.*

Elizabeth planned to take Katie Hamilton to Glamis with her. So Katie, who had been staying with the Hardinges at Altnaguibsach, came to lunch at the castle on 23 September. Mindful of the monarch's dislike of modern fashion, she perched her hat on her toupée, scraped her hair back behind her ears and let her skirt down. She began her visit, terrified, in the equerries' room, with Sir Sidney Greville, Lord Stamfordham and the Archbishop of York.

In due course she was ushered up to Elizabeth's room, rushed in, embraced Elizabeth with affectionate familiarity, but failed to notice 'something massive in the corner – the Queen knitting a voluminous pink woollen garment!'. In the other corner sat Princess Helena Victoria whom Katie described as 'trout major'. She was soon reduced to sitting trembling on a hard chair, answering 'Yes, Ma'am' when addressed.

At lunch Lady Bessie Dawson, Queen Mary's lady-in-waiting, took her in and to her horror she found herself seated at a round table with the King and Queen and the Yorks. But it went well. Elizabeth kept the conversation buzzing and the King enjoyed himself, talking about harems! Later the Duke of York told her she had 'got off with the old man'! When Katie prepared to leave with Elizabeth no one could find her bag and everyone waited about, until at last a footman arrived carrying her old mackintosh with her knitting sticking out of the pocket.†[48]

On the way to Glamis Elizabeth told Katie that this year at Balmoral

* Maureen Stanley and Dorothé Plunket did indeed look alike. They were half-sisters, Dorothé being the illegitimate daughter of Lord Londonderry by the actress Fanny Ward.
† Katie Hamilton clearly impressed the King and Queen Mary. In 1927 she was appointed a Woman of the Bedchamber to Queen Mary, serving until 1930, when she married the King's widowed equerry, Lt-Col. Sir Reginald Seymour. At the time of her appointment, she was described somewhat unfairly as 'the first Bright Young Thing at Court'.

had been much better than the first year, and everyone had been very understanding. They drove to Glamis in the mountain mists, and during their stay they all went to the Forfar County Ball, Elizabeth adorned in pink satin.

Hardly had the Duchess of York and Katie left Balmoral than the King's Scottish domain became the scene of a grim drama. On 6 October, the kind lady-in-waiting Lady Bessie Dawson fell on her morning walk at the top of the hill behind Craigowan and had to crawl back, to be rescued by two gardeners who carried her into the castle. A surgeon and a nurse arrived and she was diagnosed with an intracapsular fracture of the left femur. Being Spartan by nature, she lay in bed in her room, and, despite being in great pain, caused no fire to be lit and left the window wide open. Nor would she have her twenty-four-year-old daughter Kaitlin informed of her plight. The King declared that Lady Bessie would certainly catch double pneumonia and die, so the Queen obliged Princess Helena Victoria to go and tell the nurse to close the window and light the fire.

After dinner Princess Helena Victoria went on her mission, in which she was successful, while the King spluttered: 'Her father* was the most *obstinate* man I ever knew – and I expect her mother was the same.' Meanwhile, Queen Mary worried about the daughter, and pointed out that Lady Bessie was seeking to give no trouble, but that if only she would do as she was told then it would all be much easier for everyone.

The King then read about a woman who had suffered a similar accident and had needed both legs amputated. This led to a long conversation about people who had come to untimely and unlikely ends, the Queen ending with the complaint: 'It all comes from this mania for exercise.'

Sir Derek Keppel, the Master of the Household, was due at the castle. Since he was suffering from lumbago, he wanted to retire to bed on arrival. The King thundered: 'Why should they all want to come here to be ill!' He launched into a tirade about how Lady Bessie had been dressed when she fell. 'Of course the shoes ladies wear nowadays I don't wonder they fall down & a silly little umbrella about one foot long which could not support anybody or keep the rain off either . . .'[49]

The saga ended tragically. Lady Bessie was taken into an Aberdeen nursing home. The King and Queen went south on 9 October, the Court Circular announcing that Lady Elizabeth Dawson was unable to attend Her Majesty on her return to London. The unfortunate lady-in-waiting

---

* Admiral of the Fleet 4th Earl of Clanwilliam.

then died in the nursing home of a cerebral embolism on 13 October, aged fifty-five. Hopes that Queen Mary might do the honourable thing and relieve Elizabeth of Lady Katharine Meade, Lady Bessie's sister, by taking her on as lady-in-waiting, came to nought.

There is a curious postscript to this saga. Lady Bessie's daughter was finally informed of her mother's accident and death. Her woes were not over. In 1929 she married Captain Lord Bingham, MC, and went on to be the mother of the 7th Earl of Lucan, who murdered the family nanny and disappeared in 1974.

7

Africa and Australia

'Everybody understands that North Island was too strenuous'
– the Duke of York

The Yorks soon became the most hard-working members of the Royal Family. The Prince of Wales may have been more glamorous and outwardly charming but he was often away, while Princess Mary undertook fewer duties in this phase, being preoccupied with her two small sons,* and living mainly in Yorkshire. Prince Henry and Prince George were serving in the armed forces. Sir Herbert Morgan, chairman of Macfisheries, declared that 'the Duchess of York as a Royalty goes, she is still a novelty & has not worked herself out'.[1]

After a visit by the Duchess of York to Queen's College, Harley Street, the Bishop of London pronounced: 'I do not think that any one has ever won such amazing popularity so soon as the Duchess of York. It is only equalled by Queen Alexandra who, when she came from Denmark, had the world at her feet in five minutes.'[2]

On 1 December, the eightieth birthday of Queen Alexandra, the Yorks departed for East Africa. Seen off by Elizabeth's siblings, Rose, Michael and Jock, and by Mrs Greville, the Duchess looked 'very gay and smiling in a becoming costume of Havana-brown',[3] it was reported in the press. They were accompanied by Captain Basil Brooke, Lady Annaly (the former Lady Lavinia Spencer, a childhood friend, to whose daughter Elizabeth† the Duchess had lately become godmother) and Colin Buist. They were to be away until 19 April.

King George VI's official biographer states that both the Duke and the Duchess were 'badly in need of a holiday from the gruelling round of their official duties'.[4] Sister Catherine Black who nursed George V from 1928 wrote that it was 'a significant fact' that the Duchess 'seriously taxed' her health following her marriage, such were the demands of royal life.[5] Wheeler-Bennett also pointed out that the Yorks were keen

---

* George, the eldest, had been joined by Gerald Lascelles on 21 August 1924, Elizabeth and the Prince of Wales standing as godparents.
† Hon. Elizabeth (Patsy) White (1923–2004) married 1945, Lt-Com. James King.

to see something of the British Commonwealth before settling into the more accepted routine of married life. At the 1923 Imperial Conference the Duke had hinted to one of the Dominion Prime Ministers that he would like to visit his country, but the King vetoed this, saying 'the young people had just been married and must settle down'.[6]

There was a further unstated reason for this visit. Dynastic thoughts were never far from the forefront of courtiers' minds and while the British court was not as demanding in this respect as the Japanese Imperial Court, an heir in the male line was required. The Royal Family and the Royal Household had not quite despaired of the Prince of Wales, but they were heading towards that despair, and inevitably hoped that the Duchess of York might soon produce a child. Some time before George V died, and after the birth of Princess Elizabeth in 1926, the King declared that he hoped nothing would stand between Bertie, his daughter Lilibet (the present Queen) and the throne. Such conclusions were not formed overnight. There was more pressure on the Yorks than was ever directly expressed.

That there was a more intimate reason for the trip is not mere speculation. After the trip, Colin Buist, the equerry, asked in despair: 'Is there anything one can do to make her have a baby?' To which the lady-in-waiting, Lady Annaly, said she longed to reply: 'Well, if you don't know what it is, I'm not going to tell you.'[7]

The East African Tour was to be a mixture of official engagements with a considerable amount of big-game hunting. Such trips did not take place without complaints in Parliament. The Labour MP Commander Kenworthy (the Willie Hamilton of his day) enquired whether any expenditure from Colonial Government funds had taken place in connection with the visit. As Chancellor of the Exchequer, Winston Churchill informed him that the visit 'although of undoubted value in the public interest' was 'intended from the first to be unofficial in its character', and there were therefore no charges on the Exchequer. However, he added: 'When the Duke of York arrived in Kenya, the Legislature (including all the elected members) spontaneously expressed the wish to entertain his Royal Highness as their guest. In these circumstances his Royal Highness gratefully accepted their kindly offer.' This was greeted with 'ironic Opposition cheers'.[8]

The trip was a success and in later years, if the equerries were stuck for conversation, they had but to mention Africa and the Queen Mother's eyes would light up. She kept an album of photographs and loved looking through it and showing it. She travelled with the same vanity case that had accompanied her through the long journey, borne on the head of a bearer. One of her abiding memories of the trip was meeting a man who proved to be a murderer on the run.[9]

The Yorks travelled via Paris, staying in Lord Derby's apartment on Avenue d'Iena, to Marseilles, where they sailed on 5 December. They continued by sea to Port Said, Aden and reached Mombasa on 22 December, crossing the equator, and the Duke thus taking part in the King Neptune ceremony.

They were greeted by Sir Robert Coryndon, the Governor of Kenya, with whom they stayed at Government House, Mombasa. Sir Robert was a man much respected by the natives not only as a determined ruler, but also a first-class shot. After a garden party the Yorks saw tribal dances performed by five thousand natives. They then travelled to Nairobi in the Governor's train through jungles, mountains and plains, through land which man could not otherwise reach. Christmas was spent with Sir Robert at Nairobi, and there followed six weeks of safari, during which the Duchess, employing a 0.275 rifle, shot a great number of wild animals, including rhinoceros, buffalo, waterbuck, oryx, Grant's gazelle, dik-dik, Kenya hartebeest, steenbok, wart hog and jackal. The days were long and hot, the nights exciting under tents. Sometimes they heard animal charges in the night, and on one occasion a sudden storm wrecked the entire camp.

Both the Duke and Duchess loved Kenya and were sorely tempted when the colony offered to give them a farm. The Duke was keen to accept it, but the idea found no favour at Sandringham. Hardinge explained:

> Both the Colonial Office and the King was against it, for certain political reasons connected with the grant of land out there to ex-Service men, and also because it would both set an awkward precedent and would mean that he would frequently have to go out there and see how it was getting on. He was therefore told that he must refuse the offer, but that there was no objection to his buying a ranch if he cared to. From what I know of him he will not want to fork out![10]

The Kenyan holiday ended suddenly when Sir Robert Coryndon suddenly died following an emergency operation for pancreatitis. The Duke of York cancelled the rest of his holiday and attended the Governor's military funeral.

The Duke and Duchess left Kenya earlier than planned and went to Uganda. The Duke found Uganda less attractive, but they were seeing it in the dry season. Nevertheless he shot a magnificent elephant with ninety pound tusks, a second elephant in the long grass and a lion. He also bagged a white rhino, whose skull he later presented to the Natural History Museum in South Kensington. Having shot one white rhino herself, the Duchess made a 'favourable impression' by declining to shoot another, on being told they were rare, in danger of extinction and comparatively harmless beasts.[11]

They entered the Sudan at Nimule and embarked on a river steamer called *Nasir* to sail down the Nile. They exchanged their Uganda wardens for the official Game Warden to the Sudan Government, Captain Courtney Brocklehurst, and his assistant, Major Walsh.

Brocklehurst was an intriguing figure and he was not a stranger to the Duchess. She had met him in Scotland when he married Mabell, Countess of Airlie's war-widow daughter, Helen.* Some time before the trip, the Duke of York had invited him to lunch in London to discuss plans.

Nobody knew the Sudan better than 'Brock'. The game ranges were the largest and most varied of all the British possessions. To the east were the dry and stony mountains of the Red Sea, there were gorges near the Abyssinian frontier, and to the west the great Sahara. There were great swamps in the south through which the Situtunga and Nile Kob passed. There was parkland near the Congo border as well as thick tropical forest. The white rhinoceros could be found there, and great bull elephants lived in the extreme south near the Ugandan border.

'Over this great range of sun-parched land, Captain Courtney Brocklehurst has kept a watchful and experienced eye for many years,' wrote the big-game traveller, author and artist, J. G. Millais. 'His journeys to-and-fro have been constant and tireless – Captain Brocklehurst has never spared himself in finding out all that was necessary to protect and improve the status of various rare species.'[12]

Sir Geoffrey Archer, the Governor-General, was impressed by his great knowledge of the wilds and his personal bravery:

> He was a very gallant man, and one for whom I conceived a great liking and regard. It was delightful going round the Khartoum Zoo with him – he was officially in charge – and observing his gentle way with animals, and how his pet chimpanzee, seeing him coming,

---

* Lady Helen Ogilvy (1890–1973), married first Hon. Clement Freeman-Mitford, who was killed in action in 1915; second Lt-Col. H. C. Brocklehurst, divorced 1931, and third, Lt-Col. Harold Nutting. She was the mother of the politician Sir Anthony Nutting. She later became a campaigner on marriage issues, the status of women and divorce law reform.

would waddle along the path on his hind legs chattering and gibbering and at full speed to hurl himself into his arms.[13]

Refreshingly ahead of his time, Brocklehurst took the view that: 'A good photograph of a wild animal in its natural surroundings is of more interest than all the heads, and is often a sign of great patience, courage and skill in bushcraft. Record heads mean nothing and are purely luck. Above all, don't kill just for the sake of killing!'[14]

The Duchess of York was delighted to see Brocklehurst again. She was fond of him, and he was the kind of man who encouraged all ladies to flirt with him. Used to figures such as James Stuart, she knew how to respond, but his wild, free life disconcerted her for a while, as it made her life as the Duke of York's wife in England appear constricted and conventional. She confided her excitement at having him as their guide to Katie Seymour in London on her return. Years later she wrote to a friend: 'I adored hearing about your thrilling adventures with B---k . . . Somehow it took one's mind back to a happier and more "jolly" world.'[15]

She was right to admire Brocklehurst as was proved by his courageous end. In 1940 he rejoined the 10th Royal Hussars and served in the Middle East and Burma. On 28 June 1942 he was carried away and drowned while attempting to save the lives of his coolies who floundered, unable to swim, while crossing a river in spate.

Because water was scarce, herds of game, including white-eared kob, came to the riverside to drink. Every now and then the Yorks disembarked and went for a two-day excursion to shoot, accompanied by the Game Warden. They witnessed a tribal gathering at Talodi with 12,000 natives, saw a display of Nuba dancing, and eventually arrived in Khartoum. There they stayed in the palace that Lord Kitchener had built to replace the one in which Gordon had been killed, and which the Mahdi had destroyed less than thirty years before.

In Khartoum their host was the Governor-General, Sir Geoffrey Archer, who had been appointed following the murder of his predecessor, Sir Lee Stack. Sir Geoffrey was a celebrated ornithologist, whose book *The Birds of British Somaliland and the Gulf of Aden* is still a recognised classic. With him, they saw the battlefield of Omdurman, which Churchill had described in his book *The River War*.

The Yorks were easy guests. Exhausted after their trip – 'we were all feeling too tattered and burnt and dirty for words'[16] as Elizabeth put it – all they wanted was a peaceful time. When pressed, Elizabeth asked only for a large jug of iced shandygaff (beer and ginger beer) to be sent up to their room. The Duke asked that there should be no official visits, and the only official engagement was an evening party in the palace grounds where the Yorks chatted with representatives of Khartoum society. One present was the Duchess's old admirer from 1922, Archie Clark Kerr, then serving as acting Counsellor at the British Embassy in Cairo.

Presently they embarked in the P & O liner *Majola* at Port Sudan, returning to England ten days later. From the ship the Duchess wrote to thank the Governor-General:

> Today we had our last glimpse of Africa which is terribly sad, as we really have had a wonderful time. I expect we shall be at Rowland Ward (the taxidermist in Piccadilly G.A.) for the next three weeks![17]

During their absence the King had been seriously ill with bronchitis and, on doctor's orders, had undertaken a recuperative cruise in the Mediterranean. It was this trip to which Queen Mary had so looked forward and which was ruined for her by the presence of the King's spinster sister, Princess Victoria, who goaded the King to silly jokes and destroyed the cultural possibilities of the voyage. The King and Queen arrived back on 25 April.

In May the Duchess of York opened the sale of works for the Royal School of Needlework, inspiring the normal bad behaviour from the charity ladies – 'the cow-like women of ill will who block Elizabeth's stall on the pretence of buying & drift away after a prolonged gaze at Royalty, without buying anything'.[18]

One of the projects to which the Duchess devoted much time was the Mothercraft Training Society at Cromwell House, in Highgate, regularly attending their various events. She was President of this society, which had been founded by a New Zealander, Dr (later Sir) Truby King, Director of Child Welfare in New Zealand, a kind of Dr Spock of his day.*

On 27 May the Duchess of York dined with her cousin, Lord Henry Bentinck, and his wife at Queen Anne's Gate. The other guests were Lady Salisbury, Mr & Mrs Jasper Ridley, Lord and Lady Islington, Lord and Lady Mildmay of Flete, Lord and Lady Howard de Walden, Ruby Peto and Lord Henry's sister, Lady Ottoline Morrell (unkindly nicknamed 'Lady Utterly Immoral' by some of Elizabeth's girlfriends). Lady Ottoline recorded:

---

* She met him in New Zealand in 1927.

Elizabeth Bowes-Lyon – a star even as a child, 1904

The Earl of Strathmore in the robes of the
Order of the Thistle by Philip de László

The Countess of Strathmore
by Philip de László

Glamis Castle, 1927

Elizabeth, pensive in the woods

'The Two Benjamins' – Elizabeth, aged nine, with her younger brother David

Elizabeth, aged 2, at St Paul's, Walden Bury

Prince Albert of Wales

Elizabeth and David acting at Glamis

Elizabeth growing up

Elizabeth with her parents, 1919

Elizabeth with Elphinstone nieces and nephew

The Strathmore family. Standing (left to right): Fergus, John, Lord Strathmore, Mary (Elphinstone), Patrick and Alexander. Seated: Rose (Granville), Lady Strathmore with baby David, Elizabeth and Michael.

Elizabeth Bowes-Lyon and her sister, Rose Leveson-Gower (later Countess Granville), with a wounded soldier, convalescing at Glamis in 1916

Hon. James Stuart in the uniform
of the Royal Scots

Elizabeth as debutante

St Paul's, Walden Bury

The balcony scene after the wedding, 1923. Extreme left: Princess Louise, Duchess of Fife (The Princess Royal), with her daughter, Princess Maud. Centre: Queen Alexandra, Queen Mary, the bride and groom, King George V. Extreme right: The Dowager Empress of Russia.

The Bridal Group. Standing (left to right): Lady Mary Cambridge (later Duchess of Beaufort), Elizabeth, The Duke of York and Lady May Cambridge (later Abel Smith).
Seated: Hon. Diamond Hardinge (later Abercromby), Lady Mary Thynne (later Alexander), Lady Katharine Hamilton (later Seymour) and Betty Cator (later Bowes-Lyon). Seated on the floor: Hon. Elizabeth Elphinstone and Hon. Cecilia Bowes-Lyon.

Helen Hardinge

The young Duchess of York

Prince George (later Duke of Kent), Queen Mary and the Duke and Duchess of York
at Balmoral in the summer of 1923

We all had to line up in a semi-circle to be presented to her & make our Curtseys. She is a 'sweet' little thing appealing & charming, but not with great originality. She has quite adopted the Royal Manner. I talked to her about her Mother, & she said 'Yes, isn't she a dear'.[19]

In June, the Yorks went to stay at Bishopthorpe with the Archbishop of York, Cosmo Gordon Lang, who had married them. They undertook a tiring day in York and slept all the way home. At about this time the Duchess found she was pregnant.

The Queen Mother strongly disapproved of personal medical matters being aired in public. Suffice it to say that pregnancy did not come easily. Her gynaecologist was Sir Henry Simson, who had been connected to the Hospital for Women in Soho like the famous Dr Jervois Aarons.* Simson became an obstetric surgeon, writing many articles on the Caesarian section and other gynaecological matters. A man with strong ascetic features and an unfailingly courteous manner, he worked quietly and efficiently. He had been knighted in 1925 for his 'professional [gynae-cological] services' to Princess Mary, not long after the birth of her second son. When he died,† the Duchess said publicly: 'No man worked harder or more unselfishly to reduce maternal mortality.'[20]

Queen Alexandra had been deteriorating throughout the year. Throughout Ascot week in 1924, while the King and Queen and Royal Family enjoyed their racing, Sir Dighton Probyn, Queen Alexandra's trusty old Comptroller, languished near death at Sandringham and finally died on 20 June, aged ninety-one. Sir Henry Streatfeild, the Private Secre-tary, remained in charge of the Household, while Charlotte Knollys, Queen Alexandra's closest lady-in-waiting, turned ninety at the begin-ning of the year.

Both Queen Alexandra and Charlotte Knollys were becoming forgetful and failing to recognise people. Queen Alexandra deteriorated fast after

---

* Dr Jervois Aarons (d. 1923), of 17 Harley Street, London. A picturesque and brilliant figure and successful gynaecologist, to whom would-be mothers would apply if they had difficulties conceiving. The results were known as 'Aarons' babies'. Lady Diana Cooper consulted him and recalled later that the joke was that 'they were all his . . . He may have had a stud of handsome footmen lined up outside, but he claimed that they were a genuine case of artificial insemination. Stephen Tennant was one and so were both the Roxburghes [the 9th Duke and Lady Mary Crewe-Milnes] and they couldn't have children' (Lady Diana Cooper to author, 21 March 1980). Clementine Churchill consulted Aarons in 1912 and 1915. He was an expert on Dysparennia in the male caused by a condition in the female. He died 'by misadventure' following an operation on his bladder on 20 April 1923.

† Sir Henry Simson died suddenly on 13 September 1932, while awaiting the arrival of a patient upon whom an operation was to be performed.

Probyn's death and mumbled so badly that it was impossible to understand what she was saying. Queen Alexandra's bad cough and Miss Knollys's heart troubles laid them both low early in 1925.

By 14 November Queen Alexandra was failing rapidly and it was thought unlikely that she would last the winter. Five days later, the King was summoned from his shooting, driving to the Big House by Norwich Gate. Queen Alexandra had had a heart attack that morning, but rallied during the day, so the King returned to his sport.

That evening Queen Alexandra's condition became critical and she sank throughout the following day. The Prince of Wales and the Duke of York were summoned but arrived too late. Nor were the King and Queen with Queen Alexandra when she died. They had been there all day, but had retired briefly to York Cottage. When they attempted to return, their car broke down, and Queen Alexandra slipped away in their absence at 5.25 p.m.

Charlotte Knollys was distraught. Now nearly ninety-one, she had been taken in to see the dying Queen and had become 'hysterical and could not stop laughing', a nervous reaction. When the coffin was taken to All Saints Church, she howled at an open window, and, despite attempts to get her away, refused to move. The King then took her down to the church where she kept handling the coffin as if she could not believe it contained the Queen. Touchingly, she walked to Queen Alexandra's pew, picked up her prayer book, kissed it and put it down again.[21]

The King forbade his sons to hunt for a whole month out of respect for their grandmother, which caused a blistering row at a time when everybody was keyed up. The King cancelled the guests who normally shot with him, but by forbidding his sons' hunting he was able to get sufficient guns at York Cottage during the phase of mourning when his larger shooting parties were inappropriate. Certainly all the sons came down to Sandringham early in December.

Queen Alexandra's death provoked different reactions. The Home Secretary wanted no general mourning since this would be bad for trade. The Dean of Windsor complained that the burial being declared private meant that the remaining glory had been removed from St George's Chapel. He wrote an article about this, which irritated more than a few.*

The public part of the funeral was held at Westminster Abbey. Snow fell for two hours before the funeral procession from the Chapel Royal, making Queen Alexandra's last journey almost as memorable as her arrival in 1863. Snow covered the streets and the gun carriage. The Duchess of

* St George's Chapel was in the middle of its decade of restoration. There was no organ, which explains why the funeral was held at Westminster Abbey.

York was present with the rest of the Royal Family. The second part took place in the Albert Memorial Chapel at Windsor on 28 November, where the coffin then rested for a while.*

By this time it was known privately that the Duchess was expecting a child in 1926, though this was not announced in the press.

As early as Christmas 1925, a month after Queen Alexandra's death, the King and Queen were busily perusing her effects and sorting through her jewellery. By March they were hanging pictures and moving furniture around, as they prepared for their long-delayed move to the Big House. Queen Mary spent every day there between 10 a.m. and 6 p.m., obsessed by the operation but complaining daily about her horror of the house itself.

In January 1926 the Duchess of York suffered a car accident, but not a serious one. The next month, dissatisfied with White Lodge, Richmond, which was a huge financial burden and neither comfortable nor convenient, the Yorks searched for a country house. They entered a nomadic phase, and for country life the Duchess frequently retreated to her old family home, St Paul's Walden Bury, soon to be handed over to her brother David.

For the birth of their baby, the Yorks took over the Strathmores' London house, 17 Bruton Street. It was there that Princess Elizabeth of York was born at 2.40 a.m. on 21 April 1926. The Duke was in the room, as was Elizabeth's mother, Lady Strathmore. Sir Henry Simson, who was in attendance, announced that 'previous to the confinement a consultation took place at which Sir George Blacker† was present, and a certain line of treatment was successfully adopted'.[22] This indicated Caesarian section. The King and Queen were awakened at some time between 3 and 4 a.m. to be told of the birth of this princess, third in line to the throne.

As prescribed by ancient custom, in order to prevent baby swapping and upsetting the line of succession, the Home Secretary, Sir William Joynson-Hicks, was present in the house. Formal messages arrived from nine reigning Kings, a reigning Queen (the Netherlands) and a reigning Emperor (Japan). Ministers and chargés d'affaires from many lands kept the Foreign Office busy sending courteous acknowledgments.

According to the Duke of York in a letter to his parents, Elizabeth had always wanted a daughter. He hoped they were not disappointed that this

* Later King Edward and Queen Alexandra were buried in the special sarcophagus created for them on the south side of the altar, an effigy of the King's favourite dog, Caesar, being placed at his feet. Queen Alexandra has no animal at her feet. (King George V and Queen Mary reverted to the more traditional lion and unicorn.)

† Sir George Blacker was a Consulting Obstetric Physician to University College Hospital, London.

was not a third grandson. 'We always wanted a child to make our happiness complete,' he wrote, '& now that it has at last happened, it seems so wonderful & strange.'[23]

Princess Elizabeth was born just before the General Strike, which immobilised the country but inspired those with initiative to rally to the cause. She was christened Elizabeth Alexandra Mary by Cosmo Lang, Archbishop of York, in the private chapel at Buckingham Palace, with the King and Queen, Princess Mary, the Duke of Connaught,* the Earl of Strathmore and Lady Elphinstone as godparents. In June the Duchess took her daughter up to Glamis with her for a long holiday.

The birth of Princess Elizabeth provided the Duchess with an excuse to dispense with the services of Lady Katharine Meade and replace her with Lady Helen 'Nellie' Graham, the tall spinster daughter of the 5th Duke of Montrose, then aged forty-seven, who was a much greater help and remained with her until her death in 1945. Among her duties she had to answer considerable correspondence concerning the upbringing of the little princess, since members of the public liked to proffer advice or to ask for details that they could then apply in their own households.

In the autumn of 1926 the Duke of York spoke several times in public during the Imperial Conference.† Stanley Bruce, the Prime Minister of Australia since 1923, had wanted one of the King's sons to come to the federal capital when Parliament convened for the first time in its new legislative buildings.

Since July 1925 negotiations had been opened with the Duke of York, the obvious choice, but there was understandable concern as to whether he would be able to cope with such a long tour. Bruce had heard him speak and was distressed by the inhibition caused by his stammer. It was agony to listen to him as he hesitated and stumbled over his words, with long, anxious pauses between his words. He had been to a variety of specialists in the past, to no avail, and he began to fear that his affliction was not physical but caused by the mind.

Lionel Logue was an Australian speech therapist who had discovered

---

* In appointing the Duke of Connaught, the last surviving son of Queen Victoria, an historical link was forged, for the Duke, born on 1 May 1850, had been a godson of the great Duke of Wellington, victor of the Battle of Waterloo and an ancestral great-uncle of the Duchess of York. He had served as Colonel of Grenadier Guards since the death of the Duke of Cambridge in 1904. In this post, Princess Elizabeth would succeed him in 1942.

† This was the first Imperial Conference since 1923. Six of the Dominions were represented – Canada, Australia, New Zealand, South Africa, the Irish Free State and Newfoundland. Stanley Bruce told the Conference that the great problem for the Empire was one of men, money and markets. He said that the development of the Dominions depended absolutely on the purchasing power of Britain.

he had the gift of healing speech defects during the war, and had come to London to practise in 1924. He was recommended to the Duke, and the Duchess insisted her husband should overcome his initial reluctance and make one more attempt.

Logue's methods were to inspire confidence, encourage correct breathing and convince his patients that they could heal themselves. It was therefore a collaboration, and one into which Elizabeth entered wholeheartedly, coming often to Logue's Harley Street consultancy rooms or working at home with the Duke, the pair lying on the floor, learning to get the breathing right so that speech could follow. The Duke was aware that it was hard to alter a defect of many years standing, but he was soon singing Logue's praises and wishing he had met him years earlier. Public speaking would always be a burden to him, and till the end of his life, his more sympathetic audiences went through agonies on his behalf, but Logue gave him the necessary confidence to undertake the Australian trip. Presently he found he could even converse in a relaxed manner with his father, whose lack of patience with him had contributed to the stammer in the first place.

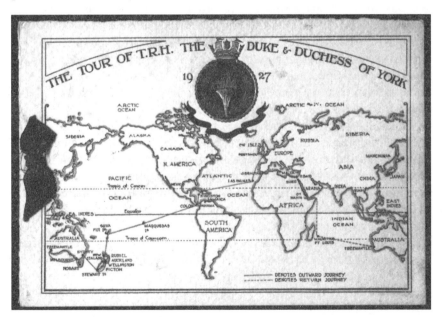

New Zealand and Australia

The Yorks' trip to New Zealand and Australia greatly enhanced their popularity on the world stage. It was demanding and meant that they were away from home for over six months, by which time they had travelled right round the world, rendering, as one who accompanied them put it: 'so signal and unselfish a service in the glorious cause of empire'.[24]

The captions in Ian Lucas's account, *The Royal Embassy*, give an indication of what they went through: 'At Jamaica's cenotaph: The Duke's tribute', 'The Duchess is initiated into Neptune's kingdom', 'A cheery word for a crippled soldier at Auckland', 'The Duchess inspects the wolf cubs at Wellington', 'An old pensioner amuses the Duke with a whip-cracking display at Christchurch', 'The Duchess with the mothers and widows of fallen soldiers at Hobart', and many similar ones.

The tour was not without controversy, taking place at a time of industrial depression. On 14 March, the First Lord of the Admiralty, William Bridgeman, informed the House of Commons that the Duke was undertaking a heavy responsibility and a replica of the Speaker's Chair was being placed in the new Parliament building in Canberra. He thought that the £7000 supplementary estimate for the trip was money well spent.

Some members of the Labour Party went into the attack, saying that it would have been more beneficial had the Yorks travelled 'in the ordinary way in passenger steamers', in order to glean the view of regular passengers, instead of being 'practically wrapped in cotton wool'. Nor was this the right time for 'a pleasure trip of this kind'. David Kirkwood, a particularly rebellious Labour MP, who had once been deported under the Defence of the Realm Act (admittedly only to Edinburgh), went so far as to say that 'It would not matter one iota to the welfare of the country if they never returned.' This was greeted with ministerial cries of 'Silence' and 'Withdraw'.[25]

Since the whole purpose of the tour was for the Duke to open Parliament in Canberra, the decision to visit New Zealand first caused annoyance in Australia. The reason for this depended on climate and 'the demands which would be made on the powers of endurance of the Duchess of York',[26] a hint that the Duchess might not be able to bear the strain, as proved to be the case.

The Yorks embarked in the battle cruiser *Renown* on 6 January 1927, with General Lord Cavan as Chief of Staff (giving orders from bed or a bath chair due to a broken leg). Lady Cavan and Tor-Tor Gilmour were Elizabeth's ladies-in-waiting. Thirteen hundred officers and men made up the ship's company.

They sailed via Las Palmas, across the Atlantic in rough seas to Jamaica, and after two tempestuous days at sea reached the Panama Canal, through which *Renown* was pulled by electric trolleys. They arrived at Balboa and sailed on to the Marquesas Islands, the Duchess's cabin made livelier by two parakeets purchased for her in Las Palmas, one of which sadly died, whereupon its grief-stricken mate plunged to its death in the sea.

The visit to the Marquesas Islands was informal, there being only two white officials on the island and no troops to form a guard of honour. Cannibalism had only been eliminated here some forty years earlier, and they met one man who could remember, 'seemingly not without delight',[27] the taste of human flesh. They visited Fiji in a downpour of warm rain, which hid the crowd of five thousand under a sea of prettily coloured umbrellas.

On 22 February they reached Auckland and began their tour of New Zealand. Elizabeth put on a delphinium-blue georgette dress with flowing gown and matching hat for the arrival and first round of receptions. Then they set off for a ten-day tour of North Island by road and rail, considered the most arduous part of their trip, seeing more of New Zealand than any other royal visitor in the past. Ian Lucas observed: 'Every one seemed to fall in love with the Duchess at first sight, and so overwhelming is her beauty and the sweet goodness of her nature that one was sometimes inclined to forget the fine human qualities of her husband, of which we were to have such convincing proof a few weeks later in the South Island.'[28]

Even in those days it was considered that the Maoris were getting a little Westernised and their dancing less practised. These men with their painted faces and primeval cries were shopkeepers and lawyers in everyday life, yet there was plenty of grimacing, sticking out of tongues, stamping of feet and gruff shouting.

Scarcely had they embarked on the South Island Tour when Elizabeth fell victim to what was described as a bad attack of tonsillitis and was forced to take no further part in the tour. It was suggested that Elizabeth's illness was due to dust encountered on the motor journey and a chill caught while waving goodbye on the wharf at Wellington before *Renown* sailed. She was said to have a temperature as high as 102, as a result of which she spent four days in bed. Presently she retreated quietly to Wellington to recuperate at Government House, as guest of the Governor-General and his wife, General Sir Charles and Lady Alice Fergusson.*

Back in London, the First Lord of the Admiralty told the House of Commons: 'I am sure the House is very sorry to hear that the Duchess is suffering from even a slight indisposition, and, being interested in the *Renown*, I cannot help feeling some satisfaction that she is on shore and not in that ship.'[29] This was greeted with laughter in the House.

* General Sir Charles Fergusson (1864–1951), a Grenadier who broke the Hindenburg Line in 1918. Governor-General of New Zealand 1924–30, a position held by both his father and father-in-law, 7th Earl of Glasgow. His third son, Bernard (1911–80), was Governor-General 1962–67. He became Lord Ballantrae and was a friend of the Queen Mother.

The Duke continued without her, refusing to curtail his plans or to disappoint any part of New Zealand that was expecting him. This placed a great burden on him, for he relied on his wife for confidence and was happily convinced that the crowd loved seeing her. This did not worry him in the least, but as he now pressed on alone, he feared whether he would be able to get through his programme.

While in Christchurch the Duke received a morale-boosting letter from Elizabeth. To this he replied at once, addressing her as his own little darling 'E.' The letter reveals that Elizabeth's illness was not a chill, but exhaustion. She could neither cope with nor face the second part of the tour. The Duke reassured her that everyone understood that North Island had been too much for her.[30] The Duke missed her dreadfully.[31]

As it happens, he acquitted himself supremely well and ended the tour of South Island with a surge of new confidence.

Finally, on 22 March, he reached the southerly port of Bluff, where *Renown* sailed as close in as possible in heavy seas. The Duke had to leave in a harbour tug which eventually reached *Renown* after much buffeting about. He leaped from the tug into the arms of officers and blue jackets and was safely aboard. The Duchess, who had sailed from Wellington, watched the complicated manoeuvres from the scuttle of her sitting room. To Lady Alice Fergusson she wrote: 'I was glad to be on board when I saw my husband being thrown (literally) from the bridge of the tug on to our quarter-deck at Bluff. It looked most unpleasant, but he did not seem to mind much.'[32]

In his farewell message the Duke said: 'It was a most bitter disappointment to the Duchess and myself that she was unable to accompany me on the South Island tour. I trust that on some future occasion she may be able to visit with me those districts which she was unfortunately prevented from seeing this time.'[33]

The couple then sailed to Australia, arriving in Sydney and staying at State Government House. They were met and entertained by Lord Stonehaven, the Governor-General.* Regrettably, John Lang, the Labour Premier of New South Wales, felt the need to insult the royal guests by turning out with his ministers in lounge suits and soft hats rather than morning dress. The residents of Sydney later complained that the processions had moved too quickly, denying them much chance to see the visitors. One report said they 'whizzed through the city'.[34] The crowds were phenomenal, nonetheless, a sea of people everywhere, since in those

---

* Viscount Stonehaven (1874–1941), a former Conservative Minister of Transport. Governor-General of Australia 1925–30.

days there was no television and if people wanted a glimpse of the Yorks into the streets they had to come.

Another long tour followed. In Victoria, on 21 April, a salute was fired at 8 a.m. (rather than interfere with reception ceremonies) to mark the first birthday of Princess Elizabeth, then living with her grandparents, so far away in England.

In Brisbane, on the way to the theatre, the royal car was surrounded, so that the Duke could not get out, while members of the public climbed on to the running boards and poked their heads through the window to get a better look at him. In an attempt to clear a path for the royal car, General Sir Brudenell White, who was in charge of the Australian part of the tour, pushed forward and was so crowded that the gold studs of his evening shirt were squashed flat into his chest, while Colin Buist was pinned between a plate-glass window and the flank of a policeman's horse. Lord Cavan fell over in the rush and cut both his knees. Tor-Tor Gilmour, the lady-in-waiting, inadvertently blocked a member of the public's view of the Duchess. A hatpin was prodded into her bottom to make her move.[35]

In Melbourne the arrival of the Yorks was overshadowed by a fatal accident in which two of the forty Royal Australian Air Force planes providing an air escort collided during a saluting dip. Although the Yorks did not see the accident, they heard the crash and saw the thick column of blue smoke rising from the ground.

And so the trip continued, punctuated by rare tragedy but more often by humorous episodes, made of nervousness and misunderstanding. Before they left Melbourne, an overexcited woman in Bendigo tried to shake the Duchess's hand, failed but seized the bouquet instead. Almost instantly she repented and threw it into one of the other cars in the procession.

Finally they reached Canberra for the inauguration of the new Parliament building, the climax of the trip. Fear of the occasion gave the Duke a restless night of nerves, and on the day the Duchess looked scared, not her normal relaxed self.

The Duke wore full-dress naval uniform with GCMG riband and the collar of the Garter. They were conveyed to the Parliament building in a state carriage with out riders and an escort of the 7th Australian Light Horse. On their arrival, a fanfare of bugles was sounded by eight Royal Marine buglers from *Renown* on silver bugles specially lent by the officers for the occasion. There were royal salutes; the National Anthem was played.

Eventually the Duke and Duchess processed up the steps of the

Parliament building, led by the Gentleman Usher of the Black Rod. At the top of the steps, Dame Nellie Melba sang the first verse of the National Anthem, which was then repeated by the choir of the Canberra Philharmonic Society. Evidently Dame Nellie did not sing it very well: 'not until some bars were over did her voice attain its full silvery sweetness to send a visible thrill through the crowd'.[36] The Prime Minister, Stanley Bruce, spoke and the Duke was invited to open the glass-panelled doors of the Parliament House with a special key. He then addressed the crowds, telling them that the occasion marked the beginning of a new era in the history of Australia.

There was a short religious ceremony and finally the Yorks went inside. The Duke unveiled a statue of the King and they went into the Parliament chamber. The Duke duly opened Parliament and read a telegram from the King. As he finished, the clock began to strike midday. According to the official report: 'the whole ceremony was most impressive and perfectly organised. It passed off without a hitch of any kind, exactly according to the time-table arranged . . . The loyalty and enthusiasm of those present left nothing to be desired. The enthusiasm though very real was of a restrained character befitting the dignity of the occasion.'[37]

After an investiture ceremony and lunch, there was a review, which gave precedence to two hundred local returned soldiers who headed the march past. There was also a fly-past, which resulted in a fatal aeroplane accident, a single-seater suddenly nose-diving from about one thousand feet and crashing to the ground in front of Parliament House. The pilot died in hospital two hours later.

The Yorks then sailed in exceptionally rough seas in *Renown* to Fremantle, to tour Western Australia. Most on board were seasick, but Elizabeth was unaffected and made several visits to the bridge to watch the fiercely breaking waves. When they sailed from Australia, the Duke left a farewell message: 'We have been greatly impressed by the general appearance of virility and well-being of the people of this great Continent . . .'[38]

It took six weeks to get home, a not entirely event-free voyage. On 26 May a serious fire broke out in the boiler room, due to oil overflowing when it was being transferred from one tank to another, and then igniting. This put the ship and all on board in grave danger for a time. Elizabeth remained calm throughout. As the voyage drew to its close the Yorks dined in the wardroom, and after dinner there was a singsong, during which the tunes they had learned en route were sung, and the officers re-enacted Maori *hakas* and Marquesan pig dances.

At Portsmouth they disembarked with a menagerie of cockatoos, parrots and two kangaroos. Most went to zoos, but Jimmie, the favourite parrot, whose phrases included 'Hullo, Jimmie, have a drink?' made his home at 145 Piccadilly.

The King and Queen were at Victoria Station to greet them, the King having instructed his son not to embrace him at the station as they were in public and to remove his hat before embracing his mother. After more guards of honour, the Yorks and their party took their places in several semi-state landaus and processed to Buckingham Palace by the traditional ceremonial route. Here they were reunited with fifteen-month-old Princess Elizabeth after a long separation.

The King bestowed the Grand Cross of the Order of the British Empire on the Duchess in recognition of her achievements during the trip. The last word came from Sir Tom Bridges, Governor of South Australia, who wrote to the King: 'His Royal Highness has touched people profoundly by his youth, his simplicity and natural bearing, while the Duchess has had a tremendous ovation and leaves us with the responsibility of having a continent in love with her.'[39]

In 1928 the Yorks' engagements were low-key. On 16 July they stayed at Lumley Castle with the Scarbroughs, the Ridleys and Roger and Katharine Lumley (eventual heirs to the Scarbroughs, and to whom Elizabeth had acted as bridesmaid in 1922). The Bishop of Durham, Herbert Hensley Henson, dined there 'most agreeably', noting that the Duke was growing very like his father in 'aspect and manner', and had 'quite mastered his stammer, and now talks freely'.[40]

The next day, the Duchess launched the cruiser *York* at Palmer's Shipyard in Jarrow. Many children lined the route, waving Union Jacks with great enthusiasm. 'The "Little Duchess" is an extremely charming person,' noted the Bishop, 'and the only witcheries which she employs are those of her own simplicity, goodness and beauty.'[41]

8

The King's Illness

'The human frame is not made for this violent and exhausting modern life' – the Duchess of York

The illness of the King was of grave concern to the Royal Family in the closing months of 1928. As so often, the doctors hesitated to tell the public the truth.

On 22 November it was announced that he had been suffering from a cold which had turned into a fever. Queen Mary opened the extension to Spitalfields Market on his behalf. That evening the King's condition took a turn for the worse, the King suffering from congestion of one lung.

Over the next days, the bulletins gave little joy. A slight extension of mischief on the lung, pleurisy, a disturbed day, a restless night, a high temperature, and decline in the strength of the heart, produced the fear that the King was likely to die.

Further alarm was caused by a cruiser being sent to Dar-es-Salaam to hurry the Prince of Wales home from an African safari. On 3 December, the Bishop of Durham noted: 'The news about the King's illness this morning is grave, and it is evident that we must contemplate the contingency of a fatal termination.'[1]

Meanwhile the King's pleurisy did not get worse, but on 4 December the Privy Council met in the room adjoining his bedroom at the Palace and the Duke of York was one of those appointed to act as Counsellor of State with Queen Mary, the Prince of Wales, the Archbishop of Canterbury, the Prime Minister (Stanley Baldwin) and the Lord Chancellor (Lord Hailsham).*

The Prince of Wales had the most to fear from the King's death. Captain Alan ('Tommy') Lascelles was with him at Dodoma, Tanganyika Territory, when news of the King's illness reached them. Lascelles recorded that the Prince refused to believe the telegrams, which he

---

* The new Archbishop of Canterbury was Cosmo Gordon Lang, the former Archbishop of York, who had conducted the Yorks' wedding in 1923. He was enthroned in Canterbury Cathedral on 4 December.

described as 'just some election dodge of old Baldwin's'. Lascelles was livid: 'Sir, the King of England is dying; and if it means nothing to you, it means a great deal to us.' The Prince said not a word, and proceeded to seduce the wife of the local commissioner.[2]

Then they sped home, arriving on 11 December. By this time the doctors knew that the King had septicaemia, but did not want to announce it. Despair set in but Lord Dawson had one more try. He found the elusive fluid and removed this from the King's lung. An operation was performed to drain the right side of the chest. The King's 'whole body and mind were one battle-ground',[3] as his doctor recorded. He gradually improved, but on 27 December he was declining food. Calcium was administered.

Improvement was gradual but sustained. On 9 February 1929 the British public saw the King driven to Bognor by motor ambulance, occasionally raising his hand and smiling to the cheering crowds. He settled at Craigweil House, Bognor, from where, on 26 February, Queen Mary noted that in spite of the tremendous cold, the fresh air was reviving the King.[4]

By 27 March the King was well enough to receive the new Archbishops of Canterbury (Cosmo Gordon Lang) and York (William Temple) so that they could swear allegiance. He returned to Windsor on 15 May, but at the end of that month fell victim to a fever, an abscess having formed under the site of his old scar. It burst on 31 May. There was to have been a national service of thanksgiving on 16 June. This was postponed until 7 July. A week later portions of two of his ribs were removed so that the abscess could drain.

By 20 August the King's wound was healing and 'bodily and mental activities were undertaken without undue fatigue'.[5] The King and Queen then retired to Sandringham for several months, where, as his biographer, Harold Nicolson, put it: 'The chaff in which [the King] indulged so gaily sometimes assumed during those weary months an irascible tone.'[6] He only resumed shooting in October.

Sister Catherine Black, of London Hospital, came to nurse him and stayed for the rest of his life. Effectively the King had been out of action for the best part of a year.

The King's illness meant a disjointed time for the rest of the Royal Family. Queen Mary showed the full degree of her stoical courage, frequently standing in for him and presiding over the courts in London. The Duke of Gloucester and Prince George both returned home in December (1928). The older members of the Royal Family rallied round.

Elizabeth led a quiet, domestic life, having friends to lunch and spending time with the little Princess Elizabeth. The Duke played a lot of tennis. In February Elizabeth herself fell ill with influenza.

In March, accompanied by Elizabeth, the Duke of York went to Norway to act as best man to his first cousin, Crown Prince Olav of Norway, when he married Princess Märtha, second daughter of Prince Carl of Sweden. The King's health was stable enough for the trip to proceed. Prince Olav was the only son of King Haakon, the Danish prince who had been chosen to be King of Norway in 1905, and his wife, Queen Maud, the youngest sister of George V. Rather like the Duke's recent visit to Copenhagen the previous October to attend the funeral of the Dowager Empress of Russia,* the Duke and Duchess's travel plans were of great concern to the Foreign Office. To arrive through Denmark was to risk the inefficiency of German ferry boats, other routes were subject to delays and a great number of changes, while flying was hazardous, if not impossible, due to fog.

The best route was by train via Sassnitz Tralleborg, and this was the route chosen. The Yorks arrived on the morning of 17 March, with Lady Annaly and Rear-Admiral Basil Brooke in attendance, and were met by the King and Queen of Norway and others at the station.

During their stay there were dinners, a ball for six hundred and a gala performance of *Geography and Love* by Björnstjerne Björnson, described by the Ambassador as 'a long and old-fashioned production which did not seem to appeal greatly to the audience'.[7] Some choral performances were then given which lasted till midnight.

The day of the wedding dawned dull, but nevertheless 1600 guests took their places in the church, the Duke arriving with the Crown Prince. The service was over by 1 p.m., and there was a wedding breakfast for two hundred at the Palace. The worst fears of the Ambassador were fortunately allayed:

> Wedding feasts in Norway are formidable entertainments. They last usually for five to six hours; during which time songs are sung in honour of the bride and bridegroom and of the victuals provided for their delectation; and a stream of sentimental speeches, poured over the heads of the devoted couple, reduces the bride to tears before the fish is well disposed of. Having heard that it was proposed to follow Norwegian customs at breakfast, it was not without some apprehension that we took our seats. Our fears were soon dispelled.

---

* The Dowager Empress died at Hvidore on 13 October 1928, aged eighty-one.

The breakfast was not too long and was expeditiously served; and only four short speeches were made, respectively by King Haakon, the President of the Storting, the Crown Prince and Prince Carl of Sweden in the order named. Mr Hambro's speech was delivered even more effectively than his reputation of being the best speaker in Norway led one to expect; and there were passages in each of the other three which moved some of the ladies to tears. The breakfast was over by 4.15 . . .[8]

Members of the Norwegian Labour Party had seemed to want to attend, but the Muscovites had poured such abuse that the Labour leaders forbade them to do so. Many rows ensued, and, while most did stay away, those who had married 'determined women, refused, and went to the wedding with their victorious wives'. As to the Yorks, they 'seemed to have enjoyed their visit, to which many eulogistic references were made in the press'.*[9]

They returned via Berlin, staying with Sir Horace Rumbold at the British Embassy. Harold Nicolson was the Counsellor. He took them to lunch at the Golf Club and was impressed that the Duchess had read and appreciated his book, *Some People*. He found her so delightful and intelligent that he bemoaned her royal status as a waste:

> She and Cyril Connolly are the only two people who have spoken intelligently about the 'landscape' element in *Some People*. She said 'You choose your colours so carefully – that bit about the palace in Madrid was done in grey and chalk-white, the Constantinople bits in blue and green, the desert bits in blue and orange'. Of course, that may be second-hand, but I don't think so – and even if I am making a mistake about her intelligence, I am making no mistake about her charm. It is quite overwhelming.[10]

About the Duke, Nicolson was dismissive: 'He is just a snipe from the great Windsor marshes. Not bad-looking – but now and again there is that sullen, heavy-lidded, obstinate dulling of the blue eyes which is most unattractive.'[11]

The summer of 1929 was the first time that Balmoral remained closed for the season, the King and Queen resting at Sandringham instead. But

---

* The Duchess of York may not have enjoyed this trip after all. She found herself 'indisposed' in January 1930 when they were invited to the wedding of Prince Umberto, son of King Victor Emmanuel III, to Princess Marie-José, daughter of King Albert I of the Belgians. The Duke of York went to Rome alone. Or this may have been morning sickness.

the Yorks went to Scotland, greeted by flags and bunting. First they stayed at Abergeldie Castle and then took Birkhall, a few miles along the road.

Birkhall had been built by Charles Gordon of Abergeldie in 1715, and bought for the Prince of Wales (later Edward VII), his guests being considered too rowdy for Balmoral. It was partly on a hill and partly in a hollow.* It had been the home of Sir Dighton Probyn, and later of Sir Frederick Ponsonby.

The Yorks entertained a shooting party there, which proved a success. From 1932 the King loaned the Yorks Birkhall every summer; it was to be the start of a long and happy association with the house.

Anyone minded to write a thesis on the public engagements of the Duchess of York in the year 1930 would find the material limited.

Early in the year Elizabeth's brother, John ('Jock') died at Glamis, just after midnight on 7 February. According to Queen Mary, he had had bronchitis and went up to his parents to recuperate. A Scottish castle may not be the ideal place in which to recuperate. Jock caught pneumonia, gradually becoming weaker and weaker. He died from an abscess of the lung, aged forty-three. A stockbroker with Rowe & Pitman, he normally lived at 36 Curzon Street in London, and left estate of £103,974 6s 5d, no mean fortune. It was noted that he was a keen cricketer and fisherman and an excellent shot.

On 10 February the Yorks attended Jock's funeral at St Paul's Walden Bury, as did his parents, his widow, Michael, David, May Elphinstone and Rose Leveson-Gower. The death of Jock prompted Lady Strathmore to write to Lady Ottoline Morrell: 'My darling Jock being taken is more than I shall ever bear patiently.'[12] And after Jock's death, his widow Fenella was left to cope with the desperate problem of her two mentally deficient daughters.

Queen Mary was worried that the shock of Jock's death might upset Elizabeth, particularly since her daughter-in-law was again pregnant. Princess Elizabeth had been born in April 1926, since which time no grandchildren had been born to the King and Queen. There were several theories for the lack of children appearing in the York household (discounting the tales bandied about in the clubs of St James's), but none is particularly convincing. Only during the long New Zealand and Australia trip would the added burden of pregnancy have been inconvenient. The succession had remained static since 1926. The Prince of

---

* Prince Charles later described it as 'a house halfway down the slope of a teacup'.

Wales was still a bachelor. Thus Princess Elizabeth followed her father, the Duke of York. And then came two more bachelor brothers, the Duke of Gloucester and Prince George, after which came Princess Mary and her two Lascelles sons.

Again the Duke and Duchess of York did not easily win the conception of a child. Nevertheless the Duchess had become pregnant towards the end of 1929, and, once the dates were examined, it was apparent that the child would be born during their summer holiday in Scotland. What better place to give birth than Glamis Castle, the family home? Maybe Elizabeth thought that the excitement of the arrival of a new child would also help her mother in her sorrow following the death of Jock.

On 18 February Elizabeth cancelled all her engagements due to family mourning, which was fair and correct, and nicely disguised the pregnancy.

Shortly after spending Easter at Windsor, and when family mourning was over, Elizabeth made a further announcement that she was 'not undertaking any further functions during the summer'.[13] That was a coded message that a baby was expected. Besides the occasional visit to the theatre, or meetings with family and friends, the Duchess led a quiet existence until she retreated to Glamis on 15 July.*

Princess Margaret was a late arrival. Due between 6 and 12 August, she was not born until 21 August. This caused particular complications for the Home Secretary, Mr J. R. Clynes, and the Ceremonial Secretary, Mr Harry Boyd, 'a small, anxious-looking man, meticulously neat in his dress and movements',[14] who were bound by law to be present. Mr Boyd, who had been *en poste* in China, was suspicious about the birth taking place in Scotland, and was afraid that people might think the whole affair had been conducted in 'an irregular, hole and corner way'. To support this, he raised the historical example of a baby substitution in the case of James II and Mary of Modena.

Lady Airlie agreed to give lodging to the Home Secretary and his stooge. There followed an amusing phase during which the baby did not appear, while Mr Clynes was richly entertained in many a Scottish castle. Sir Henry Simson assured them that the baby would arrive on the 11th, so the two men drank coffee all night with Lady Airlie. By the 14th Mr Boyd was in a state of abject panic and refused to allow the Home Secretary to go out for so much as a drive. Still nothing happened.

---

* The Duke of York remained in the south, staying one weekend at Polesden Lacey. Osbert Sitwell recorded that at a lunch in July 1930, the Duke 'was out of temper and on his dignity', though 'cocktails and champagne restored him by the fall of night' (quoted in Philip Ziegler, *Osbert Sitwell* (Chatto & Windus, 1998), p. 235).

On the evening of 21 August, the long-delayed telephone call came from Glamis. Mr Boyd took the call dressed in his blue kimono and then had to dress hurriedly. Armed with sandwiches, the two men reached Glamis by car with half an hour to spare.

The Duchess's second child, a six-pound eleven-ounce daughter, was born at 9.22 p.m., the first royal child to be born north of the border since Charles I in Dunfermline in November 1600, and his brother Robert, Duke of Kintyre, in February 1602. The child was fourth in line to the throne. Rumours circulated in the press that 'twilight sleep' – the injection of morphine to provide painless birth – had been employed during the confinement. This was denied in a statement by Sir Henry Simson on 25 August.

Soon after Princess Margaret's birth, the Duchess wrote to thank the Archbishop of Canterbury for his good wishes, showing astute awareness of the future character of her new-born baby:

> Daughter No. 2 is really very nice, and I am glad to say that she has got large blue eyes and a will of iron, which is all the equipment that a lady needs!
>
> And as long as she can disguise her will, and use her eyes, then all will be well.[15]

The Duke of York was bedazzled by this child. He could not believe he had given birth to such a beautiful creature. As she grew older, he looked on her in amazement. He used to say 'Lilibet is my pride, Margaret my joy'.[16]

The Duchess wanted her daughter christened by the Archbishop of Canterbury in the private chapel at Glamis, during his annual pilgrimage to Balmoral. But this idea was stamped upon with some indignation by the King's Private Secretary, Lord Stamfordham, who informed her that the two churches were too separated 'liturgically'. The Duchess thought it would have given 'pleasure' in Scotland, and was surprised when this created trouble at Balmoral, with the King insisting that the Archbishop would be 'appalled' by the idea. So she renounced that particular plan.[17]

Instead the christening was delayed until the Duchess took her baby south towards the end of October. The infant princess was baptised in the names Margaret Rose by the Archbishop on 30 October in the private chapel at Buckingham Palace. Her godparents were the Prince of Wales (represented by Prince George), Princess Victoria (the King's sister), Princess Ingrid of Sweden (granddaughter of the Duke of Connaught, and later Queen of Denmark, represented by her aunt, Lady Patricia

Ramsay), Lady Rose Leveson-Gower and Hon. David Bowes-Lyon (her maternal aunt and uncle respectively). The choir of the Chapel Royal sang. There remains a persistent myth that Mrs Greville was one of the godparents, but this was not so.

In the late autumn, the Duchess resumed her public engagements, taking Princess Elizabeth to see Titania's Palace on show in aid of the Children's Union. And she congratulated Osbert Sitwell on a volume of short stories, with its 'pleasant-sounding words strung pleasantly together and entrancing to read or listen to'.[18]

During these years, a surprising number of books were published about the Duke and Duchess of York, none of lasting merit, but suitable to the readership of the time. Subtly they stressed the quiet domesticity of the York family.

The leader of the field was Lady Cynthia Asquith, friend of J. M. Barrie, whose first biography, *The Duchess of York*, came out in 1928. Lady Cynthia made a lucrative living out of a succession of such books and articles designed variously for adult and child readers. In 1927 she was asked by her agent to tackle the Duchess for a serialised life in *The Women's Pictorial*. She did not know the Duchess but was allowed access to her, to her mother, her nanny (by then looking after Princess Elizabeth) and to an ex-governess.

Having met the Duchess and duly fallen under her spell, she faced new problems: 'How, unless I deliberately went in for understatement, could I hope to escape the charge of sycophancy? Unrelieved praise makes monotonous reading.'[19] Her problems were made harder when she found that Lady Strathmore had failed to keep any record of Elizabeth's childish sayings or doings, while her experience with childhood friends, teachers and others left her complaining: 'All were kind; few very communicative.'[20] Despite this, Lady Cynthia held the field with Queen Elizabeth rewrites and stories about the daughters until 1937, but dropped from the picture after the Second World War when Marion Crawford, the governess, was tricked into her outpourings about the family.

In 1932 the Hon. Mrs Francis Lascelles published *Our Duke and Duchess*. Mrs Lascelles was born Gertie Stradling, from Knowle, Bristol, and was the widow of the ninth son of the 4th Earl of Harewood by his second marriage. She was therefore technically a half-aunt to the Lord Harewood who was married to Princess Mary,* and to Tommy Lascelles,

---

* Viscount Lascelles succeeded his father as 6th Earl of Harewood in 1929. Princess Mary was declared 'The Princess Royal' on 1 January 1932, in succession to her aunt, Princess Louise, Duchess of Fife.

though her book contains no inside information. Whether Mrs Lascelles had fallen on hard times is not clear but monetary reward was her likeliest motive. She also wrote a book called *Five Roads to Royal Exile*.

Then there was Alys Chatwyn, better known for girls' adventure stories, who produced *H.R.H. The Duchess of York* in the late 1920s. This sported a number of coloured prints, and ended with the prophecy: 'The little Duchess is in her glorious spring, and every augury points to her enjoying a summer fair and an autumn sweet.'[21]

It was this phase that gave the Yorks the reputation of leading a dull life in comparison to that of the Prince of Wales. But Elizabeth was masterly at creating a life for her burgeoning family which bound them together as a strong unit, enjoying lunches and teas together, the children playing with their friends, the Duke happy in a cocoon of contented domesticity. As she informed the Archbishop of Canterbury in January 1933, she was fortunate to enjoy an especially happy family life from which she drew great strength. Without that, she thought, the 'hurry and rush' of life would be too arduous.[22]

It was not thus for the others of the family. The Prince of Wales was forced to assume some additional duties such as holding levées to lighten the load of his father. Throughout the 1920s he had travelled ceaselessly, one contributing reason to his inability to settle down and forge a proper relationship. Freda Dudley Ward had been his principal mistress throughout the 1920s but how much of a relationship that was remains in some doubt. Elizabeth commented at one point in the early 1920s that Mrs Dudley Ward must be a remarkable woman since 'certain things had not happened'.[23]

There had been others who flitted through his life during those years. By the early 1930s he was a lesser man than he had been at the beginning of the 1920s. Worn out, fed up, reluctant at the prospect of the approaching burden of kingship, it is hard to find much to say in his favour. But he was kind to his brother, Prince George, who had become a drug addict, lured into this by the ministrations of 'Kiki' Preston, dubbed 'the girl with the silver syringe', who was eventually ordered to leave the country.

Prince George had retired from the Royal Navy due to 'ill health' in March 1929, after which he was attached to the Foreign Office, but he relinquished his duties 'suffering from digestive trouble' in July that year. When he left the Navy, he moved in with his brother, the Prince of Wales, at York House.

Both the Prince of Wales and Freda Dudley Ward took a close personal interest in the rehabilitation of Prince George, helping him with his treatment at considerable personal trouble. Freda Dudley Ward knew a particular doctor who could help him, and recalled that he was '*narcissiste*' and if the nurses in the nursing home adored him, then he was happy and would go and see them again.[24] Years later, after the Duke of Kent was killed, Queen Mary wrote to the then exiled Duke of Windsor, commending him for his kindness to his brother at a time when he gravely needed him.

There were few other such testimonials. His legendary charm was wearing thin and it would not be long before he fell under the spell of Mrs Ernest Simpson, the American who arrived in London, and who was soon his major preoccupation. The Prince first met Wallis Simpson at Melton Mowbray in January 1931.

The other concern that gave him pleasure and an element of security was Fort Belvedere, near Sunningdale. This he took on and it became the one home where he was settled and happy.

The King's health stabilised and he resumed his duties as constitutional Head of State. On 4 January 1931, his sister, the Princess Royal (Princess Louise, Duchess of Fife, whose finances had suffered due to Lord Farquhar), died suddenly of heart failure in her sleep after a short illness. Elizabeth attended the private funeral at St George's Chapel on 10 January, the Princess later being buried in the private chapel of St Ninian at Mar Lodge, her home near Balmoral, on 22 May.* The court went into mourning for six weeks.

For the Yorks there was at last a home in the country, which they would enjoy as much if not more than the Prince of Wales loved Fort Belvedere. Royal Lodge stood in the heart of Windsor Great Park, about four miles from the Castle. It was rebuilt as a cottage orné by John Nash for the Prince Regent (later George IV), who first occupied it in 1815. When he was King, and was undertaking major alterations at Windsor Castle, he spent three and a half years there. After his death, William IV set about destroying it, but the Prince Consort rescued what was left, and housed his new secretary there. In 1865 Queen Victoria tried to persuade the Prince and Princess of Wales to accept it as a base for Ascot, but they declined and from 1873 until 1931 it was the residence of a succession of members of the Royal Household, the last occupant being Major Frederick Fetherstonhaugh, Manager of the

* In the late 1980s Mar Lodge was sold to an American tycoon called John Kluge. Thus he presumably bought the chapel, where the Princess Royal, Princess Arthur of Connaught and others were buried. It is now the property of the National Trust of Scotland.

King's Thoroughbred Stud, who lived there from 1926 until his death on 29 July 1931.

In the same year the King granted Royal Lodge to the Yorks and they kept it as a retreat even after they became King and Queen, spending as much time there as possible. It remained the Queen Mother's country home throughout the long years of her widowhood. They painted the drawing room green – 'very modern at the time', as the Queen Mother liked to point out. Later the Duke found heraldic shields in a cupboard at Windsor Castle and these were placed round the cornice.[25]

In 1932 the Yorks moved in and on Princess Elizabeth's sixth birthday, 21 April that year, the people of Wales gave her Y Bwythyn Bach, or 'The Small House', a miniature Welsh cottage with thatched roof and latticed windows, which soon became the favourite haunt of both the children. The cottage had four rooms, a small hall and a landing, with furniture and fittings made to scale. As they grew older, the princesses were able to bake scones on the kitchen stove, there was hot and cold running water and the cottage was surrounded by its own garden, and thus a secluded location on the south side of Royal Lodge's gardens.

The Yorks commissioned Eric Savill to help them create the gardens at Royal Lodge, turning this into a beautiful sanctuary, bursting with rhododendron and azaleas in springtime. From this they derived enormous enjoyment.

By tradition the Royal Family do not get involved in politics, which does not mean that they may not hold private political views. When Duff Cooper stood as the official Conservative candidate for the St George's Westminster seat in March 1931, Elizabeth could not resist supporting him from the wings. This was an important by-election in which the press barons Lord Rothermere and Lord Beaverbrook supported an 'Empire Free Trade' candidate, Sir Ernest Petter, an Independent Conservative. Baldwin contemplated resigning his seat to tackle this one, but in the end Duff Cooper stood as his official Conservative candidate. Had Petter won, Empire Free Trade would have become the accepted policy of the Conservative Party.

It became a heated business in Mayfair. Election posters appeared in the windows of stately houses, dinner parties were held at Londonderry House and elsewhere, and, while Duff Cooper found it hard to lure the rich to his meetings or to know if he should approach their servants, he was glad of the support of the *Daily Telegraph* since most other papers were against him. He won with 17,242 votes to Petter's 11,532.

Only at this point did the Duchess show her hand. She wrote to Duff

Cooper from Thornby Grange in Northampton, where the Duke was hunting with the Pytchley:

> I feel that I must write and congratulate you on your most excel-
> lent victory over Lords Rothermere & Beaverbrook. After what you
> told me at Lady Astor's party,* I have taken a violent interest in
> your campaign, and was so very pleased at your courage in taking
> on St George's.[26]

The Duchess dispatched a busload of servants to London, bearing slogans of support, to ensure they voted for him. Meanwhile all she could do was to thrust Petter's election communiqué into the waste paper basket.

In September 1932 the Duchess wrote to Duff Cooper: 'I hope you have had a restful month or two before our L............l† friends plunge us once more into sordidness this week.'[27]

Religion was a safer matter, with the Archbishop of Canterbury occa-sionally asking for royal support. The Duchess was fond of Cosmo Gordon Lang, a great church orator and a master of the moving address at wedding, funeral or memorial service. Some compared him favourably to F. E. Smith. In the days before microphones, he could be heard in every apse of the cathedral. Alan Don, his astute chaplain,‡ noted that he could turn on 'the wedding address tap . . . with the usual happy results'.[28] His chaplains considered him an enigma and enjoyed exam-ining him. He could depart for his annual holiday in Scotland with an absent-minded wave of the hand, and not a backward glance, just as if he were simply on his way to evensong at Westminster Abbey, rather than departing for several weeks.

He lived ascetically, in a room with no carpet, a small table and chair, a jug of water and a basin. One of his chaplains spent a night in his room and vowed never to do so again. 'The bedstead was of iron with a chain mattress covered only with a blanket and a sheet. The chaplain was so uncomfortable he spent the night on the floor.'[29] Yet the Archbishop liked the friends with whom he stayed to live in spacious surroundings. At Lambeth Palace he joked that his annual holiday was a 'Snob's Progress',

---

* This ball took place on 21 February 1931. Elizabeth, dressed in pink, had danced with Anthony Eden, George Gage and Duff Cooper.
† Liberal – there had been a National Government since August 1931, reconstructed in November 1931 and to be further reconstructed in October 1932.
‡ Revd Alan Don (1885–1966), Chaplain and Secretary to Archbishop Lang 1931–41, Chaplain to the Speaker of the House of Commons 1936–46, Dean of Westminster 1946–59 (having been Canon and Sub-Dean earlier). He was unhappily married but made a point of lunching with his wife every Friday, more or less their only point of contact.

as he made his way to the stately homes of Lord Spencer, Lord Halifax and Lord Scarbrough, the Dukes of Portland and Northumberland, the Princess Royal and, at last, the King.

George V considered him a personal friend, while the Prince of Wales thought him 'almost too polished, too worldly'.[30] Several times painted by de Laszlo, he was portrayed by Sir William Orpen in 1924. He commented: 'They say in that portrait I look proud, prelatical and pompous.' The Bishop of Durham riposted: 'And may I ask Your Grace to which of these epithets Your Grace takes exception?'[31]

Occasionally he received fan letters, only a few of which the chaplains allowed him to see. One distracted lady wrote to him: 'I want you so, my beloved. I long to possess something of your very own – a lock of hair – to have it ever with me.' As Alan Don commented: 'She would be heartbroken if she knew that C. C. [Cosmo Cantuar] hasn't a lock of any sort left.'[32]

The Archbishop was an ardent promoter of the cause of Reunion in the churches, achieving a major hurdle with the union of the Wesleyan Methodist Church, the Primitive Methodist Church and the United Methodist Church, which was celebrated at the Albert Hall on 20 September.

Thanking Duff Cooper for a copy of his biography of *Talleyrand*,* the Duchess wrote from Birkhall that she had found it there on her return from London. She had been obliged to go south in order to help with what she called: 'consummating the union' between some low churches.[33]

The event in the Albert Hall apparently demonstrated 'complete unanimity and an enthusiasm which was somewhat restrained by a sense of the solemnity of a memorable occasion in Methodism'.[34] It was a drawn-out proceeding at which the Duke of York and many Methodists spoke in turn. The Duchess was glad to get back to Birkhall, but that was not the end of the matter, as she explained to the Archbishop 'daily I receive one or more requests from Methodist parsons from every corner of these Islands! However, up till now, I have battled bravely against their onslaught – I am sure you are glad to hear this, as it was through you that I have become fair prey!!'.[35]

The mischievous side of the Duchess was apparent when the Yorks were invited to the International Colonial Exhibition in Paris in July 1931. After inspecting replicas of bazaars in Morocco, Tunis and Algiers, where the Duchess risked a cup of Arab coffee, and visiting a model of the

* *Talleyrand* (Jonathan Cape, 1932).

Temple of Angkor Wat, the Duchess turned to Marshal Lyautey and said: 'Monsieur le Maréchal, you are so powerful, you created the beautiful country of Morocco and you have made this fine exhibition. Would you do something for me?' He was surprised: 'But what can I do for Your Royal Highness?' She said the sun was in her eyes: 'Will you make it disappear?' At that moment the sun retreated behind a cloud and the Duchess said: 'Thank you, Monsieur le Maréchal, I knew that you could do anything.' She then turned to André Maurois and whispered: 'I saw the cloud coming . . .'[36]

A similar visit was paid to Brussels in July 1935 for British Week at the International Exhibition. They lunched with the new King, Leopold, and his young wife, Queen Astrid, and noted how charming the couple were with one another. They saw a recreation of eighteenth-century Brussels, mixed with the crowds (perhaps the first real royal walkabout), saw the sword swallowers and the performing monkeys. There was a dinner and a ball for 1500. They visited the British Pavilion where Lord Lytton greeted them.

Having so recently spent time with the Belgian King and Queen, they were particularly upset to hear during their Scottish holiday later that summer that Queen Astrid had been killed in a road accident. The tragedy was made worse by King Leopold having been at the wheel. The Duke went over to represent the King at the funeral, a particularly poignant occasion, King Leopold following his wife's coffin, with a scar on his face and his broken arm in a sling.

These rare overseas visits by the King's second son were more stimulating than the round of engagements in England. There were occasional day trips to English cities, and tours of industrial areas, in which the Duke took a keen interest, but it must have been hard to muster much enthusiasm for a visit to a shoe factory in Kendal, a concert for the Red Triangle club, the unveiling of a tablet to commemorate the abolition of certain tolls or a visit to the Tower of London pageant. These were among the Duchess's other engagements in 1935.

Often they combined official visits with a weekend away. When due for an evening engagement in Leicester, they stayed with the Duke and Duchess of Rutland at Belvoir Castle. For fear of fog a special Pullman train was arranged to take them there. Laura, Duchess of Marlborough, recalled: 'We boarded the train in evening dress at Grantham, where a considerable crowd had gathered. The Duke was very shy and rushed along the carriage, pulling down the blinds. I was very impressed by the way the Duchess snapped them up again immediately, saying to her husband: "Bertie, you must wave".'[37]

Their duties had the merit of leaving many days free and they were not onerous, but as the King grew more tired and the Prince of Wales's character showed no sign of improvement, there must have been odd moments when they wondered if a more significant destiny awaited them.

In June 1932, they were able to escape for what the Duke of York considered one of the best weeks in their married life together,[38] to Rest Harrow, Lady Astor's seaside home in Sandwich. The Duchess relished it since they had not had the chance to escape as a family and felt all the better for it.[39] Even Alah Knight liked it, expressing rare enthusiasm by declaring that she wished they could stay the entire month.[40]

On Christmas Day 1932, the King had made his first Christmas broadcast from Sandringham, and was 'rather hurt' when the Prince of Wales went out for a round of golf rather than listen to him. He loved the times when the Yorks left their 'sweet children' with him.

In the summer of 1933, the King missed one of the courts and then the Trooping the Colour. Nor was he at the Cenotaph in November. The Duchess of York persuaded him to come to open the new St Mary's Hospital Medical School on 12 December, which brought out his well-known character traits. He vetoed the state trumpeters because one had once blown in his ears, and criticised the very modern common room as 'too horrible'. The Duchess advised Dr Charles Wilson (later Lord Moran) that the King was not interested in buildings but liked 'medicolegal things like Crippen relics'. He was shown a patient suffering from leprosy, which he talked about all through lunch.[41]

The Yorks were hardly overworked, but still the Duchess jested with the Archbishop of Canterbury that modern life was too exhausting. She recommended a complete day of silence.[42]

As 1934 dawned, Elizabeth wrote to the Archbishop again: 'One cannot help worrying over the misery and hardship suffered by so many good people, and their courage in facing hardship is the thing that I admire most in them. It is a great example to us luxurious minded creatures – not you, but us – I mean!'[43] When the Duke of York suffered from a poisoned hand, the Duchess was able to duck out of a trip to Edinburgh with the King and Queen.

The prolonged state of bachelorhood of three of the King's sons was the cause of much discussion behind the scenes. In November 1932, King Gustav V of Sweden made tentative approaches in diplomatic services towards a union between his granddaughter, Princess Ingrid, and the heir to the British throne, firm in the conviction that Princess Ingrid 'was clearly made to be Princess of Wales'. He was not convinced that he welcomed the alternative plan, then gaining popularity, that she might become the wife of Prince George.[44]

Prince George's disagreeable aunt, Princess Victoria, had been convinced that Princess Marina of Greece was meant for the Prince of Wales, and that Prince George would marry Princess Irene of Greece, daughter of King Constantine, and first cousin of Princess Marina.*

The Prince of Wales remained unengaged, but on 28 August 1934 the betrothal of Prince George and Princess Marina was announced. This was the result of a whirlwind romance during the summer holidays. The Prince's bride arrived in London on 16 September, receiving a welcome similar to that accorded her great-aunt, Queen Alexandra, in 1863. She went to stay with the King and Queen at Balmoral. The King was very keen on Princess Marina, though Queen Mary observed her very red nails and said to her: 'I'm afraid the King doesn't like painted nails. Can you do something about it?' To this Princess Marina replied: 'Your George may not, but mine does.'[45]

Some of the courtiers thought that Prince George was not in love with her, though Freda Dudley Ward said he was, though he worried she was too 'bossy'.[46] Prince George himself sounded ecstatic when he wrote to Prince Paul of Yugoslavia, pointing out that the British were expecting 'a dowdy princess, such as unfortunately my family are', but that when they saw 'this lovely chic creature, they could hardly believe it & even the men were interested & shouted "Don't change – don't let them change you!".'[47]

The newly created Duke of Kent was married to Princess Marina at Westminster Abbey on 29 November, Princess Elizabeth and Princess Margaret serving as bridesmaids.

The only member of the Royal Family not wholly entranced was the Duchess of York, who was displeased to hear herself described by this new arrival as 'not even mediatised', a remark never forgiven. More appealing to her was her fellow debutante, Lady Alice Montagu-Douglas-Scott, another Scottish aristocrat, who married the Duke of Gloucester the following year, leaving the Prince of Wales as the only unmarried brother in the family.

---

* Princess Victoria told Princess Marina so when she met her after her engagement to Prince George, which was tactless, but in character. Princess Irene was invited to be a bridesmaid as a conciliatory gesture. In 1939 she married the Duke of Aosta.

9

End of a Reign

Sister Black – *'Feeling a little better, Sir?'*
The King – *'No!'*

At Easter 1933 Marion Crawford joined the Household as governess to
the little princesses, Elizabeth, then just six, and Margaret, not yet quite
two. She was a Scottish girl, the daughter of a mechanical engineer's
clerk, born at Gatehead, in Ayrshire, who had trained at the Moray House
Training College in Edinburgh, and had worked as temporary governess
first to the children of Lord Elgin and then to Mary Leveson-Gower,
daughter of Lady Rose Leveson-Gower, Elizabeth's sister.

While she was with the Leveson-Gowers at Admiralty House, Rosyth,
she met the Duchess of York, who persuaded her to come to her, pleased
to find a governess young enough to share the youthful games of her
daughters.

At Royal Lodge, the Yorks had their bedrooms on the ground floor,
and to these rooms their daughters ran eagerly each morning. The
Duchess's was misty blue, the Duke's more like a cabin on board ship.
Princess Elizabeth now entered the care of her governess from 9.30 till
6, while Princess Margaret remained in the nursery. Princess Elizabeth
had already begun riding lessons, which she greatly enjoyed. She had
been taught to read by her mother.

'Crawfie' admired the Duchess of York and came to associate her with
the pleasanter aspects of a peaceful life, in particular the scent of fresh
roses which adorned Royal Lodge and 145 Piccadilly. She was pleased
when the Duke joined in his daughters' games in the garden during the
morning break. The Yorks liked to dine alone together. There were rarely
dinner parties and they seldom went out. Occasionally they went to the
cinema or theatre. Crawfie accompanied the family to Royal Lodge, to
Glamis and to Birkhall, still lit only by oil lamps. In bleak weather smelly
oil stoves were carried up to the bedrooms.

When the family was in London, lessons were undertaken in the
Duchess's boudoir, off the big drawing room. The parents were much in
evidence, bath hour and bedtime being a sacred time for both of them.

But Crawfie was not impressed by the way that the Yorks approached the education of their children, a complaint supported by Princess Margaret, who, in later life, wished she had had an education more suited to her undoubted intelligence. To Crawfie the Duchess appeared disinterested and gave little guidance.

Queen Mary was concerned about this and pressed people such as the Archbishop of Canterbury to her cause. She became conspiratorial with Crawfie about expanding the education of her granddaughters. Crawfie described Queen Mary as 'a rock of strength and wisdom' to whom she could turn 'in moments of doubt and difficulty' – of these there were plenty.[1] Queen Mary was anxious that French lessons should continue during the holidays, as her own had done in her youth. She was disturbed that there were no family prayers, though she appreciated that the Duchess had read Bible stories to her children, and taught them their collects and psalms, much as Lady Strathmore had done for her in her childhood.

In 1935 King George V celebrated his Silver Jubilee. He was in imperfect health, spending a while at Compton Place in Eastbourne in January, and suffering from a bad cough in April, but he was still alert, discussing various topics such as the personalities of Hitler, Goering and Ludendorff, and the vexed issue of women sunbathing.

The central event of the Jubilee was the Thanksgiving Service at St Paul's Cathedral on 6 May, which affirmed the affection in which the King was held by the many who came to cheer him. The general public had the chance to see the Royal Family en masse, particularly admiring the Duke and Duchess of York and their two little daughters, dressed for the day in identical pink. In the evening the King broadcast to his people across the Empire, pressed a button which ignited beacons across the land and was cheered on the balcony of Buckingham Palace. There was a rare spate of banquets and a magnificent court ball for two thousand, but in June the King developed bronchial catarrh and was ordered to take a two-week rest at Sandringham, as a result of which he missed Ascot. From this time, Queen Mary worried deeply, if silently, about the King.

There were so many Jubilee engagements that summer that Elizabeth looked forward to a luncheon with the Archbishop of Canterbury as 'an oasis in a desert of dreary functions!'[2]

As the celebrations drew to their close, the King escaped to Balmoral, where he arrived on 21 August, looking well. He was met by brightly clad Highlanders out in force. The Yorks, then staying at Birkhall, were at lunch at the castle the following Sunday, on which occasion the King was 'in excellent form & very kind'.[3] At Birkhall there was much playing of a game called 'Kick the tin'. Ramsay MacDonald, Sister Agnes, Lady Patricia Ramsay and King George II of Greece came to stay at different times, and there were many picnics and much stalking.

During the summer holidays in Scotland, the engagement was announced of the Duke of Gloucester and Lady Alice Scott. This surprised and delighted the Royal Family, who had only focused on her when she had dined in the Waterloo Chamber in Ascot week the previous June. Lady Alice arrived with the Duke in time for the Ghillies' Ball on 20 September.

One Sunday the King spoke about the first volume of Duff Cooper's biography of Lord Haig, which had just been published, and of the complications caused to the author by Haig's widow. She had rejected the first candidate for the book, John Buchan, and then tried to reclaim a copy of Haig's diary from the Committee of Imperial Defence. Duff Cooper had almost given up, but eventually the problems resolved themselves. The book received hostile notices from many of the London critics, most of whom were military correspondents who believed Haig was wrong and would not countenance a word said in his favour.

As ever Cooper sent a copy to Elizabeth who found it a fascinating study, a great work and marvelled that he could have written it so quickly:

> The few critics have been quite idiotic in writing about the book. Their only cry being 'why is it not more sensational,' which is too foolish to even speak about. The only people I have seen up here who have read it, are the King & one or two tough Scottish Majors & Captains (ex), & they are all enthusiastic. Being sane because they do not live too much in cities, they are grateful to you for giving a true picture of Haig, & for writing a very difficult book so brilliantly. I do hope that you are pleased with its reception & great success. Are you calm about it, or are you a cauldron, seething and boiling? . . .

She added that the Archbishop of Canterbury had come to luncheon with her, 'and instead of the comfortable heart-to-hearter that I had been looking forward to after luncheon, pounced on your book with a cry of joy, & then there was silence only punctuated by "ah those were the days" (he was at Oxford with Haig) & "dear old So & so" & other old-time remarks – not at all the sort of thing that had been expected by his lonely & forgotten hostess.'[4]

By the end of September, when he went south for the last time, the King was looking tired. The Yorks stayed in Scotland a little longer, Lord and Lady Plunket* remaining with them. At length, the Scottish holidays were over, something Elizabeth always dreaded:

'The desolate autumn hurries through the fields apace, to nodding flowers the winds cold breath betrays', and soon we must leave this peaceful place & return to London. It is so lovely now, the birches are turning from silver to gold, the air is cold & the sun shines, so that I am sorry to go.[5]

The autumn of 1935 was surprisingly busy, with happenings both good and bad. On 9 October the Duchess of Kent gave birth to her first son, Prince Edward of Kent (the present Duke of Kent). On 19 October, the Duke of Buccleuch, father of Lady Alice Scott, died aged seventy-one. The next day, Fritz Ponsonby, Lord Sysonby, one of the mainstays of George V's court, died aged sixty-eight. The Gloucester wedding took place quietly in the private chapel at Buckingham Palace on 6 November, due to the death of the bride's father. Both Princess Elizabeth and Princess Margaret were bridesmaids. On 11 November the King asked the Duke of York to lay the annual wreath on the Cenotaph as the weather was too unsettled for him to do so. On 20 November young Prince Edward was christened with the King and Queen as his principal godparents.

The Yorks returned from St Andrew's Day dinner in Paris on 1 December, the day on which the King undertook what proved to be his last public engagement – a visit with Queen Mary to the Chinese Art exhibition at Burlington House. Then the condition of Princess Victoria, who had been in poor health for three weeks, took a turn for the worse. She suffered a severe haemorrhage.

Princess Victoria's illness upset George V, who had always been close to her. There was the well-known story of their daily telephone calls and how an operator had heard her say: 'Hullo, you old fool' and had been forced to say: 'I'm sorry, Your Royal Highness, His Majesty is not yet on the line.' Less well known is the occasion when Princess Victoria rang.

---

* Teddy and Dorothé Plunket were close friends. In February 1938 they were killed in a needless air accident in California, failing to heed the advice not to fly after noon for fear of the sudden descent of thick fog. They left three sons, Patrick, Robin and Shaun (a godson of the King), ranging from fourteen to six. They were discreetly adopted by Lord Londonderry (their natural grandfather). The Yorks kept a close interest in their upbringing. The eldest son Patrick became equerry to George VI, and later an inspired courtier to the present Queen, introducing considerable flair to many a royal occasion. He was also to be one of the present Queen's most intimate friends, sometimes described as the brother she never had.

The King answered angrily: 'Damn you, what do you want? . . . Oh, Victoria, is it you?' He heard his sister say: 'I only want to know if you feel like a bloody King today!!'[6]

Princess Victoria did not respond to a blood transfusion. The State Opening of Parliament, planned for the following day, was cancelled. She died at Coppins at 3.35 a.m. on 3 December, at the age of sixty-seven. Six weeks of court mourning were declared, to end on 14 January 1936.

Princess Victoria's death caused the King to decline sharply. He attended his sister's funeral in St George's Chapel on 7 December. His doctor hoped to see a draft of the service to 'secure its brevity', but this was not done and Dawson watched the King 'standing bent, weighed down in body and mind, for far too long a period'.*[7]

On 11 December Elizabeth went to a dinner party given by the Hardinges, at which her old suitor, James Stuart, was present. So too was Katie Hamilton, who, after missing her chance to marry Harold Alexander (later Field Marshal Earl Alexander of Tunis), was now rather belatedly married to a widowed courtier, Reginald Seymour.† He too was present, and Elizabeth was 'in marvellous form'.[8] But six days later she retreated to her room at Royal Lodge with a chill.

It has long been suggested that Elizabeth's health was a matter largely under her own control, that her illnesses were psychosomatic and occurred at times when it suited her to avoid unpleasant issues. If so, it shows some prescience for she escaped a harrowing phase for the Royal Family.

On 17 December the Duchess handed over an engagement to attend a Thé Divertissement in aid of the Not Forgotten Association to Princess Alice, Countess of Athlone. Her chill soon turned to influenza, her homeopathic doctor, Sir John Weir, nevertheless asserting that she was making good progress towards recovery. Elizabeth was not at Sandringham with the Royal Family for that last post-Silver Jubilee Christmas. She and the Duke stayed at Royal Lodge, though the princesses joined their grandparents, which kept them from her sick room.

By 31 December it was made clear by Weir and Lord Dawson that the Duchess had suffered 'an attack of influenzal pneumonia' which was

---

* There is some symmetry in the King being present for his last official outing at a private royal funeral in St George's Chapel. The Queen Mother's last such outing was the funeral of Princess Margaret, again at St George's Chapel, in 2002.

† Lt-Col. Sir Reginald Seymour (1878–1938) was first married to Winifred Boyd-Rochfort. She died in 1925. He married Lady Katharine Hamilton in 1930, and they had a son and two daughters. Seymour served as equerry to George V 1916–36, and continued to serve Queen Mary as such 1936–8. He had been knighted in 1935 for services to Queen Mary. By his first marriage, he was the father of Raymond Seymour, Assistant Private Secretary and Equerry to the Queen Mother.

'resolving'. Her general condition was 'satisfactory'.[9] As the New Year dawned, she made slow progress.

Meanwhile, at Sandringham, those curiously mistimed clocks* were chiming the last days of George V. He made his annual Christmas broadcast to the Empire, his gruff old voice now familiar in homes across the world. He rode in the park, and a series of guests came and went, including Field Marshal Sir Philip and Lady Chetwode, Lord Clarendon, the Bishop of Chester, David Bowes-Lyon and his wife,† and Marshal of the RAF Lord Trenchard with his. When Lady Algernon Gordon-Lennox left Sandringham, the King said to her: 'Goodbye, my dear old friend. I know I am done for.'[10]

Just as the royal party began to disperse, so the King slipped into terminal decline. On the day the court came out of mourning for Princess Victoria, he became breathless, lost energy and began to be sleepy during the day. Bronchial catarrh was soon followed by cardiac weakness. There was disquiet among those who watched.

The Duke of York took the train to Wolferton, in the same compartment as Captain Alan Lascelles, who was just taking up his appointment as Assistant Private Secretary. The Duke alarmed Lascelles with news of the King's health, and indeed Lascelles never saw the King during his duty at Sandringham. They arrived on the 16th, followed by the Prince of Wales on the 17th.

A strange atmosphere prevailed in the house, whereby the King languished in his room, Queen Mary presided over the house party, anxious, but maintaining the stance that all was well, and games were played with the young princesses. On 18 January the hovering journalists spotted the girls making a snowman outside the house in freshly fallen snow, until summoned inside by a nanny. They were sent back to their mother by train that day, by which time it was clear to all that the King was dying.

Partly to dispel public anxiety, both the Prince of Wales and the Duke of York felt able to motor to London on the 19th. There was a meeting with the Prime Minister. On the same day the Duke of Kent returned to Sandringham, and the Archbishop of Canterbury arrived, not without misgivings but feeling that the people of Britain would expect him to be there. Shadowing every move the Archbishop made, this time from afar, was Revd Alan Don, a fine witness to these next years. He put it thus: 'I do not envy C. C. for one knows only too well the attitude of those

* Queen Alexandra having been consistently unpunctual, the clocks at Sandringham were always kept half an hour advanced.
† David Bowes-Lyon had married Rachel Spender-Clay, a niece of Viscount Astor, in 1929.

who regard the parson as the forerunner of the undertaker and while welcoming his sympathy deprecate his ministrations in such crises.'[11]

On 20 January the King held his last Council, appointing Counsellors of State.* He also made his famous remark to Lord Wigram: 'How is the Empire?' Sister Black, who had been with the King since 1928, asked him: 'Feeling a little better, Sir?' To which the King replied: 'No!'[12]

On the same day, a rumour circulated in London that the Prince of Wales might renounce his right of succession or even swiftly marry a Catholic wife to escape the throne. This was told to the Archbishop of Canterbury's chaplain by a Diocesan Bishop, who heard it from an ex-Cabinet minister. Even at that critical hour, Don could record: 'That the P. of W. would like to make way for the Duke of York and his charming Duchess I do not doubt, but that there is truth in this rumour I refuse to believe. The next few hours may enlighten us.'[13] In the confusion of the moment, the Prince of Wales seemed to think that his imminent accession might speed his marriage to the still married Mrs Simpson. He wrote as much to her before heading to Sandringham.

That evening, at 9.25 p.m., Lord Dawson of Penn issued his celebrated bulletin: 'The King's life is moving peacefully to its close.' Dawson might more reasonably have stated that the King's life was being nudged towards that peaceful close, as his diary (kept secret for more than fifty years) recorded:

> At about 11 o'clock it was evident that the last stage might endure for many hours, unknown to the patient but little comporting with the dignity and serenity which he so richly merited and which demanded a brief final scene. Hours of waiting just for the mechanical end when all that is really life has departed only exhausts the onlookers and keeps them so strained that they cannot avail themselves of the solace of thought, communion or prayer. I therefore decided to determine the end and injected (myself) morphia gr. ¾ and shortly afterwards cocaine gr. 1 into the distended jugular vein.[14]

Dawson acted independently, in the uneasy presence of Sister Black, and without consulting the other doctors in attendance, so that news of the King's death could be reported first in the morning edition of *The Times*.

---

* The Archbishop of Canterbury, Viscount Hailsham (Lord Chancellor), Ramsay MacDonald (Lord President), Lord Dawson of Penn (the King's Physician-in-Ordinary), Lord Wigram (Private Secretary), Sir John Simon (Home Secretary) and Sir Maurice Hankey (Clerk of the Council) were assembled in the King's room to see him make his mark, with Dawson guiding his hand. Then, according to the Archbishop, the King smiled and said, 'I am sorry to have kept you waiting so long.'

To this end, he telephoned his wife and asked her to alert *The Times* of the imminent final announcement.* At 11.55 p.m., the King expired, with Queen Mary, the Prince of Wales, the Duke of York, the Princess Royal and the Duke and Duchess of Kent at the bedside.† The Archbishop led some prayers and conducted a short service in the King's room.

In the darkness of the early evening of the next day the coffin was escorted to Sandringham church by the Grenadier Guards, Queen Mary, the Princess Royal, the Duke and Duchess of Kent, and Lord Harewood, following on foot. Tommy Lascelles was impressed by the cloaked vicar silhouetted in the light of the church door, and recalled this as the most poignant and moving moment of the prolonged obsequies. Over the next days thousands passed the coffin, guarded by four foresters from the estate.

The Duchess of York, still second lady in the land, arrived at Sandringham with the Duke and the Gloucesters on 22 January. Hardly had the King died than the clerics began to discuss whether, now that the Duke of York was heir to the throne, both he and the Duchess should be included in the prayers for the Royal Family. The new King wished this. By the end of the month the wording had been settled: 'Our gracious Queen Mary, Albert, Duke of York, the Duchess of York, and all the Royal Family.'[15] On 23 January Elizabeth was in the carriage with Queen Mary and the Princess Royal as the coffin departed for London. The fine lying-in-state at Westminster Hall attracted a vast pilgrimage of mourners and the famous midnight vigil of the four Princes.

On 28 January the Duchess was well enough to take her place in the funeral procession, again in a carriage with Queen Mary and the Princess Royal and now accompanied by the King's only surviving sister, Queen Maud of Norway. They followed the coffin to Paddington, where little Princess Elizabeth, dressed in deep black, joined them. They accompanied the coffin on the train to Windsor and followed it to St George's Chapel.

At the top of the steps, Albert Baillie, the Dean of Windsor who had been so annoyed that Queen Alexandra's funeral had been held in West-

---

* J. H. R. Ramsay, writing in the *British Medical Journal*, gave his opinion that Dawson wanted the death sooner rather than later as an harmonious sequitur to his earlier bulletin, and that it would enable him to return earlier to his busy London practice. Ramsay decried his description of the King's death as 'a facet of euthanasia or so called mercy killing'. Rather, he thought it 'convenience killing', and concluded that the likely verdict was that Dawson was 'guilty of the besetting sin of doctors and that is arrogance' (*British Medical Journal*, 1994; 308: 1445 (28 May)). It would also have helped sell the memoirs that Dawson fully intended to write.
† The Duke of Gloucester was absent due to a sore throat.

minster Abbey, awaited the coffin, silhouetted in the Great West Door. He had succeeded in getting his Canons out of the way so that he would be centre stage in the press photographs. Not for nothing was he known in ecclesiastical circles as 'Albert the Magnificent'.[16]

The mourners within, a great many of them the victims of head colds, heard the coffin's approach to the sound of bands and pipes outside. At the chosen moment in the service, the coffin slowly descended by the special lift down into the Royal Vault, and the new King, Edward VIII, stepped forward to scatter a little earth on top of it. The Lord Chamberlain broke his ceremonial wand of office as is prescribed when one reign ends and another begins.

At Lambeth, the Revd Alan Don was but one who had misgivings: 'And now a new reign starts with a king very different in temperament and outlook. May he prove himself worthy of his heritage. If only he had a good wife! One trembles to think of the loneliness of his position.'[17]

10

The Abdication

'It's bad whichever way one looks at it' – the Duchess of York

The life of Elizabeth Bowes-Lyon, Duchess of York, would scarcely have merited telling but for the changes wrought in 1936. In that year of three Kings, she was propelled from being the daughter-in-law of one King, briefly sister-in-law of another and finally Queen Consort to the third.

There has always been intense interest in the role she played in the Abdication, but the simple truth is that she played none at all. This is not to say that she played an insignificant role in the events that followed it.

At no point was the Duchess of York involved in the decision taken by Edward VIII. She talked to no politicians and throughout the year she kept her opinions largely to herself. Occasionally she confided in Queen Mary, having taken the view that she would never talk about Royal Family matters outside that family. The one ally she had was the Archbishop of Canterbury who was equally sidelined, while, as Primate, he felt he should have been more consulted. As Alan Don put it: 'The truth is that C. C. has taken no part in the business except when he has been invited by Baldwin to talk things over.'[1] Edward VIII distrusted the Archbishop, as a personal friend of his father, surmising correctly that George V had confided his worries to him. With Edward VIII, the Archbishop found conversation rare and unsatisfactory. He worried about many liturgical aspects of the Coronation and the oath the King would take.

There was more than a little disquiet about the new King. He upset those at Sandringham by putting the clocks back to normal time, an exercise which occupied several professional clock engineers for several days. He then flew to London, taking the Duke of York with him. It was remarked that this was foolhardy: had there been an accident, Princess Elizabeth, not yet ten, would have succeeded to the throne.

A crisis was looming, but it was not reported in the British press, and though the name of Mrs Simpson was known to the inner few, it was largely unknown to the general public. Even in a photograph of the King skiing with her in February 1935, Mrs Simpson was merely captioned as 'an unknown American woman'.

News was strictly controlled. When unsavoury reports about the Royal Family appeared in foreign newspapers or magazines, these were excised with scissors by the distributors before they reached the news-stands. One such concerned a speculative report in *Time* magazine that Princess Marina was conspiring to have the Duke of Kent made King of Greece in lieu of the exiled King George II. It was suggested that she had been in consultation with Greek Premier, Tsaldaris. This page was cut out on account of a passage describing Marina as 'a clever, ambitious, little minx bent on jacking up her husband into something more of consequence than the youngest and willowiest son of Britain's George V'. The piece also included a derogatory reference to Queen Mary as 'the forbidding Queen-Empress'.[2]

There was considerable interest in the new reign overseas, particularly in America. Hardly had King George V died than the *New York Times* pointed out that the accession of the Prince of Wales 'brings a woman of non-royal blood within sight of becoming Queen of England for the first time in 250 years'.[3] While describing the Duke of York as 'dull and uninspiring' compared to his elder brother, his decency was applauded: 'There has never been a breath of scandal about him or his family. As far as the public knows neither he nor his wife ever made a single false step to impair their usefulness or popularity.'[4]

As early as 25 January, a mere five days after the death of the King, Charles A. Selden was wiring the *New York Times* to the effect that the Britons were 'anxious about new monarch'. The worries were listed as follows: some opinions and actions were more admirable in a prince than a king, where they risked being too radical or unconventional; that he lacked a wife; that he had no great friends among the politicians to guide him; that he took unnecessary risks with his life (e.g. flying from Sandringham to London with the Duke of York); that he was too outspoken in denouncing the meagre living conditions of miners; and that he was bored by ceremonial. The correspondent considered that Stanley Baldwin, the Prime Minister, was issuing something of a warning to the 'young King' (as he called him somewhat patronisingly). The correspondent concluded that among the King's 'qualities' was 'a quick temper and a capacity for impatience'.[5]

By the end of the month, their correspondent Frederick T. Birchall was commending the new King on the warm welcome he had given, at the first state reception, to Baron Constantin von Neurath, the German Foreign Minister, and the German Ambassador, Leopold von Hoesch. Not only was he 'more Left and less Conservative in his predilections than any British monarch within living memory', but Germany had been feeling 'isolated and friendless, and here unexpectedly a new and powerful friend may have come into her orbit'.[6]

By March interest was growing in Princess Elizabeth, and one headline proclaimed: 'May Rule Britain as Elizabeth II.'[7] On 11 March the traditional request was made to Parliament for the renewal of the Civil List. The King excited newspaper readers by asking that 'the contingency of his marriage should be taken into account, so that, in that event, there should be provision for Her Majesty the Queen and the members of his family corresponding to the provisions which the House of Commons has been willing to make in like circumstances in the past'. Will Thorne, a Labour MP, rose to enquire: 'May I ask whether His Majesty has given any guarantee that he is going to get married?' This was greeted with a roar of laughter.[8] In the same request for finance, the King made it clear that he would continue to receive the revenues of the Duchy of Cornwall but would use these, if sufficient, to pay the new Civil List annuity for the Duke of York as heir to the throne.

Humour was in short supply as the greatest crisis in the recent history of the monarchy unfolded. Towards the end of May came the first mention of Mr and Mrs Ernest Simpson in the foreign press as having attended a dinner at St James's Palace for the aviator Charles Lindbergh and his wife: 'Mrs Simpson is an American. She is the daughter of the late S. Davies Warfield* of Baltimore and has long been celebrated in London society for her charm and beauty and the distinguished friendships she has made here.'[9]

The Duchess of York began to throw off the ill effects of her pneumonia. She was still at Royal Lodge when the King died, but was able to take part in all stages of the funeral. In the days immediately following, she and the Duke and the Kents twice supported Queen Mary when Prince Paul of Yugoslavia, who had represented his country at the funeral, dined at Marlborough House.

Elizabeth minded the death of George V, as she explained to Lord Dawson, describing his earlier vitality and her relief that his end had come so quickly:

> He was getting so tired, and though occasionally he was his old delightful self, those moments seemed to be getting more rare, and no man deserved rest more than he. I miss him dreadfully. Unlike

---

* Wallis Simpson was in fact the daughter of Teakle Wallis Warfield.

his own children I was never afraid of him, and in all the twelve years of having me as a daughter-in-law he never spoke one unkind or abrupt word to me, and he was always ready to listen and give advice on one's own silly little affairs. He was so kind and *dependable*. And when he was in the mood, he could be deliciously funny too![10]

Those who saw the Duchess at this time described her as 'delicious' or 'the most perfect person'.[11] When she lunched with Maureen Stanley, Harold Nicolson failed to recognise her – 'a dear little woman in black', but reported to his wife: 'She is charm personified.'[12] It was all a contrast to the description of Edward VIII by George V's unlikely friend, Jimmy Thomas,* 'this obstinate little man with 'is Mrs Simpson'. As Thomas put it: 'I know the people of this country. I *know* them. They 'ate 'aving no family life at Court.'[13]

Presently the Duke took Elizabeth to Compton Place, the Duke of Devonshire's house at Eastbourne, where George V had spent a fortnight the year before. She remained there until March. From Eastbourne she wrote to Lord Dawson of Penn:

> I am really very well now, and, I think, am now only suffering from the effects of a family break-up – which always happens when the head of a family goes. Though outwardly one's life goes on the same, yet everything is different – especially spiritually and mentally. I don't know if it is the result of being ill but I mind things that I don't like more than before. But it will be very good for me to pull myself together, and try to collect a little will power.[14]

What concerned her most was the growing unease over the King and Mrs Simpson. It is always said that the Yorks had no idea that they might have to take over the throne until November 1936, but the possibility must have loomed in their minds, as it had in the minds of those who watched from afar. The fear must have intensified as spring turned to summer.

It was a strange business. The King had been an immensely popular Prince of Wales, full of charm and charisma, adored wherever he went, with the notable exception of his own home. He lived life at a fast pace, steeple-chasing, hunting, dancing into the small hours of the night,

---

* J. H. Thomas (1874–1949), engine cleaner and Labour MP, who rose to become Lord Privy Seal. In June 1936 he was found guilty of leaking Budget secrets and resigned as Secretary of State for the Colonies.

pursuing flirtations of one kind and another. He was his own master until he met Wallis Simpson, a brittle American woman, without particularly good looks nor, at first, any elegance. By 1931 the Prince was exhausted by his unsettled life and his extensive travels. He dreaded inheriting the throne and subconsciously sought a means of escape. He could not admit this to himself but he found it in Mrs Simpson.

Wallis Simpson was quick witted and could be funny. She was adept at wisecracks. 'The room sharpened up when she came in'[15], according to Lady Diana Cooper. The Prince of Wales was soon captivated and subjugated to her ways. She did not defer to him, but offered him a challenge that intrigued him. She may have dreamed distantly of being his queen. In her American way she failed to understand the bonds that constrained a constitutional monarch. She enjoyed being his favourite, his best friend, with whatever connotation that implied. What she did not want was to be the cause of the Abdication, or to become his wife in exile.

It is more than possible to see Mrs Simpson as the victim of the obsession of an unhappy and spoilt man, determined to have his way at any cost, a man seeking a route of escape. In retrospect, it is hard to support the line almost universally taken at the time – that she was the woman who stole the King.

The relationship between the Prince of Wales and Mrs Simpson had caused much private grief and concern to his parents, King George V and Queen Mary, and the problem remained unresolved by the time George V died. The new King may have thought himself a moderniser, flown his own aeroplane, walked bare-headed through the streets of London, but everything he did or wished to do was eclipsed by the problem of his obsession with Mrs Simpson.

At the time of his Accession, the King thought he might be able to marry Mrs Simpson with fewer problems than in his father's lifetime. He soon realised that he could not. Besides being King, he was Head of the Church of England, and he learned that at his Coronation he would be obliged to take the Coronation Oath, in which he would swear 'to maintain and preserve inviolably the settlement of the Church of England, and the Doctrine, Worship, Discipline, and Government thereof, as by Law established in England . . .'[16] Effectively, this would prevent him from marrying a divorced woman with two previous husbands living, whoever she was and whatever her merits or de-merits. He failed to confront or resolve the issue, though it worried him.

Newspapers abroad reflected disquiet about the King, as did the courtiers. Alec Hardinge had taken over as the King's Private Secretary, and almost from the start found it difficult to work with him. The King was not practical, and he was inclined to talk without thinking. When courtiers gathered there was 'nothing but ghastly conversation about how awful the new king is'.[17] On the evening of 28 March, the King brought his party from Fort Belvedere to Windsor Castle to see a film of the Grand National and another with Eddie Cantor. In the group were the Simpsons, and an American later identified as the woman chosen to be Ernest Simpson's next wife, Mary Kirk Raffray. Helen Hardinge was there and became convinced at that time that the King meant to marry Mrs Simpson.

This drama hung over the Royal Family and the court throughout 1936, and none of the King's actions gave them cause to be other than increasingly concerned. The Duchess of York had declined to meet Mrs Simpson in the last years of the previous reign, though inevitably there had been some impromptu meetings. Again, in the new reign, there were some dinners, and an uneasy afternoon when the King brought her over to Royal Lodge. Nothing had occurred that eased the minds of either party.

During the rest of the summer, the Duchess of York was living in a kind of limbo, with little to do. Her illness kept her out of the public eye in the first months and there were not many engagements in the summer, the court being in mourning until 20 October. On 7 May the Duke of York opened the Royal Tournament, and the Duchess and their daughters went with them. Four days later, she and Queen Mary looked round Canterbury, with the Archbishop as their guide. Later in the month they were both in the royal party that toured *Queen Mary*. Other than that there was the occasional court and a few undemanding ceremonies.

Thus she was able to relax at Royal Lodge, surrounded by her favourite sweet-smelling roses. She did not discourage a streak of laziness in her character, and she welcomed the time to read.

At Royal Lodge she enjoyed Duff Cooper's second volume on the life of Haig which she thought must have been hard work since, as he had put it: 'greatness of character is something different from greatness of mind or of intellect – it is a quality that does not dazzle men'. Meanwhile, she was very happy doing nothing, but using the time to look back and assess herself.[18]

In June the Yorks attended Trooping the Colour, the Duke riding behind the new King, and on 1 July they visited the Royal Show in Bristol. On 16 July the Duke was riding behind the King with his brothers, the Duke of Gloucester and the Duke of Kent, on the return journey from the presentation of new colours to the Brigade of Guards in Hyde

Park when a revolver was seen flying through the air to land at the King's feet. If some of this happened without the King's immediate awareness, the Duke of York saw it all. A man called George Andrew Mahon was arrested. A week later, the Duke and Duchess with their daughters and her parents attended the wedding of her niece Jean Elphinstone to John Wills, a Life Guards officer. The Archbishop presided, so, as his Scottish chaplain noted, 'Angus was well represented'.[19]

On 29 July the Yorks paid their key visit to colliery villages in Durham, even descending into a pit to see the working conditions of the miners. This affected the Duchess sharply.

In August she wrote again to Duff Cooper, thanking him for a copy of a speech he had made in Paris, which she agreed 'in no part of it did you say anything that could have raised ire . . . a dashed good speech', thanking him further for the translations of three 'romantic & exquisite' Japanese poems, her introduction to 'so enchanting a person as Prince Genji', and then she addressed him on her thoughts concerning the visit to Tyneside:

> I went to Palmers Shipyard, Jarrow's sole means of employment – a horrible scene of desolation, & then out through the streets – driving through large crowds of emaciated, ragged, unhappy & *undaunted* people, who gave us a wonderful reception. It made me weep – their courage is so high. I hope that you do not think that I am carried away by just a glimpse of the tragedy up in the North. I often think about it all, it seems terrible that such good material should be wasted.
>
> It is *such* a pity that the Trades Union officials etc are so foolishly anti-military – it would solve the problem of these young boys – if they could join the Army.[20]

The atmosphere in Scotland was different that summer. With King George V dead, Queen Mary did not go to Balmoral. Instead she stayed with Princess Mary at Harewood House. The Yorks were happy to be able to borrow Birkhall from the new King as usual. While the King set off on his controversial *Nahlin* cruise,* they settled into the life they so relished. The Gloucesters were nearby, at Abergeldie Mains in August and September.

The Archbishop of Canterbury was on his usual peregrination around the stately homes of England and Scotland, but he was pointedly not

---

* The King was away from 8 August until 14 September, travelling via Corfu, the Dalmatian Coast, Yugoslavia, Greece, Turkey, Bulgaria and Austria. Mrs Simpson and others were with him.

invited to Balmoral this year. Aware of this, the Duchess of York asked him to Birkhall for a night in September. She gave him a cocktail, warning him that there was 'a little gin in it'. He accepted with the words: 'I'm sure you would not give me anything that was bad for me.'[21] This harmless invitation caused the King great annoyance. He chose not to see it as an act of courtesy to a prelate and friend, but as an attempt to establish a rival court.

The King arrived in Scotland on 19 September, the Duke of York, briefly in London, travelling north with him. The King received the traditional welcome at Ballater and then at Balmoral. The castle was awash with Dukes and Duchesses – the Kents, the Buccleuchs, the Sutherlands and the Marlboroughs – with the Mountbattens, Roseberys, Colin Buists and others.

Mrs Simpson was due to arrive on 23 September, a day when the King had been asked to open the new wing of the Aberdeen Royal Infirmary. He had declined on the specious grounds that the court was in mourning and so the Yorks (who were equally in mourning) were bidden to undertake this duty instead. They did so with their customary zest. Regrettably the King was also in Aberdeen that day, greeting Mrs Simpson at the station. Photographs of the dutiful Yorks and the holidaying King were printed side by side in the Scottish papers on the next day. By that one discourtesy he lost the loyalty of the Scottish people forever.

Not unnaturally, the Duchess of York was annoyed about this incident as she wrote to Queen Mary: 'I do wish that David could have done it, as they have all worked so hard for so long, and it will be one of the best in Scotland, and it would have given such enormous pleasure to the countryside.'[22]

Mrs Simpson's arrival at Balmoral was reported in the Court Circular, which the Revd Alan Don noted in London: 'Everyone now knows of Mrs S. and talks freely about her – it is a thousand pities, and yet the King seems determined to have his way. I do pity his entourage, for they must cordially dislike the whole business.'[23] One who weighed in was Mollie Buccleuch, staying at Balmoral. She attempted to warn Mrs Simpson of how unacceptable the situation was. She made no headway.[24]

Three evenings later, the Yorks went to dine at Balmoral. The King burst into the room alone as was his habit as host, they saw the film *Swing Time* and there was a buffet afterwards. (There is a story that Mrs Simpson attempted to act as hostess, which did not suit the Duchess as senior female Royal Highness present. She swept past her saying that she had come to dine with the King, and they left as soon as possible after dinner.*) Whatever happened, it was an uncomfortable evening. The next

* This is a story that has possibly been exaggerated over the years. For example, it is not mentioned in the diary of Helen Hardinge, who was present.

day the King and Duke of Kent were observed talking all through matins, which made a bad impression.

On her return to London at the end of October, Elizabeth wrote to thank the King, telling him that they had enjoyed six weeks of complete peace at Birkhall, saying it was angelic of him to let them have it.

On 11 October the Duchess warned Queen Mary that Balmoral could never be the same again. The new King had failed to make people feel wanted, and she was forced to blame much of his attitude on Mrs Simpson. She did not feel able to invite Mrs Simpson to her house, which naturally led to strained relations with the King.

Writing to the King a while later, the Duchess again involved herself in a social concern, this time appealing to him on behalf of the workers of St John Ambulance Brigade. She told him that the Order hoped that he would perform a function for them the following summer, possibly a review or an inspection in Hyde Park. By the time her letter arrived, the bachelor King had greater issues weighing upon him.

In the weeks that followed it became clear that the press silence that had protected the King and Mrs Simpson could not be sustained indefinitely. The overseas press was filled with articles under headlines such as 'A Yankee at the Court of King Edward'. Letters of concern poured into places like Lambeth Palace expressing disgust and horror. 'We felt we were sitting on a volcano,' wrote Alec Sargent, another of the Archbishop's chaplains. 'At any moment the whole thing might flare up.'[25]

The crisis deepened when Mrs Simpson entered divorce proceedings against her husband in October. On 3 November the King attended the State Opening of Parliament, and went one step down the path towards his Coronation. As required of a new Sovereign, he made and signed the Declaration prescribed by Act of Parliament. Dr Don noted that the King had 'signed the "Protestant" oath declaring himself to be a "faithful Protestant"!' and that he had read his speech 'without any trace of nervousness'. The King also promised 'to secure the Protestant Succession to the Throne of my realm, uphold and maintain the said enactments to the best of my powers according to law'.[26]

This declaration was required by the Bill of Rights of 1689. More serious would be the Coronation Oath, taken and signed at Westminster Abbey which, as previously related, would effectively prohibit his marriage to Mrs Simpson. Don continued: 'It must have been an ordeal for him after all that has recently happened. I was standing within two feet of Baldwin and wondered what was passing through his mind.'[27]

Mrs Simpson watched the proceedings from the Royal Gallery, causing Don to comment further: 'She must be a brazen faced woman to appear thus among the assembled aristocracy within a week of the divorce which has set everyone talking.'[28]

It fell to Alec Hardinge to warn the King that press silence could not last and to urge him to take action immediately. Much has been written of the role of Hardinge. He has been roundly criticised, even castigated for imparting this news to the King in a letter. Effectively he was the messenger and the messenger is frequently blamed.

It is true that Hardinge transferred his loyalty, gradually and imperceptibly, from the person of the King to the institution of monarchy during that autumn. That he did so was one factor which helped smooth the difficult transition from one living monarch to another. The King claimed that he had no further dealings with Hardinge after the letter. This is all but true. He acknowledged receipt of it, and he took action, if not the action that Hardinge sought. He denied Hardinge any further confidences, though these had already dwindled to a minimum.

To Edward VIII's credit in these weeks, he did not create a constitutional crisis, though pressed by Winston Churchill to put his case to the country. He summoned the Prime Minister, Stanley Baldwin, and asked his views about marriage with Mrs Simpson and the possibility of her becoming Queen. Baldwin conferred with his colleagues and the Dominion governments and came back with a negative answer. The King then suggested a morganatic marriage, in other words one in which he married Mrs Simpson and she did not take the title of Queen. Again this was discussed privately, and rejected by Baldwin.

King Edward had made his position clear. In those circumstances he would abdicate. By this time, Mrs Simpson was in France, and she appealed most urgently against his decision, but his mind was resolved. The British public came to hear about it, but by the time it became a public issue the matter was all but decided.

The Duke of York was unaware of the gravity of the crisis until he summoned Hardinge in November. Hardinge warned the Yorks that the King would almost certainly abdicate and they must prepare themselves to take over. It came as a terrible realisation to the Duke that he might suddenly have to succeed his brother as King. He had undergone no training for the task ahead, and was a shy and retiring person. Both he and the Duchess were not at all sure whether the British public would accept them. They genuinely enjoyed their quiet, domestic life with their two daughters, and were daunted by the task ahead. They continued to hope for a reprieve up until the last moment.

Years later, Martin Charteris (by then Private Secretary to the present Queen) put it thus: 'It is hard to believe that Queen Elizabeth did not want to be Queen in 1936, but in my reading of history she did not. She was happy to be the Duchess of York with her two young children.' He paused: 'That's not to say that she would not be extremely reluctant *not* to be Queen now . . .'[29]

The autumn was stressful. The Yorks were present at the Cenotaph on 11 November, the Hardinge letter was delivered to the King on 13 November, soon after which, on 17 November, the King told his brothers in turn of his plight and intention to marry at any cost. The Duke of York tried to be supportive and the Duchess wrote secretly to the King urging him to be kind to Bertie, and assuring him how 'loyal and true' her husband was to him. 'I am terrified for him,' she wrote, 'so DO help him, and *for God's sake* don't tell him that I have written.'[30]

On the same day, 23 November, the Duchess wrote to Helen Hardinge:

I would love to see you, because there is nobody that I can talk to, & I know that you understand the horrible complications of the situation. It's bad whichever way one looks at it, both from our point of view, & the country's, and the *only* thing that matters is the support & sympathy of one's friends. I feel very depressed & miserable, & so am extra grateful for your support.[31]

The Yorks were completely excluded from the drama that followed. It was possibly even a relief to go to Edinburgh on the night of 29 November for two formal Scottish ceremonies. The Duke was installed as Grand Master Mason of Scotland, and the Duchess was given the Freedom of the City on 1 December. They returned to London on 3 December, the day after Bishop Blunt had attacked the King in an address to his Diocesan Conference in Bradford. They were confronted with placards openly referring to the crisis regarding the King's marriage.

For four long and anxious days the Duke of York was kept waiting by his brother, who prevaricated about seeing him. Finally on the evening of 7 December, the King rang and invited him to come to Fort Belvedere after dinner. The Duke said he would come immediately, and ten minutes later he found his brother pacing up and down and heard his final verdict that he would go.

By this time the Yorks were resigned to their fate but beginning to see the positive side of it. Helen Hardinge's mother, Lady Milner, recorded in her diary of 8 December that the Duchess has told her 'in a way that was most touching, that she and her husband were looking forward to be of service to "this dear country"'.[32]

Frances Donaldson, Edward VIII's inspired biographer, wrote more sharply of the Queen-to-be waiting in the wings: 'She cannot have been entirely cold to her opportunity.' The phrase is memorable, but it reads unkindly if taken out of context. Lady Donaldson had a more important point to make about the new Queen's character:

> Yet it cannot be said too soon or too often that what has distin-
> guished her throughout her life from many people of like
> temperament is that, entirely serious in purpose, she is invariably
> light hearted in approach. She suffers not from self pity, that most
> moving and enervating of emotions, and, since she is capable of
> great feeling, she is never under the necessity of assuming it. She
> has responded to all moments of crisis in her own career with the
> light and under stated answer.[33]

What of the future King George VI? At last able to consult Walter Monckton, the King's chosen adviser, he did his best to mediate and to give support where he could. He called regularly on his distraught mother at Marlborough House. He dined at the Fort on the evening of 8 December, where the King, his decision made, his anxieties over, spoke movingly of his recent trip to the unemployed centres in South Wales. The Duke leant over to Monckton and whispered: 'And this is the man we are going to lose.'[34]

After further discussions and pleas at the Fort, the Duke drove to London and went to see Queen Mary at Marlborough House. In his own words, he 'broke down & sobbed like a child'.[35]

The Instrument of Abdication was drawn up and signed at Fort Belvedere on the morning of 10 December. Meanwhile the Duchess succumbed to influenza. She was in bed at 145 Piccadilly while her husband moved between Royal Lodge and the Fort. Nor was she present at the dinner at Royal Lodge, following which the ex-King was driven to Windsor Castle to make his Abdication broadcast. It was a convenient time to be ill. She was able to escape a lot of Germanic emotion between mother, son and brothers.*

Of all Edward VIII's sisters-in-law, Elizabeth had been the closest and

---

* The new Queen was only well enough to go to Royal Lodge for the weekend by 19 December. She was better by 22 December, going to Sandringham to spend Christmas there with the King, the princesses, Queen Mary, the Duke and Duchess of Gloucester and the Earl and Countess of Athlone. The Duke and Duchess of Kent were not there, as the Duchess was expecting a baby – Princess Alexandra, born in London on Christmas Day.

most supportive. Only when Mrs Simpson arrived in the King's life in 1931 was a wedge driven between them. She had many reasons to regret the Abdication. The most pressing was the life-long burden that would now fall on to her husband's shoulders and indeed her own. The other was that she genuinely loved Edward VIII, admired him and had hoped for so much from him. She had sustained him in small ways in his uneasy struggles with his father, noted his restlessness and on many occasions sought to raise his spirits. In his early, more charming days, his company must have been as much a relief for her as hers was for him.

From her sickbed, the Duchess of York, so soon to be Queen Elizabeth, wrote to the departing King to say:

'God bless you' from my heart. We are all overcome with misery, and can only pray that you will find happiness in your new life. I often think of the old days, and how you helped Bertie and I in the first years of our marriage – I shall always mention you in my prayers.[36]

This is probably the last letter that the new Queen Elizabeth ever wrote to the ex-King, though she never failed to send him her Christmas card, one of which included a handwritten line about a recent equestrian victory, of which she was proud.*

The reaction of the other members of the Royal Family to the abdicating monarch is significant. They all wrote to wish him well, but some of them bade him farewell as though he were now no longer a part of their lives. In later life, his cousin the Duchess of Beaufort invariably spoke of him in the past tense, even though he was still alive.

Each varied a little in their reaction. His mother, Queen Mary, suffered deeply from the Abdication, placing the love of Britain and duty to her country first. His sister, the Princess Royal, could not understand his actions, but made it clear that they were still friends. His admired old great-uncle, the Duke of Connaught, felt sorry for him and told the new King, George VI, that he had sent the Duke of Windsor his Christmas card as usual.

* In 1961, the Queen Mother sent a card with photographs of Laffy, Double Star and The Rip, captioned: 'This is a picture of my "treble" at Lingfield.' In 1968, she added 'with my love', having seen the Duke (for the last time) at Princess Marina's funeral. She sent a card to the Duchess the year of the Duke's death, 1972, signed 'Elizabeth', but thereafter the Duchess was dropped from the Queen Mother's Christmas card list, while the Queen continued to send them, formally signed 'Elizabeth R' (Johanna Schütz, the Duchess of Windsor's secretary, to author, Paris, 13 March 1973, and 14 September 1976; also *Property from the Collection of the Duke and Duchess of Windsor* (Sotheby's, New York, 1998, Lot 171)).

The dinner at Royal Lodge took place, with the new King as host, duly addressed as 'Your Majesty'. Queen Mary, the ex-King, Princess Mary, the Duke of Gloucester, the Duke of Kent and the Earl and Countess of Athlone were there. After the Abdication broadcast, the ex-King returned to Royal Lodge to bid farewell to family. There can be no scene so poignant as the lone figure making his way to Portsmouth to embark for France and to an uncertain future. As he sailed away, he had renounced the position of King and Emperor, reigning over a large percentage of the population of the world.

The following day, the new Queen (signing herself 'Elizabeth R' for the first time) wrote in more upbeat tone to the Archbishop of Canterbury about the great task to which they had been called:

We both feel our responsibilities very deeply, and though quite prepared for a difficult time, are determined to do our best . . .

We were so very unhappy over the loss of a dear brother – because one can only feel that exile from this country is death indeed. We were miserable, as you know, over his change of heart and character during the last few years, and it is alarming how little in touch he was, with ordinary feeling – Alas! He had lost the common touch.[37]

To another she wrote: 'The melancholy fact remains still at the present moment, that he for whom we agonised is the one person it did not touch.'[38]

The new King, pale and exhausted, addressed his Accession council and spoke of the heavy task that lay before him. He announced that he was creating his brother Duke of Windsor. In the same afternoon, 12 December, he was proclaimed King by heralds, lord mayors and mayors across the land.

Two days later, on 14 December, George VI celebrated his forty-first birthday. His spirits rose when he realised that he was now Sovereign of the Order of the Garter. He commanded that a Garter service should be held the following summer, and he bestowed the Order of the Garter on Queen Elizabeth.

11

The Coronation

'The little Queen, so serious, quiet and unaffected' – Mrs Bell

A wave of relief followed the departure of Edward VIII. Alan Don noted: 'The Latin for Prince of Wales is Walliae Princeps – mercifully these words drop out of the Latin liturgy wh[ich] will be said at Convocation next week – Wally's Prince!'[1]

New prayers for the Royal Family were devised for use in church: '. . . our gracious Queen Elizabeth, Mary the Queen Mother, the Princess Elizabeth and all the Royal Family'. The Duke of Windsor was dropped from the prayers of the nation for the first time since 1910.* The Bishop of Aberdeen was keen to press for the presence of a priest to celebrate Holy Communion at Crathie Church, which, it was hoped, would find favour with Queen Elizabeth as a Scottish Episcopalian. Sir John Simon, the Home Secretary, confirmed without hesitation that, there being two daughters of the King, the one senior in age was first in line to the throne.

More immediate changes brought reality home. On the day of the Abdication, Lady Cynthia Asquith happened to be going to tea with the little princesses and their governess. The attention of the media was focused on 145 Piccadilly, and there was a huge crowd outside the house. Princess Elizabeth could not resist sneaking looks through the window as each new figure of importance arrived or a particularly loud cheer went up. The visitors were photographed in turn, though the new Queen's mother, Lady Strathmore, urged the photographers: 'I should not waste a photograph on me.'[2]

When Lady Cynthia was leaving, Princess Elizabeth escorted her to the door. A solitary letter was lying on the hall table, addressed: 'Her Majesty The Queen'. 'That's Mummy now,' said the Princess with a solemn face and a slight tremor in her voice.[3]

The next day, when King George VI returned from the Accession Council, both his daughters swept to the floor in a graceful curtsey as they had always done to King George and Queen Mary, but never before

* The same fate attended Diana, Princess of Wales, after her divorce in 1996. Camilla Parker Bowles was added to the prayers when she became Duchess of Cornwall in 2005.

to their parents. Crawfie observed that he was surprised: 'He stood for a moment touched and taken aback. Then he stopped and kissed them both warmly.'[4]

By such small signs are the changes wrought.* Presently the King and Queen Elizabeth, Princess Elizabeth and Princess Margaret, left the quiet domesticity of 145 Piccadilly to take up residence in the Edwardian hotel grandeur of Buckingham Palace and that great fortress on the hill, Windsor Castle. The King and Queen loved Royal Lodge so much that they kept this on as their retreat, a point of stability in changed circumstances. They also retained use of Birkhall.

The date for King Edward's Coronation had been set for 12 May 1937, and some souvenirs, even official ones, were already in production. There seemed no reason to choose another date; the only major alteration to the service then planned concerned the additional presence of a Queen Consort, for whom provision was easily made.

Cosmo Gordon Lang, the Archbishop of Canterbury, was the man who would crown the King. He had remained at Lambeth Palace during the Abdication crisis, but he now moved out of the shadows into the limelight of controversy. A few days after the Abdication, he made his infamous broadcast at the BBC, denouncing Edward VIII, his 'craving for private happiness' and 'his social circle'.

The Archbishop had not composed his words lightly. He had been encouraged to speak out against the ex-King's friends by communications from men he respected, such as the distinguished Cambridge theologian Revd Dr A. C. Bouquet, and he was further inspired by his interview with Queen Mary in which she had told him that she and others had made a last-ditch attempt to persuade King Edward to change his mind, and he had 'stormed & raged & shouted like a man demented'.[5] Alec Sargent prevailed upon the prelate to remove a line about the ex-King departing 'into the night', on the grounds that the 'association with Judas Iscariot was altogether too obvious'.[6] Having composed the oration, the Archbishop knelt beside his desk in prayer seeking strength to deliver it, in which pose he was interrupted by Sargent.

Following the broadcast, he received a considerable post. Sir John Reith, Lord Salisbury and Lord Astor were supportive, but the majority of letters were abusive, if not openly vituperative. In the press, H. G. Wells called it 'a libellous outburst'.[7] The Archbishop was nicknamed 'Auld Lang Swine' in a popular piece of doggerel. Alan Don judged that

---

* It was not until 26 April 1937 at a dinner at Windsor Castle, that the men of the party first kissed the Queen's hand.

the rebuke to the King's circle was more than justified, but wondered if the Archbishop had not been 'a little unfair to the poor King in attributing his decision, the surrender of his trust, to a "craving for private happiness". His motive was not so simple as that – it included, I believe, a recognition that he never could be a successful King, and that for the Empire's sake as well as for his own, he had better renounce the Throne.'*[8]

The Archbishop of York (William Temple) then joined the fray with a declaration on the evils of men falling in love with other men's wives, which he inserted into his diocesan letter. Concerned that all the Bishops in the land would add their baying cries, the new King caused Lord Wigram to ring Lambeth Palace at 11 p.m. to say that he was 'put out about this recrudescence of newspaper publicity' and to 'exhort the leaders of religion to reticence, so that the rumpus in the press could die down'.[9] Reticence was imposed.

On the same Sunday night as the broadcast, 13 December, Osbert Sitwell, by now a firm friend of the new Queen, filled his pen with purple ink and wrote the satirical poem *Rat Week*, which circulated privately in and around Sitwellian society. Sitwell had been irritated by the speed with which the friends of Edward VIII and Mrs Simpson deserted them, in particular – and mentioned by name in the poem – Lady Mendl, her cohort, Johnnie McMullin, and Lady Colefax: 'What do they say, that jolly crew, who must make even Judas queasy?'[10] Sitwell did not mention figures such as Lady Cunard or the Duff Coopers, though with more courage he might have done.

Sitwell gave copies to Mrs Greville, Lady Cholmondeley and Lady Aberconway. Sybil Cholmondeley showed it to the King and Queen, who enjoyed it so much that they passed it on to Queen Mary, who relished it. Such was its currency that when Lady Diana Cooper stayed with the King and Queen in the spring of 1937 she said to him: 'I'm afraid I'm a Rat, Sir.'[11]

The Archbishop of Canterbury was quick to visit the new King and Queen to discuss the Coronation. He saw them on 21 December. They agreed instantly to attend a great Empire service in St Paul's Cathedral, something King Edward had refused to consider. They were both happy for the Coronation service to be broadcast, at least up to the 'Sanctus' in the Communion. They did not mind photography or filming, as long as there was no additional noise, nor extra strong lighting. Queen Elizabeth particularly did not wish to be filmed during her anointing,

---

* It has been suggested that King Edward knew himself to be unable to produce descendants, thus making his reign somewhat pointless.

the most sacred part of the Coronation service, and wished the process to cease as soon as the canopy was placed over her head.

The Archbishop sent Queen Elizabeth a book about the Coronation, which sharpened her awareness of the history behind the forthcoming ceremony.[12] Queen Elizabeth was feeling 'as if I was coming to after a heavy blow on the head'. Looking back on the Abdication, she considered: 'I think that the shock of those terrible days in December was literally stunning, and a merciful numbness overcame one at the time. The return to life is rather unpleasant . . .'[13]

Lang was more than happy with his dealings with the new King and Queen: 'What a relief it was, after the strained and wilful ways of the late King, to be in this atmosphere of intimate friendship, and instead of looking forward to the Coronation as a sort of nightmare, to realise that . . . to the solemn words of the Coronation there would be a sincere response.'[14]

This atmosphere of friendliness was the key to the success of the new King and Queen. Gone were the brittle cocktail shakers and the night-club life of the previous reign. In its place came Sunday lunch, long walks in the park, bicycle rides, afternoon tea and the domestic monarchy whose appeal soon found a secure nest in many a British heart. The King's tastes were modest. He loved to shoot and relished nothing more than a day on the grouse moor, or a long afternoon lying, rifle in hand, in a freezing field of kale. He loved to come home at the end of the day, and instilled into Princess Margaret his recipe for warming up – 'a cup of tea, a hot bath and bed'.[15]

George VI was a different man from his brother. Thus the new court was a throwback to that of George V, yet the austerity of that bearded monarch and his stately consort was now replaced by a kinder, younger, simpler, more smiling pair. If the new King was not a sparkling conversationalist, he was a sincere and dutiful man, and any lulls in the conversation were easily filled by Queen Elizabeth, who, despite her angelic smile, was more than capable of a remark that proved sharper on reflection than it seemed at the time of delivery.

By now, this marriage was not dissimilar to many aristocratic marriages in history, the man the holder of the position, the estate, the office, and the wife the one who sustained the show, bringing in a breath of realism from the outside world. Lady Diana Cooper, who had known most of the Royal Family since Edward VII, was convinced that it was always those who married into the Royal Family from outside who made the greatest positive impact.*

---

* Lady Diana might have revised her opinion had she lived into the 1990s.

In later life, Queen Elizabeth maintained the staunch line that she had always deferred to the King. When people were sent to see her ladies-in-waiting, such as Patricia Hambleden, the message was always the same: 'The Queen Mother always deferred to the King.'[16] But this was not the case. Queen Elizabeth was well aware that any edicts should come from the King and not from her. She knew that in such a way they bore more weight, and that it was more correct. She was more than capable of agreeing the line with the King in advance and letting him put it out. Indeed, she seldom acted independently.

The King was grateful for her help and her advice. Later in the reign he used to irritate his second Private Secretary, Sir Alan Lascelles, by telling him, 'I will just keep these papers, and let you know what I think in the morning.' Lascelles knew that he would be consulting the Queen. She brought to all such matters a wiser and worldlier eye than that of her husband. And she acted with personal disinterest, only with the desire to come to the right decision – that the best should prevail.

Some have questioned her values. Lascelles used to say that her philosophy of life was best summed up in Mrs Alexander's well-known hymn 'All things bright and beautiful' and in particular in the politically incorrect verse now no longer sung:

> The rich man in his castle,
> The poor man at his gate,
> God made them, high or lowly,
> And order'd their estate.

When Queen Elizabeth wanted something done, her method was to invoke the King's name, and she continued to do this even after his death. 'The King would not have liked that' was the last card she would play to resolve a difference of views.[17]

The Queen had already made herself immensely popular as Duchess of York. To support the King, she had to draw on considerable reserves of inner strength. While the newspapers wrote daily of her sweetness, there were those who, like Stephen Tennant, detected a different character beneath. She was, as one observer put it 'a marshmallow made on a welding machine'.[18] The ever outspoken Margot Asquith spoke of her 'circulating smile, flannel flowers, & Neapolitan ice underneath the flounces & frills of cloth'.[19]

When Lady Londonderry invited the King and Queen to a magnificent ball three weeks after the Coronation, she submitted the list of proposed guests. The Queen replied:

I know that you will not mind my telling you that Lady Cunard is really the only one that we do not want to meet just now. The bitter months of last autumn and winter are still so fresh in our minds, and her presence would inevitably bring so many sad thoughts, that we should prefer not to meet her.

I can say this to you as a friend for so long, and feel sure that you will understand our feelings. (Private, of course). There is nobody else on your little list, except possibly poor Mrs Corrigan, who one could take exception to . . .[20]

In the weeks before the Coronation there were a number of developments which established the new King among his people. On New Year's Day 1937, he sent a greeting to the Empire declaring that he would do all in his power to strengthen the trust between himself and the peoples of the British Empire. His brother, the Duke of Gloucester, sacrificed his Army career in order to help him, thus foregoing a life-long ambition to command his regiment. When the King received delegations of foreign Ambassadors and ministers at Buckingham Palace, Ribbentrop, the new German Ambassador, gave the Nazi salute, presaging problems to come.

On 15 February the new Royal Family moved into Buckingham Palace, and they visited the Peoples' Palace in the East End and the British Industries Fair. Queen Elizabeth accompanied the King to Aintree. In April she and the King and Princess Elizabeth sailed down the Thames in the Royal Barge to Greenwich to open the National Maritime Museum.

Queen Elizabeth then created her own court. She made good choices, surrounding herself with figures on whose loyalty she could rely. That she chose well was vouchsafed by the fact that almost all of them stayed with her until death or infirmity brought their service to an end. Two of them* survived well beyond the age of one hundred, setting the pace, as it were, for their royal mistress.† The new court was announced on 5 March.

The Earl of Airlie, son of her old friend and adviser, Mabell Airlie, became her Lord Chamberlain. Sir Basil Brooke served as Treasurer, and

---

* Hon. Lettice Annesley (1885–1988), daughter of 11th Viscount Valentia (Comptroller of the Royal Household), married (1911) Captain Geoffrey Bowlby, who was killed in action in May 1915; and Lady Victoria Wemyss (1890–1994), a cousin, being a daughter of 6th Duke of Portland, KG. She was a goddaughter of Queen Victoria.
† Interestingly, she did not choose Lady Annaly. Other names mooted in the press were her London neighbour, Lady Allendale, and Lady Plunket.

Captain Richard Streatfeild as Private Secretary.* Helen, Duchess of Northumberland, became her Mistress of the Robes. She was the tall and handsome daughter of the 7th Duke of Richmond and therefore aunt of Lady Doris Vyner. She had married the 8th Duke of Northumberland, who had died aged fifty in 1930. She was a keen horsewoman and took a great interest in the poor of Northumberland.

Then the Queen surrounded herself with her best friends as ladies-in-waiting. Countess Spencer, the former Lady Cynthia Hamilton, sister of Katie Hamilton; Viscountess Halifax, the wife of the Lord President of the Council, who presently became Foreign Secretary, and daughter of the 4th Earl of Onslow; Viscountess Hambleden and the tall and beautiful Lady Nunburnholme (respectively Lady Patricia Herbert and Lady Mary Thynne, whose coming-out balls she had attended in the early 1920s) became Ladies of the Bedchamber, or senior ladies-in-waiting.

The Women of the Bedchamber were the two ladies-in-waiting already in place, Lady Helen Graham, tall and gaunt, and the Hon. Mrs (Geoffrey) Bowlby, short and dark, who had twice been mentioned in despatches for her war work as commandant of an auxiliary hospital. She served until 1944. These were joined by Lady Katharine Seymour (Katie Hamilton, who was rescued from Queen Mary's household) and Lady Hyde. Marion Hyde was the daughter of the 4th Lord Wolverton. She had married Lord Hyde, heir to the 6th Earl of Clarendon (who presently became Lord Chamberlain), but her husband had died in a shooting accident on safari in April 1935.

An extra Woman of the Bedchamber was also appointed – Queen Elizabeth's Cavendish-Bentinck cousin, Lady Victoria (Vera) Wemyss. An Austrian Countess described her as 'the salt of the earth made up of the finest qualities and no faults'.[21]

The ladies-in-waiting took it in turns to deal with the Queen's correspondence and to accompany her on royal engagements. Katie Seymour introduced the idea that some of the Queen's letters could go out typed rather than hand written. There had always been a large amount of correspondence. This now increased considerably.

The selection of these ladies was warmly applauded by the Queen of Spain's lady-in-waiting, 'Baba' Brougham, who wrote: 'I'm so glad the Queen has chosen such nice women to be around her. They – the Duchess of Northumberland, Lady Hambleden etc – are all saints. The sort of women who ride in buses, pay their bills, and are nice to old servants.'[22]

---

* Richard Streatfeild (1903–52), a cousin of Sir Henry Streatfeild, Queen Alexandra's Private Secretary. He left in 1945, having been on active service for most of the war. Later a brigadier.

Alec Hardinge was confirmed as Private Secretary, and he took up his duties on 28 March, on his return from a holiday in India following the exhaustion of the Abdication crisis. Hardinge had known the King for many years, since his sister Diamond and his wife Helen were among the Duchess of York's closest friends. He had seen him when on duty with George V, and on summer holidays in Scotland they had met regularly, his daughters being close friends of the princesses. Hardinge had heard that the Duke of York was known not to be generous by nature, and at times had heard him make disparaging remarks about his staff.

Hardinge was astonished to find how little the new King knew about public affairs, how the business of the Sovereign was conducted and the constitutional limitations of the crown. He was cautious to take no important steps without the King's previous approval. He was anxious to make no mistakes, and surprised that the King rarely expressed any opinions of his own. Hardinge made most of the important suggestions.

Even so, the King did not like to be run by any member of the House-hold, a position with which Hardinge had some sympathy. In his Svengali role, Hardinge encouraged the King to see his ministers often in the hope that they would get to know each other. He regretted that the King would not give a record to his Private Secretary afterwards, as sometimes the ministers and the King came away with different impressions of what had been said. And he encouraged the King to meet as many different types of people as possible.

Over the early years of the new King's reign hung the sinister shadow of the Duke of Windsor. That exiled former King caused his successor great anxiety. Hardinge tried to persuade George VI to take as little notice of his elder brother's activities as possible and to concentrate on securing his own position with his people. As his hold on them became stronger, so the spectre of the Duke of Windsor would gradually fade.

To this end, Hardinge was keen that the King and Queen should be seen in as many different parts of the country as possible.

Preparations for the Coronation were long and detailed. Queen Elizabeth approved the Bishops of St Albans and Blackburn as her supporters, the see of the former including her childhood home, St Paul's Walden Bury, and the latter as a representative of the Northern Province. Garter King of Arms, mindful of an unfortunate muddle at the Coronation of Queen Victoria, asked about the ring. It was to be placed on the fourth finger, but was the thumb to be considered a finger in this reckoning? The answer was that there are five fingers to the normal hand. Queen Mary asked the Archbishop of Canterbury whether he and his dignitaries would be by the altar when her procession arrived. The royal ladies were proposing to make him 'an obeisance as Head of our Church before going to our places'. They did not wish this to be taken as a bow to the altar – 'not being Papists!'[23]

A rare feature was the inclusion of the Declaration prescribed by Act of Parliament normally made in the House of Lords at the State Opening. Edward VIII had made this declaration on 3 November, but there would be no State Opening before this Coronation, so the Archbishop would administer it in the Abbey.* How would the sacred oil be dried? The Archbishop did not like cotton wool, but would use a fine cambric material. The six Free Churches would be present, but take no part in the service.

As the Coronation approached, the Archbishop instructed the King and Queen about the intricacies and meaning of the ceremony. He stayed with them for Easter at Windsor, and read the service with them, finding them 'most appreciative and fully conscious of its solemnity'.[24] On the Sunday before the ceremony, he gave them a more spiritual preparation at Buckingham Palace. The King and Queen chose 6 p.m. for this, the time when many Christians would be attending Evensong in different parts of Britain. The Archbishop prayed with them and blessed them. When they rose from their knees, all three had tears in their eyes.

On 12 May itself, the Bishops, the Royal Family, the representatives of foreign royal houses, the peers and peeresses and other invited guests took their appointed places at Westminster Abbey. There were witnesses both inside and outside the Abbey who left accounts. The young Cecil Beaton was outside. Nothing did he miss:

> The stream of cars bringing the guests to the Abbey had long since started, & there were many people to be watched on foot – A dignitary of the Church in purple cassock with purple velvet tam o'shanter looked like a figure from a Giotto fresco, the consort of some King from Fiji was in Paris clothes but looked as if she had come straight from Harlem. An increasing variety of uniforms hurried to the Annexe entrance & the crowd cheered at incidents of varying importance. A Field Marshal in plumed helmet would be the only person not to notice he dropped his Abbey invitation as he saluted, a dog unloosed ran out dazed into the empty roads

---

* The present Queen made hers on 5 November 1952, so that part was not included in her Coronation.

. . . Princess Juliana received a greater ovation than the Pauls of
Yugoslavia & any black face with turban was the signal for thunderous cheers . . .[25]

Presently the royal coaches arrived, and Beaton was amazed by the sights
before him:

The glass coaches, the gilded woodwork, the jewellery all add magic
to a magic complexion & today the loveliest ladies were those with
lovely skin. The effect of the jewellery, fur & velvet on a startling
skin was dazzling & all those like the Queen, Queen Mary, the
Duchesses of Kent, Gloucester, Devonshire, & Portland looked like
goddesses.[26]

And at last the King and Queen hove into view:

Eventually further storms of cheering could be heard approaching.
In Whitehall specks were fluttering & the high edifice of dolphins,
neptunes & palm trees that is the Royal Glass coach could be seen
preceded by the platoon of red-bobbled Greys. Inside sitting high
on crimson satin cushions sat Their Majesties, white & waxen, the
King slightly deathlike with cadaverous face leaning forward with
an ermine cap on his head. The Queen looked much lovelier than
any of her photographs & her unaccustomed pallor was very
moving.[27]

Inside the Abbey, the Archbishop of Canterbury's account contained this
description of the King and Queen:

The little Queen, the only woman present with an uncovered head
awaiting its anointing and its crown, advanced with a real poetry of
motion, her dignity enhanced rather than diminished by the tall
and beautiful figure of her Mistress of the Robes (the Duchess of
Northumberland). The King (as many said afterwards) looked like
a medieval knight awaiting his consecration with a rapt expression
in his eyes, which turned neither to the right nor to left. Their
demeanour, sustained through the whole long ceremony, seemed
from the first to invest it with a spirit of reverence.[28]

For her anointing, Queen Elizabeth was attended by four Duchesses all
of whom survived the occasion by more than fifty years: the Duchess of

Buccleuch (her old rival in love, Mollie Lascelles), the Duchess of Norfolk, the Duchess of Roxburghe and the Duchess of Rutland.*

The service was described by Henrietta Bell, wife of the Bishop of Chichester. In particular, she loved the diversity of races, tongues and experience that gathered in the Abbey:

> All this heterogeneous assemblage concentrated with such intensity and emotion on these two young, quiet, grave figures who seemed verily and indeed to be offering themselves, their Souls and bodies, to be a reasonable, holy and likely sacrifice to be used in God's service for all those multitudes within and without the Abbey, who were following the day with such vivid interest.[29]

Mrs Bell relished the arrivals: 'Wonderful Arabs *so* grave and immobile. Eastern potentates blazing with jewels, and splendid turbans. Headdresses of pearls, a blaze of diamonds in front and fringe of emeralds. Deputy Lieutenants with unruly swords and spiked helmets which were a danger to their neighbours. Peers struggling with their robes all bunched up anyhow and their coronets full of spectacle cases and sandwiches . . .'[30]

The Bishop of Durham was one of the King's supporting Bishops. He was grateful for the sustenance when, before the service, a Presbyterian divine shared his sandwiches with him. But then a Scottish peer offered him 'a draught from the flask which he had concealed under his robes'. The Bishop 'thought it prudent to decline since the comfortable exhilaration might be too dearly purchased by the suggestive aroma!'[31]

Besides the King and Queen and the little princesses, the figure who attracted the most interest was Queen Mary. Tradition ordained that no other crowned head should be present,† but Queen Mary had asked to be allowed to attend, and she presided over the Royal Box. Everyone wanted to cheer her but could only greet her by rising silently to their feet.

The King's daughters entered either side of their aunt, the Princess Royal, 'very demure with diminutive trains'. They were well rehearsed and when the moment came to sit next to Queen Mary they gathered up their trains with admirable competence. Then Princess Margaret 'wrig-

---

* Duchesses traditionally hold the Canopy at the anointing of a Queen Consort. These Duchesses were Mary Lascelles (1900–93), wife of 8th Duke of Buccleuch, Lavinia Strutt (1916–95), wife of 16th Duke of Norfolk, the Earl Marshal, Lady Mary Crewe-Milnes (b. 1915), wife of 9th Duke of Roxburghe and Kathleen Tennant (1894–1989), wife of 9th Duke of Rutland.

† Therefore no foreign kings and queens were present, though there were many crown princes. However, Queen Mary was accompanied by her sister-in-law, Queen Maud of Norway.

gled back into her chair and was much tempted to swing her legs, but Princess Elizabeth glared at her severely from the other side of the Princess Royal'.[32]

The King's procession was preceded by that of his Queen. She entered between the tall figures of her two Bishops. Mrs Bell described her:

> A very touching figure, very grave, very still with her little smooth brown head among all the tiaras and her long purple train, borne by six such graceful girls in simple white satin dresses and followed by a matchlessly dignified figure, the Dowager Duchess of Northumberland and her youngest son as her quite delightful page . . .
>
> As she passed to her seat just in front of the Royal Box, the Queen and all her ladies bowed to the Altar, and then came a gleam of a smile across her serious face as she saw the two eager little faces looking out at her from the Royal Box.[33]

At the moment of crowning, the peers, who had emptied their coronets of sandwiches and other refreshments, put their coronets on in unison, but this did not compare with 'the similar moment when the Queen was crowned and the graceful white arms of the peeresses all flashed together'. After her coronation, performed by the Archbishop of York, wrote Mrs Bell, 'it was beautiful to see her reverence to the King as she passed before him to her Throne rather lower than his'.[34]

Osbert Sitwell thought the most moving moment was not when the sea of peeresses curtsied to the Queen, or the congregation shouted 'God Save the King' or even when they put on their coronets, but when the King himself was actually crowned: 'He looked like a medieval missal, grave, white & lean, & went through his duties with the simplicity of movement & gesture of a great actor.'[35]

Not everything went according to plan. The Duke of Portland was forced to apologise afterwards: 'The only hitch was my stupid Garter chain [collar] getting hitched up with the cushion of the Queen's crown.' He enquired nervously of the Archbishop: 'I trust I did not betray either by look or by word my feelings of annoyance.'[36] The same had happened to Lord Salisbury with the King's crown, and on both occasions, Garter King of Arms had had to tear the fringes of the cushions. The Archbishop had his own problems with the King's crown, since a tiny thread of red cotton which would indicate the correct way for the crown had been removed. He appeared to fumble in the dramatic moment before placing it on the King's head.

When the great colourful procession had departed, Mrs Bell recorded her sense of awe, commending in particular 'the slim straight figure of the King, solemn in manner, his firm deliberate voice and mien', and 'the little Queen so serious, quiet, and unaffected'.[37] Back at the Palace, Alah Knight and the Queen's maid were happily in tears.

When it was all over, the Countess of Strathmore wrote to the Archbishop:

> Now that this great Coronation is past & that we are all quiet and composed once more, I want to write a few words to thank you from the bottom of my heart for the wonderful help that you gave to my little Queen all through that great and magnificent service, for I felt that without your spiritual aid she could not have carried it through so calmly & beautifully as she & the King did, for it was a great & awe-inspiring ordeal for them both.
>
> I think that nearly everyone felt the great *spirituality* of this Coronation, & this I know is entirely due to *you*, & I shall ever remember this with real gratitude.
>
> I hope you were not unduly tired out by the strain, but Portland wrote me the same evening that you were not.[38]

Queen Elizabeth herself found that of all parts of the Coronation it was the Communion that meant the most to her.[39]

Cecil Beaton made an acute observation which would be confirmed by other accounts in the days that followed:*

> It is interesting to notice how as soon as someone becomes loved they blossom. Since the King has become so universally loved & his duties of kingship have been taken up with such devotion, he has acquired an added beauty & nobility. It is the same metamorphosis that comes to a cinema star. It is for all to notice. As with his beauty, so with his speech. The technical difficulties have been overcome & his voice is solemn, deep & emotional. It is psychologically interesting, the fluke that is never a fluke, that in the broadcast speech, the only word over which he stumbled was 'distress' & the dramatic effect could not have been better produced by a Reinhardt.† He has become King now.[40]

---

* Cecil Beaton also recorded three joke Coronation nightmares that circulated at this time:
1. Princess Elizabeth dreamt that she was invisible.
2. The Duchess of Kent dreamt that she had to wear her mother-in-law's hats.
3. The Archbishop of Canterbury dreamt that he had to crown Mrs Simpson (Cecil Beaton unpublished diary, May 1937).
† Max Reinhardt (1873–1943), director of *The Miracle*.

If the new King and Queen had been hesitant on their accession, they were immeasurably strengthened by the anointing and crowning, as much by their own quiet acceptance of the great destiny given to them, as by the response of all the peers and peeresses, foreign princes, representatives of military and civilian life and the crowds that waited in inclement weather to cheer them in their coach on the long ceremonial procession through the streets of London.

The King and Queen sailed through the rest of the Coronation summer, with drives through London, a court ball with floodlit balcony appearances, a luncheon with the Lord Mayor and Corporation of London, the Coronation review of the Fleet at Portsmouth and that Thanksgiving Service at St Paul's Cathedral so earnestly requested by the Archbishop of Canterbury.

On 18 May the King and Queen and Queen Mary attended a ball given by the Duke and Duchess of Sutherland at Hampden House, where the overseas royal representatives at the Coronation were entertained. Because King George V had disliked and refused to attend such balls during his reign, it was the first time a reigning King and Queen had honoured such an occasion since at least 1910. The Sutherlands converted their tennis court into a ballroom. The walls of the tent were hung with tapestries from Sutton Place and filled with fresh flowers, also from Sutton Place. As the Duke of Sutherland noted, there was universal admiration for 'the Queen's vivacity and obvious enjoyment of life'.[41]

When Ramsay MacDonald retired from politics, he told the Queen that he thought the King had 'come on magnificently since his accession'. She asked him how he thought she was doing. 'Oh you . . .' he said with a sweep of the hand that took her part for granted.[42]

The King led his Guards at Trooping the Colour, and then went to Windsor for Ascot week which some people called a 'rest!!'[43] as he joked to Prince Paul of Yugoslavia. At the Castle, on 14 June, with great relish he installed six new Knights of the Garter at St George's Chapel. These were Lord Clarendon, the Duke of Norfolk (Earl Marshal and organiser of the Coronation), the Marquess of Exeter, Lord Strathmore (his father-in-law), the Duke of Beaufort (Master of the Horse) and Lord Baldwin of Bewdley (the recently retired Prime Minister). Queen Elizabeth walked with the King, and Queen Mary 'swept along by herself'. The procession was held up 'by a Duke* who could not be persuaded to remain at home and had insisted on taking part, though he leant on a stick and could scarcely toddle'.[44]

---

* Probably the 11th Duke of Bedford (1858–1940). He was appointed KG in 1902.

During that week, Windsor Castle and St George's Chapel were floodlit and the King and Queen liked nothing more than to come into the chapel lit only from the lights outside, and to listen to the organ being played.

On 5 July the King and Queen and two princesses arrived in state in Edinburgh, where two days later Queen Elizabeth was installed as the first ever Lady of the Thistle. Thus she joined her father and her brother-in-law, Lord Elphinstone, in the Order. Her stall plate was affixed in her stall that December, displacing that of the former Prince of Wales, fixed there in 1922, which was removed.* The occasion was photographed. Lady Strathmore cut a picture of the King and Queen at St Giles's Cathedral from the front page of a magazine and pinned it to the wall between her sitting room and the telephone alcove, a reminder for a proud mother to see daily from her writing table.[45]

Lord Crawford, one of the Knights of the Thistle at St Giles's, considered that the visit had gone well: 'Edinburgh was more forthcoming, more vocal than ever before – attributed in a casual way to the Scottish extraction of the Queen, but actually arising from a personal respect for the domestic life and basis of their personalities, with a profound sense of thankfulness to Providence for the catastrophe we have escaped'. Crawford thought the King much improved since 'his glum and dejected demeanour' at the Coronation. 'I am astonished at his sprightliness and vivacity, and what is nice is their modest recognition of the fact that all goes well.'[46]

The King and Queen also visited Wales and Northern Ireland. Nor did the King neglect his boys' camp at Southwold.† On the Queen's thirty-seventh birthday they were finally able to escape to Balmoral for the summer. White heather was growing again on the estate for the first time for many years and seen as a good omen. Soon after his arrival, the King walked over the hill from the Guelder, 'his hair ruffled & gleaming, his humour delightful'.[47] A few days later, he went on a twelve-mile walk.

There were a great number of house guests during that Balmoral summer – Bowes-Lyons and Elphinstones, James Stuart with his wife Rachel, the Beauforts and the Archbishop of Canterbury, his Balmoral holiday happily reinstated. Rachel Bowes-Lyon found Balmoral lacking in the charm of Birkhall with pages in every passage ready to open the door for her. She became flummoxed and asked for a bottle of 'Lyon' to be put in Mr 'Vichy's' room. Rachel found the staff happy, the new Queen

---

* Lord Elphinstone had been appointed by George V in 1927, and Lord Strathmore in 1928. There is no stall plate of any kind for the Duke of Windsor in the Thistle chapel, the only Knight to suffer that fate since the chapel was built in 1911.
† Sir Denis Thatcher, for one, attended these camps as a boy.

spreading fun and silly jokes everywhere, so that the chauffeur was invariably forced to suppress his smile.[48]

Even under the new regime, however, Queen Mary did not come. She went to Sandringham, then Althorp, Harewood and Holker, but she enjoined the Archbishop to say something to the King and Queen about her grandchildren's education, where she had detected lacunae.

By the time that Rex Whistler and Obsert Sitwell came to stay, the King was worn out again. According to Whistler, the King and Queen opened the Ghillies' Ball and 'hopped and skipped and capered in the wildest way the entire time we were there'. But after the ball, Whistler heard the King complaining next door: 'I've never been so tired in all my life!' In most versions of this story, the King added: 'It's these bloody guests!'[49]

Despite this, it was a happy summer. The Coronation was safely behind them, and the threat of war was not yet acute. No King ever has a trouble-free existence, but at Balmoral, with the walking and stalking, strawberry picking, climbing of hills, film shows at the castle, Braemar Games and Ghillies' balls, King George VI and Queen Elizabeth had reason to relax with pride and enjoyment.

12

The King Across the Water

'What a curse black sheep are in a family!' – Queen Elizabeth

The Duke of Windsor was an ever-present spectre that hung over the new reign, alive and well, but causing trouble in Europe. Gradually he dug himself deeper and deeper into a hole of his own making, until a final break with his family occurred in the spring of 1939.

The image of the ex-King sailing from Britain on a cold December night in 1936 was filled with pathos. That, however, is not how the departing Duke of Windsor saw it. First, he was convinced that he was laying down his burden in exchange for a lifetime of domestic happiness. Though the love of Edward for Mrs Simpson was often described as 'the greatest love affair of the century', those who knew both parties closely were more reserved.

At Lambeth Palace Alec Sargent wrote: 'It is not a case of normal love, but an obsession.'[1] Recent reports released from the National Archives suggest that, as recently as 1935, Mrs Simpson had a lover called Guy Marcus Trundle, unfairly described as 'a motor engineer and salesman'.[2] Many choose not to believe this, but in 1938 Sir Edward Peacock told the American Ambassador, Joseph Kennedy, 'that they all had evidence Wallie was having an affair with a young man, and of course, this embittered the Cabinet more than ever'.[3] Trundle was clearly an attractive figure. He was based in Mayfair and was later the lover of Vera Emanuel, the sister of Clare, Duchess of Sutherland.

A perceptive observer was Sir Godfrey Thomas, who had served as his Private Secretary from 1919 to 1935. He had watched the Prince of Wales in his decline and regretted seeing seventeen years of trying 'to keep his flag flying' crumble 'into dust in the humiliating way it did'. Thomas thought Edward VIII had played a lone hand and played it badly:

> I wouldn't mind so much could I convince myself that the step which he has seen fit to take were likely to lead to his real & eventual happiness. But I view the future with considerable misgiving . . .

He, at any rate, seems to have no regrets for the past. And he certainly has no qualms about the future. He is certain, in his mind, that he is booked, from now on, for a life of perpetual married bliss. Long may it last, is all one can hope for him.[4]

The Duke of Windsor left England in a kind of daze or a state rightly described by Queen Mary as 'absolutely unhinged'.[5] Stanley Baldwin and Lord Wigram both thought him 'almost mad'.[6] The Duke of Windsor assumed he would be abroad for a while, kick his heels, get married to Mrs Simpson after her divorce became absolute and then return to Britain with his new Duchess at his side. He would settle once more at his beloved Fort Belvedere, re-invent himself as a younger brother of the King and perform some useful role within the Royal Family – on terms that suited him.

After the Abdication, Alan Don spoke for many in the sad words he confided to his diary:

> Thus it came about that a King with an Empire at his feet nine months ago, has gone into the wilderness as an exile from his native land for the sake of a woman who has already made a failure of two marriages!
>
> Here is a theme for a dozen tragedies. Here too is a demonstration for all the world to see that the British Democracy demands from those in high places an exacting standard of life and character. It is that and that alone which counts in the long run.
>
> Tonight there is almost everywhere at any rate among responsible people, a sense of relief. The crisis is passed. We have weathered another storm and we can now settle down to try to recover what has been lost. I believe the new King with his Scottish Queen, will prove equal to the task.[7]

Unfortunately for the new Duke of Windsor, he had not organised matters as he would have wished before going. Nor did he appreciate fully the shock that his actions gave to his family, to the Establishment, to the people of Britain. If he thought he could return to be welcomed back with open arms, he was in for a nasty surprise.

His decline was a form of death by a thousand cuts. He learned that his wife was not to receive the title of Royal Highness, something he minded more than she did. He was confident that his family would come to his wedding, but this was not to be. He insisted that before coming to Britain, the Duchess must be created a Royal Highness, and they must both be received by the King and Queen and that this fact be recorded in the Court Circular.

None of these demands appealed to the new incumbents of Buckingham Palace. It is wrong to suggest that Queen Elizabeth was actively hostile to the Windsors. If they had left the King alone, then they too would have been left alone. Hatred was not part of Queen Elizabeth's nature, and she did not hate the Duchess. She thought her an adventuress, but she did not consider her significant enough to 'hate'. Indeed, the ever-widening rift between Buckingham Palace and the Windsors in the late 1930s owed nothing to what the Duchess of Windsor did, but was caused by the repeated interventions of the Duke, acting of his own accord.

If Queen Elizabeth did not give much thought to the Duchess of Windsor, she gave a great deal of thought to anything that might stand in the way of her husband being a 'good king' and the Duke of Windsor gave too many examples of ways in which he could prove a threat to this. For the peace of mind of the new King, the Windsors were left to freeze.

At one exasperated moment, when the new King was being besieged by ever-more unwelcome advice and demands from his brother, he complained that usually his predecessors became King because the previous monarch had died. The Duke of Windsor was all too alive and causing trouble in France. Likewise, one wise commentator wrote that it was just about acceptable that Edward VIII should go and dwell in a garden with Mrs Simpson, but less so if he intended to return home.

The Duke of Windsor had time to ponder perceived slights. Whereas during his years as Prince of Wales and King, there was scarcely time to pack everything into the day, and his hours were mapped out for him, now he had nothing to do. It was the sad lot of the Duchess of Windsor to keep him entertained and to fill his long hours of exile with amusing diversions. In her smart, good-hostess, wise-crack American way, she did a better job than many would have done, and she continued to do so, for better and at times very much for worse, for the next thirty-five years.

The Duke of Windsor gradually deteriorated from having been a romantic man of stature, the main protagonist in a great love story, into a pathetic, crumpled figure, who had captured 'the Woman he loved' and then failed her. He was unable to secure for her the few things he wanted – the title and the royal meeting. Pointless and trivial they might seem to us now, but they were deeply important to him then. Furthermore, he realised he had consigned her to a role in history as a hated woman. This was most unwelcome for the Duchess, since her self-perception was as the heroine of 'Rebecca of Sunnybrook Farm'.*[8] To be a hated person, and unfairly so, was something she minded deep in her heart.

* *Rebecca of Sunnybrook Farm*, a popular American children's classic by Kate Douglas Wiggin, later made into a movie with Shirley Temple, playing the little girl manipulated into being a radio star.

Following his Abdication the Duke of Windsor made himself a great nuisance to the new King, telephoning him with unwelcome advice and demands. In the early days of his exile, he thought that his brothers would attend his wedding and serve as his 'Supporters', two royal princes by tradition acting jointly as best men to their brother.

The Duke was determined to be married 'before May was out'. Lord Louis Mountbatten encouraged him to believe that the King and Duke of Kent wanted to attend his wedding. He gave him a long list of Coronation engagements,* and told him that the King preferred the date of Friday 4 June. All seemed to be proceeding well, until Mountbatten's letter of 5 May, in which he told the Duke of Windsor that a complication had arisen. He had tried to put this right but he was not very hopeful of success.

Mountbatten no doubt acted with the best intentions and, being more forward-thinking than many of the Royal Family and also a man of strong family values, he would have preferred the Royal Family to support the Duke of Windsor on that day. He was also an old friend of the Duke's and owed him much. But he was also a personally ambitious man. If he got the hint that he would harm himself by taking an independent line, then he would back away. He did not attend the wedding.†

The most intriguing line in Mountbatten's letter concerned other people stepping in. This suggests that it was not the King himself, but points to Queen Elizabeth and Queen Mary. They were surely the two members of the family who decided that no one should attend the wedding.

It would have been in the nature of George VI to have attended the wedding. The Princess Royal would have followed suit happily, her genial husband in tow. The Duke of Gloucester would have done as the others did, without enthusiasm. So too his Duchess, who admitted she had not

---

* Mountbatten mentioned the Naval Review on 21 May, a Thanksgiving Service at St Paul's Cathedral on 24 May, a court ball for Queen Mary's birthday on 26 May and the evening party given by the LCC for the entire Royal Family on 27 May. The Jockey Club dinner was on the night of 2 June.

† In later years Lord Mountbatten told several biographers, including Sir John Wheeler-Bennett and Frances Donaldson, that he had offered to be the Duke's best man, but that the Duke had told him that he would be having Supporters. In 1968 or so, Lord Mountbatten took his film *My Life and Times* out to Paris to show the Windsors. This was screened in a small studio in Neuilly near their home in the Bois de Boulogne, and the Duchess served a dish which included hot caviar.

After dinner, the Duke sat Mountbatten down, and raised with him the old issue of the wedding. 'Dickie, why would you not be my best man?' The answer was not one that Mountbatten could have given him. His attitude following the Abdication was 'The King is dead. Long live the King!' He had to ally himself to the new court. In old age, after the Duke of Windsor died, Mountbatten made several unwelcome appearances in the Duchess's house. Her attitude was 'The Duke always called him "Tricky Dickie" and that's good enough for me.'

disliked Mrs Simpson: 'She was all right as Mrs Simpson, less so as Duchess of Windsor or whatever she became.'[9] The Duke of Kent had many reasons to be grateful to his elder brother, though he was less enamoured of Mrs Simpson, and the Duchess of Kent had no time for her at all, and was not keen to be present.

In fact, in April 1937, Lord Wigram, who had been Acting Private Secretary to the King for the first months of the reign, wrote to the Archbishop of Canterbury that he had informed Monckton that it would be the end of the monarchy if any of the Royal Family attended the wedding. He would shelter the King behind Baldwin and the various Dominion Prime Ministers. A few days later Wigram wrote again to say that the Duke of Windsor was going to be informed that none of the Royal Family would be there, nor would any royal chaplains officiate.[10] There were no circumstances in which either Queen Mary or Queen Elizabeth would have agreed to be there.

The question of the Duchess being created a Royal Highness was never brooked at court. Whatever the legal ramifications so often discussed, there is nothing more to be said on this subject. The new regime could do as it pleased and it chose to withhold the title. The Duke of Windsor was livid. The reason that the King and Queen were late for the court ball on 14 May 1937 was said to have been due to him telephoning 'a tirade' just before the ball.[11] The King made the perfectly reasonable point to the Duke of Windsor that he had granted his wife the highest rank in the Peerage of Britain, the status of a Duchess.

The issue of a meeting between the Windsors and the Royal Family was explored in various ways, and eventually went wrong. This is worth examining.

Immediately after the Abdication, the Duke of Windsor settled in the Ruritanian-style Schloss Enzesfeld, replete with pseudo-Louis XV decor and American-style bathrooms, which belonged to Baron Eugen de Rothschild. There he spent Christmas away from his family (reading the second lesson at the English Church in Vienna), and away from Mrs Simpson, who stayed with her friends, Mr and Mrs Herman Rogers, in Cannes, awaiting her divorce.*

The first member of the Royal Family to go to Europe was the Duke of Kent, to attend the wedding of Princess Juliana of the Netherlands on 7 January. The new King decided that George should not visit his brother. However, the Princess Royal and Lord Harewood did stay with the Duke at Enzesfeld in February, a difficult time, as the *Daily Mirror*

* The courts forbade couples to meet until the divorce became absolute, in other words for six months.

printed a suggestion that the Princess had been sent out by George VI to dissuade the Duke from marrying. Lord Harewood noted that the Duke was dwelling under the misconception that Mrs Simpson was to be welcomed with open arms by the Royal Family as soon as they were married, and that he feared his whole future would be jeopardised should she discover that this was not to be so.

The wedding, eventually held at the Château de Candé on 3 June 1937, was boycotted by the Royal Family, a few of whom did write to him wishing him well. The Duke of Kent wrote of his disappointment at not being there, but affirmed it was impossible. The Duchess of Kent wished him all possible happiness. The Duke of Gloucester sent him a present. Even Hitler sent a cordial message.

Not long afterwards, in August, the Duke and Duchess of Kent were staying with the Duchess's sister, Princess Paul of Yugoslavia, and the Duke of Kent suggested a visit from himself to the Windsors at Schloss Wasserleonburg, which they had rented from Count and Countess Munster in Austria. Unfortunately, the Duke of Windsor sniffed a slight in Princess Marina not accompanying him, and pressed his brother. Did Marina not want to come, or was she forbidden to do so? Equally unfortunately, the Duke of Kent confessed that his wife did not want to meet Wallis, and that this had been accepted in discussion with the King and the Queen. Her reason, it would appear, was largely for fear that a meeting with the Duchess of Windsor might make her unpopular in Britain.

The Duke of Windsor was not prepared to accept that, but even when the King upset the Duchess of Kent by telling them both to go together, no visit took place. Princess Marina wrote to the Queen at once on the matter, confident of sympathy from that quarter. Meanwhile the King warned Queen Mary that at some point they would have to deal with his elder brother, other than through lawyers or Household officials. The Duke of Windsor later commented that on account of all this, the ice between himself and his family was not broken.

In October, there was a new crisis when the Duke of Windsor decided to visit Hitler in Germany, on an ill-conceived mission to urge the German Chancellor to keep the peace, though he described this as a mission to study housing and working conditions. Following this trip he planned to go to the United States.

Sir Ronald Lindsay, the British Ambassador in Washington, visited the King and Queen in Scotland to discuss the implications of the forthcoming visit. He argued that if the Duke was not put up in the Embassy, official coldness towards him would be inferred. This would create a bad impression. But the King and his advisers were not going to be moved.

The Duke of Windsor was behaving badly and stirring up trouble. Sir Ronald was prepared to argue with the King and his Private Secretaries. The Queen was a different matter:

> While the men spoke in terms of indignation, she spoke in terms of acute pain and distress, ingeniously expressed and deeply felt. She too is not a great intellect but she has any amount of 'intelligence du coeur.' Her reactions come straight from her heart and very strongly and a heart that is in the right place may be a very good guide. In all she said there was far more grief than indignation and it was all tempered by affection for 'David'. 'He's so changed now, and he used to be so kind to us.' She was backing up everything the men said, but protesting against anything that seemed vindictive. All her feelings were lacerated by what she and the King were being made to go through. And with all her charity she had not a word to say for 'that woman'. I found myself deeply moved by her, and when midnight came though my flag was still flying, it was really but a battered bit of bunting . . .[12]

As it turned out, the American tour did not take place, which would have pleased the 'senior palace official', almost certainly Tommy Lascelles, who gave his opinion that he hoped the British public would soon cease to take the Duke of Windsor seriously and realise that his mental and moral development had ceased when he was about fifteen, that he was a sad figure, but 'no longer a particularly interesting one'.[13]

Queen Elizabeth remained nervous about her brother-in-law, telling Helen Hardinge during these days that she thought he 'plays with the idea of becoming dictator'.[14]

In June 1938 there was an exchange between Queen Mary and the Duke of Windsor. The Duke asked his mother point-blank to clarify her position. This she did in a letter that is well known: she informed him that she had implored him not to abdicate for the sake of the Royal family and of Britain. She made the devastating point: 'It seemed so inconceivable to those who made such sacrifices during the war that you, as their King, refused a lesser sacrifice.' She told him that his marriage had not changed her views and that she was sorry not to see him, but, 'all my life I have put my Country before everything else, and I simply cannot change now'. If he returned to England, there would be 'division and controversy'.[15]

The Duke was disturbed by his mother's attitude. In particular he resented the implication that he had not been prepared to make sacrifices. In the Great War he had been all too willing to give his life in the service of England. He reiterated that he could never have served as King without Wallis and concluded by suggesting that many problems could be solved if his mother now accepted Wallis as her daughter-in-law.

The question of a visit to Britain by the Windsors, or indeed their return to live there, was one that preoccupied the Duke of Windsor throughout these next years before war broke out in September 1939. He made sure that it was never far from the agenda of George VI and Neville Chamberlain.

Lord Beaverbrook mounted a campaign to get the Windsors back to Britain, the Duke pressed hard, irritating his family and pressing the Prime Minister, Neville Chamberlain, to attend to his plight, when there were many more important calls on his time.

In October 1938 the Duke seemed set on coming over, and had his eye on some accommodation being made available for him and the Duchess in Windsor Castle. The King decided that, before anything else was fixed, the Gloucesters should test the water with a visit to the Windsors in Paris on their way back from Kenya. This took place at the Hôtel Meurice on 11 November, and was followed by the Duchess of Gloucester receiving hate mail from deranged members of the British public. This reaction was the excuse for further delays.

Neville Chamberlain also called on the Duke in his rooms at the Hôtel Meurice that same November. He advised against a visit in 1939, as did the Earl of Harewood. The Duke pressed on, advancing the idea that only if the Royal Family refused to receive them would any disharmony occur as a result of their proposed visit.

By February 1939 both sides were getting angry. George VI urged his mother to make it clear through a third party that she could not receive both the Windsors if they came to Britain. The Duke informed the Prime Minister that he blamed the Royal Family for their attitude towards himself and his wife, and stressed that he would never permit this to keep him away from his former country.

The King and Queen were due to pay an important visit to Canada and the United States, another reason to postpone a visit to London by the Duke, and the Duke told Lord Beaverbrook that he had agreed to this one final postponement lest the position taken by Queen Mary and Queen Elizabeth towards the Duchess might cause trouble in England or America. The Duke further protested that he had remained out of England only to allow his brother time to establish himself as King, which had now been achieved, and despite earlier statements, now declared that whether the Duchess was made a Royal Highness or not, he would return.

There was more trouble in store, this time concerning the tomb of King George V, designed by Sir William Reid Dick and destined to stand in a bay in the west end of the Nave of St George's Chapel. The Duke used this minor drama as an excuse to take offence, whereas his real anger was directed at the Royal Family's non-acceptance of his Duchess.

The Duke had paid for half the tomb, and he realised now that he could not be present at its dedication. Queen Mary had assured him there would be no dedication and that she would let it be known publicly that he had paid his share. The Duke then read in the paper of all the Royal Family other than himself being present at exactly such a ceremony. He wrote to his mother:

> Your letter of March 20th is extremely illuminating, although I greatly regret that it should have taken so sacred an occasion to disclose so much that is unpleasant, and to destroy the last vestige of feeling I had left for you all as a family. It was of course obvious, that neither you nor Bertie could notify me yourselves of the dedication of Papa's tomb in St George's Chapel. You by your final refusal to receive Walter Monckton last month . . . have made further normal correspondence between us impossible.[16]

The summer of 1939 saw war approaching in Europe, and the problem of the Windsors still loomed. It was inevitable that they would return. On the eve of the outbreak of war, Queen Elizabeth was exasperated by the Duke's demands and the strain he had placed on her husband, not to mention Queen Mary. Before his proposed return, she wrote to her mother-in-law:

> What *are* we going to do about Mrs S? Personally I do not wish to receive her at all; tho' it must depend on circumstances, what do you feel about it Mama?[17]

Queen Elizabeth feared that the Windsors would infiltrate social occasions. She predicted only problems.

There were many further dramas involving the Duke of Windsor, his plight, his demands, his involvement with the British Expeditionary Force in France, his virtual abandonment of his post when he tired of his new duties, and finally an ugly exchange with Winston Churchill, who in 1940, as near as made no difference, threatened him with court martial for disobeying military orders while being, by his own volition, a serving major-general in the British Army.

The Duke and Duchess did come to England in September 1939 and stayed with 'Fruity' and Lady Alexandra Metcalfe in Sussex. He had a meeting with the King, but he saw no other members of the Royal Family. The Duchess of Windsor was not received. Then the Windsors returned to France.

No one was more relieved than Queen Elizabeth. She told Prince Paul of Yugoslavia:

> I had taken the precaution to send her a message before they came, saying that I was sorry I could not receive her. I thought it more honest to make things quite clear. So she kept away, & nobody saw her. What a curse black sheep are in a family![18]

When the Duke of Windsor sailed from England in December 1936, Queen Elizabeth had assured him that she would always mention him in her prayers. It is unlikely that she devoted much time to him in those prayers by the onset of the Second World War.

State Visits

'I have a hard time fitting into these chairs with these new dresses'
– Queen Elizabeth

The two years before the war constituted a period of high diplomacy for the King and Queen. They received many state visitors to Britain and undertook their own important visits to Paris, and then to Canada and the United States.

They continued the policy of being widely seen in Britain, touring industrial districts in Yorkshire, visiting Hull, York, Bradford, Halifax, Leeds, Batley, Barnsley, Wakefield and Sheffield.

On her return to London the Queen became assertive. Using the issue of her Coronation robes being sent to the Dominions when she needed to pose in them for Frank Salisbury, she complained that in future she wanted a note to be sent to her or her Private Secretary when the King arranged anything that concerned her.

In November their first state visitor arrived, the widowed King Leopold of the Belgians, upon whom the King bestowed the Order of the Garter. Between his ceremonial duties King Leopold proved himself nothing if not a Coburg. 'The K[ing]'s lovely looks & gentle melancholy caused many hearts to flutter,' wrote Lady Juliet Duff. At the ball in his honour, he danced with Lady Elizabeth Paget, the most beautiful of Queen Elizabeth's maids of honour at the Coronation. He invited her to go to the Four Hundred with her when he came back in December. 'It would solve so many problems,' continued Lady Juliet, 'but as the poor girl is "not even mediatized", marriage is out of the question, & we fear his intentions can not be honourable.'*[1]

In November, on the advice of Lady Helen Graham, Queen Elizabeth went privately to see the paintings of Gluck, a lesbian painter, at the Fine Art Gallery. The ambitious painter's mother then began a convoluted campaign to get one of her daughter's pictures into the Queen's collection. As Gluck had painted a scene from the Coronation from a window

---

* The following year, Lady Elizabeth married Raimond von Hofmannsthal, son of the librettist Hugo von Hofmannsthal.

of the Cumberland Hotel, called *They Also Serve* . . . (1937), the ruse worked.[2] Within the month Queen Elizabeth attended a charity perform-ance of *Macbeth*, seated in the Royal Box, while Lady Cunard, erstwhile friend of the Windsors, was spotted in the stalls. Laurence Olivier 'ranted atrociously' according to Juliet Duff, while 'the witches had cardboard faces & Hitler moustaches'.[3]

In the New Year, fulfilling a promise to the celebrated manager of the Old Vic, Lillian Baylis, who had died the previous November, she took her daughters to Shakespeare's *A Midsummer Night's Dream* with costumes and décor by Oliver Messel, and the outrageous Robert Help-mann performing opposite Vivien Leigh. The presentations were memorable, since the elaborate coronet and beaded headdress of Vivien Leigh became inextricably entwined with that of Helpmann as the one curtsied and the other bowed. They were forced to retreat backwards locked together like stags in combat.

The Royal Family spent Christmas and the New Year at Sandringham. Charades were played which caused the unlikely spectacle of Queen Mary placing a jaunty hat on her tiara and acting being coy in a restaurant and being jolted about on a merry-go-round. Whereas in the days of George V guests had been forced to perch on a piano stool to read, there were now comfortable arm chairs. But guests such as Rachel Bowes-Lyon found the presence of a host of footmen intrusive. David became sleepy in the evenings and resented having to stay up till 12.30 a.m.

Rachel observed how Princess Margaret, then aged seven, would appear towards the end of lunch, drop a very dignified curtsey to Queen Mary, then prod the King in the ribs before drawing up her chair. One afternoon Queen Mary took the house party sightseeing in King's Lynn, oblivious to the cold and the crowd that followed. Rachel described the group as being like the Pied Piper of Hamelin, walking down the streets at great pace, darting into churches and shops and most particularly that of a cabinet-maker who made miniature reproductions of old furniture.[4]

The King was feeling more confident now that the early strains were over, and was glad that his Christmas broadcast, written by Alec Hardinge, had proved not too great a trial, even if it spoilt his lunch.[5] The Royal Family returned to London on the last day of January 1938.

The King and Queen were also Emperor and Empress of India. Early in the New Year, they suffered a major and lasting disappointment, the second cancellation of their Delhi Durbar, the magnificent coronation ceremony in India which had been such a feature early in the reign of King George V and Queen Mary.

Alec Hardinge had been keen that they should go, aware that in India the King-Emperor was perceived to possess divine attributes, and it seemed to him important that the Indian people should have the opportunity to express their undoubted loyalty to the new sovereign, for thus he would assume a form of reality.

To their lasting chagrin, neither George VI nor Queen Elizabeth ever visited India. Sir Edward Ford, who became Assistant Private Secretary in 1946, recalled the King's disappointment:

> The King used often to speak of this – with *deep* resentment at the negative advice of his Ministers and the Viceroy. According to the King, the main objection to his showing himself to his Indian subjects was not security, but finance; and he had told the representatives of the Indian Govt (especially P. J. Grigg,* the Finance Member of the Viceroy's Council) that he did *not* want a lavish show, but the opportunity to see, and be seen by his Indian subjects.[6]

A later plan to visit India towards the end of the war would also fail. In later life, the Queen Mother sometimes ventured that, had she gone to India, the outcome might have been different, and, given her magical effect overseas, it is a shame that she was not given the chance to exercise it in the Subcontinent.

On 28 April the King and Queen gave a dinner at the Castle for the French Prime Minister, Edouard Daladier, the Foreign Secretary, Georges Bonnet, and the French Ambassador, Charles Corbin. The ladies wore tiaras, the gold plate was out, the Band of the Grenadier Guards played and the guest list included the Halifaxes, the Desboroughs, Lord Wigram, Helen, Duchess of Northumberland, the artist Gerald Kelly and the architect Lord Gerald Wellesley (later 7th Duke of Wellington).

This dinner was in advance of the King and Queen's visit to Paris scheduled for June. Already, however, the trip was in jeopardy since, towards the end of April, Lady Strathmore was taken ill. There was a strange suggestion by the French aristocratic writer Elisabeth de Gramont, Duchesse de Clermont-Tonnerre, that Lady Strathmore became ill because she was convinced that her 'little Queen' was going to suffer the same fate as King Alexander of Yugoslavia, who had been

* Rt Hon. Sir (Percy) James Grigg (1890–1964), Finance Member of Government of India 1934–9.

assassinated in France less than four years before,* while on a visit to Marseilles. Madame de Clermont-Tonnerre wrote: 'The Countess of Strathmore would have been less worried if she had known the Prefect of Police, Roger Langeron, who would oversee the security of the King and Queen.'[7]

Lady Strathmore had come up to London from Woolmers Park, in Hertfordshire, to attend the wedding of her granddaughter, Anne Bowes-Lyon, daughter of Jock, at St Margaret's Westminster, on 28 April.† She suffered a slight heart attack. The wedding took place in her absence, Lord Strathmore giving the bride away, the Queen in a three-quarters length coat of ice-blue wool, with an ice-blue straw hat, and the princesses in pink.

Lady Strathmore appeared to make a good recovery from this heart attack, but nevertheless it was a worrying time for the Queen. By 30 April no further bulletins were being issued, and the King and Queen continued their duties including a visit to the Home Fleet. By 22 June Lady Strathmore's condition was again a worry. Bravely, Queen Elizabeth visited the Mothercraft Training Centre at Cromwell House, Highgate, the organisers spiriting her away as soon as they could.

That evening, after dinner, the King and Queen were called to 38 Cumberland Mansions, Bryanston Street, where at 2 a.m., on 23 June, Lady Strathmore died. It was a moment that the Queen had dreaded since childhood.[8] Later that day she wrote to the Archbishop of Canterbury, asking him to speak at the memorial service in London and to say a few 'lovely words' about her mother. She told him that they only wanted him, and would ask no other, and craved forgiveness for adding to the many burdens of his life.[9]

The Archbishop told the congregation in St Martin-in-the-Fields that it was 'like attempting to describe the fragrance of a flower or putting music into words' to speak of Lady Strathmore, but he had been bidden to say these words by 'a special person'. Having paid tribute to Lady Strathmore's dignity, grace, charm and graciousness, he concluded: 'She raised a Queen in her own home simply by trust and love, and as a return the Queen has won widespread love.'[10] Thanking him for his 'perfect'

---

* King Alexander was shot dead in Marseilles on 8 October 1934, when a Yugoslav assassin, Vladimir Tchernozemsky ('Vlado the Chauffeur', a seasoned assassin), broke through the security, leapt on to the running board of the King's car, shouting 'Vive le Roi', and promptly fired three shots at him. Louis Barthou, the French Foreign Minister, seated next to the King, threw himself across his royal guest, but the King died instantly. Barthou died later of his wounds, and the assassin was struck down by a stroke from a guardsman's sabre.

† Anne married Viscount Anson, heir to the 4th Earl of Lichfield. They were divorced in 1948. She had two children, the present Earl of Lichfield and Lady Elizabeth Anson. Major John Wills, Jean Elphinstone's husband, was best man.

words, the Queen also thanked him for his friendship at the time of their marriage, at their Coronation and at this time of sorrow.[11]

There was no court mourning since the Queen did not wish to disrupt long-planned social events at the height of the London season. But there was family mourning, and while the Queen did not attend the Red Cross Conference garden party at Buckingham Palace on the day her mother died, Queen Mary took her place, dressed in white.

Among those who sent messages of sympathy to Queen Elizabeth was Emperor William, as she called the Kaiser, and the Duke of Windsor. Even at this time of grief, she was relieved that the Duke had only signed from himself, and was grateful that he had not included '*her*' (the Duchess).

The King and Queen took the Saturday night train from Euston and arrived next day at Glamis. The last of the ten coaches contained Lady Strathmore's coffin, draped in blue and gold brocade. On the Monday, in heavy rain, the coffin was placed on a carriage bedecked with flowers, drawn by two horses and led by estate workers to the church for the family funeral. On top of the coffin were lilies-of-the-valley from the Queen and a small white cross of carnations from the princesses. The King walked bare-headed behind the coffin, and Queen Elizabeth travelled by car with her father, then aged eighty-three.

After the service, Queen Elizabeth retreated to Birkhall to answer her letters.

The King and Queen had been due to leave for Paris the next day, on 28 June. After urgent consultations between Lord Cromer, the Lord Chamberlain, and Lord Halifax, it was decided that the visit should be postponed until between 19 and 22 July. While sorry to postpone the visit, the Queen was aware that it had to be thus, and that to have attended a series of galas, banquets and garden parties would have been a 'mockery'.[12]

At first there was some doubt as to whether the Queen should go at all. At court it was thought that if she could proceed with the visit, the British would consider her brave and doing her duty to support the King. Nor would the death of Lady Strathmore have made a big impact in France. Katie Seymour was one who subscribed to this view. Queen Elizabeth was determined to go.

There then arose the vexed question as to how she should be dressed. Black seemed too dismal a colour for Paris, that most fashion-conscious of cities, and the solution was found by the couturier Norman Hartnell who altered the entire trousseau to white, an accepted colour of mourning, as had been demonstrated by Queen Mary at the Palace garden party.

The Paris trip was an important milestone in the creation of a new sartorial image for the Queen. In her younger days as Duchess of York, she had not attempted to compete with the silver brocade elegance of Queen Alexandra or the more stately magnificence of Queen Mary. The Duchess had dressed prettily, but there was a distinct mousiness to her.

Virginia Woolf had observed her at the theatre one night in December 1929, and described her as 'a simple, chattering, sweet hearted little woman in pink: but her wrist twinkling with diamonds, her dress held on the shoulder with diamonds'.[13] Her wedding dress had been abysmal in its dowdiness, designed by Madame Handley Seymour. Nor was she in any way coordinated in her fashion sense. When she toured old Brussels in 1935, she wore a long lace dress, but ruined the impact with a routine black umbrella. She needed a fashion Svengali, and she found one in Norman Hartnell.

Hartnell had been sketching fashion designs since childhood, and was much influenced by the Russian ballet of Diaghilev and Bakst. He had designed for the stage, dressing Alice Delysia and Gertrude Lawrence. Presently he opened his own fashion house, and in 1934 he moved to 26 Bruton Street. He was taken up by many society ladies, and in 1935 Lady Alice Scott became his first royal patron. He designed her wedding dress.

The Duchess of York met him when she brought Princess Elizabeth and Princess Margaret to have their bridesmaids dresses fitted. In 1936 she asked him to run up some black outfits for court mourning. Clearly she longed to move to him, but, with characteristic loyalty, she asked Madame Handley Seymour to design her Coronation dress, but Hartnell to dress her Maids of Honour. By 1938, however, she was happy to escape from Handley Seymour, and to consign the whole Paris trousseau to Hartnell.

The transformation was a dual one, and would be completed in the summer of 1939 when Cecil Beaton was summoned to photograph her. The combination of Hartnell and Beaton was crucial, and is all the more intriguing since the two men had been at Cambridge together, where Beaton, at least, viewed Hartnell with fascinated suspicion. Beaton was not a dedicated fan of Hartnell's work. When the present Queen went to Paris in 1957, he wrote to the Ambassadress, Lady Jebb: 'The Queen triumphed over Hartnell's bad taste.'[14]

Hartnell himself attributed the transformation of the Queen and the 'regal renaissance of the romantic crinoline' to the King, who took him on a private tour of the Palace and showed him the Winterhalter portraits of Empress Eugénie of France and Empress Elisabeth of Austria. This, he said, was how he wanted Queen Elizabeth dressed, and Hartnell undertook his first crinoline for the state visit of King Leopold in 1937.[15] Queen Elizabeth loved her new look, though there were hazards. When she sat down to dinner at Windsor Castle in April 1939, she told Joe Kennedy: 'I have a hard time fitting into these chairs with these new- dresses, but tonight I don't seem to overflow.'[16]

Hartnell was never better than when he tackled the dozen dresses required for Paris. He adorned her in full-skirted crinolines, soon to be made further fashionable by Vivien Leigh on the steps of Tara in the film *Gone with the Wind*. He armed her with a parasol that had originally belonged to Catherine the Great, now decorated with transparent lace and tulle. When she flicked it open with a certain nonchalance at the Ile Enchanté, all the parasol-makers of Paris and London burst back into business. Queen Elizabeth sailed through the Paris state visit, in white satin, in white tulle, in white organdie, and in white crepe, every eye upon her.

On 19 July the royal party crossed the foggy Channel in *Enchantress*. Queen Elizabeth left London in deep black. When they arrived at the specially built station in the Bois de Boulogne, decorated with a Beauvais tapestry and festooned with Union Jacks, she was all in white. There they were met by President Lebrun (whom they privately nicknamed 'Brownie').[17]

The motor procession with its escort of Spahis and Cuirassiers passed through thick crowds on the Champs-Elysées, held back by equally thick rows of police and troops, which made the procession almost invisible. Lady Diana Cooper recalled the minister responsible had told her 'that their fears and safeguards were such as to put a plain-clothes policeman in every window on the route and to have hefty citizens lean in a ring against the suspect trees lest they should fall on the procession'.[18] The King and Queen attended a banquet at the Elysée Palace, at which Queen Elizabeth wore her Legion of Honour over the wrong shoulder.

The King and Queen stayed at the Palais d'Orsay, where, according to the American Ambassador, the President had installed 'two superb bathrooms containing mosaic tubs with gold faucets which, during the stay of Their Royal Majesties, were never once used!'.[19]

It was not only the French who were impressed. A section of London society – Winston Churchill, Venetia Montagu, Lady Elizabeth Paget and Lord Gerald Wellesley among them – had crossed the Channel to share the fun, many of them bidden to a gala evening organised by Contesse André de Fels, who worked tirelessly to bring French and overseas intellectuals together. She put on a ballet gala at the Opéra called *La Nuit de la Rose*, with the Diaghilev dancer Serge Lifar performing a suite of dances by Chopin. The King and Queen were led up the steps by two 'chandeliers' – valets bearing twenty-branched lit candelabra with tall white candles before them.

Throughout the visit the weather was spectacular. The Thursday morning began misty, and there was a glorious review of fifty thousand troops at Versailles. This was followed by a magnificent luncheon for 250, with eight or ten courses and different wines for each course, in the Salle de Glaces at Versailles. Oliver Harvey recorded: 'All the waiters were in eighteenth-century costume with powdered hair and indeed the guests in their black tail coats were the only discordant note.'[20]

In the afternoon there was a concert in the chapel at Versailles. This was somewhat interrupted by the fly-past, postponed due to morning mists, the military planes competing with the choir inside singing Monteverdi. Seeing the planes, Diana Cooper was afraid: 'A sinister reminder of reality clutched at all hearts, like a deathly hand, when the fog of peace dispersed.'[21] For most the state visit seemed to herald lasting peace. Churchill, who walked among the troops and hailed a hundred years of political and religious liberty in France, relished the 'flash of arms and the roar of warlike engines', but optimistically judged the visit as 'a new and additional security against the sudden onset of catastrophe'.[22]

Fearing for the safety of the royal visitors, the French authorities vetoed a balcony appearance on the Place de la Concorde and a late drive through the streets of Paris. They were not worried about the French, but, mindful of the Yugoslavian assassination, were concerned about Spanish, Italian and Russian tourists. So there was only a balcony appearance at the Palais d'Orsay, which was so popular that the King and Queen had to come out a second time. On the Friday they visited the Villers-Bretonneux War Memorial on their way back via Calais.

Oliver Harvey attributed the success of the visit to the 'simplicity and dignity' of the King and Queen.[23] Alec Hardinge described it as 'a four days' dream of beauty'. There were not even problems with the Duke of Windsor. He had angled for a meeting, but when this was discouraged, he agreed to retreat to Italy with his Duchess.

No announcement was made of the exact hour at which the King and Queen would return to London. They arrived at Victoria Station quite late at night, tired but happy, and even so, the route to the Palace was crowded with cheering people. Later Queen Elizabeth spoke of the personal warmth of the French, but Katie Seymour,* one of the many courtiers in attendance, spotted that she still missed her mother, although she was 'too brave to mention her loss'.[24]

The Queen went back into black on her return and still wore mourning when they arrived at Balmoral for their summer holiday.

This holiday was overshadowed by the deteriorating situation in Czechoslovakia, Hitler rejecting demands that he reduce the scale of his manoeuvres. Hardinge suggested to the King that he might write to Hitler 'as one ex-serviceman to another', stressing the necessity of avoiding war. He drafted a suitable letter. The Prime Minister did not endorse this plan, however, on the grounds that a rebuff to the Sovereign by Hitler would only make the situation worse. King Boris of Bulgaria and his wife, Queen Giovanna, then came to stay, affording George VI the chance to discuss European affairs with a monarch who had close experience of what was happening in Europe.

The King went south on 14 September, partly to attend the funeral of his cousin, Prince Arthur of Connaught,† at Windsor on 16 September. Queen Elizabeth stayed at Balmoral with her daughters, and the Elphinstones for additional company, until 22 September when she too went south.

The political situation was now so bad that the King was unable to travel to Clyde to launch *Queen Elizabeth* on 27 September. But the Queen went, 'dressed in grey with a smart small hat', and looking 'much thinner than in the spring'.[25] The Queen was accompanied by the princesses and made a speech before launching the ship. It was the first time that the general public had heard her voice, which was broadcast over the airwaves, and reshown in cinemas on *Pathé News*.

Queen Elizabeth looked fragile and feminine and her voice as broadcast was thin, but her words (written by Hardinge) were delivered with confidence:

> I have a message for you from the King. He bids the people of this country to be of good cheer, in spite of the dark clouds hanging over them and, indeed, the whole world. He knows well that, as ever before in critical times, they will keep cool heads and brave hearts.[26]

---

* On 2 October Katie lost her husband, Sir Reginald Seymour, leaving her to raise a son and two daughters on her own.
† Prince Arthur of Connaught, son of the Duke of Connaught (then aged eighty-eight), had died at fifty-five of cancer of the throat.

While the King remained in London, the Queen returned to her flower-filled sitting room at Balmoral. In her brief absence the princesses had created a surprise garden for her. She retained her habitual optimism, even in the face of all the odds. The Duke of Kent was one in the family who found this perpetual optimism somewhat blinkered, often quoting his sister-in-law as saying 'everything is O.K.' or 'All is well in the world'.[27]

Queen Elizabeth then rejoined the King. On 30 September Chamberlain flew back from his visit to Hitler in Munich, returning with his waving umbrella and his 'Peace in Our Time' document. The Home Secretary wanted the King to go to Heston Airport to meet him. Instead the Lord Chamberlain intercepted the Prime Minister at the airport with a letter from the King summoning him to Buckingham Palace. There Mrs Chamberlain met her husband, and the King and Queen and both the Chamberlains went out on to the balcony to be greeted by a massive crowd in the rain, convinced that all would indeed be well. There was a private suggestion that the King might offer Neville Chamberlain the Garter, as had been done when his brother, Austen Chamberlain, had returned from the successful negotiation of the Locarno pact in December 1925, but Lord Halifax vetoed this.

The photograph of the smiling group on the balcony – and the lesser known one of the same four individuals at the state entrance of the Palace, the King and Queen surrendering the central position to the Chamberlains – briefly identified Chamberlain as 'the Peace-maker of Europe'[28]

The monarch's visible support for Chamberlain was considered by some to be entering a dangerous political arena. Anthony Eden and Lord Cranborne had resigned over Chamberlain's Italian policy and the King and Queen were strongly pro-appeasement as was most of the court with the exception of the Private Secretary who found it 'repugnant . . . both immoral and inexpedient'. But many who had gone through one world war would follow any policy that prevented another.

The King and Queen were loyal supporters of Neville Chamberlain. So, from afar, was the Duke of Windsor. He maintained that there was nothing to gain from another war, which would destroy democracy along with the Totalitarian States and give victory to Communism.[29] Nor would Queen Mary hear a word against Chamberlain. She was furious with those who attacked the Prime Minister, and described the events of the previous Wednesday as 'like a miracle'.[30]

This was an unsettled period, when appeasement held sway, and yet people worried that the Czech people had been sacrificed. The *Times* correspondent Douglas Reed was asked whether peace could be maintained, and replied: 'Certainly, as long as the supply of small states lasts!'

The King and Queen returned to Balmoral on 2 October for a fortnight of stalking, after which they returned to London. They visited Norwich and the King opened Parliament. There was a state visit by King Carol of Romania, not always a popular figure with the British Royal Family due to his loose private life, his cruelty to his former wife, Princess Helen of Greece, and his association with the 'She-Wolf', Madame Lupescu.* King Carol brought his young son, Michael, with him. For the state ball, Norman Hartnell dressed the Queen in pearl-grey satin, bouffant and trailing, embroidering the dress with grey pearls, silver and amethyst. On the recommendation of Lord Halifax, the King gave King Carol the Garter, but on the same recommendation he gave it to the King of Greece a week earlier. Queen Maud of Norway, the last surviving sister of George V, died suddenly in London on 20 November.

The advancing political crisis began to tell on the King. When someone suggested to the Queen that the Duchess of Windsor should be commended for stopping the Duke from drinking, and pointing out that he no longer had pouches under his eyes, the Queen replied: 'Yes, who has the lines under his eyes now?'[31]

---

* Elena (Magda) Lupescu (1902–77), mistress of King Carol, who eloped with her in 1925. As a result the Romanians changed the succession so that his young son, Michael, succeeded King Ferdinand in 1927. In 1930 King Carol took over, promising that Madame Lupescu would stay away, but she followed him back, exerting a certain malign influence. King Carol was deposed by Hitler in 1940, and married Madame Lupescu in Rio de Janeiro in 1947, and again in Lisbon in 1949. She displayed much public grief when the King died in Portugal in 1953.

Canada and the United States

'She is in truth one of the most amazing Queens since Cleopatra' –
Harold Nicolson

The idea of an official visit to Canada had been mooted in the spring of
1937 by the Governor-General, Lord Tweedsmuir, better known as the
novelist John Buchan. At the Coronation, W. L. Mackenzie King, the
Prime Minister of Canada, presented the King and Queen with an official invitation. He alerted President Roosevelt so that he could invite the
King and Queen to the United States.

In March 1938 the new American Ambassador, Joseph P. Kennedy,
arrived in London, with his nine children in his wake, presented his
credentials to the King and met Queen Elizabeth. He soon fell under her
spell, likewise aware of her usefulness to the cause of appeasement.
Kennedy was said to have been a bootlegger. He was known to have
amassed an immense fortune on the stock market, in the purchase of real
estate and in the film industry. He feared that England could not with-
stand the threat of Germany and worried that he might lose his sons and
his considerable fortune if war came.[1]

In April, the King and Queen invited the Kennedys for the weekend
at Windsor Castle with the Prime Minister, Neville Chamberlain, and
his wife, Lord and Lady Gage, the Elphinstones and the Halifaxes,
Dorothy Halifax being in waiting.

The American couple were treated to the traditional Windsor entertainment of the time, with an orchestra playing as they dined. Seated
next to the Queen, Kennedy promoted his line about non-aggression,
explaining that the American people feared a war, had gone into the last
war in order to make the world safe for democracy, and instead a 'crop
of dictatorships, quarrels, and miseries' had arisen. To this the Queen
said: 'But if we had the United States actively on our side, working with
us, think how that would strengthen our position with the dictators.'
Kennedy was yet more taken with the Queen. 'Fired by an idea, speaking
rapidly, her face acquired a charming animation that never shows in
photographs,' he recorded.[2]

Kennedy was as keen that the King and Queen should visit America as they were keen to go. 'I only know three Americans,' the Queen told him. 'You, Fred Astaire, and J. P. Morgan.'³ As the meal ended, a Scottish piper advanced into the dining room to summon the guests from the table. Kennedy then raised the American visit with the King, who seized on the idea. But when Kennedy began to talk about publicity agents, the King 'seemed to have trouble concentrating', unlike the Queen, who had impressed him at dinner with 'a fine head'.⁴

Despite a difficult afternoon during which May Elphinstone had a heart attack at tea at Frogmore, the idea of a US visit was firmly planted, though it could not be realised for the time being. When Roosevelt visited Canada in August that year, Mackenzie King was able to assure him that the Canadian visit would take place the following year and so in September Roosevelt wrote a personal letter to the King inviting him to the United States.

In April 1939 Joe Kennedy and his wife again spent the weekend at Windsor. By now Queen Elizabeth was determined that they should go to the United States, 'no matter how dangerous', since to cancel the visit would give such satisfaction to the enemies. 'What a woman,' commented Kennedy.⁵ The Ambassador amused the Queen by telling her that the Duchess of Windsor had complained that Rose Kennedy had refused to dine with her in Rome. His comment had been: 'I know of no job that I could occupy that might force my wife to dine with a tart.' The Queen laughed and said that it served her right.⁶

On 4 May the King and Queen dined with the Kennedys at the American Ambassador's residence in Regent's Park. Orchids were flown in from Paris for the evening, and after dinner the film *Goodbye Mr Chips* was shown; when it ended, Mrs Kennedy observed that Queen Elizabeth had had 'a little weep'. For this evening the Queen wore a pink satin crinoline gown with paillettes, which became entangled with Mrs Kennedy's own paillettes when they were near each other.

At dinner Virginia ham and pickled peaches were served. The Queen sat between the Ambassador and William Bullitt,* the maverick American Ambassador to France, who came especially from Paris. He had been *en poste* during the state visit the year before, and was determined to sour the American trip.

Bullitt had written to President Roosevelt informing him that Edouard

---

* William Bullitt (1891–1967), author and Ambassador, whose career was a chequered one, and whose views altered according to mood. He was Roosevelt's first Ambassador to Russia 1933–6, and then served in Paris 1936–41. He conducted an aggressive campaign against Summer Welles, the U.S. Under-Secretary of State, which Roosevelt considered an unpleasant personal vendetta.

Daladier, the Prime Minister of France, thought 'the King a moron; and the Queen an excessively ambitious woman who would be ready to sacrifice every other country in the world in order that she might remain Queen Elizabeth of England'.[7] He sent an exaggerated list of what he considered their requirements as regarded personal needs, which included an eiderdown for the King and Queen, and hot-water bottles for the ladies-in-waiting, which was hardly necessary for Washington in midsummer.[8] His only good advice was 'not to mention the Duke and Duchess of Windsor unless the King brings up the subject. He probably won't . . .'[9] Unaware of his machinations, the Queen sought his advice as to a suitable gift for the President. He suggested a Stilton.

But Bullitt did not rest there. A few days later, he wrote again to the President:

> The little Queen is now on her way to you together with the little King. She is a nice girl . . . and you will like her, in spite of the fact that her sister-in-law, the Princess Royal, goes about England talking about 'her cheap public smile'.* She resembles so much the female caddies who used to carry my clubs at Pitlochry in Scotland many years ago that I find her pleasant . . . The little King is beginning to feel his oats, but still remains a rather frightened boy.'[10]

Two days later, blissfully unaware of Bullitt's negative propaganda, the King and Queen sailed to Canada and the United States in *Empress of Australia*. Queen Elizabeth thanked the Archbishop of Canterbury for his message of Godspeed. There were times, she wrote, when it was all rather daunting, but she counted her blessings 'and then things don't seem too bad.'[11] These were sentiments that would have fitted well into the musical, *The Sound of Music*.

Having devoted three days to final fittings for her wardrobe, Queen Elizabeth travelled with an enormous number of trunks packed with dresses, coats and other outfits suitable for each city that would be visited. Two entire cabins were set aside for her clothes alone. Norman Hartnell's problem for this trip was that she could not appear in identical outfits in Ottawa and Montreal as each city would expect a new creation. There were times when the train would stop and the King and Queen would alight at perhaps four o'clock in the morning. For these brief interludes, Hartnell created what the Americans called 'hostess dresses' – 'a

* Queen Mary's page, George Armstrong, did not like Queen Elizabeth 'because she smiled too much' (Sir Michael Duff to Cecil Beaton).

long flowing *négligée* dress in nectarine velvet touched with a narrow band of sable'.[12] The climate changes also had to be considered, some coats being designed to be worn with gumboots.

Not everyone liked the bands of fur worn on her sleeves, bordering both long and short ones, but the parasols again proved popular. Hartnell created these in delicate lace handles decorated with diamonds and sapphires, the gifts of Maharajahs to the Royal Family. One of them was white silk, lined with dark green. When the Queen unfurled it in Washington, an American retail company was forced to order five thousand to match demand. *Life* magazine later wrote: 'To the makers of parasols and umbrellas the reign of George VI . . . will ever be the period when a Queen and a Prime Minister* raised the parasol and umbrella to unprecedented pinnacles of international significance and chic.'[13]

Queen Mary and the two princesses came to Southampton to bid the King and Queen farewell as they sailed to Canada. The journey, scheduled to last seven days, was prolonged to nine, due to days of thick fog. As they neared Quebec, they had to negotiate some spectacular icebergs. At least an exhausted King had the chance to rest.

It was the first time that a British King had visited Canada as King of Canada. The consequent welcome was exceptionally warm. They were in Canada from 17 May until 7 June, travelling in the Royal Train from Quebec to Montreal, to Ottawa, Toronto, west across Canada and back again. The enthusiasm of the greetings was intense, and the noise of cheers deafening, especially from the children.

Every time the Royal Train stopped, the King and Queen had to show themselves, and even when they did not stop there were flag-wavers waiting to see the train go by. The King presided over Parliament in Ottawa on 19 May, the Queen wearing a crinoline with a long train, and the following day the Queen made a speech at the laying of the foundation stone of the Supreme Court building, half in English, half in French†
– 'Dans mon pays natal, en Écosse, nous avons un Droit basé sur le Droit Humain . . .'[14]

The King enjoyed his trip but longed for it to be over. Banff he found too enclosed by mountains. He longed for Balmoral.[15] He was conscious that he was not keeping up with his papers or the world news as closely as usual. As he travelled in the train, he reported that the Canadians were all pleased, and commented that due to the fresh air, none of the party felt tired, or suffered from the 'dirty feeling' that assailed them after a long day of tedious engagements back in Britain.[16]

* A reference to Chamberlain's waved umbrella on his return from Munich.
† The King also spoke in French when so required.

Lord Tweedsmuir, the Governor-General, commended Queen Elizabeth's 'perfect genius for the right kind of publicity', adding 'the unrehearsed episodes here were marvellous'.[17] One such occurred when the Queen discovered that some of the workers on the Supreme Court building, whose foundation stone was being laid, were Scottish. She led the King down among them and there began a spontaneous walkabout. The King and Queen had done these before in New Zealand and Australia, but this was deemed to be the first royal walkabout as such. Soon afterwards the King told his private office: 'There must be no more high-hat business, the sort of thing that my father and those of his day regarded as essential to the correct attitude – the feeling that certain things could not be done.'[18]

Queen Elizabeth's personality added immeasurably to the success of the tour. Columnists vied with one another to define the magic of the visit. In Toronto, Thelma LeCocq concluded: 'We will remember her smile.' Her theme was that each time the King and Queen arrived in a new city there was awe-struck silence, broken instantly and forever when the Queen smiled. An old soldier in Toronto said she had 'the bluest eyes in the world'; a gardener born at Glamis was thrilled when, summoned to their log cabin in Jasper, the door was opened by the Queen herself. Many photographs were taken, but everywhere she went people said that the photographs did not do her justice. 'There's charm, and beauty and radiance in every one, but there's more in those smiles than any printed page can give,' concluded one columnist.[19] The visit to Canada had surpassed all possible expectations.

At 9.35 p.m. on 7 June the King and Queen entered America at Niagara Falls. They were the first reigning British monarchs ever to visit the United States of America. That the Queen and George Washington both descended from Colonel Augustine Warner, who settled in Virginia in 1628, was no hindrance.* With war imminent in Europe, they were determined to establish firm friendship with the President and Mrs Roosevelt. Likewise Roosevelt saw Britain as the first line of defence against a threat from Europe and was keen that the visit should cement friendship between the two countries.

Lady Nunburnholme, one of the Queen's ladies-in-waiting, told a reporter that the King and Queen were treating the visit as the most

---

* Queen Elizabeth was a second cousin six times removed of George Washington, through the ancestry of her paternal grandmother, Frances Smith, wife of 13th Earl of Strathmore. She was a fifth cousin four times removed of General Robert E. Lee, Commander-in-Chief of the Confederate Army in the Civil War, by the same route. [see Cavendish–Bentinck family tree, Appendix III]

important one they had ever undertaken, as full of risk and significance as the Coronation ceremony itself. Both the King and Queen studied a thirty-four-page dossier prepared for them by the Foreign Office, which enabled them to discourse with Congressmen with close knowledge of their aims and achievements.

Again there were the station stops. In Baltimore, Queen Elizabeth received a considerable shock. As she stepped on to the platform, a woman advanced with a bouquet of flowers. This woman looked the spitting image of the Duchess of Windsor. The Queen later told Joe Kennedy: 'I didn't know what to think. I knew she came from Baltimore and after I realized it couldn't be she, I thought it must be her sister.* Anyhow, I had a few uncomfortable minutes.'[20]

In Washington the prospect of the King and Queen in their midst created the traditional frenzy that percolates when royalty and Americans come into contact. This was at fever pitch by the time the Royal Train pulled in to Union Station at 11 a.m. on 8 June, the heat in society more than matched by the intense heat of Washington in June.

For his part, President Roosevelt anticipated their arrival with interest. To Bullitt he wrote: 'The little Queen has acquired a great reputation over here. It may be a difficult one to live up to. Needless to say, there is great excitement over here. However, I think we will all heave a great sigh of relief once they cross the Canadian border safely on their way home.'[21]

The King wore his senior uniform as Admiral of the Fleet and the Queen was dressed in pearl-grey. They were greeted by President Roosevelt. Having been a victim of polio (infantile paralysis) in 1921, the President was unable to walk except uneasily or to stand without support. Press photographs invariably showed him seated, but at times he stood, holding a nearby arm. Even an observant newspaper reader would probably not have noticed his plight. Presently he and the King were seated side by side, being driven through the city in the sweltering heat.

Queen Elizabeth travelled in the next car with Eleanor Roosevelt, who was transfixed by the Queen's relationship with the crowd, and in particular her way of looking into the crowd, 'so that I am sure many of them felt that her bow was really for them personally'.[22]

The Queen established a bond with Mrs Roosevelt by discussing their respective roles, telling her that she was surprised there had been criticism of her for going to a meeting of WPA workers. She said she thought it important that people should have the opportunity to air their

---

* It wasn't. The Duchess of Windsor was an only child.

grievances, especially to someone who might be able to alert the head of government.

After an informal luncheon at the White House and some sightseeing, there was a very hot garden party, followed by a very hot state dinner, at which starched shirts buckled and collars became soggy. A musical performance took place afterwards. When it was all over, the Queen still smiling, the King and President sat down to a long talk about international politics. They stayed overnight at the White House. Mrs Roosevelt was impressed by how 'completely unhurried' the King and Queen appeared, and fascinated by Queen Elizabeth 'who never had a crease in her dress or a hair out of place. I do not see how it is possible to remain so perfectly in character all the time. My admiration for her grew every minute she spent with us.'[23]

The next day there were ten engagements including a press conference at which Mrs Roosevelt spoke, but Queen Elizabeth did not. And so it continued – the Capitol, the Washington Navy Yard, a wreath laid on Washington's tomb at Mount Vernon, another on the grave of the Unknown Soldier at Arlington Cemetery, and finally a dinner at the British Embassy. At a camp at Fort Hunt, the heat began to overwhelm Queen Elizabeth, and she and Mrs Roosevelt retreated to the car for a while.

At the White House lived Diana Hopkins, the eight-year-old daughter of the Commerce Secretary, Harry Hopkins. Mrs Roosevelt took a particular interest in this child. Diana Hopkins longed to see Queen Elizabeth, who readily agreed. Dressed for dinner in a Hartnell crinoline, embroidered with aquamarine stones and Queen Alexandra roses, and wearing the diamond-fringe tiara originally designed for Queen Mary, she made an unforgettable impression on the small girl, who exclaimed afterwards: 'Oh Daddy, I have seen the Fairy Queen.'[24]

The King and Queen left Washington in the Royal Train the same night, arriving at Red Bank, New Jersey, at 9 a.m. on 10 June. They proceeded by destroyer to New York, arriving in Manhattan to a crowd only matched by the one that had met Charles Lindbergh after his transatlantic flight in 1927. They visited the New York World's Fair on Flushing Island, not an event they relished, returning via Columbia University. Mayor LaGuardia packed the day full of events, exhausting his royal guests.

The Roosevelts were expecting the King and Queen for the weekend at Springwood, Hyde Park, their home on the Hudson River. This was a key point on the trip, during which the vital friendship was cemented. It included the famous exchange about cocktails before dinner. Roosevelt said to the King: 'My mother does not approve of cocktails and thinks you should have a cup of tea.' To which the King replied: 'Neither does my mother,' helping himself to a cocktail.[25]

The evening was one of misadventure, with the sideboard collapsing, some Limoges china being broken, the butler tripping and a mass of glass crashing to the floor. More importantly Roosevelt and the King had the chance to talk, the King regretting that his ministers at home did not speak to him as frankly. He gained confidence from his encounter with the President.

It was not the role of a constitutional king to involve himself in politics, but much could be achieved by diplomacy. Roosevelt spoke to him and to Mackenzie King, the Canadian Prime Minister, in such a way as to suggest that intervention in Europe was a good plan, and that public opinion must be swayed accordingly.

During their stay at Hyde Park came the picnic at which hot dogs were served. Controversy had raged in public and private for weeks before as to whether it was appropriate to serve this traditional American fare to such distinguished guests. The hot dogs were duly eaten to wide delight in America.

After the King and Queen left for the Canadian border at 11 p.m. on the Sunday, Mrs Roosevelt wrote: 'I liked them both but what a life! They are happy together however & that must make a difference in the life they have to lead.'[26] She also described the Queen as 'gracious, informed, saying the right thing & kind but a little self-consciously regal'.[27] And yet there were worries too. Mrs Roosevelt wrote: 'One thought of the clouds that hung over them and the worries they were going to face, and turned away and left the scene with a heavy heart.'[28]

The King and Queen sailed from Halifax on 15 June, with tears flowing happily on all sides. Before they embarked, there were more speeches, the Queen thanking the Canadian people for 'the wealth of affection . . . throughout these unforgettable weeks'.[29] They had lived in a train for six weeks with only a few breaks, but were delighted with the tour, and repeated several times: 'This has made us.'[30]

The King and Queen reached Southampton in *Empress of Britain* on 22 June, where the princesses were waiting to meet them. Before disembarking, they had 'a glorious absolutely riotous lunch on board with the children & balloons & complete pandemonium'.[31] Their arrival in London brought the people out into the streets, and even the Members of Parliament from the House of Commons, among them Harold Nicolson. Inspired by the Queen's radiance, he wrote: 'She is in truth one of the most amazing Queens since Cleopatra.'[32]

In that last season before the war, there was a spate of grand balls and evening parties. It was noted that Queen Elizabeth looked slimmer than usual when she and the King dined at Ilchester House on 6 July before a dance for the coming out of Sonia Cubitt's daughter, Rosalind.* Noël Coward and the Queen of Spain were among the guests and Mrs Greville, recovering from pneumonia, was carried up the stairs in a wheelchair by two of her footmen. She wore the massive five-strand diamond necklace that she would bequeath to Queen Elizabeth.[33]

Soon afterwards, the King and Queen received an official visit from Prince and Princess Paul of Yugoslavia, who arrived on 17 July. This was to counter their recent visit to Hitler in Berlin. Prince Paul was such a dedicated Anglophile that, as an undergraduate at Oxford, he had announced his preferred career would have been as Curator of the Ashmolean Museum. But the assassination of King Alexander in Marseilles, while King Peter, the son, was still a boy at school, had propelled him into politics. He had been obliged to assume the Regency, something which he did not like, and for which, in many respects, he was ill suited.

During the state visit, Prince Paul was given the Garter. There was a state ball to which the Prince's great friend Chips Channon was not invited, since Queen Elizabeth now disapproved of her former house guest.† The stay was meant to last six days, but Prince Paul succumbed to dental problems, requiring the removal of some wisdom teeth, and in the end he and Princess Olga stayed for over a fortnight, finally leaving Britain on 2 August.

The King and Queen left their royal guests at the Palace and set off to Weymouth on Friday 21 July, to embark on the Royal Yacht for a visit to the Royal Naval College, Dartmouth. The occasion was memorable because thirteen-year-old Princess Elizabeth had her first proper meeting with her cousin, Prince Philip of Greece and Denmark, then one of the naval cadets. They had both been present at the wedding of the Duke of Kent and Princess Marina in 1934, but on that day the good-looking young prince became fixed in Princess Elizabeth's mind.

Meanwhile, there was the question of keeping Prince and Princess Paul amused. One diversion was to have Princess Olga photographed by Cecil Beaton. The best images of a long session showed the Princess wearing a huge diadem, with a necklace of diamonds 'like almonds'. He

---

* Rosalind Cubitt (1921–94), married in 1946, Major Bruce Shand, and was the mother of Camilla Parker Bowles, now HRH The Duchess of Cornwall.
† Channon's published diaries are conspicuously bereft of any details of the Regent's visit, other than at the very end, 1–2 August.

Lady Elizabeth Bowes-Lyon on the eve of her wedding in 1923

The Duchess of York (with the Duke of York – partially hidden) in East Africa, February 1925

The Duchess of York with her mother, the Countess of Strathmore, driving to the opening of the British Empire Exhibition, Wembley, May 1925

The Duke and Duchess of York with
their elder daughter, Princess Elizabeth,
Christmas, 1926

Crossing the Line. The Duchess of York
on her way to New Zealand and Australia
in February 1927.

Return from Australia, 1927. The Duke
and Duchess of York, Princess Elizabeth,
with King George V and Queen Mary
on the balcony of Buckingham Palace.

Six-year-old Princess Elizabeth standing proudly in the doorway of The Little House at Royal Lodge

The King and Queen with Princess Elizabeth and Princess Margaret in the pram, Scotland, 1931

Princess Elizabeth and Princess Margaret at Royal Lodge, Windsor

(*Above*) Queen Mary (*Right*) King George V
riding (*Below*) The Duke and Duchess in
old Brussels at the Brussels International
Exhibition, 1935. The umbrella was less
stylish than the parasol of the new reign.
(*Below right*) King Edward VIII, who succeeded
to the throne in January 1936

Wallis Simpson, a sketch by
Cecil Beaton, in November
1936 in the midst of the
Abdication crisis

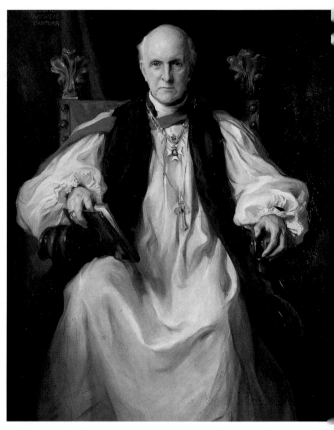

Cosmo Gordon Lang, Archbishop of Canterbury,
by Philip de László

The new Queen and Queen Mary leave for Sandringham in December 1936.
This photograph inspired Mrs Simpson to write to the Duke of Windsor: 'Really David the
pleased expression of the Duchess of York's face is funny to see. How she is loving it all!'

(*Above*) The Coronation
Procession, 12 May 1937

(*Right*) Elizabeth is crowned

(*Below*) King George VI and
Queen Elizabeth on their thrones,
awaiting the homage of the peers

The King
and Queen
prepare to
leave the Abbey

The Royal Family after the Coronation. Left to right: The Princess Royal (Princess Mary),
The Duchess of Gloucester, The Duke of Gloucester, Queen Mary, King George VI, Princess
Margaret, Princess Elizabeth, Queen Elizabeth, The Duke of Kent, The Duchess of Kent
and Queen Maud of Norway (sister of George V).

posed her against backdrops of Piranesi ruined arches and Fragonard trees, in a room with yellow silk brocade on the walls.[34] It was the first time Princess Olga had ever been photographed against anything other than a black or grey backdrop. She was impressed.

Princess Olga showed the results to Queen Elizabeth and encouraged her to send for Beaton.[35] This she did, and Beaton duly presented himself at the Palace two days later.

Just as Queen Elizabeth had relied on poor designers until she discovered Norman Hartnell, so she had relied on fashionable but uninspiring Mayfair photographers such as Bassano, Vandyk, Bertram Park and the court photographer, Hay Wrightson, a man responsible for many a stiff image. Dorothy Wilding had produced some boringly conventional official portraits for the Coronation. Only Marcus Adams took some nice mother and child portraits. Hartnell's transformation in Queen Elizabeth's style was now recorded in Beaton's most famous sitting.

Cecil Beaton went to the Palace to choose venues on Thursday 28 July, and waited in a corridor, 'hung with wonderful rose coloured tapestries & in the vitrines at the side of her door were a collection of heterogeneous objects of great beauty – lace fans, miniatures and jewellery mounted by Benvenuto Cellini'. He was ushered into her room, the walls decorated in pale blue silk with bouquets of silver and white roses. There were flowers everywhere – hydrangeas, sweet peas, and carnations, and, on the walls, a number of highly coloured paintings.

Beaton was nervous about seeing the Queen. He admired her so much that he wondered how he could ever have felt 'it was dreary & dowdy to have the Yorks on the throne . . . No-one could have done the job as well as she & one knows that there is nothing she could not succeed at if sent out for her country – she might even win Hitler to peace!'[36]

When he had first seen her at her wedding in 1923, he had thought: 'She does look sloppy.'[37] A while later, at the Ritz, he was more favourably impressed: 'She is a charming looking little person. She looks horrid from her photographs but she is really delightful with a very fresh complexion and face and charming smile.'[38] Three years passed, by which time he was captivated: 'Oh the fresh little Duchess. She has a lovely skin, like a baby's, soft & pink & white & hardly at all made up, just a little dusting of powder, like the powder that is put on a new baby after its bath.'[39]

That day she was in pale grey, with long fur-edged sleeves, an ensemble Beaton recognised from the Canada trip. Norman Hartnell had been in the Palace that very morning, and had spotted Beaton. With a twinkle the Queen told Beaton: 'I expect he had visions of his lovely dresses appearing again.'[40]

Examining the Queen with a photographer's eye, Beaton was concerned:

> The face looked very dazzling, white & pink, & the complexion flawless but as a photographer I was anxious at the lack of defini- tion in it. It is a face I know so well from the millions of pictures, but here in reality it seemed so negative. The eyes pretty but pale, very few eyelashes, a pale mouth & the lips surprisingly thin, & a vast expanse of cheek that might be difficult to light . . .
>
>   Her arms & wrists were white & rounded, with diamond bracelets & perfumed with tuberose. She is very short & her heels are very high. I liked her, but I feared for the camera results. In the glaring light from the garden windows she looked flat & shadowless . . .[41]

Beaton said he would bring Queen Elizabeth a different lipstick. Nervously, she agreed to try it.

The afternoon session began at 3 p.m. in the Bow Room, where Beaton's backdrops were set up, and continued in the Yellow and Blue Drawing Rooms. The Superintendent warned Beaton that he would be lucky if he were granted twenty minutes. After three hours they were still at work, both very happy. The daylight pictures worked and when the electric lights went on:

> To my utter amazement & joy, the Queen looked like a dream, a porcelain doll, with flawless little face like luminous china in front of a fire. Her smile as fresh as a dewdrop, her regard uncompro- mising & kindly, altogether a face that reveals what the owner is – someone with the best instincts, strict in her likes, gay, sympathetic, witty, shrewd, wistful & so well educated that she makes one full of admiration rather than shame. She is a great lady, & childish, an angel with genius & she makes every man feel she needs his protec- tion though she can well get along on her own merits.[42]

Beaton succeeded in persuading Queen Elizabeth to put on eye shadow for the next photographs, something she did in his presence. The sitting continued.

> The Queen's hands & wrists are full of character, & country hands & wrists. The nails are shortish & without enamel. They are delicate

& early Victorian. Her hair seems to belong to another woman, a more conventional elderly woman & though the coiffeur had been there this morning it was hopelessly & very charmingly formless on the forehead & temples. Her mouth forms a smile with the minimum of effort & creases are not found at each side. It is no hardship for her to smile. In fact she said 'It is so hard to know when *not* to smile.' I apologised for my over-enthusiasm & said I hoped so much the results would warrant this behaviour but that they should be so much better than those awful 'camera portraits'* that were taken at the time of the Coronation. 'Yes, & they went all over the world. It is a pity as it's so important, & they were so bad. In fact it is so distressing to me that I always photograph so badly.' I commented that the improvement in the way she photographed lately was astonishing & that it was a great feat to be able to look into the cameras & cinematographic apparati with such a clear regard. 'It isn't so difficult you know when there are forty of them. Then they seem to merge into one big fog of mechanism.'[43]

Queen Elizabeth changed into a tulle dress and her diamond-fringe tiara, with a necklace of two rows of enormous diamonds given her by the King at the Coronation. At one point the Superintendent came in and announced: 'Your Majesty, it's lovely. It's just like a Winterhalter picture.' Queen Elizabeth beamed like a child.

Then the Queen disappeared to change into a pale pink garden party dress for some photographs in the garden. The Superintendent was astonished: 'Do you mean to say she's gone off to change once more? Why, she hasn't had her tea yet has she? Well, it means the poor King will have to have his tea alone!'

They went out into the garden, where Beaton observed the Queen again: 'Her face is full of unexpected formations & contours & the effect is created by no simple straightforward means though the face we know is so easily recognisable. Yet one side the nose is quite beaky – the other retroussée.'

The photography continued, her Catherine the Great parasol was furled and unfurled, the Queen posed in front of the tridents of the Admiralty summerhouse and in front of the vast Napoleonic vase. The sitting finally ended at 7 p.m., after which the King and Queen and princesses went to Royal Lodge.

The results did not disappoint – a glorious portfolio of a romantic

---

* These were the portraits by Dorothy Wilding.

Queen in the tranquillity of the Palace rooms and garden, as Britain hovered on the eve of war. They were the photographic version of portraits by the court painters of olden times. Everybody was delighted, no one more so than the Queen. But they were not published, due to the uncertain political situation.

A gloomy forecast by the Belgian Ambassador haunted the summer holiday at Balmoral; 'You might get the grouse shooting, but not the partridge season.'* He was right.

The King had loaned Abergeldie Castle for boys attending what would be his last ever summer camp. During the next days, the Royal Family drove the short distance from Balmoral to spend time with the young men, the King sometimes having supper in camp and enjoying the evening bonfires. The press wanted to take photographs of the hill walks, but when they heard that they would have to carry their heavy cameras fifteen miles uphill, they settled for camp photographs only. This greatly amused the King.

For the King it was to be an interrupted holiday. On 8 August he went to Weymouth again, to inspect the Reserve Fleet, boarding six ships including a submarine. On 10 August he returned to Balmoral, where he was described as being 'in tearing form'.[44]

The King lost two days in Scotland when he inspected the Reserve Fleet at Weymouth. Then, on 24 August, as the political situation worsened, he went south. He held a Privy Council meeting and saw the Prime Minister. On 29 August Queen Elizabeth joined him, and on 2 September Balmoral was closed, the princesses moving to Birkhall.

On 1 September the King visited the Prime Minister at 10 Downing Street, the first time a monarch had ever been there. On the same day German troops invaded Poland on all fronts, advancing further the next day. They gave no undertaking that these troops would withdraw, and therefore, on 3 September, at 11.15 a.m., Britain declared war on Germany. The Prime Minister, Neville Chamberlain, broadcast to the nation, a more sombre note in his voice than after Munich. Soon afterwards, the first air raid was sounded because unidentified aircraft were detected approaching the coast. And then the all-clear was sounded. These sirens would be a feature of London life in the coming years. That evening the King too broadcast to the nation:

> In this grave hour, perhaps the most fateful in our history, I send
> to every household of my peoples, both at home and overseas, this

---

* Partridge shooting officially begins on 1 September.

message, spoken with the same depth of feeling for each one of you as if I were able to cross your threshold and speak to you myself.

For the second time in the lives of most of us we are at war. Over and over again we have tried to find a peaceful way out of the differences between ourselves and those who are now our enemies. But it has been in vain. We have been forced into conflict . . .[45]

15

The War

'If one did not love this country and this people with a deep love, then our job would be almost impossible' – Queen Elizabeth

The moment that war broke out, the King and Queen threw themselves into hard work. On 2 September the Queen had visited the headquarters of the Women's Voluntary Service. In the month of September alone Queen Elizabeth visited the ARP units at Westminster Control Centre, their London Defence units and the headquarters of the Red Cross and St John. She visited the City of London Headquarters of the ATS, Middlesex Hospital and St Mary's Hospital, Paddington, Bermondsey's civil defence posts, the headquarters of the YWCA and the London Volunteer Ambulance Station.

On 15 September she assumed the position of Commandant of the Women's Auxiliary Air Service, the ATS and the WRNS, though remained resolutely civilian in wartime, never wearing any form of military uniform. Between 20 and 26 September, she managed a quick visit to Birkhall to see her daughters, who had been left there with cousins and friends.

On her return to London, she called in on the headquarters of the Personal Service League, visited the Depot of the Black Watch, the Women's Voluntary Services (ARP), and she saw army troops training. This would be the pattern of life for the next five years. She told the Archbishop of Canterbury:

> I must admit I have had to call up all my reserves of strength and faith to cope with these last few days . . .
>
> I *know*, as do all our people, that we are fighting evil things, and we must face the future bravely.
>
> I shall try with all my heart to help the people. If only one could do more for them. They are so wonderful.[1]

The Queen hoped that the Archbishop had adequate air raid protection at Lambeth Palace.* She greatly resented having to rise from her bed and retire to the basement.[2]

Queen Mary was 'begged to leave Marlborough House', as she put it, and went to spend the war with her niece, the Duchess of Beaufort, at Badminton, arriving with an entourage of more than fifty people and numerous vans of luggage. Thereafter she waged her own war against the ivy on the estate, and almost succeeded in felling an historic cedar tree beside the house. She was able to get about the area, but her place of residence was never revealed in the press.†

There was some discussion as to what to do with the princesses. They remained in Scotland but many children were being evacuated to Canada and this option was considered. However, in due course, the Queen made her much-quoted remark that the princesses would not go without her, that she would never leave the King and the King would never leave Britain.

Meeting the King and Queen on 10 September, Joseph Kennedy concluded that the King's main worry was that 'within a relatively brief period, possibly three or four weeks, Poland will have been liquidated by Herr Hitler and then certainly a proposal will be made by him to France and England to put a stop to this war and to arrive at some understanding'. Kennedy noted that Queen Elizabeth's prime concern was the threatened return to Britain of the Duke and Duchess of Windsor, which she justified as 'worrying the King'. She made it clear that she was refusing to receive the Duchess. Kennedy reported this to Cordell Hull, the US Secretary of State, and President Roosevelt 'because it will have a certain effect subconsciously on the King and Queen both in arriving at a conclusion as to what answer should be made to Hitler'.‡[3]

To Prince Paul Queen Elizabeth expressed her feelings about the war, explaining that once they had got past the terrible shock that war was unavoidable, Britain had sat down to the grim task of ridding the world of the new terror unleashed upon it by the Germans. Truth, justice and

---

* On the morning of 6 September, the sirens wailed loudly at 6.40 a.m. Alan Don hurried to the Archbishop's room and found him 'in his pyjamas, fumbling his way into a purple cassock'. Don exhorted him to haste, but suggested that he put his false teeth in. 'He proceeded to pour some water over his dentures, and then just as I hoped he was ready, he decided (wisely, no doubt) to relieve nature. That done I escorted him to the crypt' (Alan Don diary, 6 September 1939, Lambeth Palace Library).

† A perceptive reader of the Court Circular might have divined that she was at Badminton from engagements reported in Bath (regularly), as well as Cheltenham and Malmesbury. Queen Mary would have preferred to remain in London and confessed that she felt rather out of it all.

‡ The Duke of Windsor did come (see p. 172). He then left for France to serve as a liaison officer.

liberty were fighting their evil, arrogance and nationalism. She and the King were calm and confident that they would win through eventually:

> What breaks one's heart, is to see yet another generation going cheer-fully off to face death. I went to see the Black Watch the other day, one of my regiments, and suddenly saw my nephew John Elphin-stone* among the officers. I had not seen him before in uniform, and received a great shock, as I thought for one awful moment that it was my brother Fergus who was killed in France when serving with the same regiment. It was only for one second, a flash, a family likeness, but how tragic to think of all that ghastly waste. And yet, is it waste?

Queen Elizabeth stressed that humanity must fight, and believed in the ultimate superiority of the spiritual things. She felt that it was as though the last twenty years of peace had never been, and that somehow the last war had never been finished and had joined up to this one. Peace was the ultimate goal of most people. Even at this time of worry, she could conjure a light image of what they were enduring:

> Everything in this country is completely upside down. All the big houses are either maternity homes or hospitals or schools, London is completely black at night & united as never before, and the balloon barrage swimming over our heads like pretty fishes when high, & very like elephants & sheep when low![4]

On 3 October the Archbishop of Canterbury lunched alone with the King and Queen, reporting that the King looked 'thin', but the Queen was 'as fascinating as ever'. They discussed the amount of 'junky' corre-spondence they each received. Alan Don commented: 'I have no doubt C.C. made the most of it – of course he sees very little of the stuff that reaches us.'[5]

The King's reassuring presence in the capital city was of vital impor-tance. He was never seen in public other than in uniform, wearing, in rotation, his uniforms as Admiral of the Fleet, Field Marshal and Marshal of the RAF. When he travelled from county to county he was not received by the Lord-Lieutenant but by regional commissioners and naval, mili-tary and air force commanders. It was the fighting people that he had come to see.

* Hon. John Elphinstone (1914–75), later 17th Lord Elphinstone, then a captain in the Black Watch. He was captured in 1940 and was imprisoned in Colditz.

At home the Queen's main concern was continually to boost the King's morale. She took on the role of representing the women of Britain, and to some extent of all women suffering under Hitler's afflictions. She was greatly supported by the Princess Royal who took on duties as Controller-Commandant of the ATS, the Duchess of Gloucester concentrating on the Women's Auxiliary Air Force, and the Duchess of Kent making a very stylish Wren as Commandant of Women's Royal Naval Service, glamorising the service by continuing to wear high-heeled shoes, silk stockings and earrings with her uniform.

In October the Queen invited the cameras into Buckingham Palace to film and photograph her sewing group at work, knitting for the troops. In November she conceived the idea of a broadcast and consulted the Archbishop of Canterbury at lunch at the Palace, later sending him a draft for his approval.

The purpose of the speech was to reassure women about their importance in the war effort. Concerned that her words might sound too 'homely', she asked his advice as to how to bring God into her few words.[6]

The Archbishop made a few alterations and additions, and on Armistice Day the Queen made her broadcast from a small room in Buckingham Palace, speaking for seven minutes. The King listened from a room next door, the National Anthem was played as were the 'Marseillaise' and the national anthem of Poland. She spoke of how everyone had believed that 'strife and bloodshed' were impossible, how this day of remembrance had been kept as one 'consecrated to the memory of past and never-to-be-forgotten sacrifice', and then expressed her sympathy for the women of Poland and 'the gallant womanhood of France':

> War has at all times called for the fortitude of women. Even in other days, when it was an affair of the fighting forces only, wives and mothers at home suffered constant anxiety for their dear ones, and too often the misery of bereavement. Their lot was all the harder because they felt that they could do so little beyond heartening, through their own courage and devotion, the men at the Front.

The Queen spoke of the vital work to be done. She contrasted the excitement of 'new and interesting duties' with the daily tasks that women had to do in wartime, spoke of those who were separated from their children, many of whom had been evacuated to homes in the countryside: 'It is, after all, for our homes and for their security that we are fighting, and we must see to it that, despite all the difficulty of these days, our homes do not lose those very qualities which make them the background, as well as the joy, of our lives.'[7]

The broadcast was well received and clearly heard as far away as in Australia. The traditional ceremony at the Cenotaph had not taken place, though wreaths were laid on behalf of the King and Queen and Queen Mary, and many others paid their respects.

In October Lord Halifax lunched with the Archbishop of Canterbury and confessed that he had never read *Mein Kampf*. He repeated this at lunch with the King and Queen on 15 November, and she promptly sent the Foreign Secretary a copy:

I send you *Mein Kampf* but do not advise you to read it through, or you might go mad, and that would be a great pity.

Even a skip through, gives one a good idea of his mentality, ignorance, and obvious sincerity.

I forgot to ask you today whether you were comfortable at the Dorchester?

It's so exciting, & sounds so rackety & gay![8]

Parliament was quietly re-opened without its normal State Opening on 28 November, the King reading a very short speech in a House of Lords thinly attended by peers and peeresses. Admiral of the Fleet Lord Chatfield carried the crown 'like a cigarette girl carries her tray'.[9]

Shortly afterwards Joseph Kennedy lunched with the King and Queen before returning to Washington for Christmas. He found the King looking unwell, 'thin and drawn', and stuttering more than usual. Hare was served but Kennedy confessed he did not like it. 'What an honest man,' said Queen Elizabeth and ordered him some pheasant. Her message to the Ambassador was that the British Empire was fighting for its life, but Kennedy noted that she 'tried to add the high moral tone of fighting for all other countries'.[10]

When she was being photographed by Cecil Beaton in the summer before war was declared, Queen Elizabeth had told him: 'I think we live in a very barren age artistically, but perhaps it [the war] will produce something later, for history shows us that all suffering & periods of anxiety & terror have produced great art, & that smug contentedness & over-eating produces nothing.' With this in mind she supported culture throughout the war, attending concerts and exhibitions and buying pictures.

The National Gallery closed on 23 August, just before war was declared, and all the paintings were removed for safety. The pianist Myra

Hess conceived the idea of daily midday concerts, which proved an important morale booster in London, and ran for six and a half years until repairs to war damage at the Gallery brought them to an end.

Queen Elizabeth described these concerts as 'some of the happiest hours of the dark times' of the war. Looking back on Dame Myra's contribution, she said: 'Indeed in her "sweet music was the art which killeth care and grief of heart" – and what gift, in days of war, could be more timely?'[11]

On 26 October, the Queen paid an informal visit to a concert by the Spanish cellist Gaspar Cassado and the pianist George Moore. On 16 November she returned with the Duchess of Gloucester to hear choral music by Tudor singers, a harpsichord recital and Cuthbert Bates, the organist, perform 'The Agincourt Song'. Osbert Sitwell was at the latter concert. He wrote to the Queen that he noticed that 'Ris K', as he called Sir Kenneth Clark, 'now blew his own trumpet quite openly'.[12]

Clark, the young Director of the National Gallery, and Surveyor of the King's Pictures,* inspired these concerts and also the exhibition of works by war artists. Before the main floor of the gallery was judged unsafe due to the increased bombing of London, the Queen supported Clark by lending works of her own and visiting.

Among Queen Elizabeth's various muses in the world of art, Clark became a friend, and, in old age, brazenly announced that she had been a bit in love with him. She had telephoned him the night that war was declared and invited him to dinner. 'We had a jolly time, drank lots of toasts. I think we were a bit in love with each other.' A notorious ladies' man, who may well have chosen to consider that every woman he met fell for him (as indeed many did), he went on to describe the royal marriage as having been no love match. 'Her husband was a very stupid man. He got a bit jealous and made one jealous scene at Windsor and one at Buckingham Palace.' Clark did not elaborate. He dismissed the King as 'so stupid. He would have a few kind thoughts about the unemployed but didn't do much about them.'[13]

Clark considered the Queen had 'quite a good eye for pictures', in consequence 'quite a good collection', for some of which he took credit. He certainly commissioned John Piper to make a record of Windsor Castle. Anthony Blunt, who succeeded Clark as Surveyor of the King's Pictures in 1945, was more reserved. He said that Queen Elizabeth 'aspired to taste' and was 'apt to suggest changing the traditional hanging

---

* Clark was Director of the National Gallery, and Surveyor of the King's Pictures 1934–45, accepting the latter appointment reluctantly at the express wish of George V.

of certain pictures for no better reason than that they might look prettier in the Blue Drawing Room'.[14]

The King was less artistically inclined than the Queen. Before their collection was despatched to various safe hiding places in the summer of 1939, he visited the Tate Gallery and asked the Director, with cheerful innocence: 'I thought I'd have a look at them before they go, although if it weren't for those labels of yours I wouldn't know one from another. Would you?'[15] This was in tune with his admission to Anthony Blunt,* that 'when he saw a name under a portrait he was not always sure whether it was of the artist or the sitter',[16] and his comment to Piper about the poor weather he must have endured when painting his wartime images of Windsor Castle under lowering skies. In 1946, when his pictures were shown in an important exhibition at the Royal Academy, the King confined his comments to his delight 'at the arrangement of the pictures and in particular with the artificial lighting of the exhibition'.[17]

The Queen let it be known that she was collecting contemporary art. She had acquired Wilson Steer's *Chepstow Castle* (1906) for 1000 guineas, Augustus John's *When Homer Nods* (a 1915 portrait of Bernard Shaw) for £750 and Dame Ethel Walker's *At Sea on an October Morning* (1938). In November 1939 she bought two works by Duncan Grant from Agnew's – *Newhaven Pier* and *St Paul's*. In January 1940 she and the Duchess of Kent were shown round the United Artists Exhibition at the Royal Academy by Sir Edwin Lutyens. A few weeks later she returned with the King, and bought *The Orchard* by E. Beatrice Bland. The purchase of these pictures was her way of indicating that life must go on despite the war, and indeed that there was a future to which to look forward when war was done. The pictures were also conveniently cheap.

In 1939 Queen Elizabeth bought Sisley's *The Seine near St Cloud*; in the same year she bought Matthew Smith's *Jugs and Apples*; before 1941 Sickert's *Ennui* and in 1941 *A Lady in a Pink Ballgown*. In 1942, on Clark's advice, she bought William Nicholson's *Gold Jug*. She also bought Augustus John's drawing, *Ida Nettleship and Dorelia*.

Another aspect was recording public monuments and private buildings. During the war Queen Elizabeth asked Cecil Beaton to come to Buckingham Palace to record its wartime face, the rooms deserted, buckets placed strategically, the pictures removed from the walls. She also commissioned John Piper for his famous set of images of Windsor Castle. He had been sent to paint the bombed Coventry Cathedral and to draw blitzed churches in Bristol. When Queen Elizabeth visited a 1941

---

* Anthony Blunt (1907–83), Surveyor of the King's Pictures 1945–52, and of the Queen's Pictures 1952–72. KCVO 1956, stripped of his knighthood when exposed as 'The Fourth Man' in 1979.

exhibition at the National Gallery devoted to 'Recording Britain', she approved the idea of commissioning Piper partly out of fear that Windsor Castle might not survive the war. Kenneth Clark told Piper that he would be paid £150 (including expenses) for fifteen watercolours. As Piper wrote: 'I follow unworthily in the footsteps of Paul Sandby, who did two hundred watercolours for George III, which I am instructed to look at earnestly before starting.'[18]

More important as an artistic mentor to the Queen was Jasper Ridley,* Trustee of the National Gallery, Chairman of the Tate Gallery and the British Museum, and a friend from her early days. He had built up a collection of contemporary pictures starting as early as 1909, and owned works by Dame Ethel Walker, Walter Sickert, John Piper and Matthew Smith. Sir John Rothenstein attributed much of the Queen's interest in contemporary art to Ridley who 'sedulously fostered her artistic and intellectual predilections'.[19] On account of Ridley, Queen Elizabeth became a regular visitor to the Tate Gallery.*

Queen Elizabeth gave her name to *The Queen's Book of the Red Cross*, which was published in November, with contributions from fifty of Britain's best-known authors, from A. A. Milne to Walter de la Mare, and artists from Edmund Dulac to Dame Laura Knight. The book was sold in aid of the Red Cross to 'forward the great work of mercy on the battlefield'.[20] The cover was adorned with one of the Cecil Beaton's photographic portraits, showing Queen Elizabeth against an Arcadian backdrop, wearing a Hartnell state gown, tiara, rubies, Garter riband and star and the Garter itself on her left arm.

This heralded the wider publication of Beaton's portraits. The Duchess of Kent had told him that they were considered a success and early in November he presented himself at the Palace to hear their fate. He hoped they would be published as the public was 'so in need of a fillip, & these pictures would be a sop if they were allowed'.

Beaton found that the Palace still had its Victorian pictures and tapestries while Queen Elizabeth's room was stacked with pictures and flowers. He was not overly impressed by the Queen's appearance:

> The Queen was in her pretty blue room, in a granite grey dress, with steel bead embroideries bordering an edging of astrakhan. It was an ugly dress & very dowdy, & her shoes were too elaborate, &

---

* In 1951 she visited the Turner, Hogarth and Henry Moore exhibitions, and admired a recent acquisition, Graham Sutherland's striking portrait of Somerset Maugham, with its famous down-turned mouth.

too pale a grey felt, & her jewellery was messy, rather too many little bits, three rows of small pearls, two small pearl clips, a very ordinary diamond bracelet, but does it matter *what* she wears, or even what she looks like, for her aura is one of such goodness & sympathy, her charm so overwhelming. She seemed to have a slight cold & kept holding a crumpled handkerchief to her nose, but her voice was as plaintive & clear as ever. It is like a sad child's voice, infinitely moving & appealing. She held her head on one side, looked very wistful & yet managed the interview in quite a businesslike way, not in a hurry, willing to linger & gossip, to admire the pictures (for she did like them very much), but also not wishing to be rushed into any commitment. 'Would you perhaps go & see Eric* about their publication? I think it would be alright, but if you'd just speak to him!'

The Queen makes quietly witty remarks with each breath. I would not go as far as David [Herbert]† in saying that she is 'camp', but she certainly has a great sense of humour & is full of quiet fun, & very shrewd. She sums up people in a brilliant & penetrating way, appreciates the sterling qualities that are so often not easily discernable. She appreciated Betty Cranborne,‡ a most difficult person, who one grows to know & admire by slow & painful degrees, at once, in a flash. She refuses to have anything to do with 'Chips' Channon.

The Queen is a genius, her instinct helps her each time. Her technique, or her education, is so sure that she is like a great artist. Knowing her limitations she makes an asset of them, appealing for protection from the lack of her gifts, talents, without compromising herself & pretending to be different from the person she is, she is able to get along well with every sort of different strata of person, not by feigning interest but by being interested in them in spite of the fact that you know she knows she is right in her calling of life, but that she sees the fascination, the excitement, say, of being a painter or a writer.

She is ideal as Queen of England for she is the personification of all that is best & a 'real' Lady.

* Sir Eric Miéville (1896–1971), Private Secretary to the Duke of York, 1936, and Assistant Private Secretary to the King 1937–45.
† Hon. David Herbert (1908–95), bachelor son of 15th Earl of Pembroke. He gravitated to Tangiers, a happy home for a man of his proclivities.
‡ Elizabeth Cavendish (1897–1982), married to Viscount Cranborne, later 5th Marquess of Salisbury, KG.

The Queen was decisive in her choice of pictures, told Beaton that she had liked some photographs of war work at Wilton and urged him to get a propaganda job, which he did. She told him that many Americans had written to say they were sorry for the British. She maintained that the British felt far from sorry for themselves. When Beaton suggested that the Americans were 'brutes', she laughed and said, 'Yes, I know what you mean.' He concluded that she disliked them 'as much as all of us do'.

The approved pictures were published to great acclaim all over the world, even in Bulawayo. A photograph was sent as a Christmas card to every soldier, sailor and airman in the British forces. The *Daily Sketch* hailed them as 'the best pictures ever taken of our Queen'.[21] More were released in March 1940.

The photographs evoked an image of peace, the civilian Queen in her drawing room or her garden, a gentle contrast to the sinister images of black-booted Nazis that emerged from Hitler's Germany. They were one of several masterly strokes of genius in the field of propaganda.

Thelma Cazalet-Keir and Hugo Pitman are both credited with having been responsible for one of Queen Elizabeth's more bizarre forays into artistic circles. Thelma claimed to have sixteen letters from Augustus John to her mother trying to arrange sittings with the Queen for him. She wrote that when her mother suggested it, Queen Elizabeth replied: 'Oh, do you think he would care to paint me? I don't think I have a very interesting face.'[22]

Hugo Pitman* had served with Queen Elizabeth's brother, Michael, in the Royal Scots in the Great War. As early as 1937 he had introduced Augustus John† to her, exhorting the artist that he must arrive unaccustomedly sober for the meeting. The idea of a portrait of the Queen was mooted though nothing happened.

Two years later, the idea was raised again. Queen Elizabeth saw the war as no hindrance and hoped for an important portrait of herself in Garter robes to inspire people as Beaton's photographs had done. Augustus John was still keen to paint her, but hoped she would be décolleté, and would wear a pretty hat. He thought the final work would end up in Hollywood.

---

* Hugo Pitman (d. 1963), a businessman married to Reine Ormond, niece of the artist John Singer Sargent. He was a keen patron of the arts and a Trustee of the Tate Gallery. He lived near Augustus John at Odstock, Salisbury, and was a keen collector of John's works. Of him it was said: 'Beauty came first – in his wife and daughters, in art, in nature, and in music' (*The Times*, 30 July 1963).
† There had been a proposal that Augustus John might paint George V in 1925, but the answer came from Lord Stamfordham that the King would not look at John so the artist would not be able to look at the King.

John was summoned to Buckingham Palace on 30 October 1939, but cried off in a fit of nerves, claiming influenza. Unfortunately his letter declared he was suffering from 'the influence'.

All manner of problems frustrated the project. John wanted a platform, an easel which leant forward and electric daylight to illuminate the Queen's skin. Then the Palace became too cold. In February 1940 the Private Secretary reported: 'The temperature in the Yellow Room is indistinguishable to that in Finland.'[23] When the sittings resumed, tapestries were brought in for backdrops.

Augustus John loved the Queen, describing her beauty as 'one of those fine English skins with watery, translucent shadows and pearl highlights',[24] but he was perpetually nervous that he was failing to do her justice. She sat for him with infinite patience, in one of her sequin-covered crinolines, her rubies and the Oriental Circlet.* At one point he took Matthew Smith's painting *Peaches* to her in the hope that she would buy it, but she did not take the bait. *Peaches* went to the Tate Gallery instead.

At a later sitting Queen Elizabeth invited Pitman to see the work in progress, telling him: 'Mr John is quite cross with me because I have been away on holiday and changed colour.'[25] The Queen then offered Pitman a glass of sherry. There was a tray with a decanter and two glasses. She explained: 'Mr John has a bottle of brandy in the cupboard and he can help himself when he wants to.'[26]

On another occasion, to put him further at his ease, she asked the Griller Quartet to play works by old English composers in a neighbouring room. But John thought she said 'Gorilla Quartet',[27] and his nerves got out of hand once more. The Blitz intervened and the portrait went down to Fryern Court, John's home at Fordingbridge.

By 1942 it seemed that the project would have to be abandoned. John showed Beaton a letter that Queen Elizabeth had written saying that she had preserved a hat that John had once seen flying by in a car when they went to inspect some troops in his part of the country. She knew that John wanted to draw it and offered to come to his studio in it 'as her home was dirty & dark'.[28]

The unfinished portrait remained hidden away, unseen and incomplete. There it stayed until it was discovered in 1961 by the West End dealer Arthur Tooth 'under thick dust and massed cobwebs, in a world of rats and spiders' in the cellar below John's studio. The shipping company Vickers Armstrong bought it and presented it to the Queen

* The Oriental Circlet was a tiara made for Queen Victoria in 1853. Queen Alexandra replaced the opals with rubies. It was a special favourite of Queen Elizabeth's.

Mother when she launched SS *Northern Star*. She hung it in the Garden Room at Clarence House.

Of this oddly two-dimensional portrait, John's biographer, Michael Holroyd, wrote: 'It is no masterpiece. Stern critics have condemned it.'[29] Nicolette Devas, who knew John well as a child, believed that there were too many problems. 'If the public and the sitters, understood more of the portrait painter's problems they would get better pictures.'[30] In the 1970s, her long-serving Private Secretary, Sir Martin Gilliat, tried in vain to get it off the drawing-room wall.[31]

The King and Queen continued to entertain friends such as the Halifaxes, Oliver and Maureen Stanley, Tor-Tor Gilmour and Henry Hopkinson. 'This was a quite delicious evening & did us all a power of good,' noted Helen Hardinge. 'The Queen's personality is the delight of these parties, her goodness, gaiety & originality of mind. Everyone expands & gives of their best & the King most of all.'[32]

Meanwhile the princesses were still at Birkhall, the King and Queen telephoning them every evening at the same hour. Crawfie was with them, and there were many children on the estate, evacuated from Glasgow. The princesses did not know when they would next see their parents, and were excited when the Queen announced they could go to Sandringham for Christmas as usual. This was a brave decision as the Norfolk coast was hardly inaccessible to German bombers. But all was well. That Christmas the King made his best-remembered broadcast, quoting 'The Gate of the Year' by Marie-Louise Haskins:

> I said to the man who stood at the Gate of the Year 'Give me a light that I may tread safely into the unknown'. And he replied: 'Go out into the darkness, and put your hand into the Hand of God. That shall be to you better than light, and safer than a known way.'
> May that Almighty Hand guide and uphold us all.[33]

Then Sandringham was closed. If the Royal Family went there, they stayed in Queen Maud's former home, the much smaller Appleton House.

In February 1940 Queen Elizabeth appeared unannounced in Edinburgh, with Katie Seymour in attendance. The King joined her and they toured Clydeside, Glasgow, Dundee and Aberdeen. A man-of-war, HMS *Duke of York*, was launched with considerably less ceremony than *Queen Elizabeth* the previous year. For Queen Elizabeth it was the chance to spend a few days with her old father at Glamis, and to lay a wreath on her mother's grave. Lord Strathmore was about to reach his eighty-fifth birthday.

On 13 April the Queen made a second broadcast, this time to the YWCA. She made this broadcast at a time when she was feeling less than usually optimistic. The first years of the reign had given her neither real peace, or peace of mind. She began to wonder if there would ever be better days ahead, but was determined to strive for a better world for her children, the next generation. Her message was: 'We've got to beat the Germans.'

The YWCA seemed a good organization to address because it was international in character, and its members in America and Canada included many working class people. By speaking at the Central Club, she could include a message for American co-workers, slipping this in almost imperceptibly.

The speech was broadcast from the YWCA Central Club in Great Russell Street, London, to which she had been bidden by her lady-in-waiting, Lady Helen Graham, who was also President of the YWCA. The religious message was duly delivered:

> Yours is the task of fitting youth for the responsibilities of tomorrow. For this you have to keep abreast with modern thought and, at the same time, to give the young that Christian purpose and direction in life without which no real betterment is possible.[34]

Following the failure of Britain's Norwegian campaign in May, there was a debate in which the Government was defeated. Neville Chamberlain then tried to form a National Coalition Government with himself as the leader. He was soon informed that this would not happen. Under increasing pressure to surrender the seals of office, he resigned on 10 May.

The King and Chamberlain both wanted Lord Halifax to succeed him as Prime Minister. Alec Hardinge described Halifax as 'always the court favourite', but Halifax dropped out on his own accord. The King then called for Winston Churchill, not without a little reluctance, largely because of Churchill's misplaced support for the Duke of Windsor during the Abdication.

The King and Queen had liked Chamberlain. Queen Elizabeth wrote to commiserate with him at his departure. 'You did all in your power to stave off such agony, and you were right,' she wrote. 'We can now only do all in our power to defeat this wickedness and cruelty. It is going to be very hard.'*[35]

---

* In October Chamberlain's health caused him to resign from the War Cabinet. He was offered the Order of the Garter, but declined. On 14 October the King and Queen motored over to Highfield Park, Heckfield, near Reading, to see him. He died there on 9 November.

Soon after Churchill took office, Queen Elizabeth complained to her lady-in-waiting, Lady Hyde, that she and the King were 'ruffled by the off-hand way' in which Churchill treated them. Whereas Chamberlain had appeared promptly for his weekly audience, Churchill often said he would come at six, then postponed the meeting till 6.30, and finally turned up 'for ten hectic minutes at 7'. Marion Hyde was able to register the Queen's concern about Churchill with John Colville, his Private Secretary, who was convinced that 'however cavalierly he may treat his sovereign' Churchill was 'at heart a most vehement Royalist'.[36]

The relationship between the King and Churchill took some time to develop, but in the end proved strong and durable and they became great friends. But Alec Hardinge believed that Queen Elizabeth never became such a friend of Churchill's as the King.

As the Germans overran Europe, so Buckingham Palace was soon awash with foreign Sovereigns. George VI did not suffer from the xenophobic fears of his father who had been afraid of being considered of German origin or too involved with German or Russian relations. George VI actively sought a role as intermediary with other monarchs in Europe, keeping in touch with those who were threatened by the German advances. He resented his Government forbidding him from making appeals to alien heads of state, in particular to Hitler, and later to Emperor Hirohito of Japan.

In the summer of 1940 he rescued Queen Wilhelmina by sending a destroyer to bring her from the Netherlands. Three weeks later King Haakon fled from Norway and spent several months at Buckingham Palace. George VI had hoped that King Leopold III of the Belgians would set up a government in exile in Britain. Instead the Belgian King surrendered to Hitler, feeling he had no choice. He then lived in captivity.

While Churchill criticised King Leopold, George VI stood by him to the extent of refusing to have him struck off the roll of the Order of the Garter, as was the fate of King Victor Emmanuel III of Italy in 1940, and the Emperor of Japan in 1942. The King was supportive of King Boris of the Bulgarians, hoping that he would make a stand against Hitler. But he had stern words for old King Gustaf V of Sweden when he tried to have King Haakon replaced by his young grandson, Harald.*

Nothing would induce the King to leave London. Though he was prepared to give sanctuary to overseas monarchs, he admired those who remained in their countries. Queen Elizabeth told Harold Nicolson at

---

* Prince Harald of Norway (b. 1937), the present King of Norway.

lunch in July that she would die if she had to leave England and was taking revolver lessons: 'I shall not go down like the others,' she declared.[37]

In June Queen Elizabeth received a letter of support from Mrs Roosevelt to which she replied at considerable length in her own hand, anxious to foster the personal link made between the King and herself and the Roosevelts the previous summer:

> Sometimes one's heart seems near breaking under the stress of so much sorrow and anxiety. When we think of our gallant young men being sacrificed to the terrible machine that Germany has created, I think that anger perhaps predominates, but when we think of their valour, their determination & their *grand* spirit, their pride and joy are uppermost.
>
> We are all prepared to sacrifice *everything* in the fight to save freedom, and the curious thing is, that already many false values are going, & life is becoming simpler and greater every day.[38]

The Queen was encouraged to know that the United States were becoming aware of the menace of the Nazis. Even in Britain, where they had lived near it for so long, the true horror was only now becoming clear. Many Americans, even quite poor ones, had sent small sums of money for the use of the wounded and others, which was most sustaining. The Queen told her how grateful she was that the Americans had an understanding of what the British were fighting for.

This was the beginning of an important campaign to interest Mrs Roosevelt in the problems of Britain, and thus to reach the ear of the President himself.

Soon after Dunkirk, Queen Elizabeth visited the French wounded, then in hospitals in the south of England. She found that even the most seriously wounded gave her the encouraging response, 'Ça va.'

On 13 June she summoned the French author André Maurois to Buckingham Palace to ask him to help her with a broadcast to the women of France the next day: 'I want to be a woman talking to other women. I will tell you what I would like to express, then you will return to your hotel, write the speech, and when it is ready you will bring it to me.'

Maurois brought it back an hour later and they rehearsed it together. He found it strange that while France had been invaded and his wife was languishing in occupied Paris, and he was 'miserable to the point of tears', with only his uniform and two shirts as possessions, he was sitting opposite the 'sympathetic' face of Queen Elizabeth in a room filled with roses, instructing her about French grammar. 'I know you have lost everything,' she said 'but do you not find that when one has lost everything, almost everything still remains?'[39] The Queen broadcast in French:

> I who have always loved France so warmly, I share your suffering today and feel it. Ever present in my thoughts are those beautiful summer days when, not quite two years ago, Paris adorned itself with all the charms to receive the King and Queen of England . . . I felt then the heart of the women of France beating close to mine.[40]

Listening at home, Bishop Hensley Henson described it as 'effective and well delivered. We are certainly fortunate in Their Majesties. The Duke of Windsor is forgotten.'[41]

The Duke of Windsor was not forgotten at Buckingham Palace, however. When France fell in 1940, the Windsors retreated to the Château de la Cröe on Cap d'Antibes. Then they gravitated to Lisbon, where many rumours soon surrounded them, most of them far-fetched but which have provided fodder for tabloid speculation ever since. The most extreme theory was that they would ally themselves with Hitler in the hope that he might eventually place them on the British throne.

The Duke's plight, and his continuing demands about the title of his wife and that she be received by the King and Queen in Britain, diverted Churchill from the rather more serious matters with which he was preoccupied. On 27 June the Duke wrote to Churchill from Madrid stressing the old theme that he was not prepared to find his wife and himself treated differently to other members of the Royal Family.[42]

Churchill remained firm with the Duke, though in his reply he excised a drafted reference to the 'great deal of doubt as to the circumstances in which Your Royal Highness left Paris'.[43] Alec Hardinge was dead set against the Duke returning to Britain and suggested that perhaps he might be appointed to Lord Wavell's staff in Egypt. He could envisage no possible future for the ex-King in Britain.[44]

Churchill then drafted a circular letter to the Commonwealth Prime Ministers, of which this was the first draft:

> The activities of the Duke of Windsor on the continent in recent months have been causing HM and myself grave uneasiness as his inclinations are well-known to be pro-Nazi, and he may become a

centre of intrigue.* We regard it as a real danger that he should move freely on the continent, even if he were willing to return to this country, his presence here would be most embarrassing both to HM and the Government.

In all the circumstances it has been felt necessary to tie him down to some appointment which might appeal to him and his wife and I have decided with HM's approval to offer him the Governorship of the Bahamas. (I do not know yet whether he will accept). Despite the obvious objections to this solution we feel that it is the least of all possible evils.[45]

The idea of the Duke of Windsor being appointed Governor of the Bahamas was anathema to Queen Elizabeth. On 7 July Alec Hardinge sent the Colonial Secretary, Lord Lloyd, some notes on the matter written by the Queen, pointing out that she wished him to have them, even though she realised that it was a fait accompli.[46] Queen Elizabeth wrote from Windsor Castle, making the following points – that she was sure that if the Duke of Windsor was appointed Governor of the Bahamas, there would be difficulties with his wife, that because she had three husbands living, she was unsuitable as the wife of a Colonial governor, that her presence there threatened the church's position that family life was essential to the stability and happiness of the community, and that the people of the Empire were accustomed to look up to the King's representatives.

Of course, the Queen pointed out, these objections were not personally directed at the Duchess of Windsor, they were written on moral grounds, fearing the disapproval of the Americans, and the danger that might ensue. Such an appointment may lead to great troubles. In practical terms she wondered if perhaps the Windsors should be sent to the Bahamas first to test the people's reaction before the appointment was sanctioned.[47]

Like the Archbishop of Canterbury in his post-Abdication broadcast, Queen Elizabeth was inspired to write those notes by letters she had received from the general public. These the Queen also sent to Lord Lloyd. A thirty-year-old married American woman from Boston had described the Duchess of Windsor as 'not the sort of woman of whom we are proud . . . One hopes that she will not be forced on you (you should never receive such a person) and that she will not achieve an H.R.H. as an undeserved reward for her bad behaviour.'[48] An old lady

---

* The final version was changed: 'though his loyalties are impeccable, there is always a backlash of Nazi intrigue which seeks to make trouble about him . . .' (Churchill to the Commonwealth Prime Ministers, 4 July 1940, Churchill Archives Centre, Churchill Papers, CHAR 20/9).

from Sevenoaks denounced the Duchess as a pro-Nazi sympathiser and trouble-maker and begged the Queen 'to exclude her from court circles.'[49] There were many more, even a letter from an upper class lady to the King: 'We can not bear to think that our beloved Queen Elizabeth too, may suffer in the eyes of the lower classes, who take an unhealthy interest in all this woman's doings.'[50]

Churchill secured the Duke of Windsor's acceptance of the Bahamas by virtually threatening him with court martial, reminding him that by his own volition he was a serving major general in the British Army, and of the dangers inherent in disobeying military orders. There was only a short delay between this threat and the offer of the Governorship.

On 31 July the Duke accepted Churchill's offer, though he pointed out that the Governorship of the Bahamas was by no means of first class importance. He could not resist returning to his well-tested theme – that since the King and Queen did not wish to end the differences between them, which effectively prevented him accepting a post in Britain, then this would serve as a temporary solution to the problem of his wartime service.[51]

A few days later a telegram from the Duchess of Windsor to Gray Phillips, their equerry, was intercepted, causing Hardinge to write to Churchill's Private Secretary that it was not the first time that the Duchess had come under suspicion for her 'anti-British activities'. He warned that they must never underestimate the power she could exercise over the Duke in her wish to take revenge on Britain.[52] A hint of this was relayed to the Duke of Windsor by Churchill.

The Bombs Fall

'Oh, curse the Germans' – Queen Elizabeth

At the beginning of June 1940, the military situation looked bleak. The Germans attacked Dunkirk, forcing 335,000 British and French troops to evacuate in all manner of vessels, leaving thirty thousand British dead or missing. Churchill declared that Britain would never surrender: 'We shall fight them on the beaches . . .' Italy declared war on Great Britain and France, and on 14 June France collapsed. This put Britain firmly in the sights of the Germans, and on 11 August the Battle of Britain began. London and other parts of the country were subjected to intense bombing, raids lasting as long as six hours, sometimes assailed by as many as four hundred aircraft at a time.

In September, Buckingham Palace was damaged by a delayed-action bomb and the King and Queen went out to inspect the damage. Two days later the Palace was bombed again and the Royal Chapel destroyed by one of the five bombs that fell on or around the Palace. On 15 September, for the third time, the Palace was hit and some of Queen Elizabeth's apartments damaged. Buckingham Palace was hit nine times in all, which identified the King and Queen with the plight of so many other Britons. The Queen made her famous remark about being able to look the East End in the face. After the King's death in 1952, Churchill paid tribute to the courage of the King and Queen:

On one of the days, when Buckingham Palace was bombed, the King had just returned from Windsor. One side of the courtyard was struck, and if the windows opposite out of which he and the Queen were looking had not been, by the mercy of God, open, they would both have been blinded by the broken glass instead of being hurled back by the explosion. Amid all that was then going on – although I saw the King so often – I never heard of this episode till a long time after. Their Majesties never mentioned it, or thought of it of more significance than a soldier in their armies would of a shell bursting near him. This seems to me a revealing trait in the Royal character.[1]

It may be that the King was less resigned about the damage to the Palace. One diarist recorded: 'During the Blitz, when he and the Queen had been out visiting bombed-out areas of the East End, very gracious and kind and sympathetic, they came back to find that his own Buckingham Palace had been hit by a bomb: sudden switch to red-faced spluttering fury.'[2]

By the time the war ended, someone had told the King that 'one of Ali and Baby Bee's boys'* had bombed the Palace, and asked the diplomat Charles Johnston to investigate this when he took up his post in Madrid. The King wanted to know if this was true. The discussion with Johnston took place at Balmoral in the summer of 1948, the King dressed in a kilt, seated on the arm of a chair, whisky in hand. 'Evidently the damage to his house was still on his mind,' noted Johnston.[3]

During the Battle of Britain, the King converted his traditional Tuesday audience with the Prime Minister into a lunch. This they served themselves from the sideboard, the King having dispensed with the servants so that the two men could talk more freely. Sometimes Queen Elizabeth joined them. Churchill found this 'a very agreeable method of transacting business'.[4] So successful were these lunches that they took place regularly over the next four and a half years, whenever the King and the Prime Minister were both in London.

These meetings gave the King the chance to be of real use to his Prime Minister. He and the Queen were travelling the length of Britain regularly, and so he was able to give Churchill first-hand reports of the public mood in the country. In 1941 Churchill wrote to the King: 'I have been greatly cheered by our weekly luncheons in poor old bomb-battered Buckingham Palace, & to feel that in Yr. Majesty and the Queen there flames the spirit that will never be daunted by peril, nor wearied by unrelenting toil.'[5]

If the King and Queen had taken a while to get on to terms with Churchill, the depth of their mutual respect was the deeper for the reserved way in which it was achieved. One day the Queen wrote out a poem in her own hand and had it sent round to Churchill to boost his

---

* Infante Don Alfonso of Spain (1886–1975) and his wife, Princess Beatrice of Edinburgh (1884–1966), daughter of Prince Alfred, Duke of Edinburgh (son of Queen Victoria), had three sons, Alvaro (1910–97), Alonso (1912–36) and Ataúlfo (1913–74). There is no evidence of either of the two sons living in 1940 taking part in any bombing. From this story there has emerged the suggestion that the bomber might have been Prince Christopher of Hesse-Cassel, but papers in the possession of the family (seen by the author) wholly exonerate him.

morale, lines from Wordsworth's poem, *The Excursion*, which, she suggested, must have been written at a time when Europe was terrified of Napoleon:

> At this day
> When a Tartarian darkness overspreads
> The growing nations; when the impious rule,
> By will or by established ordinance
> Their own dire agents, and constrain the good
> To ask which they abhor; though I bewail
> This triumph, yet the pity of my heart
> Prevents me from not owning, that the law,
> By which mankind now suffers, is most just.
> For by superior energies; more strict
> Affiance in each other; faith more firm
> In their unhallowed principles; the bad
> Have fairly earned a victory o'er the weak,
> The vacillating, inconsistent good.[6]

Churchill, a man with a strong sense of romance, chivalry and history, appreciated the Queen's trouble. He framed the poem and hung it at Chartwell.*

The King and Queen spent her fortieth birthday at Windsor Castle on 4 August. Sometimes she bided her time playing consequences, and in the early autumn she presided over groups of children collecting conkers and picking damsons in an attempt to impose some normality on childhood in wartime. On 1 October, a day when in happier times the menfolk would pick up their guns at the beginning of the pheasant season, a Messerschmitt 109 was brought down in Windsor Great Park.

The King and Queen and princesses were now mainly at Windsor. Here too was the artist Sir Gerald Kelly, permanently settled in the Castle, working on the state portraits which he had begun in 1938. He posed the King and Queen in a setting devised by Lutyens, based on Vice-Regal Lodge in Delhi. Kelly's stay was to last the entire war, so happily cocooned into Castle life did he become. Some joked that each night, as in a fairy story, he picked off the labours of the day, ensuring that the portraits were never finished. Even when the princesses made fun of him in one of their pantomimes as 'Sir Kerald Jelly', he failed to take the hint to leave.†

---

* It is now in the possession of the Churchill family.
† The Kelly state portraits were finally shown at the Royal Academy Summer Exhibition in 1945.

Windsor Castle was fortified by barbed wire, which, as Princess Margaret pointed out, 'would never have kept the Germans out, but certainly kept us in'. The King and Queen lived at Windsor at night, going up to London each day, though the impression was given that they were permanently in London, and at times they flew the Royal Standard over the Palace when in fact they were not there.

Some light relief for the princesses was brought by members of the King's guard, figures such as Hugh, Earl of Euston, who were partly deployed to keep the princesses amused. Years later, Princess Margaret joked: 'I was brought up by the Grenadier Guards – men from "Munchester" and the Duke of Grafton.'[7] Throughout the war, there were film shows at the Castle, often attended by the King and Queen, princesses and other Castle residents. On 13 October, Princess Elizabeth made a broadcast on *Children's Hour*.

In November 1940, Coventry was bombed and the Cathedral destroyed, one of the greatest acts of destruction by the Germans. The King and Queen were quick to visit the site. Lord Harlech told Harold Nicolson that when Queen Elizabeth visited Sheffield the car would stop and the Queen nip out into the snow and head straight into the crowd. 'For a moment or two they just gaze and gape in astonishment. But then they all start talking at once. "Hi! Your Majesty, look here!!" She has that quality of making everybody feel that they and they alone are being spoken to.' Nicolson attributed this to the Queen's 'very large eyes which she opens very wide and turns upon one.' Lord Harlech told him that these visits did 'incalculable good'.[8]

The Queen made her visits in stylish civilian clothes. She discussed the colours she should wear with her couturier, Norman Hartnell. Black was rejected as too gloomy and not representing 'the rainbow of hope'. Green was never worn. She chose gentle colours – dusty pinks, blues and lilacs. As Hartnell observed: 'She wished to convey the most comforting, encouraging and sympathetic note possible.'[9] The dusty blue colour was a particular favourite in the Dominions when illustrated in magazines.

This was another subtle emphasis on her position as a figure of peace. She wanted to put on her best clothes, explaining that if members of the public came to see her, that is what they would do, and she wished to reciprocate. The brighter colours and crinolines were not appropriate, and these were consigned to the wardrobe. Not once in wartime did the Queen wear uniform, though the Princess Royal and the Duchesses of Gloucester and Kent were obliged to wear theirs.

This wearing of civilian clothes inspired Mary A. Winter of Chicago to pen a little poem in honour of the Queen. It was first published in the *Daily Colonist*, and later sent to *The Times*. So popular did it become that it was soon on postcards and is remembered to this day:

> London Bridge is falling down
> My fair Lady!
> Be it said to your renown
> That you wore your gayest gown
> Your bravest smile, and stayed in town
> When London Bridge was falling down
> My fair Lady.[10]

At much the same time, Joseph Kennedy was describing Queen Elizabeth as 'having more brains than the cabinet',[11] a view to which he adhered but which he was not pleased to see quoted in the press.

As important as the visits was the way these were reported in the newspapers. Sometimes the royal press officer found himself overruled by an officer from the local military police, who would appear 'scared stiff' of letting the press anywhere near the King and Queen. On one occasion the press wanted a photograph of Queen Elizabeth at a military hospital, but the photographers were not allowed in. So the press officer went in and whisked half a dozen wounded patients in hospital blue on to the pavement outside, placing the press opposite. When Queen Elizabeth emerged, she at once spotted the plan and deliberately paused to talk to the men, while the cameras clicked away. On this and many other such occasions the press were grateful and declared: 'She's a brick!'[12]

Similarly, at appropriate moments during the war, pictures were released of the Queen and her daughters at Windsor Castle, in the family circle, the two daughters cycling behind the Queen as she drove a pony cart. She tried to learn to ride a bicycle and one visitor arrived as she was being rescued from the rhododendrons.

Soon after the bombing of Coventry, Bristol was the Germans' target, and in December the Guildhall, eight Wren churches and several commercial buildings in the City of London were destroyed by the showering of incendiaries. St Paul's Cathedral was damaged by bombs but fortunately spared. There were attacks by the British on German cities, and 'a victory of the first order', as Churchill described the advances into the Western Desert, but at the end of 1940 the situation looked bleak.

The King felt guilty to be spending Christmas with his family at Sandringham rather than sharing the plight of Londoners in the capital city. He relished the change of scene and the chance for some outdoor exercise, which he described as a form of 'medicine'. He told his Prime Minister that he hoped to return to London, fresh for the next onslaught against the enemy.[13]

Aware that the Queen might make more speeches, Churchill had sent her Fowler's *Dictionary of Modern Usage*, telling her that it had liberated him from many literary pitfalls.[14] The Queen thanked him, taking a less guilty approach to Christmas. In fact she was pleased that the weather had been so bad, as a result of which they had been detained at Sandringham longer than planned, able to enjoy walking in the fields of Norfolk, as opposed to being 'cooped up' in the grim wartime rooms of Buckingham Palace or the gloom of 'dear' Windsor Castle.[15]

The problems of Prince Paul of Yugoslavia tested George VI severely, in his dual role as British Head of State and close personal friend of the Prince. Of all the European heads of state, the King and Queen knew Prince and Princess Paul best.

Following the assassination of King Alexander of Yugoslavia in 1934, Prince Paul had served faithfully, if reluctantly, as Regent of his country. Geographically he was dangerously situated with more to fear from Hitler than many. Before the war he had done his best to warn the British of the dangers in Europe, though his words fell on stony ground.

On 3 July 1940 the King wrote him a long personal letter, mindful of the new problems faced by Yugoslavia as a result of Italy joining the war against the British. He told him that he admired his neutral stand, and was 'much touched by the evidence which reaches us of the warmth of Yugoslav opinion'. He gave him a detailed report of the progress of the British war effort in respect of the Army, Navy, Air Force and British factories:

> We may have grievous trials to face, but there will be no question
> of faltering. We remain determined to achieve that victory without
> which the peoples of this continent would for an indefinite period
> be exploited and dominated by Nazi masters.[16]

The King wrote again in November 1940, this time in his own hand. He was aware that the situation in Prince Paul's part of the world was now more critical, following Italy's attack on Greece. The King trusted that Prince Paul would never give over the sovereignty of his country. He suggested that Prince Paul might now talk to Greece and Turkey and seek cooperation with those countries. He apologised that Britain could not help with much-needed armaments, explaining that they had lost so many in the fall of France, but he hoped soon to be able to help:

> I wish you could see the spirit of the people here, which despite the violence & indiscriminate bombing of the last two months is truly wonderful. You, who I know are so fond of England, will appreciate the truth of what I say.[17]

The King enclosed an encouraging eight-page summary of the war effort. Prince Paul's brother-in-law, the Duke of Kent, was also in close touch throughout these difficult times, sympathising with him over what he called his 'wobbling neighbours'.[18]

For Yugoslavia the watershed came between January and March 1941. Prince Paul was determined to preserve a united Yugoslavia and to sign no pacts with any other country. In January he was horrified to discover that Churchill intended to send a mechanised force to Greece in order to form a united Balkan front with Yugoslavia as a pawn in a larger game. This plan Prince Paul thought was doomed to failure. Churchill, on the other hand, described the Regent as 'an unfortunate man in a cage with a tiger, hoping not to provoke him while steadily dinner-time approaches'.[19]

In March Prince Paul visited Hitler, spending five hours with him. He returned determined to fight. On 23 March George VI appealed to him in some desperation:

> Reports are reaching me that You are being particularly hard pressed by the Germans to sign an agreement with them which, whatever the reservations, will certainly, if recent history is any guide, mark the first and fatal step in the loss of Your country's independence and integrity.[20]

On his return to Belgrade, there was an uprising in Belgrade and on 27 March the Regency was overthrown. The seventeen-year old King Peter was placed on the throne. Prince and Princess Paul departed into exile, going first to Cairo, and on 28 April they arrived in Kenya to begin a prolonged and depressed existence in that country.

Prince Paul was vilified in the British press, Churchill leading the cry against him and calling him 'Prince Palsy'. Following the line of his Government, the King went silent. Nor did Queen Elizabeth send any messages of support or encouragement. She had learned to subordinate private feelings to duty. But one favour extended to him was the retention of his stall as a Knight of the Garter in St George's Chapel.

The Duke of Kent remained fiercely loyal and supportive. In July he hinted that the King and Queen might do something to ameliorate his plight, explaining that '"they" couldn't find anything else for you at short notice'.[21] Blame continued to rest on Prince Paul, and the Duke explained to him that his name had been blackened by 'the fat one',* who had gone around advancing the unlikely theory that Prince Paul had wanted the Yugoslavian throne for himself. He explained that Churchill thought it better that they stayed in Kenya and that Eden was not going to help, since he felt snubbed that Prince Paul had refused a meeting with him in February 1941.[22]

Governments wasted little time on the plight of individuals in wartime, especially those princes who no longer exercised any political influence. As with the Duke of Windsor, the main consideration was to keep them out of the way. This was the attitude applied to Prince Paul by the British Government, and in this neither the King or Queen Elizabeth was minded to interfere.

Prince Paul wanted to leave Kenya for South Africa, but the Duke of Kent told him: '"They" think it better that you should stay where you are for the present & not go farther south.'[23] Prince Paul felt completely abandoned, forced to live on what capital he could muster, and, unlike most prisoners of his standing, with no one to rely on – neither the Red Cross, nor an ambassador, nor even a foreign consul.

The Duke of Kent was beginning to make some headway when he died on active service. His death in August 1942 removed Prince Paul's only true ally in Britain. In the spring of 1943 General Smuts allowed Prince and Princess Paul to come to South Africa, and, although his liberty was not officially restored until June 1946, the worst of his ordeal was over. But Queen Elizabeth did not resume friendship until the war was won.

More was done for Queen Marie of Yugoslavia, who had been living in England since 1937, first in London and latterly at the Old Mill House, Grandsden, near Cambridge. Now exceptionally fat, and with a tendency to wear military clothes, she shared her home with a 'life-long' lady friend called Rosemary Creswell. Lady Reading was alarmed when Queen Marie announced her wish to drive a mobile canteen for the WVS. Queen Marie was a troublemaker, much disliked by the British Royal Family.

---

* Queen Marie of Yugoslavia (1900–61), daughter of Queen Marie of Romania, widow of King Alexander and mother of the young King Peter.

In June 1941 King Peter was forced to retreat to Britain, and the King, as his 'Koum', or godfather, took some care of him. But Queen Marie was a bad influence, keeping the young King under her wing, as the Duke of Kent reported in November 1941: 'She really is a bitch & we can never see the boy [King Peter] alone.'[24] Lady Astor entertained him at Cliveden, and in 1942 he fell in love with a fellow exile, Princess Alexandra of Greece,* who had left Athens for London with King George II and other members of the Greek Royal Family, when they were forced into exile in April 1941.

King Peter and Princess Alexandra became engaged and wanted to be married. He asked George VI's permission, but was told that he must wait until the King of Greece returned from the USA before proceeding.

When the Greek Royal Family were forced into exile in 1942, the King told the Foreign Office that he would give sanctuary to the exiled King, but not to any heirs to the throne – in other words, not to Crown Prince Paul and Princess Frederika, a granddaughter of the former Kaiser (who had died in exile at Doorn in 1941). Nor would he allow Princess Marina's imperious Russian mother, Princess Nicholas of Greece, to come to England. She was sympathetic to the Nazi generals in Greece and the mother-in-law of Prince Paul.† King George II arrived in London with members of his Government on 22 September 1941, and was publicly greeted by the King and Queen and Winston Churchill. Queen Elizabeth considered the King of Greece a friend.[25]

Predictably, the Duke of Windsor did not remain mute during his exile in the Bahamas. He complained to Lord Halifax about the Duchess's title, suggested he might go so far as to drop his own royal status, and took exception to an article in *Life* magazine‡ in which Queen Elizabeth was quoted as describing the Duchess as 'that woman'. In a message to Churchill he described the remark as a direct insult to the Duchess.[26] Sir Eric Miéville assured Churchill's office that the article was certainly not written with the Queen's knowledge.[27]

In October 1941 the Duke complained to Lord Halifax, by then British Ambassador to the United States, that he had 'done his best to play the game and avoid making difficulties, but that his family had not responded,

---

* Princess Alexandra of Greece (1921–93), posthumous daughter of King Alexander of Greece and his morganatic wife, Aspasia Manos.

† Princess Nicholas remained in Athens throughout the war, as did Princess Andrew of Greece, the mother of Prince Philip, taking a contrasting attitude to the Germans.

‡ The article was written by Alan A. Michie, and published on 17 March 1941.

and he never wanted to see them again'. He went on to say that 'he was completely happy with the most wonderful wife in the world'. Halifax confirmed that the Duke looked very well and was 'much less nervous and much less on edge'. In reporting this to Churchill, he said: 'I have written a bowdlerised account of all this to the King, giving him the general picture, but rather softening down the Duke's observations (so don't show him this letter!).'[28]

The King and Queen maintained as normal a life as possible. They walked together on the terrace of Windsor Castle, talking to the Castle residents. The Queen would give a gardenia to a friend for the lapel, and summoned holy pictures from the Royal Collection for the York Club in the Home Park. Films were shown, Laurence Olivier and Vivien Leigh in *Lady Hamilton* proving as popular in the Castle as it was with Winston Churchill.

Queen Mary remained anxious about the education of the princesses. Crawfie reported to Badminton that the working days were full and began punctually at 9.15. Henry Marten, the Provost of Eton, came up to teach Princess Elizabeth and saw what he called 'great stuff' in her. Before Christmas (1940) he had instructed her in all the explorers and their various discoveries from Columbus to the present day, and the Princess had delivered a lecture on these for an hour, with the aid of a map. The Provost was impressed and paid her the high compliment that she 'compared well with Eton boys a year older than she is'.

Marten then covered the entire history of America, and set the Princess an essay on this. Crawfie enjoyed listening to the Provost as much as Princess Elizabeth did, feeling that she too was learning a lot, and was amused at the way he perambulated up and down the room asking them: 'Is that clear to you gentlemen?'

Crawfie reported that both princesses were playing the piano 'delight-fully and willingly'. They often entertained the Royal Household with duets after lunch on Sundays, without in any sense showing off. Regular tours of Windsor Castle were undertaken. The princesses and their governess assembled in the office of the royal librarian, Sir Owen Morshead, who told them what they would be going to look at, and then conducted the tour. Canon Crawley did the same with St George's Chapel.

Crawfie reported that Princess Margaret was developing 'wonderfully' and becoming 'much more of a companion now for Princess Elizabeth'. She thought Queen Mary would be 'delighted at the change in Princess Margaret', which hints at the desirability for some improvement. The younger princess was full of questions during their lessons. French was also coming along well, and both princesses spoke only French during lunch with a certain Mrs Smith. The conclusion was that both children were 'happy and well; and are having knowledge poured in as fast as I can pour it in'.[29]

In September 1940 and February 1941, Arthur Penn, the Queen's Acting Secretary, told the Astors that it was too difficult for the Queen to visit Plymouth. Lady Astor, their MP, was having none of that. 'Her Majesty promised to come here last year while Waldorf was Lord Mayor, and His Majesty, when he came down, promised that she should too. So don't tell me about a difficult programme,' she retorted. 'Her Majesty has not been here since she was Queen.'[30]

On 20 March the King and Queen visited Plymouth. Just as they were leaving, the sirens sounded. A reconnaissance plane was flying over, and that night the sirens sounded again and the anti-aircraft guns went into action. Bombs and incendiaries fell, subjecting Plymouth to bombing only comparable with that meted out to Coventry.[31] Immediately the Queen wrote to Lady Astor:

> Since early yesterday morning when I first heard of the savage attack on dear Plymouth, I have been thinking of you all without ceasing. I have been praying that the people may be helped to find courage, and ability to face such a terrible ordeal, and I am certain that they have all this spirit already.
>
> Words are not invented to say even mildly what one feels, but having just left you after such a happy and inspiring day, one feels it all so bitterly, and so personally. My heart does truly ache for those good mothers and children and all the splendid workers.[32]

The King and Queen returned to Plymouth on 7 May 1942, a visit deemed 'a howling success'.[33]

On one of these visits, a young Canadian, Bombardier James, locked himself in because he could not bear Queen Elizabeth to see his disfigured face. Lady Astor discovered that his parents were dead, and he only had a half-sister living. He was sent to the Neurological Hospital at Basingstoke for 'appalling operations' to create a new nose, ears and mouth for him, with extensive work on both hands.[34] She asked if the Queen would send him a photograph. Queen Elizabeth duly sent him one with the message that she expected to see him when he was better.[35] Lady Astor reported to the Queen that the arrival of the photograph had caused such excitement that the other patients 'almost wish they had had their faces burnt!'.[36] This consideration by Queen Elizabeth was no isolated incident.

Queen Elizabeth sometimes returned from visits such as the one to Plymouth feeling unaccountably cheerful. She derived comfort from the spirits of the people, who were tackling whatever had to be done, working well as a team and not complaining.[37] This was confirmed by the Duke of Grafton, who, as Earl of Euston, was stationed at Windsor:

> They left the castle at eight in the morning and they used to get back at eight in the evening . . . The staff had their dinner . . . and at about ten o'clock the King and Queen used to join them. And there she was as bright as a button after the most harrowing day, where she had exhausted herself exuding sympathy. But she was always amusing, making jokes and larking around until midnight, and then she was off again the next morning. It was a most extraordinary experience. The King was very highly strung and, I think, exhausted by it and she absolutely kept the whole thing going . . .[38]

On 10 May many historic buildings in London were damaged. Two days later Winston Churchill informed Queen Elizabeth of the safe arrival of a vital convoy of tanks in Egypt under the name of 'Operation Tiger'. Entering into the wild beast analogy, the Queen replied: 'Even though he lacks a claw or two, it is to be hoped that he will still be able to chew up a few enemies'.[39] The Queen was sorry about the damage to the House of Commons and to Westminster Abbey. On 14 May the King and Queen visited the Abbey and the King was shown the damage at the Palace of Westminster. The following month they inspected the damage to St Paul's Cathedral.

When the Queen had visited the bombed house of Beatrice Guinness in Great Cumberland Place in 1940, 'Gloomy Beatrice' sent her to see a housemaid who had worked at Glamis. Queen Elizabeth invited Mrs Guinness to tea. 'At times of stress you must eat chocolates,' she said, helping herself and throwing the wrappers over the back of the sofa. According to the story, she did not offer them to her guest.[40]

In August the Queen prepared a broadcast to the women of America to thank them for their support and to goad them to further efforts. She sent the Prime Minister a draft, explaining that it was largely her composition.[41] Churchill thought it was exactly what was needed, and only made a few changes.[42] The broadcast was delivered on 10 August.

Her text conceded that the enemy had wrought terrible destruction on the cities of England. She spoke of houses ruined, ancient buildings destroyed, women and children killed, and 'even the sufferers in hospital have not been spared'. She thanked the women of America for clothes, food, comfort, canteens, ambulances and medical supplies. She described them as showing 'that compassion of the Good Neighbour'. Her message was as determined as ever:

> Yet hardship has only steeled our hearts and strengthened our reso-
> lution. Wherever I go I see bright eyes and smiling faces, for though
> our road is stony and hard, it is straight, and we know that we fight
> in a great cause.
>   We, like yourselves, love peace and have not devoted the years
> behind us to the planning of death and destruction. As yet, save in
> the valour of our people, we have not matched our enemies . . .[43]

President Roosevelt wrote at once to the King: 'Will you be good enough to tell the Queen that her radio address yesterday was really perfect in every way and that it will do a great amount of good.'[44]

In the latter part of August the Royal Family were able to retreat to Balmoral for a proper break. The King sent Churchill four brace of grouse, which he received 'with great appreciation', and later some venison, which he received with 'pleasure and gratification'.[45] Queen Elizabeth paid a rare visit to her old father at Glamis, taking the princesses with her.

At the end of August, the Canadian Prime Minister, W. L. Mackenzie King, paid them a visit at Balmoral. Mackenzie King was taken to a little cottage on the estate with two rooms where the princesses were playing. He observed Beating the Retreat by the band of the Cameron High-landers on the front lawn, and there was some discussion as to whether Queen Mary should leave Badminton to spend the rest of the war in Canada.

The visiting Prime Minister was intrigued by the Moderator of the Church of Scotland wearing knee breeches at dinner, and the pipers marching round the table. When he left, Queen Elizabeth 'walked alone into a small sunken garden filled with most beautiful roses'.[46] The King reported that Mackenzie King had been on his best behaviour.

17

Deaths and Diplomacy

'Why do I have to pretend I know nothing about
Mrs Greville's will?' – Queen Elizabeth

On the night of 7/8 December 1941 Japan bombed Pearl Harbor and declared war on the United States and Great Britain. Britain and America immediately declared war on Japan, and within the next few days Germany and Italy declared war on the United States.

A peripheral side effect of Japan's entry into the war was that Emperor Hirohito lost his rank as a field marshal in the British Army, one of those curious appointments that had been made for diplomatic reasons. On 26 January 1942 it was announced that his name had been struck from the roll of the Order of the Garter and his banner was removed from above his stall in St George's Chapel.*

During those dark days, the King and Queen lived a Spartan existence at Buckingham Palace with most of the rooms closed. They organised a small flat on the fourth floor of Fitzmaurice Place, near Curzon Street, to which they could retreat in secret if need be. This was partly for safety and partly because so many of the Palace staff had been called up to active service. In practice they only saw it once, and after the bombing of Schomberg House in Pall Mall it became the home of the spinster princesses, Helena Victoria and Marie Louise.

In March 1942 Cosmo Lang retired as Archbishop of Canterbury. When he told the King and Queen he was going, Queen Elizabeth told him that this was 'no time for the leadership of elderly gentlemen'.[1] He settled at the King's Cottage, Kew Green,† with a generous financial settlement of £15,000 from his American friend and benefactor, J. P. Morgan, and was created Lord Lang of Lambeth.

---

* The Emperor himself seems to have been unaware of this, since presumably he did not read *The Times* during the war. In 1952 he made enquiries as to whether he should wear what he called his 'Garter rosette' when receiving the new British Ambassador. He was not restored to the Order until 1971 when he came on a controversial state visit to Britain, but even then the fuss was minimal compared to that made in the press when his son, Emperor Akihito, was given the Garter in 1998.
† This house was formerly leased to 'Baby Bee', Infanta Beatrice, one of whose sons, the King believed, might have bombed Buckingham Palace (see footnote, p.217).

Though some wanted Geoffrey Fisher to succeed him, William Temple, the Archbishop of York, was the obvious successor, despite his adherence to left-wing politics. Temple was only there a short time, dying in October 1944, at which time Fisher succeeded him.

Throughout the war Queen Elizabeth continued her cultural programme, attending concerts by Myra Hess at the National Gallery,* visiting galleries and buying more pictures, among them *Martigues* by Arnold H. Mason and *Yachts in the Cutting, Blakeney*, by Sir Walter W. Russell. On 20 May she visited the Tate Gallery to see their wartime acquisitions and in June she loaned her John Pipers of Windsor Castle to an exhibition at the National Gallery.

In August 1942, the Royal Family were able to steal a summer holiday at Balmoral. It rained every day, but on 24 August the Queen reported: 'The sun shone and the hills looked gloriously beautiful & the heather was dry & one felt a little balm from such beauty steal into one's soul.'[2]

On the same evening, following a cold, dark and wet day, the Royal Family were at dinner when the King was called to the telephone. The first thought was that Queen Mary must have died, but it was the Duke of Kent, who had been killed in an air crash in thick fog at Berriedale in Sutherland, on his way to a military duty in Iceland.† A few days later, the family gathered at St George's Chapel, Windsor, for the funeral, and the Duke's coffin was lowered into the Royal Vault.

The death of the Duke of Kent was a great sorrow to the Royal Family, primarily to his young widow, who was now left to bring up her young family, including the baby Prince Michael, born that July. The King was only comforted by the fact that, technically, his brother had died on active service.‡

The grief of Princess Marina so affected the King and Queen that the King asked Churchill's permission for Princess Olga to come to England to comfort her younger sister. The request was controversial since Prince and Princess Paul were still at the height of their unpopularity.

---

* Following one such visit, an acerbic critic wrote of Hess's collaboration with the Central Band of the RAF: 'Orchestral concerts are rare at the National Gallery and should remain so – brass and drums were mercifully absent' (*The Times*, 13 June 1941).

† The cause of death was given as 'due to war operations, compound fracture of skull, flying accident'. Hon. Michael Strutt (brother of Lavinia, Duchess of Norfolk) was also killed, as was Squadron Leader A. J. Law, RAF.

‡ Princess Marina was the only war widow in Britain whose estate was forced to pay death duties. The King said he would take care of the Kent family financially, particularly since he was not entertaining in wartime and funds were available. Princess Marina was never given a Civil List allowance, despite undertaking a full round of royal engagments. In March 1947 she sold furniture, porcelain, pictures and drawings at Christie's, in more than four hundred lots.

Princess Olga's arrival in England was spotted by the maverick M. P. Alec ('Bobbie') Cunningham-Reid, a former brother-in-law of Edwina Mountbatten, who made several parliamentary interventions, stirring up yet more hostile feelings in Britain towards Prince Paul. He went so far as to suggest that, on her return to Kenya, Princess Olga might 'be able to convey information to her quisling husband which might be invaluable to the Axis'.[3] Despite this, Princess Olga stayed with her sister until December and had several private meetings with the King and Queen.

When she left, Princess Olga took with her a letter from the King to Prince Paul inviting him to send an account of what had happened to him, if he so wished.[4]

On 19 September 1941 tragedy hit the Strathmore family when Queen Elizabeth's nephew, John, the Master of Glamis, eventual heir to the Earldom of Strathmore, was killed in an action at Halifaya Pass serving with the Scots Guards.* In due course, the Queen was glad to hear that the Germans marked his grave well.

The Queen's nephew, John Elphinstone, was captured and incarcerated in Colditz, where he was later joined by the King's nephew, Viscount Lascelles, wounded and captured in 1944. On account of their connections, they were among 'the Prominenti'. Martin Gilliat, later to be the Queen Mother's Secretary, was also an inmate. Of John Elphinstone he wrote: 'He was probably the kindest, most undemanding and most understanding friend one has ever had.' Gilliat commended 'how totally good he was in captivity . . . When the moment came he took command and almost certainly saved the lives of the other Prominenti.'[5]

Hardly had the Duke of Kent been laid to rest than Mrs Ronnie Greville died on 15 September, aged seventy-eight, appropriately at the Dorchester, where many of her ilk, such as Lady Cunard, were living during the war. Mindful of their close friendship, the King and Queen sent Sir Eric Miéville to represent them at her funeral in Great Bookham Church. 'I shall miss her very much,'[6] wrote Queen Elizabeth to Osbert Sitwell. Mrs Greville was then buried in the Lady's Garden at Polesden Lacey.

Her obituary stated that 'it pleased her to use the great wealth which she inherited for the purposes of a wide but discriminating hospitality'.[7] In death she continued to give to the rich. From her fortune of £1,564,038 8s 3d gross (reduced to £1,505,120 5s 10d net),[8] she bequeathed to Queen Elizabeth 'with my loving thoughts all my jewels and jewellery except

* The new heir after Lord Glamis was John's younger brother Timothy, who was attached to the Black Watch, but retired due to ill health in 1944.

such as is hereby or by any Codicil hereto specifically bequeathed', and a legacy of £20,000 to Princess Margaret, a sizeable sum.

Mrs Greville had owned a fantastic collection of jewels. She wore jewels to impress, preferring size to quality and provenance. She was disparaging about the jewels of others. When a rich American lady lost the principal diamond of her necklace, and the guests scrambled for it on the floor, Mrs Greville was heard addressing a footman: 'Perhaps this might be of assistance?' She proffered a magnifying glass.[9] When asked what she thought about Lady Granard's fabulous pearls, she was dismissive: 'I thought it better not to look.'[10]

James Lees-Milne, one of those involved with the bequest of Polesden Lacey to the National Trust, wrote in 1942: 'Mrs Greville has left Marie Antoinette's necklace to the Queen',[11] and others have written of Empress Josephine's emeralds and diamonds, and a diamond ring that had belonged to Catherine the Great.

The bequest to the Queen included the openwork diamond tiara, designed by Lucien Hirtz, which Mrs Greville had ordered from Boucheron in January 1921.* There was a magnificent five-strand diamond necklace, a set of diamond earrings (worn by the Queen Mother in the open landau on her 100th birthday on 4 August 2000), a set of heavy chandelier earrings later given to Princess Elizabeth as a wedding present from her parents, and much more besides.

When these jewels were handed to Queen Elizabeth at Buckingham Palace towards the end of 1942, she said to Gerald Russell, Mrs Greville's solicitor: 'Why do I have to pretend I know nothing about Mrs Greville's will, when everyone I meet informs me that she has left her property to the National Trust?'[12]

For many years these jewels remained in their boxes.† First, it was wartime, and, secondly, the King may have had reservations about the bequest. Queen Elizabeth wore the Boucheron tiara in South Africa in 1947, and when dining at the return banquets for the French and Dutch state visits in 1950 and the Danish in 1951. Only after the King's death, in the latter months of 1953, did she have the tiara remodelled, adding some diamonds (given by de Beers to Edward, Prince of Wales, in 1900), in order to give it additional height and to make it look more regal. It lost style in the transformation.

* Mrs Greville wore this at her party for the King of Italy at her Charles Street house in 1924, when it was described as 'platinum in the favourite Empire shape' (*Tatler*, 1924 – quoted in Geoffrey C. Munn, *Tiaras* (Antique Collectors Club, 2001), p. 153).
† Chips Channon thought that the 'splendid rubies' Queen Elizabeth wore at an Ascot ball in June 1949 were Mrs Greville's (*Chips*, p. 438), but they were the rubies that a Maharajah gave to Queen Victoria.

Queen Elizabeth seldom wore the five-strand Cartier necklace of brilliant and baguette diamonds in public. But it came out in Rhodesia in 1957 and for General de Gaulle's state visit in 1960.* She sometimes wore it for private engagements, where it did not fail to impress even those who did not normally notice such things. By then she had reduced it to three strands.†

The acceptance of gifts is always a problem for the Royal Family. In 1947, Queen Elizabeth accepted the magnificent Mecklenburg service (shown in The Queen's Gallery from 2002 to 2005) from a certain James Oakes, a well-known industrialist in the pottery business in Derbyshire.

Queen Elizabeth's old father was living in retirement at Glamis, cared for by a nurse and gradually declining into senility. Her brothers were too old to play an active part fighting, and the only brother who played a significant role was her younger one, David Bowes-Lyon.

David was closest to Queen Elizabeth in age and companionship. They had been inseparable as children. When he died, he was afforded a fulsome obituary in *The Times*, which paid tribute to his contributions as a financier in the City of London, in Hertfordshire, in the world of horticulture, at the British Museum, of which he was a Trustee after 1953, and indeed as a director of *The Times*.

Bowes-Lyon was described as having a never-failing sense of humour, being genial and kind, and 'perhaps the most humorous and delightful person that many of us have ever known or probably ever will know'.[13] His charm and gaiety 'never clouded his judgement, nor prevented his acute mind from seizing upon the over-riding consideration in any issue'.[14]

Among his qualities was his ability to deflate overpersistent arguers at meetings by 'some lightly barbed comment' from which it was impossible to take umbrage. The Bishop of St Albans wrote of his strong faith and how he had given himself to God.

Yet not everyone liked him. One courtier described him as 'a man of extreme right wing views and a baleful influence at court'.[15] He was mistrusted as being likely to tell his sister all manner of things. He was inclined to extreme views, describing Robert Birley, headmaster of Eton, as 'a Communist'.[16] Though married, he was primarily homosexual. Cecil Beaton recorded a strange tale about an all-male weekend at St Paul's when a young man was bidden to wear football shorts, a

---

* For de Gaulle's state visit, the Queen Mother summoned her circlet with the Koh-i-noor diamond. It arrived under escort from the Tower of London.
† The author photographed Her Majesty wearing it at a private dinner party in March 1994 – see illustration.

sweater and heaving hobnail shoes, 'in which he subsequently ate his dinner before the long built-up defiling act took place. Where do surprises end?'[17]

James Lees-Milne confirmed the liking for shorts. In 1948 he described Bowes-Lyon as dressed in a blue shirt with no collar, bare neck, suede shoes and 'tight trousers'. The next day Bowes-Lyon enquired of the young diarist: 'Did I not think women's thighs ugly? Men's figures more aesthetic? Did I like wearing shorts? He did not approve of any sexual practices – and so on.'[18] Within the year, Lees-Milne again met the Bowes-Lyons, 'he insinuating all sorts of forbidden things in veiled terms and proposing a trip with me in the spring . . .'.[19]

In 1940 Bowes-Lyon was employed as press officer at the Ministry of Economic Warfare, where he remained until 1941. He made sure that favoured correspondents were invited to Buckingham Palace for tea with Queen Elizabeth. An unlikely assignment was to play a cameo role in the 1941 film *The Big Blockade*, directed by Charles Frend, which gave the propaganda message that Britain was isolating Germany and hampering their efforts.

Bowes-Lyon then joined the Special Operations Executive (SOE), a new organisation established by Churchill for sabotage and subversion. He worked directly under Rex Leeper who was in charge of 'Country Operations' at Woburn Abbey. Here, on 19 November 1941, the King and Queen visited the operations.

Bowes-Lyon dreamed up the name of Political Warfare Executive (PWE) for this and served under Robert Bruce Lockhart, Rex Leeper and Dallas Brooks. This was an organisation which broadcast to enemy countries and occupied territories. In November 1941 Bowes-Lyon took over at the SOE's office in the United States until he was recalled in May 1942.

In March that year he presented President Roosevelt with a long personal letter from the King, thanking him for his plans to help Britain and proclaiming his confidence that Britain would eventually win the war. Bowes-Lyon forged good relations with the President. Before he left in May, he thanked him for sparing him personal time to discuss affairs of mutual interest and to support his organisation. He apologised for the occasional argument, though added: 'I cannot deny that I enjoy a good argument.' He left Washington having made a great number of good friends there 'and no man can ask more than that'.[20]

In June 1942 there was a Foreign Office plot to prevent him from going back to Washington. Lord Halifax had to intervene and to soothe the furious King by warning him 'how ready ill-deposed Senators would have been to say that we were trying to cash in on the affection felt for the King and Queen by such an appointment'.[21]

Halifax considered Bowes-Lyon useful to the King and Queen for news they might not obtain elsewhere. He was able to warn the King that Lord Beaverbrook was intriguing to have Sir John Dill removed as Churchill's special emissary in Washington.

Thus Bowes-Lyon returned to Washington as Head of the Political Warfare Mission. His task was to establish relations with similar American agencies on a confidential basis, and to establish an organisation which would coordinate Anglo-American relations. When he died, *The Times* wrote that some of this work had remained secret and that Bowes-Lyon had extended the work beyond his brief: 'At one stage he took a particular interest in Far Eastern affairs as well as those in Washington. He himself never talked very much about the work he did in the war years.'[22]

Bowes-Lyon established a strong social position and engaged in 'functions far beyond the range (limited) of his ability'.[23] But there were assertions that he had been 'irresponsible',[24] and talk of 'indiscretions in Washington',[25] and in July 1942 there was a crisis involving a clash between the SOE and the PWE.

Robert Bruce Lockhart was suspicious of him. He recorded a description of him as 'pleasant but highly unintelligent'.[26] In March 1942 Brendan Bracken criticised his 'intriguing'.[27] By May 1943 Bruce Lockhart thought he had 'grown in political stature and self-control',[28] wanted all intelligence to go through him, and was puzzled by his remark: 'The trouble about me, Bertie, is that I am not ambitious.'[29]

There was then a move to appoint Bowes-Lyon Governor of Bermuda, but his wife Rachel told Churchill that she 'could not think of anything more ghastly'.[30] Bowes-Lyon himself schemed to have the Duke of Windsor moved from the Bahamas to a post further from the United States. Bermuda, the island he himself had turned down, was one possibility. Bowes-Lyon remained in Washington until the autumn of 1944, after which there was some talk of his becoming High Commissioner in Canada.

By November 1944, John Wheeler-Bennett was telling Bruce Lockhart of his 'low opinion' of Bowes-Lyon's character, and that 'his capacity for intrigue and untruthfulness has almost no limit'. He reported that Bowes-Lyon used to take photostats of secret documents that he was allowed to see but not keep, including those of the European Advisory Commission. Bruce Lockhart concluded: 'If this were known in London, David would be sacked, King's brother-in-law notwithstanding.'[31]

Queen Elizabeth's invitation to Mrs Roosevelt to see the war efforts of British and American women in England was of supreme importance. The Queen wanted her to see what Britain was enduring so that she could report directly to the President. To this end she and the King had written regularly to the Roosevelts.

In 1942 it took time for the images of war to reach the United States. In the days before television, news photographs, books and magazines sometimes arrived many weeks after the event. A prime example is the haunting photograph of the bombed-out child in hospital, taken by Cecil Beaton, which became the front cover of *Life* magazine in September 1940. It was instantly adopted as the poster for the William Allen White Committee in the United States and can still stir hearts to this day.

Queen Elizabeth was recovering from bronchitis (which gave her the first enforced chance of relaxing since the outbreak of war) when she accompanied the King to Paddington to greet Mrs Roosevelt, who finally arrived on 23 October after a journey delayed by fog. The Queen said: 'We welcome you with all our hearts. We have been looking forward to your visit with the greatest pleasure.' Anthony Eden, the Foreign Secretary, General Dwight D. Eisenhower, and the redoubtable Stella, Marchioness of Reading,* were also on the platform to greet her.

At Buckingham Palace Queen Elizabeth showed Mrs Roosevelt to her sitting room with but one small fire, the bath marked with a black line to permit no more than five inches of water, the windows covered in wood, isinglass with tiny panes of glass, and heavy curtains to be closely drawn at night. The Queen showed her where a bomb had destroyed some of their private rooms.

Queen Elizabeth smiled blandly while Cecil Beaton photographed Mrs Roosevelt with the Royal Family that afternoon. Mrs Roosevelt, 'enormous, over life-sized . . . elephant coloured . . . her hair nondescript',[32] was posed in front of bare cupboards which annoyed the King, but gave a good wartime message. After the sitting the Queen told Beaton that she thought Mrs Roosevelt was perpetually animated, and no doubt thinking she was still performing for movie cameras.

After dinner attended by Churchill, Smuts and Mountbatten, they screened *In Which We Serve*, a fictionalised account of the sinking of HMS *Kelly*, for their American guest.

---

* Queen Elizabeth described Lady Reading as 'a born leader whose courage and unflagging energy have never failed to sustain all who have worked for her' (opening of WVS Club at 41 Cadogan Square, 4 June 1947). She was once sitting at Buckingham Palace with Lady Reading during one of the air raids on London. She longed to retreat from the window, but the presence of this doughty figure inhibited her from so doing.

During the next days the King and Queen gave Mrs Roosevelt a personal tour of war-torn London, showing her St Paul's Cathedral with its nave open to the sky, and the devastated East End of London. Mrs Roosevelt continued her tour of Britain until mid-November. Before leaving, she visited Queen Mary at Badminton and called to see Queen Elizabeth at Windsor Castle. When Churchill met Roosevelt at Casablanca in January 1943, he took with him a letter from the King, who wrote: 'The Queen & I were so delighted to entertain Mrs Roosevelt here last October, & we hope that she returned to you none the worse for her strenuous visit.'[33] Mrs Roosevelt herself concluded that the King and Queen were 'doing an extraordinarily good job for their people in the most trying times'. She admired 'their character and their devotion to duty'.[34]

18

The Tide Turns

'It really is rather a bore to feel that one might be blown to pieces at any moment' – Queen Elizabeth

In March 1943 Queen Elizabeth worried over a broadcast to the Women of the Empire. Her aim was to congratulate the women of Britain for their tackling of jobs usually undertaken by men. She realised that after the war their roles would revert to being wives and mothers, which might not be easy.

The Queen settled on Sunday 11 April as the most appropriate date for the broadcast. One of those whose advice she sought was Winston Churchill. She sent him a draft and asked for stern criticism.[1] He read it 'with agreement and admiration', adding but a few lines: 'The important thing is to have Your Majesty's own words and feelings'.[2]

Queen Elizabeth's theme was 'the case of right against wrong'. She spoke of her constant travels the length and breadth of England with the King, and how this gave her 'a clear picture of the astonishing work' that women were doing everywhere. Often they told her: 'Oh well, it's not much. I'm just doing my best to help us win the war.' The Queen ended with the message: 'It is the creative and dynamic power of Christianity which can help us to carry the moral responsibilities which history is placing upon our shoulders.'[3] Churchill congratulated her: 'The Broadcast was an outstanding success. Your Majesty's voice was clear and captivating and I heard from every side nothing but praise and expressions of pleasure and high sentiment.'[4]

The Queen also thanked Archbishop Lord Lang for his congratulations: 'The moment I had finished, I thought of so many things I would have liked to say . . .' She wanted to stress the importance of war work but remind them of the greater importance of a Christian home: 'I felt that some of it was naïve and simple, but if you approve, well, I feel happier.'*[5]

---

* This was the last of Queen Elizabeth's letters to Lang. On 5 December 1945 he was hurrying to catch a train at Kew to keep an appointment at the Natural History Museum. He stumbled and fell, dying soon afterwards of heart failure. He was eighty-one.

Queen Elizabeth worried about the absence of press attention concerning the King's activities, a matter of concern throughout the war. They minded the lack of photographs and the brevity of reports of their activities. In July 1942 Sir Eric Miéville enumerated the problems. The newspapers were smaller than in peacetime, two pages as opposed to four, and breaking war news inevitably took precedence. There was too much sameness to many of the King and Queen's activities. The King made eleven troop visits in four months, but one division of troops looked much like another, especially when the War Office forbade shoulder badges to be reproduced in the papers. Visits to Scotland, Northern Ireland and the provinces received good local coverage, but were of less interest to London readers.

The King and Queen wanted to employ a journalist to take charge of all press arrangements. There was a plan to consult Robert Barrington-Ward, editor of *The Times*, about this appointment, the man going ahead to deal with press arrangements in advance of royal visits.

In March 1943 Queen Elizabeth complained that the King's visits were either being completely ignored or placed in what she called the 'snippets' columns in national newspapers. Queen Elizabeth was gravely irritated and suggested that a tame press man might be employed to smooth the path. These plans to control and manipulate the press were no more successful during the war than they would be in later years.

Meanwhile Queen Elizabeth continued her cultural activities which, that summer, included visits to Lady Cripps's exhibition at the Wallace Collection to raise funds for her United Aid to China Fund, a trip to the ballet, and a visit to the Strand Theatre with the princesses to see *Arsenic and Old Lace*. Osbert Sitwell prevailed on her to be patron of an event at the Aeolian Hall on 14 April – a poetry reading organised by himself and his sister, Edith, in aid of Lady Crewe's French in Britain Fund. He persuaded Beatrice Lillie to be a celebrity programme seller. The Queen brought the two princesses with her. It was an uncomfortable occasion. Sitwell had found a large Victorian lectern in the Caledonian Market, which impeded vision of the readers and impaired the sound. The poets filed in – John Masefield, T. S. Eliot, Gordon Bottomley, Arthur Waley, Edmund Blunden, Vita Sackville-West and others.

As Poet Laureate, John Masefield paid tribute to Laurence Binyon, who had died in March. Then Eliot read his 'London Bridge is Falling Down' from *The Waste Land*, which caused the princesses to giggle. Walter de la Mare, unable to reach the height of the lectern, read 'The Listeners', and W. J. Turner went on too long and had to be silenced. In the interval the Queen met the poets informally in an anteroom while an incident occurred in the hall.

The poet Dorothy Wellesley* was sitting in the audience during the first half, and intended coming up to the platform for the second. But she was drunk and told Sitwell that she would not read. Then she changed her mind and created a disturbance in the main hall. There are many versions of what happened next. Beatrice Lillie attempted to establish order by enfolding her in a jujitsu grip and pinning her to her seat. Then the poet Stephen Spender tried to knock her down, the critic Raymond Mortimer lured her out into Bond Street where, according to Edith Sitwell, she sat down on the pavement, banged her stick and used 'frightful language about A the Queen and B me'.[6] Harold Nicolson and Vita Sackville-West forcibly prevented her from taking the stage, while she belaboured Nicolson with her stick in the belief that he was Osbert Sitwell.

Queen Elizabeth was not unaware of this commotion. When Rex Whistler came to stay at Sandringham soon afterwards, they discussed 'that fantastic *Poetry-reading orgy*',[7] and all bellowed with laughter. Whistler found the King in good form and observed that the Royal Family gave the impression 'they hadn't a care in the world!'[8]

In fact the King was planning his trip to North Africa. Churchill did not want the Foreign Secretary, Anthony Eden, to go and there was the question of who would be in attendance besides Alec Hardinge. Dermot McMorrough Kavanagh,† the Crown Equerry, was considered and rejected in favour of Piers Legh,‡ the Master of the Household, who had more experience, was a good traveller, and whom the King knew better.

The Queen then heard that Hardinge was intending to send Kavanagh on ahead to make the necessary arrangements, and expressed her concerns. She was far from pleased to hear that Kavanagh had been dispatched ahead to Gibraltar.

The King left for North Africa on 11 June with Hardinge and others in attendance. In his absence the Queen's standard (the Royal Arms halved with those of the Bowes-Lyons) flew over Buckingham Palace, and she acted as Counsellor of State.

---

* Dorothy Wellesley (1889–1956), estranged wife of Lord Gerald Wellesley. She became Duchess of Wellington in September 1943. She was an alcoholic and spent some time in her later life at a Catholic residential home with an alcoholic unit, Iden Manor, Staplehurst, Kent.
† (Sir) Dermot McMorrough Kavanagh (1890–1958), equerry to the King 1937–41, Crown Equerry 1941–55.
‡ Hon. (Sir) Piers (Joey) Legh (1890–1955), equerry to the King 1936–46, Master of the Household 1941–54. Equerry to the Prince of Wales 1919–36.

It was an exhausting trip, the King and his party visiting Gibraltar and Tripoli, inspecting the victorious 8th Army and seven thousand of the Western Desert Air Force. They went to Malta, the island to which the King had given the George Cross, and eventually the King's plane touched down at RAF Northolt at 6 a.m. on the morning of 25 June.

Three hours after they landed, Tommy Lascelles, the Assistant Private Secretary, informed the exhausted Hardinge that he intended to resign due to their approach to matters being at variance, thus making further cooperation between them untenable. Lascelles made it clear that his decision was not based on a particular incident.[9] The root of the problem was that Lascelles had felt unable to advise the Counsellors of State in Hardinge's absence because he had not been shown the Letters Patent. Hardinge maintained that as the King's Private Secretary, he was serving the King. Lascelles felt that he should have been given more responsibility.

The King had tried to move Hardinge on as early as Christmas 1938, offering him the Governorship of Madras. Though Hardinge had guided the King through the early days after the Accession, they had disagreed over appeasement and Churchill.

There followed an angry exchange of letters between Hardinge and Lascelles, and even when it seemed that some rapport was being re-established between the two men, Lascelles informed Hardinge that he was still unable to work with him.[10] Worn down by the complaints, tired, and aware that he was due to retire soon, Hardinge wrote to the King offering his resignation. The King accepted it, writing him a letter assuring him of continued warm feelings to him and to his wife, Helen.*[11]

The question remains as to which forces had operated to remove Hardinge. David Bowes-Lyon had been conspiring for his removal since 1941, even when away in Washington. Mrs Greville, an aggressive pro-appeaser, had frequently blackened his name to the Queen. The King was not involved in his departure in any way, but the Queen and Lascelles may well have conspired in his absence. If so, her tracks were well covered though Oliver Harvey, then Anthony Eden's right-hand man at the Foreign Office, detected her hand:

H. was the perfect Private Secretary for the King. He had a mind of his own and didn't hesitate to state it. But there has been friction for some time (beginning from Munich and Neville

---

* Hardinge had served three Kings. His resignation was said to be for 'ill health'. He was appointed GCB.

Chamberlain), largely caused by the Queen who was determined to get him out . . . The King is fundamentally a weak character and certainly a rather stupid one. The Queen is a strong one out of a rather reactionary stable.[12]

Helen Hardinge thought the Queen might have been involved and said as much to her on 8 July. She was rebuked: 'She's very angry with me for believing they could have ill-wished Alec.'[13]

Lascelles was probably not the instigator even though he effected the resignation. He could be 'a dour figure' at breakfast at Balmoral, he was sometimes 'irascible',[14] and he could be ruthless, but those who worked with him do not recall him as a conspirator. He now took over as Private Secretary and remained in position until some months after the Accession of the present Queen.

When Montgomery won his victory at El Alamein in 1942, Churchill told the King and Queen: 'This means we will win the war.' But as the Queen Mother mentioned at her last lunch party in March 2002: 'We did not dare believe him.'[15]

Meanwhile, the King and Queen continued their visits to the bombed areas, often going to Clydeside, attending appropriate thanksgiving services when victories were won, inspecting parades, the King issuing medals such as the African Star to all those who had fought in North Africa, and other such activities.

In November 1943, for the first time since the outbreak of war, an Armistice Day service was held at the Cenotaph attended by the King and Queen, the Duke and Duchess of Gloucester, the Duchess of Kent and the Regent of Iraq (then in London, visiting the King and Queen).

On 18 December, the princesses performed in *Aladdin* at the Castle, Princess Elizabeth taking the lead male role, while Princess Margaret played Princess Roxana, and the young Duke of Kent and Princess Alexandra were in the supporting cast. The King and Queen came to the performance with the Duchess of Kent, Princesses Helena Victoria and Marie Louise, and, significantly, Prince Philip of Greece, then on leave from the Navy, and a regular visitor to the Castle.

In May 1944 there was an extraordinary clash of wills between the King and his Prime Minister over the proposed Normandy landings. They both contemplated the idea of sailing in one of the bombarding warships on D-Day. In this there was an element of schoolboy bravado. Lascelles succeeded in dissuading the King by asking him to brief Princess Elizabeth (then just of age at eighteen) as to who she should appoint as

Prime Minister in the event of the King and Churchill being killed. This focused the King's mind on the recklessness of the escapade.

Churchill, however, was determined to sail and brushed aside arguments about the gravity of finding a new wartime Prime Minister if he were killed. He bridled at the King's description of the trip as 'a joy ride'.

Churchill headed to Portsmouth by train. The King contemplated going to Portsmouth and commanding him not to embark. But finally Churchill succumbed to a telephone call from Lascelles. Even then he wrote to the King, complaining about unnecessary curbs on what he called 'my freedom of movement when I judge it necessary to acquaint myself with conditions in the various theatres of war'.[16]

The King was able to go over to Normandy on 14 June, eight days after the successful landings, to visit General Montgomery and to decorate officers and to visit Naples on 23 July. Further landings were successfully made in the South of France on 15 August, and Paris was liberated from its long years of German occupation on 25 August. In September Allied forces advanced into Germany. In October the King went to the Dutch/Belgian front for five days. The war was entering its final stage.

The King had kept a benign eye on young King Peter of Yugoslavia since his arrival in London in May 1941. As he was his 'Koum', he assumed responsibility for his education and the issue of his marriage. The young King had fallen in love with Princess Alexandra of Greece, another royal exile, who had likewise arrived in London and settled into a flat in Mayfair, which she shared with her mother, Princess Aspasia, who was said to possess the evil eye.

The King had insisted on a delay in the marriage since the couple were so young, and since King Peter's difficult mother, Queen Marie, was set against it. Churchill was for the union, declaring: 'Nothing could be more becoming than that a young king should marry a highly suitable princess on the eve of his departure for war. Thus he has a chance of perpetuating his dynasty, and anyhow of giving effect to those primary instincts to which the humblest of human beings have a right.'[17]

In 1943, after winning his wings in the RAF, King Peter had gone to Cairo, from where, King George VI hoped in vain, he might regain the throne of Yugoslavia. In February 1944 the King was told that King Peter was attracted to Alexandra, fond of her, not deeply in love but in honour bound to her. The King invited the young couple to Windsor and formally gave his permission for the wedding to take place in London.

On 20 March 1944 the King served as King Peter's best man at the wedding at the Yugoslav Embassy. Queen Elizabeth attended, as did Princess Aspasia, King George II of Greece, King Haakon of Norway, Queen Wilhelmina of the Netherlands, Prince Bernhard of the Netherlands, the Duke of Gloucester, the Duchess of Kent, Anthony Eden and others. Queen Marie, the difficult mother, was 'indisposed'. The time and place of the wedding were kept secret until after the event.*

Princess Elizabeth reached her eighteenth birthday on 21 April 1944, which meant that she was of age and could succeed as Queen without the regency of her uncle, the Duke of Gloucester. There was a family celebration at Windsor, to which Queen Mary came from Badminton, and the Princess took the salute as Colonel of Grenadier Guards in which she had succeeded the Duke of Connaught after his death in January 1942.

In advance of this birthday, Cecil Beaton was summoned to photograph the Princess. He went to the Palace to discuss the sitting with the Queen, finding her in her sitting room: 'cascades of spider chrysanthemums, a Richard Wilsman on easel, with a large Paul Nash propped beneath it, early Victorian pictures on the brocade walls, poor furniture, awful upholstery, a mass of photographs of the family & books'.[18] Queen Elizabeth was reading a book on Cézanne and Renoir, and her table was covered with war books. On some papers was a printed notice in red: 'Do it now.'

She came in from listening to the six o'clock news on the wireless, 'fresh & fat & leisurely, exuding serenity'. Beaton pressed for Windsor Castle as a setting as this would appeal to the Americans who were always demanding something original. 'May I ask the King if that would be alright?' asked the Queen. In a conversation that roamed over the merits of men being better dressmakers than women, Beaton finally said he would hate not to be outside the railings of the Palace when the armistice was signed to cheer her on the balcony.

'The balcony – since the bombing – isn't really safe,' said Queen Elizabeth.

'But the news, Ma'am, is so good, shouldn't it be reinforced at once?'

---

* King Peter and Queen Alexandra had one son, the present Crown Prince Alexander of Yugoslavia, born in 1945, to whom Princess Elizabeth was godmother. King Peter never regained his throne and roamed the world after the war as an unhappy exile. After moving restlessly between Paris, St Moritz and Monte Carlo, the couple moved to America in 1948. King Peter lost all his money, and became involved in a series of extra-marital entanglements. The marriage declined into a series of suicide attempts by Queen Alexandra, separations, periods of reconciliation and more separations. King Peter died aged forty-seven in 1970, Queen Alexandra lived in Venice until being brought back to England by her son. She died in a nursing home in Sussex in 1993 at the age of seventy-one.

'Wouldn't that be courting a setback? Perhaps we'd better have all the materials ready – standing by – the cement & stones piled in a corner.'

The Paul Nash painting was on loan from Arthur Tooth for a week, on the recommendation of Sir Jasper Ridley; the Queen was not sure if she would buy it. Beaton thought *The Landscape of the Vernal Equinox* (as it was then called),* a work rather hard to define, but presently the Queen did buy it.

At this meeting the Queen asked Beaton if he thought that, with all this suffering, the French would experience 'a tremendous new renaissance of painting'. He said he thought it a shame that the French currently in Britain squabbled and played politics to such a degree. The Queen laughed 'wistfully' and commented, raising her eyebrows in mid-sentence: 'But they're – so French!'[19]

The sitting at Windsor gave Beaton the chance to take in something of the royal life there even if he was disappointed that the princesses did not seem to have had their hair washed in honour of his visit. In particular he observed Sir Gerald Kelly 'who has been in the household painting one bad picture after another for the last 4 years. Everyone groans at his continual presence but seem incapable of ousting him.' Kelly kept his elbows on the table throughout lunch, and, after the Royal Family had filed out, 'rushed back to finish his coffee and port'.[20]

One of the books in the Queen's sitting room was *Darkness over Germany* by Amy Buller,† a book recommended by Edward Woods, Bishop of Lichfield. It opened with two images of Hitler from 1935 and 1937, showing his descent into madness. Amy Buller was born in London in 1891, but raised in South Africa. She studied in Germany and took a post with the Student Christian Movement. In 1931 she became Warden of University Hall, Liverpool, visiting Germany often and witnessing the rise of the Nazi Party at first hand.

She wrote her book to try to find out why so many Germans, coming as they did from such a cultured and civilised nation and passing through the great German universities, could have been lured into supporting the philosophy of Nazism. She was horrified that they did not use their critical judgement to assess what was happening under their very eyes. She concluded that due to the weakening hold of Christianity people were seduced by false gods.

---

* It was a spring fantasy in which the idea of equal day and night was represented by the sun and moon shining at the same time. Some of its features were taken from the Berkshire Downs, with Wittenham Clumps in the background.
† *Darkness over Germany* (Longmans, Green & Co., 1943).

Amy Buller feared that if that happened in Germany, it could happen in Britain too. She sought a tranquil place where students could go with their teachers to discuss ideas and ideals and 'examine the fundamental assumptions underlying the springs of political or economic or scientific action; and in so doing be given an opportunity of examining the Christian philosophy of life in relation to all this'.[21]

After reading *Darkness over Germany*, Queen Elizabeth invited Miss Buller to come and see her. Amy Buller did not quite know what to expect when she left Liverpool on a dark night in December 1943. The Queen asked her about her plans and Miss Buller outlined her vision of a residential discussion centre.

The war was still blazing, but it says much for the confidence of Queen Elizabeth that she did not lose sight of what Britain might be when the war was won. She was particularly concerned by the role of the next generation. She asked Miss Buller to keep in touch and over the next few years helped her in many ways, 'writing a letter here, placing a word there, facilitating negotiations, and strengthening Amy's resolve by her own vision'.[22]

The project came to be called St Catharine's, and fundraising proceeded with vigour. The Queen kept a helpful eye on developments. The new Archbishop of Canterbury, William Temple, was a help and his early death in 1944 a consequent blow. There were further delays after the war, but in 1946 Amy Buller made friends with Elizabeth Elphinstone, Queen Elizabeth's niece, who became a staunch supporter. The search for a suitable place continued in vain.

Cumberland Lodge in Windsor Great Park suddenly became vacant when Lord Fitzalan of Derwent, who had been loaned the house by George V, died there in May 1947. Before he moved there in 1924, Cumberland Lodge had been the home of Princess Christian, Queen Victoria's daughter. In July 1947 Elizabeth Elphinstone was discussing the problem of a suitable house with the King and Queen at Royal Lodge. The King pointed in the direction of Cumberland Lodge and said: 'Now I think that's the house you ought to have for your experiment. It's not a house anyone is likely to live in as a private house any more. I think it might suit very well.'[23]

The Queen summoned Amy Buller to Buckingham Palace where the formal offer was made. Thus the St Catharine's Foundation* was created in August 1947 with Lord Halifax as Chairman of the Council. Queen Elizabeth clarified its purpose as follows: 'In this quiet and relaxed

---

* The name was changed to the King George VI and Queen Elizabeth Foundation of St Catharine's in 1968.

atmosphere students and teachers can come together to examine the fundamental assumptions on which their studies are based and to explore the contemporary nature of mankind and his society. St Catharine's, established in the beauty of Windsor Great Park, is an ideal setting for this purpose.'[24]

The Foundation needed a great deal of support and help particularly in the early, sometimes faltering years. This Queen Elizabeth gave in many ways from holding fundraising parties, obtaining furniture and furnishings, to adding a special dimension to the sessions held there by entertaining the groups that came.

On a more personal level, there were times when Queen Elizabeth spotted the need to invite her niece, Elizabeth Elphinstone, over to Royal Lodge to ensure she got a square meal. There were risks involved in throwing open a private house in the grounds of the Great Park to a potentially disparate group of students. These were considered worth taking, the King and Queen having seen enough of the world to appreciate the importance of putting their trust in the young.

Gradually the Foundation developed and it has prospered over fifty years. Queen Elizabeth continued to take a lively personal interest in its welfare. She became its Patron in 1968, and last visited it officially on 24 June 2001, shortly before her 101st birthday.* (In 1984 Princess Margaret became its Visitor.)

In October 1944, the court was in mourning for Princess Beatrice, who had died on 26 October aged eighty-seven. Hardly had this ended when the Queen suffered a more personal loss. At 6 a.m. on 7 November, her father died from bronchitis at Glamis, also at the age of eighty-nine.

Queen Elizabeth had last seen her father when she visited Glamis in March for his eighty-ninth birthday. Now she and the King travelled to Glamis for another feudal funeral. The coffin, covered with the Union flag, was carried by three foresters and three gamekeepers. Then it was drawn on an estate cart by two horses, and piped to the family graveyard by four pipers of the Black Watch to the tune 'Flowers of the Forest'.

Princess Elizabeth was particularly upset by the death of her whiskery old grandfather, who had been suffering from senility for some years. Viewing the death from a more distant view, Chips Channon, a one-time guest, now out of favour, remarked: 'Lord Strathmore has died

* This was one of the rare patronages that the Queen assumed after the Queen Mother's death.

aged 89. I am surprised he was not more, for I stayed for a week or more with him at Glamis in 1922 once, and he seemed to me a very old man then.'[25]

Churchill expressed his sympathy: 'Even the venerable age Lord Strathmore had attained, while it accepts and exceeds the natural span of human life, in no way weakens the pangs of separation in a happy family.'[26] Thanking him, the Queen took the opportunity to ask about the progress of the war: 'Do you think there is any chance of London being "liberated" in the coming months? My heart aches for our own wonderful brave people, they have been tried so high, & of course can go on, but it really is rather a bore to feel that one might be blown to pieces at any moment.'[27]

In November 1944 the King mooted the idea of going to Burma to visit his troops the following February. With a wink he told his Private Secretary that this would take him to India. But Churchill vetoed this plan, unwilling to face the political implications. There may have been an element of revenge, since Churchill was still seething quietly about Normandy earlier that year. The King was disappointed.

On 6 December the Queen made a speech to representatives of all classes of women war workers, thanking them for the invaluable help they had given the war effort. On Christmas Day, the King again broadcast to the Empire, with Queen Elizabeth and the two princesses in the room beside him. 'The lamps which the Germans put out all over Europe, first in 1914 and then in 1939, are being slowly rekindled,'[28] he said.

Old Bishop Hensley Henson observed: 'I doubt if any of his predecessors . . . drew to the throne so great a volume of affection and respect . . . and he owes very much to the sweetness and steady persistence of Queen Elizabeth.'[29] But Queen Elizabeth was less confident: 'In some ways, this last year has been, for us, the most worrying of all these terrible years of war, but I have great faith that good is stronger than evil, & I pray with all my heart that 1945 will bring better days, & a return of law & order to poor tortured Europe.'[30]

In January 1945 Princess Elizabeth joined the ATS as a second subaltern and began a course at a driving training centre, while on 12 April President Roosevelt died. In the last months of the war, the King and Queen's engagements resumed their former peacetime style. Finally, the Germans surrendered on 8 May 1945. The years of combat were over.

The King and Queen, the two princesses and Winston Churchill appeared together on the balcony of Buckingham Palace to be greeted with rapturous applause. It had been a long and draining war. The King and Queen had visited innumerable bomb sites, troops in training, homeless people and air raid shelters. They had lunched with armed forces in all kinds of canteens the length of Britain. The King had personally decorated 32,000 men. Between the two of them, the King and Queen had undertaken some 4,766 public engagements.[31]

On Sunday 13 May they attended a thanksgiving service at St Paul's Cathedral, with Queen Mary (in London for the first time since the Blitz), the Kings of Greece and Yugoslavia and the President of Poland. At this hour of victory, the King and Queen became the focal point for widespread demonstrations of affection and took quiet satisfaction in the knowledge that they had fulfilled their duty from the very first to the very last moment of the conflict.

The King was deeply conscious of the magnificent support he had been given by Queen Elizabeth. He owed her every grain of his self-confidence, having depended on her in many ways, both publicly and privately. Whatever else they achieved, it is as a wartime team that they should be remembered. The British love their national characters for a reason, and the love that Queen Elizabeth inspired in the hearts of the British was fired in the years between 1939 and 1945. The affection never dimmed.

From the war the King emerged strengthened in confidence but weakened in health. As Churchill put it: 'No British monarch in living memory has had a harder time . . .' The King, he said, had lived through the war 'with a heart that never quavered and with a spirit undaunted'.[32]

Just before the end of the war, the King and Queen attended a ceremony in the Royal Gallery at the Palace of Westminster, where the King spoke in what Harold Nicolson described as his 'really beautiful voice', yet with that stammer that always made it agony to listen to him. Nicolson commented that the Lords and Members of the House of Commons listened in silence, which seemed ungrateful after all the excellent work he had done throughout the war:

But Winston, with his sense of occasion, rose at the end and waved his top hat aloft and called for three cheers. All our pent-up energies responded with three yells such as I should have thought impossible to emanate from so many elderly throats.[33]

I WISH TO MARK, BY THIS PERSONAL MESSAGE, my appreciation of the service you have rendered to your Country in 1939.

In the early days of the War you opened your door to strangers who were in need of shelter, & offered to share your home with them.

I know that to this unselfish task you have sacrificed much of your own comfort, & that it could not have been achieved without the loyal co-operation of all in your household.

By your sympathy you have earned the gratitude of those to whom you have shown hospitality, & by your readiness to serve you have helped the State in a work of great value.

Elizabeth R

Mrs. Penny.

19

Peace

'So much has happened to this poor battered world'
– Queen Elizabeth

Peace brought some respite and repose to the King and Queen. There were more joyous services of thanksgiving, more medals to be distributed, and, at the end of May, the chance for a short holiday at Balmoral. In the ensuing months the King and Queen gave numerous receptions and afternoon parties to thank the many organisations whose sterling efforts had helped the war effort. There was a tour of Northern Ireland, and a meeting on board HMS *Renown* with the new American President, Harry Truman. The King's nephew, Lord Lascelles, was released from Colditz on 5 May, as was the Queen's nephew, John Elphinstone. Some degree of normality returned to all their lives. But they were tired. 'We felt absolutely *whacked*,'[1] recalled the Queen.

On 11 June Queen Mary returned to Marlborough House, grateful to be back in the capital she loved, yet in part regretful to be leaving the more leisured life of Badminton.* To her surprise, she found herself saying: 'Here I've been anybody to everybody, and back in London I shall have to begin being Queen Mary all over again.'[2] She thought: 'How difficult the future appears to me, not at all the Peace we had been looking forward to. It is a trial to work with allies . . .'[3]

It was not long before the King had to face new problems with the Duke of Windsor. His term of office in the Bahamas came to an end in May 1945. In 1943 the Duke had been offered the Governorship of Bermuda but had declined this. He would have declined it the more speedily had he known that the preferred choice was the Queen's younger brother, David Bowes-Lyon.

In 1944 there were discussions as to what public service the Duke might now undertake. At Buckingham Palace Tommy Lascelles addressed the issue after a request from the Prime Minister's office and a meeting

---

* The British public now learned for the first time that Badminton had been Queen Mary's wartime retreat.

with Edward Stettinius, America's next Secretary of State. Lascelles made it clear that no problems in his life had given him as much anxiety as had those of the Duke of Windsor over a period of a quarter of a century.

Lascelles outlined four possibilities – that the Duke undertake some kind of ambassadorial or pro-consular role abroad, that he return to work as a quasi-younger brother of the King, that he live in Britain privately, devoting his considerable wealth to some useful cause in which he took an interest, or that he devote that wealth to some cause in the United States.

Lascelles rejected the first idea, not only on the grounds that he was an ex-King who had personally renounced the British crown, but because he would almost certainly not be safe in such a role. He seemed always to place his private desires before the public good, and, like Rehoboam, he consorted with unsavoury characters such as Charles Bedaux and Axel Wenner–Gren.*[4]

Lascelles rejected the second and third on the grounds that there was no room for two Kings, that it would be injurious to the present King's health, and would cost the Duke of Windsor some £20,000 a year in tax. He preferred the idea of the Windsors settling in the USA, in a home of his own for the first time, and devoting his fortune to some welfare scheme of his choosing. Lascelles's last point was the most devastating. He considered that any matter concerned with the Duke of Windsor held dangerous consequences for the health and well being of the present King.[5]

On 3 October the Duke of Windsor wrote to Churchill expressing his surprise and interest at the emphasis he placed on this last point. He did not consider himself a threat to them in their now assured position, and he reminded Churchill that it was usual for retiring Colonial Governors and their wives to be received by the monarch.

He thought such a meeting would anaesthetise the problem and urged Churchill to arrange it.[6]

Advice given to the Prime Minister stressed that 'H.M. would not be sorry if his brother did not come to England for the next ten years.'[7] The last word went to Lascelles, who made it clear that the King and Queen and Queen Mary were quite happy to see the Duke – but not his wife.[8]

---

* Charles Bedaux, a 'time and motion' millionaire who loaned the Château de Candé to the Duke for his wedding, and then masterminded the Duke's visit to Hitler in 1937. In 1944 he was arrested for treason and committed suicide. Axel Wenner-Gren, a Swedish multi-millionaire industrialist, and Chairman of Elektrolux. He spent the war in the Bahamas. Lascelles described both men as German agents.

Churchill was forced to pass this not wholly surprising news to the Duke of Windsor and to advise him to remain in the United States for some time longer before returning to his villa in the South of France, which was still a place of 'fights and skirmishes' and 'plenty of murders and reprisals'.[9]

The Windsors left the Bahamas for Miami in May 1945. The Duke came alone to Britain in October, had a meeting with his brother and stayed with Queen Mary at Marlborough House. Lascelles called on him and stressed the fact that George VI had taken on 'the most difficult job in the world' (for which he, unlike the Duke, was wholly untrained), so that the Duke could marry Mrs Simpson and enjoy his life with her.[10] He therefore urged him to renounce his continual demands about his wife. Presently the Windsors settled in France, undertaking no further public duties on behalf of Britain or any other country.

Hardly had the war ended than a General Election was called in which the British behaved with traditional ingratitude and ousted Churchill in favour of Clement Attlee. The King offered Churchill the Garter but he replied that, since he had just received the order of the boot, this did not seem appropriate. On 27 July a Labour administration was formed.

As a constitutional monarch, the King would deal with the elected Government whatever their political persuasion. Tommy Lascelles was instrumental in smoothing the path where needed, though he worried that Queen Elizabeth was influencing the King against his Labour ministers.

In 1946 Lord Wakehurst was due to retire as Governor of New South Wales in Australia. Although there was no particular reason for the King and Queen to become involved in the choice of his successor, this is what happened. The Duke of Glouester had recently returned from serving as Governor-General of Australia. Now the King promoted the bizarre plan of sending his brother-in-law, Michael Bowes-Lyon, to serve as Governor of New South Wales in Wakehurst's place.

The Labour Premier of New South Wales, William McKell, was determined to appoint an Australian to govern New South Wales. The British were equally determined that he would not. Before the Coalition Government fell, Lord Cranborne, then Secretary of State for the Dominions, proposed General Sir John Kennedy. McKell, who was far from being a Republican, countered with a list of fifteen Australians who were all senior servicemen. Cranborne rejected them all.

Lord Addison, the Labour successor to Cranborne, invited McKell to suggest some names, stressing that they 'should be generally acceptable to all sections and parties in New South Wales'.[11] McKell then proposed Captain John Armstrong, of the cruiser HMAS *Australia*, as his sole nomination. Addison felt he was not of sufficient calibre and asked for more names. Six of the previous fifteen were then submitted, the only one that appealed to Addison being the Australian General John Northcott, but he was about to become Commander, British Commonwealth Occupation Force in Japan.

In January 1946 Michael Bowes-Lyon was suggested. 'With the King's approval, His Majesty would be prepared to make available for this appointment The Queen's brother – the Honourable Michael Bowes-Lyon.'[12] This was deemed an insult, and in February Bowes-Lyon was dismissed by McKell as 'unacceptable'.*[13] The Labour Prime Minister Ben Chifley complained about Bowes-Lyon to Clement Attlee. Despite this, on 26 February 1946, the *Sydney Morning Herald* 'leaked' the story about Armstrong, Bowes-Lyon and the controversy. Chifley then released Northcott from his duties, and he became the first ever Australian State Governor.†[14]

However well intentioned the idea of Bowes-Lyon, it showed a lack of understanding on the part of the King and Queen, who may have thought their post-war standing so firm that they could trade on Queen Elizabeth's undoubted and well-earned popularity to secure such a post for her brother.

The work of visiting parts of England to hold local investitures and to say thank you continued through 1945 and into 1946. On 8 January 1946, the King gave the Order of Merit to Winston Churchill. The Royal Opera House reopened in February, and on 3 May the King's filly Hypericum won the 1000 guineas at Newmarket. On 8 June the King took the salute at the Victory Parade in the presence of most of the Royal Family. There were formal visits to Scotland and Wales, and the Queen took the princesses to Glamis, now the home of her eldest brother. In August 1946 Queen Wilhelmina of the Netherlands thanked the King for refuge in wartime and gave him thirty Dutch horses, some of which pulled the Gold State Coach at the 1953 Coronation.

Occasional appeals came from distressed German princes. These were ill received at the Palace, for by now Queen Elizabeth's dislike of the

---

* McKell's biographer summed Michael Bowes-Lyon up as 'an otherwise obscure, asthmatic businessman' (Christopher Cunneen, *William John McKell*, p. 175).

† Rt Hon. Sir Isaac Isaacs (1858–1948) had been the first Australian Governor-General of Australia 1931–6.

Germans was ingrained for life. In the case of Prince Bernhard Friedrich of Saxe-Weimar the Foreign Office was adamant that 'there is nothing whatever that Her Majesty can do about it', nor 'any good reason' for the prince 'expecting Her Majesty to interest herself in his distressed mother and sister'.[15] Nor were the King or the Foreign Office prepared to help the Kaiser's widow, who had been captured by the Soviets.[16]

Any hopes that the Royal Family may have entertained for adopting a quieter routine after the war were undermined by their popularity and the relentless demands for their presence. When the King made his broadcast on Christmas Day in 1946, he declared that the past year had not been an easy one: 'We cannot expect a world so grievously wounded to recover quickly . . .'[17] The King's habitual optimism was dimmed and Bishop Hensley Henson thought he sounded tired: 'It made a good start, but did not live up to it. Probably His Majesty is really rather shaken and tired by the abominable weather, the ill and uncertain courses of politics, and his own incessant exertions . . .'[18]

The occasional presence of Prince Philip of Greece at the royal table had been noted by those who monitor such things. The idea that he had been selected as a future consort to the Heir Apparent had been mooted as early as October 1941, when he was on leave from the Royal Navy. The King had written to his grandmother: 'What a charming boy he is.'[19] Since then he had served gallantly with the Mediterranean Fleet and the British Pacific Fleet. He reappeared in London in 1944, by which time Lord Louis Mountbatten was busy preparing the way for a marriage with Princess Elizabeth by getting him naturalised as a British citizen.

An eventual union was in the minds of a number of relations particularly on Prince Philip's side, but wisely they refrained from pressing him too closely on the matter. By the time Prince Philip returned from active service in the Far East, the naturalisation question had been solved.

If the eventual outcome was not in doubt, the timing was vague. By September 1946, Sir Shane Leslie, a somewhat maverick character (and also a cousin of Sir Winston Churchill), was writing to his wife: 'I understand that Philip, son of our old friend Andrew of Greece, is being groomed for Prince Consort, but the men think nothing of him . . .'[20] His close presence to Princess Elizabeth at the wedding of Lord Mountbatten's daughter, Patricia, to Lord Brabourne on 26 October was further confirmation.

Prince Philip had to face some opposition from the more insular elements at court, who considered him a foreigner, and a German to boot. Queen Elizabeth's dislike of Germans extended to the concept of his German relations. The King's concerns were those of a devoted father. He wanted Princess Elizabeth to be sure of her feelings. Thus, while HRH Prince Philip of Greece and Denmark was translated into Lieutenant Philip Mountbatten, RN, on 28 February 1947, the King made it clear that no decisions were to be made until the Royal Family returned from their visit to South Africa.

In these post-war years, the Royal Family's life was enriched by their liking of the young RAF equerry who had joined the Household in 1944. This was the Battle of Britain war hero Group Captain Peter Townsend, who had been mentioned in despatches, won the DFC and bar in 1940 and the DSO in 1941. He was destined to become closely involved with Princess Margaret. At the time he was married to a brigadier's daughter, Rosemary Pawle,* a girl with vivacious good looks, much liked by the Household staff.

Rosemary Townsend was a great hit with the King, as was the good-looking Countess of Eldon. With both of them the King allowed himself harmless flirtations. According to Veronica Maclean, the Countess's sister, Magdalen Eldon had a host of admirers: 'Bobbety Salisbury and King George VI adored her.'[21] Duncan Grant wanted to paint her, the producer Max Reinhardt wanted her to take over from Lady Diana Cooper in *The Miracle*, but, wrote her sister, she was 'diffident and genuinely modest about her appearance'.[22]

She was born as Magdalen Fraser in 1913, the elder daughter of 16th Baron Lovat. In 1934 she married her first cousin, the 4th Earl of Eldon, a lord-in-waiting and close friend of the King, who had 'no ambitions other than to farm, fish, shoot, hunt and take photographs – all of which he did exceptionally well – and to live the life of a good and placid country gentleman'.[23] Lady Eldon had wished to be a nun when young. Instead she married, had two sons and later adopted two little girls. Always deeply religious, she ran retreats, illustrated religious books for children, worked for the Red Cross with a zeal that matched Edwina Mountbatten's, and was a prison visitor. One friend wrote of her: 'Tall and strikingly beautiful, with sparkling blue eyes, her outstanding characteristic was her gaiety and bubbling sense of fun, which made what for others could be rather dreary committee meetings amusing and enjoyable.'[24]

Neither of these romantic friendships caused harm or censure, since

---

*Rosemary Pawle (1921–2004), married (1) Group Captain Peter Townsend, divorced 1952, (2) John de Laszlo, divorced 1977, (3) 5th Marquess Camden (1899–1983).

Queen Elizabeth handled the situation adroitly by befriending both ladies. When the Countess of Eldon died in 1969, she was represented by Sir Ralph Anstruther at her Memorial Mass at Farm Street.

South Africa

*'I saw the Queen's parasol, broken in two, disappear over the side
of the car'* – Peter Townsend

There were a number of contradictory reasons for the King and Queen
to visit South Africa in the spring of 1947. They were both in need of a
rest, especially the King, worn out by the war. A visit to one of his colonies
in the sun would be a tonic. The King and Queen also wished to thank
the South African people in person for their help during the war.

The family unit – the famous 'Us Four' as the King would later
describe them to Princess Elizabeth – had stayed closely together
throughout the war in a way that would not have been possible in peacetime. There would have been state visits and overseas tours and many
absences from home. This unit was about to be broken by Prince Philip.
The princesses had never been abroad and, before this happened, the
King wanted to take his family abroad.

As far as Field Marshal Smuts and South Africa itself were concerned,
the plan was more political. Smuts saw the opportunity to unite his
country under a monarch they had never seen. He had taken South Africa
into the war as an ally of Great Britain, as a result of which his rival,
General Hertzog, had broken away to form the small Afrikaner party.
Had the Germans won against Britain, South Africa would have become
a republic. While Smuts was a well-respected figure internationally, he
was less loved in his own country, where he lacked the ability to address
local issues. Yet he had been the dominant figure in South African politics for a generation, 'a great tree under which too little else could grow'.[1]
Smuts had no particular policy regarding black Africans and whites, but
the official opposition, the National Party, headed by Dr Malan, wanted
complete separation of the colours, and was busy playing on the racial
fears of the white people.

An election was due in 1948 and Smuts saw the royal visit stirring
public opinion in his favour. He saw the King as a reconciler above politics. He also wanted to stress the importance of South Africa's continued
allegiance to their King – 'to bind your peoples by a link the more' as

John Masefield expressed it in his poem bidding the King godspeed. By showing the South Africans this popular family, so well known for their wartime strength, Smuts was sure that nothing but good would follow.

Therefore what began as the alluring prospect of a holiday in the sun soon turned into a major political tour, with an exhausting schedule of visits, which would further sap the energies of a tired monarch and exhaust all four of the travellers.

The King was beset by problems at home and abroad. Britain had been virtually bankrupted by the war, rationing was still in force and a severe winter was about to descend with gales, floods and deep snow. There were power cuts, the British people were freezing, and, as factories closed, many were thrown into unemployment. India, Burma and Palestine were all in quest of independence from the crown.

The King and Queen felt uneasy about sailing away from Britain when it was wracked with economic hardship. Princess Elizabeth was undergoing the traditional reluctance of a bride-to-be at the prospect of a separation. And Princess Margaret, only sixteen at the time, was not overly drawn towards a gruelling tour with many civic ceremonies.

The coldest winter in living memory could not have been predicted. Used to sharing the misfortunes of his people, the King felt guilty heading for the sun while Britain froze. He went so far as to offer to come home, but Attlee judged that this would disappoint the many who were looking forward to seeing him. Even before the visit, Smuts had noted local enthusiasm that 'exceeded even my most optimistic expectations'.[2]

The procession of semi-state landaus planned to take the royal party to Waterloo Station was cancelled due to severe weather, out of consideration for the horses. They arrived in Portsmouth, where Miss Geach, one of the maids, got her first glimpse of HMS *Vanguard*: 'She was a breathtaking sight as she came into view as we turned the corner, looking like some mammoth piece of gray stagecraft with every nook & cranny of her crammed with the lads in navy blue.'[3]

They embarked at Portsmouth on 31 January, the Royal Family having their cabins and other quarters on an upper deck, with Lascelles close by, and 'The Cries of London', chosen by Queen Elizabeth, on the newly painted sea-green walls. One hundred and one officers, and a crew of 1,715 (including 189 Royal Marines) were on duty for the voyage. Queen Elizabeth inspected the quarters of the various staff in attendance.

They sailed on 1 February. The daunting schedule ahead was preceded by a long sea voyage, some of which could be enjoyed, though there were problems. Lady Harlech's porthole leaked and the lights in Princess Elizabeth's cabin fused. The ship's carpenter was kept busy replacing cupboard doors which fell off. The weather was exceptionally rough and the royal party sat in the sun lounge, watching the seas breaking against the escorting vessels. There was a scare about some mines and further heavy seas. A week after leaving Portsmouth, *Vanguard* was damaged in heavy seas in the Bay of Biscay. When, eventually, they reached calmer waters, Queen Elizabeth said: 'It's like being stroked.'[4]

Travelling with the Royal Family were three private secretaries, three ladies-in-waiting, a medical officer, a press secretary and two equerries. There was a full personal and clerical staff from London, including police officers, clerks, clerical assistants, dressers, maids, valets, footmen and hairdressers.

This team was augmented in South Africa by a considerable number of Cabinet ministers, provincial administrators and Union Government officials. And there was the accredited press team. Some of the reporters were figures who would later write best-selling books about the King and his family – Louis Wulff from Reuters, L. A. Nickolls and Betty Spencer Shew, from the *Exchange Telegraph*, and Dermot Morrah, from *The Times*.* Frank Gillard, the former war correspondent, came as commentator from the BBC and Mr G. H. Rottner, his 'televisionist'. On the whole, the royal tour was well served by these reporters, though Miss Geach was unimpressed by Gillard: 'When broadcasting *Vanguard*'s departure from Portsmouth, in his efforts to be spectacular rather than strictly truthful, he declared that *Vanguard* was under way with smoke pouring from her funnels, thus, according to one indignant rating, disgracing her in the eyes of the entire British Navy.'[5]

There were nightly concerts and the latest films on the quarterdeck. The ship's padre joined in 'lustily' with the wardroom officers as they sang a sea shanty, and on other evenings they saw *Wonder Man* with Danny Kaye, and Carol Reed's *Odd Man Out*, with James Mason, which Princess Margaret found 'very harrowing'.[6] Shortly before arriving in Cape Town, *Notorious* was shown, starring Ingrid Bergman, Claude Rains and Cary Grant, but the reels broke and they never saw the end.

They crossed the equator on 10 February, the princesses undergoing

---

* Louis Wulff wrote *Queen of Tomorrow*, *Silver Wedding*, *Her Majesty Queen Mary*, *Elizabeth and Philip*, and others; L. A. Nickolls wrote *Royal Cavalcade* and *The First Family* and later works early in the present Queen's reign; Betty Spencer Shew produced *Mid Pleasures and Palaces*, *Royal Wedding*, *Queen Elizabeth The Queen Mother*, and others; and Dermot Morrah wrote *Princess Elizabeth* in collaboration with Betty Spencer Shew, in advance of the tour, and *The Royal Family in Africa* after it.

Dermot Morrah (1896–1974), journalist, historian, herald and former Fellow of All Souls, leader writer of *The Round Table* (1942–4) and leader writer of *The Times* (1931–61). He suffered from a paralysed vocal chord that caused him to speak with a distinctive croak. Appointed Arundel Herald Extraordinary, he occupied a prominent position at the 1953 Coronation.

the traditional ceremonies, though not being ducked. They were bidden by King Neptune:

> Elizabeth and Margaret Rose
> Accept some powder on each nose
> And after that my doctors will
> Administer a little pill.[7]

The pill was a cherry, and the effect for those watching hilarious.

At 9.40 a.m. on 17 February *Vanguard* berthed at Cape Town. The Governor-General and Field Marshal Smuts went on board, and at 10 a.m. the Royal Family disembarked. They then began a programme which took them to forty-two locations between 17 February and 24 April with very few breaks. There were guard inspections, receptions, parades, addresses of welcome by the dozen, garden parties, balls, followed by more of the same in each new location.

In Cape Town the King opened the Union Parliament, his most important constitutional duty on the tour. Normally this ceremony was performed by the Governor-General, but the presence of the King was significant, not only because he was performing a role as King of South Africa, but because this was the first time a Sovereign had ever opened a Parliament outside Britain. The King wore the white tropical uniform of Admiral of the Fleet, with the Garter riband. Not only did he perform the ceremony in English, but also in halting Afrikaans. A low murmur of parliamentary approval greeted his linguistic attempts.

For this ceremony Queen Elizabeth wore one of several new Hartnell evening gowns, again with the Garter and a tiara. She still favoured full crinoline gowns for state banquets often with the actual Garter on her left arm. Two unusual tiaras were produced. At the State Opening in Cape Town she wore a high Russian-looking concoction, and at the Durban Ball she wore Mrs Greville's Empire-style Boucheron tiara, possibly for the first time. On one evening the Royal Family sat in full evening dress, in huge brown leather armchairs, Queen Elizabeth with tiara and white mink stole, the King in a black dinner jacket, the chairs on a single carpet, outdoors on the grass, fully exposed to the open air. It made an unusual sight.

At garden parties Queen Elizabeth wore long gowns to the floor, often bedecked with ostrich plumes at the sleeves, with parasol in hand. When wearing knee-length day-dresses, she adopted crisscross scarves across the bodice, which sometimes fell over the shoulder ending in flowing tassels. The colours were the traditional pastels, blues and pinks.

Queen Elizabeth's hats were designed by Aage Thaarup, the Danish-born milliner, whom she had favoured since soon after he set up shop in 4 Berkeley Street in 1932. He was responsible for the wide-brimmed hats with veils that she favoured into old age. On this trip, Thaarup's creations (some of which looked like kettles or twisted sausages) were carefully synchronised with the dresses, Hartnell dress No. 1 being matched to Thaarup hat No. 1 and gloves and shoes No. 1. Thaarup promoted ostrich plumes as these represented a major South African export. He avoided materials that attracted fabric-eating insects or pins that might rust in the humidity. He also took into account the broiling heat or the possibility of 'windy reviewing stands'.[8]

After the State Opening, they set off in 'The White Train', made up of some fourteen carriages, with a proper suite for the Royal Family, a dining room, sitting room with large and comfortable armchairs, and telephones. From this train the King could keep in touch with the Duke of Gloucester and his ministers in London, and elsewhere in the world if necessary, and Dermot Morrah even revealed that Princess Elizabeth sometimes made calls to Philip Mountbatten. Eight carriages were built in England, some arriving by ship, causing great local interest as they were unloaded in Cape Town. Six were taken from 'The Blue Train' which ran between Cape Town and Johannesburg. The complete train was a third of a mile long and would travel some 6944 miles around South Africa, the Royal Family spending thirty-five nights in it.

In 'The White Train', they travelled from Cape Town to Port Elizabeth, Grahamstown, East London, Kingwilliamstown, Bloemfontein, Ladysmith, Pietermaritzburg, Durban, Vryheid, Kruger National Park, Pretoria, Johannesburg, Mafeking, Kimberley and back to Cape Town once more. As in Canada, so in South Africa, the King and Queen made many impromptu stops in order to be seen.

One of the secretarial assistants to the Prime Minister travelled on 'The White Train' and reported to a friend:

All along the line, even at crossings, small wayside halts where we take on water, hundreds gather and what a reception – the coloureds and natives are particularly well-mannered. The King and Queen get out at every stop and talk to many people and walk right down the platform passed the coloureds; during the night one is awakened at some stop by singing – believe it is the way the natives show their welcome. However, I can assure you their behaviour and decorum were far above a large percent of the so-called top-notchers of either Cape Town or Port Elizabeth; I have in mind the disgusting behaviour at the garden parties at these towns.[9]

On 11 March, they entered Basutoland, escorted by thousands of native horsemen. The next day they were welcomed by a hundred thousand Basutos. On 13 March Field Marshal Smuts greeted them at Ladysmith, having kept away from the Orange Free State, a predominantly Afrikaans province. In the middle of the trip, between 13 and 17 March, they were able to take a four-day break in the Natal National Park. Smuts invited them to spend these few days at a favourite hotel of his, in northern Drakensberg, later known as the Royal Natal National Park Hotel.*

At the camp the King was given the newspapers from London. The next moment he appeared at the entrance of Lascelles's makeshift office in a thatched native hut in a towering rage. 'Look at that', he said flinging the Windsor newspaper which told of the flood devastation in the town. 'There are my people in Windsor enduring the most dreadful suffering and nobody tells me about it. Get on to London at once,' he thundered. 'I want a full report.'[10] He had not forgotten his people at home.

During these few free days Smuts arranged a secret meeting between the King and Queen and Prince and Princess Paul of Yugoslavia, so secret that even some members of the Royal Household were unaware of it. Since the summer of 1943 Prince and Princess Paul had been living quietly in Johannesburg. There had been some concern that Prince Paul might be summoned to trial at Nuremberg, but this did not happen.

Before the King and Queen's visit Lascelles had arranged with Harold Nicolson that Prince and Princess Paul should be out of Johannesburg when the King and Queen were there on 1 April. But the King and Queen were determined to see them. And so their private friendship was resumed, this display of friendship giving Prince Paul a much-needed boost from a phase of intense depression. When he died in 1976, Queen Elizabeth described him as 'one of my oldest friends and a most loyal friend to England'.†[11]

The ugliest incident of the tour occurred on the morning of 2 April as the royal car made its progress from Government House, Pretoria, towards Johannesburg. This involved an exhausting drive of 120 miles in intense heat, the King and Queen seated in the back of an open Daimler. In the front of the car Peter Townsend, who was on duty as the King's

---

* The hotel was originally built for hikers by Walter Coventry in 1919. The royal visit made it famous. The 1963 film *Zulu* was filmed in the nearby mountains. The hotel has now fallen into disrepair with weeds and wild grass growing in what was the dining room.

† After his death, Princess Olga returned to her most of the Queen Mother's letters to Prince Paul and she kept them on her desk.

equerry throughout this tour, recalled: 'Hundreds of thousands of sweating, screaming, frenzied blacks lined the route, pressed about the car, waved frantically and hollered their ecstatic joy at the sight of this little family of four, so fresh and white and – apparently – demure.'[12]

But the King was far from demure that day. Worn down by his travels and his many worries, and fractious in the heat, he suffered one of the nervous outbreaks which occurred when his fragile temperament was tested. This took the form of berating the chauffeur, who soon became 'rattled'.

As the 'incessant tirade' continued, the Queen tried to soothe the King, and the princesses tried to make light of it, but to no avail. Finally, Townsend could stick no more, and acting somewhat out of character, turned round and shouted at the King: 'For Heaven's sake, shut up, or there's going to be an accident.'[13]

Worse was to follow. Just as the royal procession reached Benoni shortly before 11 a.m., they saw an agitated policeman running anxiously towards the King's car. Looking around, they saw another man, 'black and wiry, sprinting with terrifying speed and purpose' in the direction of the car. He was clutching something in one hand, while with the other he seized hold of the side of the car. Townsend described what then happened:

> The Queen, with her parasol, landed several deft blows on the assailant before he was knocked senseless by policemen. As they dragged away his limp body, I saw the Queen's parasol, broken in two, disappear over the side of the car. Within a second, Her Majesty was waving and smiling, as captivatingly as ever, to the crowds.[14]

This shocking incident was made worse when it was presently discovered that this man was one of the King's loyal subjects. He had been calling out 'My King! My King!' and in his hand he clutched a ten shilling note as a birthday present for Princess Elizabeth. Townsend told Lascelles that he felt like resigning, but when the King expressed remorse and apologised, Townsend wrote: 'More than ever before, I realised how lovable the man was.'[15] He recorded no apology from Queen Elizabeth.

A more positive view of the Queen was given by the author Enid Bagnold:

> I must tell you I'm swept into the upward rush about the Queen. She is now surrounded by an actress-aura. She is like Irving after a First Night and oneself at the stage door. I watched her closely . . . when she was inspecting ex-servicemen right under my nose

. . . She has an extraordinary control of every facial muscle, a very delicate control, so that she makes valuable every look and half smile in a very expressive way. We others, and the princesses, just smile or don't smile, but the queen has a much bigger range and a delicacy of holding or tilting her head or casting a small look for an instant that gives a rain of pleasure here and there and on whoever gets one of the fragments.[16]

On 7 April the Royal Family flew from Pretoria to Salisbury, Rhodesia, where the King opened the new session of their Parliament. Onwards they went, crossing the Zambesi to Livingstone, seeing the Victoria Falls, visiting Matabeleland, and Cecil Rhodes's grave in the Matapos. On 17 April they were greeted by 25,000 natives of Bechuanaland at Loatsi, and on 20 April they arrived back in Cape Town.

Next day Princess Elizabeth celebrated her twenty-first birthday, reviewing a parade of troops and a youth rally, and delivering her famous speech of dedication to the service of what she called 'our great Imperial family'. On the same day Queen Elizabeth was given an honorary degree at Cape Town University.

On St George's Day, the Royal Family ascended Table Mountain. Soon afterwards the trip was over and they rejoined HMS *Vanguard* for the long voyage home.

When they reached Portsmouth on 11 May, a crowd of five hundred thousand gathered to greet them and all manner of little boats took to the sea at Portsmouth. The Duke of Gloucester came aboard and dined with the Royal Family. The voyage had come to a successful conclusion, prompting John Masefield to pick up his pen once more:

> The world has watched your going and has seen
> How true a friendship serves our King and Queen.[17]

The Times concluded: 'The crown hereafter will always be much more than a constitutional abstraction in South African life.'[18]

On 12 May, the tenth anniversary of the Coronation, the royal party disembarked to a naval and civic welcome. Their return to London was marked by more enthusiastic greetings, loyal addresses, appearances on the Palace balcony, and, a few days later, the traditional drive to Guildhall for a magnificent luncheon.

In 1976 the Queen Mother's spontaneous memories of this tour were that it was 'a very happy time',[19] but while on the tour she described it to Queen Mary as 'very strenuous'.[20] As for Smuts, his party was defeated in the General Election of 4 June 1948, Dr Malan took over and Smuts even lost his seat. He died from a heart attack soon after his eightieth birthday on 11 September 1950.

When the Royal Family returned to Buckingham Palace, the Household and staff, together with favourite pets, were assembled to greet them. Crawfie recorded the shock of seeing them. Princess Elizabeth looked 'pale and drawn', but happy to be back, Princess Margaret looked 'ill and tired out' and the King and Queen looked 'positively worn out'. She thought the King's hair had gone grey, but it was only bleached by the sun.[21] He had lost a stone in weight. At the civic welcome in the war-scarred Guildhall, many noted that his voice was hoarse and grew hoarser as he spoke. The tour had gravely undermined his health.

There was to be no respite to the problems political and personal that confronted the King and Queen on their return. Even as they sailed into Portsmouth, the Duke and Duchess of Windsor were heading to Britain from America, after finally leaving the Bahamas. Among those at the Palace to greet the King and Queen were the Princess Royal and Lord Harewood. A few days later Harewood was suffering from cardiac complications and bronchial asthma, and on the morning of 24 May he died at Harewood House, at the age of sixty-four. The Duke of Windsor did not join his brothers, the King and the Duke of Gloucester, at Lord Harewood's private funeral in York-shire. Nor did he join the Royal Family, which for some unexplained reason did not include Queen Mary, at the memorial service at St Mark's, North Audley Street.*

Nor was the Duke of Windsor invited to lunch at Buckingham Palace for the eightieth birthday of Queen Mary, on 26 May, two days after Harewood's death, though young Lieutenant Philip Mountbatten was there. The Duke had to confine his participation in this landmark birthday to visiting his mother at Marlborough House the same evening. The Duke visited the King privately the following evening, before departing for France on 4 June.

By now the Duke of Windsor needed no further assurance that his presence in England was unwelcome. He settled in France, though he did not take on his last house in the Bois de Boulogne or buy his mill

---

* Queen Mary had attended the London memorial service for King Christian X of Denmark on 1 May, but she was not even represented at Lord Harewood's service. There may have been a want of sympathy between them, though she remained close to her daughter, the Princess Royal. The King ordered that only family mourning was to be observed but the Royal Family were not expected to wear black when attending public functions. This was the height of the social season.

outside Paris until a few years later. A more public affirmation of the intransigence of the Royal Family came later in the year when he was not invited to the wedding of his niece, Princess Elizabeth.

Wedding and Silver Wedding

'A shot of wardroom heartiness into the existing atmosphere of a
Scotch house-party' – Charles Johnston on the Royal Wedding

Princess Elizabeth's wedding was the first major occasion after the war
when a little colour returned to Britain. Though 20 November 1947 was
cold, with battle dress the order of the day rather than full ceremonial
military uniforms, the youth and beauty of the bride stirred many hearts.

The King announced the engagement of Princess Elizabeth to Lieutenant Philip Mountbatten on 9 July. The young naval officer was swiftly
co-opted into the royal way of life, the happy couple presented together
at a garden party the next day, and summoned to the Palace balcony that
evening.

Philip Mountbatten then accompanied the Royal Family to Holyroodhouse on 15 July to witness his bride receive the Freedom of the
City of Edinburgh, looking bored, with set jaw and arms crossed. After
a lengthy tour of Scotland, the Royal Family settled into Balmoral for
their annual Scottish holiday.

The King adored his elder daughter and only wanted her to be happy.
A good rapport was created between the King and his son-in-law, based
on mutual respect. The King admired the way that the young man had
coped with the disharmony of his early life, his father, Prince Andrew of
Greece, by then deceased, having drifted away while his mother, Princess
Alice of Battenberg, who had suffered years of instability and indifferent
health, returning from time to time to the family fold to reassume her
position as his mother. He had served gallantly in the Royal Navy in the
war, being mentioned in despatches and serving in the Far East until the
end of hostilities.

The King was aware of the distrust of members of his Household and
entourage. Figures such as Lord Eldon, the King's lord-in-waiting, and
Queen Elizabeth's brother, David Bowes-Lyon, were hostile to Prince
Philip. Fears that the Duke of Edinburgh, as he was presently created,
was too closely identified with German royal relations meant that none
of his three surviving sisters were invited to the wedding.

But it was not a Ruritanian influence that Prince Philip brought to the marriage, as was noted by the perspicacious Charles Johnston.* He observed the contrast between the two families: 'the deer-stalking, grouse-shooting, ultra-autochthonous, Anglo-British, Picto-Scot side, which is dominant and determines the surface impression, but is from time to time broken through, shown up and let down by something which couldn't be less English: the international side, the unmentionable, Russian and German connexions, the awkward Greek ones, the acutely embarrassing Jugoslav ones,† the whole European Royal trades union with its special language of schoolroom nicknames and enthusiastic gutturals.'‡

As for Prince Philip himself, Johnston concluded that in him the Mountbatten element dominated the Greek royal background. The Mountbattens had become English very fast. The arrival of Prince Philip into the life of King George and Queen Elizabeth introduced 'a shot of wardroom heartiness into the existing atmosphere of a Scotch house-party'. Johnston cited the best example of this as 'the whole party, bridesmaids and all, egged on by the Mountbattens, chasing the going-away carriage out across the forecourt. Comment by Zoia:§ "I wonder what *la Reine Victoria* would have said."'[1]

Just before the wedding, the King appointed Princess Elizabeth a Lady of the Garter, and a few days later he bestowed the same honour on the groom, who, like those Schleswig-Holstein and Battenberg princes who had married daughters of Queen Victoria, was magically transformed into an Englishman of status – Royal Highness and Knight of the Garter on 19 November, Duke of Edinburgh, Earl of Merioneth and Baron Greenwich on 20 November.¶ He was granted a £10,000 a year Civil List allowance, and received into the Church of England by the Archbishop of Canterbury at Lambeth Palace. His name was added to the prayers for the Royal Family.

Queen Elizabeth asked Norman Hartnell to submit possible designs

* Sir Charles Johnston (1912–86), diplomat, poet and translator of Pushkin. He was married to Princess Natasha Bagration, a Georgian cousin of the Duchess of Kent.
† Prince Philip was a great-nephew of the murdered Tsarina. None of his sisters were invited to the wedding on account of being married to Germans, some of whom had been linked to the Nazi Party, Queen Frederika (a grand-daughter of the Kaiser) was considered questionable, and King Peter and Queen Alexandra of Yugoslavia were in a difficult political situation. There were further complications such as King Michael of Romania, who lost his throne soon after the wedding.
‡ There were those called 'Missy' and 'Uncle Goggie', while Princess Marina and her family often commented: 'Och, poor thing!'
§ Zoia Poklewska-Koziell (d. 1974), daughter of Baroness Agnes de Stoeckl (1874–1968), Irish-born lady at the Russian court, and author. In later life, the Baroness lived in a cottage on the estate at Coppins, the Duchess of Kent's home in Iver.
¶ Despite his legendary enjoyment of styles and titles, the King failed to make his son-in-law a Prince of the United Kingdom and Northern Ireland, which was not achieved until 22 February 1957.

for the wedding dress. He sent twelve ideas, one of which was accepted. Inspired by a Botticelli figure in clinging ivory silk, Hartnell created the wedding dress in three months. His manager brought ten thousand tiny pearls from the United States, declared them at Customs and paid the requisite duty. The dress itself was made of satin, from a firm in Dunfermline, spun by silkworms from Nationalist China. The satin for the train came from Lullington Castle in Essex. Hartnell also designed the dresses for the eight bridesmaids, in ivory silk tulle, the apricot and golden brocade outfit for Queen Elizabeth, and the magnificent dress and coat of gold tissue, embossed with sea-blue chenille that Queen Mary wore so strikingly at the Abbey. Both queens wore their Garter insignia over these ensembles. The hats were again the dashing prerequisite of Aage Thaarup.

Sir Michael Duff, son of Lady Juliet, a man who was fascinated by royalty, left his own characteristically naughty account of the day:

> Queen Mary in ice blue, shimmering in the iciest of ice blue, nodding away like a contented potentate, so ancient that she scarce held together. You felt that Pussy, Lady Cynthia, and Bertha Dawkins* were supporting her with unseen hands. Occasionally this ageing mammal, whirled her hand about, as though a plague of flies had been let loose . . . Grinners herself [Queen Elizabeth] looked like an inflated tangerine, her hat resembling a Don's, perked up with ill-gotten plumage. She looked *IMMENSE*, and even her grin damped to the minimum by the gigantic contours of her face, it was like the sun trying to shine through clouds. The King looking unbelievably beautiful, like an early French King, and HRH the bride a dream, and like a fairy tale princess.[2]

After the wedding the King wrote to his daughter to tell her that when he gave her hand to the Archbishop of Canterbury, he felt he had lost 'something very precious'. Touchingly, he added:

> Our family, us four, the 'Royal Family' must remain together with additions of course at suitable moments! ! I have watched you grow up all these years with pride under the skilful direction of Mummy, who as you know is the most marvellous person in the World in my eyes, & I can, I know, always count on you, & now Philip, to help

---

* Lady Constance (Pussy) Milnes-Gaskell, Lady Cynthia Colville and Lady Bertha Dawkins, ladies-in-waiting to Queen Mary. Lady Bertha had died in 1943, which says something for the elements of fantasy in Duff's account.

us in our work. Your leaving us has left a great blank in our lives but do remember that your old home is still yours & do come back to it as much & as often as possible. I can see that you are sublimely happy with Philip which is right but don't forget us is the wish of Your ever loving & devoted

  Papa.[3]

Eleanor Roosevelt did not attend the wedding but sent towels and kitchen clothes from Lord & Taylor. On her 1946 visit Queen Elizabeth had welcomed her, observing that so much had happened 'to this poor battered world'[4] since her wartime visit. Eleanor Roosevelt had told the Queen her mission was that her husband's plans for peace be realised. On a Sunday meeting they discussed a London memorial to the late President.

In April 1948 Mrs Roosevelt came over for the memorial's unveiling in Grosvenor Square. She stayed at Windsor, submitting gracefully to the charades that Queen Elizabeth so richly enjoyed, while Churchill, another guest, did his best to sidestep them. The handsome statue by Sir William Reid Dick was unveiled on 12 April, the third anniversary of the President's death. The King wrote to Mrs Roosevelt afterwards to say 'how much the Queen & I admired your quiet & calm bearing at a moment when your heart must have been so full of thoughts & memories'.[5]

Soon after this came the great ceremony to mark the 600th anniversary of the Order of the Garter. The King revived the full medieval ceremony at Windsor for the first time since the reign of George III. Many of the Knights present were worthy successors to the heroes of Crécy and Poitiers, and the ceremony was made the more special by the installation of Princess Elizabeth and the Duke of Edinburgh, along with thirteen new Knight Companions, one after another. Since 1946 appointments had been the sole prerogative of the King, a change which was commended, though his later choice of Knights was disappointing, displaying a preference for personal friends (such as Viscount Allendale and Earl Fortescue) over men of national distinction.

Hardly was that over than the King and Queen were processing in a state landau to St Paul's Cathedral to celebrate their Silver Wedding. The days of Cosmo Gordon Lang were over, and it fell to Geoffrey Fisher, the ninety-seventh Archbishop of Canterbury, to preach the sermon in which he gave marriage, the home and the family as basis for the security of the soul:

The Royal Family has borne with all other families its own share of domestic griefs and burdens. But in days when reassurance of life's true and lovely things has been so greatly needed, the God of all comforts has given to us in our King and Queen and their daughters a sure comfort indeed. The evidence and the example of their steadfastness, rooted in the serenity of a happy home life and expressed in selfless service to their people, has steadied and encouraged the whole nation and all through these years has stood as a living symbol in our midst of those simple sanctities wherein man's true life consists.[6]

In the afternoon they were driven in an open car through the streets of London and that evening the crowd demanded numerous balcony appearances. After the eighth, the King complained: 'Why can't they leave us alone?' To which Queen Elizabeth riposted: 'One day they might *not* want us.'[7] Out they came again.

The Silver Wedding was swiftly followed by a sharp decline in the King's health. Since January he had been experiencing cramp in both legs and as the summer wore on the condition got worse. Nevertheless, in March it was announced that the King and Queen and Princess Margaret would pay a visit to New Zealand and Australia early in 1949, to cement relations with the Antipodes.

In the summer the King and Queen stayed at Holyroodhouse. One day the King and Peter Townsend climbed up Arthur's Seat. In the evening, the King kept muttering: 'What's the matter with my blasted legs? They won't work properly.'[8] By the time of his holiday at Balmoral he was in almost permanent discomfort. Exercise helped a bit, but by October his left foot was permanently numb and then his right foot began to hurt.

The autumn was filled with a daunting schedule of engagements for a man in pain – the African Conference, the State Opening of Parliament with full ceremonial for the first time since 1938, the King and Queen of Denmark staying at the Palace for an exhibition of Danish art treasures at the Victoria and Albert Museum, and the King reviewing eight thousand Territorial Army men and women in Hyde Park.

On 20 October the King summoned his Manipulative Surgeon, Sir Morton Smart, to look at his right foot. Smart, in turn, called in Sir Maurice Cassidy, the heart specialist. On 23 November the King cancelled his Antipodean tour on medical advice, causing great disappointment to the people of Australia and New Zealand and to himself. The official statement explained that he was suffering from an obstruction to circulation through the arteries of the legs which had become acute, the defective supply to the right foot causing anxiety.

This threw the Palace into a state of alarm. A close observer of royal life at this time was Dermot Morrah, *The Times*'s respected correspondent and leader writer, who had been much looking forward to accompanying another royal tour. He had occasionally written speeches for the King, and had assisted Princess Elizabeth with her twenty-first birthday broadcast from South Africa.

During the South African tour, he had established a good rapport with Queen Elizabeth.* He was on close enough terms with her to advance the opinion that the Australians could not quite think of themselves as equal subjects to the British if they only saw their King and Queen flashing by once in a lifetime in a train. 'Well, they aren't quite, are they?' was her reply.[9] Of the King's illness Morrah wrote:

> I'm sorry to say the King's condition is really serious and everybody at the Palace is much worried. There is a real danger of losing the leg – it's the same he had in splints when he was a child, and now it's getting only 40% of its proper blood supply with consequent risk of gangrene. The foot turns black on occasion. One special source of anxiety is his personal physician – a homeopathic quack with a fascination for women, some of whom planted him on Edward, Prince of Wales, who bequeathed him to his successor as official medical officer. Of course they've called in good men as consultants, Cassidy and Learmonth especially, but this old menace is there all the time, and it was he who let the trouble go this length before sounding the alarm.[10]

Morrah's 'homeopathic quack' was Sir John Weir, the Scottish physician who had veered to homeopathy because it had cured his youthful boils where traditional medicine had failed. The Royal Family had long been beholden to homeopathy, Queen Alexandra, Queen Victoria's uncle, Leopold of the Belgians and even Queen Adelaide having privately consulted homeopathic doctors. In 1923 Weir was appointed physician-in-ordinary to the Prince of Wales, and he continued to be consulted by

* One evening his daughter was going to a function at which Queen Elizabeth was to be present. Joking, he said, 'Give the Queen my love'. He was horrified to hear that this message had been relayed as given, though it gave him the chance to write a prosaic letter of apology, for the impertinence of its delivery, but not for the sentiment of love, which as Her Majesty knew, was shared by all her subjects, not least her humble and obedient servant, etc, etc (Mrs T. E. Utley to author, 18 July 1976).

the Royal Family until his retirement in 1968, being physician to George V's sister, Queen Maud of Norway, Queen Mary, King George and Queen Elizabeth, and later to the present Queen. He was knighted in 1932, promoted GCVO in 1939 and, on the King's recovery in 1949, awarded the rare Royal Victorian Chain.

Weir was a bachelor. He never lost his Scottish accent, he enjoyed golf and was an inveterate teller of 'pawky jokes' and 'wee stories'.[11] He had a notebook filled with them. He was said to have advised the Prince of Wales: 'No cigars, four cigarettes a day, and not more than two small slices of beef for lunch.'[12] He paid great attention to the wording of bulletins issued about the state of health of his royal patients.

Significantly, the great homeopathic doctor Margery Blackie never cared for him. Though he was deemed kind, and something of a father figure to homeopathy, he was an autocrat who got his own way too easily. He frequently asked for a second opinion on his diagnoses which hinted at 'fundamental diffidence due to a lack of understanding'.*[13] At royal banquets he was in his element, the GCVO stretched across his ample girth.

This is not the place to discuss the merits or de-merits of homeopathy. It says something that two of its adherents within the Royal Family, the Queen Mother and Princess Alice, Duchess of Gloucester,† lived comfortably beyond their 100th birthdays. The King remained a staunch supporter of Weir until his dying day and called him his friend. Yet the views of Morrah and the veiled hints about Weir in the various biographies cannot be laid aside lightly.

The other doctors were Sir Maurice Cassidy and Professor James Learmonth. Cassidy served under Weir as Physician to the King. He died in October 1949, aged sixty-nine. Learmonth was the outsider called in to advise. Much younger, he had served as Regius Professor in Clinical Surgery, based in Edinburgh, and was the country's top expert in vascular disease. He quickly diagnosed an early form of arteriosclerosis, with fears of gangrene leading to possible amputation. Also consulted was the Australian surgeon Sir Thomas Dunhill, who specialised in thyroid disease. He had been surgeon to George V, and was based at St Bartholomew's Hospital, London.

* Dr Blackie much preferred Dr Douglas Borland, as she made clear at an annual staff dinner at which she was invited to lampoon the doctors in some home-devised doggerel. Her lines on Weir implied that while he had a memorable personality, he was unable to identify the malady. Weir was livid and never forgave her (see Constance Babington-Smith, *Champion of Homeopathy*, pp. 65–6).
† In 1967, the Duchess of Gloucester succeeded in shaking Weir off and switched to Dr Blackie, explaining that it was no longer fair on Weir, at his 'great age', to expect him to 'come at once and struggle up our long staircase' (*Champion of Homeopathy*, p. 131).

The King was anxious that details of his illness should be kept secret, especially from Princess Elizabeth, who was entering the last days of her pregnancy that autumn. There was joyous news for the House of Windsor, when on the evening of 14 November she gave birth to Prince Charles at Buckingham Palace. But the baby was neither seen in public nor photographed for a month, which kept a bevy of press photographers outside the Palace, and more or less tethered Cecil Beaton to his telephone at home in anticipation of a summons.

Beaton had been due to photograph Queen Elizabeth, but she had not only succumbed to a rare bout of influenza that kept her from the Cenotaph, but was preoccupied with the health of the King. Only on the King's birthday, on 14 December, was Beaton suddenly called for, first to photograph the Queen and then her new grandchild.

Beaton photographed Queen Elizabeth in a black velvet dress specially commissioned for the sitting from Norman Hartnell. He had long wanted to take these portraits to contrast the pre-war white lace dress images on the lawn. He had suggested that 'a black velvet crinoline might make a great effect, with crimson curtains festooned around a column in a somewhat Regency atmosphere'.[14] When Beaton saw Queen Elizabeth, he realised that she was 'entirely different from her aspect before the war',[15] but the portraits succeeded spectacularly. The effect was to create the most majestic images of Queen Elizabeth taken in her long life, and assured Beaton of his position as the photographic incarnation of the court portrait painter. That these pictures were achieved at a time of such stress is a further tribute to sitter and photographer.

By the end of November Lascelles's message to the Foreign Office was that there was unlikely to be any quick development or improvement in the King's condition, and that patience must be exercised.[16] Privately he was more forthcoming, reckoning that all that could be said was that the King's circulation had not deteriorated.[17]

When news of the illness spread, messages of sympathy poured in from all corners of the globe. King Haakon of Norway sat by his wireless late into the night in quest of news, upset to have heard nothing direct from the Royal Family. In due course Queen Elizabeth sent him a detailed report.[18]

The Maharajah of Nepal expressed his 'deep concern',[19] the Shah of Iran hoped the King would make a 'complete and early recovery',[20] the Emperor and Empress of Japan sent 'sincere sympathy to the King and Queen' on the King's indisposition. As diplomatic relations between Britain and Japan had been suspended due to the war, these messages could only be accepted 'privately' and 'informally'.[21]

The Foreign Office and Buckingham Palace were bombarded by 'shoals' of communications 'from well-wishers in all quarters who desire to put their personal experiences and their recommendations of the physicians responsible for their cures at the disposal of His Majesty's medical advisers'.[22]

A man in Sweden had suffered severe blood poisoning due to infected teeth, which were removed. Later his blood was thinned by sulphonimide tablets and he was completely cured. A 'warm-hearted lady' living near Boston, Massachusetts, who had suffered from 'venous ligation' recommended her surgeon, Robert R. Linton. In Paris the Embassy was approached by everyone from astrologers to vendors of patent medicines. A Mr Goldberg in Milan urged the King not to allow his leg to be amputated. He had muddled along with the use of warm linseed poultices and, by giving up smoking, and was still alive twenty years later.

The distinguished Argentine doctor Mariano Castex sent his medical works to Professor Learmonth, and the equally distinguished surgeon Dr Maurice Tussau in Paris, who had been consulted about George V in 1929, put forward his diagnosis. And so the well-meant recommendations flooded in from Washington, New York, Copenhagen, Vienna, Jerusalem and Warsaw. By and large these offers were not welcomed by the King's medical team, yet all were acknowledged in the manner deemed appropriate.

The King remained in bed until the middle of December, evidently a difficult patient, disinclined to read a book, hard to keep 'amused & occupied' and lacking in 'resources'.[23] But he was well enough to go to Sandringham for Christmas, and even to shoot a bit. At the end of the year, Tommy Lascelles reported: 'The K. continues to please his doctors, but he won't be out of the medical wood for many weeks yet.'[24] Early in the New Year he took his first drive since the illness.

During his recuperation Sir Gladwyn and Lady Jebb went to stay a night at Sandringham, in order that the King could knight him.* Queen Elizabeth met Cynthia Jebb in the hall, who described her: 'She has very dark hair which I imagine must be dyed; blue eyes; a pretty skin, with very little make-up on it; a very charming smile which, even in repose, remains in her expression of serenity and agreeableness. This, enforced by a soft voice and considerate, sympathetic and tactful words, produce an effect of great charm.'[25]

* Sir Gladwyn Jebb (1900–96), later Lord Gladwyn. Appointed KCMG 1949.

The King appeared alert and in better health than press reports had suggested. He was cracking jokes and, as at Glamis in the 1920s, 'if it borders on improprieties such as lavatories, all the better.' He called the Queen 'Ducks', noticed Lady Jebb. A piper circled the table twice when dinner was ended and the Queen withdrew, in her 'very beautiful dress, unmistakeably Hartnell, of black net richly embroidered with coloured paillettes, very much crinolined'.[26]

By 24 February the King and Queen were back in London. It was at Buckingham Palace that Learmonth and James Paterson Ross carried out a right lumbar sympathectomy operation. The only reason for the delay was the need for the King to gain strength to face the knife. Learmonth pepped him up with iron pills, and set about the hard task of getting him to cut down on his smoking. The operation was finally undertaken in a specially created surgical theatre in the Buhl Room on 12 March and was considered a success. The leg was saved and there was a wave of relief across Britain. Yet when Harold Nicolson called on Queen Mary to talk about his book on George V, she told him in a sad voice: 'The present King . . . now he is so ill, poor boy, so ill.'[27]

Learmonth warned the King that he must now reduce the tempo of his life since thrombosis could occur if he was stressed either psychologically or physically. These warnings the King heeded, though he did not find it easy. His Hanoverian temper remained a problem. He had been known to kick a Corgi across the room at Windsor.[28] Group Captain Townsend recorded that during one of the King's 'gnashes' Queen Elizabeth held the King's arm high, appearing to take his pulse, and saying 'tick, tick, tick' to lighten the moment.[29]

During his recuperation, the King took little part in public life, so that until May Queen Elizabeth led the engagements with the rest of the Royal Family supporting where necessary.

In the midst of this, on 25 May, Queen Elizabeth's oldest brother, Patrick, 15th Earl of Strathmore, died at Glamis, having been seriously ill for some months. The Earl had been a widower since the death of his wife, Dorothy, also after a long illness, in June 1946. The Royal Family had not attended Dorothy Strathmore's funeral, which took place in Ascot week, but for her brother Queen Elizabeth took the special train to Scotland, with Katie Seymour in attendance, for the second feudal funeral at Glamis in five years. The estate now passed to Timothy, Queen Elizabeth's then unmarried, increasingly alcoholic and reclusive nephew. Thus Glamis entered a strange, isolated phase which lasted until Timothy's death in 1972.

The King was not well enough to go to the Derby on 4 June, but five days later he attended Trooping the Colour in a carriage, while Princess Elizabeth, who had lately moved into Clarence House, rode to the Parade as Colonel of Grenadier Guards with the Duke of Gloucester beside her. The King was able to enjoy Royal Ascot, especially when his horse Avila won the Coronation Stakes. The King and Queen then retreated to Balmoral for a few days.

In July they were back in London, and it was considered noteworthy that the King stood throughout several investiture ceremonies. When in evening dress, he wore black suede shoes for the comfort of his foot, which surprised some who met him.[30] Eleanor Roosevelt had read that the King had returned to public duties and wrote to Queen Elizabeth to say how pleased she was. Queen Elizabeth replied:

> I am glad to tell you that he is *really* better, and with care should be quite well in a year or so. It is always a slow business with a leg, and the great thing is not to get overtired during convalescence. You can imagine how difficult this is to achieve with the world in its present state, & worries & troubles piling up![31]

Hoping that Mrs Roosevelt would soon visit Britain again, Queen Elizabeth told her: 'I am sure that you will find that people are recovering very quickly from the effects of that long and agonizing war. One feels that the anguish & worry reveals itself long after, & last year was bad, & now one feels a divine revival of spirit & serenity.'[32]

Whatever concerns she may have had, Queen Elizabeth's Voltairian optimism was undented.

22

'Crawfie'

'No No No to offers of dollars'
– Queen Elizabeth to Marion Crawford

As the King's health stabilised, the Royal Family might have hoped for less anxious times. But in 1948 they had embarked on a seemingly harmless course of allowing press access to Princess Elizabeth for a series of articles about her upbringing to be written for an American magazine. This exercise got out of hand, leaving Queen Elizabeth feeling betrayed.

Bruce and Beatrice Blackmar Gould, joint editors of the *Ladies' Home Journal* in the United States, wanted the articles to show how a princess was trained to be Queen in the middle of the twentieth century. The plan was a long time gestating.

The Goulds, who both lived from 1898 to 1981, were ambitious editors who had emerged from relative poverty in Iowa and risen through the tough school of reporting, short-story writing and even play-writing to running the *Ladies' Home Journal*, resurrecting a flagging magazine in a few years and assuring it the largest circulation of such a magazine in the world.

They achieved this by audacity, inspiration and downright ruthlessness. They employed guile and charm. They flattered world statesmen, they lured innocent sources into exposing their secrets. Shamelessly, they rewrote copy to suit what they decided their readers wanted. They had an eye for a good story and took time and skill to 'develop' it. During their co-editorship, which lasted from 1935 until 1962, they commissioned many top literary figures and addressed numerous social issues. They hailed their readers as 'Ladies of America'.

They professed devotion to Anglo-American relations, and made friends with influential figures such as Eleanor Roosevelt, whose badly written memoirs, *My Story*, they serialised, while in England they forged links with Lady Astor, Stella, Marchioness of Reading, and Kay Elliot (later Baroness Elliot of Harwood).

In the war they hit on the idea of a series of articles by 'Women of the World' – influential women writing on behalf of their countries. They enlisted Mrs Roosevelt for the United States, and set about targeting the doughty Queen Wilhelmina of the Netherlands, Madame Chiang Kai-shek for China, Madame Pandit for India, Eve Curie for France, and for Britain Queen Elizabeth. 'Each would do an article about the bonds of sympathy which unite women everywhere, their concern for the nourishment, health, and education of children in their own lands and in every nation. They would suggest a universal spiritual Esperanto – philosophical, nonpolitical, but promising sympathy and, if possible, aid in the postwar years.'[1]

To this end the two editors travelled to England at the time of Mrs Roosevelt's wartime visit in the autumn of 1942. They later claimed that Mrs Roosevelt had put their idea to Queen Elizabeth, who said she needed to take advice. They further claimed that during a stay at Cliveden with Nancy Astor there had been a luncheon attended by Queen Elizabeth and Princess Elizabeth, and that, after lunch, Lady Astor had given Beatrice Gould the chance to outline her plan in person to the Queen. 'The Queen listened with warm concentration,' wrote Beatrice, 'but with non committal ease, explaining again that she would need to consult her advisers.'[2]

The plan failed, and evidently Tommy Lascelles called on Mrs Gould at the Ritz to explain that Queen Elizabeth was 'above and beyond politics' and 'could not speak to this matter to other nations'.[3] Mrs Gould sailed home.

In 1948 the Goulds returned to the fray, with Princess Elizabeth as their new target. They approached Buckingham Palace, harnessing all their allies to their cause. Ambassador Winant was involved, Brendan Bracken was consulted, and finally, in 1948, the Foreign Office. Ambitiously, the Goulds wanted to commission their series to be written by Princess Elizabeth 'as told to' an author of their choosing.

This idea was quickly squashed by Mary Agnes Hamilton,* at the Foreign Office. The Goulds then proposed that Rebecca West write on the Princess, but Mary Hamilton warned them that only an approved writer would get their articles for them and expressed some surprise that the Palace 'was willing to fall in with the plan',[4] at all.

The Palace's man was none other than Dermot Morrah, who had become a close friend of Lascelles, with whom he had played chess on the long journeys in South Africa. Taking the line of least resistance, the Goulds commissioned him for the enormous sum of $2,500 for some articles and brought him over to the States. The Goulds concluded: 'He

---

* Mary Agnes Hamilton, CBE (d. 1966), a former Labour MP, had been a Governor of the BBC. She was a novelist and biographer, and was at the Foreign Office between 1940 and 1952.

deeply respected the monarchy, the Roman Catholic Church, and good wine, though not necessarily in that order.'[5] But they feared that his pieces were likely to be too formal and dry: 'While they may be excellent for English readers who take royalty and a reverence for royalty for granted, this is not likely to be the best treatment for Americans.'[6]

Morrah soon became a staunch ally and an informant on matters royal. He told them that Queen Elizabeth was keen for him to produce the articles. He mentioned that Prince Philip understood the needs of the American press, but that the Prince did not wish to be interviewed himself. 'This is all good as far as it goes,' he claimed, 'particularly because I know the Prince is the one person who can bully the King and Queen when they are inclined to be stuffy. But I do want to see the Queen, if I can, myself.'[7]

Morrah was soon busy working his way 'through a long list of court worthies, all of whom have been most anxious to help'.[8] One figure eluded him, the one person that all the courtiers recommended – Marion Crawford, until lately the royal governess.

In January 1949 Morrah had approached Crawfie through Lady Cynthia Colville, one of Queen Mary's ladies-in-waiting, acting spontaneously, and as a good friend of Morrah's, since his wife was Chairman of the Metropolitan Juvenile Courts, in which Lady Cynthia served as a magistrate. Despite this, Crawfie 'gracefully evaded' Morrah's requests to see her.

It may be thought that Crawfie was adhering to the rule of reticence implicit in royal service. She appeared to be regarding even formal requests with royal backing as unwarranted intrusions. This was not the case. Crawfie had a plan. She had just retired as governess to Princess Margaret, having stayed on after Princess Elizabeth's wedding.

Crawfie had lived with the Royal Family on intimate terms. She was adored by their friends, had been involved with their pantomimes and even captained the Buckingham Palace Troupe of Girl Guides. All had gone well until, in 1947, two months before Princess Elizabeth's wedding, Crawfie had married George Buthlay, a divorced major, who had served in the Middle East in the war with an outfit called UNNRA, several of whose members were court-martialled for some shady business in Albania, which almost certainly involved smuggling. Out of work at the time of his marriage, Buthlay had appealed to Sir Ulick Alexander, Keeper of the Privy Purse and a Director of the Scottish Union Insurance Company, who secured him a job with the Bank of Scotland, which enabled him to suggest he was a bank manager.

In 1949 Crawfie had retired to Nottingham Cottage, a charming grace-

and-favour residence at Kensington Palace opposite the apartment of the Dowager Marchioness of Milford Haven, Prince Philip's grandmother.*

There is no question that Buthlay was a bad influence on Crawfie. We can but speculate how this thirty-eight-year-old spinster adapted to married life with such a man. He was a philanderer, both before and after the marriage, he manipulated her and fueled her anger. Prodded by him, she became irritated by her pay, felt that her pension was inadequate,† was unhappy with the meagre wedding presents she had received from the Royal Family,‡ and even became dissatisfied with the CVO she was given on retirement in January 1949, apparently feeling a DCVO would have been more appropriate.§

Until her marriage Crawfie had never considered telling her story. The idea of helping Morrah did not appeal. Meanwhile, Buthlay sniffed the chance that his wife might make a lot of money telling her own story in her own words. So she kept Morrah at bay.

Meanwhile, the Goulds heard from Dorothy Black, a successful novelist who wrote a letter column for the *Ladies' Home Journal*, that Crawfie 'had been more or less retired and that she was definitely huffy – if not absolutely angry – with the Palace. We were informed that she was more or less ready to tell her story with or without the Palace sanction.'⁹

Dorothy Black discovered that Crawfie was hoping to be allowed to write her own story about the education of the princesses, under her own name, and that she had been to see Queen Elizabeth in February to discuss this idea. She hoped to obtain the full approval of the Queen, and had appointed the agents Pearn, Pollinger & Higham to represent her.

Queen Elizabeth was not happy about this plan. She delayed a while and then made her position clear. In April 1949 she wrote to Crawfie in a letter marked 'Private':

---

* Many years later, Nottingham Cottage was the home of Sir Philip Hay, Private Secretary to Princess Marina, Duchess of Kent, which gives some idea of its status as a grace-and-favour home.
† All Royal Household salaries were low because the Civil List, agreed in 1937, was proving inadequate due to post-war inflation. Her pension may have been modest but she lived in a rent- and rate-free cottage in a sought-after area of London.
‡ In *The Little Princesses*, Crawfie lists her presents as a coffee set from Princess Elizabeth, three bedside lamps from Princess Margaret, a 'complete and very beautiful' dinner service from Queen Mary and a visitors' book from the Princess Royal. She mentions nothing from the King and Queen, which may be significant.
§ The King appointed only ten lady CVOs in his reign, most of them ladies-in-waiting, one the Private Secretary to the Prime Minister, and another the Chief Clerk in his office. Crawfie was appointed 'for personal services'. He only appointed nine DCVOs, who were either relations, or ladies-in-waiting, and one Vice-President of Queen Alexandra's Army Nursing Board. Crawfie's CVO was exceptional and she should have been well pleased with it.

My Dear Crawfie,

I am so sorry to have been so long in giving you my views about the questions you asked me, but, you know, they were extremely difficult to answer especially as I fear that the answers are still the same as I gave you when you came to see me. I do feel, most definitely, that you should not write and sign articles about the children, as people in positions of confidence with us must be utterly oyster, and if you, the moment you finished teaching Margaret, started writing about her and Lilibet, well, we should never feel confidence in anyone again. I know you understand this, because you have been so wonderfully discreet all the years you were with us. Also, you would lose all your friends, because such a thing has never been done or even contemplated amongst the people who serve us so loyally, and I do hope that you will put all the American temptations aside very firmly . . .

Queen Elizabeth offered to help Crawfie get another teaching job. She concluded:

Having been with us in our family life for so long, you must be prepared to be attacked by journalists to give away private and confidential things, and I know that your good sense & loyal affection will guide you well. I do feel most strongly that you must resist the allure of American money & persistent editors, & say No No No to offers of dollars for articles about something as private & as precious as our family.[10]

This was sound advice, which was not taken. All its dire prophecies eventually came to happen. In the same month, Dermot Morrah went to see Queen Elizabeth, and she said of Crawfie: 'She is a bit wrought up just now, but I don't think she will always be like this.' He concluded that there was 'still ill-feeling on the part of both Crawfie and her husband, Major George Buthlay, about the terms of the financial settlement on her retirement from royal service'.[11]

In May Sir Arthur Penn wrote to Morrah on the Queen's behalf making two points, that any of Mrs Buthlay's recollections could be incorporated into his articles on Princess Elizabeth, but that it was undesirable that articles should appear under Mrs Buthlay's by-line since this might lead to embarrassment.[12] Undeterred, in May the Goulds came to London in ruthless pursuit of Crawfie, full of flattery, professing friendship and trustworthiness, dropping into the conversation, and later their letters, snippets of homespun philosophy recalled from famous figures. They were more than a match for the then innocent Crawfie. There were meetings with Crawfie and her husband. On 25 May Crawfie signed her contract with them. It was a grim document.

The contract recognised that Queen Elizabeth did not favour the proposed articles, but accepted that Crawfie's reminiscences could be given to Morrah. It commissioned Crawfie to produce a manuscript of forty thousand words or more with the help of a secretary-journalist, provided by the Goulds. It hoped that Queen Elizabeth's approval would be granted, in which case Crawfie was to obtain permission from the Queen, Queen Mary and the princesses to reproduce facsimile copies of their letters to her.

Point 4 addressed the issue of the Queen's endorsement being withheld, in which case Crawfie would agree to consider the incorporation of her material into articles by Dermot Morrah or another writer. Point 5 suggested she would consider producing them under her own name on terms to be arranged. Point 6 promised that the editors would not publish anything without the written agreement of Crawfie or her agents, and point 7 covered the 'complete discharge of the *Ladies' Home Journal*'s financial or other obligations' to Crawfie for two payments of £250. Point 8 opened the way for further negotiations over money should the articles be published either under Crawfie's name or someone else's.[13]

On 27 June 1949 Crawfie sat down with Dorothy Black, who, the Goulds assured her, would be 'immensely helpful in making your story a story which will enlist the sympathy of the Queen as well as our readers, not an easy thing to accomplish'.[14] Crawfie did so in the belief that she could still control her story. In letters to the Goulds, drafted by Buthlay, Crawfie told them she would have preferred to dictate to her husband, that she resented Dorothy Black being cut in on the deal, hated the 'alarming' headings suggested, and was scared stiff by telegrams from the Goulds, which had her name on them. But she retained 'abundant faith on your word and great journalistic & editorial experience'.[15]

The Goulds sent nasty newspaper cuttings about the Royal Family from the States to show Crawfie the ill-informed and hostile rubbish that only she could refute. They sent an American stenographer to type the work confidentially. The Goulds agreed to pass $300 to Kenneth Buthlay, George's son by his first marriage, who was then in the States. Meanwhile Buthlay dispensed with Crawfie's agents and put himself in charge. Bruce Gould arrived at the Dorchester on 18 August. The work was done.

Back in the States, and with the typescript safely in his hands, Bruce

Gould wrote to Crawfie: 'I hope you will trust Beatrice and me to take fullest advantage of your rich material in a way which will give it the broadest possible appeal.'[16] This was ominous.

Once the Goulds had finished their editing, they enlisted the help of Lady Astor in getting a fair copy of the script delivered to Queen Elizabeth. This was done through David Bowes-Lyon, conveniently married to Nancy Astor's niece, and ever eager to dabble in court affairs.

Meanwhile, Crawfie and her husband took a holiday at the Caledonian Hotel in Aberdeen, confident that the text would please Queen Elizabeth. By the time Crawfie came south, she was so imbued with the Goulds' propaganda that she (or rather George Buthlay) wrote that she was sure that 'my story will bring America & Britain closer together in real friendship & understanding. I feel that our Foreign Office will welcome the chance. Like you, we pray all will go well & that the Queen will not only agree but also write a preface in her own handwriting.'[17]

Queen Elizabeth received the latest version of the script from her brother towards the end of her Balmoral holiday. It appeared to be the work of Crawfie, but in fact it was the Goulds' final version, which Crawfie had not yet seen. With it came an unctuous letter from the Goulds addressed to the Queen, assuring her that 'the American public will get a story that will enthrall them & endear the Princess & the Royal Family to them beyond measure'. They requested that Queen Elizabeth 'give the project your blessing by briefly prefacing the articles over Your Majesty's photograph'.[18]

The King had gone south earlier and Queen Elizabeth had plenty of time to read Crawfie's articles. She completed her reading in the first two weeks of October. She was nothing short of horrified. On 19 October she left Scotland, inspected the Queen's Bays in Chester and arrived back at Buckingham Palace. She wasted no time in informing Lady Astor of her feelings:

> Perhaps you have heard that the whole thing has been a great shock to us, and I wonder whether Mr & Mrs Gould would consider taking out some of the inaccurate or dangerous bits, which would indeed be a *great* relief.
>
> We have worried greatly over this matter, and can only think that our late & completely trusted governess has gone off her head, because she promised in writing that she would not publish any story about our daughters, and this development has made us very sad . . .
>
> We have to trust our people completely, and such a thing has

never happened before, & is a bad example to others, as I am sure you understand.[19]

Lady Astor cabled Bruce Gould to say the King and Queen were horrified. The following day she elaborated:

You can have no idea what a shock it is to Their Majesties. I thought it would be, because their personal staff are always so loyal, and I may add Their Majesties are so trusting. I do hope you will be able to take out what they wish. You see how helpless they are about it all, and how hurt, and I think too if you do this it will give them so much confidence in anything else that we wish done in reference to the USA and Great Britain . . .

I do feel for Their Majesties, & apparently Princess Elizabeth is deeply shocked & hurt & furious.[20]

Shortly afterwards Nancy Astor went to the Palace to see Queen Elizabeth's Private Secretary, Major Thomas Harvey. Instead she was ushered into Queen Elizabeth's room: 'She was so understanding about it all, but deeply distressed by Miss Crawford. She thinks she must have gone queer, for it was not too long ago that they saw her, and then they felt she was not quite her old self.'[21]

Queen Elizabeth had charged Tom Harvey to address the points she disliked. Harvey wrote to Lady Astor. He did not mince the words of official disapproval he was bidden to express. He stressed the distress that had been caused to the King and Queen by a trusted member of the Household breaking silence to deliver herself of her personal reminiscences. This was alien to the spirit of the Royal Household, and furthermore a breach of decency and good taste.

Then he made his first tactical mistake. He told the Goulds that there was nothing much that Queen Elizabeth could do about it. He asked for thirteen points to be addressed on the grounds that they were either distorted, untrue, would cause pain or would dig up matters best left undug. He hoped that by removing these points, some of the damage would be mitigated, though, even so, publication of the articles would be absolutely 'repugnant', to the King and Queen.

His points were as follows: offence had been caused by the implication – believed by Crawfie – that the King and Queen were not greatly concerned with the higher education of their daughters, that Queen Mary had intervened to improve matters (which was true), or that it was she, Crawfie, who had asked Georgina Guérin to help with holiday work and who had allocated a private sitting room to Princess Elizabeth.

Queen Elizabeth objected to the implication that she did not like scenes, and that therefore things were kept from her. She was cross at a story that Princess Elizabeth had scratched from her lesson books the name of Dr Simpson,* who had invented chloroform, and at another that the King, Queen and Princess Elizabeth had stood on the Brunswick Tower, watching an air raid destroying London, and resisting appeals to come down. This, he claimed was untrue and offensive. There was also the story that, in a game of charades, the Duchess of Kent had drawn 'Royal Flush', and pretended to pull a lavatory plug. Harvey described this as a silly story and hoped it be excluded. There were a few other points.[22]

Although Lady Astor sent the Goulds a copy of Harvey's letter, they withheld it from Crawfie, stating that it was confidential to Lady Astor. Dermot Morrah was taken into their confidence. He advised the Goulds that Queen Mary's lady-in-waiting, Lady Cynthia Colville, took a rather dim view of Queen Elizabeth's attitude towards education: 'According to her no Bowes-Lyon ever cared for things of the mind – rather a harsh judgement considering that the family has produced three not negligible poetesses in the last twenty years. (One of these, however, disgraced herself two years ago by marrying a Papist, so we don't mention her at Court).'[23]

From afar Crawfie begged that any points raised by the Palace be addressed since in that way she would have fulfilled her obligations to the Queen. Gould warned Crawfie that Queen Elizabeth was 'likely to be rather cool to you, at least until after the story is published and she begins to realize how much good it has done the Royal Family in this country'.[24] The ultimate fate of Crawfie was of little concern to him.

Here lay cause for misunderstanding. Queen Elizabeth believed that Crawfie had promised not to publish under her own name. Crawfie believed that she had only promised to submit her text for approval. In Crawfie's mind, guided by Buthlay, the removal of the thirteen points effectively gave that consent. It was a misinterpretation that would never be resolved, as Dermot Morrah recognised:

> The Queen has dug her toes in firmly and is not going to budge on the principle that all former royal servants are forbidden to write under their own names about the royal family. This means, I fear, that Mrs Buthlay has blotted her copybook for good and all. On the

---

* Sir James Simpson (1811–70), Professor of Medicine at Edinburgh University. His paper advocating the use of chloroform was delivered in 1847.
† Lady Cynthia Colville was annoyed that a private letter she had written on behalf of Queen Mary was to appear in these articles. In *The Little Princesses* it was paraphrased.

other hand they go out of their way to say that you and Mrs Gould are in no way to blame.[25]

Furthermore, he wrote:

It's an interesting dispute about Crawfie's alleged promise to the Queen, but I'm rather glad that my interest in it need be no more than academic. The background of it is evidently two women who, after long years of association, have got on one another's nerves; and when that happens they are likely, with the most honest intentions in the world, to put opposite interpretations on the plainest documentary evidence. I'm prepared to believe that the production of the letter may settle the question for you and me and Lady Astor, but don't expect it for a moment to do so for the two principals.[26]

Queen Elizabeth was overgenerous in her interpretation of the role of the Goulds. They had been unscrupulous in luring Crawfie with offers of money and leading her to believe that she was contributing to the good of Anglo-American relations. Queen Elizabeth does not appear to have considered the odious role of Crawfie's husband. Some will argue that she was unduly harsh on the governess herself.

Now the long ostracism of Crawfie began. She began to fear that 'the Queen's displeasure' might soon extend to 'the Household and then to the social circles outside the Palace which have embraced me up to now'. She feared for her grace-and-favour house and her pension (or, rather, Buthlay led her so to do). Buthlay also encouraged her to consider a lecture tour, though she was horrified at the idea of crossing the Atlantic, but again in his words, she wrote: 'Whatever way the wind may blow, I would be wise to make as much as I can while the going is good as (a) I shall certainly require every penny I can earn if the Queen's displeasure is brought to bear against me, and (b) if events cause Her Majesty to smile upon me, whatever I do to make *The Little Princesses* more popular, will only add to my favour in the Queen's eyes.'[27]

Crawfie never heard a direct word from Queen Elizabeth, then or later. When Christmas came, there was the usual card from Princess Elizabeth, sent from Malta, and a card, but this year no present, from Queen Mary. The Royal Household remained friendly a while longer. Lady Mary Alexander* came to a cocktail party given by the Buthlays, central heating

---

* Lady Mary Alexander was formerly Lady Mary Thynne, whose dance in 1922 Queen Elizabeth had attended just before her engagement. She married Lord Nunburnholme, divorced in 1947, and then married Sir Ulick Alexander.

was put into Nottingham Cottage, and when she needed a car the House-hold provided one.

In Buthlay's words, Crawfie kept her chin up as best she could:

I have no fear of what might be called 'consequences' because I have adhered to the terms of my understanding with the Queen, and if she decides to be unfriendly, or worse, she will be the loser. If any action on Her Majesty's part is brought to bear on me to my detriment, I shall not hesitate to expose it in the Press if necessary, and if an attempt should be made to eject me from this house and/or deprive me of my pension, I shall fight in Court and have the facts made public if I am driven to do so. All this is not likely to happen, however, as I have earned both house and pension, and in any case I feel that, as you have already said, the Queen will merely feel she should show a certain amount of disapproval, and the non-arrival of the usual card at Christmas may be the first sign of it, absolutely childish as it is.[28]

Here the drama ends in so far as it affects Queen Elizabeth. The Goulds took a week off to alter Crawfie's prose 'word by word, line by line until we had it, finally to our liking'.[29] This resulted in Crawfie being livid to find herself suggesting that the Duchess of York might attend a function in Edinburgh, dressed in 'agreeable old tweeds, & sensible shoes', or describing the Duke of Windsor as 'golden-haired, glamorous Uncle David'. Incidents were inserted which never happened and words put into the mouths of those who never said them. Crawfie feared 'serious innuendoes & implications, most especially as far as I am concerned'.[30] The Goulds did not care. They would be neither the first nor the last editors to rewrite copy.

The Buthlays realised that the game was up, and the best they could do was to get as much money out of the Goulds as possible. This is the explanation for many plaintive letters typed by Buthlay and signed by Crawfie. There is a difference in style between her naïve and childlike writings and the bitter missiles that he wrote in her name. In the end the Buthlays gained about $80,000, which the Goulds instantly recuperated by selling overseas rights for $90,000. A little tax notwithstanding, the Goulds had obtained Crawfie's tale at no cost to them. They remained in touch with Crawfie throughout 1950 as the articles appeared, and fifteen million readers lapped up the governess's account of life with the royal children. After that, Crawfie had served her purpose. They suggested she might write some pieces on the King, but rejected her preference to write about Queen Mary.

The *Ladies' Home Journal* put another five hundred thousand on its circulation, reaching two million, Buthlay was sent a gold watch that he wanted, and Crawfie a ham. They were invited to the royal garden party at Buckingham Palace in July 1950 and were pleased when Sir Eric Miéville, the King's former Assistant Principal Secretary, greeted them warmly. They did not stay long.

In November 1950 the Buthlays had enough money to buy a large house in Aberdeen, 60 Rubislaw Den South, to which they retreated. For by now the Queen's displeasure had indeed permeated throughout court circles, and, in the words of a courtier of the time, 'they were shunned by colleagues from top to bottom'.[31]

Crawfie went on to publish a life of Queen Mary (*The Queen Mother*) in 1951, and sold her name to a further series of articles on Princess Elizabeth in *Woman's Own*, which emerged as *Queen Elizabeth II* in May 1952, and went into six impressions by February 1953. *Happy And Glorious* and *Princess Margaret* also appeared that year. All these were written by whoever was delegated the task in the offices of *Woman's Own*.

Crawfie's story ended badly. On 16 June 1955, *Woman's Own* published a gushing account of Trooping the Colour and Royal Ascot. Unfortunately these events were cancelled due to the National Rail Strike between press date and publication six weeks later. Crawfie became a figure of public mockery and was never heard of again. Despite provocation she remained loyal to Buthlay until his death in 1977, and she stayed on in Aberdeen, making at least one suicide attempt in old age. She died at Hawkhill House, an Aberdeen nursing home, on 11 February 1988 at the age of seventy-eight. The press made much of her lonely funeral, with no wreathes from the Royal Family. Her Royal Household pension, which she thought might have been rescinded, was paid until she died.[32]

Queen Elizabeth never forgave the betrayal and was wary about future lapses. The Royal Household were obliged to sign confidentiality agreements, which almost did for Major George 'Hoppy' Hopkins, Superintendent at the Royal Mews, who had a little book up his sleeve. He got round this by putting it into the name of his wife, Phyl.*

As to the Goulds, they were more than satisfied with the exercise. Nor did they cease to blow their own trumpets. They were delighted when, in August 1950, Crawfie's book became the top best-seller in non-fiction

---

* *Village Royal*, by Phyl Hopkins (Angus & Robertson, 1955). It was a harmless enough effort, though occasionally sharp: 'It would be idle to pretend that Queen Elizabeth's countless attractive qualities included the flair for classical elegance . . .' (p. 97).

in the United States. They wrote to Major Harvey to inform him of the good effect the articles were having for the monarchy in the minds of the American people. Harvey conceded politely that although none of them could 'approve or condone' the conduct of the writer, they could recognise the fact that 'good may come out of evil!'[33] They then pursued the idea of Queen Mary publishing her diaries, an idea which did not materialise.

In 1950 the Goulds failed to persuade the theatrical agent and producer Leland Hayward that *The Little Princesses* would make a great Rogers and Hammerstein musical.

Throughout 1956 they were hot on the plan that Queen Elizabeth should write her memoirs, or that Dermot Morrah (helped by Dorothy Black) should write a 'serial biography'. They tried to engage Lady Astor as go-between. At first she refused outright but later approached David Bowes-Lyon, who warned her that his sister was 'notoriously evasive'[34] when it came to this sort of matter. In their memoirs, the Goulds claimed that Queen Elizabeth 'dallied for months with our proposal that she write her story'.* They concluded somewhat archly:

> She preferred her endless games of solitaire. 'The truth is,' one of those close to her confessed at last, 'she's too lazy' – an integral part, no doubt, of the Queen Mum's plump, enduring charm.[35]

The more likely truth is that the Queen Mother wished to have nothing more to do with the machinations of those unscrupulous editors.

---

* In October 1956 Bruce Gould went to see the American Ambassador, Winthrop Aldrich, who appeared so keen that he was prepared to approach Eisenhower to support the project. Aldrich was clearly admiring of the Queen Mother – 'I do believe she has quite won his heart as, apparently, she does everyone's,' wrote Gould (Bruce Gould to Lady Astor, 30 October 1956 – Astor papers, MS 1416/1/2/532 – Reading University). Cass Canfield, publisher at *Harper's*, was also keen on a book.

The Death of George VI

'I am sure that he was looking forward to some slightly less anguished years' – Queen Elizabeth

The last years of the King's reign were overshadowed by fears for his health, though not, at first, specific ones. There were occasional chills that confined the King to his room, but he led a reasonably normal life. He was then in his early fifties.

The General Election of 23 February 1950 returned Clement Attlee with an overall majority of eight. On 6 March the King opened Parliament in state, Queen Elizabeth wearing the circlet with the Koh-i-noor diamond in it. The Korean War was a major issue preoccupying the new if limping Government. The uncertainty of their tenure of parliament worried the King, and in due course led to a further General Election in October 1951 in which the Conservatives regained power, and returned Churchill to Downing Street.

The first battle between the two parties, which might have caused the Labour Government to fall, occurred on the evening of the gala performance at Covent Garden during the state visit of President Vincent Auriol of France and his wife, in March 1950. The Government survived by a slender majority, and rival Members of Parliament were able to rush to the Royal Opera House and take their respective places in seeming amity. The King played a full part in the French President's visit, and he and the Queen went to Victoria Station to wave them farewell. On 27 April there was a Garter ceremony at Windsor, and the King was able to walk in the procession down the hill.*

During the year it was often the Queen who led the royal party. When the King did appear, he looked frail and grey, lined of face and forehead. At the 1950 Trooping the Colour, he drove to Horse Guards Parade in a carriage, though he stood to take the salute.

In July Queen Elizabeth toured north Nottinghamshire and opened

---

* A few days earlier, in true kingly manner, he had shown himself at his most animated when informing the actor Anthony Quayle that, when portraying Henry VIII on stage, he was wearing his Garter incorrectly.

Hesley Hall, a home for disabled children near East Retford, pointing out that those who most deserved 'agility of mind to compensate them for the disability of a bad body' would now be well cared for in this new, specially equipped home.[1] She dined with the Duke and Duchess of Portland at Welbeck Woodhouse, and stayed with the Duke's mother, Duchess Winifred, widow of her mother's first cousin, at Welbeck Abbey.

Both the King and Queen maintained their well-tried routine, the King keeping abreast of news and Cabinet papers. Dermot Morrah wrote: 'He is not a quick reader, and he never skips; but he has the reward of the conscientious labour he devotes to these tasks in that he always remembers what he has read.'[2]

Every morning Queen Elizabeth was occupied with her Private Secretary over public engagements and her lady-in-waiting over private correspondence and household matters. Some mornings were devoted to dressmakers or shopping, and then private luncheons. Like the King, she had audiences to give. She tried to temper the more solemn role of the King with informality. Morrah explained:

The Queen works by persuasion rather than by command. She is always calm and gentle; as a parent she seems easy-going . . . While now with a grandmotherly hand she once more rocks the cradle, she sways, by an influence unobtrusive yet palpable, the affections and affairs of the people of the British Commonwealth.[3]

This was the working Queen at fifty. Other writers described her as 'a matron, dignified both in face and figure' with 'no streaks of grey in her soft chestnut-brown hair'. She occasionally used glasses for reading or writing, and her 'fresh Scottish complexion' remained 'so pleasing that many younger women envy it'.[4] Her love of chocolates was no secret. The Queen's plumpness was noted and her friends wrote of 'contours', while Cecil Beaton suggested she was now so fat that she could not cross her hands over her waist, a wicked exaggeration.

On 14 August the King arrived alone at Balmoral, while Queen Elizabeth waited in London until Princess Elizabeth gave birth to her second child, Princess Anne, who was safely born at Clarence House the next day. She and Princess Margaret then joined the King in Scotland.

A curious domestic crisis preoccupied Queen Elizabeth during this holiday. Her niece, Anne, had married Viscount Anson, a Grenadier Guards officer, in 1938. Anne was the eldest surviving daughter of Queen Elizabeth's brother, Jock, from his ill-fated alliance with Fenella Hepburn-Stuart-Forbes-Trefusis, a 'magically dotty woman',[5] as her grandson put it. Unlike two of her sisters, who were confined in a state mental hospital, Anne had been born sound in mind and limb, but was flighty by nature.

Her marriage had produced a son and daughter, Patrick and Elizabeth,* but during the war Anne had been less than faithful to her husband, and when he returned home little rapport was left between them. When he wished to divorce her, he was informed by his commanding officer that he must step forward as the guilty party. Obligingly, he did so, and in March 1948 they were divorced on the grounds of his desertion, Anne claiming that he had left her in January 1945.

For a time she had floundered about in London, precariously short of money, resorting to occasional employment, one occupation being to demonstrate refrigerators at the Ideal Home Exhibition for a welcome £19 a week.

None of this was especially satisfactory, so Queen Elizabeth then found Prince Georg of Denmark, a lofty figure of no great spark, aged thirty and serving as Military Attaché at the Royal Danish Embassy, first in Paris and then in London. This description is supported by Patrick Lichfield, who described his new stepfather as 'a middle-aged and rather strait-laced career diplomat with an endless appetite for military music'.[6]

It was arranged that the pair would be married in the chapel of Glamis Castle on 16 September 1950. Canon H. G. G. Rorison, Lord Strathmore's chaplain, was set to preside when he was suddenly forbidden to do so, 'because the bride had been party to a divorce'.[7] Into his place stepped Revd Mogens Buch, pastor of the Danish Seaman's Missions in Newcastle upon Tyne, who performed the marriage ceremony.

Various royal figures attended the marriage, including Crown Prince Olav of Norway, his two daughters, and Prince Carl Bernadotte of Sweden. But Queen Elizabeth stayed away in order to avoid allegations of supporting the celebration of a divorced woman marrying in church. She and Princess Margaret confined themselves to attending the luncheon party afterwards.

Queen Elizabeth prevailed upon King Frederik of Denmark to allow her niece to be styled HH Princess Georg of Denmark, whereas many similar such unions had ended with Danish princes renouncing their titles and becoming Counts af Rosenborg, as Prince Georg's younger brother, Flemming, had been obliged to do when he married a commoner. The Denmark–Anson union was a matter handled deftly, diplomatically and subtly by Queen Elizabeth, without her own position being tarnished.

The Archbishop of Canterbury (Geoffrey Fisher) referred to this

---

* Patrick, 5th Earl of Lichfield (b. 1939), the well-known photographer, and Lady Elizabeth Anson (b. 1941), who runs Party Planners, which organises all the grandest parties in London.

incident when talking to James Pope-Hennessy some years later. He described Queen Elizabeth as 'a profoundly religious woman', but doctrinally, he believed, there was 'little impact'. He cited the non-attendance of the wedding as evidence for this. Queen Elizabeth had not disapproved, but she did not want to get 'muddled up in it'. The Archbishop then listed the things he believed the Beaverbrook press hated most, above all else the Archbishop and the Church of England. He thought they loved divorce. 'So they thought they could get us all at once over Prince George of Denmark – Queen Mother, myself, Church of England, marriage in Scotland – the whole bag of tricks.'[8]

On 21 October 1950, the King and Queen were present at the christening of Princess Anne, and Queen Juliana of the Netherlands paid a state visit. The following year the Festival of Britain was celebrated, and London's South Bank burst into post-war regeneration. The King was well enough to open proceedings on the steps of St Paul's Cathedral on 3 May. There were plans for a royal visit to Northern Ireland in June, and the cancelled tour of Australia and New Zealand was rescheduled for December.

In March 1951 the King and Queen invited the Churchills to dinner, and Queen Elizabeth told her friend Audrey Pleydell-Bouverie on the telephone that they had enjoyed every minute of it. Audrey urged Churchill: 'Do ask them to come & have drinks with you one evening because I know they would love it – they so rarely go out unofficially & love it when they do.'[9]

But the King was getting increasingly tired and looking visibly ill. He had restricted his public engagements to those of maximum importance, with the fear of thrombosis ever-present. In May he was well enough to preside over King Frederik of Denmark's state visit to London and to invest him with the Garter and install him at a Garter ceremony at Windsor. Again the King processed down the hill.

A visit to the Chelsea Flower Show one day and to the London Stock Exchange another was followed on 24 May by the first ceremony of the Order of the Bath since 1935. At all of these Queen Elizabeth was present. The King was clearly ill when he installed the Duke of Gloucester as Great Master and twenty-seven other GCBs at Westminster Abbey. On that occasion, the last great ceremony he attended, he was, 'to the great distress of all present . . . obviously ill and in such pain that the procession had to be considerably curtailed in an endeavour to spare him fatigue'.[10] Even so, in the afternoon he and the Queen visited the Imperial Institute.

The next day, with a high temperature, he took to his bed, or, as the bulletins stated, was 'confined to his room' with 'a mild attack of influenza'.[11] After being examined by the doctors, the King was relieved to learn that he had a catarrhal inflammation on the left lung, known as pneumonitis. He thought a week of penicillin would remedy this. In fact, he was suffering from cancer of the lung, but there was some delay in diagnosing this. The King's radiologist, Dr George Cordiner, had diagnosed it correctly, and was worried that his advice was ignored. Apparently he brooded on this to the point that he took his own life with an overdose of barbiturates in April 1957.[*][12]

The King's visit to Northern Ireland was cancelled, and soon afterwards all his engagements were cancelled for the next four weeks. There was concern that the King's illness was more serious than was being stated.

While the King was resting in his room, the burden of his duties again fell on Queen Elizabeth. She hosted the traditional family party for Queen Mary's birthday, her eighty-fourth. She took Princess Margaret to Northern Ireland with her and they toured Ulster, staying with her sister, Rose Granville, whose husband was now Governor of Northern Ireland. Katie Seymour was in attendance, but it was a sadder trip than the joyous visit of 1924, when the Yorks were setting out on their married life.

The King was not able to greet King Haakon on his state visit, and his place was taken by Queen Elizabeth and the Duke of Gloucester. Queen Mary made a special effort to come to the state banquet at which Princess Elizabeth was 'charged' to read her father's speech. Princess Elizabeth led the Birthday Parade and took the salute at Trooping the Colour for the first time.

The King was still in his room at the Palace when Queen Elizabeth and the Royal Family presided over Royal Ascot. Only at the end of that week was he well enough to travel down to Royal Lodge. He remained there until 9 July, presiding over a meeting of the Privy Council on 29 June. He was not well enough to attend the garden party, but on 31 July he held an investiture at the Palace, when, dressed as an Admiral of the Fleet, he knighted thirty-four men, including the actor Godfrey Tearle and the composer William Walton.

On 2 August the King and Queen retreated by the evening train to Balmoral, taking Prince Charles and Princess Anne with them. Here the King was able to enjoy something of the open-air life he so relished,

---

* Dr George R. M. Cordiner, CVO (d. 1957), hon. radiologist at St George's Hospital, London. He was given a CVO in June 1951 for personal services to the King. Many tributes were paid to him when he died.

including some shooting. Having scarcely been seen in public for more than three months, he was photographed with his family, but looked pale and thin at the Braemar Gathering on 6 September.

He then developed a chill and a sore throat. Sir Horace Evans, his physician, and Clement Price Thomas, a leading specialist on malignant diseases of the chest, came up to Balmoral on 1 September for what was described as a routine inspection. The King was also seen by Dr Cordiner and the chest specialist, Dr Geoffrey Marshall. They decided that the King should come to London for a bronchoscopy, described as 'a more thorough examination'.[13]

The King had not been expected south until 10 October, but two days later he went down to London by train and visited Dr Cordiner's rooms at 7 Upper Wimpole Street. Only then, after numerous reports had been filed and the traditional second opinion sought, was a tumour discovered at the root of the King's lung.

The King returned to Balmoral for a final week, and then flew down to London, again without the Queen, on 15 September. Three days later the bronchoscopy was performed. The bulletin, signed by nine doctors, spoke of 'structural changes' having developed in the King's lung. Churchill summoned his doctor, Lord Moran, to Chartwell to explain the situation. As soon as Moran heard that one of the doctors was a chest surgeon, he translated 'structural changes' as cancer. He was also worried by the lack of reassurance in the bulletins, the news that Queen Elizabeth was flying down and that Queen Mary had been to visit the King. This he believed was to prepare the public for the worst. On hearing this, Churchill brooded 'darkly' on the matter and went silent. 'Poor fellow,' he muttered. 'I'll pray for him tonight.'[14]

Immediately the Queen, Princess Elizabeth and the Duke of Edinburgh flew to London, the Queen wearing her habitually reassuring smile. The tumour was discovered to be malignant and the King's left lung was entirely removed in an operation performed at the Palace on the morning of Sunday 23 September.

Queen Elizabeth and Princess Margaret were at the Palace, Princess Elizabeth and the Duke of Edinburgh at Clarence House and Queen Mary with the Duke of Gloucester and the Princess Royal at Marlborough House. A huge crowd waited nervously outside the Palace gates. Finally the King regained consciousness, and the crowd outside was marshalled to file past the bulletin attached to the gates: 'The King underwent an operation for lung resection this morning. Whilst anxiety must remain for some days, His Majesty's immediate post-operative condition is satisfactory.'[15] The doctors did not say that the King's other lung was infected and that he could not live more than two years.

Meanwhile the King's engagements were all cancelled, and on 27 September, Princess Elizabeth's proposed visit to Canada between 2 October and 5 November was postponed. The reticence of earlier bulletins was criticised in the press.

Queen Elizabeth and her daughters carried on the business of monarchy. On 27 September she and her daughters were appointed to serve as Counsellors of State, along with the Duke of Gloucester and the Princess Royal.* On the same day, perhaps to show that all was well, or due to a strong urge to be there, Princess Elizabeth went to Ascot with the Duke and Duchess of Norfolk, and again the next day, with Princess Margaret and the Princess Royal.

During these worrying weeks Queen Elizabeth was a lone figure visiting the WVS, schools, hospitals and exhibitions, and present at the dedication of a new chapel for the Manchester Regiment, engagements so special for them, so usual for her and made additionally difficult by her concern for the King. By 6 October the King was deemed to be over the worst and the postoperative period to have passed without complication. He held a bedside Privy Council meeting and signed the proclamation dissolving parliament.

The Royal Family spent their weekends in London. Because the private chapel at Buckingham Palace had been destroyed in the war and had not been rebuilt, and because the Chapel Royal at St James's Palace admitted the public, Queen Elizabeth chose to go to the Archbishop of Canterbury's private chapel for at least three Sundays running. 'I am sure it has helped her not a little to find herself in a family group here with everything completely private and simple,'[16] explained the Archbishop.

Princess Elizabeth and Prince Philip departed for their Canadian tour on 8 October. In their suitcases were emergency clothes of mourning (which was not unusual), and accession documents that might be needed should the King die in their absence. The next day it was announced that the Princess would undertake the Australia and New Zealand tour the following year on behalf of the King.

The King carried out as much business as he was able from within the confines of the Palace. He was well enough to receive the Prime Minister, Clement Attlee, on 26 October, when he resigned following his defeat at the General Election, to receive Mr Churchill, and presently the first eight new ministers as they took office. On 5

---

* Usually six Counsellors of State are appointed, and these are traditionally the six next in line to the throne, over the age of twenty-one. Effectively a quorum of two act at any time. Counsellors of State are appointed if the Sovereign cannot undertake his duties due to illness or absence abroad.

November the King again received Mr Attlee, bestowing on him the Order of Merit.

Queen Elizabeth watched the Duke of Gloucester lay the King's wreath at the Cenotaph on Remembrance Sunday, accompanied on the Home Office balcony by Queen Mary, Princess Margaret and other members of the Royal Family.

The King was not well enough to come to Euston Station to greet Princess Elizabeth and the Duke of Edinburgh on their return from Canada on 17 November. Much has been written of Princess Elizabeth's supposed formality when greeting Prince Charles, then two years old. However, *The Times* recorded:

> When the royal train stopped, Princess Elizabeth and the Duke of Edinburgh could be seen smiling through the window of their carriage. Prince Charles began to skip joyfully as he caught sight of his parents. Within a few seconds the people gathered on the platform were witnessing a happy family reunion.
>
> Princess Elizabeth stepped out of the train and kissed her mother on both cheeks, then knelt down and hugged Prince Charles affectionately. The Duke of Edinburgh saluted the Queen, and then turned at once to greet his son, who smiled up at him . . .[17]

The Duke of Windsor had recently published his memoirs, *A King's Story*, a further source of annoyance for the Royal Family. He had intended to be present at a dinner in London given by the Book Publishers' Association, but cancelled it when the King became ill. Now he appeared in London for a lunch given by the Association at Claridge's. He also lunched with Queen Mary and visited the ailing King before returning to Paris. Lascelles's line was that the less attention paid to 'these blasted memoirs', the better.[18]

On 27 November Queen Elizabeth succumbed to one of her rare colds and had to cancel two engagements. But she was in the car with the King when he was driven to Royal Lodge on 30 November. A small crowd saw him as he emerged from the Palace, looking grey and dressed in a heavy grey overcoat. On Sunday 9 December special prayers were said throughout the land to give thanks that the King had been brought 'in safety through the dangers of a severe operation to daily increasing health and strength'.[19] The next day the King revoked the warrant appointing the Counsellors of State and resumed his constitutional duties.

A cough which developed early in December required a second bronchoscopy to help relieve it. On 21 December the King and Queen went to Sandringham for a Christmas party which included Queen Mary, the Edinburghs and their children, the Gloucesters, and the Duchess of Kent and her three children. Queen Elizabeth was still smiling and waving from the car, giving no sign of inner fears.

The King's traditional Christmas Day message was recorded this year to save him the strain of having to deliver it live. The explanation given by Buckingham Palace was: 'The King's voice has not yet regained its normal strength and is still liable to be a little uncertain.'[20] As usual, he and the Queen worked on the speech together to get it as he wanted it. The King took the opportunity to express his 'deep thankfulness' to the 'faithful skill' of his doctors, surgeons and nurses for getting him through his illness. He told his listeners how disappointed he and the Queen were to be 'compelled' to cancel their Australian trip for the second time.

While the general public remained optimistic about the King, the experts were unhappy. Obituaries had been commissioned and updated, and those with medical knowledge expected the worst. Staff who saw him at Sandringham distributing gifts were shocked by how ill he looked.[21] The King himself was in the band of the optimists, unaware of the extreme gravity of his health.

The King stayed at Sandringham in January 1952, making plans for a recuperative visit to South Africa with Queen Elizabeth, departing on 10 March. There were shooting parties at the Bircham, Harpley, Shernbourne areas, Appleton and elsewhere, the King going out with the guns from time to time and taking an occasional shot. Only on 16 January, the day of the funeral of Alfred Amos, the former head keeper, was shooting cancelled as a mark of respect. Queen Mary left for London on 14 January and figures such as Lord Dalkeith came to stay.

On 28 January the King and Queen and Princess Margaret returned briefly to London. The King had a check-up, invested the New Zealand Finance Minister, Sidney Holland, as a Companion of Honour, gave an audience to Churchill, and the whole family went to see *South Pacific* at the Drury Lane Theatre.

The next day, the King, his immediate family and the Prime Minister were at London Airport to bid farewell to Princess Elizabeth and Prince Philip as they set off to fulfil the twice cancelled tour of Australia and New Zealand, stopping in East Africa on the way.

One of those present was Oliver Lyttelton, Secretary of State for the Colonies. Later he expressed the concerns felt by many who saw the King that day:

I was shocked by the King's appearance. I was familiar with his look and mien, but he seemed much altered and strained. I had the feeling of doom, which grew as the minutes before the time of departure ebbed away. The King went on to the roof of the building to wave good-bye. The high wind blew his hair into disorder. I felt with deep foreboding that this would be the last time he was to see his daughter, and that he thought so himself.[22]

The King and Queen and Princess Margaret went to Sandringham, taking Prince Charles and Princess Anne with them. The King resumed his quiet days as best he could, while Queen Elizabeth and Princess Margaret did likewise.

On 5 February 1952, the King went out shooting in a group of twenty including tenants, police and visiting gamekeepers. The bag was 280 hares, four rabbits and two pigeons. Of these, nine hares fell to the King's gun. On the last drive there were a great many hares. The King teased his neighbour, saying he would get any hares before they crossed the hedge to him. Aubrey Buxton described what happened as the hares appeared to see the King and headed towards the next gun:

The first was bowled over by His Majesty on the crest of the bank. His friend looked across and was greeted with a gleeful grin. The second was far out in front when it made the hedge, but the King got it none the less. The third, and the last, was at full speed, for the drivers were close in, but His Majesty killed it cleanly against the hedge.

It was his last shot.[23]

Queen Elizabeth and Princess Margaret had gone cruising for an hour and a half on the Norfolk Broads with the artist Edward Seago, lunched with him at Ludham, went to Barton Broad with him, and then on to tea at Barton Hall with Mrs (David) Peel,* widow of Lady Delia's nephew. The artist sent some pictures back in the Queen's car. She and the King looked at them in the hall, before and after dinner. 'He was enchanted with them all, and we spent a very happy time looking at them together,'[24] she later wrote.

In the evening, Phil Haywood, one of the Sandringham gardeners, brought flowers up to the Big House to be arranged next morning at 6.30 a.m. He happened to see the King in conversation with Lord Fermoy.[25]

---

* Her son, Jonathan, was a page of honour to the King.

There was no reason to note anything unusual. The family dined together and the King retired to bed. The night watchman heard the King open the window of his downstairs bedroom for fresh air before retiring. He went to bed and died quietly and peacefully in his sleep.

Queen Elizabeth was served her morning tea by her dresser, Gwen Suckling. Shortly afterwards, the King's equerry, Captain Sir Harold Campbell, asked to see her. He informed her of the King's death. She was stoic from the first, and, after visiting the King's room, ordered that a constant vigil be kept there.

Later she spent part of her day playing with her grandchildren. Queen Mary was told at Marlborough House; Churchill was informed at 10 Downing Street. When his Private Secretary, Jock Colville, visited him later in the day, he found him 'sitting alone with tears in his eyes, looking straight in front of him and reading neither his official papers nor the newspapers'.[26] The Princess Royal, recuperating from fibrositis at St James's Palace, cancelled a visit to Switzerland. The Duke of Gloucester, who was leaving Barnwell Manor for an engagement, drove over at once to Sandringham. The Duchess of Kent flew home from a family visit in Germany and the Duke of Windsor sailed from New York.

The King's death was announced from Sandringham at 10.45 a.m., and was broadcast to the world on the BBC at 11.15. In 1837 Queen Victoria had been told she was Queen when in her nightgown. In 1952 Princess Elizabeth had become Queen while perched in a tree house at Treetops, in Kenya. It was an extraordinary way to begin a reign, watching a glorious day dawn over the wide landscape of Africa, the heralding of a new age. She was told of her father's death by a stunned Duke of Edinburgh, and began at once the journey home.

The next days were ones of inestimable sadness for the British people. Some worried about the new young Queen, still out in Kenya, and were happier once she had made her confident if poignant descent of the aircraft steps, dressed in black, and was safely back in Britain.

The King's family was as shocked as anyone. Patricia Hambleden telephoned the Queen Mother (as she was now to be)* who 'said it had been the most dreadful shock to them all, for he had seemed so well and happy the day before'. Queen Mary was 'heroic beyond words, but heartbreaking to see'.[27]

---

* Queen Elizabeth was thereafter always known as Queen Elizabeth in court circles to differentiate her from The Queen. But more widely she was called 'the Queen Mother'. Her official title in widowhood was 'Her Majesty Queen Elizabeth The Queen Mother'. A distinction could be made whereby the cognoscenti used 'Queen Elizabeth' rather than 'the Queen Mother'.

The coffin of George VI made the same journey as that of his father sixteen years before, first to the little church at Sandringham, then by train to London.

There was the dramatic photograph of the three Queens awaiting his arrival at Westminster Hall for the lying-in-state, which said more about the transition then taking place than any of the many images of that time – Queen Mary, upright and grim, in full Tudor mourning, a figure from another century; the distraught widow in her veils; and the slim-waisted young Queen, on the brink of her destiny.

Churchill's voice spoke movingly to the nation of the King who had walked so nobly with death at his side and the people watched and wept silently for the King they loved so well. The gun carriage conveyed the King's coffin through London's streets. And so he was borne to Windsor.

The diplomat Charles Johnston was present in St George's Chapel. He witnessed the pageantry:

> There was genuine emotion, but it was certainly helped by superb stagecraft. The crowded, silent nave and the first faint hint of the approaching bagpipes. There was a primitive, anthropological quality, all the stranger from the unfamiliarity of the ingredients. The tribal wail and drumbeat of the lament. The timeless, deadpan shrillness of the bosun's pipe as the coffin was taken off the gun carriage. The ritual, clockwork slowness of the Heralds in their court-card get-up pacing in ahead of the procession. The Pharaonic attributes of majesty on top of the coffin as it came in at the West Door. The courtiers on each side of it, familiar figures quaintly holding bearskin or braided brodrick headgear, and Lord Clarendon [the Lord Chamberlain] like a lame witch doctor limping in front with his wand.
>
> The tiny veiled figures of the Queens, the Duke of Windsor as an Admiral of the Fleet and Lord Mountbatten as a Personal Naval ADC (two curious bits of ceremonial fantasia), then the foreign potentates* all yellowed and pinched with the appalling cold of this remote Hyperborean Kingdom . . .
>
> Here was something very old and strange and not at all artificial and in a way pathetic. It was the machinery of the nation state putting on the best show it could.[28]

At the appropriate moment in the service, the coffin was lowered into the Royal Vault and the lame Lord Chamberlain broke his wand of office.

---

* Sir John Weir, the King's homeopathic doctor, claimed a record in having prescribed Ignatia for five kings and three queens during their visits to England for the funeral.

The twenty-five-year-old Queen sprinkled earth on her father's coffin as it gently descended out of view. On the lawn outside rested Churchill's wreath with the simple words: 'For Valour'.

The presence of the Duke of Windsor was another of those 'black sheep' occasions that had haunted Queen Elizabeth with intolerable regularity throughout her husband's reign. He had followed his brother's coffin with the Dukes of Edinburgh, Gloucester and Kent, but was criticised by one observer for his swaggering walk, 'talking and looking around, gesticulating and almost waving to the huge and completely silent crowd'.[29] The Duke went to see Queen Elizabeth briefly, when, according to his notes at the time, she 'listened without comment & closed on the note that it was nice to be able to talk about Bertie with somebody who had known him so well'.[30] He concluded that it was the Queen Mother and Princess Margaret who minded the King's death the most, and that the new Queen and her consort represented a 'Brave New World. Full of self-confidence.'[31]

Many tributes were paid to the King and, in these tributes, Queen Elizabeth was not forgotten. In the House of Lords, Lord Salisbury, Leader of the House, spoke of 'the Queen Mother, who trod with him so radiantly the way of life, and who will forever be linked with him in our hearts'.[32] Lord Jowitt, the Lord Chancellor, described her as having 'shared with him the anxieties of the age, sustained him in his trials, and supported him in all his endeavours'.[33] In the House of Commons, Churchill spoke:

> I have said his was the hardest reign of modern times. He felt and shared the sufferings of his people as if they were his own. To the end he was sure we should not fail; to the end he hoped and prayed we might reach a period of calm and repose. We salute his memory because we all walked the stony, uphill road with him.
>
> This ordeal he could not have endured without the strong, loving support of his devoted and untiring wife and Consort.* To her we accord, on behalf of those we represent, all that human sympathy can bestow.[34]

Many wrote to Queen Elizabeth to express their sympathy, including Mrs Roosevelt and even the playwright Tennessee Williams. The Prime Minister, Winston Churchill, wrote privately and he was one to whom

---

* This was greeted with 'Hear, hear' in the chamber of the House of Commons.

King George VI – Colonel-in-Chief, Grenadier Guards

The Royal Family
at Royal Lodge, 1937

The King and Queen arriving
at St Giles Cathedral, Edinburgh,
for the Order of the Knights of
the Thistle service, 9 July 1937

The Royal Procession passing through the Place de la Concorde, 19 July 1938.
Note Police balloon overhead.

Queen Elizabeth in Paris, 1938

Queen Elizabeth with Mrs Roosevelt,
driving from Union Station to the
White House, 1939

The King and Queen with
Mackenzie King in Canada during
a weekend in Banff

Queen Elizabeth, photographed
by Cecil Beaton, in the garden at
Buckingham Palace, July 1939

The controversial photograph of
Mr & Mrs Neville Chamberlain with the
King and Queen at Buckingham Palace
after Chamberlain's return from seeing
Hitler in Munich, 30 September 1938

The King and Queen
visiting a north western shipyard
during their tour of the North,
29 August 1940

The King and Queen visiting
a bombed area in south west
London, 19 September 1940

Queen Elizabeth with the widowed
Duchess of Kent (Princess Marina) on the 18th
birthday of Princess Elizabeth, 21 April 1944

Queen Elizabeth inspecting the one
thousandth tea car, named *America*, given by
the American people to the British people

Queen Elizabeth broadcasting from Buckingham Palace, 12 November 1939

The wedding of King Peter of Yugoslavia and Princess Alexandra of Greece: (*Left*) Queen Elizabeth kissing King Peter. (*Right*) King George VI and Queen Elizabeth with the bride, 1944.

The King and Queen, Princess Elizabeth and Princess Margaret with the Prime Minister, Winston Churchill, on the balcony of Buckingham Palace on VE Day, 1945

The Royal Family in South Africa in 1947: Evening dress in the open air; Queen Elizabeth photographing in Kruger National Park; Queen Elizabeth accepting an honorary doctorate at the University with Jan Smuts; Queen Elizabeth wearing an Aage Thaarup hat with the King and others at Tafelberg.

The King looking ill at the end of the South Africa trip

The newly wed Duke and Duchess of Edinburgh in Paris, May 1948

A medieval scene.
Three Queens at Westminster Hall for the Lying-in-State of King George VI in February 1952
– Queen Elizabeth II, Queen Mary and Queen Elizabeth The Queen Mother.

The King's funeral procession passing through Hyde Park Corner, February 1952

The new Queen Elizabeth II, wearing Queen Victoria's circlet and the riband of the Order of the Garter, 1953

Queen Elizabeth The Queen Mother and Princess Margaret in their Coronation robes at Buckingham Palace, 2 June 1953. Photographed by Cecil Beaton.

she replied personally, telling him how pleased the King had been to have him back as his Prime Minister. She wrote of the hopes that were now dashed:

> It is very difficult to believe the King has left us. He was so well, the day before he died, so gay, & so full of plans & ideas for the future. I am sure that he was looking forward to some slightly less anguished years, with perhaps a little time to give to fairer things, such as making gardens, which he loved, planning vistas and rehanging the pictures at Windsor, and other very English things which he never had time for.[35]

The New Elizabethan Era

'Life is immensely dull without him' – the Queen Mother

The death of the King effectively ended the political life of Queen Elizabeth, forcing her into a kind of retirement. She had sustained the King for many years, and latterly she had borne the burdens of Head of State, leading the nation when he was ill. Though his death was not completely unexpected, it was nevertheless a deep shock. The King and Queen had been looking forward to a period of recuperation in South Africa in March, with none of the demands of the 1947 tour.

Now everything changed. The new Queen, Elizabeth II, 'in the great and lonely station to which she has been called',[1] was the person to whom everyone turned. There was no defined role for Queen Elizabeth, a widow at only fifty-one. Her skill was to create a new role for herself.

There had never been a working Queen Mother before. Queen Alexandra, elegant, beautiful and deaf, had restricted her widowhood years to occasional appearances, notably her Alexandra Rose drives.* Though the popular belief is that she retreated permanently to Sandringham, she was frequently in London, living at Marlborough House. Queen Mary had played a more prominent role, especially in the early years of the reign of George VI when her presence forged a direct link between George V and his second son. She represented the stability that had been briefly threatened by the trauma of the reign of Edward VIII.

While Queen Mary was again a respected and much-loved figure, her later engagements were relatively limited. Neither Queen Alexandra nor Queen Mary ever played any part in the constitutional aspects of the next reign. They were never Counsellors of State in widowhood.

Queen Elizabeth did not seek to be a political influence. She would never occupy the kind of role that Queen Frederika of Greece played in

---

* Alexandra Day was instituted in 1913, the fiftieth anniversary of Queen Alexandra's arrival in Britain. Drives took place in June with roses as the outward, visible sign. Myriad flowers were sold in aid of British hospitals and, when able to, Queen Alexandra took a carriage drive in London so as to be seen.

the reign of her son King Constantine in the 1960s. She now retired from the political fray. Like many a widow, she found that she had the chance to do as she pleased, and not to have to subjugate her personal interests and tastes to those of her husband. She had done her bit, especially in the war, and she had earned her repose in her widowhood. When she recovered from the shock of the King's death, she created a very pleasing new existence.

However, this was no instant transformation. Queen Elizabeth minded greatly the loss of her power base as wife of the King. At first she found it hard to accept her daughter in her new role. As with many difficult figures who needed support, the loss of the King was acutely felt. She and the King had spent almost every day of their married life together, only being separated on the rare occasions when he visited troops overseas or she spent a few days with her father at Glamis. She missed him, and now she could see only his good qualities, and let slip the occasionally difficult times, the gnashes, the tensions and the frustrations. She adopted the line that she loved to talk about the King with old friends who knew him well. As the years went by, and these died off, she welcomed the chance to reminisce with any who remembered him. She held him in increasingly affectionate memory.

From the first moment of widowhood, the posthumous reputation of the King concerned her. They had reigned side by side, but she was anxious to stress that she had not been the dominant partner in the marriage and that she had not made political decisions for him.

Nor did she want the King portrayed as a man who could not cope or was in any way a feeble character. Any influence she had exerted had been done privately, with the King taking the credit. It had been subtle, understated, gracefully employed. She knew well that power was more effectively wielded behind the throne. Stories about the King's health worried her.

Queen Elizabeth was disturbed when a book about the King arrived in the post in April 1952. *His Majesty King George VI** was a study by John Pudney, the poet, best remembered for his famous ode to British airmen, 'For Johnny'.† Also a novelist, essayist and journalist, Pudney had been commissioned to produce this quick, well-illustrated commemorative volume, which contained good photographs and a well-written text.

* Published by Hutchinson, 1952.
† John Pudney (1909–77), author of *Spring Encounter* (1933) and of the poem 'For Johnny' (1941). The latter begins with the lines 'Do not despair/For Johnny-head-in-air –' and was broadcast by Laurence Olivier and declaimed by Michael Redgrave in the film *The Way to the Stars* (1945). In the mid-1950s he became an alcoholic, but recovered from his addiction.

Queen Elizabeth asked her Private Secretary, Oliver Dawnay, to address her concerns. First, she objected to the use of certain sources, which were not always considered 'as being completely accurate'. This was a veiled reference to quotes from Crawfie's book. Then she felt that 'undue stress' had been laid on the King's ill-health, and the 'recurrent allusions to gastric pain etc' might have suggeted 'a perennially unfit person'.

Dawnay pointed out that the King took part in every possible type of sport and exercise, and added, as an aside: 'I can tell you that up to the last year of his life, many young visitors – half His age – to His estates have been practically walked off their legs by their Sovereign!'[2]

In contrast, Queen Elizabeth was delighted to commission Aubrey Buxton, a shooting friend of the late King, to produce a book about his sporting life entitled *The King in His Country* (1955). This remains the most personal account of the last years of the King's life, though not everything the author wished to put in was passed for publication. Likewise, it has been widely hinted that Sir John Wheeler-Bennett's official biography of the King, *King George VI: His Life and Reign* (1958) suffered excisions made by the Queen Mother. It is an admirable work, but lacks illuminating anecdotes.

At the beginning of the new reign Queen Elizabeth was granted a Civil List Consolidated Fund annuity of £70,000, the same as that given to Queen Mary on 28 April 1936, which had never risen since then.*

The Queen Mother now had to decide where to live. She retained Royal Lodge at Windsor, and returned to Birkhall near Balmoral, lately the Scottish home of the Edinburghs. She still went regularly to Sandringham, which was a great solace, as she explained to Prince Paul of Yugoslavia:

> As the time goes on I miss him more & more – he was always so good & loving & thoughtful, & so much *fun* to be with.
>
> You knew him well, & of course he had developed & strengthened his already strong character through those long years of war, and life is immensely dull without him.[3]

The usual home for a Dowager Queen in London was Marlborough House, but Queen Mary was still alive and might occupy it for some

---

* Queen Elizabeth's Civil List annuity did not change until 1972, when it was increased to £95,000. By the time of her death, linked to inflation, it had risen to £643,000.

years to come. So, for longer than was usual, Queen Elizabeth remained at Buckingham Palace.

Presently it was decided that she would take over Clarence House, where neither Princess Elizabeth nor Prince Philip had felt especially at home, though it had been made more comfortable since the days of the Duke of Connaught, when it sported but one bathroom and indifferent lighting.

Clarence House was built by John Nash for the Duke of Clarence, later William IV, in 1825. He continued to use it as his London residence even after he became King. Later it was the home of Queen Adelaide, Princess Augusta (sister of George II), the Duchess of Kent (mother of Queen Victoria) and then two sons of Queen Victoria – the Duke of Edinburgh (until 1900) and the Duke of Connaught (until his death in 1942). From 1942 until 1947 it was the headquarters of the Red Cross and St John Organisation.

Clarence House had lacked unity and individuality when the Edinburghs lived there between 1947 and 1952. Only the Princess's desk reflected her individuality, with a profusion of family photographs (mostly of Prince Philip, but a snap of her mother and a Hay Wrightson of Queen Mary), while opposite, a Cecil Beaton of Prince Charles, his christening group, and a small oil painting of three ballerinas – *Le Lac des Cygnes* by Oliver Messel.

Princess Elizabeth had modernised the kitchen, introducing stainless steel units and daffodil-yellow tiles, but as a young couple they had few possessions and had relied on pictures borrowed from the Royal Collection, and the wedding presents given them in 1947. As the distinguished architectural historian Christopher Hussey wrote: 'As the years pass, and Their Royal Highnesses have the leisure to exercise their tastes in supplementing the present collection, most of the components of which have been gifts, no doubt personal preferences will become more marked.'[4] In other words, they had failed to impose any style on the place.

Queen Elizabeth was more confident in her taste. She set about stripping the walls and deciding which pieces of furniture she would take from her rooms at Buckingham Palace. She hung her collection of pictures. There were traditional works by Sir David Wilkie, Sir Allan Ramsay, Sir Peter Lely, and others of that ilk. To these she added the contemporary works she had bought in the war, which included, in addition to those already mentioned, a Simon Elwes of the Garter investiture of Princess Elizabeth and a James Gunn of Field Marshal Montgomery and officers in a mess tent in Belgium (1944) (bought direct from the artist), in the hall. The Morning Room sported two Sickerts, one of which was *Conversation Piece at Aintree* (1927), depicting George V and his stud manager, Major Fetherstonhaugh, her predecessor at Royal Lodge. Showing guests this picture, she would invariably remark of George V's unsmiling face: 'Not a day when he had a winner, I think.'[5] Here too hung Lowry's *A Fylde Farm* (1943).

The dining room was hung with Beecheys and copies of Hoppners (William IV and his brother, the Duke of Kent). Augustus John's *Ida Nettleship and Dorelia* hung on the lower half of the staircase, while his *Edith and Caspar*, a beautiful John Piper of the *Church of S.S. Giovanni e Paolo in Venice* and some Edward Seagos hung on the upper half.

The Ethel Walker, some sugary Savely Sorine portraits, two 1931 de Lászlós of herself and the Duke of York, two heads of George VI (by Simon Elwes and F. Hodge) and a Charles Sims of George V were hung in the Queen's Corridor. The drawing room with its Nash ceiling had early family portraits and a Brock of Princess Margaret as a small girl in white muslin dress, while the Small Drawing Room had a Simon Elwes of George VI at Princess Elizabeth's Garter investiture, a de László of Princess Elizabeth dated 1933, and a Rodrigo Moynihan of the Princess in a blue dress, painted in 1946.

The John Pipers of Windsor Castle, many of them still in their simple wooden wartime frames, were hung in the Lancaster Room, where visitors would wait before being summoned into the Queen Mother's presence in the Morning Room.

Then there was the Side Passage, known as the Horse Corridor, in which various Herrings and Stubbses competed uncomfortably with more modern interpretations of Queen Elizabeth's racehorses, many of which were of more sentimental value than artistic merit.

Clarence House was also filled with fine furniture, silver, china and Fabergé. The Queen Mother had made post-war purchases of furniture at house sales at Wentworth Woodhouse, buying a fine set of twelve eighteenth-century gilded chairs and sofa from Preston Hall, Midlothian, and pieces from her parents' later home at Woolmers Park, Hertfordshire. She bought a fine mirror from Ditchley Park. There was a mass of important plate, along with gifts acquired on royal tours, kept in the Plate Room. In her bedroom she placed Raffaelino del Garbo's *Madonna and Child* above the mantelpiece, and moved her bed in, which had a bedhead specially painted for her by Riccardo Meacci in 1923, a wedding gift from her aunt, Violet Cavendish-Bentinck.*

* This bedhead bears the Strathmore arms and the Royal Arms, without the differencing label of the Duke of York, above a flaming cauldron.

The Queen Mother had a large collection of clocks, from a massive Chippendale grandfather to a small Sheraton on a painted pedestal. There was a three-faced 1804 musical clock in the entrance hall, and two from the time of Louis XVI, made by Ragot and Dubois. There was a French gilded wall clock in the boudoir, and a Parliament clock from 1797, the gift of Coutts.

In the hall hung a 1600 Brussels tapestry bought in 1950, and presently a portrait of George III, bought one day with Queen Mary and only retrieved from Marlborough House after her death. Elsewhere was a cabinet filled with the Hanover service, many pieces of which the Queen Mother bought over the years, and another filled with Fabergé.

When eventually she moved in, Queen Elizabeth gave to Clarence House the charming ambiance of a country house in the middle of London. She opened a way through the rooms from the Morning Room through the small library to the rather dark dining room, which no one ever much liked, it being too closely overshadowed by Lancaster House.* She seldom used it, preferring to lunch at a round table in the small library, unless there were too many guests.

Princess Margaret also moved to Clarence House, her home until 1960. She was allocated her own drawing room overlooking the garden.† It was fitted with copious cupboards to house her gramophone records of ballet and Broadway musicals. The reconstituted Household was established there, including the Queen Mother's office, which was now run independently from the secretariat at Buckingham Palace.

As soon as all the kings and presidents left London after the King's funeral, the Queen Mother retreated to Royal Lodge. There was a small memorial service in the Royal Chapel in the Great Park.

She played no part in the Queen's decision, at the bidding of Winston Churchill, to declare on 9 April that she and her children should be called the House and Family of Windsor, thus denying the Duke of Edinburgh the chance to perpetuate his name.‡ This came about because Queen Mary heard that Lord Mountbatten was boasting that the House of Mountbatten now reigned since the death of the King. After a sleepless night, Queen Mary asked John Colville to consult Churchill. As a result, the Cabinet declared 'unanimously that they would tolerate no such thing'.[6]

* This dining room better suited the Duke of Connaught, who was used to wintering in Bath, and residing at the Pulteney Hotel.
† After Princess Margaret's marriage in 1960, Queen Elizabeth turned this into the Garden Room, and later hung her Augustus John portrait there.
‡ It is, of course, the anglicised version of Battenberg, the name of Prince Philip's mother, and not that of his father, that was in question.

Prince Philip wrote 'a strongly, but ably worded'[7] memorandum protesting against this, which annoyed Churchill, but in vain. Not until February 1960 was a further change made, giving to those descendants of the Queen and the Duke of Edinburgh as require surnames the name 'Mountbatten-Windsor'. It is not hard to detect pressure from Lord Mountbatten in the realisation of that change.*

The Queen Mother spent that Easter with her family at Windsor Castle, at which time she was still receiving messages of sympathy. An Australian Bishop sent a report on how sad the Australians felt at the King's death. Acknowledging this, the lady-in-waiting allowed herself a personal note: 'Her Majesty is wonderful, but these are indeed sad days for her, & one can hardly bear to see the happy family circle no longer complete.'[8]

After the Easter court, the Queen moved into Buckingham Palace and though the Queen Mother stayed on until April 1953, it was not long before visitors found her cared for by a skeleton staff. Another lady-in-waiting said: 'We're picnicking here.'[9]

The Queen Mother's first solo engagement in widowhood was to inspect the 1st Battalion Black Watch at Crail Camp, Fife, on 13 May, before they set off for Korea. She flew from Windsor for the occasion, dressed in the deepest black, made a speech about the regiment, but was still too shaken to make mention of the King. Five hundred men paraded past her as she stood dramatically on a hillside.

In May the Queen Mother and Princess Margaret went to Hatfield for a flight in a BOAC De Havilland Comet airliner. Lord and Lady Salisbury accompanied them, and at the last moment the Queen Mother suggested her chauffeur come too. This was their first jet flight and in the course of four hours they flew 1850 miles over France, Switzerland, Italy and the northern tip of Corsica. The speed of the flight reached 500 mph. Then the Queen Mother asked if they could fly faster than a meteor. The test pilot, John Cunningham, suggested that the Queen Mother push the control column forward and hold it there until the needle touched the red danger section. They achieved 525 mph.

At that point the Comet began to 'porpoise', or pitch up and down like a boat in rough sea. This indicated that the aeroplane was at the limit of its aerodynamic stability. Eighteen months later a series of fatal crashes would reveal fundamental weaknesses in the Comet's design. Had the 'porpoising' gone on much longer, the racking on the structure might have caused a rupture of the plane's skin. Blissfully unaware of this, the

---

* The Queen's descendants do not yet quarter Prince Philip's arms with the Royal Arms, which would be the normal result of a double-barrelled surname. An esoteric point.

Queen Mother's comment was: 'The Viking will seem a little slow after this.'[10] Sir Miles Thomas, Chairman of BOAC, who was also on board, recalled: 'I still shudder every time I think of that flight',[11] aware of how he had nearly escorted the Queen Mother and Princess Margaret on a celestial journey to rejoin the King.

On 26 May, Queen Elizabeth was among the royal visitors to Queen Mary on her eighty-fifth birthday, and even gave tea to the Duke of Windsor when he was briefly in London to visit his mother. She received General Eisenhower and his wife, and she paid a soothing visit to the Chelsea Flower Show. She attended Trooping the Colour, but, unlike the Queen and other members of the Royal Family, she avoided Royal Ascot, retreating to Balmoral instead where she enjoyed a holiday with her grandchildren, Charles and Anne.

The Castle of Mey

Before coming south again on 26 June, Queen Elizabeth flew from Aberdeen to Wick to stay with Commander Clare Vyner and his wife, Doris, who were living at the romantically named House of the Northern Gate,* on Dunnet Head, with commanding views over the red-cliffed Orkneys, fourteen miles across the sea. She arrived on 18 June, still wearing mourning for the King† and draped in furs. Here she could relax with one of the rare couples with whom she had sometimes stayed without the King. Lady Doris was one of her oldest friends and she particularly liked Commander Vyner, rich from coal mining, whom she remembered as 'such an energetic man, always doing something'.[12]

During her marriage, in her flower-filled drawing room Queen Elizabeth had spent much time alone, quietly playing patience or enjoying her thoughts and interests, her reading and her love of art and poetry. Now, at this time of bereavement, part of her wanted to retreat from the world. She was drawn to the northern shores of Caithness and fell for the one home among many that she could call her own.

The Vyners first took her to see Barrogill Castle (as it was then called). They arrived unannounced at the derelict sixteenth-century Z-plan castle. The castle had been occupied by the coastal defence troops from the Ministry of Defence during the Second World War, and important maintenance had been neglected because most of its staff had been called up.

* The Vyners had owned 8500 acres there, including the estates of Dunnet, Freswick and Keith, with rough shooting, trout fishing and loch fishing. Their house had eight bedrooms and dressing rooms.
† The court officially came out of mourning on 1 June, but she wore black for a whole year.

After the war, rates were high, but if roofs were left off, nothing needed to be paid. Thus Barrogill's roof was left with tiles missing, leading to extensive rain damage. Shortly before the Queen Mother's impromptu visit, a storm had further devastated part of the roof.

The Vyner party approached the front door and the commander rang the bell. There was no reply. But the door was not locked. In they went to find two pairs of shoes on the staircase 'green with mould', as the Queen Mother put it.[13] Eventually the owner appeared, finding the visitors walking outside again.

Barrogill belonged to Captain F. B. Imbert-Terry, MC, of the Devonshire Regiment, remembered in Mey as 'a somewhat enigmatic figure', whose wife had died a few years before.* He owned a cow and hens, liked shooting with his friends, and had recently sold off some land in lots. The Queen Mother was horrified to learn that there was real danger that Barrogill might be pulled down, the fate of so many small castles in Caithness. 'Never! It's part of Scotland's heritage. I'll save it,'[14] she declared.

The castle was almost certainly built between 1566 and 1572 by George, 4th Earl of Caithness. Ownership remained in the Sinclair family until 1889 when the 15th Earl died without issue, leaving it to a friend, P. G. Heathcote, whose widow, Mrs Gerold Sinclair, sold it to the Imbert-Terrys in 1929. As both the captain and his wife suffered from heart conditions they installed a lift.

The Queen Mother liked Captain Imbert-Terry. He would happily have given it to her but members of the Royal Family cannot accept such gifts. So he sold it to her for the nominal sum of £100.[15] Even after the sale, they kept in touch. The captain occasionally lunched with the Queen Mother, and when he died (on a cruise in 1963), she was represented at his memorial service.

The Queen Mother loved the castle's remoteness and found that she slept well in the far north. Not long afterwards she told Cecil Beaton that she had bought a castle 'in the most remote part of the world'. She told him her plan was 'to get away from everything', adding 'but I don't expect I shall ever be able to get there'.[16]

This was the line soon adopted by the press. They decided that she had bought the castle on an impulse, at a time of intense grief. As she recovered her spirits, so the Castle of Mey (to which she restored its original name) would surely be forgotten. Extensive restoration was required so that it was not until October 1955 that the Queen Mother spent her first night in the castle. This fuelled press speculation that her

* Captain Frederic Imbert-Terry (1887–1963), served in the First World War, married 1917, Lilian Hickman (1872–1949).

interest had declined. This was far from the case: from 1956 until the last autumn of 2001, she enjoyed holidays at that romantic castle on its bleak promontory.

In the restoration work, a new dining room was created, oil lamps were replaced by electric lights, a telephone line (with a scrambler) was installed, the captain's hipbath was removed and new bathrooms were installed. A hideous old yellow pine bird-case at the entrance made way for a jardiniere in the form of a huge shell bearing flowers, supported on coloured rocks, over a cave for a crouching blackamoor. The lift was eventually made to work once more.

Caithness was not to everyone's taste despite the cornfields and grass-land and the inquisitive seals peering from the breakers, but if the castle looked austere from the outside, this belied the style and comfort within. There was an emphasis on 1950s comfort, with chintzes and soft furnishings. Visiting just before the Queen Mother took up residence, Loelia, Duchess of Westminster, described its simplicity and comfort: 'From the moment a visitor enters the stone-flagged walls, the atmosphere of a well-loved house is continuously apparent.' The Duchess was pleasantly surprised to find 'such unashamed femininity, colour and comfort north of the Tweed'. She even took a look at the Queen Mother's bedroom, with its panelled walls painted in aquamarine, the white cornice, the grey carpet and cretonne curtains with pink rose and blue-leaf design.[17]

Sir Arthur Penn also approved. He loved Caithness with its vast skies, high above the turbulence of the Pentland Firth, and was quick to point out: 'They were wearing velvet and drinking claret in Caithness before they did so in the south.'[18]

Another challenge was the garden with its twelve-foot-high Great Wall of Mey. There had been a garden there in the seventeenth century, but by 1952 the kitchen garden was a tangle of overgrown hedges, with some old fruit trees and herbaceous material. David Bowes-Lyon, President of the Horticultural Society, was convinced that it was a lost cause, but the Queen Mother appointed Charlie Tate as her first gardener and went round the garden with him. 'The Queen Mother was interested in every small detail,' he said. 'She asked all sorts of questions, but I thought she probably knew more than I did.'[19] Hedges were reshaped, dividing the rose garden from the kitchen garden, shells were laid along the paths, and there was much experimenting since, though the great wall was a help and the warm current from the Gulf Stream deterred frost, there were occasional gales of great ferocity. The kitchen garden burst into life at the beginning of August, when fruit and vegetables, including rasp-berries and globe artichokes, were needed for the house parties.

As early as September 1952, the post office at Mey was bombarded with requests for postcards to be mailed to them all over the world, bearing the local postmark. 'It is a grand thing for the county,' declared the postmaster, George Laing. 'This is the first time Mey has really been on the map.'[20] David Banks, the estate contractor, told the press: 'To be sure the old folks of Mey are thrilled at the revival of the Auld Hoose. It will make a great difference to the county too.'[21] Journalists snooped about and one unearthed the Barrogill Castle time book, which recorded the daily history of the place, including 'oiling thè castle' every five years or so, a thirteen-day process during which it was brushed with linseed oil to prevent water entering cracks.[22]

That same summer a rumour emerged that the Queen Mother might be appointed Governor-General of Australia, which had some foundation as Churchill had discussed it privately in April.[23] When it was announced that the Queen Mother would be going to Southern Rhodesia the following year to open the Central Africa Rhodes Centenary Exhibition, the rumour began to gain credence. It was stated that the Queen Mother was planning an active future, and, whether or not that appointment came to fruition, she would be undertaking 'lengthy tours of the Commonwealth'.[24]

This was premature. Queen Elizabeth was still depressed and uncertain about what to do. When the Royal Family went to Balmoral for the summer, moving in for the first time, she retreated to Birkhall, her summer house most years since 1929.*

At Birkhall (which Churchill would presently describe as her 'remarkable abode'),[25] the Queen Mother employed a Glasgow architect to install new kitchens. In 1956–7 she added a granite wing with a high sloping roof of blue-grey slates from a neighbouring quarry, built at right angles to the house, which included four guest suites. There was a substantial Victorian porch, later painted white, with sturdy columns made of rustic, rough-hewn pine trunks, and the building was covered with ivy. The Queen Mother now implemented the garden plans which she and the Duke of York would have undertaken but for the Abdication. One of these involved a yew hedge planted many years before which had now grown high enough to serve as a new garden entrance and was adorned with a gate, latticed with iron-work flowers and fruits, bought at a Royal Highland Show.

In 1960 she bought a small cottage on the Invercauld estate for use as a picnic place. At one time there was a white caravan formerly used by

* The Edinburghs had used it between 1947 and 1952.

Lord Mountbatten in Burma, and loaned by him for young royal guests, and also a dirty green truck, which the young Duke of Kent sometimes used when in Scotland.

In that summer of 1952 the Queen Mother remained much on her own, unwilling to see anyone. She received *Closing the Ring*, the fifth volume of Churchill's *The Second World War*. In thanking him, she wondered if 'Providence' had been 'kinder to us than we realised' in providing him with time out of office to write 'this wonderful history of those glorious & anguished years of War'.[26]

After the King's death Churchill had promised to come and see her. She was glad to hear he was soon to stay at Balmoral, 'for it was always the King's ambition to get you there. He particularly wanted to hang your photograph with other Prime Ministers, & I hope that it will now occupy a place of honour in the Ministers' room.'[27]

Churchill paid the Prime Minister's traditional summer visit to the Sovereign between 1 and 3 October. He sent a message to Birkhall asking if he might make an appointment. Lady Jean Rankin, then in waiting, sent a message back: 'Don't ask. Tell him to come over.'[28] So Churchill arrived unannounced and had a talk with Queen Elizabeth.

Whatever Churchill said it had a salutary effect. Lady Jean thought 'he must have said things which made her realise how important it was for her to carry on, how much people wanted her to do things as she had before'.[29]

As her depression began to lift, the Queen Mother was pleased when Edith Sitwell sent her a copy of *A Book of Flowers*, an anthology she had published that year. She wrote to thank her:

> It was so very kind of you to send me a copy of your *lovely* book. It is giving me the greatest pleasure, and I took it out with me, and I started to read it, sitting by the river, & it was a day when one felt engulfed by great black clouds of unhappiness & misery, and I found a sort of peace stealing round my heart as I read such lovely poems & heavenly words.
>
> I found hope in George Herbert's poem, 'Who could have thought my shrivel'd heart, could have recovered greennesse? It was gone quite underground'* and I thought how small & selfish is sorrow. But it bangs one about until one is senseless, and I can never thank you enough for giving me such a delicious book wherein I found so much beauty & hope – quite suddenly one day by the river.[30]

* From 'The Flower' by George Herbert.

At Christmas Queen Elizabeth stayed at Sandringham with the Queen and the immediate Royal Family. Prince Paul of Yugoslavia, who had attended the King's funeral the year before, sent her some chocolates. She wrote: 'The extraordinary thing is, that they are *all* good! I have never had a box of chocolates before which didn't have pink flavoured with bath-salts, or nougat made of iron filings & sand, and it is so exciting to *know* that yours are all delicious.'[31]

Her sense of humour was returning.

Coronation and Crisis

'He has Theudas trouble' – Tommy Lascelles on Townsend

Christmas at Sandringham without the King had its own sadness. This was accentuated by the realisation that Queen Mary was fading fast. She only got up in the late afternoon and stayed mostly in her room. On her return to London she enjoyed being driven out to see the stands being erected for the Queen's forthcoming Coronation. She took her last such drive on 9 February 1953.

Queen Mary had hoped to see her granddaughter's Coronation, either from a special stand erected in the garden of Marlborough House, or at least on television. But she left instructions that, in the event of her death, court mouring was not to cause a postponement of the ceremony. At 10.20 p.m. on 24 March she died peacefully in her sleep at Marlborough House. The Queen restricted court mourning to one month.*

Queen Elizabeth had just come out of mourning for the King after a year. Now she was again dressed in black, as she 'gently acknowledged the crowd's silent waving with a nod of the head',[1] arriving at Marlborough House. Queen Mary had encouraged her marriage to the Duke of York, and to Queen Mary the Queen Mother had always been a dutiful daughter-in-law, keeping her informed and in touch, particularly during the war. Of her mother-in-law, Queen Elizabeth wrote: 'It was her mingling of stateliness and innocence, of a sense of enjoyment and a sense of duty, that made Queen Mary's character such a feature and support of contemporary English life.'[2]

Though Marlborough House became vacant, there was no change in the planned move of the Queen Mother to Clarence House, which took place on 18 May.

On 1 May, shortly before the move, on a day when the Queen Mother

---

* During the present Queen's reign, mourning has been curtailed to suit the royal programme. In October 2004, when Princess Alice, Duchess of Gloucester, died, there was 'royal mourning' only on the day following her death, and on the day of her funeral. This was so that the Queen did not have to wear black during a state visit to Germany.

and Princess Margaret were attending the British Industries Fair, the Queen Mother's brother Michael died at his Bedfordshire home at the age of fifty-nine. His health already damaged by his time as a prisoner of war in the First World War, he had long suffered from asthma, which greatly curtailed his activities. Death came from heart failure, chronic myocardial degeneration (fibrous), emphysema, asthma and bronchitis.

Michael had been heir to the Earldom of Strathmore since 1949, his nephew Timothy, the 16th Earl, being then unmarried. The Queen Mother and Princess Margaret flew up to the funeral at Glamis, returning the same night. Once again the coffin was conveyed to the family cemetery on a farm wagon flanked by gamekeepers.

Tributes were paid by old friends of the family. James Stuart wrote of his 'exceptional charm, manners and generosity in its best sense' and considered that he had such a closely united family 'due in large measure to his tactful handling of the normal problems of family life'.[3] His brother-in-law, Colonel Harry Cator, another shooting friend of the late King, opined: 'He had the countryman's patience and calm, common sense, sound judgement, and stored wisdom, the harvests of experience in the fields of life he understood and loved, and in addition the integrity and fastidiousness of a man of moral courage and taste.'[4]

Soon after this, on 2 June, the Coronation of Elizabeth II took place in Westminster Abbey. Norman Hartnell designed the Queen's Coronation dress, and battled with Garter King of Arms to be allowed to depict a daffodil to represent Wales. 'No, Hartnell, you must have the Leek',[5] Garter told him.

Following the precedent set by Queen Mary in 1937, the Queen Mother attended the Coronation. Hartnell designed her a gown of 'white satin, bordered with gold tissue and embroidered in a feather design of crystal, gold and diamonds'.[6] This dress hung limply at first, but he added an underskirt of ivory taffeta laced with horsehair and a great many strands of whalebone. Over her dress she wore the riband and star of the Garter,* the Royal Family Orders of the Queen and George VI (but no longer of George V), her three-strand diamond necklace (given by the King), and the circlet with the Koh-i-noor diamond, adapted from the crown with which she had been crowned in 1937. She wore a long and wide purple velvet train, adorned with gold, which was carried

---

* Coronations are 'Collar Days' but, apart from the Queen, none of the royal princesses wore their GCVO collars.

by four pages, the Earl of Erne, Viscount Carlow, Michael Anson and Jonathan Peel.*

Members of the Royal Family were allocated seats in the Royal Boxes on the north and south sides of the Abbey. Queen Elizabeth invited twenty-one guests (not including any Bowes-Lyons, who were invited by the Queen). Among Queen Elizabeth's guests were Nancy Astor, Audrey Pleydell-Bouverie (the former Audrey Coats, who would bequeath her a Fantin-Latour in 1968), Sir Osbert Sitwell, Lady Victoria Wemyss (her Bentinck cousin), the Vyner family and Katie Seymour, together with other ladies-in-waiting, the mothers of her four pages, and Sir Eric Miéville, who had worked for the King.

She travelled to Westminster Abbey with Princess Margaret in the Irish State Coach, and processed up the aisle alone, preceded by her Lord Chamberlain, the Earl of Airlie, and followed by the magnificent Dowager Duchess of Northumberland, Sir Arthur Penn and Countess Spencer.

Seated in the front row of the Royal Box, she watched a service similar to that in which she had taken part fifteen years before. During the ceremony she was joined by the four-year-old Prince Charles, who came to the Abbey just long enough to see his mother being crowned. Afterwards Cecil Beaton captured the burgeoning relationship between grandmother and grandson in a memorable photographic portrait at Buckingham Palace.† Beaton was quick to identify a new role for the Queen Mother 'so basically human and understanding'. He wrote: 'The great mother figure and nannie to us all, through the warmth of her sympathy bathes us and wraps us up in a counterpane by the fireside.'[7]

Hardly was the Coronation over than the Royal Family had to face the first major crisis of the reign. In the annexe of the Abbey, Princess Margaret had been spotted removing a piece of fluff from the shoulder of Group Captain Peter Townsend's jacket. Though the incident was not photographed, it was reported in the foreign press, where, as with the Abdication in 1936, speculation was already growing about the romance between the Princess and the former Battle of Britain pilot. The news broke in Britain in the *People* on Sunday 14 June.

* All were pages to the Queen and came from broken homes – 6th Earl of Erne (b. 1937), a godson of George VI, whose father had died of wounds in France in 1940; Viscount Carlow (b. 1938), grandson and successor to 6th Earl of Portarlington – his father had been killed on a secret air mission in 1944; Michael Anson (b. 1937), a former page to the King, the grandson of Captain Sir Harold Campbell – his parents were divorced; and Jonathan Peel (b. 1937), another page to the King, whose father, Major David Peel, had been killed in north-western Europe in 1944.
† An attempt to portray Princess Anne with the Queen Mother was less successful, because the relationship was not so close.

Peter Townsend was originally appointed temporary equerry to the King in 1944, but had made such an impression on both the King and Queen that he was continually asked to stay on. In 1950 he was appointed Assistant Master of the Household. In the last years of the King's reign, he was good at keeping his morale high. After the King's death he was chosen to accompany Queen Elizabeth to Clarence House.

His wartime marriage to Rosemary Pawle, so liked by the King, had collapsed by 1952, as a result of an affair she had (the Guards officer in question not taking her on), and later her adultery with John de László. Townsend's prolonged duties at court and his own religious fervour and dreams for his future had not helped matters. Their marriage ended in divorce at the end of the year.

When he realised his predicament, he went to see the Queen and told her how devoted he was to the Royal Family and asked if he could stay on in the Household. She agreed. What he failed to mention was that by then he was in love with Princess Margaret and that she was in love with him.

At Balmoral in the last summer of the King's life, Townsend had stretched out on the heather to doze. He became aware that someone was covering him with a coat. It was Princess Margaret with her face rather close to his. He noticed that the King was watching, half-amused, and warned the Princess. She laughed and walked away with her father. Soon afterwards Lady Jean Rankin tackled him: 'I think you're falling in love with her.' He replied: 'That's the first I've heard of it.' But he was drawn to 'her dazzling façade, the apparent self-assurance', combined with 'if you looked for it, a rare softness and sincerity'.[8]

The King's death was the greatest tragedy in Princess Margaret's life. She lost her mainstay, a father who adored her, and she was forced to become a guest in the homes she had taken for granted. She was disorientated, without, at that time, strong artistic or intellectual resources on which to rely. Though surrounded by the eligible suitors who comprised 'The Margaret Set', she found herself drawn to her father's equerry whom she had known for nine years. Some say she had been in love with him since the age of fourteen. One afternoon he confessed his feelings to her and she replied: 'That is exactly how I feel too.'[9] Townsend described this as 'an immensely gladdening disclosure, but one which sorely troubled us'.[10]

Townsend and Princess Margaret carried out a relatively discreet courtship at Windsor, Sandringham and Balmoral. Then came the turning point, in Townsend's words: 'How to consummate this mutual pleasure was the problem.'[11]

Townsend wrote that the Queen was informed and appeared to accept the situation. She was torn between a human sympathy for her sister and the wish that she could be happy, with the dilemma of her role as Head of the Church of England, which did not tolerate divorce. The timing was unfortunate coming so soon after the euphoria engendered by the Coronation.

His version of the Queen Mother's reaction was that she was considerate without giving the impression that she acquiesced in any way. He maintained that she was 'wonderful all the way through, and most sympathetic', if 'extremely concerned and worried'.[12] The more accepted view is that the Queen Mother did not address the issue. She 'ostrich-ed'.

When Townsend put his plight to Tommy Lascelles, still briefly Private Secretary to the new Queen, he told him, 'You must be either mad or bad.'[13] Consultations took place behind the scenes. Michael Adeane discussed Townsend with Lascelles, who said: 'He has Theudas trouble.'[14] Lascelles then quoted the Acts of the Apostles: '. . . For before these days rose up Theudas, boasting himself to be somebody.'[15] Churchill made it clear that the Queen could not give her consent to such a marriage, least of all in the year of Coronation, and that Princess Margaret would have to wait at least two years, until she was twenty-five. Lascelles wanted Townsend to leave his post as Comptroller of the Queen Mother's Household, but neither the Queen nor Queen Elizabeth would sanction that.

Townsend maintained that Commander Richard Colville, the Queen's Press Secretary, a man of such glum manner that Martin Charteris, one of the Queen's private secretaries, had dubbed him 'Sunshine', was either unaware of what was being said in the foreign press or failed to address the question. Then came the Coronation and the fluff incident, and, twelve days later, the story burst.

One day at Royal Lodge the young couple came in to find Queen Elizabeth reading one of the press reports. The affair was becoming dangerous, and Lascelles and Colville now insisted that Townsend must quit the Queen Mother's Household. The Queen and the Prime Minister decided on a year's trial separation.

In later life Princess Margaret maintained that no one, not least Lascelles, explained the dangers. 'Had he said we *couldn't* get married, we wouldn't have thought any more about it. But nobody bothered to explain anything to us,'[16] she told her biographer. She never forgave Lascelles (who lived near her at Kensington Palace). When she saw him shuffling to post a letter in later life, she told her chauffeur: 'Run the brute down.'

Townsend had been due to accompany the Queen Mother and Princess Margaret on their tour of Rhodesia on 30 June. He was relieved of that responsibility and Lord Plunket went as equerry in his place. Princess Margaret knew that Townsend would be leaving England presently, but neither of them thought that it would be before her return from Rhodesia. Thus they said goodbye in the belief that they would see each other again within three weeks.

The next day Townsend flew to Belfast as equerry to the Queen and Prince Philip. While they were undertaking their engagements, Colville announced his appointment as Air Attaché to the British Embassy in Brussels. The *London Gazette* then announced that he had been appointed an Extra Equerry to the Queen 'on being released to resume duty with the Royal Air Force'.[17] His post as equerry was taken by Viscount Althorp (later Earl Spencer).

Lascelles informed Townsend that it had been decided he would be leaving on 15 July, two days before Princess Margaret's return. As he departed to his new sinecure, he felt thoroughly deflated.

Townsend's memory of those events was recorded in his book *Time and Chance*. He chose to bathe the story in roseate tones. The truth is rather harsher. Before she left for Rhodesia, Princess Margaret was informed by the Queen and two of her ministers that she had been born to a responsible position and 'must do her best to forget this man'. Townsend was sternly reprimanded by the Queen's advisers in the following terms:

> There would be far more sympathy for you if you had been a young man, say of 27, honestly and passionately in love.
>
> In that case one could not have done much about it because young love is a fundamental emotion of young people.
>
> But you are not a young man. You are 38. You have two children. You have been through the divorce court. You are an officer and you knew your duty. You took on a job and you should not have allowed your personal feelings in any way to affect it.[18]

The Queen Mother and Princess Margaret arrived in Salisbury on 1 July, took the train to Bulawayo, where the Queen Mother opened the Central Africa Rhodes Centenary Exhibition, visited the grave of Cecil Rhodes, left for Gwelo on 6 July, and then visited Umtali, the Nyanyadzi irrigation farms for Africans, and the Zimbabwe ruins, before returning to Salisbury where the Queen Mother laid the foundation stone of the Rhodesian University. Not happy that the stone was properly aligned, she called for a spirit level, checked its position and gave it a sharp tap with her trowel.

The Queen Mother stressed the forthcoming union of Southern Rhodesia, Northern Rhodesia and Nyasaland into a Federation. She praised the 'great spirit' of Rhodes, 'the man of whom all that is left that is mortal lies in the granite tomb in the Matopos so near to us here'.[19] At the African village of Mrewa, Chief Magwande's jester held up her car flourishing assegais and a battle-axe and an octogenarian chief, 'hoary headed and white bearded', performed a short dance of welcome, after which he 'tottered breathlessly back to his place amongst his fellow chiefs'.[20]

In the midst of the tour, Princess Margaret was told that Townsend would have left England by the time of her return. This caused her to suffer from 'a cold', in fact Bulawayo flu and a temperature of 103, in the middle of the tour. While her mother continued with her engagements, she was flown back to Salisbury. She was well enough to attend a ball in her honour at Government House, to which eight hundred young people were invited, and on the Sunday morning she took Holy Communion, accompanied by the Governor, Sir John Kennedy, and his wife.

On the day that Townsend was departing into exile, the Queen Mother and Princess Margaret were attending tobacco auctions, with a wild auctioneer conducting his business in a frenzied high-pitched singsong voice, and then a civic garden party. The next day they flew home via Entebbe, arriving back in a Comet on 17 July.

Before long the Townsend affair dropped from public consciousness though the young couple wrote to each other almost every day, Princess Margaret sometimes covering many pages. They did not meet for another year.

But there was a sequel. Sir David Maxwell Fyfe wasted no time in addressing the question of revising the Regency Act of 1937. This Act had been drawn up hurriedly after the Abdication and had various shortcomings. If the Queen died, Princess Margaret would become Regent. On 22 July a new Bill was introduced by R. A.('Rab') Butler, the Chancellor of the Exchequer. Though it was stressed that this had been something on ministers' minds since shortly after the Accession, no one failed to connect it to Princess Margaret's private life. Lieutenant-Colonel Marcus Lipton asked about this in the House of Commons, and Butler said he sincerely hoped 'the present deplorable speculation and gossip' would now be brought to an end.[21]

A *Times* leader on 24 July (almost certainly written by Dermot Morrah) decried the way that the recent 'remarkable weeks' in the Queen's reign had been saddened by 'the bandying about of her sister's name in public gossip'. Taking the moral high ground, it suggested that 'the appearance of scandal' was based on 'the flimsiest structure of supposition'. The faults in the Regency Act were addressed. To have an aunt rather than a widowed father take charge of an infant nephew was 'a curious arrangement'. And it was suggested that 'everyone will want to see the name of the Queen Mother included' as a potential Counsellor of State.[22] When the Bill was debated in Parliament in November, the identical points were made.

Following the State Opening on 3 November, the Queen sent a message to Parliament via the Lord Chamberlain and Maxwell Fyfe to effect the various changes predicted in the *Times* leader. She asked that if the Heir Apparent or Heir Presumptive were of age, then he should be able to act as Regent; that the Duke of Edinburgh should be Regent 'and be charged with the guardianship of the person of the Sovereign', and finally addressed the role of the Queen Mother:

> Consideration of the affection and confidence which you and all my peoples have evinced for, and in, her leads me to recommend that you should take into consideration also the expediency of securing to her the opportunity of rendering as a Counsellor of State further service to you and to them.[23]

Maxwell Fyfe made it clear that Princess Margaret 'shared the desire of the Queen'[24] in the Regency matter. No official Opposition amendments were tabled. Patrick Gordon Walker, the Labour MP, suggested that Counsellors of State were outdated, and that there should be a Governor-General during the absence abroad of a Sovereign. Cuthbert Alport, MP for Colchester, looked ahead and anticipated that if the Queen lived as long as Queen Victoria, then Prince Charles might be in the wings for forty-two years after achieving his majority at eighteen.* His plan was that he should serve as a kind of 'deputy' monarch.

In the House of Lords, Viscount Samuel rejected Gordon Walker's suggested amendment:

> By the Act of Succession, the Crown was vested in the Royal Family. The Royal Family were resident in the United Kingdom. When the

---

* By his fifty-sixth birthday on 14 November 2004, Prince Charles had been in the wings for thirty-eight years after attaining his majority. Alport's plan might be perceived to have had some merit. It was rejected. Alport's arithmetic was based on the length of life not of reign.

Sovereign was absent it would be natural for his or her functions to be put into commission and be exercised by other members of the Royal Family who were resident here. No such conditions existed in any other part of the Commonwealth.[25]

The new Regency Act became law on 19 November 1953, the Duke of Edinburgh becoming Regent-designate and the Queen Mother being given her new role within the Constitution as a Counsellor of State.

Two days later, on 20 November, the Queen Mother assumed this role, which she exercised until the Queen's return on 15 May 1954. She and Princess Margaret went to London Airport on 23 November to bid farewell to the Queen and Duke of Edinburgh as they set off in a BOAC Stratocruiser aircraft on their Commonwealth tour. In so doing the Queen became the first monarch of any nation to circumnavigate the globe. The Queen Mother also took care of Prince Charles and Princess Anne.

The Queen Mother was the senior of five Counsellors of State,* invariably acting in tandem with Princess Margaret, once joined by the Duke of Gloucester, and only on one occasion in May delegating a duty to the Duke and his nephew, the Earl of Harewood.† Usually the Queen Mother and Princess Margaret conducted their business at Clarence House. Thus, effectively, the Queen Mother resumed the role that she had undertaken on behalf of the King during his periods of illness as a kind of deputy Head of State.

With Princess Margaret, she presided over several meetings of the Privy Council, which brought a variety of Government ministers to Clarence House, usually with the Lord President of the Council, the Marquess of Salisbury, in attendance. They jointly signified the Queen's approval in Council, issued commissions giving the Royal Assent in Parliament, approved and signed proclamations, warrants and other documents that required the Queen's approval, and generally exercised the royal prerogative and 'any statutory or other powers enabling The Queen to act for the safety or good government of the United Kingdom and Colonies'.[26]

They received addresses from the House of Lords and the House of Commons. They received incoming Ambassadors to Britain (usually at Buckingham Palace) and new Ambassadors 'kissed hands' on their appointments overseas. At Buckingham Palace the Queen Mother undertook six investitures, at one of which she knighted the actor George

* The five Counsellors of State were Queen Elizabeth The Queen Mother, The Princess Margaret, The Duke of Gloucester, The Princess Royal and the Earl of Harewood.
† They received Wilfred Gallienne, our new 'man in Havana', on 12 May 1954.

Robey. Privately she gave the badge of Companion of Honour to Rab Butler and invested Countess Alexander of Tunis with the GBE. In March she picked the List of Sheriffs.

On two occasions, on 10 March and 4 May, she received the Prime Minister, Sir Winston Churchill, in private audience, and once, on 12 March, the Foreign Secretary, Anthony Eden.

She would have gone to Norway for the Silver Wedding celebrations of Crown Prince Olav and Crown Princess Marthë, whose wedding she and the Duke of York had attended in 1929, but the Crown Princess fell gravely ill and the celebrations were cancelled. The Duke of Gloucester represented the Queen at the Crown Princess's funeral following her death on 5 April.

She also undertook some of the social roles that would have been done by the Queen. She and Princess Margaret hosted the Royal Household Social Club's dance at Windsor Castle on 15 December. And on two consecutive days in March 1954 she presided over Presentation Parties at Buckingham Palace, in which mothers brought their debutante daughters to court. In these she was supported by other members of the Royal Family, Princess Margaret, the Princess Royal, the Duchess of Kent and Princess Marie Louise at the first, and Princess Margaret, the Duchess of Gloucester and again Princess Marie Louise at the second. The Gentlemen-at-Arms and Yeomen of the Guard were on duty, and a string band from one of the Guards regiments played.* In April she took the salute at the march past of Boy Scouts at Windsor.

The Queen Mother had Mrs Greville's Boucheron tiara remodelled, put on a series of Hartnell crinolines for a succession of evening engagements, appeared at a number of racecourses and kept the monarchical flag flying, a role in which she was deft and experienced. To all these duties, be they political or social, she brought an extra touch, introducing a little element of fun wherever possible. Now she had the time to linger.

As Queen Mother, she was a tremendous performer. She chatted to people presented to her, listening to what they said, often turning to someone else standing nearby as if sharing the information proffered. When meeting a line-up of men, she would talk to one man, move on and then glance back, which made that man feel he had scored a particular hit. There was inevitably a formula to these things, one that worked well, and she was unfazed when the crowds pressed close, or the lenses intruded, when the wind threatened her hats, or dislodged a feather.

To those she met she gave much. To win them over was her challenge.

---

* After 1958, on the advice of Prince Philip, these Presentation Parties were abolished as outdated.

Arguably they took with them more than she gave from herself. Her philosophy on public and private engagements was that when people came into her orbit, their lives must get better. She too enjoyed these occasions, perhaps not in the same way as those she met. She liked individuality and sparky characters, she disliked the pompous, of whom there were many, and for all the repetition and similarity in the duties, for all the mayors and presentation lines, there was satisfaction in knowing that by her mere presence, suitably adorned, and a few easy words, she could give intense pleasure.

On the domestic front Queen Elizabeth had guardianship of Prince Charles and Princess Anne from November until they left for Gibraltar to rejoin their parents the following April. In the absence of the Queen, they continued to live with their nannies at Buckingham Palace, where their grandmother visited them regularly from Clarence House, often being there to tuck them in at bedtime if her duties permitted. She invariably took them both with her to Royal Lodge for the weekend with Princess Margaret (though on at least one weekend she went racing at Lingfield Park), and she made the best of Christmas for them at Sandringham, a holiday which lasted from 23 December 1953 until 9 February 1954.

The Christmas party also included Princess Margaret and the Gloucester family, and they were joined after Christmas by the Kents and Prince and Princess Paul of Yugoslavia in the days before New Year. They gathered to listen to the Queen's Christmas broadcast from New Zealand, and then enjoyed the rare treat of talking to her over a 'radio-telephone', trans-global links in those days being reserved only for special occasions.

A strong bond was formed between grandmother and grandchildren, Prince Charles being the more reliant of the two. He adored his grandmother from his earliest days and snuggled close to her, while Princess Anne appeared less dependent and was closer to Nanny Lightbody, whose favourite she was. Their mother had so many duties as Queen and had to balance the disposition of her time between being Queen and mother. But the Queen Mother was able to devote any amount of time to these two small children.

She soon detected in her grandson sensitivity and need for protection. To him she gave the same unquestioning devotion as she had given to the King. She bolstered his fragile confidence and boosted his sometimes failing morale. While the Duke of Edinburgh was anxious to instil confidence into this oversensitive child, his methods were interpreted as overly tough. Prince Charles never felt this about his grandmother. A child's growing character can be compared to a plant. Some plants need stressing in their pots to bring them to flower, others gentle nurturing each day. Prince Philip was a stresser, and Queen Elizabeth a nurturer. She was critical of Prince Philip's methods, letting slip to Cecil Beaton (in 1968): 'Now he doesn't need to be toughened any more . . .'[27]

On 14 April the Queen Mother and Princess Margaret took their young charges to Portsmouth, where they embarked in *Britannia* on their way to join their parents in Malta. A month later, on 15 May, the Queen Mother was to the fore in greeting the Queen and Duke of Edinburgh after *Britannia* arrived in the Port of London, and they undertook the last lap of their long journey with them in the Royal Barge, alighting at Westminster Pier, where the Duke and Duchess of Gloucester, the Princess Royal and the Duchess of Kent were waiting to greet them.

With the Queen back, the Queen Mother could retreat into the new life she was establishing for herself. One of the first big gatherings of royalty after the Queen's short holiday at Balmoral was the wedding of Viscount Althorp and Hon. Frances Roche at Westminster Abbey on 1 June. The Queen Mother joined the Queen and eight members of the Royal Family to see this pair united, little knowing how the union would impact on all their futures.

26

The Queen Mother's Team

'He fitted into the job like a prawn into aspic'
– Martin Charteris on Martin Gilliat

The Queen Mother brought a particular aura with her to Clarence House. That she had been Queen Consort for sixteen years gave her an unassailable position and a mystique which never left her. Though her new home was smaller than Buckingham Palace, it was run as a grand Edwardian court with private secretaries and equerries, ladies-in-waiting and uniformed staff. By and large it was a happy Household and the spirit of welcome and sense of fun permeated every level of the building, emanating directly from Queen Elizabeth herself.

The hierarchy was complicated. The Lord Chamberlain and Mistress of the Robes appeared on state occasions, the Ladies of the Bedchamber on national ones, while the Women of the Bedchamber took it in turns to be in waiting. The Private Secretary, Treasurer and Permanent Equerry did the day-to-day work, assisted by the Women of the Bedchamber.

Below them was a network of Household figures – the Officials, the Clerk Comptroller, the Information Officer, and secretariat. And then there was the domestic staff, headed by the Steward and Page of the Backstairs, while, confusingly, the Deputy Steward held the title of Page of the Presence.

The Earl of Airlie was the Queen Mother's Lord Chamberlain until 1965,* and her loyal band of ladies-in-waiting, overseen by Helen, Duchess of Northumberland, until her retirement in 1964,† included Countess Spencer, the Dowager Viscountess Hambleden, Lady Harlech and the Countess of Scarbrough for the important engagements, and the more regular ladies, Katie Seymour, Lady Hyde, Lady Jean Rankin and the Hon. Mrs John Mulholland.

---

* He was succeeded by the Earl of Dalhousie, who served from 1965 until 1992, and then by the Earl of Crawford and Balcarres. All were Knights of the Thistle.
† She was succeeded by the Duchess of Abercorn (formerly Lady Kathleen Crichton). She described her job as being 'the Head Girl'. She organised the rota and accompanied Queen Elizabeth on her most important engagements. After her death in 1990, no new Mistress of the Robes was appointed, and the rota was arranged by Lady Grimthorpe.

The key men of the Household from the mid-1950s were Sir Martin Gilliat, who took over as Private Secretary from Oliver Dawnay, Sir Ralph Anstruther, the Assistant Private Secretary, Lord Adam Gordon, the Comptroller, and the only Press Secretary, Major John Griffin. There was a succession of young equerries, always from the Irish Guards, and a team of Extra Equerries.

Sir Arthur Penn was the mainstay during the 1950s to the point where, to the chagrin of both himself and Queen Elizabeth, he was suddenly promoted in the press as a man she might be intending to marry. Penn may have been a little in love with her back in the 1920s, but since that time he had served her with loyalty only. Independently rich, he had numerous interests which served him well as courtier and friend. He knew about painting, music and gardens, and enjoyed the rural pursuits of shooting, fishing, golf and tennis. He even knew how to lay bricks. It was a great sorrow to Queen Elizabeth when he died on 30 December 1960, aged only seventy-four. His job was taken by Sir Ralph Anstruther, while Captain Alastair Aird, equerry in 1960, joined as Assistant Private Secretary in 1964.

Ruth, Lady Fermoy was an important addition to the Household in 1956, and Lady Elizabeth Basset joined the ladies-in-waiting in 1958. They all proved long-serving.

The Household at Clarence House was run on old-fashioned lines, and the courtiers led an unhurried life. They frequently lunched with Queen Elizabeth, either in the little room between the dining room and the morning room, or in the summer, if it was fine and sunny, at a table laid in splendour in the garden. If there was no luncheon at Clarence House, Sir Martin Gilliat lunched at Brooks's, usually with one of his many friends. Every afternoon the courtiers settled down to have tea together and to mull over the events of the day. A certain amount of alcohol was served at the appropriate hour, and the atmosphere was such that no crisis was allowed to disrupt the time-honoured schedule.

All letters came direct to Queen Elizabeth and were directed to the appropriate officer by the ladies-in-waiting. Correspondence was answered promptly and politely, employing phrases redolent of old-world courtesy. 'I have laid your letter before Her Majesty who bids me tell you . . .' was the traditional tone of such things. When engagements were accepted, they were done so with great joy. But the Queen Mother could not always oblige. When she said no, it was up to Sir Martin to deliver the news as gently as possible: 'Queen Elizabeth has given very careful and sympathetic thought to the enquiry you have conveyed . . . The Queen Mother is most attracted by the suggestion but to her Sorrow fears that she must decline the invitation . . . Would you be good enough to explain . . . how sorry Queen Elizabeth is to have to reach this necessarily disappointing decision . . .'¹ Recipients of such letters were made to feel that special attention had been given to their requests.

Queen Elizabeth's court was not as preoccupied as the more frenetic world of Buckingham Palace. Courtiers did not have to make political decisions and were not concerned with constitutional matters. Their duty was to arrange the official life of the Queen Mother, to keep her diary full, to emulate her example of courtesy, kindness and consideration to the world, and to stimulate her quieter moments.

Lieutenant-Colonel Martin Gilliat arrived for a trial period in 1955 and was still serving, his appointment never officially sanctioned, until his death at the age of eighty in May 1993.

Born in 1913, he followed in the tradition of bachelor courtier, polite and brave, ever-courteous yet protective, himself the scion of two rich landed families, and fulfilling the concurrent roles of courtier and friend. An Old Etonian, he had served in the King's Royal Rifle Corps. Early in the Second World War he was captured, twice slipping away from the column on its way to captivity, but both times being recaptured. He tunnelled his way out of Eichstadt, and when caught again for the fourth time was declared 'a persistent escaper' and incarcerated in Colditz Castle for two years until the end of hostilities. One of his fellow escapers was David Walker,* later a successful novelist in Canada, who also ended up in Colditz and described him as 'the wit of our mess . . . you might take him for a smoothie unless and until you knew more about him'. He dubbed him 'unflappable'.²

Gilliat worked for Mountbatten in India, where he witnessed the Delhi riots in 1947, observing 'such scenes of inhuman cruelty that I should think have seldom been rivaled even in Germany and Russia. Women & children lying in the streets dead or dying having been mutilated in the most fantastic way – children in all the hospitals with either their legs or their arms cut off . . .'³ He then served Malcolm Macdonald in Singapore, and Field Marshal Sir William Slim in Australia. While in Singapore, there had been a sticky moment when the young King of Thailand came to lunch and was paralysed into silence by his shyness. Gilliat rescued the party by saying to King Bhumibol: 'Your Majesty,

---

* David Walker (1911–92), served in the Black Watch in India and Sudan, ADC to Lord Tweedsmuir, Governor-General of Canada, served in the Second World War, but captured 1940, briefly Comptroller to Lord Wavell in India 1946–7, emigrated to New Brunswick 1948, author of nineteen novels, some of them set in the Scottish Highlands or involving adventures in and out of prisoner of war camps.

rumour has it that you are extremely good at standing on your head: do please show us how you do it.'[4] The King obliged and the party went with a swing.

At the suggestion of Martin Charteris, Gilliat joined Clarence House in 1955, and took over as Private Secretary the following year. In Charteris's words, he 'fitted into the job like a prawn into aspic.'[*5]

Executive and efficient, he organised the tours and the entertainments, shared the Queen Mother's interest in racing, selected suitable plays for her to attend† (being the backer of some thirty plays in London) and sought out prominent figures from the theatre, services and business for her to meet and entertain. He helped to spread the atmosphere of bonhomie that permeated directly from her. Dame Frances Campbell-Preston described him as 'a very able mirror to his employer', with 'a boundless capacity for friendship across the world'.[6] If someone sent the Queen Mother a racy book, he was not beyond excising offending pages with a razor blade before giving it to her.

Gilliat could be seen in the salesrooms waving his catalogue as he made the occasional purchase for her collection; he could be seen representing her at memorial services when he assumed an unapproachable air (he almost became the Queen Mother); and he could be seen two steps behind her, an increasingly angular and Dickensian figure, who, as he aged, would have made a perfect subject for the cartoonist Spy. A tall man, his years of bending to the diminutive height of his royal 'employer' left him with a figure like a question mark.

Gilliat was a stalwart figure at Clarence House and Royal Lodge, and a favourite at the Castle of Mey. He knew the rules and knew when to waive them. When the difficult Parsee, Bapsy, Marchioness of Winchester, signed the Queen Mother's book at Clarence House, in the hope of an invitation, he commented; 'She'll be lucky!' and when a young guest, expected at the Castle of Mey for the summer, announced his engagement, Sir Martin rang him to cancel the invitation, saying he was sure he would now wish to spend time with his fiancée. He trained the young equerries with a light touch, and he was expert both at putting people at their ease and occasionally disconcerting them. Lord Charteris said:

Many will remember with gratitude being instantly put at ease on their arrival at Clarence House or Royal Lodge and having a fortifying drink pressed into their hands. And I may say that dear Martin

* Charteris was quoting P. G. Wodehouse.
† This task became harder as the years went by, particularly when the Lord Chamberlain surrendered his 'blue pencil' in 1968, and stage language became consequently bluer.

was as generous in dispensing his own alcohol as he was in pouring Queen Elizabeth's.[7]

The inner man was secretive, some said selfish and overly considerate of his own needs. A reserved man, something of a loner, a bit of an actor, occasionally duplicitous, Gilliat had been damaged by his wartime experiences. At Fairlawne, staying with the Cazalets, he could be heard in the next room, restless and anxious, moaning with nightmares through the small hours.[8] But few would disagree that he could not have been better chosen to serve Queen Elizabeth during those thirty-seven years.

Gilliat's number two in the Household for many years was Sir Ralph Anstruther, a baronet twice over, and a more Edwardian character. Opinions vary about him, some holding him in high esteem, others with suspicion. Sir Ralph relished court life.

If Gilliat had a tweedy attitude, Anstruther adhered to the stiff-collar approach. Gilliat favoured a pale grey morning dress suit for racing, Sir Ralph the black silk hat. The two men were not always in sympathy with each other, though they worked side by side for many decades.

Sir Ralph served as the Queen Mother's equerry from 1959, was Assistant Private Secretary from 1959 to 1964 and Treasurer from 1961. His most public duty on the Queen Mother's behalf was to lay her annual wreath at the Cenotaph on Remembrance Sunday. In military greatcoat Sir Ralph took his place each year behind the Queen and the Duke of Edinburgh.

Sir Ralph had lost his father soon after his birth in 1921, while his mother, a formidable influence, would live with him until her death at a great age in 1995. He was a Scottish baronet and a considerable landowner in Scotland in his own right, living at Balcaskie, the family estate in Fife (in the family since 1698), and Watten Mains, consisting of nearly seven thousand acres in Caithness, and what his successor as Treasurer called 'a grouse-less grouse moor'.[9]

Educated at Eton and Magdalene College, Cambridge, he served in the Coldstream Guards, where he won the Military Cross in 1943. During the war he was Private Secretary to Harold Macmillan, accompanying him to Italy and Greece. Not a man fond of culture or the arts, he was a stickler for protocol. His international contacts were impeccable, and he was a guiding force in the Queen Mother's private visits to France and elsewhere, being able to converse fluently in French and other languages.

Sir Ralph oversaw finances, though he was scarcely trained for this, and had but a hazy idea of costs. He could also be fierce.

At his memorial service, Natalie Brooke said: 'Many an equerry felt the lash of his tongue.'[10] He berated Martin Leslie, the Factor at Balmoral and later at the Castle of Mey, for appearing at the Royal Smithfield Show without a furled umbrella or a bowler hat, neither of which Leslie possessed. He often bullied the equerries, and tore strips off Jeremy Stopford, who, on assuming his post, accompanied the royal party to church at Sandringham in a tweed suit and brown shoes. After the service, Sir Ralph ushered him into the library for a wigging. A dark suit and stiff collar were required, Anstruther informed him.[11]

He forbade photography at the Castle of Mey, insisted on dinner jackets in the evening and did not hesitate to report what he perceived as errant equerries, or to get people into trouble if it suited him. There were dark hints about his private life, and he was to be seen in London restaurants with a bevy of young men, and occasionally forged regrettable alliances. Equally, he could be benign and gentle.

Lord Adam Gordon left a less lasting mark on the Household, since he served as Comptroller and Assistant Private Secretary for only nineteen years, which in terms of service to Queen Elizabeth was relatively short. Born in 1909, he was a younger brother of the 12th Marquess of Huntly. He served as a major in the Royal Artillery before succeeding Group Captain Peter Townsend in 1953. A mild, courteous and charming man, he worked closely with Sir Martin Gilliat (who sometimes referred to him as 'my colleague') and no enquiry was too trivial or unimportant for him not to give it his fullest attention. He retired in 1974 and died ten years later.

Major John Griffin joined the Household as an Extra Equerry in 1956, and became her first and only Press Secretary. It fell to him to handle the press interest during Princess Margaret's marriage to Antony Armstrong-Jones. Being of the old school, bluff, genial and friendly, he was reluctant to release any more information than was absolutely necessary and given to old-fashioned quotes such as: 'The Princess is a little under the weather.'

Born in 1924 Griffin served in The Queen's Bays, and in 1962 married Henrietta Scott, daughter of Brigadier Andrew Scott, who commanded the Irish Guards, and a cousin of the Duke of Buccleuch. When he strolled with her in St James's Park before the marriage, he still wore his bowler hat and carried his furled umbrella.

Like Sir Martin Gilliat, Ruth, Lady Fermoy joined Queen Elizabeth's Household in 1956, and served to the end, dying a few weeks after him in July 1993. Appointed soon after she became a widow at the age of forty-six, she began as an Extra Woman of the Bedchamber, and was promoted Woman of the Bedchamber in 1960.

Ruth Fermoy lived at Hillington, near Sandringham, and was a cultured musician and Chairman of the King's Lynn Festival. She secured the Queen Mother's attendance at every festival from 1951 until she retired in 1988. Having trained under the great Alfred Cortot in Paris from 1927 to 1931, she frequently played the piano in public, notably with Josef Krips at the Royal Albert Hall in 1950, and with the Hallé Orchestra conducted by Sir John Barbirolli at King's Lynn in 1966. She used to accompany the Prince of Wales when he was learning the cello, and once endured him scratching his way through an entire piece, at the end of which he discovered he had been following the first violin part.[12] Once she had finished with the King's Lynn Festival, she helped the Prince of Wales launch 'Music in Country Churches'. Raymond Leppard described her as 'strong, gentle, firm, but endlessly considerate and aware of others, unshakeably loyal to those she loved and direct in her approval and disapproval'.[13]

Lady Fermoy played a key part in the Queen Mother's week at Sandringham towards the end of July. She also accompanied the private expeditions to France and elsewhere, and, like Gilliat, was an important figure at the Castle of Mey. She and Gilliat were the prime movers in enlivening Queen Elizabeth's cultural life, and, while Gilliat had the theatre contacts, her world produced musicians such as David Willcocks and Raymond Leppard.

Ruth Fermoy had been a friend of the Royal Family for years, her husband, Lord Fermoy (who died in 1955), having been a shooting friend of the King's and with him at Sandringham on the evening before he died in February 1952. She was considered to be socially ambitious and keenly interested in her royal life. She had also taken the unusual step of siding against her own daughter, Frances, at the time of her divorce from Viscount Althorp. Later she was to play a key role when her granddaughter, Diana, married the Prince of Wales.

Olivia Mulholland became a lady-in-waiting as a widow in 1950. She was a daughter of 1st Viscount Harcourt, a prominent member of the Liberal Cabinet in the First World War. Her mother had been a neighbour of the Bowes-Lyons at St Paul's Walden Bury. She had a degree from Lady Margaret Hall, Oxford, and upheld the beliefs of the old Liberal Party, silently disapproving of Queen Elizabeth's more right-wing approach. She was the intellectual in the Household, urged the other ladies to read the last paragraph of every letter first, as they would find the gist there, and she often helped write the Queen Mother's more important or demanding speeches. She died in 1985.

Lady Elizabeth Basset became one of the inner court in later life. She was invited to join the Queen Mother by Sir Arthur Penn and served as Extra Woman of the Bedchamber from 1958. Only in 1982, when some of the older ladies had died, did she become a Woman of the Bedchamber, and thus more actively involved. She conceded that it was more fun to be a lady-in-waiting than to have one.

Lady Elizabeth was the second daughter of the 7th Earl of Dartmouth, a former Lord Great Chamberlain. Born in 1908, in 1931 she had married Ronald Lambert Basset, the descendant of an English family said to have come to England with the Conqueror. They had two sons, the younger of whom, Peter, tragically shot himself at the age of nineteen, having been bullied to an extreme point during training for a commission in the Welsh Guards.

She was kind, well read, intelligent and soft spoken, and she developed a strong religious devotion after her son's death. She led retreats and meditations at the Royal Foundation of St Katharine in the East End of London, some of which lasted three days, and she involved Queen Elizabeth in aspects of her religious life.

Lady Elizabeth compiled several anthologies, to one of which, *Love is My Meaning: An Anthology of Assurance*, the Queen Mother contributed an introduction, recommending it to those 'who will find in the pages what in our hearts we believe but find hard to say'.[14] Lady Elizabeth was assisted in its compilation by Sir John Betjeman, and she donated all the royalties to Feed the Minds.

There until she died in 1994 was Patricia, Viscountess Hambleden, the longest serving lady-in-waiting in history, achieving fifty-seven years. Though ladies-in-waiting are anxious not to cite favourites and describe themselves as a team with equal status, Lady Hambleden was probably the closest to Queen Elizabeth. She had known her since her coming-out ball at Wilton in 1922, and had served her since 1937.

Lady Jean Rankin had joined the Household in 1947, having been approached by Lady Delia Peel. The elder daughter of 12th Earl of Stair, she had spent much of her married life on the Isle of Mull, where her husband established a successful collection of rare ducks. She held a pilot's licence and was a no less determined driver, believing, even in old age, that the fast lane was the place to be, since time on the road was thus minimised. A forthright character, it was she who had urged Churchill to make his 1952 visit to Birkhall. It was her idea that Queen Elizabeth should always have a lady-in-waiting with her, as so often there was bad news to contend with, and it was good to have someone to talk to.

Like Patricia Hambleden, she regularly accompanied the Queen

Mother on overseas trips, and, when in London, tended to serve two weeks on and then six weeks off. Her assessment of the Queen Mother was that she was an easy boss to work for, and she considered her character 'a positive force'.[15]

Lady Katharine Seymour, her old friend Katie Hamilton, was custodian of secrets from the days at Glamis. Always shy, she had a tragic later life. In December 1953 her nineteen-year-old daughter, Cynthia, a goddaughter of the Queen Mother, caught her dressing gown against a gas fire in a flat she shared with a girlfriend in Glebe Place, Chelsea. Gravely burned, she survived the shock but died of toxaemia in Park Prewett Hospital, near Basingstoke, on 9 January 1954.* Katie Seymour veered towards religion in later life, but continued to do periods of waiting, resuming her duties in May 1954, when she wept throughout it. She became a prison visitor and once asked permission for time off to attend a wedding. It transpired she was to be a witness at a ceremony in prison.

In 1965 Clarence House was joined by Frances Campbell-Preston. Her late husband, Patrick, had served in the Black Watch and had been an inveterate escaper. He was finally imprisoned in Colditz alongside Sir Martin Gilliat. She was to prove a stalwart member of the team, and, as some of the older ladies declined and died, Gilliat wrote of her: 'She, anyhow, goes from strength to strength and has a most splendidly stimulating and down to earth outlook on all our activities – bringing any form of overt pomposity very quickly down to earth.'[16]

Besides the ladies-in-waiting, there was the Household staff, notably the team of pages, led by William Tallon and Reginald Wilcock.

William Tallon was born above his grandfather's hardware shop in Birtley, Co. Durham, in 1935. When he was one the family fell on hard times and moved to Coventry. He came to the Royal Household by writing directly to the King as a very young man, and asking for a post. He was surprised to receive a summons to serve at the Easter Court at Windsor in 1951. He was then employed at Buckingham Palace and was supposed to go on the Commonwealth tour in 1954. Instead he was kept back, then told he must go on national service, serving in the RAF. Later he asked the Queen Mother if he could come to her. He stayed at Clarence House until the end.

Tallon dedicated his whole life to her, and had a special role in helping her to be what she was to the outside world. As page, he could enter her rooms without knocking – the door was never closed unless the doctor was there – so he was a familiar and intimate presence in her life.

* The Queen Mother and Princess Margaret were in charge of Prince Charles and Princess Anne at Sandringham at the time. They did not attend the funeral, but sent flowers.

William (the pages were called by their Christian names) was a wizard with a drink. Empty glasses mysteriously filled, and he was adept at overcoming reticence in guests. Dame Frances was convinced that he made a rather grim afternoon gathering of veterans at St James's Palace go with a particular swing by adding whisky to the tea. Those not used to his interpretation of the strength of a drink sometimes left the worse for wear, and Kenneth Rose, a lunch guest, recalled: 'No use putting your hand over the glass, he pours it through the fingers!'[17]

William was also knowledgeable about theatre and art. He spotted some unusual paintings on the railings at Piccadilly, bought one, and recommended that the artist present one to the Queen Mother. She received him and commissioned him for various presents. The Duchess of Kent also bought one,* and presently the artist, Roy Petley, was being exhibited at the Marlborough Gallery and went on to have his own highly successful gallery in Cork Street.

These and other skills made him a considerable impresario in the Queen Mother's life. 'My role,' he said, 'was to keep her smiling.'[18] That in turn made him unpopular with some of the Household – he was more an Anstruther than a Gilliat man. He rescued the Chelsea Pensioners from behind a cordon during the Queen Mother's birthday walkabout at Clarence House, knowing that she would wish to see them. He was an integral part of the Household, assuring a warm welcome to generations of royalty and guests when they arrived to see the Queen Mother in her various homes.

If William Tallon was extrovert and ebullient, his friend Reginald Wilcock was the quieter counterpart. He was another stalwart member of the staff, who began royal service as a footman at Buckingham Palace between 1954 and 1957, and worked as the Duke of Windsor's valet in Paris from April 1957 to June 1959. He then came to Clarence House in June 1960, rising from footman to Senior Queen's Footman in 1975, and then Deputy Steward and Page of the Presence from 1978 until his death in 2000.

Reg was born in 1934, his father running a popular fish and chip shop in Wakefield, Yorkshire. Like William, Reg was a cultivated man. He was much respected at Clarence House, loyal in service, and discreet in all his duties. Lady Elizabeth Basset described him as 'self-effacing but always full of jokes and laughter'.[19] He contributed to her anthologies.

The pages worked long days, often finishing at 11 p.m., and were most visible when guests came to see the Queen Mother. They travelled with

---

* She signed her cheque 'Katharine' which worried the artist, but that is how royalty sign.

the Queen Mother, their quiet organising behind the scenes adding immeasurably to the success of royal tours. On one overseas visit, the Queen Mother's hostess was amazed, on opening the wardrobe to show her royal visitor where her clothes would hang, to find that Reginald had them unpacked and in place. 'I'm here already,' she said.[20]

The Queen Mother and Princess Margaret had varying approaches to their staff. On 21 May 1977, the Queen Mother's Protection Officer, Chief Superintendent Richard Sumner, had a sudden heart attack on the top of Lochnagar, and despite an attempt to rescue him by RAF helicopter, he died. Being driven to Holyroodhouse, Edinburgh, the next day for the ceremony to install Prince Charles as a Knight of the Thistle, the Queen Mother never once mentioned Dick Sumner, though she had been devoted to him.

In December 1959, the Queen Mother and Princess Margaret were about to leave Royal Lodge for London when they were told that the forty-two-year-old Clerk Comptroller, Allan Wickens, had been found dead in his office from an overdose of barbiturates. As a chief petty officer, Wickens had joined Queen Elizabeth's office as Clerk to her Private Secretary, Major Tom Harvey, on the royal tour of South Africa in 1947. She took him to Clarence House where he worked for Sir Arthur Penn and Lord Adam Gordon. He was a perfectionist, whose only wish was to serve the Queen Mother as well as he could. He suffered from a duodenal ulcer and a nervous breakdown, was given three months leave, but, according to a note eventually found under the cover of his typewriter, everything had got on top of him. He came into Clarence House late on Saturday night and disposed of himself with the help of pills and whisky. At the inquest the reason for the suicide was attributed to 'his mental condition', Arthur Penn adding that he was 'unfailingly competent'.[21] The real reason was marital difficulties.

The Queen Mother said: 'I wish he had come to talk to me about his problems.'[22] She cancelled the staff Christmas party out of respect to him and dined alone in her room. Hearing that the staff were now free, Princess Margaret promptly invited fourteen friends for dinner. Instead of the party, they had to work.

Clarence House was largely a happy Household, but there were the inevitable incidents when hierarchies clashed. Sir Ralph did not like the lady clerks being addressed by their Christian names and he kept a vigilant eye to see that while they were served afternoon tea, they were not allowed cakes or biscuits, which were slipped to them by the ladies-in-waiting if he was called to the telephone. The pages were reluctant to serve the lady clerks in the same way as the ladies-in-waiting. The private secretaries resented the intimacy of the pages, who could circumnavigate official channels.

When one member of the Household wished to see the Queen Mother but was anxious not to alert the interest of Sir Martin or Sir Ralph, he asked William Tallon's help and was spirited to the Queen Mother's presence via an underground corridor from Tallon's lodge house, and then a lift from the basement. His presence was undetected.

On a later occasion, when there had been a fracas and the private secretaries were urging the removal of one of the pages, the Queen Mother called the Household in and told them in no uncertain terms: 'Their jobs are *not* negotiable. Yours are.'[23]

27

Ambassador for Britain

'The Queen Mother has brought us rain at last' – Masai warriors

The Queen Mother was determined to give the Queen the freedom to be a constitutional Head of State without maternal interference. However, having acted as senior Counsellor of State, Queen Elizabeth had more than proved her worth as a working Queen Mother. This new role developed imperceptibly. She was able to serve in a diplomatic and ambassadorial capacity, and thus fly the flag for Britain.

This was never so well demonstrated as when she set off to the United States at the beginning of 1954 for her most important trip in widowhood. Had the King lived, he would have gone to America to thank them for their help during the war. But now he was dead, as was President Roosevelt. The Queen Mother crossed the Atlantic alone.

She sailed in *Queen Elizabeth*, occupying a three-room suite on the promenade deck, and arrived at Pier 90, New York City, on 26 October, in such bad weather that disembarkation was delayed by twelve hours. On arrival she declared: 'Ever since our happy visit in 1939 I had always hoped that one day I might be able to come back and stay a little longer in your great country.'[1] She took up residence at Wave Hill, the home of her friends Sir Pierson Dixon, the United Kingdom Delegate to the United Nations, and his wife, Ismene.

Her stay was a mixture of formal luncheons and receptions, interspersed with sightseeing and visits to places such as the Metropolitan Museum of Art. She went shopping and was seen to spend hundreds of dollars in two hours, making swift decisions at various counters. She was fascinated by the ingenious gadgets at Hammacher Schlemmer on East 57th Street, buying a thermos ice bucket in the shape of a red apple, a magnetic bottle opener, a combination beer can and bottle opener, and various unusual cocktail glasses, mixers, whisky decanters and plastic trays. At Saks she bought the Queen a jewelled sweater and a number of accessories. And at FAO Schwarz she moved happily among the whirring electric trains and chose some particularly American items for her grandchildren.

Elizabeth, The Queen Mother

The Queen Mother saw a performance of *The Pajama Game*, and was cheered to her seat by the other theatre goers. Then, because the weather was favourable, she made a spontaneous trip to the 102nd floor of the Empire State Building, enjoying the view so much that she lingered there for three cups of tea. When she came down, though her visit had not been announced she found a huge impromptu crowd had gathered, which 'cheered, applauded, honked automobile horns, and almost swept over the police barricades to get within touching distance of her'.[2] Several admitted they were risking censure back at the office for skiving for so long. After the visit, William Keary, President of the Empire State Building, said: 'As a goodwill ambassador she would be hard to excel.'[3]

Huge crowds, swelling to five thousand, soon became a feature of her New York visit, Manhattan grinding to a contented standstill whenever she was in the vicinity.

On the evening of 30 October the Queen Mother, in pink satin ball gown with Garter riband and tiara, attended the Charter Dinner of Columbia University, at which distinguished world figures such as the Belgian statesman Paul-Henri Spaak joined the 2600 guests. She spoke at this dinner, standing on a special stool in front of the podium.

The Queen Mother spent most of the following day in church. On her way to morning service at the Cathedral of St John the Divine, she met a crowd of five thousand including British West Indians living in Harlem, gathered outside St Martin's Church, on Lenox Avenue and 122nd Street. At the cathedral she unveiled the Motherhood Window, and listened to a sermon preached by Rt Revd Horace Donegan, Bishop of New York, who, from that moment, became an unusual friend and later a persistent annual visitor to Royal Lodge.

Donegan was the son of a Derbyshire doctor, and a contemporary of Queen Elizabeth's. It is said that he had trained for the stage, but had fallen in love with his landlady's daughter. The landlady in question had been so shocked at the prospect of an actor as a son-in-law that instead he entered the priesthood. In fact he remained unmarried, and in later life travelled with a priestly acolyte. A worldly man, he was a keen denunciator of racism in America, and acutely conscious of the stark difference between the wealth of some of his parishioners and the poverty of others. In the mid-1950s he opposed McCarthyism and in the 1960s was prepared to leave his cathedral covered in scaffolding 'as a symbol of the anguish of the surrounding slums'.[4]

On this day he spoke on themes close to the Queen Mother's heart decrying the deterioration of home life and the breakdown of the sanctity of the family. Unworthy literature, the disintegrating influence of much popular entertainment, the 'false social standard which subtly persuades a mother to go out of her home in order to increase the family income' were all themes upon which he heaped his disapprobation. Divorce, he said, led to 'broken children who become unstable, undisciplined men and women'.[5] The Queen Mother warmed to him, and, once he had found her, he never let her go.

The Queen Mother visited a day care centre, where her manner was deemed 'too motherly and friendly to give the children any inkling of her importance'.[6] But one three-year-old boy was upset by the flashlights, and, when the Queen Mother tried to feed him his macaroni and cheese, he refused loudly, and it required Lady Jean Rankin, trained in nursery schools, to pick him up and hold him in her arms. Meanwhile the Queen Mother sailed on, patting the odd child on the head.

A postponed visit to the Cloisters took place on 1 November, there was a ball at the Seventh Regiment Armory in Park Avenue,* and a private lunch at Hyde Park given by Eleanor Roosevelt. This meeting had been long in the planning. Well in advance of the trip, Mrs Roosevelt had written to invite the Queen Mother for 'a very quiet few days in the country', or a dinner or theatre visit in the city, but received no reply. In May she wrote again to ask if the Queen Mother might attend Mrs Lytle Hull's ball† in aid of therapeutic music services at the Waldorf Astoria. Again she received no reply.

In August Mrs Roosevelt approached the British Ambassador to ask where the Queen Mother was staying so that she could send flowers.[7] This provoked a response from Captain Dawnay, who told her that Queen Elizabeth would be 'most distressed' to hear of 'this apparent discourtesy', but that no trace could be found of her letters. Nevertheless Queen Elizabeth was looking forward to seeing her 'enormously', and hoped to come to lunch on 2 November if Mrs Roosevelt was not too busy.[8]

Mrs Roosevelt's flowers arrived at Wave Hill and were enthusiastically acknowledged by Olivia Mulholland, the lady-in-waiting, as 'another proof of the friendship which Queen Elizabeth values so greatly'.[9] The lunch on 2 November took place, Mrs Roosevelt serving traditional Thanksgiving fare of roast turkey and candied sweet potatoes, but a proposed visit to the Roosevelt Library and the laying of a wreath on the President's grave were dropped on account of potential political repercussions due to it being the day for off-year elections.

---

* The Bishop of New York and his mother, Mrs George H. Donegan, were seated in Box 5 at this occasion.
† Three British hospitals benefited from the scheme being supported – the Star and Garter at Richmond, Stoke Mandeville, and Grove Park in London.

Mrs Roosevelt was also a guest at Mayor Wagner's lunch at the Waldorf Astoria the next day. The Queen Mother spoke warmly of her visit, contrasting 'the beauty of your great city, with its dramatic perspectives and exhilarating air', to 'the soberer contours and softer skies of London'.[10]

That evening after a dinner at the same hotel given by the English-Speaking Union, she made her most important speech, which was relayed across the United States on television. The English-Speaking Union had raised considerable sums to establish the King George VI Memorial Fund to provide scholarships to encourage the British young to study in the United States, to learn about America at first hand. The Queen Mother told her audience:

> The King was always deeply interested in everything that could make life a better and a worthier thing for young people. He would, I know, share to the full the conviction which animates all of us here tonight, and all those many other members of the English-Speaking Union who cannot be here; the conviction that the most important factor in world affairs is understanding between the English-Speaking peoples, and that there is no better method for the furtherance of goodwill between our countries than by the interchange of young people. For without goodwill and understanding there can be no harmony, or true partnership. And without partnership there can be no peace, no security, no prosperity, no freedom in the world today.[11]

She ended with the memorable words: 'The Atlantic, once a wide gulf between us, is surely now a lake that links us.'[12]

While in New York, she attended a dinner given by the former US Ambassador to Britain, Lewis Douglas. It was slightly sticky, so she was relieved when Patricia Hambleden's son Harry arrived and sang some homespun calypsos, though she urged him: 'Remember who I am and where I am.'[13]

The next day, 4 November, the Queen Mother flew to Washington in President Eisenhower's special plane. As in 1939, she stayed at the White House, lodged in the Rose Room, which had been redecorated by President Truman, for better or worse. While in the nation's capital, the Queen Mother met Alice Longworth, young Senator Richard M. Nixon and that vicious scourge of Communism, Senator Joseph R. McCarthy.

After Washington the Queen Mother went to Annapolis, Maryland, and Richmond and Williamsburg, in Virginia, sitting by her own request in George Washington's pew, walking through the Capitol of the Governors by candlelight, and remarking: 'I seemed in truth to step back into the 18th century.'[14]

She went to Jamestown, the small river island where adventurous Englishmen had founded a community which became one of Britain's most important colonies. In Virginia, she detected a close bond with Britain in common heritage, but also in 'a gracious way of living'.[15] On 12 November she flew to Ottawa.

Canada

The Queen Mother's arrival in Canada was preceded by press criticism, not of her, but of the suggestions in the British press that she was to be their Governor-General. The press considered this 'solely the responsibility of the Canadian Government'.[16]

The Canadians had not forgotten the Queen Mother from her 1939 visit and gave her a tremendous welcome, waiting for hours in the freezing cold to see her arrive. The streets were packed and the bunting was out. Sir Archibald Nye, the High Commissioner, had no hesitation in reporting: 'The visit was a triumph from start to finish and not the slightest incident marred its success.'[17] The Queen Mother's few days in Canada contrasted with the glitz of the American visit by being more formal yet giving the impression that she was on home soil. Arriving in the dusk of a November evening, her first words were: 'It's nice to be back.'[18] She was soon spotting faces she apparently remembered from 1939. Nye commended 'her unique gift for projecting the warmth of her personality and her smile to people at a distance from her'.[19] When she left, Vincent Massey, as Governor-General her host in Canada, said: 'it seemed as though the lights had dimmed'.[20]

Speculation that the Queen Mother might become Governor-General of Canada persisted. Though she laughed it off at the time, a secret file emerged in September 1957 listing her likes and dislikes and alterations that would need to be made at Rideau Hall, the Governor-General's residence, if she were appointed. During the Queen's visit in October 1957 the question was revived. The Queen threw back her head and laughed: 'What a novel idea. I'm afraid we would miss her too much.'[21]

Looking back on the Canadian visit, Sir Archibald Nye paid the Queen Mother the highest tribute:

I have on occasion emphasised the necessity for positive action on our part if the ties of Commonwealth are to be maintained with Canada. It is a striking fact – and a sobering one for politicians and diplomats – to realise that a few days' visit by this gracious lady has probably done more for this great objective than all our own efforts for the past year.[22]

The Queen Mother's American visit was also hailed as a success. After she sailed, her eighty pieces of luggage now escalated to 149, with twenty-nine additional packets and cartons. Edward L. Bernays, later dubbed 'The Father of Spin',* wrote that the British were 'stuffy, snobbish, snooty and unapproachable'. It therefore followed, in his opinion, that these qualities would be 'exaggerated in the Queen Mother'. So he was delighted that the Americans had discovered in her 'warmth, sincerity, frankness, democratic bearing and interest in American institutions and a vigour that no one had imagined a Queen could have'. He concluded: 'Undoubtedly she has been a most potent symbol for Britain in this country, not excluding Ambassadors, Generals and Prime Ministers.'[23]

This view was shared by Anthony Nutting, then Leader of the UK Delegation to the UN General Assembly. When briefing the Queen about United Nations matters, he told her that the Queen Mother 'had taken New York by storm. She could run for President tomorrow whether Republic or Democrat.'[24] He also tried to tell the Queen Mother that it had been a great success, but she would hear nothing of it. Nevertheless, in reply to a letter from Churchill she wrote:

> Everybody was most welcoming, from the President, to the taxi drivers in New York, who stuck their heads out of their cabs, and with kindly smiles, said: 'Hi ya queen'. I have a sort of feeling that the Americans rather like us, and a strong feeling that nothing can divide us.
>
> It was rather exhausting, but I am very fond of those warm 18th century people, and one knows that if we are together the world will be safer.[25]

On the subject of taxi drivers, Cecil Beaton had also been in New York:

> The Queen Mother has, during a ten-day visit, done a wonderfully successful piece of propaganda for England. She has been loved by all who have been here, & from the newspaper stories, she has emerged as a real character, witty, tactful, amusing, dignified, &

---

* Edward L. Bernays (1891–1995), long-lived pioneer of public relations in the United States.

warm. Diane Vreeland* remarks that she has been able to 'put over the warmth while maintaining the restraint', & has pointed out that the wave, the gesture with upturned hand pointing inwards is an acclaim that is still reserved. It is unlike an actress's gesture which gives out & goes out to the people. This gesture remains contained & does not permit intimacy.

My German taxi driver, the father of a huge family in the Bronx, said he had seen the Queen [Mother] when his taxi was stuck for an hour in Broadway, when [she] went to see *The Pajama Game*. He thought her so pretty with her smile & radiance. I asked 'Didn't you consider her a bit fat?' 'Just pleasantly plump,' he said & went on to muse: 'I'm sure if she wasn't a Queen, just an ordinary woman, she wouldn't remain single for a month. There's many a man who would like to marry her, with her smile & bright eyes, & she'd be a pleasing handful at playtime.'[26]

Paris

For her trip to Paris in 1956 there survive contradictory accounts, the formal one of the Ambassador, Sir Gladwyn Jebb, and the private one of his wife, Cynthia. The Jebbs already knew Queen Elizabeth and had been received by her and Princess Margaret, as joint Counsellors of State, before they proceeded *en poste* to Paris in March 1954.

The Queen Mother flew into Le Bourget on 13 March and opened the Franco-Scottish exhibition at the National Archives the same afternoon. In the evening she met representatives of the official and literary world at the Hôtel de Rohan.

The next day she lunched with President Coty at the Elysée Palace, with Lord and Lady Ismay among the guests. The President was in mourning for his wife, but particularly wanted to entertain the Queen Mother. She then went out to Versailles, attending a reception, and there was a further dinner at the Embassy followed by a reception where leading members of 'Tout Paris' had 'decked itself out in all its finery to honour Her Majesty'.[27]

Sir Gladwyn Jebb's version was that, following the success of the 1938 visit to Paris, it was likely that this visit would go well, but that 'what was really rather astonishing was the degree of enthusiasm it evoked'.[28] Despite little advance publicity, the crowds lined the route from Le Bourget to the Embassy ten or twenty deep, maybe as many as a hundred thousand people.

---

* Diane Vreeland (1903–89), style guru, then editor of *Harper's Bazaar*.

At the Embassy receptions the Ambassador made sure that the most distinguished figures in France, excluding members of the Communist Party, were invited, and thus the Queen Mother met Labour leaders, scientists, journalists, figures in the arts and literature, those with good war records and members of the Resistance. Sir Gladwyn concluded:

> There is no doubt at all in my mind that this kind of visit has a very profound and salutary political effect. Just when the French were feeling low about things in general, and more particularly about Algeria on the eve as they are of important decisions which will probably affect most families in the country, it was heartening for them to have physical proof of sympathy from their closest ally in the person of so charming and intelligent a member of the Royal Family.[29]

On the other hand, Lady Jebb observed that the Queen Mother arrived 'all smiles and nods and beams',[30] accompanied by a considerable staff. On the second day of the visit, when there were less official engagements, she noted:

> I find her a puzzling person. So sweet, so smiling, so soft, so charming, so winning, so easy and pleasant. And yet there is another side, which sometimes reveals itself, rather mocking, not very kind, not very loyal, almost unwise.[31]

An old governess came to visit her and was mimicked before and after, yet no doubt charmed during the visit itself. The Queen Mother enjoyed mimicking herself acting her charm. She was unpunctual, making the guests at Versailles distinctly edgy at her non-appearance. As soon as Lady Jebb ventured that she hoped they would not meet André Maurois at a particular function, since his war record was considered poor,* the Queen Mother at once insisted on seeing him and did so. On the way to Le Bourget, the Queen Mother took her gloves off and had to scramble to get them on again, blaming her 'silly maid' for giving her 'tight gloves'.[32]

Dunkirk

The Queen Mother and the Duke of Gloucester embarked in HMS *Chieftain* early on the morning of 29 June 1957 for the unveiling of the Dunkirk

---

* Maurois, ostensibly a friend to Britain, had fled to America during the war and given broadcasts to the effect that Britain was finished.

memorial to the soldiers of the British Expeditionary Force 1939–40. As the Queen Mother relaxed in a chair on B gun deck, covered by a rug, *Chieftain* sailed across the Channel.

The advance planning of this essentially simple ceremony had caused an unusual number of diplomatic headaches. Every possible problem of protocol arose, largely because Dunkirk and Lille were fiercely jealous of each other, and there had been disappointment that the Queen and Duke of Edinburgh had been unable to visit the port during their state visit to France that April.

The local rivalries led the Mayor and municipal authorities to act their most self-important and to arrange social events which were quite out of keeping with a memorial unveiling. The protocol department at the Quai d'Orsay were unhelpful. In fact, their representative 'found the first meeting at Dunkirk with the local French authorities such heavy going that he never reappeared!'[33]

On the day itself the Queen Mother and the Duke of Gloucester attended a small reception and then a 'profoundly moving' service after which wreaths were laid by the Queen Mother, General Ganeval (representing the President) and a great number of Commonwealth representatives. The Ambassador reported: 'There was universal admiration for the moving manner in which Queen Elizabeth carried out Her engagements and many Frenchmen remembered gratefully also the days when England stood alone.'[34]

Lady Jebb's memories were more robust. She described it as 'the hottest day of the year' and 'exhausting under the blazing sun'. While the Duke of Gloucester was stoically buttoned into full-dress uniform, Field Marshal Montgomery wore lightweight battledress, informing the Ambassadress: 'I don't mind what people say or think. I just do as I want to do.'[35]

The Queen Mother re-embarked in *Chieftain*, which sailed past the beaches to a pre-arranged position, at which point she released a wreath into the sea by cutting the security line so that it floated off. On the return voyage, she had tea on B gun deck and visited the wardroom during the return voyage to Dover. She announced that she had been pleased to have been up and down ladders, hither and thither on board, without getting so much as a mark on her white organdie dress.

There had clearly been vicissitudes for the Royal Navy, but, at the end of it, *Chieftain*'s commanding officer, P. C. Chapman, got his reward:

On arrival at Dover I had, for the last time, changed into sword and medals at the Charterhouse before going one deck lower to report our arrival to Her Majesty. I found her watching events from the Starboard side of the Forecastle by my cabin door. When she said with evident feeling and sincerity, 'Well done, I have had such a splendid day,' the years that had been added to my natural span were removed by her smile.[36]

Rhodesia

It was not long before the Queen Mother was on her travels once more. Between 2 and 16 July, she returned to the Federation of Rhodesia in order to be installed as First President of the University College of Rhodesia and Nyasaland in Salisbury. This was the first time the territory had enjoyed a full royal visit since the Prince of Wales's visit in 1935, and it was the first time there had ever been a royal visit to Nyasaland.

The ceremony at the University on 5 July was more academic than political, with the emphasis on the 'academic commonwealth of universities', and to a colourfully robed assembly the Queen Mother was able to convey in public a message from the Chancellor of the University of London to the President of the University College, since she embodied both roles. There had been much criticism in the British press about racial segregation, but students and visitors of all races took part in the proceedings without any ostentatious multi-racialism. The local press had complained that the University was expecting too much by linking its examinations with those of the University of London rather than the South African universities. But Queen Elizabeth made it clear in her speech that the decision had been taken 'to insist that the College, from its inception, should aim at the highest academic standards and should open its doors to all who are qualified to enter, regardless of race and colour'.*[37]

During the remainder of her stay, the Queen Mother laid the foundation stone for a new cathedral at Lusaka, attended the State Assembly in Zomba, opened a multi-racial hospital at Blantyre, both in Nyasaland, unveiling a plaque at a camp for children of all races similar to the former Duke of York's camps, and opened the Rhodes National Gallery in Salisbury. All these events were for the benefit of all races, and all races were represented at the functions attended by the Queen Mother 'though this was not achieved without pressure in some cases'.[38] The civic authorities in Salisbury were subjected to considerable pressure before they would

* In July the Queen Mother thanked King Faisal of Iraq for sending the gift of a tablet with Babylonian cuneiform text to the University.

allow Africans and other non-Europeans to be presented to the Queen Mother at the civic garden party.

The Acting High Commissioner for the United Kingdom, Edwin Sykes, reported:

> For her part, Her Majesty emphasised again and again the pleasure with which she saw the representatives of all races, and this gracious influence in favour of racial tolerance cannot fail to be of effect throughout the country. Not the least of the beneficial results of the tour will, I think, be the fact that now that these barriers of race prejudice have once been lowered other people will be less fearful of trying to behave in a liberal way in future. Her Majesty arrived in the Federation at a time when the franchise proposals of the Federal and Southern Rhodesia Governments were causing heated public controversy, but even the noisy (though small) Segregation Society felt constrained to insert at the end of their Press advertisements about a petition opposing the franchise proposals of Southern Rhodesia the apologetic postscript: 'We apologise for the fact that this petition will clash with the visit of our beloved Queen Mother.'[39]

The Queen Mother was sad to give up the University College in 1970 and all connections with Rhodesia due to political differences with Britain.

New Zealand and Australia

At the end of January 1958 the Queen Mother undertook a long tour of New Zealand and Australia, calling at Montreal, Vancouver, Honolulu and Fiji on the outward journey, and returning via the Cocos, Mauritius, Uganda and Malta. In so doing she became the first Queen ever to fly round the world.

She arrived in Auckland on 2 February and toured the country, being welcomed in every city by huge, enthusiastic crowds.* From North Island she went to South Island, before flying to Canberra on 14 February. She opened the biennial conference of the British Empire Service League, dined privately with Lord Carrington and then went on to Brisbane and Sydney, passing through nine miles of crowds on her way to Government House. She made a broadcast which was relayed by 250 Australian

---

* It was during this trip that Sir Ernest Davis, the former Mayor of Auckland, spontaneously presented her with Bali H'ai III (see Chapter 35).

radio stations. She returned to Canberra for a state ball, and visited Melbourne (where the flamboyant Liberace tried to gate-crash a garden party), Tasmania, Adelaide (or 'Dear old Adeloid'[40] as she called it), and Perth, leaving Australia on 7 March.

Engine trouble delayed the Queen Mother in Mauritius, causing last-minute consternation at an unprepared Government House, and then she was again delayed at Entebbe. She was travelling in an Australian Quantas Super Constellation, but refused to swap to a British one. She had been meant to open the new Nairobi Airport on her way back, and when the delays were announced in Nairobi her non-appearance was swiftly attributed to rumours of a plot to assassinate her. The Queen Mother finally arrived home three days late, on 13 March, looking tired, thinner and strained.

The Prime Minister, Harold Macmillan, had wondered if he should go to the airport to greet her. The Queen Mother relayed a message saying she hoped he would not 'dream of going unless he particularly wanted to'.[41] Macmillan's office thought there would be some political mileage in his being there and so he made the trip to the airport. On 17 March the Queen Mother was accorded a Guildhall reception, and spoke of the flight delays, introducing a veiled reference to her 1956 Aintree disaster with Devon Loch: 'I have some experience of seeing a dazzling success snatched from one, even at the last fence, and my sympathy is much with the gallant crews, who worked so unceasingly to complete their task.'[42]

African Skies

In compensation for having missed Nairobi in March 1958, the Queen Mother embarked on a three-week tour of Kenya and Uganda on 5 February 1959.

The visit began in controversy with the African Elected Members of the Kenya Legislative Assembly declaring they would boycott the visit. This was due to the Government having banned African public meetings for the duration of the Queen Mother's stay. The Members sent a message to the Queen Mother saying that their non-participation must not be interpreted as a sign of disloyalty or discourtesy to her.

A certain Tom Mboya, the twenty-nine-year-old unofficial leader of the African Elected Members, then considered 'completely indoctrinated', on whom much of the Labour Party was relying for 'a pure black state in Kenya',[43] explained to the media that the Kenya Government had arranged the visit by the Queen Mother 'at a time when conditions do not permit full participation by African people in events of celebration and joy'.[44]

Cairo Radio declared: 'Let us show these British dogs that we are natives of Africa and that we will never receive or welcome the Queen Mother of England. We are not sheep to be driven by the wishes of the British dogs.'[45] But the Kenyans were so keen to see the Queen Mother that there were no protests and the African Nationalists had to give up any ideas of protest.*

Those accompanying the Queen Mother were warned by Dr Craig, medical officer to the royal party throughout the visit, that they would encounter humidity, crisp evenings, the danger of sunburn on the equator, in fact 'extremes of climate'. They would pass through areas where malaria was transmitted and should rely on malaria prophylactic drugs, and some might suffer from motion or travel sickness, caused by plane, train, launch or motor car, but the good news was that Dr Craig would be travelling with them and pleased to offer 'advice and assistance on health matters' at any time.[46]

The Queen Mother and her party stayed in Nairobi with Sir Evelyn Baring, Governor of Kenya, and his wife, the former Lady Mary Grey. At the Parliament building a loyal address was presented by Sir Ferdinand Cavendish-Bentinck,† Speaker of the Legislative Council, a distant cousin, who was heir to the Dukedom of Portland. Four of the supposedly boycotting Africans were present. While Tom Mboya was absent, Mr D. T. arap Moi was there and told the Queen Mother he looked forward to seeing her when she toured the Rift Valley.

When hundreds of Suk tribesmen walked miles to Kitale to see the Queen Mother, a movement called Dina Ya Yomut (Voice of the Wind) – similar to the Mau Mau and started in 1956, and who were reputed to have oathing sessions, sex orgies and to burn European farms – dissolved.

The usual daunting schedule of nearly sixty engagements followed with ceremonial drives, garden parties and receptions, long lists of people presented at each occasion. Twenty thousand children were gathered in Mitchell Park, Nairobi, to see the Queen Mother make two circuits of the arena.

The first full day was 6 February, the seventh anniversary of the King's death. At a garden party the Queen Mother was reunited with two bearers who had been with the Duke of York when he shot his first lion in Kenya

* Disappointed that the boycott was failing, Mboya made the sensational claim that certain Kenya Europeans were stockpiling arms in advance of an 'Algerian settler rebellion'. He made this claim in the NPCP's weekly news-sheet, *Uhuru*.
† Sir Ferdinand Cavendish-Bentinck (1888–1980), who succeeded his distant cousin as 8th Duke of Portland in 1977.

in 1925. One of them, Ali Mohammed, wore a faded photograph of himself with the Duke on his tunic, and carried the skin of a black and white colobus monkey. But, surrounded by eight thousand men in top hats, he lost his nerve and bolted. The Queen Mother was glad to have a talk with him when he recovered his equilibrium.

It was on the morning of 9 February, at Narok, a sun-drenched and remote quarter of the Kenya plateau, that the Queen Mother made a speech that was to become especially memorable. For weeks Masai tribesmen had been praying for rain, to no avail. At noon that day the Queen Mother arrived and inspected a Guard of Honour made up of Kenya Police and the Kenya Police Band.

For the main ceremony, the Queen Mother sat serenely opposite two half-circles of Masai elders, their chests and backs covered with red ochre, which was also daubed in the fine plaits of their greased hair. They looked ferocious, carrying shields and knobberries. They stood or crouched shoulder to shoulder and their plumes of ostrich feathers swayed as they nodded agreement to the words of greeting spoken.

Speeches of welcome were made in both Masai and English. And then the Queen Mother replied. She delivered her speech in bright sunshine, with words to the effect that she hoped that one day – soon – the rains would come. She smiled and gave a vague gesture towards the sky.

Hardly was she back in her car than a splinter of lightning crossed the sky and there was a fierce rumble of thunder. The first drops of rain fell, and then down came a deluge. The dry streambeds filled with rushing water, the red ochre on the seminaked bodies of the warriors was washed down their legs, and their two-foot-high headdresses of ostrich feathers hung limp and sodden.

'It is a good omen,' declared the warriors. 'The Queen Mother has brought us rain at last.' She was hailed as the Rainmaker.

As Queen Elizabeth settled into the back of her car, which was then winched out of the mud, she turned to Patricia Hambleden and said: 'Well, if they don't want me in England, I can always come here and be a witch-doctor!'[47]

In Mombasa the Queen Mother was welcomed by fifty thousand coastal Arabs, saw a sword dance and sailed among the dhows in the colourfully adorned Old Harbour. Forty-three sheiks and sharifs were presented. There was a reception given by women of all races, ladies of the Arab community in brilliant costumes, singing a song of welcome. The Queen Mother sat on a dais in a three-hundred-year-old ceremonial chair of ebony and ivory and later met Europeans, Africans, Indian Muslims, Arabs and Goans. Meanwhile, during rare free periods, the Royal Household staff was taken shopping, sightseeing or to swim in safe bathing places, the sea being considered too dangerous on account of sharks. She visited Nakuru and Bondeni, eventually departing in the Royal Train for a tour of Kenya.

On St Valentine's Day, the Queen Mother received a spontaneous card from seventy-one representatives from the railways:

> We railwaymen are deadly dull,
> Our lives run straighter than our line,
> Today our cup is more than full,
> For you provide our Valentine.[48]

The Queen Mother agreed to accept it – unofficially. She travelled via Naivasha, Nyeri, and over the Aberdares, arriving in due course at Tree-tops Hotel, where Princess Elizabeth had become Queen seven years before. It was not the original hotel, which had been burnt down by the Mau Mau in 1954, but a new one on the opposite side of the salt lick. Just before the visit both the power engines failed and the visit almost turned into a fiasco. They were restarted just in time.

The Queen Mother was the first important guest at the new Treetops. She met Eric Sherbrooke Walker, who had built the hotel, and his wife, Lady Bettie; they watched game and returned to the verandah after dinner to watch more game until midnight. Two baboons were repelled from the observation platform; bushbuck, rhinoceroses, buffalos and warthogs were seen.

The Queen Mother stayed the night at Treetops, with Colonel Gilliat, her equerry and two ladies-in-waiting. She relished the 'atmosphere of stillness and calm',[49] and how close she was to the animals in the wild, and yet quite safe.

On 18 February the Queen Mother flew to Entebbe where she was the guest of King Freddy, the Kabaka, and his wife. Whereas the Baganda tribe had boycotted the Queen's 1954 visit because the Kabaka was in exile, they gave the Queen Mother a huge welcome, causing her car to slow down to acknowledge the crowds. She enjoyed a visit to Uganda's National Park, seeing lionesses, nine elephants, marabou storks, pelicans and hippos. On a Nile boat trip, the Queen Mother's launch passed close by a huge crocodile snoozing on the river bank. When one of the royal party threw some waterweed in its direction, it burst into life, disappearing under the water close to the launch.

On the same evening, in Kampala, a game warden had to drive an elephant from the doorstep of the Queen Mother's lodge. Lady Jean

Rankin was rightly nervous as the royal party went out on to the veranda, announcing that she could hear breathing. Others mocked her but when the game warden shone his torch, it revealed five elephants browsing all too close to the Queen Mother.

The tour was hailed as a great success. There had been a politically inspired threat of boycott in Kenya, but she had been greeted by all Africans and all races. The strength and affection of such greetings had transcended political differences. 'The healing touch is something to be valued in those troubled parts,' declared the *Daily Telegraph*.[50]

Roman Holiday

There was further controversy when Queen Elizabeth and Princess Margaret went to Rome in April 1959, the Free Church of Scotland criticising their plan to visit Pope Pius XI.[51] Not unreasonably, the Queen Mother's office at Clarence House responded. 'You will no doubt realise that a courtesy call of this nature does not imply, or reflect any views as to the political or religious opinions of the Heads of State visitant.'[52]

This was an unofficial five-day sightseeing visit to Rome, a precursor to the Queen's state visit in 1961. There were diplomatic implications, one correspondent describing it as 'one of the most considerable moments in Italo-British relations in nearly a quarter of a century'.

They arrived in one of the worst rainstorms experienced in Rome for a long time, the welcoming party being soaked through. Princess Margaret's pink straw hat looked most inappropriate, yet, commented one observer: 'The demeanour of the Royal visitors in these trying circumstances was an object lesson in unruffled equanimity.'[53]

If they were hoping for a holiday, they were not to be left in peace, but they did not appear to resent the firework display of hundreds of paparazzi flashbulbs that accompanied their every move.

For the visit to the Pope the Queen Mother wore black with the Greville tiara, Garter riband, star and Garter on arm, and her Royal Family Orders. She sent Princess Margaret back to put on her jewels and orders, which her maid, Ruby Gordon, had to retrieve from the top of William Tallon's cupboard, where they were kept for safety, wrapped in newspaper. The dual impression made by the two royal ladies in black was nothing less than magnificent.

They spent twelve minutes with the Pope. He waived protocol by moving from his desk to the door to greet them. The conversation so feared by the Free Church of Scotland revolved around Princess Anne's chickenpox, some general words about the Queen and Prince Philip and a message of greeting and friendship from the Pope to be relayed to them.

The rest of their stay was a mixture of sightseeing and being entertained. The Queen Mother unveiled a bust of Lord Byron on the Spanish Steps, lunched with Sir D'Arcy Osborne,* a childhood friend, who once confessed that she was 'the past love of his life',[54] and visited a stud farm. She consoled a weeping mother whose son had been killed by the Allies in the war, patting her on the head, and sent a message to the Mayor of Rome asking for clemency for a woman who broke through the police cordon, baby in arms, crying out: 'My husband has no work! Give us work! Give us bread!'[55]

While she accompanied her mother by day, Princess Margaret also enjoyed Rome's legendary nightlife, in the company of her friend Judy Montagu, meeting Roman aristocrats, film stars and artists, and returning to the British Embassy in the small hours of the morning. The press became excited when she was frequently entertained by the charming Prince Heinrich of Hesse (also known as the artist Enrico d'Assia), though he was not a marrying man.

One day the Embassy Rolls-Royce was stuck at a level crossing. Enrico d'Assia was squeezed between Princess Margaret and Judy Montagu. 'Che bella la Principessa' a voice cried from the pavement. Then, thinking Judy Montagu was the Queen Mother, the same voice cried, 'Ma che bruta la Regina Madre!'[56]

As mother and daughter flew to Paris, the visit was judged to have gone remarkably well, due to the gracious behaviour of the royal ladies, the helpful attitude of the British Embassy and the political skill of various Italian ministers. It was rare to find all elements praised.

Paris in Springtime

From Rome a Comet IV conveyed the Queen Mother and Princess Margaret to Paris for the weekend, the purpose being the opening of the Floralies exhibition (a glorified flower show) at the Place de la Défense. Lady Jebb was still the Ambassadress and presumed that the visit had been inspired by David Bowes-Lyon's presidency of the Horticultural Society. Her heart sank when Queen Elizabeth said she hoped to bring Princess Margaret. The Princess's priorities soon became clear – to have her hair done by Monsieur Alexandre and to be fitted for a Dior dress.

---

* Sir D'Arcy Osborne (1884–1964), British Minister to the Holy See 1936–47. He lived in a palazzo in Via Giulia. He succeeded his distant cousin (the brother of Dorothy, wife of Patrick, Earl of Strathmore) as 12th Duke of Leeds in August 1963, but died the following March.

The Queen Mother and Princess Margaret duly arrived on 25 April, the former 'radiant as ever', the latter 'looking far from radiant', having been exhausted by Judy Montagu and her social peregrinations in Rome. With them came an entourage of eleven.

It proved a far from easy visit, not on account of the Queen Mother, who took every nuance in her stride, but because Princess Margaret veered from being overly formal to showing displeasure when bored. Nor did she mingle when asked to. After a dinner for sixty, the party went into the ballroom for a concert, and she insisted on sitting next to Jean Cocteau because he had amused her at dinner.

The next day, a Sunday, Princess Margaret was in a bad temper at church. She wriggled out of a visit to the Ganays at Courance and Madame Sommier at Vaux-le-Vicomte, claiming she had a cold. The Queen Mother appealed to Lady Jebb 'rather sadly and sweetly' to ask if it would matter. Princess Margaret remained at the Embassy, to which Monsieur Alexandre was presently summoned to do her hair.

Lady Jebb spoke of this to Patricia Hambleden who expressed no surprise, adding: 'You will see that this tiresome incident will have no effect on Queen Elizabeth at all. She will enjoy her day as much as though it had never happened. Nothing will disturb her happiness.' Lady Jebb wondered whether it would have been better had the Queen Mother taken a tougher line. She asked Lady Hambleden if the Queen Mother had always possessed this philosophical approach. 'Yes, I think she always had this quality. And a sort of serenity, and of being unhurried.'

While Princess Margaret continued to be difficult, the Queen Mother continued to enchant. She opened the exhibition, lunched with General de Gaulle, visited 'The Age of Elegance', an exhibition of eighteenth-century furniture at the Musée des Arts et Métiers, and finally left Paris 'as serene and happy as ever'.[57]

28

Princess Margaret

'Queen Elizabeth & the Queen look quite miserable'
– Helen Hardinge on the wedding

From 1953 until 1960 the Queen Mother and Princess Margaret lived together at Clarence House. This was not an unqualified success. As Queen Elizabeth grew busier, so Princess Margaret seemed to do less. Her royal duties bored her. She led a largely independent life, and notes were passed by pages from Queen Elizabeth's room to hers when they needed to communicate or make a plan. She missed her father desperately.

The Queen Mother sometimes gave in to Princess Margaret, though she would not allow her to retreat to bed until after an engagement was over, even if she was genuinely ill. She herself never disappointed the crowds and was keen that others should follow her example.

If she had no engagements, Princess Margaret would stay in bed, listening to the radio and reading the morning papers, seldom appearing before 1 p.m. She lunched with the Queen Mother in the library, taking her afternoon tea either with her mother or the Household. In the evenings she invariably went out, giving friends scrambled eggs before the theatre and returning home late.

In 1955 the second part of the Townsend saga was played out. Townsend had returned only once to England on a brief visit in July 1954, seeing Princess Margaret for two hours at Clarence House. Nothing about the future was discussed in the two-hour meeting but it was clear that their feelings for each other were as strong as ever.

During Townsend's two-year absence in Brussels, Princess Margaret had been deeply unhappy. She believed that he had been harshly treated, while she felt isolated, unable to discuss the matter either with her mother who at first refused to believe the romance and therefore would not discuss it, or with the Queen, who was happily married and busy.

In the meantime various suitors had come and gone. Some thought that if the King had lived he would have prevailed upon Princess Margaret to marry Lord Dalkeith, son of the Duke and Duchess of Buccleuch. Dominic Eliot, son of the Earl of Minto, would have made a kind and sympathetic husband. Revd Simon Phipps, who could match Princess Margaret's gift of mimicry, or Colin Tennant, son of the Queen Mother's former beau, Lord Glenconner, would both have been stimulating and unusual company. The latter was considered a suitor and would remain a lifelong friend. In 1954 she was his weekend guest in Scotland, and he was at Balmoral for her twenty-fourth birthday that August.

The press were convinced that Tennant would soon become Princess Margaret's husband, and during that summer Balmoral were besieged by reporters and photographers. Tennant became neurotic and dreaded Princess Margaret's birthday dinner because the Queen Mother decided that it would be a nice idea if they did as they used to when the King was alive, and dressed up and sang a specially made up song for her at dinner. The evening was a disaster: it highlighted Princess Margaret's plight, stressing the loss of her father and the absence of Townsend, and was not helped by the understandable tension of Tennant.

In the spring of 1955 Princess Margaret went on a solo trip to the West Indies, which was as successful as such tours tended to be. On the day that Princess Margaret went to a civic luncheon at the Mansion House there was an interview in the *Daily Sketch* in which Townsend, in Brussels, was asked if he and Princess Margaret would marry. 'Wait and see,' he was quoted as saying. Townsend rang the *Sketch* to say he had been misquoted, but enquiries to Lord Rothermere proved that he had invited the journalist for the interview.

Princess Margaret reached her twenty-fifth birthday at Balmoral on 21 August 1955, and Townsend reappeared on British shores on 12 October, going to stay in the Lowndes Square flat of the Marquess of Abergavenny.

He failed to understand why he could not go immediately to Balmoral. He spoke to friends about God's will making the marriage happen. He rang Balmoral several times through intermediaries and, finally, he telephoned himself. A page startled Queen Elizabeth and the house party by announcing: 'Group Captain Peter Townsend is on the telephone for Princess Margaret.'

Before Princess Margaret came south from Balmoral, she prevailed on a friend to discuss her crisis with the Queen, but nothing came of this as the Queen was anxious that her sister must never believe that she had been forced by her into taking one action or another. Nor did the Queen Mother help her, since she made it a point not to interfere in the lives of her daughters.

On 13 October Princess Margaret went to Clarence House and Townsend came round for tea. Queen Elizabeth had gone to the Castle of Mey for her first visit* and she arrived later in the day, immediately launching herself into a series of dinner parties. A media scrum went on outside, while inside Clarence House all was seemingly serene.

The group captain was besieged by the media at Lowndes Square and it continued when he took refuge at Allanbay Park, the home of the Queen Mother's niece, Jean Wills.

Queen Elizabeth spent that weekend at Royal Lodge, feeling guilty that she had not done anything to help, though now it was too late. By this time mother and daughter were scarcely on speaking terms and on one occasion Princess Margaret had even thrown a book at her mother's head.

There was so much press interest in the whole affair that Commander Colville, the Queen's Press Secretary, issued a statement to the effect that no announcement concerning Princess Margaret's future was at present contemplated. Princess Margaret had much to think about. As Townsend put it: 'Mr Eden had only recently brought home fully to the Princess the consequences of her marrying me. The brave Princess had a huge load on her mind.'[1]

Royal engagements continued as normal throughout the crisis. The Queen, the Queen Mother, Princess Margaret and other members of the Royal Family gathered at Carlton Gardens for the unveiling of the King George VI Memorial. Then the President of Portugal arrived on a state visit. There was a gala for him on 27 October, and, the next day, Princess Margaret made her celebrated visit to the Archbishop of Canterbury.

Unbeknown to her, there had been much activity behind the scenes. Before Anthony Eden had gone up to Balmoral for the Prime Minister's annual visit, the Lord Chancellor, Lord Kilmuir, had proffered his advice on the marriage question in a handwritten document. The Lord Chancellor's options were:

1. To proceed as per the Royal Marriages Act.
2. To legislate for Princess Margaret's renunciation of her rights to the throne.
3. To legislate for exclusion from the Royal Marriages Act only.[2]

---

* On 12 August she had been able to invite the Royal Family to visit the castle, all the work finally being complete. There was further confirmation that she would use the castle regularly when flying space between Wick and Aberdeen was declared a purple passage (a special royal route) joining London to Aberdeen and London to Marham, near Sandringham.

The Royal Marriages Act of 1772 stated that, after the age of twenty-five, if one of the descendants of George II (other than those descending from princesses who had married into foreign royal houses) persisted in wishing to marry without the Sovereign's consent, they would have to submit such a request to the Privy Council, at which time their marriage could be solemnised 'unless both Houses of Parliament shall, before the expiration of the said twelve months, expressly declare their disapprobation of such intended marriage'.[3]

It was thought unlikely that ministers had been consulted about royal marriages such as Lord Harewood's in 1949, but in 1955 the civil servants drew up a draft procedure to deal with Princess Margaret's possible marriage.

The Princess would formally request the Queen's permission, recognising that it would be hard for her to give consent due to the Royal Marriages Act, and state that she wished to renounce her rights to the throne for herself and her children. The Queen would then seek the advice of all the Commonwealth Governments concerned with the succession to the throne, in other words all except India. The Queen would also consult the British Prime Minister. The Royal Marriages Act would be altered to restrict it to 'marriages of children and grandchildren of the Sovereign and marriages of the Heir Presumptive'.[4] Once the various Commonwealth Governments had agreed, the Queen would deliver a 'Royal Message' to Parliament 'to consider the expediency of giving effect to Princess M's wishes and of otherwise amending the law relating to Royal Marriages'.[5] Princess Margaret would cede her rights to the throne.

Despite no longer being in the Succession, Princess Margaret was hoping to go on living in the United Kingdom and carrying out royal duties. She would keep her title and her Civil List annuity would be increased by a further £9,000 a year.

There was much discussion about the Royal Marriages Act itself, in respect of how badly drafted it had been, and how much opposition it had attracted in both Houses of Parliament back in 1772. It had even been attacked by Charles James Fox.* There was an argument for its abolition, but it remains on the statute books to this day.

When advising the Prime Minister, Lord Kilmuir pointed out that

---

* A legal pedant even suggested that the only person to whom the Act now applied was the Duke of Connaught's grandson, Captain Alexander Ramsay. He based his argument on the descendants of Edward VII being also descended from 'the issue of a princess who had married into a foreign royal family', Queen Alexandra descending from Princess Louisa, daughter of George II and the wife of Frederik VII of Denmark. Excluding the descendants of King George V of Hanover and the Duke of Albany (later Saxe-Coburg), Ramsay was the only man, though this was not the spirit of the Act.

unpleasant questions would undoubtedly be asked in the House of Commons should Princess Margaret ask the Privy Council for permission to marry. Ministerial advice would have to be given to the Queen, and would inevitably involve her position as Head of the Church of England. There was the question as to whether the groom-to-be would be given a title. What would his status be if, as the result of a series of tragedies, Princess Margaret became Queen? Kilmuir stressed: 'This is a matter on which the wishes of the Queen would be of the highest importance to Ministers. The Queen should be respectfully asked to consider the points which I have raised and to be graciously pleased to express her views.'[6]

The Government did not want to introduce legislation solely to facilitate a royal marriage with a divorced person. Yet Kilmuir concluded that it was his belief that '75% of the electorate would be in favour of the marriage being somehow allowed'.[7]

Despite the negotiations of the civil servants and Government lawyers, neither Princess Margaret nor Group Captain Townsend was kept in the picture. It seemed to them that the choice was either marriage – which meant loss of rights to the throne, title, royal duties and Civil List, 'conditions which, frankly, would have ruined her',[8] as Townsend put it – or renunciation. No one advised them and there were hints that Lord Salisbury might resign from the Government over the issue. Lady Patricia Ramsay, a granddaughter of Queen Victoria, who had renounced her royal styles and titles in 1919, when she married a naval officer, Alexander Ramsay, apparently warned Princess Margaret that the loss of royal status was not very enjoyable.* There is no question that the fear of losing her income also played on Princess Margaret's mind.

The Church of England began to menace and the press became more frenzied, while the British Ambassador in Paris wrote to say that the favourite subject of the French press was now Princess Margaret's 'supposed romance with Group Captain Townsend and on this topic they are prepared to go to almost any extreme of fantasy or expense'.[9]

Princess Margaret and Townsend met at Clarence House on Saturday 22 October, after which she left for Windsor Castle. They were both worn out by the pressure of the situation. At Windsor there occurred a discussion within the family about the future. The Queen, Prince Philip, the Queen Mother and Princess Margaret were all there. Queen Elizabeth volunteered that Princess Margaret had not even considered where she was going to live. Prince Philip then said, not without sarcasm, that it

---

* Nevertheless, Lady Patricia insisted on wearing the robes and coronet of a Princess of the Blood at the Coronations of George VI and the present Queen.

was not impossible to buy a house even in these days, and the Queen Mother left the room, slamming the door behind her.

Just as the general public was convinced that the Margaret–Townsend romance was one of the great love stories of the century, so, in reality, the romance had run its course. Princess Margaret had sunk to the nadir, and, during a long, sleepless night, came to the conclusion that she must renounce Townsend. When he came round the next day, they both agreed that this was the only solution. They continued to maintain that their love was on a higher plane than anyone else's, and that their mutual renunciation had lifted it above the reach of the squalid media.

On the Thursday, Princess Margaret went to Lambeth Palace to see the Archbishop of Canterbury. She told him she had no need of his books. She would renounce Townsend. His reported reply was: 'What a wonderful person the Holy Spirit is!' And when he received members of the NATO Staff College in audience, the Pope spoke of his 'deep thankfulness for the news which has just been received by your beloved country'.[10]

There was a last weekend spent with Lord and Lady Rupert Nevill at their home at Uckfield. Evidently this was a happy occasion for them, released from the tension of their decision. They returned separately to London and, on Monday 31 October, Princess Margaret's official statement was released. 'Mindful of the Church's teaching that Christian marriage is indissoluble, and conscious of [her] duty to the Commonwealth,'[11] she would not be marrying Group Captain Townsend.

That night Princess Margaret was at Clarence House, while Queen Elizabeth was due to keep an evening engagement at the University of London. The Queen Mother set off for this, unaware or unconcerned that her daughter would be having dinner alone on a tray.

Townsend left a slightly bitter postscript to this, pointing out that, despite the Church's resounding victory, little good came from it. Public morality continued to decline, the process of divorce was much facilitated. Princess Margaret was held in high esteem, but to what end? 'Her decision was undoubtedly right. But the example it set seems to have been in vain . . . For people who like fairy tales, our story had a sad ending.*[12]

All over the world, different countries and different religions reacted differently. The *Daily Mirror* in America sent this message:

---

* Princess Margaret lived long enough to see a divorced Princess (Princess Anne) marry an unmarried equerry (Timothy Laurence). By 2005 it was considered acceptable for a divorced Prince of Wales to marry his mistress, likewise divorced.

We can say to the Princess – speaking for most Americans: 'We're mighty sorry, girl.' And we can add with the same authority: 'When some of the heartache wears off, why don't you come and see us. Pay us that long-delayed visit. You'll be so welcome.'[13]

Princess Margaret's Wedding

After Townsend's departure, Princess Margaret continued to live at Clarence House with her mother, drifting towards an uncertain future. Sometimes this found outlets in posing for the unhappy sculptor Sir Jacob Epstein and in her exploration of the arts, the ballet and the theatre. She regularly attended performances by Marlene Dietrich, Frank Sinatra and Danny Kaye. She mixed with Noël Coward and others of that world. She posed for Annigoni. As always there was capricious selectivity. 'I like angry young men,' she told Cecil Beaton in 1958. 'They're not nearly angry enough. If they're angry, I'm furious. But I hate squalor! Tennessee Williams makes me feel ill.'[14]

Then one of her closest friends, Lady Elizabeth Cavendish, who also served as her lady-in-waiting, took it upon herself to try to lift the Princess out of her post-Townsend gloom and to ensure that she met interesting new people from the world of the arts. Without considering the possible outcome, she produced an up-and-coming young photographer, Antony Armstrong-Jones. He became known in royal circles when he photographed the Duke of Kent in 1956, and then the Queen and her family in the grounds of Buckingham Palace in 1957, bringing him considerable publicity.

A day came in 1959 when Group Captain Townsend called at Clarence House for tea, a last goodbye. Normally the Queen Mother and Princess Margaret waited in the chosen sitting room until a guest was brought in. This time they were coming along the Horse Corridor to greet him, Princess Margaret running forward to embrace him. They then retreated to her sitting room for tea. According to an ex-footman, Princess Margaret required all her royal training not to break down when he took his final leave. And that night she told her servant: 'I shall be dining with Her Majesty tonight', a unique dinner during this man's tenure of employment, since she went out every night.[15]

Shortly afterwards Townsend announced his engagement to a Belgian girl, Marie-Luce Jamagne, curiously similar in looks to Princess Margaret but of a gentler beauty. According to the same footman, Princess Margaret hurled the newspaper confirming the stop-press news into a far corner of her sitting room. That night she dined with Billy Wallace, a putative candidate as husband, in whom the press was taking interest.

In 1959 the key members of the 'Princess Margaret Set' were less in evidence, and gradually she saw more of Armstrong-Jones. His Bohemian lifestyle intrigued the staff. When he stayed at Royal Lodge, a brown zipped bag revealed clothes rolled into a ball, all previously worn. Sometimes she visited him at his little Thameside flat.

Armstrong-Jones went to Balmoral, where he was not especially at ease, the tweedy or tartan image of the Royal Family and their friends holding little appeal for him. He wore thin socks and suede shoes with his plus fours. He was not an early riser. When it became clear that he was keen to marry Princess Margaret, her uncle, the Duke of Gloucester, is said to have greeted Harold Macmillan, as he arrived for the traditional Prime Minister's stay, with the line: 'Thank Heavens you've come, Prime Minister. The Queen's in a terrible state; there's a fellow called Jones in the billiard room who wants to marry her sister . . .'[16]

Finally, on 26 February 1960, the Queen Mother announced 'with the greatest pleasure' the engagement of her 'beloved daughter' to Armstrong-Jones. It was an unconventional union, but after the chaos of Townsend there was no reason why it should not proceed. Armstrong-Jones was the son of Ronald Armstrong-Jones, a QC, Deputy-Lieutenant and JP in Caernarvonshire, who had served as High Sheriff in 1936. His mother, Anne Messel, sister of the ballet and stage designer Oliver Messel, had married, as her second husband, 6th Earl of Rosse. If the father was serious-minded, the mother was flighty, fey and pretty. She had inherited a beautiful garden at Nymans, in Sussex, and lived her life in a self-imposed haze of fairy-tale romance, with many a wistful gesture, many a pose struck. When the Queen Mother first dined with the Rosses at their house in Stafford Terrace, she arranged a red carpet at the front door to welcome her.

Anne Rosse had been in society for a long time, and was known in certain mischievous circles as 'Tugboat Annie' – because she drifted from peer to peer. Lady Diana Cooper recalled that when one summer in Venice in the mid-1930s Lord Rosse had kissed her on a balcony, it was suggested that her honour had been impugned, and that he should marry her. This he was happy to do.[17]

Due to long-held jealousies over a 1930s affair between Oliver Messel, Lady Rosse's brother, and Peter Watson,* Cecil Beaton chose to spend his later years exploiting his dislike of Anne Rosse for his own enjoyment and the edification of his friends. His papers are filled with references

---

* Peter Watson (1908–56), rich man about town, later a considerable art patron and financier of *Horizon*.

to her and sightings by friends, and he amused himself by painting a series of brilliant yet vicious caricatures of her, one of which shows her in the foyer of the Royal Opera House, sinking in a curtsey to the floor to the Queen Mother, who gazes elsewhere over her head. In his diaries, which were notably lacking in reticence, he produced this description of her at a ball at Windsor in 1970:*

Her manner was the 'prettiest' you have ever seen, a sorbet wouldn't melt in that cat-smiling mouth, no evil thoughts would ever come through those girlish starry pupils, yet she was dividing her interests, regarding the silver and porcelain services in the glass cupboards through which we passed, observing who was here, and at the same time keeping a close watch on herself.[18]

When Beaton announced the engagement to his Wilton neighbour, Lord Pembroke, the latter responded: 'Then I'll go and live in Tibet!'[19]

Since leaving university, where he had coxed the Cambridge crew to victory in the 1950 Oxford and Cambridge Boat Race, Armstrong-Jones had carved out a name for himself as a photographer. He held his first one-man exhibition, 'Photocall', in London in 1957, and published two books, *Malta* (1957), a collaboration with Sacheverell Sitwell, and *London* (1958). He worked for magazines and newspapers and was much in demand as a society photographer. Beaton felt threatened by him, and, while Beaton had no wish to be described as the court photographer, he was equally reluctant to surrender the role to anyone else, and in particular not to the nephew of Oliver Messel.

Queen Elizabeth and Tony Armstrong-Jones got on well together from the first. 'My dear and talented son-in-law', she used to call him.[20] He was the type she liked – amusing, artistic, forever alive with new ideas, gadgets, inventions and subtle forms of design – an individual with the confidence to express himself, giving little care to what others thought of him. He was destined to make a considerable impact in the artistic field, almost in spite of this marriage. Part of his struggle in the early 1960s was to balance his career with the restrictions that the royal union imposed upon it.

There was nothing arranged about this marriage. It was a love match. And the British public responded with their traditional adoration of a royal romance.

At the wedding on 6 May 1960 the Queen looked glum. At her home

* See *The Unexpurgated Beaton*, p. 72.

in Kent, with her husband dying,* Helen Hardinge observed: 'Queen Elizabeth & the Queen look quite miserable really which is not surprising. I hope it's all better than it seems. Princess Margaret v. pretty but Princess Anne I thought the star performer actually – so quiet & efficient.'[21]

Because it was not a dynastic alliance, the wedding was treated as low-key by the Royal Houses of Europe. In the front rank of royalty, only Queen Ingrid of Denmark, Princess Margaret's godmother, travelled to London for the event.† But Jean Cocteau, such a hit on the visit to France in 1958, was at the Abbey with the Duchess of Buccleuch.

The Queen Mother's brother David and sister May Elphinstone (both of whom would die the following year) were at the wedding breakfast, as was the other surviving sister, Rose Granville. The reclusive head of that family, the Earl of Strathmore, was not. The Queen's table had ten seated; from her right: the bridegroom, the bride, the Duke of Edinburgh, the Queen of Denmark, the Duke of Gloucester, the Countess of Rosse, David Bowes-Lyon, Queen Elizabeth, and Ronald Armstrong-Jones.

The wedding dress was designed by Norman Hartnell, provoking from the obsequious journalist Godfrey Winn a barbed comment that he would have preferred John Cavanagh – 'by far the chic-est of the younger school of English designers'.[22]

The press implied that when the vows were exchanged the Queen Mother's smile vanished and she lowered her eyes, 'recognising, it seemed, all the implications of that hallowed moment . . . including the bitter-sweet prospect of an increasingly solitary future'.[23] Like all such pronouncements, this was simplistic. The Queen Mother and Princess Margaret had been leading detached lives. The Queen Mother could not rely on her daughter for company. There were stories of Princess Margaret returning to Clarence House after an engagement, to be asked by the Queen Mother if she had enjoyed herself and replying: 'Honestly, Mummy, I was bored stiff.'[24]

By the time Princess Margaret married in 1960, the Queen Mother's life was exactly as she wished it to be.

---

* Alec Hardinge died on 29 May 1960, having received a visit from the Queen Mother during his final illness.
† Princess Alexandra's wedding to Angus Ogilvy in 1963 was much more glamorous in this respect, with Queen Frederika of Greece, Queen Ena of Spain, Queen Helen of Romania, and others.

The Routine Established

'We all had to do our best to be bright and gay on orange juice'
– the British Ambassador in Tunisia

The Queen Mother's life was aristocratic and her annual programme almost as inflexible as that of 'Master', her old friend and contemporary, the 10th Duke of Beaufort, who fished on exactly the same weekend each year with the Duke of Northumberland. The Queen Mother punctuated this routine with official visits abroad, whereas the Duke only went abroad when obliged to do so as Master of the Horse – for the state visit to Paris in 1938, or the installation of Queen Juliana ten years later – or, rarely, to a sporting fixture.

The Queen Mother's year began at Sandringham, where she had spent Christmas. The Norfolk winter invariably gave her a cold. She remained there until mid-February, her principal engagement a visit to the Sandringham Women's Institute (the only WI which had restricted membership). Later, she made it her habit to return to Royal Lodge in time for the anniversary of the King's death, spending that time quietly, with only close family, Princess Margaret, Rachel Bowes-Lyon, and later her Elphinstone nieces. There was a simple service in the King's memory in the chapel at Royal Lodge.

In March she enjoyed the racing at Cheltenham and in the early years she would stay nearby with Captain Frank and Lady Avice Spicer, or later drive over from Royal Lodge with her house party. She presented the Cheltenham Gold Cup. This became an annual fixture, rarely missed until 2002.

Easter she spent with her family at Windsor Castle, moving in from Royal Lodge for some days. Then she spent most of the summer in London until the end of July, punctuated by occasional visits to Birkhall, to the House of the Northern Gate to stay with the Vyners, to inspect work on the Castle of Mey, and occasionally to stay with friends elsewhere. In the early summer, from 1962 until 1992, she travelled abroad for pleasure.

State visitors always came for tea on the first afternoon of their state visits, affording the Queen Mother the chance to entertain them privately and talk to them informally in her own home. This became a regular practice which continued to the end, even if in her last years the Queen Mother was not strong enough to attend the state Banquet the same night. Thus, over the years, she received successive Kings of Sweden and Norway, three Presidents of France, Emperor Haile Selassie of Ethiopia, the soon-to-be murdered boy King, Faisal II of Iraq, and, less agreeably, in 1978, the Ceauşescus of Romania. When Emperor Hirohito of Japan went to St James's Palace in 1971, she came out on to her balcony to wave to him.

The Trooping the Colour in June (in those days on a Thursday, but from 1958 always on a Saturday out of respect for London traffic jams) was followed by the Garter ceremony on the first Monday in June, and a week at Windsor for Royal Ascot. During that week there were entertainments at the Castle and sometimes the house party went to the Theatre Royal in Windsor. In later life, the Queen Mother did not disguise her dislike of certain nationalities, notably the Germans. When Crown Prince Naruhito of Japan, son of Emperor Akihito, was staying for Ascot, she insisted that the Japanese sword of surrender be put on display in the Royal Library for his special interest. The Queen vetoed this, the Queen Mother countermanded the veto, but eventually the Queen won and the sword stayed in its cupboard.

As the royal party processed into dinner, the Queen Mother said: 'Come on everybody – Nip on! Nip on!'

The summer holidays, which lasted until early or middle October, were always spent in Scotland. Once the Castle of Mey was ready, she would go there in August and September, spending the end of August and early September at Birkhall.

The Queen Mother then came south to London for the autumn, with weekends at Royal Lodge, and Christmas, in the 1950s, spent at Sandringham. Her engagements were of the traditional royal kind. She received numerous freedoms of cities, there were visits to regiments, charity events, appearances at the opera, ballet and the Royal Variety Show, hospital openings, statue unveilings (especially war leaders), dinners with worthy bodies, church services and tours of London gardens.

The Queen Mother was patron of the London Gardens Society, which promoted the beautification of London by the growing of flowers, provided a 'healthy and civilising interest for those who have little opportunity for self-expression' and encouraged 'the humblest citizen' to improve his surroundings. She visited many private suburban gardens in places such as Stepney, Bethnal Green, Deptford and Greenwich, sharing a cup of tea with a selected couple in the front room of their homes.[1]

There were regional engagements. One such was her visit to the Peterborough Agricultural Show on 18 July 1956, a long day among everyday country folk. In partly wet, partly fair weather, the Queen Mother toured the show, accompanied by men in dark suits and bowler hats. She watched show jumping and four-in-hand driving, a procession of Aberdeen Angus, Lincoln Reds and other prize cattle, from a Royal Box heavily banked with hydrangeas. She admired floral displays, presented bouquets, walked through the ranks of show-goers, inspected the work of the Territorial Army and various nursing brigades. She presented cups and rosettes. Her energy never flagged. When she was not smiling, she was quizzically interested in what she was being shown.[2] Occasions such as these inspired Stephen Tennant to muse: 'She is marvellous – still inspecting prize pigs today'.[3]

In April 1955 Churchill retired as Prime Minister to be succeeded by Sir Anthony Eden. On 23 April the Queen Mother made her first helicopter flight, travelling from Windsor to Biggin Hill. This was soon to become a favoured method of transport. 'The chopper,' she said, 'has changed my life, much as it did that of Anne Boleyn!'

On 24 November 1955, as the Townsend drama subsided from the public's consciousness, the Queen Mother was installed as Chancellor of London University, to which she devoted much time. She attended two presentations a year at the Royal Albert Hall, the university's Foundation Day, and visited two or three colleges a year. She supported the university publicly and promoted it privately.

The Queen Mother's philosophy was that for those who came into her orbit, life must get better. She had a particular knack of winning people over by a shared joke, a telling glance, or by showing consideration unusual in a royal figure. At this she became exceptionally polished, honing the skill to a fine art. When the Queen Mother's car was waiting at traffic lights in the Mall, a pedestrian on the pavement suddenly sneezed. She wound down the window and said 'Bless you!'. The lights changed and the car sped off with laughter all round.[4]

Many people, including the Queen, recognised the Queen Mother's talents as an actress. Like any good performer, she understood her audience. It could be argued that she did not exist unless she was on show. Her engagements, whether private or public, were like performances. Privately, there was less going on, since between these performances she rested. At home she 'made an art of doing nothing' as her page, William Tallon, put it.[5] She would read books or poetry, or write letters. She would play patience or simply relax on her chaise longue. She never kept a diary, preferring to live her life and leave the recording of it to historians.

But when it was time to perform, she engaged her thespian qualities to put on a wonderful show, whether for one person received in audience, whether for a lunch or dinner in her home or at someone else's, or out on a public stint among the thronging crowds.

Dame Frances Campbell-Preston was a perceptive judge of her character. She wrote:

> It is impossible to define the Queen Mother's character and I don't claim to have ever really known her. The outlines are obvious – her enjoyment of people of all sorts, her sense of fun and funniness, her skill at communicating, all wrapped up in her overriding sense of duty and service. She certainly had a firm will, but that could also be described as courage. As well as faith – not only in a religious sense although that was a major ingredient, she had faith in people but particularly the British people. She wasn't a starry-eyed optimist. There were other qualities, rather paradoxical in nature. She had dignity but never pomposity or pretentiousness. She could be quite forceful in mocking people who she suspected of this . . . She had great intuitive powers, reacting quickly to a mood or atmosphere . . . She wasn't always punctual at arriving for an engagement, but she was never late if it mattered. Engagements usually ran late as she engaged more people for longer in conversation than had been reckoned . . . She was a very human person.[6]

The Queen Mother rescued a moment at a Royal Variety Show when the audience failed to clap in tune with Tommy Steele. She paused for press photographers to ensure they got their pictures without apparently noticing them. She broke new ground by agreeing to meet lady reporters at the Women's Press Club, chatting informally to them. 'She seems such fun,' wrote Nancy Spain.[7]

At the Ghillies' Ball at Balmoral in 1958, she sent Lord Plunket over to ask her chauffeur to dance with her. He protested that he could not dance. 'Now is your chance to learn,' replied the Deputy Master of the Household alarmingly. He protested again to the Queen Mother, but she said she would guide him: 'The next dance is a quick-step and all you have to do is walk to the music. I'll see that you get round all right.'[8]

On her return to London in October 1958, she visited Morley College where Harold Nicolson observed her:

> She was in her best mood and spirits. She has that astonishing gift of being sincerely interested in dull people and dull occasions. Really the woodwork, the pottery and the drawings with which these Morley students occupy themselves in the evening are horrible objects. But the Queen Mother seemed really interested and spoke to almost all of them, putting them instantly at their ease.[9]

The press reported incidents such as a dog-walking expedition from Windsor Castle when the Queen Mother and Princess Margaret emerged from a side door of the Castle, heavily muffled up on a particularly wet day. 'Hard luck having to exercise those dogs on a day like this,'[10] muttered a hapless sentry, failing to recognise them.

The occasional breakdown of a car, the showing of a film, a visit to a school, the eating therein of a school meal, enlivened many a news report. And there were occasional profiles, all of which followed the same favourable line:

> Only the kind of person who kicks kittens, snarls at babies and denies the existence of Santa Claus can resist her jolly face, her utter femininity, her guileless way of blandly steam-rollering through any situation.
>
> The Queen Mother is frankly, a comfortable-looking woman. Yet people who see her for the first time always come away prattling about how much prettier she is than her pictures show.[11]

Only the occasional ill-founded rumours in the press left a jarring note. She had been upset about the Arthur Penn rumour. An equally ridiculous one suggested that she might marry the widowed Crown Prince Olav of Norway. She would not remarry. She had settled into a more cosy existence of rich food, and a certain laziness. She loved her chocolates – her friend Lady Diana Cooper claimed that she even ate the Good Boy dog biscuits. She relished butterscotch, cream and butter. She punctuated the day with elevenses and afternoon tea, and she lunched and dined well. As a result, there was an unmistakeable plumpness to her figure.

She enjoyed her widowhood self-indulgences. She told David Herbert that she woke each morning and said to herself: 'And what shall Elizabeth do today?'[12] This is not to imply that she was lacking in zest or energy, or in any professionalism in her public duties. She put duty first, but saw no reason why enjoyment could not be introduced into duty. It was an effective approach.

The Queen Mother reached her sixtieth birthday in August 1960 and appeared on a balcony of Clarence House* to watch a march past of the drum and fife band of the Welsh Guards, affording the crowd the chance of a rare glimpse of the baby Prince Andrew, who had been born in March that year.

Kariba Dam and Tunisia

The Queen Mother made visits to Africa in 1960 and 1961. The first was to the Rhodesian Federation to open the Kariba Dam, a three-week visit. Despite a weekend of violence in Lusaka, she refused to moderate her itinerary. Determined to be recognised as a queen, she put her Garter riband and Royal Family orders over her pale ivory day coat when she addressed Parliament in Mongu, enjoying the sight of the Prime Minister, the Imasiku, dropping to his knees in the mud as she arrived.

The Kariba hydro-electric project had caused serious local problems, nine thousand of Chief Chipepo's subjects having been moved from the gorge to make it possible, while ten thousand of Chief Sinazongwe's subjects had also been unsettled. Before the ceremony both Chiefs of the Batonga people approached the Queen Mother with tears in their eyes to make known their woes, not least the anger of 'the River God'. The Queen Mother smiled at them dazzlingly and said: 'I am very sorry.'[13]

'Poor, godless, poverty stricken Batonga,' commented an exasperated reporter. 'I wish they knew that economically at least this is the best thing that ever happened to them.'[14] It proved a vital life source.

In April 1961 the Queen Mother visited Tunisia. The visit was planned with the proviso that it 'might have to be called off in the event of some sudden or drastic deterioration in the Tunisian or North African situation as a whole'.[15] It was not an easy time, the Algerian War being at a crucial stage; few high-ranking British visitors had been to Tunisia since it had become independent, and no member of the Royal Family. The women of Tunisia were said to have 'a lively interest in and affectionate regard for The Queen Mother'.[16] During his visit to Sandringham at the end of January, Lord Home, the Foreign Secretary, talked the visit through with the Queen Mother. Fears that if the Queen Mother embarked in *Britannia* in Gibraltar there might be a 'Spanish campaign of vexatious

---

* It would seem that the first such balcony appearance at Clarence House was in 1955, when a crowd of about one thousand gathered to sing 'Happy Birthday' to her.

restrictions' were considered groundless,[17] and Sir Pierson Dixon, the British Ambassador in Paris, was not unduly concerned by what he described as an official visit to Tunisia 'in the course of a cruise in the Mediterranean in the Royal Yacht'.[18]

President Bourguiba had steered Tunisia to independence in 1955. Originally a lawyer from Monastir, Bourguiba was an engaging figure who had survived many arrests and a period of exile to become President. He was variously described as a North African Atatürk, and 'the Charismatic Warrior'. He was considered to exert 'an important moderating influence in African councils' and frequently referred in public to the way that Britain had brought colonial territories to independence.

When he was approached, he was 'flattered and honoured' by the idea of a visit from the Queen Mother. He was told that between 23 and 28 April was the only possible time and the dates 'were not subject to variation'.[19] Eventually 24–28 April was agreed.

Bourguiba had a problem with his wife. Before the Queen Mother arrived, it was announced that Madame Bourguiba was 'ill' and would take no part in the programme for the visit. The illness proved to be due to strained relations between husband and wife. She did not appear.

This visit was not without hazard. As *Britannia* arrived, a grave crisis broke out. The French Army rebelled in Algeria, which could have led to a dangerous situation in Tunisia. The Queen Mother offered to postpone her visit, but the Tunisian Government decided it should go ahead. The Ambassador had some difficulty in delivering this message, as when he rang the Foreign Minister, he discovered that he, the President and every member of the Cabinet had gone to a football match. When he further rang the pavilion to attempt to bring the minister to the telephone, the official thought he was in quest of the score, and shouted 'zero, zero' into the instrument and hung up.

The Royal Yacht arrived in a heavy gale, nearly missing the elaborate arrival ceremonies. Plans were made at the last moment and invariably altered, which the British Ambassador hoped 'may rather have diverted than fatigued Her Majesty'.[20]

The dinner party on the first night was 'the least happy event of the tour'. The Queen Mother was nervous and needed much joking from William Tallon to stir her into the right mood. The President was tired and worried about the Algerian situation, the table plan was awkward, and 'not even Her Majesty's wonderful powers of putting people at their ease could make the conversation flow'. The President of the Chamber was there, a strict Muslim, and thus 'we all had to do our best to be bright and gay on orange juice'. On the second night the Queen Mother gave a dinner for forty on board *Britannia*, which was 'the climax of the visit'. The Ambassador reported:

> It was indeed a masterpiece, done in royal style, with more than a touch of panache, but invested with the warm and gracious personality of Her Majesty. It demonstrated to many present that in order to be great or regal, it is not necessary to be pompous or distant. For myself, who had the honour and privilege of sitting opposite Her Majesty at the centre of the horseshoe table, it was an experience which I am not likely to forget. The Belgian Ambassador who represented the diplomatic corps as doyen, whispered to me at one point 'I feel I am in a dream; so does everyone else.' A Tunisian lady said afterwards that she had not talked to her neighbours at all; she had been unable to take her eyes off Queen Elizabeth.* There had earlier been a little disappointment that Her Majesty was not to stay at all on Tunisian soil. This did not really amount to anything, but I was pleased to hear that the Minister of the Interior had said to my wife at dinner that he now understood the point of having the Royal Yacht.[21]

The dinner had a salutary effect on the President, who relaxed into his usual spirits and regaled the Queen Mother with almost his entire life story. When they visited Sousse, the Queen Mother overrode his abject terror of being assassinated and made him accompany her in an open car, no trouble befalling them.

The Queen Mother's performance at this and other events compared well to the dour visit of President Tito of Yugoslavia a week before. Unlike him, she spoke to most of the notables when confronted by a presentation line. Tito had spoken no French and passed every point of interest on the tour at disinterested speed.

The Tunisians were upset when a theatrical event proved an ambitious flop, with moments that some of the British found unintentionally hilarious. The Ambassador assured them that the Queen Mother would not judge them by their theatre and consoled himself that the audience had come to see her, not the play.

The visit ended with the Ambassador taking pride that the Tunisians had seen how a royal person could comport herself. His own standing was enhanced by the visit, the Tunisians having no previous idea of 'what the Queen's representative stands for'. He thought the visit would leave

---

* Nor did she eat so much as a mouthful.

'a lasting impression', and might 'well mark a turning point in Anglo–Tunisian relations, provided that it is not allowed to remain as an isolated episode'.[22] He concluded: 'There is not one of us, I think, in this Embassy, who does not feel a glow of pride.'[23]

Travels and Trauma

'At one moment she did a sort of African dance with John [Hope]' –
Lady Gladwyn

The Queen Mother's official life was at its most important when the Queen
was away or when she made an official overseas visit. She served as Counsellor of State when the Queen and the Duke of Edinburgh went to India
in January 1961 and to West Africa the following November, and again from
January to March 1963. In June 1962 she made the first of a series of popular
visits to Canada, a ten-day visit to the Black Watch of Canada (of which
she was Colonel-in-Chief) for their centenary celebrations. The press hinted
that this visit, and a later regimental visit by the Princess Royal, were to
'patch up relations between Britain and Canada after the fiasco of "consultations" between the two countries on the Common Market'.[1] The Queen
Mother was much commended for travelling on a commercial flight, in a
Trans-Canada DC8, her party of ten occupying the first class, while six
more went economy with thirty-six fee-paying passengers.

She never returned to the United States, though they longed for her
to come. 'I must find an excuse,'[2] she said, making no effort to do so.

A widow for ten years, she now added a new dimension to her annual
programme – travelling for pleasure.

In the early 1960s, the Earl of Euston (later Duke of Grafton) casu-
ally asked Queen Elizabeth if she had ever seen the châteaux of the Loire.
'No, I haven't,' she replied. 'Arrange it!'[3]

Besides Lord Euston, the Queen Mother's friend Sir Pierson Dixon
was involved, as British Ambassador to Paris. He was one of the most
able and charming diplomats, a scholar, a novelist and a sportsman, who
had recently served as Britain's deputy in the doomed Common Market
negotiations in Brussels.

Masterminding the trip at Clarence House was Sir Ralph Anstruther,
who had the advantage of Lord Euston in speaking fluent French. He
knew the Vicomte de Noailles, an aristocrat with a deep love of beautiful
houses and, more so, of gardens.

It might be supposed that the Queen Mother could pay a private visit to the Loire without trouble, but the visit soon became sunk in the mire of European politics. The drama of Britain and the Common Market had caused the visit to be cancelled in 1962. This only made Queen Elizabeth more determined than ever to make her trip in 1963. She would allow nothing to deflect her from gratifying her long-held desire.

Unfortunately, on 29 January, de Gaulle delivered his veto against Britain joining the Common Market, causing Macmillan to record: 'All our policies at home and abroad are ruined.'⁴ Sam Spiegel and Lord Mountbatten had fixed that Princess Margaret and Lord Snowdon would attend a gala showing of *Lawrence of Arabia* in Paris in aid of the Hertford Hospital, but after de Gaulle's rejection of Britain, the Foreign Secretary advised Princess Margaret to cancel. The lame excuse given was that she was needed in England as a Counsellor of State. This caused a furore in the British press, some considering the cancellation a slight to the French President. On 7 February Buckingham Palace announced that their visit was off.

In the wake of this, the Foreign Office was worried that the Queen Mother's visit might become the cause of political demonstration, while Sir Martin Gilliat complicated matters by stating that the Queen Mother had it in mind to spend a night in Paris in order to visit the Hertford Hospital of which she was honorary President, to make up for Princess Margaret not going. Then the Queen Mother informed Sir Harold Caccia, the Permanent Under-Secretary at the Foreign Office, that she wished to go to the Loire, but not to Paris.

She instructed Sir Martin to inform Caccia that she did not think 'the doctrine reasonable that members of the Royal Family other than the Head of State' could pay 'private visits to foreign countries without becoming involved in functions of a ceremonial and official character'. She pointed out that when George VI was Duke of York, he had been abroad privately on several occasions without 'being put under such an obligation'.

Having made her point, she conceded that if the British Ambassador was convinced that her visit would cause offence to de Gaulle, then she would 'naturally accept' his view, and 'subject to advice from the Foreign Secretary her inclination would be to call the visit off'.⁵ She could promise this with confidence since Lord Home was a personal friend, easy to bend to her will.

When the press learned of the Queen Mother's plan, matters became trickier. A slick journalist representing the *Sunday Telegraph* in Paris called the British Embassy in mock innocence to enquire whether there were plans for the Queen Mother to visit the Loire. He was told that she 'had indeed been wanting for some considerable time' to make such a trip, but that 'there were at the present time no definite arrangements'.[6] The correspondent then revealed that the Elysée Palace had told him not only the proposed dates in April, but that she might be lunching in Paris with the President.

The Queen Mother thought it a good idea to send a quick message to the Elysée Palace to say it would be difficult for her to come to Paris. She would cite the celebrations before Princess Alexandra's wedding on 24 April as the reason for shortening her trip. The French press then created mischief:

> Like a spider caught in its own web, the British Government continues at one and the same time to soothe and irritate French susceptibilities; soothes by confirming the project of the trip by the Queen Mother between April 17 and 22 to the Loire Chateaux; irritates by asserting that there had never been any question of the Queen Mother passing through Paris, that is to say, of her meeting General de Gaulle . . .[7]

Dixon happened to lunch at Clarence House on 19 February. Before his hostess appeared, he had a meeting with Sir Martin and Sir Ralph. They told him that Queen Elizabeth was keener than ever to go. He suggested it would be better if he did not go so as to minimise official involvement. The two courtiers were 'frankly appalled'. Dixon was the Queen's representative and a close personal friend of Her Majesty. As lunch ended, the Queen Mother informed him she was expecting him to join her, but, as he put it, 'I did not make any reservation on that point.'[8]

Sir Ralph drafted a prosaic letter for the Queen Mother to write to de Gaulle. The Foreign Office drafted an alternative one pointing out that Paris could not be on her itinerary. The Prime Minister said he was prepared to tell the Queen Mother in person that Dixon must not accompany her, but Lord Home decided he could go. The British Ambassador then went to see de Gaulle's protocol officer whose only stipulation was that the visit should not be 'ostentatious' and hoped the press would not suggest that, by the Queen Mother not meeting de Gaulle, 'somebody was snobbing [sic] somebody'.[9]

Once the Vice-Marshal of the Diplomatic Corps had clarified that, as this was a private trip, the Royal Household would pay the expenses of the Queen Mother and the Ambassador,[10] the Queen Mother was able to set off, accompanied by the Eustons, Sir Ralph, Ruth Fermoy, and members of her staff. They flew into the military airport at St Symphorien in the Touraine, where they were met by Sir Pierson Dixon and Charles de Noailles.

Noailles was a mixture of the conventional and the unconventional. The young Auberon Waugh described him as 'getting on in years, but . . . still quite a gay dog'.[11] The latter description was all too apt. He was primarily homosexual and largely separated from his wife, the troublesome Marie-Laure.* She never accompanied him on these royal excursions.

The royal party took over a floor in a hotel, the Château d'Artigny, an eighteenth-century-style castle, built by François Coty, the perfume millionaire, in 1912. Staying in a hotel was a novel experience, but the press also took over a floor, so hotels were eschewed in the future. They saw Chambord and visited Cheverny, the only castle on the Loire still occupied by the direct descendants (the Marquis and Marquise de Vilbraye) for whom it had been built in the fifteenth century. As they walked across the long bridge to Chenonceaux, Noailles saw the lady owner waiting to greet the Queen Mother with a man at her side. Noailles warned the Queen Mother that this was her butler – and lover.

An enjoyable aspect of these trips was Lord Euston's limited French. As the senior male of the party he always sat on the right of his hostess. He relied on two stock phrases: 'Oui, oui,' and 'Ça m'est égal', which his wife had to point out did not do full justice to the fine wines being offered to him.[12]

Charles de Noailles had to perform an extraordinary juggling act since so many people vied to entertain the Queen Mother. Thus they only went to tea at the Château d'Ussé, said to have inspired Charles Perrault to write *The Sleeping Beauty*, but saw Villandry, whose magnificent gardens were not at their best due to the severe winter, and then to the Château Rochecotte, restored by the Duchess of Dino. In Chinon the Queen Mother got out of her car and a flower-seller spontaneously presented her with a bunch of roses, she dined at a countryside restaurant with Noailles and visited Fontainebleau before flying home.

The French police kept a discreet eye on security, the press made no mention of de Gaulle and the photographers were kept away from Tours airport. The television photographer who covered it for the BBC and French TV was so annoyed that few of his films were shown in France that he accused the British Embassy of embargoing them. The welcome in Touraine was enthusiastic, the streets were crowded wherever they

* Soon after their marriage Noailles had been caught by his wife in bed with his gym instructor.

went, and the local *châtelains* more than hospitable. During the trip, the Queen Mother showed General de Gaulle's reply to Sir Pierson Dixon. He judged it 'friendly without being too warm'.[13]

The Ambassador's conclusion was that the trip had strengthened good-will towards Britain:

> I might add that I am sure Queen Elizabeth enjoyed the tour and its very informal nature, which freed her from too strict a programme and enabled her to meet large numbers of local people. It is not too much to say that she left everyone captivated wherever she went.[14]

Back in Britain, the decorator Felix Harbord saw it differently: 'The Queen Mum has gone to the Loire Valley to eat from what we can gather from the press.'[15]

During these and subsequent years, there were many cultural occasions, including visits to Covent Garden for opera and ballet. In July 1962, Lady Diana Cooper and Lord Drogheda, Chairman of the Royal Opera House, sat beside the Queen Mother during two acts of a gala performance of *Otello*. In the interval Mario del Monaco (Otello) and Tito Gobbi (Iago) were invited to the Royal Box, the former suddenly forgetting his English and falling silent. This the Queen Mother relieved by calling for a glass of champagne. Those who accompanied Queen Elizabeth to the opera were fascinated by her confidence. After acknowledging the audience, she would sit down without a backward glance. The chair was always there.

In May 1963, Lord and Lady Gladwyn (the former Sir Gladwyn and Lady Jebb) were invited to Clarence House for dinner before a gala performance of *Figaro*. Despite the champagne cocktails, Lady Gladwyn found the atmosphere a bit formal, the party consisting of the Queen Mother's old friend Malcolm Bullock, Lord and Lady John Hope,* with Countess Spencer and Major Griffin in attendance. Lady Gladwyn described the evening:

> Suddenly there seemed a movement in the air, a widening of our circle, a rustle of skirts, and in came, with the greatest informality and the highest of spirits, the Queen Mother. Sparkling with diamonds, in a pink tulle crinoline, and breaking any ice there might have been, she exuded an excited joy that was almost unqueenly.[16]

---

* Lady John Hope was the daughter of the novelist W. Somerset Maugham.

Lady Gladwyn wondered if this 'terrific amount of fun' could have been induced by 'the champagne which flowed so lavishly' throughout the evening. She was fascinated by the Queen Mother's 'inherent stoutness' which was now 'completely out of control'. She concluded that she relished her food to such an extent that she was not going to be bothered by diet or exercise.

When they got to the opera, the party settled down in the Royal Box to enjoy the Mozart. Lady Gladwyn was not convinced, however, that the Queen Mother was enjoying it:

> She sat straight as a ramrod and completely still, not moving a muscle, which must require a good deal of self-control. I thought from where I sat that I could detect a little weariness, a little sadness, in her profile. The moment there was an opportunity for applause and comment her gaiety returned.[17]

The Queen Mother urged her party to clap loudly and prompted John Hope to shout 'encore'. She gave him the cue by singing 'encore' and the applause suddenly stopped so that those sitting nearby would have heard. This she enjoyed. Later they all went back to Clarence House, where more champagne was served. Lady Gladwyn further recorded: 'At one moment she did a sort of African dance with John [Hope]. I fancied that Lady Spencer and Major Griffin didn't think it all quite so funny. Being rather serious-minded and conventional people, perhaps they feared that their high-spirited mistress might go on thus till all hours.'[18] As it happened, the party broke up soon after 1 a.m.

Some months later Lady Gladwyn had a further opportunity to observe the Queen Mother when she and Princess Margaret came through 'the hole in the wall' from Clarence House to the state rooms of St James's Palace for a charity evening in aid of the Hertford Hospital. Hers is a clinically accurate description of the Queen Mother's technique:

> Her stout glittering form moves slowly and gracefully through the crowds. One brings forward the person to be presented and tries to give some clue as to who he is or what he does or where he comes from; maybe one can't illuminate her much. She gives her hand, and then seems to pause an instant, after which she somehow contrives to say a few words which invariably are exactly fitting to the occasion, in fact, the right thing. She looks enchanted to be talking to the person, and visible pleasure glows from his face. The conversation may be short or long, but never too long, but the

difficult moment of bringing it to an end is brilliantly achieved. She just moves on slowly with a charming smile and a lingering look of reluctance at parting. So there is no more shaking hands, bowing or curtseying to be done, and the person is left with the happy impression that the Queen Mother would have liked nothing better than to remain. It is a great gift.[19]

Curiously, the Queen Mother claimed to suffer from shyness all her life, but her mother had taught her to go straight through a door and into a room as if she owned it.[20] It was an effective technique.

There was a need for the Queen Mother's face to remain animated as the eyes in repose could look cold, even glacial, and sometimes did so by design. A friend of Helen Hanff, the American author of *84 Charing Cross Road*, saw the Queen Mother shopping. She noted: 'Her public image is a masterpiece of press agentry. I once stood next to her in Harrods and caught her eye, and she has the coldest eyes I have ever looked into.'[21] Stephen Tennant, an occasionally harsh critic, for ever bitter at her rejection of his brother, observed in his particular idiom:

I worship the Queen Mother. Oh, the Queen Mother loves all children & flowers, family love at stifling point. All her days are domestic hours (She's too royal to carve the joint!). All that she clutches for turns to gold! She is kind, sweet & reliable, unless her past you unfold . . .[22]

Whether shy or confident the Queen Mother knew how to present herself to supreme advantage.

In the summer of 1963 Britain was racked with scandal. Macmillan's Conservative Government was almost felled when it was revealed that John Profumo, the Secretary of State for War, had engaged in an affair with Christine Keeler, a call girl who had at one time been involved with the Russian Naval Attaché, Yevgeny (Eugene) Ivanov.

In the midst of the unfolding drama, the Queen Mother continued to entertain, her guests including the hapless Profumos. Lady Avon reported: 'Then we lunched at Clarence House for Jock Whitney, & after waiting hours before lunch, in came the Queen & Profumo, who had been at a Privy Council together* – this was the day before the balloon went up & Val was in black with some prescience.'[23] To her credit the Queen Mother

---

* At this Privy Council meeting, on 30 May, Robert Carr was sworn in. On 26 June Profumo's name was struck off the list of Privy Counsellors.

remained a loyal friend to the Profumos, particularly admiring Profumo's wife, the former film star Valerie Hobson: 'How beautiful Valerie is! Real beauty of expression as well as glorious features, & beauty of mind & heart as well . . .'[24] When the film *Scandal* was released in 1989, a distorted, fictionalised account of the Profumo affair, the Profumos felt they should back out of a dinner being given by Lady Dufferin at which the Queen Mother would be present. She would not hear of it.

Had all gone to plan, the Queen Mother would have paid a visit to Canada, New Zealand and Australia (to open the Adelaide Festival), a thirty-thousand-mile tour, between 28 February and 25 March 1964, and thus she would have missed the birth of Prince Edward on 10 March. In the summer of 1963, the Queen told her mother that, so long as it was approved, she would like her to use *Britannia* as a floating base, a less tiring way of travelling, as she knew from personal experience. Various Government ministers were consulted about the cost of getting *Britannia* there (£30,000), and though Iain Macleod thought some MP like Willie Hamilton might ask questions, 'on the whole the answers to such questions get more cheers than the questions themselves'.[25]

However, the tour was cancelled in February 1964 when the Queen Mother went into the King Edward VII Hospital for Officers in London for an emergency operation, to remove her appendix, as was stated at the time.

Bulletins concerning royal health have frequently been misleading, partly to protect the privacy of the royal patient and partly so as not to alarm the general public unduly. The operation was almost certainly the colostomy, so often hinted at in later years.* The Queen Mother never admitted to undergoing this. She disliked any discussion of royal illness† and strenuously denied it was a colostomy when asked to send messages to fellow sufferers. 'Queen Elizabeth could lie like a trooper,' said one close friend in connection with this.[26]

Cecil Beaton sent her freesias, and, soon after her return to Clarence House on 16 February, she wrote to thank him, turning her operation into an adventure:

It is very nice to be home again, but after the first day or two at Sister Agnes', I began to enjoy being tucked away in a small cabin.

---

* Other world figures to have endured this operation included President Dwight D. Eisenhower and Moshe Dayan, Defence Minister of Israel.
† In December 2001 she was irritated by the press details concerning the operation for ectopic pregnancy suffered by the Countess of Wessex.

One felt gloriously isolated, with endless time to think, & only the *very* nicest people to peer in for a *few* minutes.* It was a truly enjoyable experience, apart from the fact that kind people sent me modern novels to read, and they were so loathsome, & so perfectly horrible, that I felt quite sick with distaste. I think that we must be living through a moment of bad taste in many forms of art, & I hope that the English will revolt soon.[27]

Britannia had reached Fiji when news of the Queen Mother's illness was announced. The Royal Yacht then made its way to Kingston, Jamaica. The Queen Mother waited until Prince Edward was safely born and then flew out to join her for a three-week convalescence cruise.† With her went the Countess of Leicester, Lady Jean Rankin, Sir Martin Gilliat and an equerry. Her only engagement was a twenty-minute visit to Government House to meet the Governor-General, Sir Clifford Campbell. But she paused to buy straw hats and bags as an astonished local band played 'Island in the Sun'. What was meant to be a rest turned into a whistle-stop voyage to no fewer than fourteen islands. The Queen Mother flew home on 2 April.

Affection and admiration for Queen Elizabeth was widespread. She had been a working Queen Mother for over a decade. She was considered dignified yet approachable, to have the common touch, and to lighten official engagements with a sense of humanity. She was known to visit open-air antique markets and bargain for small items. She had a quick and ready answer for unexpected encounters on public engagements. The feathery hat image was well in place, the lively step as she alighted from a royal car, the beaming, all-encompassing smile. Her illness was a reminder of her mortality and sharpened the respect in which she was held. Her return to good health and to public duties was welcomed.

On her regular visit to St Paul's Cathedral for the Friends' service, a housewife who had come all the way from America to see her called out to her and she broke away from the official proceedings and spoke briefly to her. As she rejoined the procession, she suddenly turned and waved goodbye. This was an art she had perfected.

Auberon Waugh, then a young journalist on the *Sunday Mirror*, was one of those assigned to assess the Queen Mother, writing before he had

* The Queen and Princess Margaret came together. The Moroccan Ambassador called, and the twenty press photographers outside clubbed together to buy her some spring flowers.
† The Queen Mother wore black as she left due to court mourning for King Paul of Greece, who had died on 6 March.

fully adopted the acerbic voice that made him so popular in some quarters and so disliked in others:

> It is difficult to imagine someone so universally agreeable as she is who is not insipid.
>
> The Queen Mother must meet horrible people in the course of her duties, just as we all do, but for some reason the fattest alderman forgets his nastiness in her presence.[28]

Waugh further noted that the Greeks had recently passed a law making it a criminal offence to be rude about their Queen Mother, Queen Frederika, whereas there had been no need for such a thing in Britain. Not even Malcolm Muggeridge had had 'a hard word'.[29]

Yet there were tensions behind the scenes. At a dinner that Lady Gladwyn gave for the Queen Mother, the Duke of Devonshire told her that she still missed not being Queen. He also said that her Treasurer could be seen 'leaving Clarence House holding his head in despair because of her extravagance, perhaps having bought a new string of racehorses'. She even spoke of the Castle of Mey which had cost a fortune to restore: 'I can't think why I ever bought the place.'[30]

If 1964 had been a year of royal births, infants being born in quick succession to Princess Alexandra, the Queen, the Duchess of Kent and Princess Margaret, so 1965 opened with deaths. Sir Winston Churchill died on 24 January, and Queen Elizabeth was present with the Queen, most of the Royal Family and many world leaders at his state funeral at St Paul's Cathedral. One of those present was her sister-in-law, the Princess Royal, who suddenly collapsed and died on 28 March while walking with her son in the gardens at Harewood House. Aged only sixty-seven, she had looked older than her years.

The Queen Mother, who so many years before had been her bridesmaid, joined the Royal Family at the funeral at Harewood House, while the Duke of Windsor, who was recovering from an eye operation in the London Clinic, attended the memorial service in Westminster Abbey, the first ceremony which he and the Duchess had attended in public in Britain.

From 1966 onwards the Queen Mother took over the Princess Royal's role in distributing the shamrock to the Irish Guards, a custom begun by Queen Alexandra in 1905 and taken over by the Princess Royal after her death. The King had done it in 1950.

*   *   *

In April 1965, soon after an official trip to Jamaica, the Queen Mother made her second trip to France for pleasure, be it cultural or gastronomic. She stayed in Provence for a week, again with Charles de Noailles in attendance and the Eustons in her party.

This time she accepted the loan of a private house from Pierre Delbée, president of the French Society of Decorators. He handed over his small eighteenth-century château, the Château Legier, for a nominal rent of one French franc. It was hoped that this would give the Queen Mother more independence and freedom. But here the hazards were worse than staying in a hotel. The royal party were horrified to discover that Suzy Delbée had descended on the château in advance of the visit to stock the larder and arrange a series of exotic menus with her Provençal chef at considerable expense to herself.

When he saw the proposed menus, Sir Ralph Anstruther vetoed all but the soupe de poisson, because the Queen Mother disliked garlic and preferred classic French dishes to a Provençal menu. Reflecting on Suzy Delbée's plans, Charles de Noailles commented: 'It is a delightful gesture, but highly embarrassing.'[31]

The house sported every possible variety of decorative frog, the owner's passion, which amused the Queen Mother and her party. From this frog-ridden abode she set out on a round of lunches and dinners with a variety of French aristocrats, and visited Jean Laffont's enormous ranch in the Camargue, where he bred bulls and horses. She went for a stroll in Aix-en-Provence, dressed in full Queen Mother guise, complete with feathery hat, veil and pearls. Extra police were called to control the enormous crowd. 'We thought she would hardly be recognised in France,' Lord Euston commented.[32]

During this tour, Charles de Noaille's difficult wife, Marie-Laure, hid in the crowd, and, after the Queen Mother had passed by, called out: 'A bas la Reine d'Angleterre!' loud enough for the entourage to hear.[33]

The Queen Mother also visited Douglas Cooper, the powerful and sinister art dealer who possessed an enormous collection of works by Picasso, Braque, Léger and Juan Gris. Cooper was not in the mould of the French aristocrats who welcomed Queen Elizabeth. In 'queenly' manner, he informed his neighbours that he had covered the gates of the Château de Castille with barbed wire to keep her away. The truth was different, as Cooper's then companion, John Richardson, recorded:

He begged Charles de Noailles . . . to bring his royal charge to dinner. In his wisdom, Noailles arranged for the Queen Mother to make what is called a 'standing visit' – minimal refreshments, no dawdling or sitting down. 'We queens are at the mercy of a very tight schedule,' Her Majesty supposedly told Douglas, apropos the brevity of her visit. Ironically, Douglas was captivated by her.[34]

More formally the Queen Mother went to Canada, to present the new colours to the Toronto Scottish Regiment, whose Colonel-in-Chief she had been since 1937. The next month she paid a rare visit to Germany, visiting the British Army of the Rhine, resisting her intense dislike of the Germans.

In the spring of 1966, the Queen Mother travelled to Australia and New Zealand. When they were in Fiji, Sir Martin Gilliat made up customarily outrageous stories about having a wife and several black babies to stir up conversation with his neighbours, while Frances Campbell-Preston was told by a local chief that he thought they might be related. The chief looked at her name card and told her that his great-grandfather had once eaten a Campbell.

This tour had the usual duties – a visit to the Adelaide Festival of Arts and the opening of the new Flinders University – but it also had a personal purpose. Prince Charles had progressed via Cheam to Gordonstoun, and in January that year had set off for a spell at Timbertop, an outpost of Geelong Grammar School in Melbourne. Separated from his family, the Prince had initially felt lonely. The Queen Mother was the only member of his family to visit him. They met in Canberra in March and spent two days together in the Snowy Mountains, something he never forgot. He was not reunited with the rest of his family until the late summer.

The New Zealand leg of the trip was memorable for the small crowd of only six hundred when she disembarked from *Britannia* at Bluff, causing organisers to wonder if they had misjudged matters. In Auckland there were signs declaring 'Oppose British Royalty' and 'Q.M. go home'. Two men were arrested. In Christchurch a shot rang out behind the crowd and police found four young boys playing with a rifle which wounded a housewife waiting in the crowd, in the left arm. Otherwise enthusiasm was strong.

The Queen Mother's host in New Zealand was Sir Bernard Fergusson, the Governor-General, and the son of the Governor-General with whom she and the Duke of York had stayed in 1927. She enjoyed some fishing, wading into Lake Wanaka wearing hip boots, Windcheater and a large string of pearls.

After her farewell reception on board *Britannia* at Auckland, the Queen Mother and her Household went down to the wardroom, she still in long evening dress and tiara, and on hearing that some of the men were hungry she hit on the idea of bacon and eggs, put on an apron and assisted them in the cooking.[35]

On 6 December 1966 the nation was alarmed to hear the news that the Queen Mother had entered hospital for observation, no further details being given. Just before she went in, she attended a reception given by the Women's Royal Voluntary Service at St James's Palace. On 10 December it was announced in somewhat vague medical terminology that she had undergone a ninety-minute operation for the relief of a partial bowel obstruction. A hospital spokesman called it 'a fairly common operation'.[36] One report described it as a lump that had formed around the scar tissue of her appendix operation and was causing partial blockage of the lower intestine. Medical experts noted that the doctors consulted were known for their work on the lower intestinal tract.

The Queen Mother remained in hospital over Christmas and did not sign her Christmas cards that year. She made gradual but steady improvement, and on 29 December she returned to Clarence House. She was soon walking about, but she cancelled her engagements for the next few months and decided, with regret, that she would not be able to serve as Lord High Commissioner to the General Assembly of Scotland the following May.

The ladies-in-waiting at Clarence House were kept busy answering about three hundred letters a day. 'We've been inundated with letters and presents,' Lady Jean Rankin told the press.[37] The Queen Mother's flowers were distributed throughout the hospital.

There has always been speculation about this operation. They thought this one was the colostomy, and members of the Colostomy Welfare Group claimed they had always known it to be such when this was published in a 1980 biography of the Queen Mother. It was declared as a fact in the Queen Mother's obituary in *The Times*.

But this was the operation that reversed the process, the earlier so-called 'appendix' operation having proved a complete success. Though the Queen Mother continued to deny the operation, apparently she sent a letter of support to World Ostomy Day, Auckland, New Zealand, in 1998.

31

Family and Fabrics

'I shouldn't in the least mind being called the David Herbert of Clarence House' – the Queen Mother

It says much for the Queen Mother's strength of character and body that she was to survive her difficult operations by more than thirty-five years. She spent quiet days recuperating first in London then at Sandringham in the early months of 1967. By 20 March she was well enough to attend a concert in St George's Chapel, and on 27 April she dined with the London Scottish Territorial Regiment in London. The only noticeable difference was that she looked thinner.

On 1 May she embarked in *Britannia* for a tour of Cornwall and Devon before sailing to northern France. The Queen Mother was meant to rejoin the Royal Yacht in Falmouth, but heavy squalls prevented this. When the barge was sent to collect her, the deputy supply officer was surprised to hear her leading a chorus of the Eton Boating Song as the barge emerged through the mist.[1] In France she visited the Normandy invasion beaches and the British War Graves cemetery at Bayeux, and afterwards she resumed her normal duties as though there had been no operation.

The hierarchy of the Royal Family changed during the 1950s and 1960s, and, as the older members died, so the Queen Mother became a more matriarchal figure within the family structure. Figures such as the Earl of Athlone, Princess Marie Louise, King Haakon of Norway and Princess Arthur of Connaught died in the late 1950s. On 21 February 1960, Edwina Mountbatten died in British North Borneo.

The Queen Mother was not an unreserved fan of the Mountbattens, nor was there a strong band of sympathy reciprocated from Lord Mountbatten, who could not combat her quiet influence. She had liked Mountbatten's mother, Victoria Milford Haven, even if she found her 'quite dictatorial'.[2] And she admitted teasing Mountbatten's sister, Princess Andrew of Greece, in her nun's habit: 'Very fetching, we said to her.'[3]

During the war, Patricia Hambleden had prevailed upon Queen

Elizabeth to let Edwina Mountbatten make an appointment in connection with the Red Cross for which she had been pressing. Queen Elizabeth sidestepped several requests, and Lady Hambleden asked again. 'Oh must I see her?' she asked. 'There's nothing more tiresome than a reformed rake!'[4]

Following Edwina's death in Jesselton, worn down, yet working to the last, her body was brought home for burial at sea off Portsmouth, and the coffin launched into the sea as is traditional with a naval burial. There were two comments made at the time. The Duchess of Windsor enquired: 'What can you say about a man who throws his wife into the sea?' while the Queen Mother's verdict was: 'So like Edwina, she always did everything with a splash!'

Members of her own family died too. In 1959 her niece, Lady Nancy Blair, twin sister of the reclusive Timothy, Earl of Strathmore, was found dead in her St Marylebone flat at the age of forty.* Her brothers-in-law, Earl Granville and Lord Elphinstone, had died, the former in 1953, the latter in 1955. Her brother Michael's widow, Betty Cator, the Queen Mother's bridesmaid, died in January 1959, the Queen Mother making another visit to Glamis for the funeral. On 8 February 1961 her sister, Lady Elphinstone died, soon to be followed by her favourite brother, David.

David and Rachel Bowes-Lyon were staying with her at Birkhall in September 1961. It was a great shock for the Queen Mother to find him dead in bed. Suffering from hemipligia, he died of a heart attack at 11.20 on the morning of 13 September. The process of burying him was prolonged, with the funeral at Ballater and committal at St Paul's Walden, made worse by flight delays.

Eleanor Roosevelt wrote to express her sympathy, but by now her friendship with Queen Elizabeth had become distant and she normally answered via her lady-in-waiting, as when Mrs Roosevelt sent some maple sugar the following Christmas. With no war menacing, Mrs Roosevelt had become more of a nuisance than a life saver. The Queen Mother's only remaining sibling, Rose Granville, survived until 1967.

Glamis was not visited by the Queen Mother because Timothy, who had become 16th Earl in 1949, was a hopeless alcoholic, later suffering from epilepsy. He spent much of his time in and out of nursing homes, and in 1958 married Mary Brennan, a member of the nursing team looking after him. She renounced her Roman Catholicism to make the marriage possible. They had a daughter, who died of pneumonia less than

---

* Nancy's second husband, John Blair, had blown his brains out in Ireland in 1955.

a month later, in January 1960. Depressed, the Countess took an over-dose of Seconal and died of acute barbiturate poisoning in the early morning of 8 September 1967, aged forty-five.[5]

Timothy gradually became a recluse at Glamis, seldom seen. On 13 September 1972 he was found dead by one of his staff, having suffered a coronary thrombosis at 1 a.m. He was only fifty-four. Five days later, more as a tribute to the incoming Earl, his cousin Fergus, the Queen and Queen Mother, who were both in Scotland at the time, drove over to Glamis to attend Timothy's funeral.

The active members of the Royal Family in these years, besides the Queen and the Duke of Edinburgh, the Queen Mother and Princess Margaret, were the Duke and Duchess of Gloucester, Princess Marina and her daughter, Princess Alexandra, who began royal duties at a very young age. The Princess Royal was dead, and the Duke of Gloucester's health collapsed after he lost control of his car on his way home to Barnwell after Churchill's state funeral in January 1965, decanting the Duchess into a field. A series of strokes followed and he lost the power of speech in 1968, retiring to Barnwell as a complete invalid. He died there in June 1974.

The Duchess of Gloucester (later Princess Alice) spent as much time as possible with him, while taking on some of his commitments and continuing with her own. After his death she remained an active member of the Royal Family into her nineties and outlived the Queen Mother, dying in October 2004, at the age of 102.

Still alive, though in failing health, was the Duke of Windsor. The Duke was seventy-three and the Duchess an elegant seventy-one. The time was approaching when the Duke would die, and, despite past bitterness, the Queen and her advisers wished to offer a tentative olive branch. The Queen therefore invited the Windsors to a ceremony at Marlborough House on 7 June 1967 to commemorate the centenary of Queen Mary. This public meeting with the Royal Family was one of the two things the Duke had craved since the Abdication.*

For the Queen Mother this was a hurdle to face. Privately, she threatened to boycott the ceremony if the Windsors were there. But as ever, on the day, she behaved impeccably. When the courtiers went to fetch her from Clarence House, expecting delays due to her habitual lateness, she was eager and waiting, and in excellent humour. There were no processions, the Royal Family arriving separately. They were organised in a

---

* The second, the bestowal of HRH on the Duchess, never happened.

line-up that broke the rules of precedence. From right to left – the Duchess of Windsor, the Duke of Windsor, the Duchess of Gloucester, the Duke of Gloucester,* the Queen Mother, the Queen, the Duke of Edinburgh, Princess Marina, and the Duke and Duchess of Kent. The Court Circular was devised to make no mention of the presence of the Duke and Duchess of Windsor.

Courtiers remained anxious as to how Queen Elizabeth would react. They were nothing short of flabbergasted when she leaned forward to kiss the Duke on the cheek. 'I felt so sorry for him,' she said. 'She would not have had him to lunch though,' recalled Sir Michael Hawkins, the Duke of Gloucester's Private Secretary. 'The Gloucesters asked them.'[6]

The Queen Mother would see the Duke of Windsor only one more time, at the funeral of Princess Marina in August the following year. As usual, the Queen led the Royal Family into the Quire of St George's Chapel, and at the end of the line was the tiny dapper figure of the Duke of Windsor, with his haunted eyes, still slim enough to wear the morning coat in which he had been married in 1937.[7]

The death of Princess Marina in 1968 removed from the Royal Family one of its best-loved and most elegant figures. Since the death of the Duke of Kent in 1942, she had been respected as a lonely figure, who continued to serve the land of her adoption while raising her family of three, more or less single-handed. The Duke of Kent and Princess Alexandra were then happily married, while Prince Michael was serving in the army.

But she had never been a favourite of the Queen Mother's. Many years before there had been the 'not even mediatised' remark, a version of 'those common little Scottish girls' so often attributed to the Princess in relation to her Scottish sisters-in-law, the Duchesses of York and Gloucester. When the remark about mediatisation was relayed to the Queen Mother, she was never forgiven. Cecil Beaton's verdict was 'The Queen Mother adored Princess Marina the moment she died. When she was alive, she hated her!'[8]

The Queen Mother derived great pleasure from being grandmother to Prince Charles and Princess Anne, sometimes spoiling them and declaring: 'That's half the fun of being a grandmother!' She played with them, even joining in energetic games of tag, took them to their first pantomime, *Cinderella*, but whether she gave them an expensive toy or sent a postcard, she expected equal gratitude to be expressed.

* This was one of the last public appearances by the Duke of Gloucester, leaning heavily on a stick.

With the Queen and Duke of Edinburgh frequently away on overseas trips, she relished the time this gave her with them. When the Queen was in Australia on her Commonwealth tour in 1954, she appeared to recognise this. When asked if she missed her children, she replied: 'More than they miss us, I'm afraid. You see, they have a doting grandmother.' She gave them chicken and ice cream for lunch and boiled or scrambled eggs for tea.[9] Key figures in bringing up these children were the Queen Mother's pages, William Tallon and Reginald Wilcock.

The Snowdon marriage fascinated society and the press. The young couple appeared to cross the boundary between official royal life and the art world, something that had not happened before. Princess Margaret made the transition well, able to be both formal and informal according to the gathering. Armstrong-Jones seemed less comfortable as a royal consort, a role against which, presently, he rebelled.

Sir Osbert Sitwell was much amused by a photograph in the *Daily Mail* of Princess Margaret staying with the Rosses in Ireland. Sir Michael Duff, Armstrong-Jones's godfather, and another tease, chided Tony for taking the title 'Snowdon' in anticipation of the birth of their first child, without asking his permission. Snowdon, he pointed out, was the Welsh mountain to the rear of his estate.

In the autumn of 1961 Princess Margaret moved back into Clarence House in anticipation of the birth of her son. Lady Rosse commissioned a wickerwork cot for her latest grandchild. It was dressed in frilly French spotted organza, mounted on cream taffeta, trimmed with yards of Valenciennes lace and could be run through with a large ribbon, while the hood sported a satin bow. The ribbon and bows were either to be blue or pink as appropriate to the sex of the baby. This confection was delivered to Clarence House soon after the arrival of David Albert Charles Armstrong-Jones, Viscount Linley, on 3 November. The names derived from David Bowes-Lyon, who had died so soon before, with Albert for George VI, and Charles for the Prince of Wales.

Meanwhile journalists loved to contrast the Queen Mother to the other grandmother, Anne Rosse. While the Queen Mother adhered to her chosen style, Princess Marina and Princess Margaret, and the Countess of Rosse moved with the fashion of the day, 1960s elegance taking over from the constrained styles of the 1950s. Lady Rosse was profiled in women's magazines as a royal granny. She 'cleverly plays up her large, dramatic eyes with skilfully applied eyeshadow and eyeliner . . . She has a small, doll-like face plus magnificent green eyes . . . Lady Rosse favours frothy turbans and hats matched with ostrich tips. She is also fond of wide, rustling silk coats and adores velvet in rich, glowing shades.' A fashion expert, Penny Knowles, gave the advice: 'The Countess of Rosse dresses in a style becoming to her, but I wouldn't suggest it as a pattern for others to copy.'[10]

Private teasing was a feature of society life. The Queen Mother was not spared this, particularly in the more artistic circles of which she was so fond. Her more aesthetic friends (as opposed to the racing, fishing and shooting fraternity) were inclined to mimic her. The choreographer Sir Frederick Ashton perfected this. Sir Michael Duff, that mischievous lover of royalty, called her 'Grinners', and even referred to the ocean liner *Queen Elizabeth* as 'The Grinning Lizzie'.

The Queen Mother was known as 'The Queen Mum' in the popular press, a nickname widely applied by all classes. Sir Michael Duff sometimes elaborated this to 'Queen Mummikins'. In the Bowes–Lyon family she was known as 'Peter', something not widely publicised, though it is referred to in an article about her fiftieth birthday. This derived from Beatrix Potter's Peter Rabbit.

Many letters exist referring to the Queen Mother as 'The Cake', and in a certain set – that of the Duchess of Buccleuch and Lady Diana Cooper, for example – she was invariably known as 'The Cake'. This was in no way pejorative. But how did it come about?

It was not inspired by the Queen Mother's flowing coats and hats, so reminiscent of a birthday or wedding cake. Alastair Forbes maintained that it was Lord Head who 'so happily, long ago, nicknamed that Winter (halter) Queen' thus.[11] The most likely originator is the (Dowager) Duchess of Devonshire.*

At a reception following a London wedding, one of the wedding party approached the Queen Mother and said: 'Ma'am, the young couple are about to cut the cake . . .'

'The cake!' she exclaimed, arms thrown upwards in delight. The Duchess overheard it and she was 'The Cake' from that day on.[12]

Houses and gardens were a great comfort and interest to Queen Elizabeth. In 1965 Oliver Ford† became her interior decorator, receiving his royal warrant in 1974. He was a camp and difficult character, a chain smoker with kipper-brown fingers, not recalled with unreserved affection by some of those with whom he dealt in Queen Elizabeth's Household.

Ford had started his career on the stage, but the actor Kenneth

---

* Hon. Deborah Mitford (b. 1920), widow of Andrew, 11th Duke of Devonshire, KG (1920–2004).
† Oliver Ford (1925–92). At his last home, Bewley Court, Lacock, Wiltshire, those who are keyed into such things claim his ghost can be seen walking at twilight.

Williams, in whom he inspired 'incredible emotion'[13] in 1948, persuaded him to study decorative arts at the Southern College in Bournemouth. He progressed via Waring & Gillow and Harvey Nichols to the Duchess of Windsor's favourite Paris decorator, Stefan Boudin of Maison Jansen, opening their office in London. He then opened Oliver Ford (Decorations) Ltd in the Bahamas, finally joining Lenygon & Morant, royal decorators since the time of Queen Victoria, as a partner in 1962. He designed state banquets for the King of Jordan and the King of Saudi Arabia, was responsible for the hall and Orchid Room at the Dorchester, and was frequently commended in the *Tatler* column 'Jennifer's Diary' by the social writer Betty Kenward.

When O. Bateman-Brown retired through ill health from Lenygon & Morant in 1966, Sir Ralph Anstruther renewed the Queen Mother's royal warrant in Ford's name confident that he would be able 'satisfactorily to give effect to Her wishes.'[14]

The appointment preceded a difficult time in Ford's private life, which came to the attention of Sir Martin Gilliat. Ford had been paying Household Cavalry corporals and guardsmen to act as procurers for him at a time when homosexuality was still illegal. One corporal had been paid £10 to drive six troopers down to Ford's country house, among other charges. In May 1968 Ford pleaded guilty to committing indecent acts with two of them between January and September 1967. He was not sent to prison since the judge declared himself satisfied that Ford had taken 'medical advice', no men had been seduced or corrupted, and that 'the public interest' would not be served by a custodial sentence. He was fined £700.*[15]

The proclivities and foibles of men did not concern the Queen Mother as long as they did a good job. She was no stranger to homosexuals. Patricia Hambleden's brother, David Herbert, by now a resident of Tangiers, lunched with her and said: 'Ma'am, I don't know if I should say this, but I am sometimes described as the Queen Mum of Tangiers.' She paused. 'Oh really? I shouldn't in the least mind being described as the David Herbert of Clarence House.'[16]

When the Queen Mother told Gilliat that she intended to retain Ford to work on Clarence House, Gilliat tried to intimate that this would be inappropriate. Aware of the circumstances and enjoying Gilliat's discomfort, the Queen Mother pressed him to explain. Finally, he spluttered:

---

* His old friend Kenneth Williams noted in his diary (7 May 1968) that some men would always pay for sex with a woman, others with a man, and that no law in the land would ever change that. John Betjeman was inspired to write a poem about the incident. See Bevis Hillier, *The Bonus of Laughter*, pp. 385–6.

'Oscar Wilde and all that, Ma'am.' To this the Queen Mother replied: 'I can't see how that could possibly harm Clarence House – or me for that matter!'[17] Ford stayed on.

In the autumn of 1966 Ford embellished the entrance hall and lobby at Clarence House in Burgundy red, with red felt from Gorringe's and a Persian carpet. He re-did the Lancaster Room, the Garden Room (introducing coral pink Thai silk curtains), chintzed the Queen Mother's dressing room and turned her bathroom sky blue. He tackled the Visitors' Suite on the second floor in 1969, and by 1970 had placed a representation of the crown, the ER cipher and two lions in the skylight, replacing the utilitarian plain glass.

In the autumn of 1972 he produced a table for lunch outside in the garden at Clarence House. 'I am determined to have a "christening" lunch,' the Queen Mother told him, 'even if one has to be wrapped in rugs and tweeds!'[18]

At Royal Lodge, he re-did the bedcovers and valances in white silk or copper-pink, put a blue speckled carpet in her bathroom and made curtains to match wallpaper of brown and blue chintz style. In 1971 he decorated the orangery. He designed Princess Margaret's bathroom and Lord Snowdon's dressing room. He repainted the Saloon in 1974, and three years later made an 'enchanting' bedroom for Lady Sarah Armstrong-Jones, also repainting the servants' wing, making it 'nice & clean & white & they are very pleased with it'.[19]

He designed the Landscape Room and the Garden Room and put new curtains in the Queen Mother's dining room to replace ones that were 'in a bad way', and turning it sky or Wedgwood blue. The Queen Mother was delighted to return from Scotland to 'a completely "New Look" dining room'.[20]

In 1971 he created a tent like an Eastern pagoda, Wedgwood-blue canvas on the outside, pink on the inside, partly inspired by a medieval jousting pavilion, under which a dozen guests could eat on the terrace without worrying about the weather.

No detail was too small not to merit personal discussion with Queen Elizabeth and he had frequent meetings with her at Clarence House or Royal Lodge, selecting the exact yellow to re-cover the Chinese Chippendale chairs, fabric for bedside tables or changes to pelmets.

While a strong sense of theatricality permeated Ford's work, this occasionally clashed with Queen Elizabeth's Scottish frugality. She preferred underfelt to be cleaned rather than replaced, and welcomed a plan that would save 'a few acres of red carpet'.[21] When 'blackamoor' wall lights arrived, some Nubian figures went off for sale, deemed too big for

Queen Elizabeth The Queen Mother arriving at Buckingham Palace for the State Banquet for President de Gaulle of France, April 1960. To impress the General she wore her circlet with the Koh-i-Noor diamond (summoned for the night from the Tower of London) and all five strands of Mrs Greville's necklace, rarely seen in public.

Queen Elizabeth The Queen Mother
at the Peterborough Agricultural Show,
18 July 1956

The Queen Mother with Commander
Clare Vyner and Lady Doris Vyner at
the Castle of Mey

The Queen Mother and The Queen
at the Badminton Horse Trials, April 1958

The Queen Mother at the Territorial
Army's table at the Peterborough
Agricultural Show

The Queen Mother presenting the
winner's cup at the Peterborough
Agricultural Show

The Queen Mother at the State Dinner at Government House, Ottawa, 18 November 1954. On her right is Rt Hon. Louis St Laurent, Prime Minister of Canada, and Mrs Kerwin. On her left is Rt Hon. Vincent Massey, Governor General of Canada.

The Queen Mother and Prince Charles in the garden of the Royal Lodge, Windsor

Wearing the robes of Chancellor of London University, the Queen Mother walks toward the Faculty of Agriculture of Makerere College, the University East Africa, 1959

The Duke of Windsor in London at the time of Queen Mary's death, March 1953

Princess Margaret and the Queen Mother at a performance of Ashton ballets at the Royal Opera House, in aid of the Royal Ballet Benevolent Fund, 10 March 1959

Princess Margaret on her engagement to Antony Armstrong-Jones at Royal Lodge, 1960

The Queen Mother and Sir Arthur Penn in the car, June 1956

The Royal Family at Princess Margaret's wedding, Westminster Abbey, April 1960. They are led n by the Lord Steward (The Duke of Hamilton), the Lord Chamberlain (The Earl of Scarbrough) nd the Master of the Horse (The Duke of Beaufort). The Queen Mother, The Queen and Prince Charles, followed by Queen Ingrid of Denmark and the Duke and Duchess of Gloucester. In the back of the photo is Sir Martin Gilliat, Private Secretary to the Queen Mother.

The Queen Mother's 60th Birthday, 4 August 1960. The Queen Mother with Prince Charles and Princess Anne, and Prince Andrew on her knee.

The Queen Mother fishing in New Zealand in 1966

The Queen Mother with Sunyboy, her 300th winner under National Hunt rules, at the Fernbank Hurdle at Ascot, 18 February 1976

The Queen Mother with her trainer, Peter Cazalet at Lingfield Park on 25 November 1955. Devon Loch had just won the Blindley Heath Handicap Chase, with Dick Francis in the saddle.

The Queen Mother and Princess Anne at London Airport awaiting The Queen's return from her Australasian tour, March 1963

The Queen Mother at the Derby at Epsom with (second left to right) Princess Marina, Duchess of Kent, The Queen and The Princess Royal (Princess Mary), 1st June 1960

(*Above*) The Queen Mother dancing an eight-some reel with students at London University Senate House on 28 November 1958 (*Right*) The Queen Mother alighting from a helicopter, County High School for Girls, Chelmsford, February 1962

The Queen Mother and Diana, Princess of Wales, on the way to a Trooping the Colour ceremony, mid 1980s

The Queen Mother, photographed by the author, with Paul Getty at his home Wormsley Park, 3 May 1987

Clarence House, and as late as 1989 the Queen Mother joked about asking Ford to Clarence House, where she would show him 'tattered chair covers etc!'.[22] She was grateful for his help and advice 'in the battle to keep these old houses alive & beautiful'.[23] On one visit Ford spotted the Queen Mother's finger playing in a hole in the fabric. 'I could re-cover that for you, Ma'am,' he offered. 'Oh no,' she said. 'I find it reassuring.'[24]

Ford was meticulous in sending her birthday lilies to greet her at the Castle of Mey each August, freesias in October to welcome her back to London and blue and white hyacinths at Christmas. 'Flowers make such a difference to one's life,' wrote the Queen Mother, 'either growing in the garden, or blooming in one's room.'[25]

After Ford's death in 1992 no work was done on the properties, unless the Queen insisted on giving her mother new chair covers. All her residences became increasingly run down and when the electrics at Royal Lodge were inspected after her death, it was deemed a miracle there had not been a fire.

In respect of supposed extravagances, Dame Frances Campbell-Preston noted: 'She certainly had a hazy idea of costs (she never carried cash or ever shopped across the counter), but greedy she was not and her extravagances as measured by those of modern celebrities could be reckoned almost modest.'[26]

Throughout the 1950s and the 1960s the Queen Mother won consistent glowing praise in the press. In the complicated game of give and take between public figures and media, she gave the reporters good angles on stories, turning routine engagements into occasions of fun, with always a new slant to report. She had a canny instinct as to when to pause to let a photographer get his picture, did not mind turning again if he claimed to have missed the shot and her ready smile was always to the fore. Following deep concern over her 1966 operation, there was widespread relief at her recovery and she was praised when she set off on another trip to Canada in July 1967, fulfilling this with no diminution of energy.

During the late sixties the Queen Mother witnessed her two older grandchildren grow up and leave school. Prince Charles had relished spending time with her as a little boy, hearing stories about her life and responsibilities, and she had awakened in him a love of the arts and music. She had told him about the paintings in the various royal residences and had taken him to his first ballet when he was seven.

The Prince laboured under the impression that his parents were out of sympathy with him, but his grandmother continued to extend to him unqualified support and devotion. She was his ally, and by living so long was able to sustain him in the travails that lay ahead of him.

After Gordonstoun and his phase in Australia, he went to Trinity College, Cambridge, where he began to emerge from his shyness. In the summer of 1968, the Queen Mother walked with him when he processed down the hill through Windsor Castle, embarrassed to the point that his face was apple-red, to be installed as a Knight of the Garter.* From then on, when he attended the Garter ceremony, he usually escorted his grandmother.

Consideration was now given to the final resting place of King George VI, and, when the time came, of Queen Elizabeth herself. Since his funeral in 1952, the King's coffin had lain in the Royal Vault underneath St George's Chapel. Now it was decided that the King needed a special burial place: 'Called unexpectedly to kingship, he led his people through fifteen difficult years of war and peace. Before and throughout these years his character and goodness endeared him not only to those who knew him but to a vast company in every land of the Commonwealth.'[27]

In 1968 work began on the King George VI Memorial Chapel. Thus the new chapel was built as 'a very beautiful little addition to the Chapel, nestling between the buttresses of the North Wall',[28] designed in a twentieth-century version of perpendicular, with a small altar, the grave itself matching the black marble tombs of Edward IV, Henry VI, Henry VII and Charles I. The Queen Mother hoped John Piper might do something. Lord Salisbury, Chancellor of the Order of the Garter, invited the Garter Knights to contribute towards Piper designing eight stained-glass lancet windows in the chapel. Prince Paul of Yugoslavia was one of the contributors.

In March 1969, the Royal Vault was opened and the King's coffin brought up and placed in the new tomb. On 31 March the Royal Family and the Knights of the Garter gathered for the dedication service. The Duke of Windsor did not come from Paris, though he was invited, but Prince Paul sat in his stall, wearing his Garter star. The Queen Mother herself was in sparkling mood, and paused so long to talk to those involved that the Queen stood smiling in the North Quire Aisle, tapping her foot, while she waited for her mother, resigned to the delay, not for the first time, nor for the last.[29]

---

* All Princes of Wales are automatically Knights of the Garter. The Prince was installed in advance of his Investiture at Caernarvon Castle the following year.

32

Birthday Cards and Horrors

'I never thought I would dance a Fandango in Pont Street'
— the Queen Mother

The film *Royal Family* was shown on television in July 1969, in advance of the medieval-style Investiture of the Prince of Wales at Caernarvon Castle, which launched him into public life. Many millions watched it, the ratings comparing favourably to those for the moon landings a few weeks later. *Royal Family* has been much criticised for letting daylight in on royal magic, yet it is hard to see how the Royal Family could have avoided confronting the medium of television.

Most of the Royal Family appeared in the film, and some viewers were surprised to hear Lord Snowdon addressing the Queen Mother as 'Ma'am'. Cecil Beaton was saddened by the Queen Mother's representation: 'The Queen Mother, very badly photographed, came out as a leftover, very sad as she is responsible for so many of the excellent qualities with which her grandchildren are endowed.'[1]

As the Queen Mother approached her seventieth birthday, overtures arrived from television companies for a similar film about her life. These she rejected, 'rightly fearing the contamination of what might seem contrived or commercial', as Kenneth Rose put it.[2] The seventieth birthday was considered a considerable milestone, though it was to be eclipsed by her eightieth, ninetieth and 100th birthdays.

The Queen gave a reception at Windsor which was shared by the Duke and Duchess of Gloucester, Lord Mountbatten and the Duke of Beaufort, all of whom, apart from the Duchess of Gloucester,* a year younger, attained the age of seventy that year. It was an evening made the more memorable by the surprise General Election victory of Edward Heath and the Conservatives over Harold Wilson's Labour Party. Heath attended the party; Wilson did not.

The eulogies poured in with the flowers and the presents. There was scarcely a hint of criticism, though Kenneth Rose ventured the sugges-

---

* The Duke of Gloucester was too ill to attend.

tion that a collected edition of the Queen Mother's speeches would make uninspired reading. 'Bland, cautious and traditional, they are elegantly unmemorable.' He quickly added: 'But in her gestures, her smiles, her conversation, her ability to radiate a sense of intimately shared enjoyment, she is enchantment itself.'[3]

Her position as a benign matriarch within the Royal Family was well established. Her nephew, Prince William of Gloucester, was interviewed:

> You only had to be loved by her – and to love her yourself – to know that no matter what, you could never let her down. If I let myself down – say I got into a mess of some sort – my first thought would be that the Queen Mother would feel I had let her down. I have always felt this, even as a young child. It isn't that she ever said anything – it's a sort of indescribable sense of dedication she gave me.'[4]

Her vigour remained unchecked. There are various vignettes recorded. At the end of 1970 she danced spontaneously at a party given by the harpsichord maker Tom Goff, an old friend: 'I never thought that I would dance a Fandango in Pont Street, and I only hope that the whole street was not kept awake by the stomping and twirling of your happy guests.'[5] A year later she lunched next to a Labour peer who said to her: 'If there was a Republic in Britain, you would be its first President!' 'Oh no,' she said. 'They would choose the Queen!'[6] At a film première in 1972 the Queen Mother met a scantily clad Susan George, whose top was a see-through tissue-thin silk. 'She didn't say much to me,' reported the actress. 'She asked if I felt a little hot.'[7]

'Every day with her is a new adventure,' wrote one journalist. 'She has such a glorious sense of humour that no engagement is a chore. People are such fun to her.'[8] At the beginning of 1971, Sir Martin Gilliat reported that she was 'raring to go. She is enjoying the best of health.'[9] Thanking some hosts for entertaining her shortly before Christmas, Gilliat described the occasion as 'a delightful prologue to the Christmas festivities'.[10] He was probably more truthful the following year when he wrote: 'Here [Clarence House] we are madly preparing for Christmas with endless rather inane celebrations and parties, and one longs for it all to be over.'[11]

Following the Marlborough House ceremony in 1967 and Princess Marina's funeral in 1968, there had been no further meetings between the Queen or the Queen Mother and the Duke and Duchess of Windsor. In March 1970, strongly influenced by Mountbatten, Prince Charles suggested that they should be invited over for the weekend. He tackled the Queen Mother and on this rare occasion she vetoed his plan. Prince Charles's authorised biographer, Jonathan Dimbleby, wrote that she found it hard 'to be reconciled with the man she held responsible for consigning her husband to an early grave'.[12]

By the spring of 1972 the Queen Mother knew that the Duke of Windsor was dying of cancer of the throat. She made no contact with him, but in May, during the state visit to Paris, the Queen paid her only visit to the Windsors' house in the Bois de Boulogne, accompanied by the Duke of Edinburgh and the Prince of Wales. Ten days later, on 28 May, the Duke died.

Some years before the Queen had agreed the Duke's funeral plans. He would be buried at Frogmore, the Duchess, in due course, beside him. His coffin was duly flown to RAF Benson and lay in state at St George's Chapel, before the funeral.

Given the long antipathy between the Queen Mother and the Duchess of Windsor, it is not surprising that the Duchess was anxious at the prospect of coming to England. Shocked by her bereavement and her mind muddled by advancing arteriosclerosis, she was particularly nervous about meeting the Queen Mother. Lord Mountbatten was sent to meet her at Heathrow Airport. He told her: 'Your sister-in-law will receive you with open arms. She is deeply sorry for you in your present grief and remembers what it was like when her own husband died.' According to Mountbatten, 'this message comforted her a lot'.[13]

The Duchess stayed at Buckingham Palace and only met the Queen Mother at the funeral on Monday 5 June. The Royal Family arrived in a relay of cars at the Deanery, the Duchess at 11 a.m., the Queen Mother at 11.02, the Queen at 11.03. Mountbatten recalled that all the Royal Family 'went up and were very sweet to Wallis'.[14]

The funeral in St George's Chapel was impressive, but before it, according to the diary of the Prince of Wales, none of his family, other than his grandmother, was in what he called a funeral mood, because the Duke of Windsor had been away so long and was therefore a remote figure.[15] For the Queen Mother the occasion had darker resonance.

The service veered between the magnificent and the simple. The men of the Royal Family, including King Olav of Norway, walked behind the coffin, the royal ladies having already taken their seats in the Quire. The Duchess of Windsor, slim in her Givenchy black coat, sat next to the Queen who helped her find her place in the service sheet. The Queen Mother was dressed in deep black with a black veil in her hat.

Afterwards there was a luncheon, the Queen Mother sitting next to the Duke's Private Secretary, John Utter, and she was full of questions about the Windsors' life in Paris. Utter detected no bitterness.[16] One lingering question remained in the schedule of the day. Would the Queen Mother go to the grave at Frogmore for the committal after lunch? She did so, and stood with the other members of the family as her difficult brother-in-law was laid to rest in the earth of the land he had rejected so many years before. The Duchess of Windsor flew back to Paris, relieved that it had gone much better than she had expected.

For the Queen Mother it was the end of a long and painful saga with many phases. She had known the young and popular Prince of Wales. She had anguished over the Abdication and seen his character deteriorate. She had had glimpses of him as a sad old man. Though she had no respect for his wife, despite everything she retained a soft spot for the Duke (the man he used to be and might have been) deep in her heart.

The Queen Mother was by now almost anaesthetised against the deaths of family and friends, the occupational hazard of old age. Within days of the Duke of Windsor's funeral, she was lunching out 'so happy and relaxed in that delicious atmosphere, that words came pouring out!!'.[17] When warned that her friend Betty Somerset was dying, she refused to be pessimistic: 'I cannot bear to think of her ill & sad . . . By now, I expect that she will be at home again . . .'*[18] The death of Prince William of Gloucester, in a flying race, aged only thirty, was harder to bear because he was so young. She wrote:

> The tragic accident was a great shock to all the family, but I feel desperately for his dear little mother. She has the courage of a lion, and has suffered so many cruel blows in the past few years . . .[19]

Lord Harewood had been excluded from the funeral of the Duke of Windsor, but later that year, the Queen Mother was one of the first of the family to meet the new Lady Harewood when she visited a Red Cross home in Harrogate. On such occasions, she extended her hand but her eyes narrowed slightly. It would be impossible to fault her, but the reservation could be spotted by the observant.†

The Queen's Silver Wedding was celebrated at Westminster Abbey in November 1972. Soon afterwards another anniversary passed, marked only in the press. The twenty-third of April 1973 would have been the

---

* Betty Somerset died a few weeks later.
† The present author observed her meeting the first Lady Harewood, by then married to Jeremy Thorpe, at a concert at St James's Palace on 20 March 1984. By this time Thorpe had been acquitted of a charge of conspiracy for murder. She kissed Marion Thorpe, and shook Thorpe's hand with an extended arm, inviting no conversation with him. It was subtly done.

Queen Mother's Golden Wedding. It marked fifty years of royal service with no relaxation in pace. The following year, when she was again a Counsellor of State, the Queen Mother wrote: 'At the moment the mornings are very crowded with Investitures & Ambassadors etc, but when the Queen returns, I shall be more free.'[20] Nor had she lost her touch with the crowds which still fell victim to her charm. Meeting a leading seaman from *Ark Royal* in Leeds in November, and finding he had lost his voice, she looked in her bag and produced a throat lozenge for him. In November she attended the wedding of Princess Anne to Lieutenant Mark Phillips at Westminster Abbey and in June 1974 the Duke of Gloucester's funeral at Windsor.

In the spring of 1975 the Queen Mother accepted a visit from the Shah and Shahbanou of Persia to visit their country for five days. She was meant to fly to Teheran by Concorde but arrived by Comet instead. She visited a school for disabled children and a crèche for 194 orphans founded by the Empress. She also visited Chiraz, Isfahan and Persepolis, the site of the great 1971 celebrations, which had been attended by most of the world's heads of state.

Such a success was this visit that the Queen Mother invited the Shahbanou to stay with her at Clarence House on her visit to Britain the following year, the only time that the wife of a Head of State stayed at Clarence House rather than Buckingham Palace. The Shahbanou came to Britain to promote various aspects of Islam's culture and heritage in the West. It was a curious few days at Clarence House, the Queen Mother warning her staff not to be surprised by the presence of 'guns in the corridors'. She arranged dinner parties so that she could meet people of special interest. A strong link was established between the two royal ladies, based on 'their shared, deep interest in the arts, in particular, and many other aspects of their queenly responsibilities', as Lesley Blanch, the Empress's biographer, put it.[21]

At the Queen Mother's insistence, there were no official celebrations to mark her seventy-fifth birthday, though a portrait photograph taken of her with Prince Charles by Peter Sellers matched the air-brushed images by Norman Parkinson, then enjoying a phase as royal photographer. There was what was described as a large crowd of 160 well-wishers gathered at Clarence House to greet her on the day and there was a private dinner party with dancing at Buckingham Palace that evening.

The Queen Mother's line about personal security was disbelief that anyone would wish to assassinate her, and, confident in this belief, she went about life with as little personal attention to security as possible. Only after Lord Mountbatten's assassination in August 1979 were television cameras and electronic beams installed at Royal Lodge.*

In 1977 the Queen Mother played a full part in the Silver Jubilee Celebrations of the Queen, 'the rush & busy-ness of the Jubilee',[22] as she described it. She appeared in Huw Wheldon's *Royal Heritage*, went to Edinburgh to see Prince Charles installed as a Knight of the Thistle, attended a banquet at Edinburgh Castle, and, back in London, the great Silver Jubilee Gala at the Royal Opera House, Covent Garden, an occasion for orders, decorations and tiaras. She was at Windsor for the lighting of the first bonfire.

On the day of the St Paul's Cathedral service, an advance party of courtiers and pages came out of the front door of Clarence House, creating an atmosphere of expectation and then she emerged into the garden shared with St James's Palace. Wishing the palace guests 'Good morning' either side of the car, she entered it and set off.[23]

The cheer that greeted the first sighting of her by the crowds outside Clarence House was nothing short of deafening. She travelled to St Paul's Cathedral in her own carriage procession. In his sermon the Archbishop of Canterbury recalled the role of George VI 'and his beloved Queen' in the 'days of war and post war stress' which had 'taught us afresh what duty means'. He continued: 'The years that followed that reign have not been easy, but the foundation then laid has proved strong enough for another sovereign to build upon; and this she has done.'[24] That day was a triumph. 'A drab day for Republicans' ran one of the headlines.[25]

In November the Queen Mother became a great-grandmother when Princess Anne gave birth to Peter Phillips. A *Daily Express* journalist, Michael O'Flaherty, claimed a unique interview with the Queen Mother as the black doors to the garden at Clarence House opened to reveal her about to get into her car. 'This is one of the happiest days of my life,' she told him. 'It's wonderful news, isn't it?'[26]

There was no more memorable reassurance that all was well in the world than the annual progress of the Queen Mother's carriage down the Mall to Horse Guards Parade for the Queen's Birthday Parade. Few could recall a time when the Queen Mother was not a part of that ceremony. By the time she died she had made nearly seventy such annual drives.

* By 1989 even the garden of Princess Alice, Duchess of Gloucester, at Barnwell sported a variety of such devices, and she had round-the-clock police in three shifts. She was quite unfazed when policemen and tracker dogs suddenly marched through her drawing room one summer afternoon, while she was serving tea.

Each year, at almost the appointed hour, she left Clarence House by car and made her way to Buckingham Palace. Invariably dressed in pale pastels, shades of lemon or lilac, soft blue, green or pink, and with one of her characteristic feathery hats, she drove past, smiling serenely, accompanied over the years by the latest most fashionable royal, and in time the young royal princes on their first royal outing. The assembled ranks of the Household Division parted like the Red Sea on Horse Guards Parade, and the National Anthem was played. Men went to the moon, in time the Internet became a feature of many a home, but this carriage procession remained the same.

Two days after the Birthday Parade came the Garter ceremony. When new Knights were to be invested, the members of the Order foregathered at Windsor at 12.15pm. After the private ceremony, there was a magnificent luncheon in the Waterloo Chamber, at which those who sat next to her were treated to that brand of boosting chatter which made them feel special. This was occasionally spiced with an unexpected observation. Looking at the Queen laughing happily in the company of the lately retired Prime Minister, Sir Harold Wilson, at his Investiture in 1976, the Queen Mother mused: 'Isn't it wonderful – how she's tamed him?'[27]

The Queen Mother never missed a Chapter of the Order, and only towards the end of her life did she miss the occasional service. After lunch she donned the robes of Queen Victoria (a slightly darker blue velvet than the other mantles, with a velvet collar and a train that required one page to carry it), and she joined the procession down the hill. She was able to walk down the hill every year until 1992, by which time she was ninety-one.

When St George's Chapel was reached, there was a daunting climb up the West Steps to the Great West Door. Lord Mountbatten used to hover at the top, looking round in apparent concern to make sure the Queen Mother was all right. In fact he was establishing what appeared to be a separate royal procession, which he then headed.

The Garter ceremony has been described as 'The Ascot Vigil', at which the Knights kneel in prayer for a winner later in the week. The Queen Mother invariably attended all four days of the Royal Meeting at Ascot, travelling up the course in a carriage and making at least one visit to the Paddock in the course of the afternoon. On one such occasion in the 1960s she spotted the flamboyantly dressed Aliki Russell, Greek-born wife of the diplomat Sir John Russell. 'Isn't she spiffing?' said the Queen Mother.[28]

Windsor Castle was usually the setting for a house party with dinners and even plays or concerts at the end of the day, an exhausting programme by any standards.

The rest of the summer consisted of normal royal engagements until the final hurdle, which she called 'birthday cards & horrors'.[29] In London she would appear at the gates of Clarence House, to be serenaded with 'Happy Birthday' from a guards band marching past her. Then children came forward bearing gifts and flowers and the Queen Mother beamed happily and pleased everybody. It was a latter-day version of the appearances that Queen Alexandra made on Alexandra Rose Day, and was first inspired by William Tallon. 'In 1970 I persuaded her to come to the gates. In 1980 Reg got her out on the balcony.'[30]

In the evening Martin Gilliat and Ruth Fermoy took the Queen Mother in a Household party to see a suitable play. In order to ensure that there was not too much swearing on stage, the hapless Sir Martin was forced to endure many an unsuitable production before settling on what was often a safe revival.*

For the birthday, for Christmas and following illnesses and accidents, the Household had to go into collective overdrive to cope with the bombardment of presents, welcome and unwelcome, which arrived at Clarence House.

Queen Elizabeth's birthday afforded the donors of a number of kindly meant (if sometimes bizarre) gifts the chance to express their affection and to make contact. For her birthday in 1963, for example, her couturier Norman Hartnell sent red roses from his hotel in Vichy, Captain Cecil Boyd-Rochfort sent toffees, Maria Floris sent a cake, while flowers arrived from the Royal Gardens and the WI at Sandringham, the National Farmers' Union, and a host of other well-wishers. A lady formerly from the Bible College at Swansea sent some lines for the Queen Mother's 'meditation' from her new home in Jerusalem.

A lady in Preston apologised that this year she could not send her habitual box of homemade chocolates because she was too ill, but she hoped to have some ready for Princess Margaret's birthday and would then start making more for Christmas.[31] Another lady sent a headscarf and some postcards, the significance of which she politely explained: 'Please excuse me for taking up your precious time, but this gives me the greatest pleasure in my life, and if God spares me, I will send you a few more lines Aug. 4th 1964.'[32]

Handwritten replies went to the inner circle, typed replies to friends from the wider group. Carbon copies were kept on thin paper, still with

---

* Some of the Queen Mother's ladies-in-waiting thought she might like to see the 1987 film *White Mischief*, with its scenes of Kenya. Fortunately they went to see it in advance and dropped the idea.

the heavily embossed Clarence House coat of arms in red. They were stamped in purple ink with the name of whichever lady-in-waiting replied.

Cranks or supposed cranks required delicate handling. One curious figure sent some sheets and other items, which were passed on to Sir Martin Gilliat's bazaar for the Save the Children Fund. When the same person sent a brocade dress and jacket and a pair of gloves, with price tags still attached, enquiries were made to see if he or she was 'mad, undesirable, or what'. The police investigated, found a woman known to them as 'of very low mentality'. She said the items were personal gifts for Her Majesty. A note was made in the file to thank her in future.[33]

No reply was sent to a disabled AFS man in Manchester, who wrote: 'I hope you keep smiling, regards to your big, lovely smile', or to a man from Fayetteville, New York, on whose letter it was noted that he wrote 'frequently', but was 'not always answered', nor to a man from the Moselle country in France, who wrote about his own health and pointed out that he was not a homosexual.

A disabled pensioner in Brixton (and branch member of the British Legion) sent a string shopping bag he had made, announcing it had taken him exactly five hours and forty-four minutes to do so. To date, he told Queen Elizabeth, he had completed 'in twelve years of this enjoyable occupation',[34] some 4135 such bags, raising £500 for various charities. The Queen Mother kept it and Patricia Hambleden noted that it was going with them to the sea for their next picnic. At Christmas another string bag arrived. The internal memo asked if they thanked every time. They did.

The courtesy extended to the general public was indicative of a friendly Household. The internal notes and replies were written with enjoyment rather than exasperation, even if on 9 December we learn that Queen Elizabeth was looking forward to using the British Commonwealth Ex-Services League's Diary, and on 16 December that the BOAC diary, another 'excellent' publication, would be of the greatest use during the coming year.[35]

The famously vulgar Sir Bernard and Lady Docker sent flowers, the Iranian Ambassador sent caviar, Elizabeth Arden sent a dressing gown and cosmetics, Charles Bolles Rogers, an industrialist and art collector from Minneapolis, and a friend of Michael Bowes-Lyon, sent two 'beautiful' boxes of chocolates from the Ritz Tower in New York. These were taken to Sandringham for the benefit of the large family party. He also sent extensive news of himself, not once but twice. It was agreed that no answer need be made to the second letter.

By 1963 Stephen Tennant was no longer the svelte figure the Queen Mother remembered from her stays at Wilsford in 1922. He was a rotund and eccentric recluse, lying in bed, surrounded by make-up and strange jewellery, at Wilsford Manor. He wrote to enquire if a porcelain jar of potpourri had ever arrived. He hoped Queen Elizabeth was well and happy. Tennant's vibrant purple ink confused the office, but his name rang a bell. Sir Ralph Anstruther tracked him down as well-known to Her Majesty, and Lady Caroline Douglas-Home* wrote to him by hand.†

Of all the correspondents, both famous and unknown, one stands out. Charles E. Locke was a First World War veteran who had charged the Prussians on the Aisne in September 1914. He was a one-time private in the Labour Corps, who later served with the 2nd Sherwood Foresters, and fought his way with them almost as far as Lille (where the Kaiser was) until they were down to thirty-five men and were rescued by reinforcements. He fought on the Somme, and at Bethune, Lens and Ypres.

He spent every winter from 1935 until his death in 1974, at the age of eighty-three, at the Queen Alexandra Hospital Home for ex-Servicemen, Gifford House, Worthing. The Queen Mother had become President in 1953, had visited it twice at Roehampton in 1928 and 1932, and first came to Gifford House in 1934. She was a keen supporter, and paid five more visits, the last being in 1992. On one visit, recalled the chaplain, 'she began talking to a resident in his room, kicked off her shoes, shut the door and talked to her heart's content, much to the anxiety of her lady-in-waiting, and the Lord Lieutenant who were concerned about the schedule she was supposed to follow'.[36]

Though Locke had never met the Queen Mother, he sent her regular cards. He made soft toys in the hospital workshop. In 1962 he made her an elephant, and in 1963 he offered a Bambi or a Donald Duck. The Queen Mother said that a soft toy would be very acceptable, leaving the choice to him. Shortly after Christmas a Donald Duck arrived with an offer of a Bambi for one of the grandchildren. The Donald Duck pleased her so much that she sent a message to the effect that a blue Bambi would also be very acceptable.'[37] The Queen Mother sent him a Pitkin book about Princess Margaret and Lord Linley.

In thanking the Queen Mother, Locke said he was sorry to hear that she had had to have an operation. 'Please your Majesty have a good rest

---

* Lady Caroline Douglas-Home (b. 1937), daughter of 14th Earl of Home (Sir Alec Douglas-Home, Prime Minister 1963–4), temporary Woman of the Bedchamber to the Queen Mother from 1963 to 1965.
† This letter survives in Stephen Tennant's papers. The Queen Mother did indeed remember him, and told the present author that she hoped she had kept the multicoloured epistles that winged their way to her from Wilsford from time to time. Some were kept.

and a nice holiday before you start on your many engagements again.' He asked if he could have a photograph of her for his workshop. He wrote: 'I have been writing to you now at Xmas over 30 years although I haven't met you yet. I think of you as an old friend . . .'[38] The Queen Mother asked Lady Fermoy to send him a photograph, something of a break from royal protocol. Locke replied at once: 'It is my most treasured possession. I am having it framed and hung amongst my Military Photos in the place of honour.'[39]

In 1963 the gifts and cards were manageable. But after 1970, when the Queen Mother's birthday appearances became an annual fixture, the ritual of gifts turned into a flood, requiring extra staff to cope. The momentum grew until the end.

33

Eighty Years On

'You may be excited about it. We are all extremely relieved'
– Princess Margaret on the Royal Wedding

The Silver Jubilee was a high point in the reign of Elizabeth II, the Royal Family seemingly unassailable. The Palace held sway and most of the press behaved with integrity towards them. The problems that caused regular trouble revolved around the Civil List and the assumed cost of the monarchy, and dramas involving the breakdown of Princess Margaret's marriage.

The Queen Mother remained on her pinnacle and even republican scourges such as the Labour MP Willie Hamilton* conceded at climacteric birthdays that she did a good job. The worst he could say was:

> She makes no speeches of consequence. She gets through her public relations by pleasing facial exercises, or by purposely chatting to 'the lads in the back row' and taking a drop of the hard stuff, her native Scotch Whisky. Yet, behind the matey tipple and the ever-ready smile, there lurks the mind of a shrewd businessman.[1]

She had earned her place in the affections of the public and, though there were jibes at the cost of her large Household and rumours of massive overdrafts at Coutts, these were usually made with a hint of envy that she should get away with it. The Queen Mother ran a large Household, employing a considerable staff.† She also had a good number of race-horses in training, but she believed that this was how a Dowager Queen should live.

The major crisis was the collapse of the Snowdon marriage, which had begun with such hopes in 1960. The couple crossed the line between the traditional aspects of the monarchy and the arts. Lord Snowdon was

---

* Willie Hamilton was taken seriously as a scourge of the monarchy for many years. But then he made the mistake of cashing in and writing a book – *My Queen and I* – after which his gun barrels were somehow empty.
† In 1972 the Queen Mother had a Household of thirty-two, of whom thirteen were salaried (including five full-time clerks). Only two of her Household occupied grace-and-favour residences.

photographing for the *Sunday Times Magazine*, designing the aviary at the London Zoo and exploring social issues in provocative documentaries, not least *Don't Count the Candles*, which examined aspects of old age. His work for the Investiture had been inspired and earned him his GCVO.

Princess Margaret was drawn to the ballet and theatre. Both parents educated their children by taking them to the National Gallery and showing them one picture at each visit so that they would remember it. But the marriage suffered from tensions early on. Throughout the late 1960s and early 1970s there were stories of rows and scenes at parties.

In 1976 a Sunday newspaper printed photographs of Princess Margaret and a young friend, Roddy Llewellyn, seated side by side in Mustique (taken at least two years earlier and cunningly cropped to excise the others from the group), prompting the Snowdons to separate.

Major Griffin issued one of his statements: 'A separation has been a possibility for some time and once the final decision had been reached, it was obviously better to implement it straight away.'[2]

Cecil Beaton amused himself with a caricature of Lady Rosse reading the headline 'Meg & Tony to split' with her false eyelashes and wig flying off, resembling the wicked queen at her dressing table in *Snow White*. The couple were divorced in 1978, making Princess Margaret the first prominent member of the Royal Family to go through the divorce courts.*

Lord Snowdon remained popular with the Royal Family after the separation and on good terms with Princess Margaret, though she was exasperated with her mother when, despite this, she suggested that he join them at Royal Lodge for the weekend as though nothing had happened. He did not come and mother and daughter were photographed by paparazzi on a grim, solitary walk together, accompanied by the ever-present Corgis.

Restless years again followed for Princess Margaret after her divorce. Her name was occasionally linked with some figure such as Norman Lonsdale, but, being deeply religious, she would never remarry and was therefore destined for a life which appeared lonely, despite the support of her family and a host of intelligent and interesting friends. There were occasional scares about her health and a serious operation to remove tissue from her left lung in 1985. Eventually she gave up smoking completely and ceased to drink alcohol in the middle of the day. There were those

---

* In 1967 Lord Harewood was divorced. He then married Patricia Tuckwell, by whom he already had a son, Mark. Following that, he was excluded from invitations to court for some years. He was not invited to the funeral of the Duke of Windsor in 1972, nor to the wedding of Princess Anne to Lieutenant Mark Phillips in 1973, despite giving her a ruby and diamond stockpin, which was displayed among the gifts from members of the Royal Family at St James's Palace after the wedding.

who were depressed by the way she could be openly rude to her mother when groups were about, though when alone with her, perhaps without an audience, she tended to be more sympathetic. But there was clearly some residual bitterness, and the Queen Mother did not always have an easy time with her younger daughter.

The post-Jubilee euphoria extending into the looming possibility that Prince Charles would soon marry, there was much to which to look forward. The Queen Mother continued her engagements unabated.

She went to Canada at the end of June 1979. In advance of the trip, which took in Halifax and Toronto, Sir Martin Gilliat wrote: 'Already it has become clear that "they" are trying to fit far more into the programme than is compatible with the Private Secretary getting away even for a few hours. On the contrary it will be hard to measure up to the demands that are made when such a greatly loved person comes on a brief visit.'[3]

Walmer Castle

Hardly was she back than the Queen Mother succeeded the late Sir Robert Menzies, former Prime Minister of Australia, as 160th Lord Warden of the Cinque Ports, Admiral of the Cinque Ports and Constable of Dover Castle. She was the first woman to hold the office, thus ending nine hundred years of male domination. For her installation at St Mary's Church, Dover, she used *Britannia* as a base, then undertaking engagements at Dover Castle and Walmer Castle, accompanied by Prince Andrew and Prince Edward.

Having assumed the ancient office, the Queen Mother made a visit to Walmer an annual date in her calendar. In 1980 she again stayed on *Britannia*, going ashore to visit the various Cinque Ports. In subsequent years, the Royal Yacht was not always available. In 1986 the Queen Mother moved her operations to Walmer Castle, announcing: 'I want to go and live there – from Friday to Monday.'[4]

Sir Robert Menzies had occupied a small flat in the castle on his occasional visits from Australia. The Queen Mother decided to take over the public rooms (to the annoyance of the Historic Buildings and Monuments Commission) if only for three nights a year, during a weekend in July. It is not everyone who took on a new home at the age of eighty-six, especially when she already had four homes. Oliver Ford was invited to undertake the necessary interior decoration. She wrote to him:

I . . . want to thank you so very much for making Walmer Castle so comfortable and charming to live in. My bedroom was really lovely, and we even managed to entertain some guests for dinner in the makeshift dining-room. The chef was very happy in his little kitchen, and the castle had a delightful atmosphere. I know it is all due to your hard & tactful (!) work there, that we were able to spend a successful weekend.

I shall hope to return there next summer.[5]

Return there she did every summer including the last, of 2001.* Chef may have been happy in his kitchen but it meant a huge effort for her Household. The castle was Spartan, one guest complained of a damp bed, while the annual visit caused a huge upheaval, with silver, glass and plate brought from London, not to mention special chairs. 'We brought everything. In the end we took the dining room table too,'[6] recalled William Tallon. Then all had to be returned, no mean operation. Some of the furniture, joked the Queen Mother, had been 'pinched from Windsor'.[7]

Walmer involved much civic entertaining, and on the Sunday night she gave a small dinner party, which invariably included Lord and Lady Northbourne, who lived near Deal, the writer Kenneth Rose, who stayed with them, Lady Thorneycroft, the young George Plumptre and others. The hospitality was as generous as ever.

The Queen Mother liked to show her guests around the castle's public rooms, filled with Napoleonic relics. One item on display was a meagre camp bed, used by the Duke of Wellington, an earlier Lord Warden. Rose commented that he had slept on such a thing during the war, to which she riposted: 'Yes, but you weren't a Field Marshal.'[8]

Not long after her 1979 installation, Lord Mountbatten and members of his family were killed at Mullaghmore on the west coast of Ireland, when the IRA blew his boat up. The Queen Mother flew from Scotland with the Queen to attend the ceremonial funeral at Westminster Abbey. She was described as the only one to smile walking down the aisle – at some ladies who had arranged the flowers. Neither she nor Princess Alice, Duchess of Gloucester, joined the funeral train to Romsey for the burial, a small concession to age.

The Queen Mother's friends died in great numbers. She described Helen Hardinge, who died on the same day as Mountbatten, as 'one of

---

* The Queen Mother's last Christmas card showed her at Walmer with her Corgis. There were cannons in the picture, which she enjoyed. 'They're pointing towards France!' she said.

my oldest & dearest friends', while regretting that 'this summer was such a nightmare that I never found a day to go & see dear Helen, which I always loved doing'.[9] The Dowager Countess of Scarbrough, to whom the Queen Mother had been a bridesmaid, died on 23 November, just past her eightieth birthday. Martin Gilliat was saddened by the death of Frances Campbell-Preston's sister-in-law, the famous Joyce Grenfell, and then of her sister Lady Ballantrae, killed by a falling tree. Both were friends of Queen Elizabeth. Meanwhile Lady Jean Rankin languished in Beaumont House after a second hip operation. Only the Queen Mother flourished, as Gilliat reported:

Happily Queen Elizabeth seems to be approaching her 80th birthday on 4 August quite undaunted by any sign of approaching old age. People often ask me why I don't retire and I can only answer that as I work for someone 13 years my senior I can not easily do so unless she wants to part with me or I become totally decrepit.[10]

In fact she approached this birthday with misgivings. Gilliat again reported:

We are hard at work on plans for the 80th Birthday on 4 August, although Queen Elizabeth herself is rather disinterested in the whole business. She so far does not think there is any point in all the fuss with Thanksgiving Service and Carriage Processions, but the People of this Country do so love her and even in this crazy modern life 'Age' is still quite venerated.[11]

The family celebrations began with a dance at Windsor Castle, coupling the Queen Mother's name with the two surviving royal octogenarians, Princess Alice, Duchess of Gloucester, and 'Master', the Duke of Beaufort. By the age of eighty, the Queen Mother was less attentive to detail than hitherto. When shown the guest list for her approval, she simply said 'How perfectly lovely!' and failed to notice the omission of her old friend, Commander Clare Vyner, who was not unnaturally somewhat put out.

The castle was floodlit and filled with the Queen Mother's surviving friends. Sir Charles Johnston,* invited due to a superfluity of widows and unattached princesses, observed the scene but found little mischief to report. He thought the Queen Mother 'radiated fun, and even her

---

* By this time, his wife Natasha had suffered a stroke and was not well enough for such occasions.

smart French racing friends, if not actually impressed by the party, at least didn't sneer visibly'.[12]

The Queen Mother asked Johnston if he had written anything lately:

As a result I am committed to sending her a copy of *Rivers and Fireworks*. I hadn't meant to do this, and am slightly nervous about the effect of 'Ruined by syphilis and high society' – which really could seem a bit steep after I've been enjoying myself like mad at her birthday party. The saving factor is that she has, quite genuinely, never thought of herself as 'high society' at all. As she once said, about Lady Cunard: 'We weren't nearly smart enough for her.'[13]

Just before he left, Johnston overheard a wife saying to her husband: 'Now you're *not* to dance with Midnight Moll – otherwise we shall never get away.'[14] The widowed Duchess of Buccleuch, who had so diverted James Stuart in the 1920s and later, was approaching her own eightieth birthday that year.

There followed the great service of Thanksgiving at St Paul's Cathedral with attendant carriage processions on 15 July, and fulsome tributes in Parliament and press. The Archbishop of Canterbury declared: 'The Queen Mother has been no stranger to suffering of a kind that comes to most of us, notably bereavement, but she has accepted what has befallen her and been able to turn it into uncondescending and lively sympathy for the misfortunes of others . . . She has occupied the centre of the stage since 1923 without suffering the fate which so frequently befalls the fashionable personality who is played out after 10 years or so in the public eye.'[15]

In the House of Commons, the first ever woman Prime Minister, Margaret Thatcher, described her as 'a Queen who had been strong with the brave, had mourned with the sad and had enchanted everyone by her grace and wit'. But a hint of the disappearance of deference was introduced by Dennis Skinner and Willie Hamilton, who sought to contrast her to other octogenarians, coping with less fortunate circumstances.[16]

There was a garden party at the Palace. One lady told the Queen Mother she had worried about her in the carriage procession with her sleeveless chiffon coat. 'I was warmed by the love of the British people,' the Queen Mother replied.[17]

On the actual birthday there were enormous crowds at Clarence House, and sack loads of gifts. Ten Jet Provost aircraft from the Royal Air Force Central Flying School flew past in an 'E' formation. There was a gala performance of ballet at the Royal Opera House, with a huge cake to be cut.

The Royal Family, the Queen Mother's friends and Household clubbed together to give her a log cabin on the banks of the River Dee at Pol Veir, one of her favourite fishing pools. It was of Scandinavian design, cost about £9,000, and was erected in time for the Queen Mother to pay it an inaugural visit in the summer when she was at Birkhall to fish. The first party there took place despite the Queen Mother hearing of the death of her niece (and bridesmaid), Elizabeth Elphinstone, that day, 16 May.

Thanking the contributors was a problem. The Queen Mother eventually sat down to write her thank-you letters during her Birkhall visit in October. Thus hundreds of more or less identical, individually handwritten letters went off with the message that the log cabin was 'a real joy', 'such a perfect birthday present', and telling the friends: 'It has settled in most happily between the river and the tall pine trees, and I have spent many blissful hours there, in fact, I cannot think what we did before it arrived!'[18] The difficulty for the ladies-in-waiting was that no list was kept of those who had been thanked, and some were overlooked. They had to devise a form of wording which would not look idiotic if a prior letter had been despatched.

The Queen Mother's Household staff were not invited to contribute to the log cabin, which caused some offence, but William Tallon went to Hancock's and arranged their own gift of fish knives, which were taken to whichever house they stayed in. One guest described these as middle class, so the Queen Mother made sure they were always out when he came to lunch.

Now that she was eighty, the Queen Mother decided to retire as Chancellor of London University. The requisite for being Chancellor did not depend on academic prowess. The first Chancellor, the 7th Duke of Devonshire, was no academic, nor was the Queen Mother's predecessor, the Earl of Athlone, who held the post for twenty-three years. And she had scarcely been to school. But she had been a success, attending two presentations a year at the Royal Albert Hall, the university's Foundation Day, visiting three or four colleges a year and places such as the marine biology station and the boat house. She averaged ten engagements a year for them, which was high by the standard of annual royal engagements. She enjoyed the role, appearing at university functions in full evening dress and tiara, and inviting elements of university life to Clarence House.

Her retirement took them by surprise and left them the task of finding a new Chancellor. She let it be known that she wanted Princess Anne to succeed her. However, 83,000 electors were allowed to put forward other candidates, and there was a distinct move that the Princess should not be returned unopposed. At the last moment two candidates were put forward, Nelson Mandela, the South African nationalist, still imprisoned on Robben Island at that time (one of whose proposers was Jonathan Dimbleby), and Jack Jones, the former Secretary of the Transport and General Workers Union (nominated by Tessa Blackstone, Lord Young of Dartington and Professor John Griffith). There was never a question of the candidates descending to the hustings.

Bernard Levin dismissed Mandela since he probably knew nothing of his proposed candidature. He accused those who nominated Jack Jones as guilty of 'an intellectual and psychological bankruptcy'.[19] Levin maintained that the Chancellor's role was largely ceremonial and that Princess Anne should be elected.

Princess Anne was elected and soon set her own style, in every sense more brisk than that of her grandmother.

The prolonged bachelorhood of the Prince of Wales had preoccupied the media as much as it had the Prince himself and his family. In the autumn of 1980 the Queen Mother attended the fiftieth birthday party of Princess Margaret at the Ritz, on which occasion Lady Diana Spencer, youngest daughter of Earl Spencer, was a guest.

There had been months of speculation that at last a bride had been found, and in February 1981 the engagement was finally announced. The accepted view was that this was a match inspired by Clarence House. Both the bride's grandmothers, the late Countess Spencer and Ruth, Lady Fermoy, were in the Queen Mother's Household, as were no fewer than four great-aunts – the Dowager Duchess of Abercorn (the Mistress of the Robes), Lady Katharine Seymour (sister of Countess Spencer), Lady Delia Peel (who died that year) and the late Lady Annaly (both sisters of Earl Spencer).* Of these, Katie Seymour and Lavinia Annaly were intimate friends. The idea circulated without contradiction that the Queen Mother and Ruth Fermoy must have plotted the whole thing. 'How those two grandmothers must have prayed for it!' was Elizabeth Longford's version.[20]

The union was promoted by Ruth Fermoy, even though she later denied it, and she convinced the Queen Mother of its merits. Though spoilt by her father, Diana Spencer had been through a miserable childhood and

---

* Lady Lavinia Spencer (1899–1955). She had been on the South African trip in 1925.

learned to make her way in life by guile. Her mother had 'bolted' and
Lady Fermoy had testified against her. There had been the resented second
marriage of her father to the flamboyant Raine, Countess of Dartmouth,
daughter of the novelist Barbara Cartland. Sir Martin Gilliat described
the reaction at Clarence House:

> We are all in a great state of excitement over *the* engagement, the
> more so as the Bride is living under this roof. Possibly I am no one
> to judge, but even the most normally cynical experts believe there
> could be no more marvellous outcome to all our hopes.[21]

Much later, when it all went wrong, Lady Fermoy claimed that she had
harboured grave misgivings, which she had kept to herself. She knew of
the instabilities in the bride's character. During the engagement, when
a friend said to her how wonderful it was that the bride loved music, she
did volunteer: 'She'll need that.'[22]

Hardly was the engagement announced than the bride-to-be dropped
hints that she was not merely a meek kindergarten teacher. She appeared
at Goldsmiths' Hall in a revealing black dress, with a deep décolleté which
almost exposed her breasts. 'Wasn't that a mighty feast to set before a
King?' exclaimed Lady Diana Cooper, present that night.[23] At a lunch at
Clarence House the bride told Lord De L'Isle that the wedding would
be at St Paul's Cathedral as there was more room than in the Abbey 'and
I don't want my friends to have to sit behind pillars'.[24]

In the mounting enthusiasm for the wedding, few would countenance
the truth, known to some, that the situation was not as straightforward
as it appeared. The Prince of Wales had been in love with Camilla Shand
for years. Jonathan Dimbleby published the approved version of this.
They met through Lucia Santa Cruz, a Cambridge girlfriend, upon
whom, as Lady Butler, the wife of the Master, put it, he had 'cut his
teeth'.[25] The Prince was drawn to Camilla Shand by her natural pretti-
ness, smiling eyes and a shared sense of humour, which was 'neither dry
nor arch, and it lacked that edge of malice required by jaded palates'.[26]
Dimbleby revealed: 'Like him, she was convulsed by the Goons, by silly
accents and daft looks, while his taste for the absurd was complemented
by her down-to-earth irreverence.'[27]

The first phase of this love affair took place during the latter six
months of 1972, at the end of which, confused, lacking in confidence
and unsure of the future, the Prince sailed in the frigate HMS *Minerva*
for an eight-month spell of duty in the West Indies. While he was absent,
Camilla Shand returned to a former boyfriend, Andrew Parker Bowles,

a good-looking officer in the Life Guards (and former escort of Princess Anne), with none of the introspection of the heir to the throne. In April Camilla and Parker Bowles announced their engagement. Prince Charles was forlorn and some would argue that he did not fully get over this for twenty-five years.

Between 1973 and 1980 Andrew Parker Bowles and his wife were frequently in royal company, staying at Windsor, Balmoral and Sandringham, and with the Queen Mother at the Castle of Mey. He rose in the Blues and Royals to command the Sovereign's Escort of the Household Cavalry and eventually to be Silver Stick in Waiting. According to Dimbleby, who is politely vague about dates, there came a point when Prince Charles was again able to count on Camilla as his best friend and 'touchstone'.[28] Their relationship concerned members of his family who warned him that 'an illicit liaison would be damaging to his own standing and to the institution of which he was so crucial a member'.[29] But he was neither willing nor able to give her up.

Prince Charles's character was different from that of both the Duke of Windsor and Princess Margaret, yet he faced a similar dilemma. By 1980 he was obsessed with the need to find a wife and do his dynastic duty. He was drawn to Diana Spencer by her obvious sensitivity towards him, her sense of 'tomboy' fun and her natural innocence.

Henry James wrote that most relationships are based on a mutual misunderstanding, and in this case Diana was in love with Charles, while he was not particularly in love with her. But, thanks to Ruth Fermoy, the Queen Mother approved, as did most of the world.

Once the media discovered Diana Spencer, the pressure intensified. The Prince felt (wrongly) that he was being bludgeoned into matrimony by his father. He interpreted a thoughtful letter from the Duke of Edinburgh, which warned him not to dally with Diana's affections and risk compromising her, as a virtual command to marry her. Even so he continued to procrastinate, confiding to a friend that he was afraid to make a promise that he might live to regret. As Dimbleby, his apologist, put it: 'Making every allowance for last-minute nerves, it was hardly the most auspicious frame of mind in which to offer his hand in marriage.'

A mere two weeks before the engagement, friends of the Prince and the Parker Bowleses were convinced of two things: the engagement would happen but Camilla was 'determined not to let the Prince go'.[30] This was the reason for the prolonged delay in the announcement.

When the engagement was announced, at least one observer noted: 'I can't help finding certain aspects deeply depressing.'[31] No newspapers printed the lines in the Palace interview about 'whatever love is' that so upset the perceptive, but Lady Diana Cooper did not miss it. She said they should have replied: 'Yes madly!'[32] The press called it a fairy-tale romance, and their only mischief was to liken the whole thing to a Barbara Cartland novel.

The night before the engagement Diana Spencer moved in to Clarence House, later transferring to Buckingham Palace, where she put on weight due to eating four meals a day.[33] In the ensuing months she saw little of her future husband, but she was at Sandown with the Queen Mother when he was thrown from his horse. Sir Martin Gilliat warned the waiting crowd outside the Royal Box: 'It'll be at least another ten minutes yet!' When the bride emerged, a voice called out: 'Good on 'yer, Di!'

'It's Diana, actually,' she replied.

'Yes,' added the Prince of Wales, 'we must get these things right.'[34]

Behind the scenes worrying stories circulated. During Princess Margaret's Mustique holiday, one of the guests said to her: 'You must be thrilled about the Royal Wedding.' To which, in her inimitable style, the Princess replied: 'You may be excited about it. We are all extremely relieved and by the way she [Camilla] has no intention of giving him up.' During that summer, the present author noted:

> The Royal Wedding is no more romantic than a picnic amid the wasps. Prince Charles has been mucking about with Camilla Parker Bowles (curiously the great-grand-daughter of Mrs Keppel, mistress of his great-great-grandfather, Edward VII) and is said to have told the Queen angrily: 'My marriage and my sex life have nothing to do with each other' . . . So what love there is emanates from Diana. And if the truth be known she is a determined character who longs to be Queen.[35]

The bride was worried about the Prince's prior relationship with Mrs Parker Bowles, and these worries came to the fore when she discovered the 'farewell' present of a bracelet with 'GF', for 'Girl Friday', on it. There was a confrontation and the Prince told his bride he would be handing the present over, in the words of Dimbleby, to 'say goodbye for what both of them intended to be the last time'.[36]

At that time the social intelligentsia wondered what John Betjeman, the Poet Laureate, would muster by way of a celebratory poem for the wedding. Lord Gowrie raised the matter when he invited Sir Charles Johnston to lunch at the Garrick Club. He suggested that Betjeman had already written about Lady Di: 'clear of eye and firm of limb'. Sir Charles mused: 'A rich man's Joan Hunter-Dunn?'*

The Royal Family and the bride-to-be appeared for the annual Birthday Parade on Saturday 13 June. This was important for two reasons, the most important being the dramatic six shots (they turned out to be blanks) fired at the Queen as she turned into Horse Guards Approach. The Queen, riding side saddle, handled the situation with great aplomb, extending her arms and thus re-collecting the horse, and rode on to the Parade Ground as if nothing had happened.†

No mention was made of the second incident. For this ceremony, as soon as the parade is over, the Royal Family leave the major general's office to return to Buckingham Palace in a series of cars, all of which happens swiftly as the Queen cannot ride off until they are well up the Mall. The Queen Mother slipped on the stairs and hurt her leg, which later caused an ulcer, giving her a temperature the week before the wedding. She was confined to Clarence House, but recovered at Royal Lodge during the weekend.

As for the bridal pair, by the end of June the Prince of Wales was reported to be 'depressed at the forthcoming wedding' while the bride was so bored that she was taking ballet and tap-dancing lessons in the Palace.[37] Charles was observed snapping at Diana at Prince Andrew's twenty-first birthday party at Windsor in June.[38]

In retrospect, the Court Circular for 29 July 1981 makes sinister reading:

> The Queen and The Duke of Edinburgh, with Queen Elizabeth The Queen Mother and other Members of the Royal Family, drove to St Paul's Cathedral in a carriage procession escorted by a Sovereign's Escort of the Household Cavalry, with two Standards, under the command of Lieutenant-Colonel Andrew Parker Bowles.[39]

Even on the day of the Royal Wedding, there was no escaping the Colonel – or his wife.

The night before, the Queen Mother and Ruth Fermoy were at

---

* John Betjeman had lately suffered a stroke. 'A Subaltern's Love-song' in *New Bats in Old Belfries* (1945) (*John Betjeman's Collected Poems* (John Murray, 1958), pp. 97–9). Despite the stroke, Betjeman produced a poem, but was criticised for suggesting that blackbirds would be hailing the city morn. One tease pointed out that July was the moulting season and, had they wanted blackbirds to sing, the royal couple would have had to marry in the spring.

† By the following Wednesday at Ascot, new security measures were in place. The police faced into the crowd in order to spot trouble-makers. Andrew Parker Bowles was instructed to ride close to the Queen's carriage in the wedding procession. He and others were issued with walkie-talkies in their saddles and commanded to surround the Queen if anything happened.

Clarence House, where Diana Spencer and her sister Jane Fellowes were spending the night. The two Spencer sisters dined alone together and were soon tucked up in bed in anticipation of the great day ahead. Meanwhile, the Queen Mother watched a rerun of *Dad's Army* before tuning in to the pre-wedding interview with Angela Rippon and Andrew Gardner. They then watched coverage of the fireworks, the Queen Mother expressing great relief at not being present on account of the proliferation of German royal guests. Spotting Mrs Reagan on the screen, she declared her 'a nice little woman'.[40]

The Queen Mother did not ask any of her friends either to the ball or to the wedding, not even Prince Jean-Louis de Faucigny-Lucinge, who masterminded her visits to France. On the day itself, she looked 'sad & tired, . . . predictably feathered in green'.[41] She was spotted dabbing a tear with her handkerchief.

What did the Queen Mother make of the wedding? Presumably she welcomed it as veering towards her world rather than to a 'high-tech' Prince Philip/Mountbatten alliance. Geographically and sociologically the wedding found its roots in a field at Sandringham. And there were many Queen Mother connections – the two grandmothers having been close friends for years – the many ladies-in-waiting in her Household who were great-aunts, Park House on the Sandringham estate, the familiar names of those who used to shoot with the King and which pepper his game book – Felloweses, Fermoys, even the bride's father, then Viscount Althorp.* The Queen Mother shared the world's hope for happy times ahead for her favourite grandson. Others held reservations. Sir Charles Johnston watched on television:

Like the whole country, we were totally bewitched by the bride. I've never seen such a strong charge of innocently provocative sex. One prays for the happiness of the couple – and there are certain doubts in one's mind which makes the prayer very much more than a formality.[42]

The present author's diary does not contradict Sir Charles:

Well, they're married. We've got a Princess of Wales at last. The week has been one of magnificence and pomp, splendour and tears, but happiness abounding. I speak of general happiness though, for I fear that the Prince himself is not a happy man. He feels pushed

* Lady Jane Spencer was married to Robert Fellowes, the Queen's Assistant Private Secretary. His father was Sir William Fellowes, the land agent at Sandringham.

into the wedding and so he wriggles. He looks bored, tortured, exasperated. He likes to think he leads a busy and fulfilled life but he doesn't – he has pomposity and in some ways he has lost his touch. And he is so resentful of his fragrant child-bride. She is lovely & has won all hearts. Her approach to the marriage is so much more sophisticated than his. She said at one point: 'You'd better like it,'* and she was right.

She offers him her life, she is sacrificing herself wholeheartedly. She offers him love & more than love – friendship. If he wants it, there is friendship there for him. He may get quite a surprise in the next few days. He may find that life is easier, that home is a nicer place to be than he has realised in the recent months. That's how she will win him, because already she is a huge asset to him. I hope he will be kind to her – it's worth it. And I hope we will see that tortured, twisted brow relax and his reactions grow more natural.

When the bride fluffed her lines and said 'Philip Charles' he followed her by saying 'thy goods with thee I share'. I said† that this was done on purpose & I hope so. For then, instead of him being fluent & well rehearsed, he was letting her off the hook and the result was that they were two young people muddling through together. If so, it is the first time he has been nice to her. The tears incident‡ the other day was, I am sure, because he was not paying her enough attention.

Then of course there are Andrew & Camilla Parker Bowles to contend with – especially the latter . . .[43]

---

* In the television interview in the summer house at Buckingham Palace, shown the night before the wedding.
† In a live studio interview for ITN.
‡ Lady Diana Spencer had collapsed in tears at the polo at Smith's Lawn at Windsor the previous Sunday.

34

Social Life

> *'What I always say is, isn't it lovely to be asked to a party?'*
> – the Queen Mother

The Queen Mother's long years of widowhood were a mixture of public duties and private entertainment. Obviously she will be best remembered for her official life, but there was much going on behind the scenes. Her social and cultural life was seen by fewer but made up a large part of her later existence.

There was considerable entertaining in her various residences, and she too was widely entertained. Unlike her neighbours, the Duke and Duchess of Gloucester,* who were shy and did not entertain much, thinking people would not want to come, she did not hesitate to pluck figures from the arts and other areas of life at will and lure them to her table. Most people greatly enjoyed these occasions, though a few were out of tune with the racing fraternity, so often found there. Lord Avon, the former Prime Minister, who was invited in retirement, begged leave to decline future invitations, which was not popular.

Clarence House

Those invited to Clarence House for lunch or dinner were put at their ease by William Tallon and Reg Wilcock, served appropriate drinks, and when the scene was set and the conversation flowing, William would alert the Queen Mother. She would come out of the lift, ask if all was well, and make her entrance. At that point the pages faded into the background and the show began. Corgis ran about and the Queen Mother greeted her guests with theatrical gestures, arms waving in greeting. There was a long time drinking cocktails before the guests went into lunch which could undermine the unwary.

The most telling accounts of these lunches came from observant outsiders whose invitations were infrequent. Cecil Beaton was, as ever, an exacting critic. He was bidden to a concert at the Festival Hall in the

---

* The Gloucesters lived at York House, St James's Palace, until 1970.

summer of 1969. 'The Queen Mother seems remarkably happy in her later years,' he noted. 'Tonight she was in fine fettle, making good out of every remark. I arrived the last. "I hope you won't mind this harpsichord concert." "No, it will be very refreshing," was greeted with gales of laughter . . ."[1]

Dinner was at Clarence House, after the concert – 'lobster mousse, fried chicken, lots of veg, avocado and salad, and Scotch woodcock (which I couldn't eat). Masses of drink of all sorts.' Sir Frederick Ashton described the Queen Mother's bosom as acquiring 'a Dry Martini flush'.[2] Beaton was impressed with how the Queen Mother discussed politics with the businessman David McKenna.

When he dined there again in 1973, before the ball for Princess Anne's wedding, Beaton thought the glamour had gone. 'It is a hideous house & the mixture of furniture makes for a rather sordid ensemble. Some of the pictures are so bad (in the dining room particularly) that it gives the impression of a pretentious hotel . . . I was even disappointed with the food and found it all too creamy. The Queen Mother enjoyed her glass of wine and held her head back each time she quaffed a glass.'[3]

Sir Charles Johnston and his wife Natasha lunched there in April 1972. Sir Charles could appear dour and reserved, but he liked to observe with the eye of a modern-day Pushkin, his prose that of an intelligent Wykehamist: 'Same cosy, unprovisional feeling as I noted at Balmoral years ago: a jolly Scotch house-party camping out in a historic monument. Not the same power of appropriating and dominating her surroundings that Princess Marina had.'[4] He was impressed when 'an unseen hand' – that of William Tallon – placed a Fabergé box with a portrait of Tsar Nicholas II at his wife's place at the table.[5] Meeting the Queen Mother after a pre-Christmas lunch at the White's staff party, she said to him: 'I hope the grub was all right?'[6] just as she sometimes referred to a party in pre-war slang as 'our Beano'.

A later guest was Roy Strong, Director of the Victoria and Albert Museum. In June 1976 the table had been taken out into the garden under two weeping plane trees. It was laid for eighteen, adorned with three large bowls of flowers, and a pair of eighteenth-century *biscuit* figures of huntsmen, given by President Le Brun in Paris in 1938. The Queen Mother sat at the middle of the table, and the guests were waited on by three men servants. William placed a Gerald Benney box in front of Strong, knowing his interest in the crafts. It was a way to make a new guest feel at ease. 'The Clarence House ritual is that of an Edwardian great house,'[7] noted Strong.

At another lunch, this time indoors in December 1977, there were twenty-five guests. Ritz Crackers were handed round in the packet, and Strong judged the lunch 'really bad; a deep-fried rissole, frozen Brussels sprouts and mashed potatoes, even if they are served on silver, don't rank in my running as even good plain food'.[8] In 1981 the food was no better: 'very indifferent: an over-decorated stodgy salmon mousse, meatballs, beans and potatoes and an ice-cream with black cherries'.[9] Two years after that Strong quoted Mark Bonham-Carter complaining about all aspects of the lunch – the chrysanthemums, the china and the 'awful food', which Strong confirmed: 'It always is! Rissoles again!'[10]

The same guests were invited to certain annual lunches. On her birthday she always asked Sir John Johnston, the former Comptroller of the Lord Chamberlain's Office, Sir John Miller, the former Crown Equerry, and for many years she entertained Major Guy Knight, a man unloved by the Royal Family for his eagerness to drink and habit of sweeping a pile of the Queen Mother's cigarettes into his pocket for later enjoyment.

The Queen Mother's last Treasurer, Nicholas Assheton, cited a strong element of Scottish frugality in the entertaining, which he admitted was 'contrary to common belief', the tabloid-reading public being convinced that she was extravagant on all fronts. The Queen Mother ran a large Household, which she considered fitting for a Queen Dowager, and she had a considerable racing stable, but, as to the food, it was 'wholesome and basic – bread and butter pudding. She had a bottle of champagne at her side for dinner, from which only she drank. If good wines were served, these were the gift of some Rothschild.'[11]

Royal Lodge

The Queen Mother's arrivals at Royal Lodge were preceded by a fleet of cars, and it is no exaggeration to say that, even though she was largely unseen, the mere knowledge that she was there bestowed an aura of warmth and happiness that reached out like a bush telegraph to the furthest corners of Windsor Great Park.

At Royal Lodge the guests were divided into two categories, loosely racing and artistic. For Cheltenham the house was filled with racing figures, Sir Michael and Lady Angela Oswald, Anne, Duchess of Westminster, Nicholas Soames, Bobby Corbett and Houston Shaw-Stewart. Over the years the artistic guests included Sir Noël Coward, Sir John Betjeman, Lord David Cecil, and Sir Roy Strong and Julia Trevelyan Oman. And there were friends such as the Duke and Duchess of Grafton, Lord and Lady Carrington and Sir Fitzroy and Lady Maclean.

Princess Margaret often spent the weekend there.

Invitations to Royal Lodge were confirmed in letters from the Private Secretary, expressing the Queen Mother's delight that the invitation had been accepted and the hope that the guest would arrive around 6.30 on Saturday evening and remain until after breakfast on Monday. Thus Queen Elizabeth, who would have been at Royal Lodge since Friday afternoon, would have had a little time to herself before the fun began.

Sir Charles Johnston was co-opted on to the weekend list in 1972, and spent seven annual weekends there in a row, before a break in 1979. Of one weekend in June 1973 he wrote:

It's an enchanted world entirely on its own – all the splendour of a Royal establishment but none of the public attention and bother and sense of strain. A broad terrace above vast lawns, noble trees, clipped hedges surrounding open-air salons bursting with roses. Sitting with Jean Rankin on the darkened terrace after dinner, we looked in through five neo-Gothic ogival windows into the long green drawing-room lit up and full of people. It was a delicious theatre-décor. Outside the locked gates at the entrance to the drive is the everyday world which has somehow ceased to be relevant.[12]

Sir Charles enjoyed the 'absolutely irresistible sense of enjoyment' that emanated from his seventy-two-year-old hostess:

After dinner we had songs and dancing and marching up and down, and I shall never forget this dynamic little figure, covered in jewels, hair tumbled, twirling round, stamping, leading the column of guests – out of one door, in at another – arms up in Highland attitudes, the rest of the party wilting before such an insatiable appetite for fun. Bernard Ballantrae* played the piano and I sang bits of *Stenka Razin*† and *Waltzing Matilda* and we all got noisy and overexcited and the ex-bish of New York began to lose his collar.[13]

The 'ex-bish' was the same Horace Donegan who had made friends with the Queen Mother on her 1954 visit to New York. He was invited every year for a quarter of a century but still became decidedly jumpy if his dates were not in the diary by the end of January. He then planned his

* Lord Ballantrae, KT (1911–1980) (formerly Sir Bernard Fergusson). Powerfully-built brigadier with moustache and eyeglass. Served in the Black Watch and was Governor-General of New Zealand 1962–7. The Queen Mother stayed with his parents when she collapsed in New Zealand in 1927.
† *Stenka Razin*, symphonic poem by Glazunov, based on the tale of a lurid seventeenth-century pirate of the Volga.

trip to London with Royal Lodge in the middle, telling friends in the first week where he was destined, and in the second from where he had just come.*

One of the Bishop's duties was to deliver the sermon at the chapel in the park, where the Queen and Queen Mother worshipped. Wisely he stuck to safe themes (the need for God's spirit in human affairs) and delivered these in an off-pat manner. After some years the Queen Mother tired of this exercise: 'We put an end to that!'[14]

In New York the gossiping community liked to joke that the Queen Mother was in love with the urbane Bishop, which was humorous nonsense. One of the problems of having him in the house was his fondness for dry martinis which left him less than articulate at dinner. In 1975 the Queen Mother took Sir Martin Gilliat aside and told him that 'on pain of dismissal' he was not to allow the American prelate more than one drink before dinner. However, the Bishop managed to get his hands on a second martini with the result that, when they gathered at the table, he lost his presence of mind and could not say grace. 'We all stood in silence for what seemed an age while the Bishop composed his thoughts,' noted Sir Charles Johnston.[15]

Sir Martin confessed afterwards that these were agonising moments. His past life flashed before him: 'Everything I did at Ludgrove, the whole of Eton, I was halfway through Sandhurst . . .', when, mercifully, the Bishop intoned: 'For Her Majesty's kindness in bringing us together in this place, for Thy bounty, O Lord . . .'[16] On later visits Sir Martin could be heard saying to him 'in his sardonic *pince-sans-rire* voice': 'Have another drink, Bishop. It will steady you for the Grace.'†[17]

Sandringham

The Queen Mother's hospitality was not the most relaxing. She was fond of guests reading aloud, or singing if they had the voice for it. There was the memorable occasion at Sandringham when she persuaded the lame Lord Chancellor, Lord Hailsham of St Marylebone, to cast aside his sticks and accompany her in a dance under the direction of Sir Frederick Ashton. There were charades and Martin Gilliat admitted to eager reporters that, yes, he had seen 'a number of jigsaw puzzles in various stages of completion'.[18]

---

* When Peter Coats, a social bachelor and inveterate weekender, received an invitation to Royal Lodge in 1979, he was 'like a dog with two tails; making people guess where he spent the weekend, he helps them eagerly to make sure they guess right' (Sir Charles Johnston diary).
† A later Royal Lodge joke was that his grace should have been 'Benedicat Benedictine'.

At the end of July Queen Elizabeth would spend the weekend at Sandringham, during which she would often entertain her French hosts from the early summer. Johnny Lucinge and Ruth Fermoy were key figures during these four days, and the Prince of Wales joined them. They attended events at the King's Lynn Festival, the Sandringham Flower Show, and invariably took a picnic of delicious food to a Swiss chalet near the beach.

Their post-prandial stroll took them close to naturist territory, some of the nudes scattering at the arrival of the royal party, others remaining distractingly in place. The Queen Mother was much entertained by the idea of the nudes.

Johnny Lucinge recalled an evening in 1988 when Ruth Fermoy played the piano and the Queen Mother and Ashton danced together:

> Freddy Ashton, dancer and choreographer, rose, took Her Majesty's hand and began a *pas de ballet* with her. He was eighty-four, she was eighty-eight, and they were grace itself. They bowed to each other at the end, and in our turn we all danced waltzes, tangoes, and *paso dobles*. If anyone had seen us, they would have scarcely believed this pastime of respectable old-timers.[19]

Birkhall and the Castle of Mey

Birkhall was reserved for May and then again September and October, guests including those who liked to fish, shoot grouse at Corndavon or shoot at Invercauld. Jean Wills, a regular guest at Birkhall, recalled a woman fishing opposite Queen Elizabeth who on noticing the royal presence curtseyed in the river, despite her waders filling with water. Royal Lodge guests were not necessarily invited to Birkhall, nor were Birkhall guests asked to the Castle of Mey. Lady Grimthorpe, a long-standing lady-in-waiting, was never invited to the Castle of Mey, which she minded.

Ted Hughes was invited to Birkhall. The Queen Mother discovered him in 1985, and asked Charles Johnston about his poems at a lunch given by Mary, Duchess of Roxburghe. Johnston resisted discussing the poems but described him as 'a fine-looking man, like Tennyson without a beard'.[20] The Queen Mother decided to invite Hughes to lunch. This was a success and he was soon a regular guest in Scotland.

He often read poetry to the guests and on 16 August 1997 was responsible for the last message signalled to the Royal Yacht *Britannia* as she sailed from Scrabster. Every summer the Queen and her guests paid a visit to the Castle of Mey from the Royal Yacht, as they ended their

Western Isles cruise, and headed to Aberdeen for the long summer holiday at Balmoral. The Queen Mother's equerry, Ashe Windham, recalled:

> It was the tradition that the local Coastguard would turn up at Mey with all the time-expired pyrotechnics from the whole of the North of Scotland which would then be let off with a terrific series of bangs and bright maroon flares in front of the Castle. The pyrotechnic response from *Britannia* and her escorting frigate was usually rather less memorable consisting of a few old Verey lights!
>
> The Mey party would then ask the Coastguard to transmit a poem, which we had written for the occasion, via their radio to the Queen on board *Britannia*. The Queen's Party would then reply in like vein . . . On this sad occasion we thought that it would be appropriate to mark the event and Ted, being a good friend of Her Majesty's and Poet Laureate at the time, was asked to write a few lines. The resulting poem caused no little surprise on board the Royal Yacht as our poetry writing skills had been diminished some-what by the death in 1993 of Sir Martin Gilliat.[21]

This was the poem sent:

> 'Farewell to *Britannia*'
> Farewell to you, *Britannia*, once more
> So many summers you have blessed this shore
> And blessed the Castle of Mey.
> This summer let us say
> Heartier farewells than ever before
> As you go on your way
>
> You go, but you go, deeper than ever
> Into our hearts this year
> With all our memories of you, so happy and dear
> Whichever course your Captain takes, you steer
> Into this haven of all our hearts, and here
> You shall be anchored forever.[22]

At the Castle of Mey the Queen Mother loved the evening skies and would lead guests from the dining-room table to admire a special one. She often sat outside watching the changing scene and sometimes the Northern Lights.

At Mey she entertained equerries past and present, overseen either by Sir Ralph Anstruther, when they were all obliged to wear black tie at dinner, or by Sir Martin Gilliat, whose attitude was more casual. Gilliat liked to take the young men on expeditions to Orkney where it became a tradition to return with ever more absurd souvenirs, which then became features of the castle – a ceramic drunk, several furry Viking bottle openers and a tartan Loch Ness monster, which found a permanent home above the drawing-room tapestry, placed there during a nocturnal revel.

The Queen Mother liked to make the parties fun. She would summon the men from post-prandial port by coming to the door and singing: 'Why are we waiting?' After one dinner she bade the ladies of the party hide with her behind a curtain. Sir Martin strode into the deserted drawing room and said: 'Thank God. They've fucked off to bed.' He got a nasty shock.

With so many youngsters confined in the limited space of a small castle, it was inevitable that high jinks would ensue. One morning the Queen Mother mentioned to Reg Wilcock that she had been 'menaced by a shadowy figure wielding a soda siphon' during the night. Two former equerries, Ian Farquhar and Jeremy Mainwaring-Burton, had hidden Ashe Windham's sheets. The escapades got out of hand and ended with a chase down the corridor, siphons to the fore.

Later Farquhar and Mainwaring-Burton rushed into Windham's room, but as he had no pyjamas on he was reluctant to get out of bed. Mainwaring-Burton emptied a bottle of Dettol over him. Windham jumped up and knocked him flat out. Farquhar said he had not seen such bad behaviour since Valentine Cecil* had shot a seal, while staying at Mey, after which he was never invited again.[23]

The next morning Windham drove the guests to Wick airport. When he returned, Reginald was waiting for him. He informed him that matters had gone too far and he would be reporting his exploits to Lady Fermoy. Windham spent an agonising day alone at the castle and was finally confronted by the Queen Mother who concluded that the guests had clearly enjoyed themselves, but added: 'It was rather like the Blitz!'[24] He atoned for his crime by going to the Caithness Glass Factory and buying some glass for Reg and other members of staff.

Despite these antics, Ashe Windham remained a favoured guest and in June 1996 the Queen Mother appointed him Chairman of the Trustees when she turned the Castle of Mey into a Trust. It was Ashe Windham who invited me to Mey in August 1998,† when I was entertained to lunch by the Queen Mother.

* Lord Valentine Cecil (b. 1952), son of 6th Marquess of Salisbury. Page of Honour to the Queen Mother 1966–7.
† I was invited to talk to the Trustees about future plans for opening the Castle of Mey to the public. I was only present during a small part of their longer meeting.

I had the chance to witness the various levels of welcome extended to guests, from the friendly equerry, Will de Rouet, who took me on tour of the castle and gardens and up the tower to see the view to Orkney, from the ladies-in-waiting (one was leaving to be replaced by Lady Penn), to William Tallon, first spotted laying the table in a bright turquoise vest, later concealed by his uniform. As has been seen, he often made a guest feel welcome by placing an object of particular interest on the table where they would sit. In my case it was a souvenir ashtray with the Queen Mother's head on it, and the wrong Coronation date – 2 October 1937. The Queen Mother had found this and it had amused her, so she bought it.

I was in the drawing room with the house party. At 12.30 the Queen Mother came in, alert, walking with a stick, wearing her habitual Scottish outfit, a pale blue woollen suit with tartan lapels. She was then ninety-eight, a tiny figure, but she never missed a nuance in the conversation. The Trustees were still in their meeting downstairs. 'They've been down there for three hours. What can they be talking about? I should hate it!' said the Queen Mother. She asked me if I had been up the tower. I said yes. 'Bad luck!' she said, stirring her drink with her finger.

Lunch was served in the dining room, due to the presence of the Trustees. Normally the house party would picnic somewhere. Oeufs Drumkilbo (egg and prawns) were followed by lamb with roast potatoes and vegetables, and a rich roly-poly pudding with golden syrup, and then cheese and coffee. White wine, claret and finally port were served, and, as expected, glasses never remained empty for long. Towards the end of lunch, the sun came round and streamed in through a window directly on to the Queen Mother at the head of the table. She was expecting it, and had a pair of commendably fashionable dark glasses which she put on for the last few minutes of lunch.

In this short of glimpse of life at the Castle of Mey I concluded that it was a happy set-up and the guests were enjoying themselves. The routine of meals, teas, drinks and dinners, followed by chocolates circulating, and reruns of *Dad's Army* might be an exacting one, but as ever the good spirit of the party emanated from the lively hostess, ably supported by her Household and staff.

At Birkhall too there were house parties, with guests of an older generation casting off the years and having fun. In the last year, 2001, a group staged a short enactment of *Dad's Army* for the amusement of the Queen Mother. It was written by Sir John Johnston. Captain Mainwaring was played by Sir Michael Oswald, Sergeant Wilson by Sir John, Corporal Jones by Peter Campbell, Private Fraser by Sir Angus Ogilvy and Private

Walker by Sir Alastair Aird. The play was spiced with well-remembered lines from the series:

> Captain Mainwaring: 'Oh my God. Do you realise what you've done Jones? You landed back in England and blew up one of *our* guns. Corporal Jones: 'Oh did I? I'm ever so sorry, Captain Mainwaring . . .'[25]

Annual lunches and dinners were given for the Queen Mother which continued until the host or hostess either died or became too infirm to entertain. There was therefore an ever-diminishing rota of such occasions. The Queen Mother loved to go out, preferring a lunch to a dinner, but there were certain hazards as these occasions were less easy to control when not in one of her residences.

One problem was the food. On 14 November 1968, she attended the Grand Day Dinner at Gray's Inn, and, not being hungry, surreptitiously placed her partridge on the plate of her host, Sir Dingle Foot, Treasurer of the Inn. He ate the brace.[26] When the Queen Mother dined with Lady Doris Vyner, she was prevailed upon to say a word to the kitchen after dinner. She popped her head round the door: 'How lovely to be a cook!'[27]

Cecil Beaton

On 10 April 1968 the Queen Mother lunched with Cecil Beaton, the second such occasion. A detective came to do a reconnoitre the day before and the police placed a 'No Parking' sign outside 8 Pelham Place. Beaton invited Lady Diana Cooper, Leo d'Erlanger, Sir John (Jakie) Astor, Christian, Lady Hesketh, the actress Irene Worth and Roy Strong, then Director of the National Portrait Gallery, in a psychedelic tie.

During lunch Diana Cooper told a story of how Ava, Lady Waverley had been dis-invited from staying with Harold Macmillan, known to Lady Diana as 'The Horse'. Beaton recorded:

> The tale was so well told that the QM laughed from the gut. The fact that Macmillan was continually referred to as 'The Horse' (reason unknown) added to her enjoyment. The little fat face crinkled except for two apples in the centre of the cheeks. These remained as round and perfect as always.*[28]

---

* A full account of this luncheon appears in *Beaton in the Sixties*, pp. 230–32.

Following these occasions, the host or hostess never failed to receive a handwritten thank-you letter on the Queen Mother's personal grey-blue writing paper, which had her 'ER' cipher on the left and was either blank or had the address of one of her houses on the right. The words spread over several pages in her generous hand. On this occasion she thanked Cecil Beaton for his delightful luncheon party, the 'charming' house and the 'charming' company:

> I adored Diana's story about Ava & Harold – she gave it such deli-cate & naughty point – And how beautiful she is!
> I am poring over that glorious magazine that you lent me. I fear my dear *Tatler* can't really compete!

And then she thanked him once more for his 'charming' hospitality.[29]

Beaton was a guest when Patricia Hambleden entertained the Queen Mother for lunch in March 1970 before she opened a nearby Women's Institute in Henley-on-Thames. He observed 'the old-fashioned car' arrive with 'a pink cushiony cloud in it'. After lunch the Queen Mother made even the signing of the visitors' book an occasion:

> When she sat with pen in hand, she did an imitation of a Helen Hokinson museum lady and the adept appearance was hilarious. Later Mary [Pembroke] told me that sometimes when playing bridge, the Queen [Mother] has taken a strip of the brown paper from a chocolate box and has done an imitation of an old general telling who should play when and what cards.
> The two ladies went off in the big car (the pink costume would make its usual great effect) and in the car Patricia would be amused by a running commentary, 'That's a good one. Look at that fat pig! Oh I say!'[30]

Of some of the hostesses to the Queen Mother I had personal experience.

Maureen Dufferin

One stalwart entertainer was Maureen, Marchioness of Dufferin and Ava, one of the many Guinnesses who had peopled the world of the 'Bright Young Things' in the 1920s. She lived in an enormous house, 4 Hans Crescent – in fact, several houses joined together. These rooms came alive intermittently for fairs in aid of Maureen's Oasthouses for Arthritics, but never more so than for her annual dinner for the Queen Mother, an event that took root in the 1950s and continued until 1994.

How much the Queen Mother looked forward to these dinners is questionable. Lady Dufferin would write to her inviting her to dine in the spring, which gave her as much scope as little chance of escape. Queen Elizabeth may have had a packed diary, but could not claim an evening engagement every day for four months. Sometimes she hesitated before committing herself, keeping her hostess on tenterhooks. This was a game played between them, recognised by both parties, but never acknowledged. Lady Dufferin knew that the Queen Mother did not want to come, but she was equally determined that she would. Letters were sent in profusion to Clarence House, listing the guests, yet the Queen Mother often found that they were not presented by name, and she feared that she would not know anyone. In the end she always capitulated and went to the dinner.

The Queen Mother would arrive with a lady-in-waiting, frequently Lady Jean Rankin, or latterly the Duke and Duchess of Grafton, to find a varied list of guests, a mixture of the exceptional with those more steady figures who were such an integral part of any hostess's life, and who were her close friends seen regularly throughout the year. The large dining room at Hans Crescent would seat twenty, Maureen Dufferin at one end of the long table, Queen Elizabeth at the other.

Lady Dufferin knew that at a certain point she would have to catch the Queen Mother's eye to get her approval for the ladies to retire. She also knew that the Queen Mother would feign not to notice until almost the point of agony. After dinner, another twenty guests would arrive from dinner parties elsewhere, and Lady Dufferin would take the chosen ones up to the Queen Mother in turn for five minutes or so.

One advantage of entertaining the Queen Mother was that almost everybody considered it a fabulous invitation, a gala night out, and, as the years went by, this was one of the last bastions of pre-war style entertaining, as the Queen Mother recognised, her habitual refrain on such occasions being how rare it was these days to go out to a 'real dinner party'. Lady Dufferin would gather figures such as the Duke and Duchess of Northumberland, Lord and Lady Home of the Hirsel, the Earl and Countess of Longford and Norman St John Stevas, and figures from the arts such as Sir Frederick Ashton, and distinguished stage actors Sir Alec Guinness, Evelyn Laye and Dorothy Dickson. Close friends of the Queen Mother such as Zara Cazalet, widow of her trainer, Peter Cazalet, were also there.

At a dinner in the 1960s, the Queen Mother was sitting next to Alec

Guinness when the lights fused and they were plunged into darkness. 'Tap once if you are all right, Ma'am, and twice if you are not,' suggested the actor. He was rewarded with a typical Queen Mother response: Tap – tap – tap.

These dinners were not without incident. In the years that I attended them (between 1984 and 1994),* I recall Lord John Manners having enjoyed the fine wines a little too freely, spontaneously kneeling beside the Queen Mother to tell her how exciting it had been to emerge from a nightclub in the middle of the Blitz to see the sky alight with Hitler's devilry. Having worked hard during the war, her finest hour, the Queen Mother listened to this dissertation with eyebrows raised in horror.

On another evening Lady Dufferin presented her grandson, who sprang forward and kissed the Queen Mother on the cheek. Faces fell and I registered private concern for the young man's eventual inheritance, but the Queen Mother passed it off as the greatest fun, anaesthetising a potentially ugly moment. The grandson later commented: 'She looked as though she needed a kiss!'

As the hostess got older, and the 'Bright Young' friends of yesteryear took to their sticks, so the dinners took on a valiant quality. 'Harold Macmillan used to say to me "Enjoy it while you can",' said Lord Home as he made an unsteady descent into the dining room on his stick. 'I'm just beginning to realise what he meant.' On the same evening, his wife and the actress Evelyn Laye, then nearly ninety, arrived with the back of their dresses undone and asked to be buttoned up before they went upstairs.[31]

After dinner Lady Dufferin took the Queen Mother upstairs but one year she treated her to a video of herself which went on so long that the Queen Mother cut this part of the evening out in future. Nor would Lady Dufferin let her go when she wanted to. From the armchair, somewhat after 11 p.m., the Queen Mother told me: 'Now, I really must be going,' which message I duly relayed to my hostess. 'She can't!' said Maureen indignantly, and marshalled more guests for presentation.

Lady Dufferin spent most of the year between each dinner in quest of a pair of star guests for the Queen Mother's left and right at dinner, producing figures such as Edward Fox and Barry Humphries. Twiggy

---

* For many years Maureen's photographs of these evenings had been taken by a waiter and were often out of focus. I offered to bring my camera in 1988, with better results, which I made sure reached my hostess early the next morning. This had the happy result that I was co-opted on to the list for dinner as a permanent fixture. It became established practice that I would go downstairs and take a posed 'snap' of the Queen Mother with Maureen before she went home. One year Maureen's maid could be spotted in one of the photos peering round a door at the royal party. Trouble ensued.

and Richard Branson also appeared, so the evenings were varied and memorable. In 1992 the Queen Mother thanked Lady Dufferin: 'You do give the most enjoyable and the most glorious dinner parties to be seen in London today! Everyone puts on their best frocks, men and women alike, and your lucky guests spend a truly happy evening, thanks to their kind and brilliant hostess.'[32]

In January 1997 Maureen celebrated her ninetieth birthday with a ball at Claridge's, to which she invited the Queen Mother. Agonising weeks passed without an answer until Lord St John of Fawsley* had his habitual pre-Christmas lunch for the Queen Mother. Lady Dufferin was a guest. Only then did the Queen Mother say she was looking forward to the party.

Guests were bidden to wear tiaras, but the Queen Mother refused to do this. Out of five nonagenarians present, the Queen Mother was the only one to dance – with Ned Ryan, a friend of Princess Margaret's. She was then ninety-six.

Only once was Maureen Dufferin invited back to Clarence House. She died in 1998 and it was not by oversight that the Queen Mother was not represented at her memorial service.†

Lady Diana Cooper

Lady Diana Cooper fared better. When she died, the Queen Mother sent flowers to her funeral at Belvoir, was represented by Angus Ogilvy at her memorial service and attended a charity event in her memory.

In later life Diana Cooper gave two parties a year, a lunch for Harold Macmillan and either a lunch or dinner for the Queen Mother. Before one such lunch in March 1981 Lady Diana was poised in an elegant black dress with a small veil on her head with black velvet ribbons, silhouetted by the door to her drawing room, pouring an entire bottle of Gordon's gin into some grapefruit juice in order to create a drink known as 'the House Poison'. Living in Warwick Avenue, she would invite her Little Venice neighbours for a drink before lunch and they would slide out just before the eight or ten guests sat down to lunch.‡

Lady Diana's approach to these occasions was as original as ever. 'The Queen Mother comes to lunch with me once a year,' she said, 'which is very nice for me – and very nice for her!'[33] At the 1981 lunch the Queen Mother wore her velvet coat of a green-turquoise colour and matching

---

* Norman St John Stevas was ennobled as Lord St John of Fawsley in 1987.
† However, she spoke warmly of Maureen at the Castle of Mey that August.
‡ In 1981 I was invited to be an honorary neighbour.

hat. Presently she removed it to reveal the dress in the frontispiece of Godfrey Talbot's 1978 biography of her.

I had lately written a book in advance of the Royal Wedding. I asked Diana particularly not to mention this as it embarrassed me. Diana led me by the arm and presented me: 'This is my great friend Hugo Vickers, who's writing the life of Cecil.' So we began on that subject. She was particularly interested in Beaton's diaries. 'How fortunate that he kept them all. Do you think it's a help to know your subject?' Then Diana continued: 'Tell Her Majesty about your latest project'.

'Ma'am, I'm afraid it's a Royal Wedding Book'.

'You must have worked very hard . . . Does it have lots of pictures? That's what people seem to like? . . . You young people pack so much into your lives – you at 16, 18 . . .' (I was then nearly thirty, but felt light of foot – blessed with eternal youth).

We spoke again of Cecil Beaton. 'What fun he was,' she said and she told me about the photographs he had taken of Buckingham Palace – 'the funny baths – people today have no idea how we lived'. But later she added: 'Of course there was another side to him. Pins going in . . . here . . . there.' She gestured to right and left.

Then it was the turn of the veteran artist Adrian Daintrey. He paid her some compliment and in a vague way went on: 'I always notice women's clothes.' The Queen Mother was kind to him: 'That's rather marvellous – To be encouraged.'[34]

To describe Diana's dinner at Warwick Avenue in April 1982, I can do no better than quote my own diary as a source, as, in this book, I have so often relied on the diaries of others:

> I was terrified I'd fall asleep and miss the Queen Mother. But I didn't. I set off in good time and waited until I saw the Berkeleys go in (Sir Lennox in a suit) and then Edward Fox and Joanna David go past. John Julius [Norwich] was greeting everyone at the door. Inside I found Kitty Farrell,* who has now become my friend: 'Don't be so nervous, Hugo,' she said as I spotted the Queen Mother in pink by the fireplace and began to retreat to the dining room part by the screen.
>
> Diana was in a long dress, given her by the Aga Khan's sister-in-law. The others in the room were Artemis [Cooper], Charles Farrell, Anne Norwich, Lord Head, Paul-Louis Weiller, Nicky Haslam and boyfriend, Cavan O'Brien, Father John Foster, 'The

---

* Lady Katharine Farrell (b. 1922), Paget niece of Lady Diana Cooper.

Last Attachment' [Nigel Ryan], Virginia Ashcombe, Charles Ritchie* and his wife and one or two others – anyway, a select group, most of whom I know.

To begin with I stayed by the dining-room table. Kitty sat me down with her and we had a long talk. Then she said it was time to take me over to the Queen Mother. In the meantime everyone who'd been with the Queen Mother came running back to relay their story. Virginia Ashcombe had said something to her about a friend and the Queen Mother had described this person as 'a good egg'. 'Talking about good eggs, Ma'am,' said Virginia, 'I do like your necklace.' The Queen Mother was wearing beautiful rubies in clusters of diamonds. They were vast and *real* (obviously) – they were the gift of a Maharajah to Queen Victoria. Father John Foster said that just *one* would permit him to buy a nice house in the country to which he could retire happily.

Over I went. Kitty would have to say: 'He also writes books about the Royal Family,' which received a polite frown, but was saved quickly by Diana saying: 'Ma'am, you know Hugo, you met here before.' So the Queen Mother beckoned me to sit beside her by patting the little stool.

She looked wonderful in a long pink dress with jewels sewn into it. It was tight fitting and then very full – the huge rubies were magnificent (I remember Caroline [Lowell] saying that at Maureen Dufferin's, St John Stevas couldn't take his eyes off them). I suppose the Queen Mother looked about 70, not nearly 82.

We started on Cecil and the Queen Mother asked: 'Was he more of a giver or a taker in life, do you think? . . . I think more of a giver – probably – really.'

Also beside her sat Cavan with Nicky on the floor. There was a long discussion about the artist Edward Seago. The Queen Mother said that she had been asked by the Tate to lend a picture and had offered one of his. They didn't want it. 'So I said – well – then I might not lend anything. Finally they took an English landscape, a large one. Really! Horrid snobs!'

Nicky discussed his giving up smoking in a somewhat indelicate way. The Queen Mother had never smoked. Nicky also told her of the spinal cancer of Rory McEwen. 'Sobering note,' he said, prejudicing the Queen Mother's reaction. 'Oh! I'm sure he'll *pull* through and get better. He has such *great* courage.'

---

* Charles Ritchie (1906–95), Canadian High Commissioner in London 1967–71, author of five books called 'the Undiplomatic Diaries'.

'I knew you would be sorry and of course he's such a great friend of Princess Margaret.'*

I told her that I'd been to Osborne. 'Oh! I love Osborne (pronounced Osb'n). I can so understand how Queen Victoria spent so much time there. Those lovely blue skies.'

Normally one does about five minutes with the Queen Mother. But John Julius chose this moment to sing his French ballads. So I stayed nearer forty minutes. At the end of each song, the Queen Mother would say 'Enchanting' or 'Wasn't that marvellous?' To which one struggles to find something other than 'Absolutely, Ma'am'. I think she was having a good time though. Occasionally she sipped her drink, but not often. Occasionally, nearer the end of the evening, she tried a surreptitious look at the clock as any of us might have done.

At one point while John Julius was singing, Diana called out 'No!' He'd got it wrong. It would have passed over our heads. Instead we all laughed but it was a bit embarrassing. Then John Julius and Anne sang a duet – a love duet – and you'd have thought no more faithful and loving couple sat side by side after thirty years of marriage.†

Nicky went on to ask the Queen Mother if she might like to 'whiz down and see the garden'. Perhaps she will. They have John Fowler's house. Finally at 11.30 the Queen Mother thought she should go so I swapped places with Kitty who could better master-mind the situation. They are great friends and they kiss on parting. So too Diana who then sank in agonized curtsey which she later imitated to me to express the pain of the act.

The room groaned as Paul-Louis‡ sidled forward. Earlier he had monopolized the Queen Mother and by his blindness approached so close that gradually she had been pushed almost into the grate. Kitty had frog-marched him away and the Queen Mother had said 'Thank you'. Now he moved in for the kill. 'Majesté,' he said, kissing her hand. 'Voulez-vous (Artemis said he actually said 'veux-tu') diner avec moi quand vous venez à Paris?'

I then witnessed a famous Queen Mother gesture. Up went the forefinger of the right hand, and with an angelic smile she said: 'Ah! Now I shall have to look in my book'. To me that meant: '*No!*'

---

* Rory McEwen jumped to his death on a train line on 16 October that year.
† They were divorced three years later.
‡ Paul-Louis Weiller (1893–1993), millionaire industrialist, with many homes in France, and a great lover of royalty. The irony of this evening was that, despite producing everything from food to flowers to wine, he was not invited to dine. Like me, he came in afterwards.

Smiling to all, she stopped particularly at Charles Ritchie. Earlier in the evening he had said how much he wished she would visit Nova Scotia again. 'Dear Nova Scotia,' she said and John Julius relayed this widely: 'Just as Charlotte Bonham Carter might say: Dear Wales . . .'

After the departure there was general relaxation. Diana hugged Paul Louis who is 88 and thanked him. He had produced champagne [Pol Roger 1975], 'whispered' wine, foie gras for twenty, flowers of great price from Fortnum's and so on. 'C'est un homme riche et c'est le seul homme riche que je connais qui est génereux,' said Diana, planting a big kiss on him.[35]

The Queen Mother came to more than one charity event for Diana Cooper. One was a poetry reading in St James's Palace for *People and Places*. 'I've got the Queen Mother, hook, line and I hope not sink 'er,' Diana announced one day.[36] After Diana died, the Queen Mother came to another such evening in her memory, again at St James's Palace. Of this, I was the Chairman.

Once again Paul-Louis Weiller was munificent, paying for the band of the Irish Guards that played and taking a table. In the morning he telephoned me to ask how to address the Queen Mother. 'Do I call her Majesté? Do I say: How do you do?' I suggested he might say 'Good evening' or 'How do you do?' 'Ah, I say: Good evening, how do you do? Majesté?'

On this evening it was possible to observe some of the travails faced by the Queen Mother on a charity evening with a social element attached. She arrived in a green sparkly evening dress, with a Star of India-style brooch and the necklace of huge pearls she sometimes wore. She wore high-heeled satin sandals. Lady Cullen of Ashbourne, involved with the charity, tried to persuade her to lunch at Edgecote again. 'Always such a treat!' said the Queen Mother, which sounded like another 'no'. One of the ardent and admittedly generous charity supporters, Mrs Anne Wall,* latched on to the informal procession escorting the Queen Mother in to the performance. Mrs Wall's arm was in a sling and in a theatrically wounded voice she told the Queen Mother: 'I'd only have turned out for you, Ma'am!'†

Sir John Gielgud introduced the programme and John Julius Norwich and Artemis Cooper read extracts from Duff and Diana Cooper's letters.

---

* Not to be confused with the Queen's former Assistant Press Secretary Anne Hawkins, who married Commander Michael Wall.
† Yuk!

Afterwards the Queen Mother said: 'The letters brought a lump to my throat. Young people today find it so hard to understand what it was like living through the war.'

Then various charity supporters were presented. One of them, 'a bore in life', now used 'his once in a lifetime opportunity to bore the Queen Mother. He got a great deal of "boring" in before he finally gave way.' Paul-Louis Weiller came up: 'I find it so hard to find the words in English to say what is in my heart . . .' (In fact he spoke faultless English.)

'Oh, mais on peut parler français,' said the Queen Mother. By the next day he had adjusted this story: 'She is very kind. She always speaks French specially for me.' This had been manipulated by him.

At the end of the evening I escorted the Queen Mother through the room of diners, through the door that leads to Clarence House and down the stairs to the Horse Corridor. I concluded: 'I suppose it's fair to say that the first genuine response to the Queen Mother occurred at this point. A fat old Corgi waddled out to greet her. I gave her back the programme she had consigned to my care and that was that.'[37]

Sir Charles Johnston

It was Lady Home* who alerted Sir Charles and Lady Johnston to the fact that people were often nervous of inviting the Queen Mother, and that, in consequence, there were times when she sat alone in front of her television. Sir Charles took the hint. He was in that curious position of being married to Princess Natasha Bagration, a cousin of Princess Marina, Duchess of Kent, so that when the Queen Mother wrote to them, she addressed them as 'Dearest Natasha and Sir Charles'.

In February 1983 the Queen Mother lunched with Sir Charles at Ennismore Gardens. Clive James was one of the guests. 'I greatly enjoyed meeting Mr James (the first Socialist Democrat that I have actually met!)', wrote the Queen Mother, 'and I *do* hope that I was not too outspoken about that particular party! One can't help feeling a bit uncertain about people who leave the good old Labour party to invent a "Social" (what's that) "Democratic" (equally mysterious) party – perhaps rather up a Don's street!!'[38]

With Sir Charles she enjoyed musing on the characters of literature: 'I was fascinated by Ammian . . . His dislike of "arrogant Grandees" is splendid. "When you come up to greet them, they lean out their heads to one side, for you to kiss them" is so like some people one knows today!'[39]

* Elizabeth Home (1909–90), daughter of Cyril Alington, wife of the former Prime Minister, Lord Home of the Hirsel, KT.

Woodrow Wyatt

There were, of course, many and varied hosts and hostesses who entertained the Queen Mother. The choice of these is by definition selective. Woodrow Wyatt left numerous accounts of these in his diaries to be published after his death, the more ironical since he had berated A. N. Wilson for revealing a conversation with the Queen Mother in print, which became something of a *cause célèbre* at the time of her ninetieth birthday.

Wyatt's daughter hinted that her father and the Queen Mother enjoyed a 'conspiratorial relationship'.[40] Others have suggested that the Queen Mother used him as a conduit to release information into the world. She might confide in him rather secretly that the Queen and Mrs Thatcher got on much better than was generally supposed. She was confident that he would not be able to resist spreading this about by word of mouth or column. What she did not perhaps anticipate, especially after the A.N. Wilson saga, was that he would consign all her supposed confidences to his diaries, and instruct that they be published, true or false, after his death.

Sir Michael Duff

An unusual party was that given for Sir Michael Duff's seventieth birthday on 3 May 1977. 'Sporting old Queen Mummy is buzzing from Clarence House *hoping* to see you,' wrote Sir Michael to Cecil Beaton.[41] The party was held at 2 Tregunter Road, the home of Patricia Hambleden's younger daughter, Kate Townend.

Sir Michael kept shouting: 'More red wine for Her Majesty', as one of the guests, Robert Heber Percy,* 'toppled off his chair on to the floor'. At this the Queen Mother turned to Sir Sacheverell Sitwell and said: 'What I always say is, isn't it lovely to be asked to a party!'[42]

---

* Robert Heber Percy (1911–87), squire of Faringdon, which he had inherited from Lord Berners. Known as 'Mad Boy'.

35

Sporting Life

'I think the world of her. Every East Ender does'
– a wartime survivor

The Royal Wedding summer had been as busy as ever for the octogenarian Queen Mother. She accepted the Freedom of Windsor, went to the Cup Final, took Lord High Admiral's orders at Dartmouth and visited Ottawa and Ontario in July. Despite the wedding Sir Martin Gilliat considered the Canadian visit the highlight of 1981. The Canadians were 'friendly, kind, enthusiastic people'. As ever, the Queen Mother was the star:

> On a tour Queen Elizabeth for all 4 score years + one is so dynamic and outgiving – combining such a youthful charm and beauty with so much wisdom and experience. The same applies in this country, but somehow an overseas visit really brings it out.[1]

Dame Frances Campbell-Preston confirmed this:

> It was always said that they welcomed any star in Canada, and that Joan Collins would get just the same reception. But as these tours continued, the crowds for the Queen Mother got bigger and bigger. One Canadian High Commissioner told me that the loyalty of Canadians was a lot personal to her, that these visits made all the difference to Canada and that the reason they kept the monarchy was largely due to them. There was none of the dissent that was prevalent in Australia or New Zealand.'*[2]

There was no doubt that Canada held a special place in Queen Elizabeth's heart. In 1976 she said of the African boycott of the Olympic

---

* Dame Frances recalled a conversation between Joyce Grenfell and Lady Astor in August 1940, published in the letters to her mother: 'Aunt N. has a good story about a Canadian she met in the street. She asked him why he'd come over to fight. Was it for England? No. For freedom? No. Did he hate the Nazis? Not particularly. Then why had he come? Because he saw the Queen in Canada last summer [1939] and by golly he'd come and fight for her'. [James Roose–Evans (ed.), *Joyce Grenfell – Darling Ma* (Hodder & Stoughton, 1988), p. 159.]

Games in Montreal: 'Oh those poor *blackamoors*, they've been practising so hard.'[3] Norman St John Stevas then asked the Queen Mother whether she preferred Canada or Australia. She was quick to reply: 'How could I *possibly* say? They're both so *wonderful!*'[4]

The pattern of engagements continued with visits to Omagh and Paris. On 21 June 1982 she was delighted to become a great-grandmother when Prince William* was born, giving the House of Windsor a male heir in the second generation.

The Queen Mother still flew about Britain by helicopter. On her way to Ramsgate for Lord Warden duties that summer, her helicopter developed a fault and had to land on the polo ground at Smith's Lawn. 'The wretched little thing has broken down,' said the Queen Mother. 'Oh well it's a lovely day for it.' She drove to Heathrow and was flown to Kent in an Andover of the Queen's Flight.[5]

A new feature of the Queen Mother's life in the 1980s was the occasional emergency trip to hospital. The first fishbone incident occurred at Royal Lodge on Sunday 21 November 1982. At dinner a fishbone became lodged deep in her throat. She tried to make little of it, but Princess Margaret took control and at 1.20 a.m. accompanied her mother to King Edward VII Hospital for Officers in London, where it was removed in an operation at 3 a.m. Queen Elizabeth left the hospital the following Tuesday afternoon, thanking well-wishers in a whisper, and was presently back in her routine.

In August 1986 there was a second fishbone incident. Her former equerry, Ashe Windham, had been present at the first fishbone dinner. This time he caught four trout in Loch Losgann. Aware of the dangers, he had taken special care in filleting them, or so he thought. 'The sequel,' he wrote, was 'less jolly and almost ended in Reginacide.'[6] The trout were cooked in butter, but at dinner he heard the beginning of some tell-tale coughs and experienced a horrible sensation of *déjà vu*.

The Queen Mother played it down as usual, but the surgeon was summoned from *Britannia*, and the next day, on the insistence of the Queen, the Queen Mother made a 130-mile flight by helicopter from the Castle of Mey to Aberdeen Royal Infirmary (which the Yorks had opened in such controversy in 1936). This time the bone had gone, and no operation was needed. Prince Charles visited her and presently she emerged, smiling to the world, the incident forgotten.

Towards the end of this holiday in Scotland, the Queen Mother was

---

* The Queen Mother was told the name before it was published. *Private Eye* suggested wickedly that Sir Martin 'Each Way' Gilliat had placed a substantial bet on 'William' in a St James's betting shop.

walking near Birkhall when she cut her leg on some heather. The leg did not heal properly. At the Festival of Remembrance at the Royal Albert Hall she was in discomfort and needed a footstool, but she was present at the Remembrance Day Service at the Cenotaph as usual. She then went into King Edward VII Hospital where she remained for several days. Sir Martin Gilliat was overwhelmed with letters due to what he called 'the Queen Mother's slight leg mishap'.[7] When asked if she were better, her laconic Press Secretary, John Griffin, said: 'Yes, otherwise she would not be coming out.'[8] After five days she did.

The Badminton Horse Trials had been a regular feature for many years for the Royal Family, including the Queen Mother. 'Master', the Duke of Beaufort, was almost her exact contemporary, and, as Master of the Horse and being married to Queen Mary's niece, he was one of the Queen's advisers during the early years of the reign. His wife Mary had begun to lose her mind in the early 1980s and once pointed at the Queen Mother, asking 'Who is that woman?' The Duke died aged eighty-three on 5 February 1984 and the Queen Mother, 'splendid in mink tippet down to the ground',[9] joined the Queen, the Prince and Princess of Wales, Princess Anne and Captain Mark Phillips at his funeral at Badminton.

This great hunting figure was extolled in magazines such as *The Field* and *Horse and Hound* as one of the great figures of hunting. He had been in the hunting field the day before he died, and the vicar noticed three foxes sitting on the graves of his father and grandfather at Badminton to herald his approaching demise. 'Thank you Master . . .' was the headline of a eulogistic tribute in *Horse and Hound*.[10] Thus ended another annual excursion.*

As more friends died – Lord Adam Gordon and Olivia Mulholland in 1984, and Katie Seymour in 1985 – the Queen Mother continued 'as active as ever'. Sir Martin Gilliat wrote that she looked at him 'with amazement' when, at seventy-one, he seemed to flag.[11]

The Queen Mother looked stunning in purple velvet and dripping in diamonds when she unveiled a memorial stone to Noël Coward in Westminster Abbey on 28 March. Seated in the congregation, Alastair Forbes attributed her lightness of foot to a win at Sandown the day before.† She looked equally good the same night at a Maureen Dufferin dinner in pale

---

* There was strong condemnation of an attempt by hunt saboteurs to dig up the Duke's body the following Christmas, in order to send his head to Princess Anne at Gatcombe Park. Following this, a substantial edifice was placed as a tomb over his grave in the churchyard of St Michael and All Angels at Badminton.

† Special Cargo had won the Alanbrooke Memorial Handicap Chase.

turquoise and pearl necklace, while two of her bachelor friends could be seen 'all over each other, almost stroking each other's tummies'.[12]

Racing

Only a serving or former officer can enter a horse to run in the Grand Military Gold Cup at Sandown. As colonel of a number of regiments, the Queen Mother was eligible. Likewise the jockeys must be serving officers – or in the Reserve or Territorial Army. The Queen Mother still holds the record of five wins in the Grand Military, having won three times in succession with Special Cargo in 1984, 1985 and 1986,* with Gerald Oxley, a lieutenant in the 13th/18th Royal Hussars (QMO), in the saddle, again in 1990 (the 150th running of the race) with The Argonaut,† who 'sailed home in splendid isolation',[13] and finally in 1996 with Norman Conqueror.

On 28 April 1984, a few weeks after his first Grand Military, Special Cargo, ridden by Kevin Mooney, gave the Queen Mother her greatest racing victory. It was the high point in her long association with National Hunt racing, and she had waited since 1949 to achieve it.

Everything about the 1984 Whitbread Gold Cup was exciting from start to finish. The celebrated former jockey and trainer Fred Winter said: 'That was the greatest race I've ever seen',[14] and John Oaksey, the distinguished racing correspondent of the *Daily Telegraph*, had no hesitation in declaring that the result was 'quite literally the most exciting finish I have ever seen'.[15] The Queen Mother was at Sandown to see the race, while the Queen was at Wood Farm on the Sandringham estate, waiting for some mares to foal and watching on television with her Stud Manager, Sir Michael Oswald.

Special Cargo had missed two seasons as a result of breaking down and his legs were so damaged that no one thought he would race again. Carbon-fibre implants were inserted. When he won the Grand Military Gold Cup at Sandown on 9 March, it seemed, in the words of John Oaksey, 'a miracle'.[16]

At Sandown, in the Whitbread, Special Cargo faced strong competition. He sat well behind the other horses. The thirteen-year-old Diamond Edge, with Bill Smith in the saddle, was never out of the first three. He ran as though he owned Sandown, jumping majestically, shirking no risks. Behind him ran Donegal Prince until he fell at the downhill fence (the third fence), obstructing the path of Robert Earnshaw on Lettoch and possibly costing Lettoch the race.

* The Queen Mother won a treble that day.
† The Queen was there for the first time to present her mother with the cup in her ninetieth year.

Various horses vied for the first six places. As they took the last fence, the battle seemed to be between the Fred Winter-trained joint favourite Plundering and Lettoch, when Diamond Edge suddenly rode through the two leaders and held the front 100 yards from home.

Then Kevin Mooney got a spectacular response from Special Cargo, who came up on the far side and thrust his head past on the line. The finish was so close that no one knew who had won, and there was a three-way photo finish. John Oaksey went so far as to suggest that the best result would have been 'a triple dead heat'.[17] But Special Cargo was the winner, and, minutes later, the Queen Mother was advancing to the winning enclosure with a speed that defied her eighty-three years to receive the Gold Cup from Colonel W. H. Whitbread, 'proud as a peacock', as he was described on the day.*

Narrowly beaten by two heads, Diamond Edge retired, his jockey confident that he had 'never run a better race'.[18] Cath Walwyn, wife of the Queen Mother's trainer, Fulke Walwyn, whose seventh Whitbread winner this was, said she hoped that Diamond Edge never realised he had been beaten.†

This victory for the Queen Mother was the more fantastic because all the leading horses and jockeys had performed so well. It was also important for National Hunt Racing – the twenty-eighth running of the Whitbread Gold Cup, which had been founded by Colonel Billy Whitbread in 1956. If proof were needed of the benefits of his sponsorship, it was well proved that day.

Only a few months younger than the Queen Mother, Whitbread‡ was not only one of Britain's best-known brewers, but an important figure in the sporting world. As a young man he had ridden twice in the Grand National, he fished, shot and stalked deer, piloted his own plane and sailed his own yacht. After the war he was anxious that British racing should return to pre-war standards. Therefore he persuaded the Jockey Club to allow his brewery to sponsor a steeplechase at Sandown. This became the Whitbread Gold Cup and one of the most important races in the National Hunt calendar. He also sponsored the Mackeson Gold Cup.

Whitbread was the man who financed Sir Francis Chichester, being persuaded, over a pint of beer, to contribute to the costs of his 1966

---

* The result of the 1984 Whitbread Gold Cup was: (1) Special Cargo (8–1); (2) Lettoch (11–2); (3) Diamond Edge (11–2); (4) Plundering (7–1, joint favourite); (5) Ashley Hall (7–1, joint favourite).
† This would have been Diamond Edge's third Whitbread.
‡ Colonel W. H. Whitbread (1900–93). Chairman of Whitbread from 1944 to 1971. He spent the last twelve years of his life in great pain, partly paralysed by a fall. The Queen Mother was represented by Major Raymond Seymour at his memorial service in March 1994.

Atlantic voyage and his solo round the world voyage. This he did 'without any paperwork or strings attached to it'.[19] He also sponsored the Whitbread Round the World Yacht Race. His sporting activities extended to a lively private life. Twice married, and despite a huge, bulbous nose, he had the habit of arriving on the racecourse with a succession of 'nieces'. The Queen Mother was not taken in. 'Billy, another niece?' she greeted him.[20]

The Queen Mother followed a long tradition of royal racing. The Royal Studs at Hampton Court dated to the sixteenth century, thus being the oldest thoroughbred stud in the world, while an astonishing 90 per cent of all thoroughbreds descend from two stallions bred by William, Duke of Cumberland, in Windsor Great Park in the eighteenth century – Eclipse and King Herod. Queen Victoria had been a keen breeder of racehorses and is still the only person to have bred a horse that won the Derby and the Oaks in the same year.

As Prince of Wales, Edward VII had founded studs at Sandringham and Wolferton in the 1880s and bred three particularly good full brothers – Florizel, the Triple Crown winner Diamond Jubilee and the famous Persimmon, winner of the Derby, the St Leger, the Ascot Gold Cup and Eclipse Stakes and four times Champion Sire. King George VI bred the classic winners Hypericum and Aureole.

Like the King, Queen Elizabeth enjoyed Flat racing and took an interest in the royal studs, but it was National Hunt racing that became her great passion. Racing was in her blood as Bowes-Lyons had raced for generations and in the mid-nineteenth century, John Bowes, the illegitimate son of the 10th Earl of Strathmore, had won eight classic races including four Derbys.

She had loved horses since she was a little girl, and enjoyed the social side of racing. By 1949 the war was over and the King's health was curtailing his activities. Perhaps in quest of a new interest in those difficult days, Queen Elizabeth was fired with enthusiasm when the well-known amateur jockey Lord Mildmay of Flete, an old family friend of hers,* stayed at Windsor for Royal Ascot in 1949 and talked with animation of racing 'over the sticks'.

Mildmay and his trainer, Peter Cazalet, had suffered a recent racing disaster. Earlier that year, when riding Cromwell in the Grand National, he had fallen victim to cramp and lost all chance of winning. This defeat was in sharp contrast to many wins, 197 out of some 1037 rides. Of this

* In the summer of 1924 his parents had stayed with the Strathmores at Glamis while the Yorks were there.

he spoke. Princess Elizabeth was already enthusiastic about racing. Now her mother was lured into sharing a horse with her. Peter Cazalet found Monaveen for Queen Elizabeth and Princess Elizabeth to share.

Monaveen was an eight-year-old bay gelding and the first horse to run for an English Queen since 1714. This 'gallant little horse',[21] as Queen Elizabeth called him, won three races in 1949 (including the Queen Elizabeth Steeplechase). He always ran blinkered. In 1950 he ran in the Grand National but made a mistake and, though he finished, was well out of the race. In February 1951 he had won the George Williamson Chase at Hurst Park, and in March had put on a bold display after being winded at a fence and finished fifth in the Grand National.

On 12 May 1950 Mildmay went for a swim, developed cramp and was drowned. As a result his horses went up for sale. Queen Elizabeth took on his Manicou as sole owner, Princess Elizabeth being preoccupied with her young family, and from these small beginnings developed her racing career. In October she registered her racing colours based on those of her grandfather, the 13th Earl of Strathmore – pale blue and buff stripes, blue sleeves, black velvet cap with gold tassel.

Having entered the sport, she proved as resilient as ever and did not allow early setbacks to deflect her. She relished every aspect of National Hunt racing. It was earthier than the Flat, less tied up with major sponsorship and the characters encountered were more durable, returning year after year. Courageous and colourful characters peopled the sport at all levels.

Steeplechasing never became as commercial and serious as Flat racing. No one made a fortune and the spirit of competition was high. The horses became well known to the punters, remaining in training for many successive seasons.

'Queen Elizabeth had a weakness for amusing scallywags,' recalled her Racing Manager, Sir Michael Oswald. 'Jump racing has remained essentially a sport and only an incurable optimist could hope to make money as an owner. It was this sporting character which Queen Elizabeth loved.'[22]

Presently Queen Elizabeth became the first Queen since Queen Anne to win under her own colours when Manicou won the Wimbledon Handicap Chase at Kempton on 24 November 1950. This was deemed to be beginner's luck, though he was certainly a good horse – the first of Queen Elizabeth's 462 winners.

But eight days later, tragedy struck. On 1 December Queen Elizabeth flew from Sandringham to see Monaveen* race in the Queen Elizabeth Steeplechase at Hurst Park. On that day Monaveen ran second with Tony

* Monaveen finished fifth in the 1949 Grand National.

Grantham in the saddle, but failed to clear the water and broke a leg in soft ground so badly that the vet had to put him down at once.

Queen Elizabeth's first reaction was to worry whether Princess Elizabeth might have heard the race in Malta. She was anxious lest the tragedy had been broadcast over the airwaves, but in those days the wireless did not reach that far. 'We are feeling very sad about it,'[23] telegraphed Queen Elizabeth in response to a message of sympathy from Churchill.

Some wondered if this accident would put Queen Elizabeth off. Yet as Ivor Herbert recorded: 'You cannot lie down and mope in the small world of racing any more than you can in the big life outside.'[24] The racing community was impressed that she was back to watch Manicou six days later.

Later he too was injured, and Queen Elizabeth acquired Devon Loch, seeing him do well on his first steeplechase on 17 January 1952, a few days before the death of the King.

After the King died, the Queen Mother's racing career went quiet for two years, but once she had recovered her spirits, she became increasingly active. If she had but one horse in training in the 1949–50 season, she had twenty-two by the 1966–7 season. There were times when she regretted that her royal duties and the long overseas tours interfered with her chance to see her horses run.

The 1956 Grand National was the most dramatic race in the Queen Mother's long racing career. Devon Loch had the race at his mercy in record time, when he sprawled a mere 50 yards from the winning post. The reasons for this have been discussed and analysed in racing circles for years (though the Queen Mother herself tried to avoid these post-mortems). Her jockey, Dick Francis, concluded that the enthusiasm of the crowd unnerved the horse and caused him to go down. For owner, trainer and jockey, it was one of the most shocking bits of bad luck to be meted out in a career in racing.

A few days later Harold Nicolson sat between Michael Adeane and the Duke of Devonshire, both of whom had witnessed the collapse. Each said 'it was a horrible sight'. The racegoers and general public were so convinced of a royal win that they had turned towards the Royal Box and were gesticulating wildly. When someone shouted out that there had been an accident, the ovation ceased and a complete hush fell. All those in the Royal Box were devastated.

The Queen Mother's first thought was to console the jockey, trainer and stable lads. 'I must go down,' she said, 'and comfort those poor people.'[25] The Duke of Devonshire said that he hoped the Russians had witnessed the scene – Malenkov, a Vice-Chairman of the Council of

Ministers of the USSR, was in a nearby box. 'It was the most perfect display of dignity that I have ever witnessed.'[26]

Peter Cazalet had trained Devon Loch as he did the winners of some 262 races, including Makaldar, The Rip, Laffy, Chaou II, Escalus, Inch Arran and Game Spirit. On 9 December 1961 three horses he trained for her, Laffy, Double Star and The Rip, won her a treble victory at Lingfield Park in the same afternoon.

She enjoyed her weekends at Fairlawne with the Cazalets, where she had stayed as a childhood friend of his sister, Thelma.* There was the cuisine of Albert Roux, the resident chef, while Noël Coward often sang after dinner. But her own staff found the haphazard service by the motley crew of extra helpers that Zara Cazalet brought in on these occasions something of a hazard. The Queen Mother was good with all the figures of the team, from Cazalet to his head man, Jim Fairgrieve, to the stable hands. Rare among owners, when she went into the winner's enclosure, she never failed to thank the handler, as well as the horse and rider.

Peter Cazalet, a keen cricketer and rackets player at Eton, was not seized by a love of the Turf until he went up to Oxford. He raced in point-to-points and between 1932 and 1938 as an amateur, which gave him good knowledge of race and stable management. Later he teamed up with Anthony Mildmay. He was a perfectionist, and his _Times_ obituary made a subtle point: 'Reserved and averse to publicity, he was admired and respected rather than loved by the racing public. The high standards he set made him at times appear to strangers as somewhat impatient and intolerant.'[27]

In December 1962, Noël Coward was a guest at Fairlawne, recording: 'The Queen Mother absolutely enchanting and particularly sweet to me. We discussed all sorts of forbidden topics such as the abdication, my long-ago refused knighthood, Tony Armstrong-Jones, etc.'[28]

The Queen Mother's important venture into Flat racing came about by accident. It was impossible for any celebrity to go to Auckland, New Zealand, without attracting the interest of the former Mayor, Sir Ernest Davis, a maverick character who had expanded his father's distillery business, Hancock & Co., into an enormous concern. He was Mayor of Auckland from 1935 to 1941, and became a noted philanthropist, giving Auckland a marine light installed at the entrance to Hauraki Gulf, and a particularly hideous fountain, with hidden coloured lights, at Mission Bay. He had extensive interests, including rowing, racing, farming and

---

* Thelma Cazalet-Keir (1899–1989), MP for East Islington 1931–45. Author of _From the Wings_ (1967).

extra-marital relationships. Of him it was written: 'His ability to juggle an astounding array of business, sporting and social priorities never faltered.'[29]

In 1962, by which time he was ninety, Davis proposed marriage to Vivien Leigh, lavished gifts on her and, even though she turned him down (a rare occurrence for him), he bequeathed her some valuable shares.* When encouraged to write his memoirs, he demurred, saying he had no wish to go to gaol. This did not stop John A. Lee, a politician (and former criminal, swagger and smuggler)† from writing a fictional account of Davis's life, called *For Mine is the Kingdom*, in which he related how the liquor trade fought prohibition, how Sir Ernest 'Booze' employed thugs to do his bidding and how, eventually, he became 'a respected philanthropist who gave a horse to Royalty and wanted to forget his past'.[30] He was, as Jack Lee put it, 'colourful in the sunlight and sinister in the shadows'.[31]

That horse was Bali H'ai III. Sir Ernest met the Queen Mother on her 1958 visit, and, before she knew it, he had presented her with a horse. By then he was Auckland's leading racing horse owner and his black gelding, Bali H'ai III, won the St James's Cup at Trentham, north of Wellington. The Queen Mother was walking with Davis to the winning enclosure. She told me:

> He was a dear old man, I do remember. He was following me down to get a prize and I could hear him saying: 'Shall I . . . Can I? No, I can't . . . I'd better not . . . Perhaps I will . . .'. Then he took the microphone and said: 'I give my horse to Queen Elizabeth' – in front of everybody! It wasn't very easy . . . One doesn't always want that.‡[32]

The crowd responded with resounding cheers, and the local press recorded that he described the Queen Mother as 'the greatest lady in the world'.[33]

* In July 1962 Davis almost set off to Britain to see her, but cried off, as he had not received a letter from her. Her letter then arrived, but the steamer had sailed six hours before. The next one was not due until October, by which time he was dead.
† John A. Lee (1891–1982). Even his entry in the *Dictionary of New Zealand Biography* describes him as a 'criminal'. He served twelve months in Mount Eden prison for smuggling. He became a Labour MP in 1921, but when he lost his seat in 1928, Sir Ernest Davis gave him the job of managing a hotel in Rotorua. Later he became an influential political journalist, and, having outlived many of his enemies, was able to settle a number of old scores.
‡ The Queen Mother asked what he did. I said I thought he was in gin. She frowned a little. I quickly added that he was a great philanthropist – always giving lighthouses to New Zealand. This seemed to reassure her (Hugo Vickers diary, 2 April 1987).

Bali H'ai came to England by ship in a specially fitted compartment, travelling with a plentiful supply of peppermints. He was trained by Captain Cecil Boyd-Rochfort and won three races for the Queen Mother, including the Queen Alexandra Stakes at Royal Ascot in 1959. He then returned by ship to retirement with Sir Ernest in New Zealand, where he ate what Davis described as 'about a bushel' of gobstopper peppermints every day.[34]

In March 1965 the Queen Mother had 'The Blower' installed in Clarence House, fitted by the Exchange Telegraph Company in order that she could listen to the racing commentaries as relayed in betting shops.

Contrary to popular mythology, she never placed a bet herself, perhaps considering that owning steeplechasers was a chancy enough business on its own. However, Sir Martin Gilliat often placed one for himself and liked to give the impression that he had been virtually ruined if the horse he backed failed to win.

In 1973 Peter Cazalet fell victim to cancer. He was too ill to go to Aintree, so the Queen Mother watched the Topham Trophy with him on television. With Inch Arran, Cazalet had trained his last winner for her. When he died a few weeks later, a phase of the Queen Mother's racing life came to an end. Staying at Royal Lodge the following weekend, Sir Charles Johnston noted: 'Overshadowing the whole week has been the death of Peter Cazalet on May 29th. It was the end of an empire and a bitter personal tragedy for the family – much worse than an ordinary bereavement because with his death a whole system has collapsed.'[35]

Cazalet's role was assumed by Fulke Walwyn, a leading amateur rider in the thirties, then training at Saxon House, Upper Lambourn, and considered the greatest trainer of steeplechasers of his generation. He trained winners of 102 more races for the Queen Mother. These included her favourite horse, Game Spirit, who won twenty-one races before dying of a massive pulmonary haemorrhage just past the post at Newbury in March 1977,[*] and Tammuz (bred by the Queen), winner of the £10,000 Schweppes Gold Trophy at Newbury in 1975, at odds of 18–1. Walwyn trained her 300th winner, Sunyboy, who won by eight lengths at Ascot in 1976. He gave the Queen Mother her best season with eighteen winners (seventeen from his stable), in 1975. And then came Special Cargo, now immortalised in a bronze statue at Sandown.

After Walwyn's death in 1990, his widow, Cath, took over as principal trainer. She was later succeeded by Nicky Henderson at Seven Barrows,

---

[*] Jack Logan wrote in *The Sporting Life*: 'We were in truth shocked by the news. Game Spirit was a well-loved horse. And if there is a shorter cut to a bloody nose in Tattersalls than to criticise the Queen Mother, I do not know it.' (Bill Curling, *Royal Champion* (Michael Joseph, 1980), p. 250)

Lambourn, who won forty-one races for her with half of the number of horses she had had in training in the 1960s and 1970s.

She had several racing managers in succession, first the Marquess of Abergavenny, later HM Representative at Ascot, then Captain Charles Moore, Major Richard Shelley, and from 1970 onwards Sir Michael Oswald, who was also Manager of the Royal Studs. He recalled that Sandown was the Queen Mother's favourite course, since she won seventy-eight races there, while she was less successful at Cheltenham, only achieving one win, a second and two thirds in the Champion Hurdle, a second and third in the Champion Two Mile Chase and a third in the Gold Cup:

> When being shown a horse in a stable or paddock Queen Elizabeth would invariably first talk to whoever was holding it and thank them; how seldom do owners do this. She was always considerate of the people doing the hard work in the background.
>
> Most of her horses in her later years were home bred and she loved nothing better than to see the mares and foals at Sandringham and young stock at nearby Raynham, to go down to Wolferton to feed carrots to her favourite stallion Bustino or to visit Lew in Oxfordshire where her old friend Captain Charles Radclyffe did the breaking in.[36]

Every March the Queen Mother attended three days of the Cheltenham Festival. In the 1950s and 1960s she stayed with Captain Frank and Lady Avice (Avie) Spicer,* a lady with a more colourful past than many of the Queen Mother's friends, at Spye Park, Chippenham, where there were lively house parties. Later she came each day from Royal Lodge. The weather could be bleak, which never concerned the Queen Mother. During those days, even in her nineties, she would attend a series of lunches that would exhaust a person half her age and entertain her own house party at Royal Lodge.

At the time of her death, the Queen Mother had eleven horses in training. She bought a few inexpensive youngsters, but most of her horses were homebred. There was plenty of optimism. In 1999 she was breeding for the Cheltenham Gold Cup nine years later, without appearing to consider that she might not be there to see the race.

Queen Elizabeth always counselled against pushing a horse too soon.

---

* Captain Frank Spicer (1893–1973) was a former Joint Master of the Duke of Beaufort's Hunt. Lady Avice (1897–1985) was the daughter of 8th Earl De La Warr, and sister of Idina, Countess of Erroll, whose ex-husband was murdered in Kenya. Lady Avice was first married to Stewart Menzies, Director of MI6.

At the age of one hundred, she said of First Love, last of her 462 winners: 'It's too early, too young. Let's wait, there's lots of time.'[37]

Although First Love was withdrawn from Wincanton immediately after her death,* there was no question of the Easter bank holiday racing schedule being cancelled. 'She would have been horrified,'[38] declared Sir Michael Oswald. However, jockeys wore black armbands as a mark of respect.

There were as many tributes in the racing pages as elsewhere in the papers. 'A bit of danger, a bit of excitement' was the Queen Mother's way of describing the lure of steeplechasing. One tribute declared: 'If racing were to choose an epithet, two words would suffice: Game Spirit.'[39] Nicky Henderson said: 'She was the same in victory and defeat, gracious, great fun and she absolutely adored her horses. Jump racing has lost its patron saint.'[40]

The Queen Mother would always take a telephone call from her Racing Manager, anxious to hear the latest news from the Stud, or the prospects for the next race.

So too she wanted to hear about her North Country Cheviot Sheep and Aberdeen Angus herd in Caithness. She took great interest in the breeding, lambing and calving and liked to show both the sheep and the cattle at the Caithness Show, the Royal Highland Show and the Black Isle Show. Martin Leslie recalled that she 'liked nothing better than walking around with farmers and stockmen, their comments welcomed – the more forthright the better!'.[41] Leslie would telephone the Queen Mother regularly about shows and sales, conscious that, while she played a large part in their lives in Caithness, they played a relatively small part in hers, and yet were never once made to feel this.

As she listened on the telephone, the Queen Mother would have her Corgis with her. The first Corgi, Dookie, was given to Princess Elizabeth by her father in 1933. In those days the Welsh Corgi was virtually unknown outside Pembrokeshire or Cardiganshire, and had only been recognised as a breed by the Kennel Club in 1928. The princesses saw one when playing with the children of Viscount Weymouth. They came home, asking for a dog, Dookie was bought from Mrs Thelma Gray, a breeder who owned the Rozavel Kennels in Surrey,† and the Royal Family have never been without Corgis since.

---

* First Love was withdrawn from Sandown on 15 February 2002, the day of Princess Margaret's funeral, but won easily on 8 March.

† By a curious coincidence, when Mrs Gray was nine, her Chow dog was accidentally run over by the Duke of York's car. He offered the child another dog, but her parents thought it better not. In his later dealings with Mrs Gray, she never reminded him of this incident.

Mrs Gray also provided a Corgi called Jane, with whom, it was hoped, Dookie would father a line of successors, but this did not happen. At Christmas 1938 Jane produced Crackers and Carol by another 'husband', and it is from Crackers and Susan (who replaced Jane when she was run over in Windsor Great Park in 1944) that over ten generations of royal Corgis descend.

The Queen had as many as thirteen at one time, and the Queen Mother never had fewer than two, concerned that during her absences abroad they would have each other for companionship. After Princess Margaret left Clarence House in 1960, these little dogs were her only constant companions, travelling everywhere with her, and encouraged to deplete the rabbit population in the policies round the Castle of Mey.

In 2000 the Queen gave her mother one of a new litter of Corgis, named after birds. He started life as Martin, became Marty and in due course Monty. But as a lively young puppy there were fears that the Queen Mother might trip over him, so he went back to the Queen. In her last years the Queen Mother had two Corgis, Rush and Minnie. Rush was born in 1990 and Minnie was her daughter, born in 1993. When the Queen Mother died, the Queen took them both over, but sadly they both died within a few weeks of each other, Minnie at Balmoral in October 2004, and Rush at Windsor, after the Queen went south, also in October 2004.

A feature of the Queen Mother's longevity was that authors became less guarded in writing about her, even if her newspaper press remained adulatory. Christopher Warwick suggested there might be another side to the sugar-coated image, and, within the year, Penelope Mortimer was more outwardly hostile, causing Lady Jean Rankin to remark at a dinner at which the Queen Mother was present: 'I want to cut her head off.'[42] Such books impacted little on the Queen Mother herself.

Nor did the many obituaries that were prepared in advance of her death. Many of her Household were filmed, dressed in the deepest black, giving their reminiscences though most of them would precede her to the grave. Interviews with figures such as Godfrey Talbot saying that her later years were made happy by the marriages of her grandchildren were presently consigned to the bin. The funeral itself was planned to the last step, and it is said that very early one morning the Queen Mother woke to see a cortège pass. Asking later whose it was, the answer was given: 'Yours, Ma'am'.*

The Queen Mother celebrated her eighty-fifth birthday with a two-hour flight round the British Isles in Concorde, invited by Lord King.

* This story must be apocryphal.

'Supergran takes off!' was the headline in the Star.[43] On the day she gave particular pleasure to a fan of hers, aged seventy-two, called Phyllis Thomas, who had been writing to her since 1934. She let it be known that she would accept a bouquet from Miss Thomas. Having done so, she asked her fan to stand with her while the band marched past singing 'Happy Birthday'. Later the press swooped on Miss Thomas, putting many words into her mouth. She wrote to apologise to the Queen Mother, and received a letter back: 'Queen Elizabeth says don't worry. She knows exactly what the press is.'[44]

Too much happened within a few days in April 1986. On 21 April the Queen celebrated her sixtieth birthday with a service at St George's Chapel,* and the 'Fanfare for Elizabeth' at Covent Garden. The Queen Mother went to both. Two days later King Juan Carlos of Spain arrived on a state visit, with attendant banquet at Windsor Castle, and the following day the Duchess of Windsor died in Paris in her ninetieth year after a long and miserable illness.†

Because of this death, the Queen did not go to Sandown Races at the last moment, but the Queen Mother attended and Princess Anne competed. Major Griffin stated: 'Her Majesty always attends this meeting. She was asked to go and she went. That's all there is to it.'[45]

On 29 April the Queen and many of the Royal Family attended the Duchess's funeral in St George's Chapel. The funeral was conducted in the same way as all private royal funerals, with fine singing and the Archbishop of Canterbury pronouncing the blessing.‡ The Queen Mother, in traditional black, attended the funeral of this unloved sister-in-law, having already been to a service at Westminster Abbey for the 900th Anniversary of the Domesday Book in the morning.

The Duchess's coffin was carried in by a bearer party of Welsh Guards. After the service, the Queen, the Duke of Edinburgh, the Queen Mother, the Prince and Princess of Wales and Princess Anne followed it to the west steps. Only then was there a concession. The Queen Mother did not go to Frogmore for the interment.

On 23 July the wedding of Prince Andrew, created Duke of York on

* Group Captain Peter Townsend was in the congregation as an Extra Equerry. He came from Paris with his wife.
† The Duchess had suffered from arteriosclerosis since the early 1970s. Since 1976 she had been imprisoned in her house by her wicked lawyer, Maître Suzanne Blum. Her death was a merciful release.
‡ The coffins of George V and George VI, the Dukes of Windsor and Gloucester, Princess Marina, Princess Alice, Countess of Athlone, and Lord Cambridge were among those that had rested in the same place in the Quire.

the day, took place. It heralded a new phase for the Royal Family, which led to its nadir in 1992. Again the Queen Mother was there, travelling to Westminster Abbey in an open landau with Princess Margaret, Lord Linley and Lady Sarah Armstrong-Jones.

On the Queen Mother's 1987 Canadian visit in June, there was an indication that too much was expected of an eighty-six-year-old lady. This was the tenth time she had gone to Canada and included an important visit to Quebec, paving the way for a later visit by the Queen.

The Queen Mother stood for half of a five-hour day, made two speeches and gave out awards. But at one point her eyes looked tired and strained. And she banged her head on a door frame and slumped into the car, before rallying with her usual smile.

Her overseas travelling had not finished. A month later she visited the Black Watch in Berlin to mark fifty years as their Colonel-in-Chief. In 1988 she visited Northern Ireland and in 1989 she was at Bayeux for the forty-fifth anniversary of the Normandy landings, speaking French to the veterans and giving no impression of being a veteran herself. As she re-entered her helicopter after a long day, she paused and waved, then made a gesture as if she had suddenly spotted some special favourites, and in she went. Soon afterwards she sailed through five days of engagements in Toronto at the height of the Canadian summer, walking with impressive youthfulness.

In March 1990 she flew to Berlin for three days to present the traditional shamrock to the Irish Guards on St Patrick's Day and to visit the 1st Battalion, the Light Infantry and she saw the lately fallen Berlin Wall. Ironically she was virtually mobbed by exultant crowds of East and West Berliners.

Not many members of the British Royal Family had attained the great age of ninety. Queen Mary's aunt, the Grand Duchess of Mecklenburg-Strelitz, had lived to be ninety-four, the Duke of Connaught and his sister, Princess Louise, Duchess of Argyll, reached ninety-one. These were remote figures. More recently, in 1981, Princess Alice, Countess of Athlone, had survived to nearly ninety-eight, and held the record as the oldest ever member of the British Royal Family.

Queen Elizabeth approached the milestone with her habitual nonchalance, still in excellent health. While the nation geared itself up to celebrate her ninetieth birthday, she refused to have another St Paul's Cathedral Service of Thanksgiving. But visits were made to Cardiff in the spring and to Scotland in July.

She went up to Birkhall for a few days in May: 'The countryside is looking so lovely here, the trees just out, and the bird cherry looking like white clouds against the green, and so far, no MIDGES! I am here for a whole week and a day or two, and it is bliss having *nothing* to do.'[46] The same could not be said of the older members of her Household, as Sir Martin Gilliat reported later in the year:

> Poor John Griffin is still recovering albeit rather slowly from a stroke he had back in June – and some of our Ladies are showing signs of wear. Happily, however, Frances is a tower of strength and keeps us all in good order.[47]

Griffin had slipped at Waterloo Station. Soon afterwards, he was the victim of an unpleasant accident at Clarence House, when, during the serious storm of January 1990, part of a chimney fell through the skylight in the Household corridor and landed on his head. The press heard of this and naturally enquired if the Queen Mother had been in any danger. In Griffin's absence, Clarence House replied: 'Not particularly. Queen Elizabeth was at Sandringham at the time.' Sir Martin was also hit on the head by some falling plaster. He described himself as 'shaken, but not . . .' 'Stirred?' volunteered the journalist who asked him about the incident.

On 29 May the Queen Mother went to the 550th anniversary celebrations for Eton College, an event to which she had not looked forward, but enjoyed. The Provost, Lord Charteris, could be heard on loudspeakers suggesting: 'Shall we stagger up the hill together?'

Having walked down the hill at the Garter ceremony, looking pale and a little out of breath,[48] she went to three of the four days of Royal Ascot, bowing out of the fourth due to tiredness. She attended the Festival of the Friends of St Paul's, and flew in secret to the Black Watch in Northern Ireland.

In London there was the traditional Guildhall lunch (to which she went with Princess Margaret) and a gala variety performance at the London Palladium (she was already ten years old when it was built). The evening was hosted by Sir John Gielgud, with appearances from Cliff Richard, Mickey Rooney, Roger Moore, Michael Caine and the perennial Dame Vera Lynn. Sheridan Morley considered this was an improvement on the usual Royal Variety Show, where 'most of the acts had risen from the grave for the honour of being there', but the best sight of the evening was the Queen Mother 'cheerfully singing along with Flanagan and Allen 'as reincarnated quite superbly by Bernie Winters and Leslie Crowther'.[49]

The most memorable and ingenious celebration was the cavalcade procession of armed services and civilian organisations with which the Queen Mother was associated, on Horse Guards Parade. This was the brainchild of Major Michael Parker, the producer of the Royal Tournament, an exuberant figure and sometime antique dealer, who had enjoyed notable success with imaginative independent celebrations at a number of royal events, notably the Queen's bonfire at Windsor to mark the 1977 Silver Jubilee. The Parade Commander was Colonel Andrew Parker Bowles, Lieutenant Colonel Commanding the Household Cavalry and Silver Stick in Waiting. The Birthday Tribute on the evening of 27 June was nothing if not unusual. An Aberdeen Angus bull could be spotted in a pen in St James's Park.

The Queen Mother arrived on Horse Guards Parade in a carriage, accompanied by Prince Charles and Princess Margaret, and escorted by the Household Cavalry. She stepped from her carriage with agility, radiant in pale blue.

There was a march past of the Royal Navy, Army, Royal Air Force and Commonwealth forces – the Black Watch (Royal Highland Regiment of Canada) so often visited, the Toronto Scottish Regiment and Canadian Forces Medical Corps, and from Australia the Royal Australian Medical Corps, and from New Zealand the 1st Medical Support Team Royal New Zealand Army Medical Corps.

These were followed by a glorious miscellany of 4,500 representatives of civilian organisations, many of whom had waited patiently all day in St James's Park before making their appearance, and then trooped past the Queen Mother, advertising their respective organisation with appropriate props and symbols, some of them entertaining and humorous. The Bursar of Cumberland Lodge was riding his fire engine, there were nurses, old folks on floats, Mayors, Fellows of the Royal Society, ladies knitting, many dressed in a kaleidoscope of historical costumes, as worn over the century. Jerry Hall and Susan Hampshire represented the National Trust, the famous racehorse Desert Orchid rode past. One holder of the George Cross got stuck behind the Chelsea Pensioners (stalwart old boys, not one of them as old as Queen Elizabeth) and was frogmarched by police into the crowd, missing his chance to march past.

More massed bands preceded an address by Sir John Mills, the only part the Queen Mother did not like: 'A mistake. I tried to prevent it. Such a pity, poor old chap, such a nice man.'[50] The veteran actor, who had spent some time patting his hair down, told the Queen Mother that he knew she wanted no fuss, but: 'Ma'am, that is one royal command that has been flagrantly disobeyed.'

After a twenty-one-gun salute and a fly past, the Queen Mother herself addressed the now massive assembled company. She then departed by carriage.[51] Privately she had been dreading the parade, but she stood valiantly through it, and was clearly deeply moved by it.* In fact she enjoyed it so much that she played the tape many times over to her guests at the Castle of Mey later that summer.

There was a review of more than a thousand yachts in the Solent, which the organisers told her was a rehearsal for her 100th birthday, the Prince of Wales gave a concert at Buckingham Palace and commissioned a new musical work,† the Queen gave a dinner on the Royal Yacht for all the Royal Family. *Britannia* was moored in the Pool of London, and Tower Bridge was lit up by fireworks afterwards.

There was a memorable return visit to the East End. One survivor, who had been seventeen when Hallsville School was bombed and seventy fellow pupils killed, said: 'She picked her way over the rubble and was an example to everyone. There were tears. You could see the look in her face. I think the world of her. Every East Ender does.'[52]

The Times reapplied Lytton Strachey's lines about Queen Victoria: 'The vast majority of her subjects could not remember a time when she was not reigning over them.'[53]

---

* The spectators could not fail to be moved, and one home viewer said: 'My television worked fine, but my vision was somewhat blurred.'
† *The Thistle and the Rose* by the young Scottish composer Patrick Doyle. It was first performed at Buckingham Palace on 2 August 1990.

36

Nonagenarian

*Nowadays one feels that the press, radio and television are sadly
lacking any respect for one's institutions & traditions*
– the Queen Mother

The ninetieth birthday achieved, the Queen Mother should have been
able to drift into the serenity of old age. But the 1990s was the worst
decade endured by the Royal Family since the Abdication. It is exhausting
to look back on this phase with its excesses, extravagances and decep-
tions, not to mention the many peripheral tragedies that came in its wake.
The worst was the collapse of the marriage of the Prince and Princess
of Wales, and the Princess's ultimate spiral into dark chaos and death.

The Queen Mother was only partially spared the media attacks directed
at the Royal Family. There was danger in living too long, since the revi-
sionists set to work prematurely, and she became the victim of previously
unthinkable satire, including spiteful caricatures and her depiction on
television's *Spitting Image*, where it became a cliché to portray her as a
gin-sozzled old granny. In 1992 the republican novelist Sue Townsend
even published a novel, *The Queen and I*, which opened with a fictional
depiction of her funeral.

During the 1990s the Queen Mother's various operations and illnesses
took a gradual toll on her strength, especially after 1992. Although the
Queen Mother was adept at rising above disaster, and negating the effects
of crises, it was nevertheless a dispiriting time. That she survived the
decade to attain her 100th birthday again says much for her determination of mind and body.

Her way of keeping going was to ignore the years. She spent little time
thinking how old she was. She was no great dweller in the past. She liked
to remain as modern as possible. She would ask her equerry if he had 'a
bird' and in her 100th year looked at his red socks and described them
as 'wicked'.[1] As Princes William and Harry grew up, they taught her
about Ali G. and his phrase 'Respec'.[2]

She was not always 'on message'. One evening at dinner, she watched
Dynasty with Lady Elizabeth Basset and Tor-Tor Gilmour. A character

announced: 'I've felt so much happier since I came out of the closet.' 'What did he say, Ma'am?' asked the rather deaf Tor-Tor. The Queen Mother replied: 'I think he said he felt much happier since he came out of the *wardrobe*.'[3]

Meanwhile the Queen Mother continued in her well-tried routine, planned ahead month by month, facing each new hurdle as it came. Privately it did not get any easier, and when close friends commended her courage, she confessed that it was not always thus. 'You don't know, . . . inside' was as close she would get to confessing to despondency.

Each summer the Queen Mother went abroad privately, exploring a new region of France. As ever her party included the Duke and Duchess of Grafton, Sir Ralph Anstruther and Ruth Fermoy. The artist Sir Hugh Casson and his wife were popular later additions.

Until 1974 Charles de Noailles organised the visits and one friend believed that these trips 'may have been the most pleasurable of his life'.[4] When Noailles became too ill, Prince Jean-Louis de Faucigny-Lucinge took over, declaring: 'I am Potemkin!'*[5] Only then did they become an annual feature. 'Johnny' Lucinge had danced with the Queen Mother at Oxford in the days before her marriage and his mother-in-law, Baroness d'Erlanger, had been a neighbour of the Yorks in Piccadilly. He was the perfect guide.

Lucinge's first experience in 1974 had shocked him greatly. Baron Philippe de Rothschild invited the Queen Mother to Mouton, but when they were planning her itinerary, he vetoed a visit to one neighbour who was angling for a royal visit. To Lucinge's great surprise, the royal party drove up to this lady's Palladian mansion. Expressing his surprise to the Baron, he was horrified to hear him reply with quiet malice: 'We are just passing by. We will not get out. It is a custom in the Bordeaux region'.[6] While the Queen Mother was oblivious to the Baron's plot, Lucinge observed a butler in a window struggling into his white jacket – pointlessly.

Strangers, admittedly rather grand ones, were ever willing to entertain the Queen Mother, though where possible she preferred to stay in *Britannia*, as it was less tiring. These excursions also signified the rare time that the Queen Mother ate a meal in a public restaurant.†

Numerous adventures befell the group on their peregrinations around

* Grigori Alexandrovich Potemkin (1739–91), organised Catherine the Great's fabulous Crimean Tour in 1787.
† The Queen Mother occasionally lunched in a restaurant in London, usually in a hotel like the Ritz or Claridge's. 'They're always full of men!' she declared after one such lunch in 1989.

Europe. There was an advance row about whether or not the Queen Mother would start an Alsatian feast with snail soup. After heated exchanges, a compromise was reached and this local speciality was offered, with melon as an alternative. The Queen Mother chose the soup: 'I'm going to take the plunge,' she said, later asking for a second helping. They visited the Cognac region during the 'guerre des moutons' between France and Britain, and on this occasion her thoughtful hosts, the Hennessys, hid their sheep from view.

At Bournel they found their host, the Marquis de Moustiers, and his family pursuing a rat round the hall, and at Hautefort, the home of the Baronne de Bastard,* the reception was such a success that none of the locals would leave. The Queen Mother had to pretend she was retiring for the night. After the exodus she redescended for dinner.

At Serrant, another year, the restaurateur shook the Queen Mother's hand with such enthusiasm that she could not write for days. After a very late dinner near Pisa, Lucinge suggested they view the floodlit baptistry of Campo Santo. When they arrived, they found a motley group of guitar players whiling away the night. A curious procession soon formed and, after seeing the sights, the Queen Mother asked them to play Neapolitan airs and the whole group (including her) sang together.

At Asolo, flowers arrived in droves at the Hotel Villa Cipriani where they were staying. One evening local singers came to sing and the Queen Mother's party sat in a restaurant, to the astonishment of Americans at the next table. The evening ended with the National Anthem. The next morning, the hotel staff was singing the National Anthem in the kitchen. 'How touching!' commented the Queen Mother.

The Queen Mother loved the French trips best, but *Britannia* took her to Sicily, and in October 1984 she went to Venice for four days for the first time since a childhood visit to the station.

She sailed in on 25 October, and her party travelled about in two water taxis as the canals were too shallow for the Royal Barge. The plan was to see churches under the guidance of John Julius Norwich and to be entertained by grand Venetians in glorious palazzi.

Sir Ralph Anstruther was determined that the Queen Mother was not going to get into a gondola despite earnest requests from photographers. Three days went by and the Household thought they had got away with it. But on the last day, as the Queen Mother left a particular church, there was a gondola hired by the press with a gondolier attired in the traditional outfit. The Queen Mother agreed to give the press the treat

* The Baron de Bastard had his coat of arms on the soles of his shoes to impress this in the sand as he trod his estate.

they sought and to do a quick round-trip. She asked Sir Paul Greening, Flag Officer of the Royal Yacht, to join her.

There was frenetic photography from the world's press but then they turned a corner where there was total peace. Behind the building, two nuns, standing on a verandah, became 'hysterical with excitement'. Then there was another peaceful section before they turned the last corner and were 'confronted by the chaos created by the press',[7] with the inevitable Cornetto, as they returned to the steps.

In 1989 the Queen Mother was planning a visit to Albi, an area of France which Lucinge did not know at all. He asked thirty-eight-year-old Bertrand du Vignaud, great-nephew of the artist Toulouse-Lautrec, to mastermind the visit, and she saw the Toulouse-Lautrec Museum, Carcasonne, Toulouse and various private châteaux. Arriving at the family home for lunch, there was a power cut, which the Queen Mother greatly enjoyed – 'The French!'*

From then on, du Vignaud was co-opted to the team, invited to Sandringham and presently took over from Lucinge, as he grew frailer. 'You will be Zubov!'† Lucinge told him, extending the Potemkin theme.[8] Though steering an elderly group about from the generation of his grand-mother, he found them spry and eager to enjoy themselves:

> The first night the Queen Mother would receive the Ambassador, the 'Prefet' and the Mayor, but after that she was on holiday, with no official engagements. She always said how much she loved to be 'in the family.' They had a lot of fun. They may have been collapsing, but in their enthusiasm they were like a group of schoolchildren on a school trip![9]

In 1990 the party visited Brittany, exploring three chapels near La Forêt-Fouesnaut, took a river cruise and were confronted by a crowd of two thousand at the Cathedral of Saint Corentin. Du Vignaud managed to fix a visit to Karl Lagerfeld's château, Grandchamps, 'not particularly easy . . . but eventually great fun'.[10] At a dinner Ruth Fermoy collapsed, and soon after the trip Johnny Lucinge suffered a mild heart attack.

Nevertheless the intrepid team set off to explore Savoy in 1991, Lucinge insisting on coming since this was the part of France from where his family came. Being very frail now (he almost fainted at one lunch), he dreaded

* When du Vignaud arrived at Sandringham that July for a return stay, there was a power cut there too, the cause of more hilarity.
† Prince Platon Zubov, the last and youngest of Catherine the Great's lovers between 1789 and 1796.

that the Queen Mother would ask to see the family fortress, a ruin on top of a hill. He was relieved when they merely looked at it from the road.

The party stayed at the Royal Hotel at Evian, a celebrated thermal spa, tackling truite en gelée, with a Reblochon cheese, and a 1934 Rezan-Segla. In a packed few days the Queen Mother inspected 105 soldiers at the military cemetery at Thorens-Glières, who survived from the liberation of Haute-Savoie in 1944. After a final lunch at the legendary Père-Bise, the local Mayor bade her farewell: 'Vous êtes ici chez vous.'

The following May Johnny Lucinge died, so Bertrand du Vignaud took sole charge. He escorted the Queen Mother to Umbria, and they visited Perugia, Assisi, Orvieto, Cortona and La Sala. The 1992 excursion proved to be the last trip. The Queen was increasingly worried about her mother travelling, not to mention her companions, and insisted they should stop. Nevertheless, with her customary spirit, Queen Elizabeth continued to suggest trips to Urbino, the Basque country and elsewhere, and on his visits to Sandringham, du Vignaud discussed these with her, though both knew they would never come to fruition.

The Royal Family's popularity was already suffering by the late 1980s. In the next decade matters deteriorated even more and the Queen Mother's long-held values were gravely threatened. As the Prince and Princess of Wales travelled the world, seemingly a dream team, behind the scenes their marriage was visibly collapsing.

In August 1989 Princess Anne and Captain Mark Phillips separated and in 1992 they divorced. The Queen Mother did not attend the marriage of Viscount Althorp to Victoria Lockwood (another doomed alliance) despite being a life-long friend of the Spencer family. Nor did Althorp's godmother, the Queen.*

The Princess of Wales became more and more popular, the media interest in her only increasing. Meanwhile the Duchess of York received grotesque publicity, which she did little to aid by headline-winning pranks.

Diana was the most enigmatic figure in the midst of this. She depended for her existence on being the 'Cinderella' choice of the Prince of Wales. She had a unique natural touch, possessing in full measure all the gifts of the best-loved princesses in history. She was good with the sick, good with children and good with old people. She became a living icon, outdistancing the Royal Family to whom she owed her public being.

But she was not happy, and simmering beneath the surface were the fires of revenge. She had never been convinced that Prince Charles loved

* The Queen normally attends the weddings of her godchildren. When Crown Prince Alexander of Yugoslavia married in Franco's Spain in 1972, she sent Princess Anne to represent her.

her, and never ceased to be suspicious of Mrs Parker Bowles.* The Wales marriage was a grim tragedy.

It is commonly said that the Princess of Wales was too young and did not know what she was going into. This is only partly true. She knew about Camilla Parker Bowles, but, not unreasonably, she thought that once she was married she had at least a chance with the Prince. As one who worked at the Palace at the time put it: 'No one told her romance wasn't part of the deal.'¹¹ Nor was she strong enough to override the problems and make the best of things. Between 1992 and her death in 1997 she delivered a series of devastating blows to her husband.

In this there is tragedy worthy of Shakespeare's pen – the young Princess convinced that her husband was still entangled with his mistress, the Prince unable to cope with the mood swings of his wife, and probably believing that she was the first to be unfaithful. One member of the Royal Family likened the Wales marriage to rescuing a dog from Battersea Dogs' Home. 'You bring it home, a shy, damaged creature. You love it and it becomes your best friend.'¹² Diana basked in no such love.

What the Queen Mother made of this is all too easy to imagine. She had relied on a devotion to duty and a steady round of official engagements, many so similar. Her philosophy was to get on with things. There was a price to pay for everything. The Royal Family was there to serve, not to dart about the world having fun.

Likewise, the Queen Mother had an Edwardian approach to marriage. Men had affairs. Women did not. When she was informed what the Princess of Wales was doing, she feared for the consequences. Hating public crises in the Royal Family, she was deeply depressed when the Prince of Wales warned her of the impending collapse of his marriage. Some noticed a marked decline after 1992. She was too old to play an active role in the discussions that took place between the Waleses and the Queen and the Duke of Edinburgh, but she could and did support Prince Charles. Throughout his life she never rebuked him. And now she remained fiercely loyal to him at a time when he badly needed an unquestioning ally. As for Diana and Sarah, she did not bother further with them. Diana had failed to make Charles happy, therefore she was in the wrong. Her name was not mentioned at Clarence House, but then, somewhat to the irritation of Prince Charles, nor was the name of Camilla Parker Bowles mentioned in the last decade of the Queen Mother's life.†

* Had the Princess of Wales been resurrected in 2005, she would have witnessed her rival elevated to the title of Duchess of Cornwall and status of Royal Highness. She would have been vindicated in her earlier suspicions, however ill-founded they may have appeared at the time.

† Several say that Prince Charles would not have dared risk losing his grandmother's friendship by marrying his mistress.

In 1992 the excesses of the 1980s unravelled in a most unpleasant way. The Duchess of York was the first to fall. Some photographs proving a relationship with a Texan, Steve Wyatt, were found on top of the wardrobe in a rented flat in London in January. Two months later, the separation of the Duke and Duchess of York was announced, and in the summer the Duchess was photographed having her toe sucked by her then lover, John Bryan, euphemistically described as her 'financial adviser'. *Paris Match* headlined the saga: 'Fragrant Delit – Comment Sarah offre son pied à son "conseiller financier".'*13

In February 1992 the Waleses were in India and the press could not fail to notice and photograph the Princess turning her head to avoid the Prince's kiss at a polo match. It was not long before a version of her story was serialised in the *Sunday Times* and then in a book, put together by Andrew Morton, a tabloid journalist to whom, by devious methods, she had spoon-fed the information. Though the Princess denied her collusion with Morton, it was a clear sign that the marriage was doomed. A troubled summer followed. On 9 December John Major, the Prime Minister, announced their official separation.

The Queen Mother was not the only grandmother to suffer from this. Ruth Fermoy was made miserable by the collapse of the Wales marriage, not least because it caused some tension between her and the Queen Mother. Relations with Diana had sunk to low ebb. During the crisis she went to Kensington Palace to appeal to her. Diana told her footman to escort her grandmother out. They seldom spoke again. All that Lady Fermoy had held sacred collapsed about her. She went into a sharp decline and died the following year.

1992 marked the fortieth anniversary of the Queen's Accession. This meant that it was also forty years since the King had died. Nigel Jaques, an Eton master, who had been co-opted on to the Royal Lodge guest list, recalled his memories of the King's funeral. To this the Queen Mother replied:

I was so interested to see that you used the words 'affectionate respect', in describing the boy's feelings on that day, especially as nowadays one feels that the press, radio and television are sadly lacking any respect for one's institutions & traditions. Perhaps the schools can make up for this lack.14

* Prince Andrew stood by his wife, and, despite their subsequent divorce, the couple remained on close and amicable terms, sometimes sharing a dwelling, sending out joint Christmas cards and showing a commendable lack of respect for the institution of divorce.

It was hardly a year for celebration. There was the grave fire at Windsor Castle, somehow symbolic of the crumbling of the House of Windsor, and the Queen's announcement that she would now pay taxes. Even the House of Hartnell collapsed, it being noted that their two staunchest surviving customers were the Queen Mother and Dame Barbara Cartland, the latter invariably clad in pink.

In May that year, the Queen Mother unveiled a statue to Marshal of the RAF Sir Arthur Harris, head of Bomber Command in the war, whose controversial bombing of Dresden in February 1945 had cost 35,000 civilian lives, with a further one hundred thousand refugees lost fleeing the approaching Soviet Army. The King and Queen had known him well during the war, and the Queen Mother held him in great respect.

'Bomber Harris' had required police protection until his death in 1984. Even before the unveiling, there was controversy. The Mayor of Pforzheim (which lost a quarter of its population) and the German Foreign Minister appealed in vain to Clarence House to have the memorial stopped.

When the Queen Mother performed the ceremony, two hundred peace protestors tried to spray paint over onlookers. On 19 October, the words 'War Criminal' were sprayed on to the plinth, and ten days later it was again vandalised, this time sprayed with red paint, and the word 'Shame'.[15] Later, Harris's daughter thanked the Queen Mother for doing the unveiling. Her response was: 'He cared so much for his boys.'[16]

The remarriage of the Princess Royal again brought the Queen Mother into controversy, acres of newsprint being devoted to the question as to whether she would be attending the ceremony in Crathie Church, near Balmoral. There seemed little mercy in expecting a ninety-two-year-old lady to leave her long-planned house party at Royal Lodge with a bad cold to fit in with plans made relatively late in the day.

The press stressed that the Queen Mother disapproved of divorce and remarriage. Therefore, to support Princess Anne, she flew to Scotland and back on the same day, Saturday 12 December, leaving at 9.40 a.m., attending the service at Crathie Church, lunching at Craigowan, flying south again and finally reaching Royal Lodge at 8.20 p.m. Her shooting party guests had decorated the hall with balloons and put a 'Welcome Home, Ma'am' banner in the drawing room.

Ashe Windham ventured to suggest that the Queen Mother had had a 'busy day'. 'Nonsense', she riposted, and stayed up till half past midnight.[17]

The Princess Royal's second husband was Commander Tim Laurence, a former equerry to the Queen. When a friend pointed out that he would know the rules, the Queen Mother observed: 'Yes, he'll know how to mix the Martinis.'[18]

The mischievous diarist Woodrow Wyatt quoted Lady Angela Oswald saying in 1994 'that she dates the deterioration in the health of Queen Elizabeth, who is now a bit doddery, from the publication of the ghastly Morton book about Diana'.[19] The Queen Mother's decline was certainly precipitated by the events of 1992. And yet, like the Queen, she kept on going regardless, conducting business as usual. She bided her time until the crises passed. It was necessary to take the long view.

Cultural Life

One way of maintaining enjoyment of life was to arrange cultural events to entertain family and guests. Concerts and readings had been given through the 1970s and even earlier. A remarkable extension of an Edwardian life, they continued into the 1990s. The Queen Mother enjoyed inviting figures from the performing arts, entertaining them and then asking them to perform. Over the years there were many such occasions and the performers had been top rate. Noël Coward was one who was despatched to the piano to perform his old favourites in the 1960s.

The evenings were the inspiration of Sir Martin Gilliat, an angel in the theatre, and Ruth Fermoy, a proficient pianist in her own right and the founder of the King's Lynn Music Festival.

One who attended many such occasions was Nigel Jaques, who received an unexpected telephone call from Gilliat in March 1979, summoning him to escort Lady Charteris to a musical evening that day at Royal Lodge in place of the Provost, who had suddenly fallen ill. Jaques was Treasurer of the Eton Beagles, which met regularly at Royal Lodge each March, and had therefore met Queen Elizabeth on several occasions. Sir Martin told him on the telephone: 'Queen Elizabeth is beside me and she is smiling with pleasure that you can come.'[20]

The Queen Mother came in with her house party and presently the Queen arrived alone from the Castle, dressed simply in green. After drinks, the assembled company sat down for an informal poetry reading by Sir John Betjeman – 'slow and sometimes faltering, but still uniquely engaging' mixed with piano duets by Raymond Leppard and Ruth Fermoy. Dinner was then served at two tables, one with Queen Elizabeth at one end and the Queen at the other, and then a round table for six. Green soup, kedgeree, cold chicken and ham, and a vanilla soufflé, was washed down with sherry, hock, claret and later coffee and port.

On 26 February 1984, with the Queen again present, there was another musical performance. Queen Elizabeth settled her guests by asking them: 'Would you, as they say, take a seat?' The two Queens sat in the front row and the performance began:

> Schubert and Britten songs by young Canadian baritone, polite but assured, accompanied by D [David] Willcocks. Readings by David Cecil, lisping engagingly & not too audible, from E. Thomas, Hans Anderson (*Tin Soldier*), Mary McCarthy's account of Q. Victoria's funeral, risky I thought but successful, and, best, Max Beerbohm 'On Going for a Walk'. Both Queens reacting with happy smiles & murmurs of delight. D.W. played Myra Hess's arrangement of 'Jesu Joy . . .' All very pleasurable & undemanding.[21]

On other occasions there were performances from Patrick Garland and Edward Fox, who paid poetic tribute to the Crazy Gang. In 1990 John Gielgud read from Horace Walpole's diaries and from Auden, a Russian pianist, Sergey Podobedov,* played Schumann, Rachmaninov, Debussy and Moszknowski, Lucy Wakeford played the harp in 1992, a violin and piano evening with a programme varying from Handel to Gershwin in 1993, and Dorothy Tutin and Osian Ellis produced a programme of words and music.

Early in 1993 the Queen Mother was described by a close friend as 'a very sad lady'. She looked vague at the Derby and had resorted to the use of a stick disguised as an umbrella, which became a feature from now on.

During her annual early summer stay at Birkhall, she had to pay another visit to Aberdeen Royal Infirmary, being admitted there on 20 May after complaining of 'a slight tightening of the throat'. This proved due to a piece of salmon. Leaving hospital a few days later, she again looked vague, but cheerful. 'How are you feeling, Ma'am?', asked a reporter. 'Very much better, thank you,' she replied. 'Will you be taking things a little easier now?' 'Everybody's been so kind,' she said, something of a non sequitur.

It would not have been surprising had the Queen Mother slipped into a decline and died that summer. She looked 'other worldly' at the Birthday Parade, and even the way she re-arranged her veil made astute onlookers fear that her soul was moving on.

---

* Sergey Podobedov (b. 1972), won a scholarship from the Royal College of Music in 1990, which was later upgraded to a Queen Elizabeth The Queen Mother scholarship. He was only nineteen when he performed at Royal Lodge on 24 March 1991.

The Queen was sufficiently worried to tackle her mother about doing too much when they repaired to Royal Lodge for their post-Matins drink the next day. An argument ensued as a result of which the Queen drove out of the gates of Royal Lodge at excessive speed, a passer-by took umbrage, and the Queen ended up on the front page of the *Sun*.

Until the last moment, the Queen Mother was meant to walk in the Garter procession that Monday. It was a rare wet day, no time for a ninety-two-year-old to walk down the hill. The Queen persuaded her to remain in the Castle. The Queen Mother protested that she had to attend because her young page, Lord Mornington,* would be so disappointed. But the Queen said: 'Don't worry, I'll take Arthur', and won the round. The Queen Mother then missed the whole of Ascot for the first time ever, due to what was described as mild flu. 'We expect her to go into bat again next week' was the up beat comment from Clarence House.[22]

Her next major engagement was the unveiling of a statue to General de Gaulle at Carlton Gardens on 23 June. In glorious sunlight, the British produced a Guards band, wondrous old Frenchmen greeted each other sonorously in perfect French, and two old French generals, who in earlier times would have been Marshals of France, wandered about draped in the bright red riband of the Legion of Honour. The British guests were distinguished figures, among them Sir Edward Heath. The Queen Mother made a valiant comeback:

Evidently she leant on an umbrella as she greeted the VIPs, but there was no sign of it on the platform. She wore pale green, almost light blue, with the pearl brooch and the badge of the Croix de Lorraine. She looked pale and frail, but serene and rather beautiful. There remains this other worldly quality about her. And like Mary Poppins, she could sail away into the sky at any moment.

Yes, she coughed & her mouth did a Princess Alice twitch – but she remained as radiant as always with a half-smile & an attention to what was going on.

Mary Soames spoke in English & French. Then a magnificently over-bedecked French Ambassador – in full Ambassadorial kit, with ostrich-plumed hat, Grand Cross of the Royal Victorian Order & at least six stars, many of which had nothing to do with Britain or France, spoke at considerable length in pure French – a joy to listen to.

The Queen Mother rose to her feet and, though holding a piece of paper with words writ large, delivered a short, perfect speech and unveiled the

* Grandson of the Duke of Wellington, KG.

statue. An old French warrior kissed her hand, not a brush of polite admiration, more a slobber. He gazed at her in abject devotion. When she left the marquee, she stood bathed in sunlight, waving to the assembled company.[23]

The Queen Mother had overcome a grave crisis. Now that she had slipped a little, she settled into a steadier routine, undertaking slightly less, pacing herself better, and in this measured way continued her nonagenarian existence.

Health and survival became the predominant issues. They would remain so till the end. She was sustained by lashings of Vitamin C, sent to her by the redoubtable Barbara Cartland, whose further offerings of strange-smelling Indian herbs were perhaps less avidly received.

In the summer of 1993 Clarence House lost two of its stalwarts in close succession. Sir Martin Gilliat died on 27 May, and Ruth, Lady Fermoy on 6 July. After their deaths, Clarence House was never quite the same again. In the immediate aftermath, there was great sadness. 'As you realise the sorrow over Martin is great – he is quite irreplaceable & at the moment a lot of the stuffing has been knocked out of all of us here,' wrote Dame Frances Campbell-Preston.[24]

On 6 July, the day of Lady Fermoy's death, the Queen Mother was present when the controversial Queen Mother Gates in Hyde Park were unveiled by the Queen. These gave her no pleasure.

Before he died, perhaps because of the pain of his terminal illness, or perhaps because, due to Queen Elizabeth's ingrained dislike of visiting dying friends, she had not gone to see him, Gilliat railed against his employer, declaring that he had wasted the best years of his life in her service. The Queen Mother did attend his packed memorial service at St Martin-in-the-Fields, at which Lord Charteris paid tribute to his devotion to her. 'He was run to a shadow, visibly dying, jaundiced as a yellow guinea, scarcely able to walk across Colour Court from his apartment to his office at Clarence House, where at his desk he found some ease in continuing with Queen Elizabeth's full understanding and blessing, to work for her as he had done for 37 years.'

Lord Charteris addressed these words directly to the Queen Mother, who sat at the front, increasingly alone, as bereavement followed bereavement. Soon afterwards, she made the day trip to Norfolk for Ruth Fermoy's funeral, returning the same day by helicopter (with the Princess of Wales) to undertake an afternoon engagement in Westminster Abbey.

By the end of August the Queen Mother was at Birkhall among her chiming grandfather clocks. That she fell asleep momentarily at the

Braemar Games was reported, so too that she wore a plaster on her leg, walked falteringly and looked frail.

Having endured a notably bad 1993, the next two years were somewhat easier, or so it appeared to the general public. In 1994 the Queen Mother continued to pace herself well.

The divorces of the previous years were balanced by the low-key but especially happy weddings of her grandchildren, David Linley (to Serena Stanhope in October 1993) and Sarah Armstrong-Jones (to Daniel Chatto in July 1994). These marriages were destined to prove more durable than those of the Queen's children, and served as a tribute to the qualities of parenthood of both Princess Margaret and Lord Snowdon. In the later years of the decade Princess Margaret was much more contented, rejoicing in the arrival of grandchildren, and all went much better until her own health suddenly declined in 1998.

Cultural events continued with others assuming the mantles of Martin Gilliat and Ruth Fermoy. Michael Wade, a successful businessman and opera lover, heard that the Queen Mother needed a cultural boost and so, through Oliver Everett, the Librarian at Windsor Castle, he brought Opera Interludes to Royal Lodge, under the direction of the baritone Philip Blake-Jones. There was a brief meeting with Sir Alastair Aird, now the Private Secretary, at which he asked who might be present. Aird told him twenty-five to thirty people, mostly local. When pressed, he added: 'The Dean of Windsor, members of the Household – and the Queen, people like that.'[25]

Thus a varied performance, ranging from Delibes and Mozart to the ever-popular Gershwin, took place at Royal Lodge on 18 February 1995. The cast changed in the nursery suite upstairs, unaltered since the days of the princesses, with the occasional book inscribed 'Love Crawfie' still on the shelf. During the performance itself, Wade observed that the light vocal music went down best with the two Queens, while during 'The Flower Duet' from *Lakmé*, the Queen looked stern and a Corgi wandered out of the room. During 'Là ci Darem' from *Don Giovanni*, the Corgi returned, enabling Blake-Jones to comment: 'Can't be too bad then!' This brought a huge smile from the Queen and general laughter in the room.

After the performance Wade talked to the Queen Mother and was amused when the steward failed to notice her drink was empty. 'Oi!' she said – 'in a stern voice that any Cockney would have been proud of', and the message went home. There was then a flurry of activity concerning the Queen Mother lowering herself into an armchair, in which the Queen took solicitous control. Wade's conclusion was that the Queen was 'immensely protective' of her mother and that the Queen Mother had a 'deep understanding of the extraordinary role that her daughter was performing [as Queen] – and knew of the challenges that were consequently made upon family life'.[26]

The Queen Mother's eyesight, which was poor, was considerably improved by cataract operations undertaken while in her later nineties. Prior to that she had only been unable to recognise house guests when they spoke. Her leg suffered from what appeared to be an incurable ulcer, but this did clear up, and by August 1995 the daily bandages were off, at least for a while.

The next problem was her hip, which gave her constant pain and meant that she slowed down considerably in the last few months of 1995, her concentration wavering at times, while she became unable to walk more than about 50 yards. She was resigned to the use of an elegant stick (which had belonged to Queen Mary). In private she used two sticks (though not yet in public), or sometimes a surgical crutch with arm support* or she resorted to a wheelchair (though these were never seen in public). She agreed to ride about in an attractive and dignified golf buggy the Queen had given her the year before.

This golf buggy, presently decorated in her blue and beige racing colours, became a hugely popular feature of the Queen Mother's public appearances, at Clarence House, Royal Ascot and the Sandringham Flower Show. Often the Queen Mother walked out first and then, after a suitable pause, the golf buggy was driven out by her chauffeur, to the delight of the crowd.

In the summer of 1995 the most memorable appearance she made was on the balcony of Buckingham Palace, with the Queen and Princess Margaret either side of her, on the fiftieth anniversary of VE Day in 1945. Despite the recent travails of the Royal Family, a reassuringly large crowd was gathered in the Mall to witness the three survivors of the war reunited there. Their dignity was enhanced not only by the re-enactment of a scene from fifty years before, but because none of these royal ladies had given their secrets to the media. It was a scene that keen supporters of the Royal Family had feared they might never see again.

In December 1995 the Queen Mother made the brave decision to undergo a hip operation. She had been in such grinding pain for months that life was becoming unbearable. No patient had ever undergone this operation

---

* In May 1995 the Queen Mother used this at the private funeral of her goddaughter (and neighbour in the Great Park), Elizabeth Johnston.

at such an advanced age, but she decided that the dangers did not outweigh the misery. When her former equerry Ashe Windham warned her of the dangers, she said: 'Quite honestly, life is not much fun at present.'[27] She survived the operation without a problem, returning to Clarence House and at once taking her place at her table for a large lunch party.

Her friends, her Household, and the general public were amazed by the Queen Mother's resilience and apparent enjoyment of life. But underneath, there was another figure: a sad and contemplative old lady, a widow for nearly half her life, if not confused, then certainly disappointed by the failing standards of modern life, the lack of commitment in some of the younger members of the family, and the overt aggression and vulgarity of the media.

37

Centenarian

Am I to be buried here?
– The Queen Mother in St George's Chapel

To list every fall at the Sandringham Stud, every fractured bone or bruise would be to create a nurse's medical report. Both hips were replaced, releasing the Queen Mother from pain. Physically she remained strong and her brain was as sharp as ever. It is impossible to ignore completely the onset of extreme old age, but she made the very best she could of it, by giving and taking as much enjoyment out of life as possible.

The grim events of the early 1990s plunged to new depths as the decade progressed with Prince Charles's ill-advised 1994 television interview with Jonathan Dimbleby, followed by the authorised biography that soon followed. In this the Prince placed his side of the story on record, not failing to deal his parents some unattractive public blows in the process. The Princess of Wales, by then distanced from the Royal Family, though still living at Kensington Palace, responded with her notorious 1995 *Panorama* interview with Martin Bashir. The combined public admissions of respective adultery received great publicity as did the Princess's assertion that Prince Charles would make an unsatisfactory constitutional king.

Despite the squabbling and covert media briefings, not to mention the recorded telephone conversations, all played out in full public glare, neither the Prince nor Princess of Wales seemed willing to be the first to instigate divorce proceedings. But, following the *Panorama* interview, the Queen took the initiative of commanding the couple to dissolve their marriage. This they did in the summer of 1996.

The Princess of Wales had but one more year of life to live. Towards the middle of 1997, she began to spiral into a form of dangerous chaos. Shunned by the Establishment, she came to rely on the kindness of tycoons, and eventually fell into the camp of Mohammed Fayed, the controversial owner of Harrods, accepting a summer holiday in the South of France with him, and later consorting with his playboy son, Dodi. To the first holiday she took her sons but they refused to go again. She went for a series of further holidays on the newly acquired Fayed yacht, openly disporting herself with Dodi, and then the couple made their way to Paris.

On the night of Saturday 30 August they dined at the Ritz, departed by a side door (the Princess looking trapped and ill at ease), and were pursued by paparazzi. The chauffeur, recalled unexpectedly to duty, had an excess of alcohol in his system. The combination proved fatal, there was an accident in the Pont d'Alma tunnel, the chauffeur and Dodi Fayed were killed instantly, and to the intense shock of the whole world, Diana, Princess of Wales, died in hospital a few hours later.

Those are the bland facts. The saga is well known. There was no conspiracy. They were not assassinated. It was a tragic and in many ways sordid and unnecessary end to a life that held so much promise.

The news broke at Balmoral and in due course was relayed to Birkhall, where the Queen Mother was staying. All the immediate Royal Family were at Balmoral, though about to disperse in different directions. All asked the Queen if they could remain. Everything was done to support the two boys who had lost their mother, and to give them strength to face the demands of a large ceremonial funeral in London the following Saturday.

At Birkhall Diana's name was not mentioned, though the Queen Mother, dressed in appropriate black, accompanied the Royal Family on their much-criticised visit to Sunday morning service at Crathie Church hours after the tragedy.

The furore in London is well etched in the public memory. There were complaints that no flag flew at half-mast on Buckingham Palace, though at Windsor Castle and Sandringham flags were at half-mast. The Queen was attacked in the press for not rushing back to London immediately. One of the problems was that the Queen had no legal or moral right to bury her divorced daughter-in-law. Diana's sons were too young to take the initiative, and the wishes of the Spencer family had to be taken into consideration.

During that week no one in television or radio studios wanted to hear a good word said in favour of the Queen, or in justification of her motives in remaining at Balmoral, though, with hindsight, her role is now better understood and respected.

Eventually, a day late, as Buckingham Palace conceded, the Queen announced plans to come down to London on the eve of the funeral, and to make a live address to the nation. Thus the Royal Family flew to RAF Northolt, the Queen Mother with them, arriving on the Friday afternoon. The Queen made her measured broadcast from the Chinese Dining

Room, with people milling about in the Mall in the background. The Queen was heard in silence in newsrooms, pubs, private homes and other places by a record audience.* Her message was to urge people to lay aside their differences and to unite for a dignified funeral the following day.

The Queen Mother did not join the group of Royal Family members that stood outside Buckingham Palace to see the Princess's cortège pass by. But she was at Westminster Abbey and received no credit for walking the length of that great aisle at the age of ninety-seven. She who had been present at Queen Alexandra's funeral over half a century before, now took part in a service, some elements of which were derived from drafts for her own funeral.

Elton John sang, the crowds outside and most of the congregation within the Abbey clapped Lord Spencer's well-crafted but ultimately wounding words†. After the service, public attention focused on the long flower-strewn drive of the Princess's hearse to Althorp for burial, while the Royal Family flew back to Scotland. Arriving at Birkhall, the Queen Mother rejoined her guests. 'Ah tea,' she said as she came in, seeing that the traditional spread of afternoon tea was still on the table.

That evening one of the guests asked her what she had made of Lord Spencer's address. 'It was very bold!' she said.

The absence of an angry and feuding Princess of Wales did not make life more difficult for the Royal Family. Despite the reluctance of the press to allow Diana, Princess of Wales, to rest in peace, and despite a plethora of books and sordid revelations, there was gradually less to say, though it must be conceded that still the revelations emerge from diverse sources.

The Royal Family went into a period of consolidation and, though the traditional carriage procession was cancelled, all were present at the service of Thanksgiving for the Queen and the Duke of Edinburgh to mark their Golden Wedding at Westminster Abbey on 20 November. The Queen Mother was there, but sitting below the steps of the sacrarium to spare her the climb after another long walk up the aisle.

That evening there was a ball in the newly restored rooms of Windsor Castle, which the Queen Mother had lived long enough to see magnifi-

* The Queen's address is easier to listen to again years later than the pseudo-spontaneous, quasi-emotional words of the new Prime Minister, Tony Blair, when he claimed her as 'The People's Princess' on the day of her death.
† Had Lord Spencer sat down after his description of his sister, 'a girl given the name of the ancient goddess of hunting was, in the end, the most hunted person in the modern age', it would have been a masterly piece, but he could not resist attacking the Royal Family, seated mutely opposite him.

cently restored after the fire exactly five years before. The Queen had considerable difficulty persuading her mother to go to bed.

After Prince Edward's wedding to Sophie Rhys-Jones in the summer of 1999, also at Windsor, the Queen Mother circled the dance floor with Prince George of Hanover. She was nearly ninety-nine.

The Queen Mother returned often to Glamis in later life though, as with St Paul's Walden Bury, she felt detached. It all belonged to an earlier age, long past. But she stayed at the castle to attend the many ceremonies at Dundee University, of which she was Chancellor, to make visits to Lord Roberts Workshop and the Royal Highland Show in Dundee, or to the Black Watch on the Capel Mount, for events such as the opening of the Tay Road Bridge, or to take a look at Falkland Palace with Lord Wemyss, milestones respected and noted, until the last visit on 20 September 1998, appropriately for the Black Watch. She remained at Glamis from 11.45 a. m. until 3.50 p.m., according to the schedule, and, as ever, was in no hurry to leave.

Another hazard of living a long time was that not everyone had the stamina to keep up. Older members of the Household had a habit of dying. The Queen Mother did not encourage retirement, taking the commendable if tough attitude that you were either alive or dead, and if you were alive, then you were working.

In the late 1990s the Queen Mother's Household was boosted by the appointment of a younger team of ladies-in-waiting, from a different generation. No Mistress of the Robes was appointed to replace the Dowager Duchess of Abercorn, who died in February 1990. After this, Lady Grimthorpe (daughter of the Queen Mother's childhood friend, Katharine McEwen, Countess of Scarbrough), appointed in 1973, ran the rota. The young Countess of Scarbrough joined her sister-in-law as a Lady of the Bedchamber in 1994.

Patricia Hambleden was still in waiting in the summer of 1993, wracked with shingles, a testament to her courage, serving the Queen Mother to the end. She died on 19 March 1994. Lady Jean Rankin also undertook occasional duties until 1994, when ill health forced her into a nursing home in Edinburgh. She died aged ninety-six on 3 October 2001, shortly before the Queen Mother.

Lady Angela Oswald, a niece of Princess Alice, Duchess of Gloucester, and wife of the Queen Mother's Racing Manager, Sir Michael Oswald, had joined as an Extra Woman of the Bedchamber in 1981 and more permanently in 1983. Jane Walker-Okeover, born in 1942, was the daughter of a baronet who owned the House of Glenmuick, at Ballater, which neighboured the Birkhall estate. Like her father she became Master of the Meynell Hounds, and the families had known each other for years.

Arguably Lady Margaret Colville, who had been a lady-in-waiting to Princess Elizabeth, was the closest family friend to join the Household. She took up her duties in 1990, having been widowed when her husband, Sir Jock, collapsed with a heart attack on Winchester Station and died in 1987. She and the Queen Mother enjoyed the long-standing joke of talking to each other with a Morningside accent: 'Och Ay, Lady Meg', and so forth.

Mrs Michael Gordon-Lennox was the former Jennifer Gibbs. The Queen Mother had attended her wedding in 1974, as she was the daughter of Hon. Vicary Gibbs, a Grenadier who was killed in the war, and his wife, Jean, who had later married Revd the Hon. Andrew Elphinstone, the Queen Mother's nephew. Jenny Gordon-Lennox's mother had been a lady-in-waiting to the Queen.

The other ladies-in-waiting were Catriona Leslie, wife of Martin Leslie, the former Factor at Balmoral, then Factor at the Castle of Mey, and Lady Penn, formerly Prudence (Prue) Wilson. The Queen Mother had attended her wedding in 1947. Sir Eric Penn had almost been a child of the Household; he had been raised by his uncle, Sir Arthur Penn, after his parents died. He had joined the Lord Chamberlain's Office in 1960, the year his uncle died, and rose to be Comptroller, retiring in 1981. The Penns were close friends of the Royal Family, and especially close to Princess Margaret.

Sir Alastair Aird took over as Private Secretary on the death of Sir Martin Gilliat in 1993, having been Comptroller since 1974. For many years he had effectively run all the residences and had covered for Sir Martin Gilliat and Sir Ralph Anstruther when their attention to detail slipped. He was not flamboyant like his predecessor, and much of his time was spent fending off questions about the Queen Mother's health, and dealing with preparations for her eventual funeral. He continued to run the office at Clarence House with legendary efficiency and friendliness, replying promptly to all communications, and taking enormous trouble to thank anyone who performed any service, however small. He changed the emphasis of the Queen Mother's engagements, wherever possible bringing groups to her rather than her going to them.

Since 1992 there was a new Lord Chamberlain, the Earl of Crawford and Balcarres, the former Government minister, Robin Balniel. His duties were not onerous, and he too was aware that one of his eventual responsibilities would be to oversee the Queen Mother's funeral.

It also fell to Lord Crawford to deal with tricky problems that arose within the Household, none so awkward as the question of the mooted retirement of the Treasurer. That old stickler for etiquette Sir Ralph Anstruther had become increasingly unwell. His mind was disorganised, he had taken to arriving at his desk on Sundays not realising that it was not a weekday, and he suffered certain indignities, which meant that on at least one occasion he who was so scrupulous about his attire was observed walking trouserless along an upper corridor of Clarence House. But when Lord Crawford suggested he should relinquish his office, he was met with a torrent of abuse, and Anstruther refused to talk to him from that day on.

This ugly situation was made no easier by Anstruther having held his office since 1961, and being, in his particular way, an integral part of the Queen Mother's team, a frequent guest at her lunch table, the mainstay of her visits to France and elsewhere, a regular at the July weekends at Sandringham and a presence at the Castle of Mey. There is no question that Queen Elizabeth was fond of him and his muddled brain miraculously cleared when he was talking to her, though clouded when he was not. By the late 1990s he was achieving nothing for the Household, and, after an idle time at his desk, would either lunch with Queen Elizabeth or go out for sandwiches, returning to yet further inertia.

The appointment of a new Treasurer was achieved with difficulty. Nicholas Assheton was about to retire as Deputy Chairman of Coutts. He was asked to come part-time to Clarence House, and finally took over in May 1999. Beforehand he took the precaution of inviting Sir Ralph to lunch at White's, with Lord Napier, Princess Margaret's Private Secretary. Anstruther feigned not to be aware of who he was or why the lunch was taking place. Assheton was then not pleased to hear that Sir Ralph was going about claiming that his job was being prised from him by 'a little clerk from Coutts'.[1] He even accused Assheton and Aird of embezzling the Queen Mother's funds.

Matters were not helped when the Queen Mother appointed Sir Ralph her 'Treasurer Emeritus' in 1998 and, when writing to him, said 'Your desk will always be here for you.' This he interpreted as a reprieve.

At one point, when he was particularly unwell, Sir Ralph even moved into Clarence House, but eventually the situation became so untenable that the Queen Mother commanded him to go to Scotland and remain there. With this command he complied.*

---

* Sir Ralph had hoped to take part in the Queen Mother's 100th birthday celebrations, but he was not well enough. Nor was he present at her funeral. He died at his home in Scotland, soon after the Queen Mother, on 19 May 2002.

More worrying was the ill health of Princess Margaret. In February 1998 she suffered a small stroke which made her forgetful. She failed to keep appointments, once leaving her cousin and lady-in-waiting Jean Wills waiting for her in vain in the Causerie at Claridge's for lunch. The following year she was well enough to go to Mustique, but scalded her feet badly in the bath. From this later setback she made only a partial recovery, her spirit being reluctant to face the challenges needed to get fully well. At first she remained in bed, depressed and low in energy.

Her friends and family had to persuade her, first to leave her bed, then to rise from her wheelchair and eventually to walk again. She was on her feet in time for the Queen Mother's ninety-ninth birthday, and went through a better year until past the 100th birthday, carrying out certain public engagements.

A precipitous exit was made by Jean Wills. She had stayed with the Queen Mother at Birkhall as usual in the summer of 1999, but was forced to go home suddenly as her husband, Major John Wills, took a turn for the worse and died at Allanbay Park on 20 September.

On 25 November there was a memorial service at Chelsea Old Church in London for Lord Dalhousie, the Queen Mother's former Lord Chamberlain, who had died that July, aged eighty-four. This service Queen Elizabeth attended. Princess Margaret had hoped to be there, but felt ill on the morning and sent Jean Wills to represent her. Afterwards there was what one of the guests described as 'a huge lunch party' at Clarence House. Towards the end of lunch, Jean Wills collapsed. She regained consciousness momentarily to say: 'I must go home to feed the chickens', and then lapsed into a coma.

Mrs Wills was then transferred to St Thomas's Hospital, and, because she came from Clarence House, special efforts were made on her behalf. But she never regained consciousness and four days later the machine was switched off.*

On 1 December the Queen Mother attended a performance of opera and ballet with the Queen and the Duke of Edinburgh to mark the reopening of the Royal Opera House, the christening of her new great-grandson, Charles Armstrong-Jones, the next day, lunched at the Ritz, the room falling silent as she entered, and dined with Fellow Benchers of Middle Temple, an occasion she always enjoyed as her concept of a perfect dinner was to be surrounded only by men, preferably without even a lady-in-waiting.

* The Queen and the Queen Mother attended her funeral at the Royal Chapel in Windsor Great Park on 6 December.

On 9 December she lunched with the Grocers' Company, causing some consternation for Sir Clive Bossom, who had anticipated pre-luncheon drink requirements and offered her gin, but she surprised him by saying 'The wine here is always so good. I'd like a Dubonnet.' A waiter was sent sprinting off down Prince's Street to get the requisite from a pub. Belgian chocolates awaited the guests on the table, and the Queen Mother polished off her bowl before the main course.[2]

Four generations of the Royal Family attended the family Christmas lunch at Buckingham Palace a week before Christmas, including the Queen Mother, and then, on 23 December, she departed for Sandringham.

The Queen Mother caught her traditional chill during the Sandringham holiday but was better by 10 February 2000. A few days later the Queen of Denmark and Prince Henrik came on a second state visit, and she had them for tea at Royal Lodge, but did not attend the state banquet.

On 17 March she made her first public appearance of the year, when she presented the shamrock to the Irish Guards in their centennial year. She was then able to enjoy Cheltenham, walk the entire length of the Guards Chapel at the memorial service for Lord Abergavenny, who had acted as her Racing Manager after the war, and her general condition was deemed good, though as one of her court warned: 'She's not getting any stronger.'

And so it continued through the early summer. She was in vivid Garter blue at St George's Chapel for Easter morning service, she presented the Whitbread Cup at Sandown on 29 April and she enjoyed her traditional mid-May holiday at Birkhall. Because it was her centennial year, she agreed to present the trophy on Derby Day, this going to the Aga Khan, whose Sinndar brought him his fourth such victory.

The Queen Mother attended the Birthday Parade in pale blue, seated next to Princess Margaret. She used two crutches to support her while watching the parade from the window of the major general's office, wearing dark glasses, rarely seen in public, on a boiling hot day.

Two days later she made her last public appearance at the Garter ceremony. The cheering which greeted her car as she arrived at the Galilee Porch was nothing short of thunderous. William Tallon was on hand to open the car door, and the bobbing ostrich plumes of her hat marked her arrival. She entered the Quire, surrounded by a great entourage of courtiers.

It had been traditional for some years to place a mounting block by the North Door of the Chapel to enable the Queen Mother to enter her

Ascot landau away from the public gaze. Thus, on leaving the Quire, she would turn right, leave by the North Door and climb into the landau at her convenience. This then followed the Queen's landau and no one outside realised that she had not walked the length of the Nave aisle and down the West Steps.

On this last Garter ceremony, she was accompanied by the Prince of Wales and the Princess Royal, both members of the Order. As she moved slowly to the North Door, she turned to the Prince of Wales who held her hand, glanced in the direction of the George VI Memorial Chapel, and asked him: 'Am I to be buried here?' He paused for a second, looked nervous and replied: 'Ye-es.' She then gave him a conspiratorial glance as if to say 'well, not for a while yet', and his face broke into a relieved smile. They proceeded to the carriage, climbed up the four steps of the mounting block and set off to face the cheering crowds.[3]

Not one of the four days of Ascot did the Queen Mother miss, this time using her golf buggy for the traditional visits to the paddock. There was an evening party for her 100th birthday at which she stayed up till 1.15 a.m.

She then entered the phase of public celebrations to mark her centenary, which continued for six weeks. A luncheon was given at Guildhall by the Lord Mayor and Corporation of the City of London. The Queen Mother, again in pale blue, her favourite colour of that summer, sat between the Lord Mayor and George Carey, the Archbishop of Canterbury. The City presented her with a picture. She had not prepared a speech, but suddenly realised the Lord Mayor was going to address her and that she should reply. She prepared her place by pushing her wine glass to the left.

In a charming impromptu speech, she said she would enjoy looking at the presented picture – 'which I'm sure will be very often' (pronounced 'orphan'). When it was time for the toast, the Archbishop inadvertently took her glass of red wine, now by his right hand. 'That's mine!' she said, which was touching, funny, and convinced everyone that this centenarian was alert.[4]

There was a Service of Thanksgiving at St Paul's Cathedral, but without a carriage procession, as a concession to the demands of the busy London traffic. The Queen Mother arrived by the door in the south transept, dressed in pink. Most of the Kings and Queens of Europe flew in for the occasion and there was an array of guests representing many areas of her life.

There were two particularly striking memories. The first was the phalanx of twelve Household Cavalry trumpeters in the Whispering

Gallery who sounded a fanfare and then moved slowly away round the inner circle of the dome, their gold tunics catching the light in turn, a movement of such grace and beauty that it would have done a choreographer proud. Then, at the end of the service, there was the Queen Mother's last courageous long walk down the entire length of the central aisle of the Cathedral, escorted by the Prince of Wales, using her two sticks as markers to guide her. As she made this progress, her eyes appeared to 'surf' the congregation without making any direct 'hits'. Many will have thought she spotted them. She was followed by the entire Royal Family and the members of Foreign Royal Houses.[5]

On 19 July there was a pageant similar to that performed a decade earlier. Again the representatives of the civilian groups were twice rehearsed and shouted at by a sergeant major figure, urging them to move along faster.

The performance began at 4.30 and the Queen Mother arrived in pink in her carriage at 5.10, with the Prince of Wales. She was on the parade ground until 6.30. Once again this was the brainchild of Major Michael Parker, who received a KCVO for his efforts, and again there were the touching figures who sought nothing more than to march past their patron.

Britain's Labour Government had done its best to denigrate this stratum of society – the kind of doughty volunteers who make tea at village fêtes and take round 'Meals on Wheels', the backbone of rural England. That evening, in the setting sun, the Queen Mother brought 'Old Britain' back to its feet. Sir John Mills made another shaky tribute from a car, and the Queen Mother spoke fluently, delivering her thanks and a blessing. They were words of valediction.

Later in the month the Queen Mother was only reluctantly persuaded to watch the parade on video at Sandringham. She found the coverage irritating. One commentator professed to know her well, causing her to comment that she did not know him at all and regretted that she never would. When the Household Cavalry was mentioned as the regiment of Andrew Parker Bowles, the Prince of Wales walked out of the room. Princess Margaret insisted that the watchers stood up whenever the National Anthem was played.

During this stay the fire alarm went off in the middle of the night, not an unusual occurrence. Corgis were led out and most of the guests were forced to assemble downstairs in their dressing gowns. The Treasurer, Nicholas Assheton, asked if the Queen Mother was coming down. The reply came: 'No, but she has put her pearls on.'[6]

A few days before her 100th birthday, the Queen Mother went to have tea with her sister-in-law, Princess Alice, Duchess of Gloucester, who was then ninety-eight and in frail health. It was the last time the two survivors of that generation of the Royal Family would meet.

The fourth of August finally dawned with the Queen Mother at Clarence House. Her page, Reg Wilcock, in his finest uniform, brought her her morning tea and the gift from the Household staff. He was accorded this honour because he was known to be seriously ill with leukemia. No sooner had he performed it than he collapsed in the corridor.

The Queen Mother went out to the gates of Clarence House with her equerry, Will de Rouet, to receive a special 100th birthday telegram from the Queen, which the young equerry opened with his sword. The Queen Mother had been reluctant to go by carriage to Buckingham Palace, saying that she would look stupid if no crowds turned out to see her. The carriage drew up, splendidly decorated with flowers in her racing colours.

A crowd of forty thousand awaited them. Mindful of the difficult times through which the Royal Family had so lately passed, this said much for the Queen Mother's enduring popularity. As William Tallon, her other page, put it: 'She's back where she belongs.'[7]

There followed a balcony appearance and a huge lunch party, and in the evening the Queen Mother, the Queen and Princess Margaret went to the Bolshoi Ballet at Covent Garden. Here the happiness of the birthday turned to sorrow. A message came through that Reg Wilcock had been taken to the Charing Cross Hospital. He died there, aged sixty-six, a week later, by which time the Queen Mother was at the Castle of Mey. Lord Snowdon, Lady Sarah Chatto, Household and friends attended his magnificent funeral in the Queen's Chapel at Marlborough House.

Her century achieved, the Queen Mother did not give up. At the Castle of Mey she still walked her Corgis alone for twenty minutes three times a day. On her return to London in the autumn she fell and appeared to have fractured her collarbone. She was confined to her room at Clarence House for some weeks. When her friend Fleur Cowles sent her some flowers, she replied that they took her mind off the American election muddles, traffic jams and the Euro,[8] not matters generally considered to worry her unduly.

But she was well enough to go to Sandringham for Christmas. A friend lunching with her before the trip asked her how she would be travelling. She would go by helicopter. Well, he said, that entails just a short drive from Clarence House to the lawn of Buckingham Palace. 'Oh no,' she replied. 'We are flying from Kensington Palace. The helicopter is for Margaret, not for me!'[9]

The Queen Mother continued her royal duties through 2001. Among the special ones was her attendance at Prince Philip's eightieth birthday celebrations at St George's Chapel, when she insisted on walking from the North Door to the nave, and back again, impressing the congregation, alarming the Queen and annoying Prince Philip.

The fast-failing health of Princess Margaret caused the Queen Mother great anxiety. In March 2001 a more serious stroke confined the Princess permanently to a wheelchair, and left her partly paralysed. The Queen Mother often visited her at Kensington Palace, emerging from the lift and announcing herself with a 'Coo-ee!' to which, from her bedroom, Princess Margaret would call out: 'Oh come in, Mummy.' On one occasion, to amuse her infant great-grandson, Charles Armstrong-Jones, the Queen Mother dropped a rose into the large pocket of her coat.

When Princess Margaret made a sad appearance at the Queen Mother's 101st birthday, wearing dark glasses and with her arm in a sling, it was a telling reminder that, as the Golden Jubilee approached, time was running out for the frailer members of the Royal Family

A few days before her 101st birthday, it was said that the Queen Mother was suffering from a heat rash. Then her blood count went down and she was suddenly taken into King Edward VII Hospital, where a room was always ready for her, for an emergency blood transfusion. There had been so many visits to the hospital in the 1990s. Sometimes the Queen Mother was the patient and Princess Margaret visited her. Sometimes it was the other way round.

The transfusion was successful, and a large contingent of press and well-wishers waited to see her come out. It was a great performance. Even if she had come down in a wheelchair, and a wheelchair awaited her at home, what the press saw was the hospital doors open and the Queen Mother step out in pale blue with hat, a three-strand pearl necklace and diamond brooch sparkling in the flashlights. She waved to the crowds and got into her car. She might have been going to the Gold Cup.[10]

The Queen Mother's last birthday fell on Saturday 4 August. She reached the age of 101. There had been fears that she would not be up to it. She was tired, but determined not to disappoint the large crowd, many of whom had been coming year after year. They were happy to be back at Clarence House, as the normal birthday walkabout had not happened the year before due to the 100th birthday carriage drive.

William Tallon was masterminding the show, as ever, and had kindly allowed one small two-year-old to be the first to present the Queen Mother with her flowers. Thus this small boy, born in 1999, met the last Empress of India, born nearly one hundred years before him. Later, after a forty-minute ride in her buggy, she spotted him again and called to him: 'Goodbye – Aged Two.' She had not lost the ability to give pleasure even at that great age and on a day which was her celebration.[11]

Back in the garden, the Queen Mother could enjoy her pre-lunch drink, but she sent it back as it was not strong enough, causing the Princess Royal to say: 'Doesn't Granny know that alcohol is bad for you!' A large lunch and an evening visit to Covent Garden followed as was customary.

The Queen Mother left for the Castle of Mey as usual, and later went down to Birkhall. At the end of August she missed the Braemar Games and went into the Aberdeen Royal Infirmary for forty-five minutes for tests. When the Prince of Wales suddenly cancelled a holiday to Jordan, a rumour spread that the Queen Mother had died. But better news followed and presently she was photographed going to Crathie Church, looking thinner but not unwell, and on 11 October she accompanied the Prince of Wales when he unveiled a statue of an Aberdeen Angus at Alford.

Back in the south, the Queen Mother undertook her last public engagement on 22 November and a memorable one it proved to be. Having launched a previous *Ark Royal*, and this, the fifth, on Tyneside in June 1981, she attended the recommissioning ceremony at Portsmouth, when the aircraft carrier was ready after a £147 million refit at Rosyth. She was tired that day and allowed herself the concession of 'sensible shoes'. Nevertheless Captain Snelson described her as 'full of life and vitality'. As the ceremony ended, she gave the mischievous call: 'Captain, Splice the main brace', well aware that the practice had been discontinued, but giving enormous pleasure (and hopefully a tot of rum) to all who witnessed it. Thereafter the Queen Mother disappeared from public view.

Yet, on 4 December, she agreed to talk to an author about Grand Duchess Xenia. To Coryne Hall the Queen Mother appeared tiny but alert: 'Her posture was still remarkably erect. In fact, I found it hard to believe that I was sitting with a lady of 101 years . . . I noted the little combs which she kept touching to make sure they were in place . . . Despite her great age, Queen Elizabeth's memory was razor sharp . . . extremely sprightly, she had retained her sense of fun and zest for life.' Recalling that when she, the King and their daughters drove past Craigowan, they always sang the 'Volga Boat Song', the Queen Mother proceeded to sing a little to the author. Eventually she began to pick up her sticks, a sign that the interview was coming to an end.[12]

The Queen Mother did not attend the 100th birthday parade for Princess Alice at Kensington Palace on 12 December, not because she was afraid of upstaging her but because she thought a line-up of wheelchairs would make a depressing image. At the parade Princess Alice (who could walk with help) sat between the Queen and Princess Margaret (who was in a wheelchair), her bridesmaids from 1935. The Queen Mother's instincts were sound. She sent flowers instead.

Later that month the Queen Mother had a fall in the night, of which she made little. She did not cancel a private lunch engagement despite being in some discomfort, and no one there would ever have guessed that anything was wrong. The following day there was the Household party at St James's Palace, which she attended in a wheelchair, rising many times from this in order to speak to the various guests. And the day after that, there was the Household Christmas lunch.

The next day, as the year before, the Queen Mother and Princess Margaret set off in the helicopter from Kensington Palace. Whereas Princess Margaret was muffled against the cold, Queen Elizabeth was in a purple coat, with pearls, and no scarf to protect her neck. Only when she arrived at Sandringham did the Queen Mother see the doctor and find she had a fractured pelvis.

The Queen was alone at Sandringham when the helicopter landed. First came her mother in a wheelchair and then her sister, also in a wheelchair. It heralded a worrying Christmas. Neither of them was well enough to go to the Christmas services, though the Queen Mother managed one visit to the royal stud. When the holiday was over, Princess Margaret, who was not entitled to a helicopter on her own, was taken back to London by car.

The Queen Mother had decided to stay at Sandringham until the spring, despite the departure of the Queen. On 6 February, the fiftieth anniversary of the King's death, one of the drawing rooms was set up for a special service, such as would normally be held at the Royal Chapel at Royal Lodge. Canon John Ovenden, her chaplain, came up from Windsor to take the service. When it came to the National Anthem, the Queen Mother made the determined effort to rise from her chair.

She was not well. During these months she was cared for by a younger team, Leslie Chappell, who had succeeded Reginald Wilcock as Page of the Presence, and Jackie Meakin, her dresser. Neither was trained in nursing care, but the Queen Mother could not have been looked after with greater devotion. It was easier for the Queen Mother to allow herself to be cared for by them as they were younger, she knew them less well and it was therefore less personal. William Tallon, for example, she knew too well.

When it was thought a good idea that she should eat yoghurt, Chappell disguised it as a strawberry soufflé so that she might try it. Neither he nor Jackie had any time off during those weeks, and Chappell slept outside the Queen Mother's room every night in case she needed him.

In February Prince Michael of Kent came to see Queen Elizabeth to ask her about Queen Alexandra. Although she was in a wheelchair and clearly not well, her mind was as alert as ever. Prince Michael recalled:

> I asked her about her memories of Queen Alexandra. She said 'I do remember being dragged over to Sandringham to meet her, and how she and her sister, who wore the same clothes – so that no one could tell them apart – played duets on the piano.' Then she pointed: 'on that piano – over there'. It was still in the same place 79 years later. She also recalled that Dagmar lived in a suite upstairs, with a huge Cossack who stood all night outside her door, arms akimbo, at attention. And how when the sisters waved, they did so with cupped hands.[13]

The Queen left Sandringham after 6 February, after which the Queen Mother invited Sir Michael and Lady Angela Oswald to move in to Sandringham with her to keep her company.

This arrangement might have continued for some time, but a mere three days after the service for the King, Princess Margaret suffered another stroke, followed by cardiac problems. She was swiftly moved to the King Edward VII Hospital, where she died in the early hours of Saturday 9 February. The Queen was in London. News reached Sandringham and it was decided to lighten the blow for the Queen Mother by first saying that Princess Margaret was desperately ill in hospital (even though she was already dead), after which the Queen telephoned her to say that she had died.

Prince Philip was at Wood Farm, to which he normally retreated for a few days after the Sandringham house party left. Prince Charles came at once to Sandringham to comfort his grandmother.

Just before Princess Margaret's funeral the Queen Mother telephoned the Archbishop of Canterbury, with whom she had bonded over the wine-glass incident, and told him that she knew Princess Margaret could not

The Queen Mother photographed in black velvet by Cecil Beaton
at Buckingham Palace, December 1948

The Queen Mother
walking on the
beach in Norfolk,
followed by one
of her Corgis,
28 July 1982

The Queen Mother
with the Princess
of Wales in an Ascot
landau at Royal
Ascot in 1987

The Queen Mother
flanked by a less
than happy looking
Prince and Princess
of Wales at the
Derby, 4 June 1986

The Queen Mother,
photographed by the
author, in her carriage at
her 90th Birthday Tribute
Parade on Horse Guards,
7 June 1990

The Queen Mother,
eventually persuaded
into a gondola in
Venice, October 1984

The Queen Mother, photographed by the author, in London, March 1994.
She wears three strands of Mrs Greville's necklace.

Three photographs of the Queen
Mother at dinners given by Maureen,
Marchioness of Dufferin & Ava:
with Richard Branson; with Sir Alec
Guinness; with Lady Dufferin

The Princess Royal and the Queen Mother, photographed by Elizabeth Vickers, as they returned from the Garter ceremony, Windsor Castle, June 1998

(*Right*) The Queen Mother, photographed by Elizabeth Johnston, on a visit to her home, Studio Cottage, Windsor Great Park, in the summer of 1994 (*Below*) The Queen Mother, photographed by the author at Diamond Day, Ascot, on 29 July 2000, a few days before her 100th birthday

The Queen Mother making
her long walk down the aisle of
St Paul's Cathedral, accompanied
by The Prince of Wales, after
the Thanksgiving Service in
Commemoration of her
100th Birthday, 11 July 2000

The Queen Mother
on her 101st birthday,
4 August 2001, after receiving
flowers from Arthur Vickers.
Looking on (left to right):
Mrs Martin Leslie, Lady Angela
Oswald, the Countess of
Scarbrough and William Tallon.

The Queen Mother being driven back to Royal Lodge by her chauffeur, John Collins after Princess Margaret's funeral at St George's Chapel 15 February 2002. This was her last appearance in public.

Lying-in-State, Westminster Hall, April 2002

have coped with another stroke. She received thousands of messages of condolence during the next days and weeks, but her staff noticed that the death did not affect her as they might have supposed. She did not seem to grieve or to mind unduly. So used to death, and so close to death herself, she rose above what was a merciful passing. And it must also be said that Princess Margaret had not always made her mother's life easy.

The Queen Mother was determined to attend the funeral at St George's Chapel on Friday 15 February, despite considerable concerns. The day happened to be the fiftieth anniversary of the King's funeral in the same chapel. To the waiting world, there had been rumours that the Queen Mother had ceased to eat and was gravely ill herself. A variety of plans were discussed as to how to get her to Windsor.

In the week before the funeral, the Queen Mother had two falls at Sandringham, one of which brought paramedics rushing to the house. But she was well enough to fly in a helicopter to Royal Lodge on the Thursday, arriving in the late afternoon.

On the day of the funeral the Queen Mother did not join the Royal Family for lunch in the Castle, but conserved her strength until the last moment. The sadness of the funeral was alleviated by it being a beautiful early spring day.

The Queen Mother was taken to Windsor in the special disabled vehicle from Motability that Princess Margaret had lately used. She did not wish to be seen in a wheelchair and so arrived at the North Door of the Chapel. Few in the Nave saw her and the choir was held back in the Cloisters until she had passed by. She was wheeled up the North Quire Aisle, dressed in deep black with jewellery, and a light veil in her hat. Though her head was leaning slightly to the left, and her very thin right leg was bandaged, her blue eyes were as bright as ever, and she was reassuringly alert. There was something strong, almost demonic in determination, in the way that she attended that service. Her energy was devoted more to the physical effort of being there than to the expression of emotions concerned with her dead daughter.

Throughout the service a doctor and a nurse kept a watchful eye on her. An ambulance was parked outside and there were supplies of oxygen. None was needed. Again she stood briefly at this service, to pay her respects as the coffin left. Afterwards she was brought out into the North Quire Aisle with the Prince of Wales and most of the Royal Family behind her. She then engaged in a spirited conversation with the Comptroller of the Lord Chamberlain's Office as to which door she would leave by, and only when she had been assured that there was no press there and that she would not be photographed did she consent to the plan. Her chair moved off in a phalanx, followed by the Prince of Wales and the Royal Family. Though an invalid, she was still thoroughly in control. It was impressive.[14]

The Queen Mother retreated to Royal Lodge, where she remained, with her faithful staff, Leslie Chappell and Jackie Meakin to look after her. She watched Cheltenham races on the television. There was the traditional party for the Eton Beagles, on 5 March, at which she presided at lunch, going out afterwards on the first beautiful day for some weeks to see the boys and the beagles. She asked Eric Anderson, the Provost of Eton, to arrange her annual visit to Eton later in the year, and later suggested a walk round the garden.

There was a party for the Grand Military at Sandown, hosted by the Queen, at which the Queen Mother was not expected to appear, though she did. To this last party William Tallon came down from London. Without quite knowing why, he kissed the Queen Mother's hand on departure. He never saw her again. One day Martin and Catriona Leslie paid her a visit. 'Not long till Mey,' she said optimistically.

In the meantime the Queen had flown to Jamaica, Australia and New Zealand on her first Golden Jubilee trip. She worried about her mother, and whenever she saw one of her Household answering a mobile phone she dreaded it might be bad news about her mother. 'I can see myself coming down those steps again,' she said, the stark memory of her father's death very much to the fore.

But the Queen Mother was determined to keep going and not to oblige the Queen to come home. Occasional visitors came from within her close court. Dame Frances Campbell-Preston was in waiting for a few days. 'It was awful really, the atmosphere quite different to the olden days. You never knew what was happening. Nobody told you anything. You would look down from the landing into the hall and see the doctor arriving.'[15]

The first signs of spring came and the Queen Mother decided to go out for a drive in her golf buggy to see the new Jubilee Hall being built next to the Royal Chapel and to inspect the greenhouses, as was her custom. She did so though she did not issue her normal instructions as to which plants should go into the cold frames. As she was being driven back, she caught sight of the statue of George III, and commented how well he looked silhouetted in the spring light. She was driven back to the front door, and Leslie and Jackie were there to take her in. She never went out again.

Only in that last week did the Queen Mother appear to accept that her long life might be coming to an end. She had said that she hoped to live to see the Golden Jubilee. At planning meetings, there were discussions as to how to get her into St Paul's Cathedral for the Service of Thanksgiving in June. Yet when she realised that she was not getting better, like Queen Mary with the 1953 Coronation she was determined not to disrupt the celebrations.

The Prince of Wales came to visit his grandmother just before taking his boys on a long-promised skiing break in Klosters. Anxious that she might die in his absence and torn as ever between duty to the old and duty to the young, he expressed the hope that all would be done to keep her alive while he was away. After he had left, the Queen Mother made the decision not to comply with these plans.

It is hard to know if people can decide to die on a particular day. There was only one day that year when the Queen Mother could have died without disruption to external plans. The Queen was back at Windsor with no public engagements planned during the Easter court. All her family was with her for Easter – except the Prince of Wales and his boys. Possibly this suited the Queen Mother, who was fundamentally private and may have wished to spare her adored grandson the torment of a deathbed vigil.

On the evening of Good Friday, 29 March, she was so weak that she could hardly raise her head from the pillow. She called Leslie in and told him to get a box out. She gave him a pair of cuff links. Then she gave Jackie a brooch. She wanted to thank them for their devoted service to her, service which is praised beyond measure by those who witnessed the last months of the Queen Mother's life. An array of Easter eggs was lined up to be given to the grandchildren, great-grandchildren and staff.

On the Saturday, the Queen was out riding when she was warned that her mother's condition had taken a sudden turn for the worse. She arrived in her riding clothes. The chaplain, John Ovenden, was at hand, as was Margaret Rhodes, the Queen Mother's niece and lady-in-waiting. Sarah Chatto was there. The Queen left for a while to change. She returned before the end.

The Queen Mother retained her presence of mind until ten minutes before she died. She just slipped away, as perfect a death as it had been a life. It was 3.15 p.m.

38

The Funeral

'We had all been expecting it for so long, but it still came as a great shock. It took us all by surprise,' recalled William Tallon, who was told the news in London. Likewise, a group of young people in Trafalgar Square at around midnight were filmed by television cameras as they read the headlines in the Sunday papers. 'Oh no!' was the touching reaction of one of them.

The day after the Queen Mother's death was Easter Sunday. The Queen had meant to attend matins with the Royal Family in St George's Chapel. Instead they went privately to the Royal Chapel at Royal Lodge.

Prince Charles and his sons flew back from Klosters. That evening he broadcast a tribute in which he said how much he had always dreaded this moment.

The Queen Mother's coffin was carried the short distance from Royal Lodge to the chapel, followed by the Queen and her immediate family, a small group walking across the lawn.* There the coffin remained until Tuesday morning, visited privately by family and the Household. This was the most informal of its resting places.

It was conveyed by hearse to London. In normal circumstances it would have been taken to the Chapel Royal, but that chapel was undergoing restoration so it rested, again in private, in the Queen's Chapel at Marlborough House.

On Friday there was the great ceremonial military procession through the streets of London, with 1,700 members of armed forces marching. These included representatives of South African and Canadian regiments, the Royal Air Force, Army and Royal Navy. The gun carriage drawn by the King's Troop, the same gun carriage on which the King's coffin had been carried, made its way from Wellington Barracks down the Mall, then turned in towards Clarence House and drew up outside the Queen's Chapel. There it was joined by the pall bearers, the male members of the Royal Family and those members of Queen Elizabeth's Household who would follow the coffin in procession.

---

* Leslie Chappell was not told that there would be press photographers. Nevertheless he stopped the undertakers from moving the coffin to the Royal Chapel on a barrow, insisting that it be carried. A grave indignity was saved.

The Royal Family went inside the Queen's Chapel, and, at the appointed moment, the coffin was brought out and placed on the gun carriage. It was covered by the Queen Mother's royal standard, as it had been since it left Royal Lodge. Now it had the crown with which she was crowned in 1937 on top of it, made fabulous by the Koh-i-noor diamond. There was also a huge wreath of white lilies and a card: 'In loving memory – Lilibet'.

No one had anticipated the crowds such a ceremony would attract in a country which had been virtually brainwashed by its Labour Government to subscribe to 'Cool Britannia'. Nor did that Government know how to respond when asked whether shops should close on the day of the funeral. Later there would be revelations that the Prime Minister sought to maximise his role in the lying-in-state, as he had done at the funeral of Diana, Princess of Wales. He was rebuffed. In the aftermath of the funeral, there was a controversial exchange about this between Black Rod at the Palace of Westminster and Downing Street.

An enormous crowd of all ages, nationalities, colours and creeds was drawn to see the Queen Mother's last major procession. They stood in silence on a beautiful April morning, the leaves just beginning to shimmer on the plane trees, and watched as the procession made its way down the Mall, taking exactly twenty-eight minutes to reach Westminster Hall. The cortège drew up outside the door of the hall as Big Ben struck the last bell of midday. In Britain the trains did not run on time but the Army was prompt to the second.

There the Queen was waiting. The Royal Family followed the coffin in, and watched as it was placed on the catafalque in the centre of the great hall. Gathered at the far end were members of the Houses of Parliament, and also in the hall the Queen Mother's ladies-in-waiting and staff. There was a short service and then four officers of the Household Cavalry took up their positions at each corner of the catafalque.

The Queen and the Duke of Edinburgh then left the hall. As they emerged into Parliament Square in the car, the crowds that had watched in silence suddenly broke out into strong but respectful clapping. It was as though affection was being transferred from one much-loved matriarch to another. The Queen was deeply touched.

The television images could not prepare people for the emotion experienced as they turned the corner and caught the first sight of the coffin so beautifully lit in the centre of the hall. The crowds that had chatted with animation in the long, slow progress to Westminster, fell silent. It was a dramatic way to bring home to those who passed by that the long story of the Queen Mother had come to its final end.

By Monday evening 170,000 people had queued for many hours in order to file past. Earlier that evening the Prince of Wales, the Duke of York, the Earl of Wessex and Viscount Linley, the four grandsons of the Queen Mother, came to Westminster Hall and replaced four members of the Royal Company of Archers to stand vigil over the coffin. The Prince of Wales and the Duke of York were in full naval uniform, Prince Edward and Viscount Linley in morning dress. They guarded the coffin for twenty minutes. The scene echoed the princes' vigil at the coffin of King George V in the middle of the night in January 1936. As six o'clock struck, and the princes prepared to move away, the Queen broadcast to the nation from Windsor Castle.

Such was the interest that Westminster Hall remained open until 6 a.m. the following morning. After the hall was closed, the four soldiers on each corner continued to stand guard over the coffin.

Arriving for the funeral rehearsal at Westminster Abbey, the Lord Chamberlain commented: 'The Queen Mother has united this country, and thus performed her last duty to the nation.'[1]

The Queen Mother's funeral took place on the morning of Tuesday 9 April at Westminster Abbey. Another procession with stirring pipes brought the full glory of Scotland to Parliament Square. Haunting sounds from the bagpipes helped move the slow procession from Westminster Hall to Abbey.

There the Queen was waiting, and many Kings and Queens and members of foreign royal houses. The surviving friends and Household were there, but most of the Queen Mother's intimate friends had long preceded her to the grave. The staff from Clarence House had arrived by bus to find themselves seated at the back of the North Transept, unable to see but the crown on the top of the coffin, an administrative muddle which caused great distress. More than any, they should have been placed near the front.

The Archbishop of Canterbury spoke, her eighth Archbishop, and after the service, as the cortège made its way up the Mall, there was a double fly-past of the last Lancaster bomber still flying, escorted by two Spitfires.

Accompanied by the Prince of Wales, at his special request, the hearse made its way to Windsor, eschewing the M4 in death as the Queen Mother had always insisted upon doing in life. At length it arrived at Windsor Castle and entered by the Henry VIII Gateway.

When the coffin was taken into St George's Chapel, it was lowered into the Royal Vault on the lift in the centre of the Quire, in order to be embalmed. This was required because its final resting place was the King George VI Memorial Chapel, and thus it would not have been sufficiently below ground. When it was brought up again, it weighed more than 36 stone and was conveyed to the little chapel on a trolley.

In the afternoon the immediate Royal Family arrived at Windsor Castle, and, in contrast to the ceremonial and pomp of earlier in the day, there was held a simple service of committal to lay her to rest beside the King. At the same time the ashes of Princess Margaret were placed in the tomb, uniting the earthly remains of three of that group of 'Us Four', which had formed such a powerful image of happy family life during the dark days of the war.

The following Saturday the choir sang Fauré's Requiem, and on the Sunday the doors of St George's Chapel were opened during Eucharist for another file of mourners to pay their respects as they walked past the simple black slab now bearing the joint names: 'George VI 1895–1952' and 'Elizabeth 1900–2002'.

Again, it was impossible to put a type to those who came. They were from all ages, all countries, all races, colours and creeds, united by one thing only, their wish to be there and their willingness to wait long hours for the privilege. Silently they came and silently they left replenished by the experience.[2]

It had been a long journey and a full century from that summer of 1900 to that small side chapel of St George's Chapel, through the long Scottish summers, the travails of the Great War, the restless months of indecision, the acceptance of the Duke of York, the unexpected call to greater service and finally the long years of widowhood, creating from a little girl with an engaging smile and endearing manner a great icon of the twentieth century in Britain.

Surely her epitaph must be this: when the Duke of York succeeded to the throne so unwillingly and with such trepidation, all he wanted to be was a good constitutional King. The times through which they lived were hard ones. By her strength and support, Elizabeth Bowes-Lyon made it possible for the King to be that man.

History will surely confirm her as one of the greatest, if not the greatest, of consorts in the long line of Kings and Queens that have reigned in Great Britain.

APPENDIX I

The Ancestry of Queen Elizabeth

The Strathmores

Queen Elizabeth descended twice from Robert the Bruce, King of Scotland, on the paternal side of the family, this descent being recognised in the escutcheon granted to Lord Strathmore, in 1938, when his daughter became an English Queen Consort.

The first descent was by the marriage of Sir John Lyon to Jean, Lady Keith, King Robert II's third daughter by his first marriage to Elizabeth Mure, and the second by the marriage of Sir John Lyon's son, also Sir John Lyon, to Euphemia, Countess Palatine of Strathern, whose grandmother, Euphemia was King Robert II's second wife.

The Lyon family had been landed in Forfar since 1372, the first Sir John Lyon being Keeper of the Privy Purse and Chamberlain of Scotland. King Robert II gave him the thaneage of Glamis. Sir James Lindsay of Crawford killed Sir John in 1382. His great-grandson, Patrick, 1st Lord Glamis, was one of the hostages for the ransom of King James I of Scotland delivered to the English in March 1424.

The Lyon family survived through the centuries, losing some of its members brutally on the way. The 4th Lord Glamis died of wounds received in a fray with the Ogilvys in 1500, and the widow of the 6th Lord was horribly burned to death in 1537 for plotting against the King. Their son was sentenced to death, but not executed, while the 8th Lord Glamis was shot through the head in a fray with Lord Crawford's men.

The 9th Lord (whose wife had been the mistress of James V) was created Earl of Kinghorne in the peerage of Scotland in 1606. The 2nd Earl died of the plague, leaving terrible debts due to his excessive style of living, while his son, Patrick, the 3rd Earl, was created Earl of Strathmore in 1677, after which time the Earls were known as Earls of Strathmore and Kinghorne combined.* He opposed the Revolution of 1688, as did his son.

In 1715 the young 5th Earl was slain at Sheriffmuir fighting for the

---

* From now on, there is one of those peerage confusions. The 3rd Earl of Kinghorne and 1st Earl of Strathmore was styled 3rd Earl of Strathmore and Kinghorne.

cause of the Stewarts, 'struck by a musket shot and sabred by a dragoon'.[1] His brother, Charles, 6th Earl of Strathmore, was killed in a scuffle in 1728 by the drunken James Carnegie of Finhaven, 'the swiftest of foot when running from the Battle of Sheriffmuir', who perpetuated the wicked deed, and 'without any previous warning ran throw and throw the body (and no sword drawn but his own)'.*[2]

Horace Walpole recorded that the 6th Earl's wife had rushed between her husband, attempting to restrain him, whereupon his rival had 'stabbed him in her arms, on which she went mad, though not enough to be confined'.[3] In widowhood she married her factor and died in a convent near Paris.

Subsequent Earls fared better and it was by the marriage of the 9th Earl to Mary, the very rich heiress daughter of George Bowes in 1767, that the name of Bowes first replaced but was later linked with Lyon. She brought a fortune of £600,000 to the family, and Streatlam Castle, Co. Durham, and Gibside Castle, near Newcastle, were added to the list of family seats. She was a flighty girl with a somewhat loose past. After her marriage she had an affair with George Grey, and even a child by him. She was deeply unhappy in her marriage. In 1785 Walpole recorded that she had eloped 'taking two maids with her; but no swain is talked of'.[4] Two years later her husband abducted her but she was rescued and they were finally divorced. She died in 1800 and, despite all this, was buried in the South Cross of Westminster Abbey.

The 11th Earl was the youngest son of the 9th Earl. He was succeeded by his grandson as 13th Earl. The Strathmores were still peers of Scotland and only in 1887 was the 13th Earl given an English peerage as one of eight Golden 'Jubilee' Barons, styled Baron Bowes of Streatlam Castle. He was the Queen Mother's grandfather.

The Queen Mother likewise descended from many splendid families including such Shakespearean forebears as Courtenays and Talbots, Howards and Percys. Through the Cavendishes, she descended from the Earls of Cork and Dukes of Somerset, and thus from the 1st Earl of Hertford, great-great-grandson of the Tudor King, Henry VII. She had Huguenot blood which joined the family through marriage with a Grinstead in 1820. She brought more Welsh blood to her grandson, Prince Charles, than had flowed in the veins of any previous Princes of Wales.

* Carnegie's kinsman some generations later, Charles, 11th Earl of Southesk, mounted the Guard of Honour at the wedding of the Duke of York and Lady Elizabeth Bowes-Lyon in 1923, and later that year married Princess Maud. He stayed at Glamis for the Duke of York's first visit in September 1920.

Through the Wellesleys she descended from Murrough 'The Tanist' O'Brien, last King of Thomond and back through the Kings of Munster to Brian, High-King of Ireland. On a more earthy note she also descended from one George Carpenter, who at the age of sixty married the eighteen-year-old daughter of a plumber who had come to repair his roof.

The Portlands

Mixed with this blood of Scotland, Ireland and Wales was her maternal descent through Cecilia Strathmore from the formidable Cavendish-Bentincks – the Dukes of Portland. It is this ancestry that accounted for the mettle in her constitution. The Dutch Bentinck ancestors made judicious marriages into the great families of England, contributing strong genes to the Bowes-Lyon family when united with them in 1881.

Horace Walpole declared that 'no wise King of England would think it for his credit that he considered himself, or was considered by others, as personally at variance with a Duke of Portland'.[5] The Bentincks, from whom the Portlands descended, were originally part of the ancient nobility of the Duchy of Guelder in Holland. One of their first known ancestors was Wicherus Benting, who witnessed the signature of Bishop Willibold of Utrecht in 1230. By the late 1400s the family were settled at The Loo (later the home of Queen Juliana of the Netherlands).

Hans William Bentinck, the 3rd son of Bernard, Baron Bentinck, served first as page to William, Prince of Orange. He became close to him, his 'favourite'. He rose to be the Prince's confidential adviser. He came to England to arrange his marriage to Princess Mary of York (later Queen Mary II), daughter of James II. He spoke little English and did not endear himself to his new country. When William became King, he was sworn of the Privy Council, appointed Groom of the Stole and created Earl of Portland (in 1689). He was installed as a Knight of the Garter in 1697, and the following year appointed Ambassador to France. To the discredit of the King, Portland received a considerable number of estates making him a very rich man, including Bulstrode Park in Buckinghamshire, once the home of the notorious Judge Jeffreys.

The 1st Earl of Portland first married Anne Villiers, daughter of Sir Edward Villiers, a gallant Civil War officer, whose wife was governess to the future Queens, Mary and Anne. Their son Henry was created Duke of Portland by George I partly because his father had supported the Hanoverian succession. He lost a lot of money in the South Sea Bubble and died in Jamaica aged forty-four. His son, the 2nd Duke, a retiring and unambitious man, nevertheless succeeded in marrying Margaret

Cavendish Harley, an heiress as well as a wit and the muse of the poet Matthew Prior, and the only daughter of the 2nd Earl of Oxford, and of Lady Henrietta Holles, daughter of the 1st Duke of Newcastle. This union brought Welbeck Abbey, the great Cavendish estate in Nottinghamshire, into the family.

Their son was the 3rd Duke of Portland (1738–1809), Viceroy of Ireland and twice Prime Minister in the reign of George III. He achieved the rare distinction of heading both a Whig and later a Tory administration. The Duke was a courageous man once enduring an operation to remove a stone without an anaesthetic, uttering not a groan. During his second administration he never made a single speech, causing Lord Rosebery to describe him as 'a dull, dumb Duke'.[6] He was deemed to have held the office of Prime Minister as the esteemed representative of 'the aristocratic theories of government for which he lived, and because he attempted to carry them out in a period of great events'.[7]

The Duke married Lady Dorothy Cavendish, daughter of the 4th Duke of Devonshire, thus uniting two great dynasties. The family were now rich and powerful, their greatest asset being the borough of Marylebone in London, many of the streets in which bear family names – Welbeck Street, Portland Place, Oxford Street, and New Cavendish Street.

That Duke's third son, Lord Charles Cavendish-Bentinck, married Georgiana Seymour, commonly believed to be a bastard daughter of George IV.[8] By his second wife, Anne Wellesley, a bastard daughter of the 1st Marquess Wellesley, he was the grandfather of Cecilia, Countess of Strathmore, Elizabeth's mother.

APPENDIX II

The Descendants of the Earl of Strathmore

The Queen Mother had six brothers and three sisters. She outlived all her siblings, the last one by more than thirty-four years. Her eldest sister died in 1893, while the youngest died in 1967, and she died in 2002. The Queen Mother had twenty-two nephews and nieces. Of these, she outlived fifteen. Many of them died at young ages, some in tragic circumstances.

Claude, 14th Earl of Strathmore, KG, KT
(1855–1944)
= Cecilia Cavendish-Bentinck
(1862–1938)

1) Patrick, 15th Earl of Strathmore (1884–1949)
   = Lady Dorothy Osborne (1888–1946)

    1) John, Master of Glamis (1910–41) (killed in war)
    2) Timothy, 2nd Earl (1918–72)
       = Mary Brennan (wife of 17th Earl) (1923–67) (committed suicide)
    1) Cecilia (1912–47)
       = Major Kenneth Harington (b. 1911)
    2) Nancy (1918–59) (found dead on a couch)
       = (1) Lance Robinson (divorced)
       = (2) John Blair (shot himself in Ireland in 1955)

2) John (Jock) (1886–1930)
   = Hon. Fenella Trefusis (1889–1966)
    1) Patricia (1916–17)
    2) Anne (1917–80)
       = (1) Viscount Anson (divorced)
       = (2) HH Prince Georg of Denmark (1920–86)
          Patrick, Earl of Lichfield (b. 1939)
          Lady Elizabeth Anson (b. 1941)

3) Nerissa
   (1919–86) (mentally deficient)
4) Diana (1923–86)
   = Peter Somervell (d. 1993), one daughter.
5) Katherine Bowes–Lyon (b. 1926) (mentally deficient)

3) Alexander (1887–1911)

4) Fergus (1889–1915) (killed in war)
   = Lady Christian Dawson-Damer (1890–1959) (remarried)

   Rosemary (1915–89)
   = Edward Joicey-Cecil (1912–85)

5) Michael (1893–1953)
   = Elizabeth Cator (1899–1953)

   1) Fergus
      17th Earl of Strathmore (1928–87)
      = Mary McCorquodale (b. 1932)

      1) Michael
         18th Earl of Strathmore (b. 1957)
      1) Elizabeth (b. 1959)
      2) Diana (b. 1966)

   2) Albemarle (b. 1940)

   1) Mary (b. 1932)
      = Sir Timothy Colman, KG (b. 1929)
   3 sons, 3 daughters

6) David (1902–61)
   = Rachel Spender-Clay (1907–96)

   1) Simon (b. 1932)
      = Caroline Pike 3 sons, 1 daughter

   2) Davina (b. 1930)
      = 13th Earl of Stair (1906–96) 3 sons

1) Violet (1882–93) (died of diphtheria)

2) Mary (1883–1961)
   = 16th Lord Elphinstone, KT (1869–1955)

    1) John, 17th Lord Elphinstone (1914–75)
       (imprisoned in Colditz)
       2) Andrew (Revd) (1918–75)
       = Jean Gibbs (b.1923) 1 son (18th Lord Elphinstone), 1
       daughter
       1) Elizabeth (1911–80)
       2) Jean (1915–99) (collapsed at Clarence House)
       = Major John Wills (1910–99)
       3) Margaret (b. 1925) (lady-in-waiting)
       = Denys Rhodes (1919–81) 2 sons, 2 daughters

3) Rose (1890–1967)
   = 4th Earl Granville, KG (1880–1953)

    James 5th Earl Granville (1918–96)
       = Doon Plunket (1931–2004) 2 sons, 1 daughter

    Mary (b. 1917)
       = Samuel Clayton (1918–2004) 1 son, 1 daughter

4) **Elizabeth** (1900–2002)
   = HM King George VI (1895–1952)

APPENDIX III

Genealogical Tables

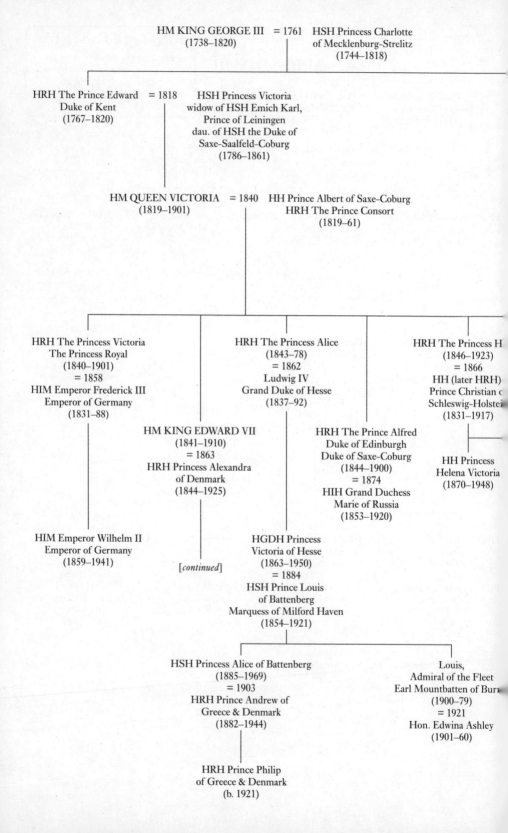

HM KING GEORGE III = 1761 HSH Princess Charlotte
(1738–1820) of Mecklenburg-Strelitz
(1744–1818)

HRH The Prince Edward = 1818 HSH Princess Victoria
Duke of Kent widow of HSH Emich Karl,
(1767–1820) Prince of Leiningen
dau. of HSH the Duke of
Saxe-Saalfeld-Coburg
(1786–1861)

HM QUEEN VICTORIA = 1840 HH Prince Albert of Saxe-Coburg
(1819–1901) HRH The Prince Consort
(1819–61)

HRH The Princess Victoria
The Princess Royal
(1840–1901)
= 1858
HIM Emperor Frederick III
Emperor of Germany
(1831–88)

HRH The Princess Alice
(1843–78)
= 1862
Ludwig IV
Grand Duke of Hesse
(1837–92)

HRH The Princess H
(1846–1923)
= 1866
HH (later HRH)
Prince Christian ©
Schleswig-Holstei
(1831–1917)

HM KING EDWARD VII
(1841–1910)
= 1863
HRH Princess Alexandra
of Denmark
(1844–1925)

HRH The Prince Alfred
Duke of Edinburgh
Duke of Saxe-Coburg
(1844–1900)
= 1874
HIH Grand Duchess
Marie of Russia
(1853–1920)

HH Princess
Helena Victoria
(1870–1948)

HIM Emperor Wilhelm II
Emperor of Germany
(1859–1941)

[continued]

HGDH Princess
Victoria of Hesse
(1863–1950)
= 1884
HSH Prince Louis
of Battenberg
Marquess of Milford Haven
(1854–1921)

HSH Princess Alice of Battenberg
(1885–1969)
= 1903
HRH Prince Andrew of
Greece & Denmark
(1882–1944)

Louis,
Admiral of the Fleet
Earl Mountbatten of Burn
(1900–79)
= 1921
Hon. Edwina Ashley
(1901–60)

HRH Prince Philip
of Greece & Denmark
(b. 1921)

Select Royal Family Tree

Royal Family tree displaying, in
particular, those members of the
Royal Family mentioned
in the text.
See continuation overleaf.

HRH The Prince Adolphus = 1818 HSH Princess Augusta
Duke of Cambridge | of Hesse-Cassel
(1774–1850) | (1797–1889)

HRH Princess Mary Adelaide, = 1866 HH Prince Francis
Duchess of Teck | Duke of Teck
(1833–97) | (1837–1900)

HSH Princess Victoria Mary =1893 HM KING GEORGE V   Alexander, = 1904 HRH Princess Alice
of Teck | (1865–1936)   Earl of Athlone | of Albany
(1867–1953)   (1874–1957) | (1883–1981)

Lady May Cambridge = 1931 Colonel Sir Henry
(1906–94) | Abel Smith
(1900–93)

HRH The Princess Louise   HRH The Prince Arthur   HRH The Princess Beatrice
(1848–1939)   Duke of Connaught   (1857–1944)
= 1871   (1850–1942)   = 1885
John, 9th Duke of Argyll   = 1879   HSH (later HRH)
(1845–1914)   HRH Princess Louise   Prince Henry
    Margaret of Prussia   of Battenberg
    (1860–1917)   (1858–96)

HRH The Prince Leopold
Duke of Albany
(1853–84)
= 1882
HRH Princess Helena of
Waldeck & Pyrmont
(1861–1922)

HH Princess
Marie Louise
(1872–1956)

HRH Prince Arthur of   HRH Princess Patricia   HRH Princess Alice   HRH Princess
Connaught   of Connaught   of Albany   Victoria Eugénie
(1883–1938)   (1886–1974)   (1883–1981)   of Battenberg
= 1913   = 1919   = 1904   (1887–1969)
HRH Princess Alexandra   Admiral Hon. Sir   Alexander, Earl   = 1906
Duchess of Fife   Alexander Ramsay   of Athlone   HM King Alfonso
(1891–1959)   (1881–1972)   (1874–1957)   XIII of Spain
    (1886–1941)

Captain Alexander
Ramsay of Mar
(1919–99)

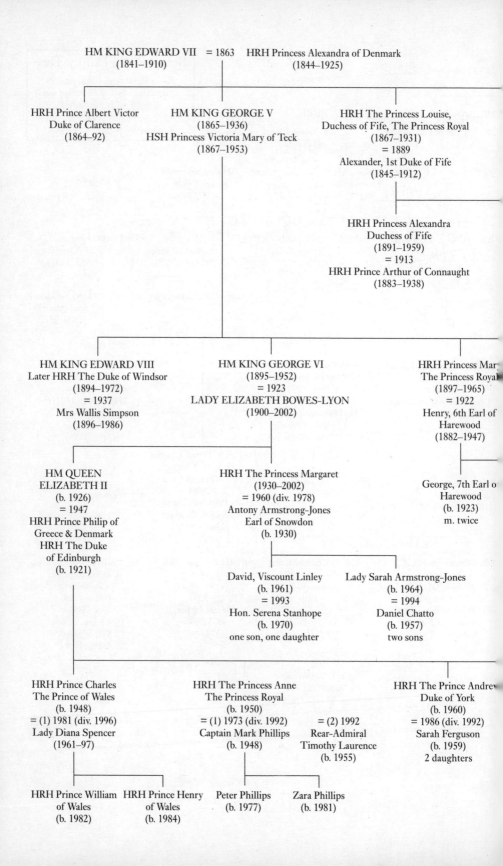

HM KING EDWARD VII = 1863 HRH Princess Alexandra of Denmark
(1841–1910) (1844–1925)

HRH Prince Albert Victor
Duke of Clarence
(1864–92)

HM KING GEORGE V
(1865–1936)
HSH Princess Victoria Mary of Teck
(1867–1953)

HRH The Princess Louise,
Duchess of Fife, The Princess Royal
(1867–1931)
= 1889
Alexander, 1st Duke of Fife
(1845–1912)

HRH Princess Alexandra
Duchess of Fife
(1891–1959)
= 1913
HRH Prince Arthur of Connaught
(1883–1938)

HM KING EDWARD VIII
Later HRH The Duke of Windsor
(1894–1972)
= 1937
Mrs Wallis Simpson
(1896–1986)

HM KING GEORGE VI
(1895–1952)
= 1923
LADY ELIZABETH BOWES-LYON
(1900–2002)

HRH Princess Mar
The Princess Royal
(1897–1965)
= 1922
Henry, 6th Earl of
Harewood
(1882–1947)

HM QUEEN
ELIZABETH II
(b. 1926)
= 1947
HRH Prince Philip of
Greece & Denmark
HRH The Duke
of Edinburgh
(b. 1921)

HRH The Princess Margaret
(1930–2002)
= 1960 (div. 1978)
Antony Armstrong-Jones
Earl of Snowdon
(b. 1930)

George, 7th Earl o
Harewood
(b. 1923)
m. twice

David, Viscount Linley
(b. 1961)
= 1993
Hon. Serena Stanhope
(b. 1970)
one son, one daughter

Lady Sarah Armstrong-Jones
(b. 1964)
= 1994
Daniel Chatto
(b. 1957)
two sons

HRH Prince Charles
The Prince of Wales
(b. 1948)
= (1) 1981 (div. 1996)
Lady Diana Spencer
(1961–97)

HRH The Princess Anne
The Princess Royal
(b. 1950)
= (1) 1973 (div. 1992)
Captain Mark Phillips
(b. 1948)

= (2) 1992
Rear-Admiral
Timothy Laurence
(b. 1955)

HRH The Prince Andre
Duke of York
(b. 1960)
= 1986 (div. 1992)
Sarah Ferguson
(b. 1959)
2 daughters

HRH Prince William
of Wales
(b. 1982)

HRH Prince Henry
of Wales
(b. 1984)

Peter Phillips
(b. 1977)

Zara Phillips
(b. 1981)

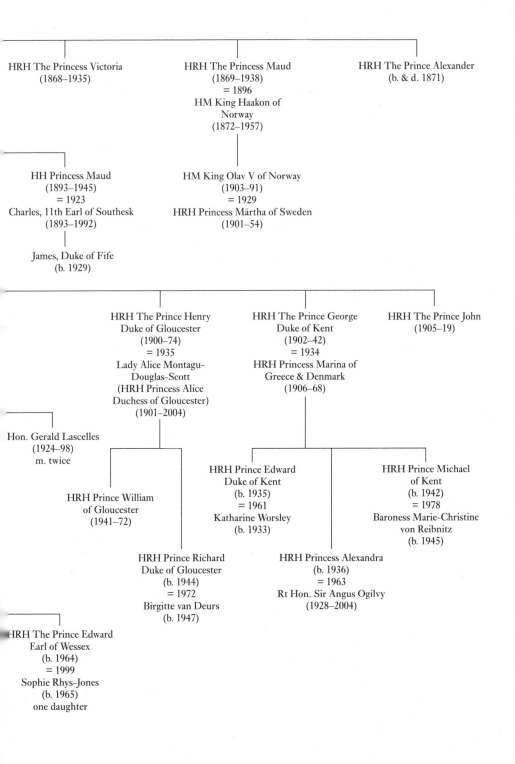

HRH The Princess Victoria
(1868–1935)

HRH The Princess Maud
(1869–1938)
= 1896
HM King Haakon of
Norway
(1872–1957)

HRH The Prince Alexander
(b. & d. 1871)

HH Princess Maud
(1893–1945)
= 1923
Charles, 11th Earl of Southesk
(1893–1992)

James, Duke of Fife
(b. 1929)

HM King Olav V of Norway
(1903–91)
= 1929
HRH Princess Märtha of Sweden
(1901–54)

HRH The Prince Henry
Duke of Gloucester
(1900–74)
= 1935
Lady Alice Montagu-
Douglas-Scott
(HRH Princess Alice
Duchess of Gloucester)
(1901–2004)

HRH The Prince George
Duke of Kent
(1902–42)
= 1934
HRH Princess Marina of
Greece & Denmark
(1906–68)

HRH The Prince John
(1905–19)

Hon. Gerald Lascelles
(1924–98)
m. twice

HRH Prince William
of Gloucester
(1941–72)

HRH Prince Edward
Duke of Kent
(b. 1935)
= 1961
Katharine Worsley
(b. 1933)

HRH Prince Michael
of Kent
(b. 1942)
= 1978
Baroness Marie-Christine
von Reibnitz
(b. 1945)

HRH Prince Richard
Duke of Gloucester
(b. 1944)
= 1972
Birgitte van Deurs
(b. 1947)

HRH Princess Alexandra
(b. 1936)
= 1963
Rt Hon. Sir Angus Ogilvy
(1928–2004)

HRH The Prince Edward
Earl of Wessex
(b. 1964)
= 1999
Sophie Rhys-Jones
(b. 1965)
one daughter

Robert I The Bruce = (1) Isabella
King of Scots   dau. of Donald,
(1274–1329)   6th Earl of Mar

Marjorie Bruce = 1315 Walter, 6th High Steward
(d. 1316)   of Scotland (d. 1326)

Bowes-Lyon

Family tree of the Earls of
Strathmore & Kinghorne, showing
the Queen Mother's dual descent
from Robert I, The Bruce, King of
Scotland. The tree also shows
her descent from the 1st Earl of
Chesterfield, and the 1st Duke
of Ormonde, and her relationship
to George Washington, first
President of the United States
of America, and to General Robert
E. Lee, Commander-in-Chief of
the Confederate Army in the
American Civil War.
See continuation overleaf.

(1) 1347   = King Robert II   = (2) Euphemia
Elizabeth   of Scotland   (d. 1387),
(d. ante 1355)   (1316–1390)   dau. of Hugh,
dau. of Sir   4th Earl of Ross
Adam Mure
of Rowallan

Jean   David, Earl Palatine
=   of Stratherne
Sir John Lyon   (b. 1356/60, d. ante 1389)
Chamberlain
of Scotland   Euphemia, Countess
(d. 1382?)   Palatine of Stratherne
                        (b. ante 1375 – d. in or post 1434)
                        = 1406
                        Sir Patrick Graham, of Kilmont

Sir John Lyon, 2nd of Glamis   =   Elizabeth
(d. ca 1435)

Patrick, 1st Lord Glamis   =   Isabel dau. of Sir Walter Ogilvy
(d. 1459)

Alexander   John, 3rd Lord Glamis   John, 8th Lord Glamis
2nd Lord Glamis   (d. 1497)   (d. 1578)
(d. 1486)   =   =
=   Elizabeth Scrymgeour   Elizabeth
Agnes, dau. of   widow of William Meldrum
William, Lord
Crichton   John, 4th Lord Glamis   Patrick,
                      (d. 1500)   9th Lord Glamis
                      =   1st Earl of Kinghorne
                      Elizabeth   (1575–1615)
                      dau. of 2nd Lord Gray   = 1595
                                                        Anne (d. 1618)
George   John, 6th Lord Glamis   dau. of John, Earl of Tullibardine
5th Lord Glamis   (d. 1528)
(d. unmarried 1505)   John, 2nd Earl of Kinghorne
                      Jonet   (1596–1646)
                      (d. 1537)   =
                      dau. of George,   Lady Elizabeth Maule
                      Master of Angus   (d. 1659)

                      John, 7th Lord Glamis   Patrick, 3rd Earl of
                      (d. 1559)   Strathmore & Kinghorne
                      =   (1643–95)
                      Janet Keith   = 1662
                      dau. of William, 4th Earl Marischal   Lady Helen Middleton
                                                        (d. 1708)

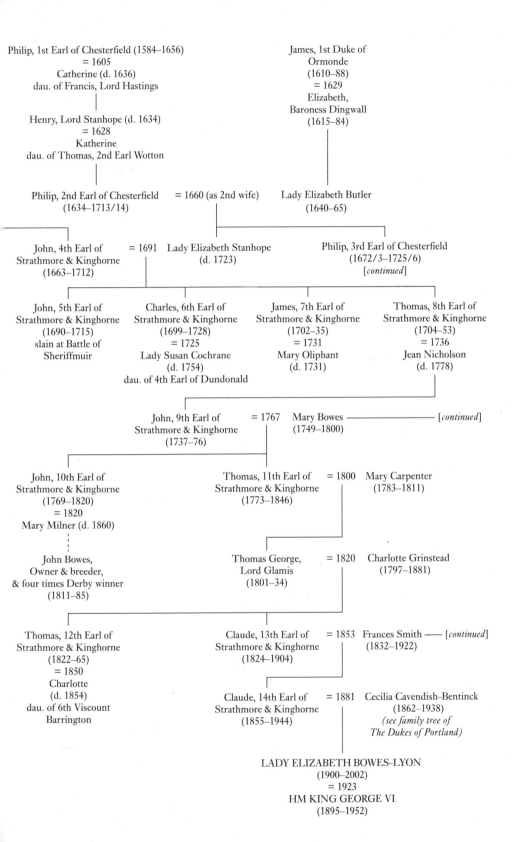

Philip, 1st Earl of Chesterfield (1584–1656)
= 1605
Catherine (d. 1636)
dau. of Francis, Lord Hastings

James, 1st Duke of
Ormonde
(1610–88)
= 1629
Elizabeth,
Baroness Dingwall
(1615–84)

Henry, Lord Stanhope (d. 1634)
= 1628
Katherine
dau. of Thomas, 2nd Earl Wotton

Philip, 2nd Earl of Chesterfield   = 1660 (as 2nd wife)   Lady Elizabeth Butler
(1634–1713/14)   (1640–65)

John, 4th Earl of   = 1691   Lady Elizabeth Stanhope   Philip, 3rd Earl of Chesterfield
Strathmore & Kinghorne   (d. 1723)   (1672/3–1725/6)
(1663–1712)   [continued]

John, 5th Earl of   Charles, 6th Earl of   James, 7th Earl of   Thomas, 8th Earl of
Strathmore & Kinghorne   Strathmore & Kinghorne   Strathmore & Kinghorne   Strathmore & Kinghorne
(1690–1715)   (1699–1728)   (1702–35)   (1704–53)
slain at Battle of   = 1725   = 1731   = 1736
Sheriffmuir   Lady Susan Cochrane   Mary Oliphant   Jean Nicholson
                             (d. 1754)   (d. 1731)   (d. 1778)
                             dau. of 4th Earl of Dundonald

John, 9th Earl of   = 1767   Mary Bowes ——————————— [continued]
Strathmore & Kinghorne   (1749–1800)
(1737–76)

John, 10th Earl of   Thomas, 11th Earl of   = 1800   Mary Carpenter
Strathmore & Kinghorne   Strathmore & Kinghorne   (1783–1811)
(1769–1820)   (1773–1846)
= 1820
Mary Milner (d. 1860)

John Bowes,   Thomas George,   = 1820   Charlotte Grinstead
Owner & breeder,   Lord Glamis   (1797–1881)
& four times Derby winner   (1801–34)
(1811–85)

Thomas, 12th Earl of   Claude, 13th Earl of   = 1853   Frances Smith —— [continued]
Strathmore & Kinghorne   Strathmore & Kinghorne   (1832–1922)
(1822–65)   (1824–1904)
= 1850
Charlotte
(d. 1854)
dau. of 6th Viscount   Claude, 14th Earl of   = 1881   Cecilia Cavendish-Bentinck
Barrington   Strathmore & Kinghorne   (1862–1938)
                                      (1855–1944)   (see family tree of
                                                                        The Dukes of Portland)

LADY ELIZABETH BOWES-LYON
(1900–2002)
= 1923
HM KING GEORGE VI
(1895–1952)

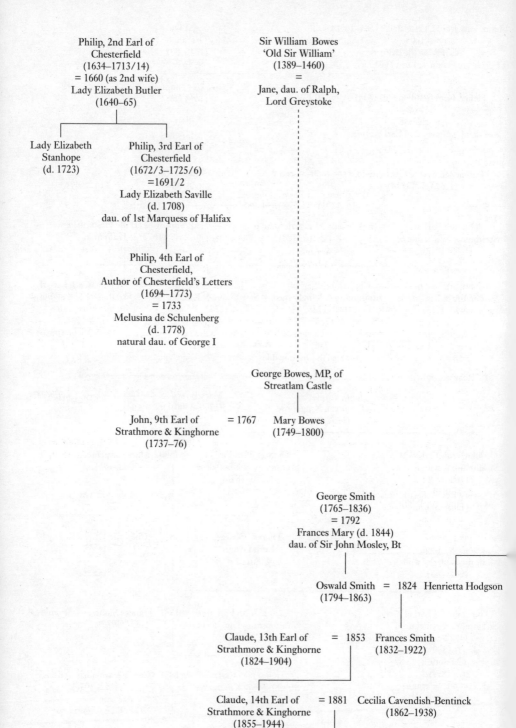

Philip, 2nd Earl of
Chesterfield
(1634–1713/14)
= 1660 (as 2nd wife)
Lady Elizabeth Butler
(1640–65)

Sir William Bowes
'Old Sir William'
(1389–1460)
=
Jane, dau. of Ralph,
Lord Greystoke

Lady Elizabeth
Stanhope
(d. 1723)

Philip, 3rd Earl of
Chesterfield
(1672/3–1725/6)
=1691/2
Lady Elizabeth Saville
(d. 1708)
dau. of 1st Marquess of Halifax

Philip, 4th Earl of
Chesterfield,
Author of Chesterfield's Letters
(1694–1773)
= 1733
Melusina de Schulenberg
(d. 1778)
natural dau. of George I

George Bowes, MP, of
Streatlam Castle

John, 9th Earl of
Strathmore & Kinghorne
(1737–76)

= 1767

Mary Bowes
(1749–1800)

George Smith
(1765–1836)
= 1792
Frances Mary (d. 1844)
dau. of Sir John Mosley, Bt

Oswald Smith = 1824 Henrietta Hodgson
(1794–1863)

Claude, 13th Earl of
Strathmore & Kinghorne
(1824–1904)

= 1853

Frances Smith
(1832–1922)

Claude, 14th Earl of
Strathmore & Kinghorne
(1855–1944)

= 1881

Cecilia Cavendish-Bentinck
(1862–1938)

LADY ELIZABETH BOWES-LYON
(1900–2002)
= 1923
HM KING GEORGE VI
(1895–1952)

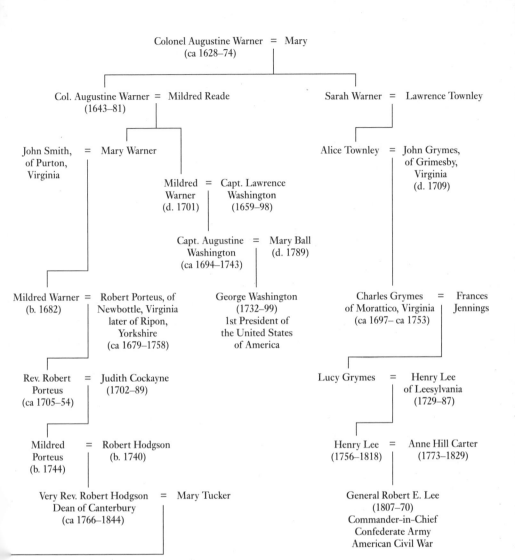

Colonel Augustine Warner = Mary
(ca 1628–74)

Col. Augustine Warner = Mildred Reade
(1643–81)

Sarah Warner = Lawrence Townley

John Smith, = Mary Warner
of Purton,
Virginia

Alice Townley = John Grymes,
of Grimesby,
Virginia
(d. 1709)

Mildred = Capt. Lawrence
Warner   Washington
(d. 1701)   (1659–98)

Capt. Augustine = Mary Ball
Washington   (d. 1789)
(ca 1694–1743)

Mildred Warner = Robert Porteus, of
(b. 1682)   Newbottle, Virginia
                 later of Ripon,
                 Yorkshire
                 (ca 1679–1758)

George Washington
(1732–99)
1st President of
the United States
of America

Charles Grymes = Frances
of Morattico, Virginia   Jennings
(ca 1697– ca 1753)

Rev. Robert = Judith Cockayne
Porteus   (1702–89)
(ca 1705–54)

Lucy Grymes = Henry Lee
of Leesylvania
(1729–87)

Mildred = Robert Hodgson
Porteus   (b. 1740)
(b. 1744)

Henry Lee = Anne Hill Carter
(1756–1818)   (1773–1829)

Very Rev. Robert Hodgson = Mary Tucker
Dean of Canterbury
(ca 1766–1844)

General Robert E. Lee
(1807–70)
Commander-in-Chief
Confederate Army
American Civil War

King Edward IV   = 1464   Elizabeth (1437–92),
(1442–83) | widow of John,
                   2nd Baron Grey of Groby
                   & dau. of Richard Woodville,
                   1st Earl of Rivers

Elizabeth Woodville = 1486 King Henry VII
(1465–1503)   (1457–1509)

Louis XII = (1) 1514 Mary = (2) 1515 Charles Brandon
King of France   (1496–1533)   1st Duke of Suffolk
(d. 1515)   (1484–1545)

Frances Brandon = ca 1534 Henry Grey, 1st Duke of Suffolk
(1517–59)   (1517–54)
                          beheaded

Lady Jane Grey
(1537–54)

James, 1st Duke of   William, 1st Duke of Bedford
Ormonde   (1613–1700)
(1610–88)   = 1637
= 1629   Lady Anne Carr
Elizabeth, Baroness Dingwall   (1615–84)
(1615–84)   dau. of Robert Carr, Earl of Somerset

Lady Mary Butler = 1662 William, 1st Duke of   William, Lord Russell = 1669 Lady Rachel
(1646–1710)   Devonshire   (1639–83)   Wriothesley
                 (1640/1–1707)   beheaded   (d. 1723)

William, 2nd Duke of = 1688 Hon. Rachel Russell
Devonshire   (1674–1725)
(1672–1729)

William, 3rd Duke of = 1718 Catherine Hoskins
Devonshire   (d. 1777)
(1698–1755)

William, 4th Duke of Devonshire = 1748 Charlotte Boyle,
(1720–64)   Baroness Clifford
                          (1731–54)

Lady Dorothy Cavendish
(d. 1794)
[continued]

See continuation overleaf.

Cavendish-Bentinck

Family Tree of the Cavendish-Bentincks, showing the Queen Mother's descent from King Edward IV, King Henry VII, The Kings of Ireland, The Dukes of Portland, Somerset, Devonshire, Bedford, Suffolk, Ormonde, and Newcastle, and The Earls of Oxford. The tree also shows her relationship to Lady Jane Grey and Arthur, Duke of Wellington, victor of The Battle of Waterloo.
See continuation overleaf.

Lady Catherine Grey (ca 1539–68) = ca 1560 Edward Seymour 1st Earl of Hertford (1537–1621)

Edward, Lord Beauchamp (1561–1612) = 1585 Honora, dau. of Sir Richard Rogers

William, 2nd Duke of Somerset (1587–1660) = 1616/17 Lady Frances Devereux (1599–1674) dau. of 3rd Earl of Essex

Lady Jane Seymour (1637–79) = 1661 Charles Boyle Viscount Dungarvan (1639–94)

Charles, 3rd Earl of Cork (ca 1674–1704) = 1687/8 Juliana Noel (1672–1750)

Richard, 4th Earl of Cork (1695–1753) = 1720 Lady Dorothy Savile (1699–1758) dau. of William, Marquess of Halifax

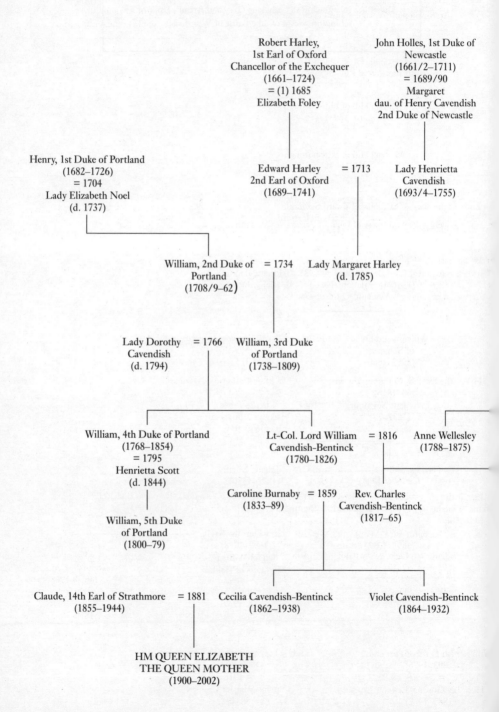

Robert Harley,
1st Earl of Oxford
Chancellor of the Exchequer
(1661–1724)
= (1) 1685
Elizabeth Foley

John Holles, 1st Duke of
Newcastle
(1661/2–1711)
= 1689/90
Margaret
dau. of Henry Cavendish
2nd Duke of Newcastle

Henry, 1st Duke of Portland
(1682–1726)
= 1704
Lady Elizabeth Noel
(d. 1737)

Edward Harley   = 1713   Lady Henrietta
2nd Earl of Oxford   Cavendish
(1689–1741)   (1693/4–1755)

William, 2nd Duke of   = 1734   Lady Margaret Harley
Portland   (d. 1785)
(1708/9–62)

Lady Dorothy   = 1766   William, 3rd Duke
Cavendish   of Portland
(d. 1794)   (1738–1809)

William, 4th Duke of Portland
(1768–1854)
= 1795
Henrietta Scott
(d. 1844)

Lt-Col. Lord William   = 1816   Anne Wellesley
Cavendish-Bentinck   (1788–1875)
(1780–1826)

William, 5th Duke
of Portland
(1800–79)

Caroline Burnaby   = 1859   Rev. Charles
(1833–89)   Cavendish-Bentinck
                                      (1817–65)

Claude, 14th Earl of Strathmore   = 1881   Cecilia Cavendish-Bentinck
(1855–1944)   (1862–1938)

Violet Cavendish-Bentinck
(1864–1932)

HM QUEEN ELIZABETH
THE QUEEN MOTHER
(1900–2002)

Hon. Mary O'Brien
sister of Murrough O'Brien, 1st Earl of Inchiquin,
French cavalry general & Viceroy of Catalonia

> Hon. Mary O'Brien traces her descent through the Barons of Inchiquin, the Kings of Thormond, the Kings of Munster, and back to Brian 'Boru' (Boruma), High King of Ireland, who was killed in victory over the Norse people in the tenth century.

Michael Boyle
(d. 1702)
Archbishop of Armagh, Lord Chancellor of Ireland

Elenor Boyle
sister of Murrough, 1st Viscount Blesinton, whose
family discovered Boyle's Law in physics

William Hill of Hillsborough
(d. 1693)

Michael Hill of Hillsborough
(d. 1699)

Arthur, 1st Viscount Dungannon
(d. 1771)
(descendant by marriage of O'Neill Barons of Dungannon)

...rret, 1st Earl   = 1759   Anne
Mornington   (d. 1831)
(1735–81)   dau. of 1st
                        Viscount Dungannon

Richard, Marquess Wellesley   Arthur, 1st Duke of Wellington
(1760–1842)   (1769–1852)
&   = 1806
Hyacinthe Roland, Common-law wife   Hon. Catherine Pakenham
(ca 1760–1816)   (d. 1831)

Elizabeth   = 1857 (1)   Lt-Gen. Arthur   = (2) 1862   Augusta, Baroness Bolsover
...kins-Whitshed   Cavendish-Bentinck   (1834–93)
(d. 1858)   (1819–77)

William, 6th Duke of Portland   Lord Henry Cavendish-Bentinck   Lady Ottoline
(1857–1943)   (1863–1931)   Cavendish-Bentinck
= 1889   = 1892   (1873–1938)
Winifred Dallas-Yorke   Lady Olivia Taylour   = 1902
(1863–1954)   (d. 1939)   Philip Morrell
                                  dau. of Thomas, Earl of Bective   (1870–1943)

...illiam, 7th Duke of Portland   Lady Victoria Cavendish-Bentinck
(1893–1976)   (1890–1994)
= 1915   = 1918
Hon. Ivy Gordon-Lennox   Captain Michael Wemyss
(1887–1982)   (1888–1982)

Notes

Introduction (pp. XXV–XXXI)

1. Hugo Vickers diary, 6 November 1976.
2. Lady Fry to author, Surrey, 5 December 1976.
3. Hugo Vickers diary, 2 April 1987.
4. Ibid., 20 February 1983.
5. Ibid., 18 March 1986.
6. Ibid., 29 March 1990.

Chapter 1: *Early Days: (pp. 1–9)*

The best and most serious history of Glamis Castle, its building and legends is Harry Gordon Slade's *Glamis Castle*. The *Complete Peerage* and *Burke's Peerage* also have good stories, both about Strathmores and Portlands. The author has paid two visits to Glamis, in September 1989 and in August 2003, where much historical information is on display, both in the castle and in the exhibition areas.

Michael Thornton's *Royal Feud* airs the question of where the Queen Mother might have been born, and chastises a number of authors who failed to check the primary sources.

1. This has to be that most boring of sources – private information.
2. Birth certificate of Elizabeth Bowes-Lyon, 21 September 1900.
3. Alison Miller article, *Sunday Times*, July 1980.
4. Dorothy Laird, *Queen Elizabeth The Queen Mother*, p. 35.
5. William Tallon to author, London, 19 January 2005.
6. Checked in *Kelly's Directory of London* (various years between 1897 and 1901).
7. Court Circular of 31 July, *The Times* (1 August 1900).
8. The Countess of Strathmore to the Archbishop of Canterbury, 1 June 1937 (Lang papers, Lambeth Palace Library).
9. *The Times*, 18 February 1904.
10. Diary of 27th Earl of Crawford, 2 October 1905 – John Vincent (ed.), *The Crawford Papers*, p. 86.

11. Queen Elizabeth to Winston Churchill, Buckingham Palace, 14 November 1944 (Churchill Archives Centre, Churchill Papers, CHAR 1/380/52–53).
12. Kenneth Rose, *Sunday Telegraph*, 1 August 1965.
13. Queen Elizabeth to Archbishop of Canterbury, Buckingham Palace, 23 June 1938 (Lambeth Palace Library).
14. Queen Elizabeth to Neville Chamberlain, Birkhall, 2 July 1938 (Neville Chamberlain papers, Birmingham University, NC7/4/8). (Quoted in Sarah Bradford, *George VI*, p. 270)
15. The Countess of Strathmore to Lady Ottoline Morrell, Woolmers Park, nr Hertford, 4 January (1937) (Lady Ottoline Morrell papers, HRC, Texas).
16. Ibid., St Paul's Walden Bury, 17 November 1931 (Lady Ottoline Morrell papers, HRC, Texas).
17. J. G. (possibly Colonel Guthrie) writing in *The Times*, 24 June 1938.
18. Virginia Cowles, 'The Queen Mother Today' (*Sunday Express*, 4 April 1954).
19. The Duchess of York to Viscountess Astor, Rest Harrow, Sandwich, 19 June 1932 (Astor papers, MS 1416/1/4/8 – Reading University).
20. Arthur Mee, *The King's England and Hertfordshire*, p. 168.
21. Queen Elizabeth to Sir Osbert Sitwell, 18 December 1944 (private collection).
22. Queen Elizabeth The Queen Mother to Sir Charles Johnston, Windsor Castle, Christmas Day, 1974 (author's collection).
23. Katharine, Duchess of Atholl, *Working Partnership*, p. 47.
24. Frances Donaldson, *King George and Queen Elizabeth*, p. 22.

Chapter 2: *Childhood (pp. 10–28)*

Some background material has been drawn from Grania Forbes's useful account of the Queen Mother's early years, *My Darling Buffy*, though some dates and information in that book have proved confusing.

1. Joan Woollcombe to Helen Cathcart/Harold Albert, 22 May 1969 (Harold Albert papers).
2. *The Lady*, 31 July 1969.
3. Elizabeth Longford, *The Queen Mother*, p. 16.
4. Hugh Cecil to author, London, 18 March 2004.
5. The Queen Mother to Nigel Jaques, Royal Lodge, 25 November 1994.
6. Kaethe Kübler, *Meine Schülerin, Die Köningen von England*, p. 8.
7. Lord Elphinstone to Nancy Shaw (later Viscountess Astor), 7 March 1906 (Astor papers, MS 1416/1/4/40 – Reading University).
8. Grania Forbes, *My Darling Buffy*, p. 54.
9. Obituary exhibited at Glamis Castle.
10. Death certificate of Hon. Alexander Bowes-Lyon (New Register House, Edinburgh).

11. Dorothy Laird, *Queen Elizabeth The Queen Mother*, p. 36.

12. Mrs Miriam E.S. Flint, schoolmistress, to Helen Cathcart, Shropshire, 16 August 1966 (Harold Albert papers).

13. Miss Dorothy M. Birtwhistle to Harold Albert, Guildford, 2 October 1966 (Harold Albert papers).

14. Mrs Miriam E.S. Flint to Helen Cathcart, Shropshire, 29 August 1966 (Harold Albert papers).

15. Kübler, pp. 7.

16. Ibid., p. 10.

17. Ibid., pp. 13–14.

18. Ibid., p. 17.

19. Revd John Stirton, *Glamis Castle*, pp. vii–viii.

20. Diary of 27th Earl of Crawford, 2 October 1905, in John Vincent (ed.), *The Crawford Papers*, p. 87.

21. Stirton, pp. 36–7.

22. Ibid., p. 49.

23. James Wentworth Day, *The Queen Mother's Family Story*, pp. 131–2.

24. Raymond Asquith to Katharine Horner, Glen of Rothes, North Berwick, 25 September 1905, quoted in John Joliffe (ed.), *Raymond Asquith: Life and Letters*, p. 134.

25. Hon. Stephen Tennant to author, Wilsford Manor, 4 October 1980.

26. Wentworth Day, p. 132.

27. Helen Hardinge manuscript (Hon. Lady Murray papers).

28. Lady Cynthia Colville, *Crowded Life*, p. 128.

29. Lady Elizabeth Bowes-Lyon to Edward Campbell, Glamis, 1 September 1913 (Nicholas White collection).

30. Ibid.

31. Kübler, p. 31.

32. Ibid., p. 32.

33. Forbes, p. 34.

34. Lady Elizabeth Anson, quoted in *Daily Telegraph*, 7 April 1987.

35. Hon. Michael Bowes-Lyon, *Three Months of War* (privately published, 1996), p. 2.

36. Ibid., p. 16.

37. Note by Hon. Michael Bowes-Lyon, displayed at Glamis Castle.

38. *Dundee Courier*, 1 September 1916.

39. Harry Gordon Slade, *Glamis Castle*, p. 82.

40. There is a reference to repair work in Helen Hardinge's diary of September 1924, when she visited Glamis (Hon. Lady Murray papers).

41. Mabell, Countess of Airlie, *Thatched with Gold*, p. 166.

42. Hon. Stephen Tennant to author, 1980.

43. Queen Elizabeth to Hon. Lady Johnston, Sandringham, 30 December 1989.

44. Ibid.

45. Helen Hardinge, *Loyal to Three Kings*, p. 28.

Chapter 3: *The 'Dear Duke' (pp. 29–43)*

1. Hon. Stephen Tennant to author, Wilsford Manor, 4 October 1980.
2. *The Times*, 30 August 1923.
3. *The Lady*, 1 April 1920.
4. Ibid., 10 June 1920.
5. Ibid.
6. Viscount Stuart of Findhorn, *Within the Fringe*, p. 57 (but giving a different occasion and date by mistake).
7. King George V to Duke of York, Buckingham Palace, 7 June 1920, quoted in John Wheeler-Bennett, *King George VI*, p. 140.
8. The Prince of Wales to Freda Dudley Ward, HMS *Renown*, Lyttelton, New Zealand, 22 May 1920, quoted in Rupert Godfrey, *Letters from a Prince*, p. 300.
9. Recorded in the private diary of Sir Charles Johnston, 24 February 1952 (author's collection).
10. Cecil Beaton diary, [Summer] 1971, quoted in Hugo Vickers (ed.), *The Unexpurgated Beaton*, p. 188.
11. Helen Hardinge diary (Hon. Lady Murray papers).
12. The Prince of Wales to Mrs Dudley Ward, 11 p.m., 23 October 1918, quoted in Godfrey, p. 98.
13. The Prince of Wales to Freda Dudley Ward, New Zealand, 24 May 1920, quoted in Godfrey, p. 304.
14. Mabell, Countess of Airlie, *Thatched With Gold*, p. 166.
15. John Balfour, *Not Too Correct an Aureole*, p. 1.
16. Lascelles diary for 21 May 1910, quoted in Duff Hart-Davis (ed.), *End of an Era: Letters and Diaries of Sir Alan Lascelles 1887–1920*, p. 81.
17. *The Memoirs of Princess Alice, Duchess of Gloucester*, p. 62.
18. Helen Cecil to Alec Hardinge, Glamis, 18 September 1920 (Hardinge papers, Maidstone, U2117 – C2/33).
19. Cecil Beaton to Stephen Tennant, revealed in a BBC documentary, July 1984.
20. Derived from a letter from Mary, Duchess of Buccleuch, 22 February 1991 (private collection).
21. Private information, 4 November 1991.
22. Lady Cynthia Colville, *Crowded Life*, p. 128.
23. Alec Hardinge to Helen Cecil, Balmoral, 14 September 1920 (Hardinge papers, Maidstone, U2117 – C1/22).
24. Ibid., 13 September 1920 (Hardinge papers, Maidstone, U2117 – C1/21).
25. Helen Cecil to Alec Hardinge, Glamis, 19 September 1920 (Hardinge papers, Maidstone, U2117 – C2/34).
26. Ibid., in the train, 13 September 1920 (Hardinge papers, Maidstone, U2117 – C2/24).
27. Helen Cecil to Alec Hardinge, Glamis, 14 September 1920 (Hardinge papers, Maidstone, U2117 – C2/28).

28. Ibid., 14 September 1920 (Hardinge papers, Maidstone, U2117 – C2/29).
29. Ibid., 17 September 1920 (Hardinge papers, Maidstone, U2117 – C2/31).
30. Ibid., 18 September 1920 (Hardinge papers, Maidstone, U2117 – C2/33).
31. Ibid.
32. Ibid., 20 September 1920 (Hardinge papers, Maidstone, U2117 – C2/36).
33. Ibid.
34. Ibid., 19 September 1920 (Hardinge papers, Maidstone, U2117 – C2/34).
35. Ibid., 20 September 1920 (Hardinge papers, Maidstone, U2117 – C2/36).
36. Ibid., Balmoral, 21 September 1920 (Hardinge papers, Maidstone, U2117 – C1/33).
37. Helen Hardinge, *Loyal to Three Kings*, p. 39.
38. Ibid., p. 39.
39. Alec Hardinge to Helen Cecil, Balmoral, 10 September 1920 (Hardinge papers, Maidstone, U2117 – C1/12).
40. Ibid.
41. Ibid., 15 September 1920 (Hardinge papers, Maidstone, U2117 – C1/23).
42. Ibid., 11 September 1920 (Hardinge papers, Maidstone, U2117 – C1/19).

Chapter 4: *The Proposals (pp. 44–59)*

1. Helen Hardinge, *Loyal to Three Kings*, p. 39.
2. John Wheeler-Bennett, *King George VI*, p. 150.
3. Mabell, Countess of Airlie, *Thatched with Gold*, p. 167.
4. Ibid.
5. Robert Sencourt, *The Reign of Edward VIII*, p. 18.
6. Cynthia Gladwyn, *The Paris Embassy*, p. 192.
7. Elsa Maxwell, *I Married the World*, p. 144.
8. Copy of letter from Dorothy ('Dickie') Fellowes-Gordon to HM The Queen, thanking her for a centenary telegram, 7 August 1991 (author's collection).
9. Mabell, Countess of Airlie, p. 167.
10. *Ibid.*
11. Grania Forbes, *My Darling Buffy*, p. 149.
12. Ibid.
13. Viscount Stuart of Findhorn, *Within the Fringe*, p. 57.
14. Sir Anthony Nutting to author, London, 12 March 1990.
15. 2nd Viscount Stuart of Findhorn to author, 27 April 1990.
16. The Duke of York to Queen Mary, September 1921, quoted in Wheeler-Bennett, *King George VI*, p. 148.
17. Account of Princess Mary's Wedding, by Revd George Bell, later Bishop of Chichester, then serving as chaplain to Randall Davidson, Archbishop of Canterbury (Bishop Bell papers, Volume 190, Lambeth Palace Library).
18. Lady Elizabeth Bowes-Lyon to James Stuart, London, 12 March 1921,

quoted back to her in a letter from Stuart to her (quoted in unpublished article by Sir Ludovic Kennedy).

19. James Stuart to Lady Elizabeth Bowes-Lyon, New York, 24 March 1922, quoted in an unpublished article by Sir Ludovic Kennedy.
20. The Queen Mother to author, London, 26 March 1981.
21. Lady Rumbold to author, Wiltshire, 25 May 2004.
22. Cecil Beaton, *The Wandering Years*, p. 154.
23. The Queen Mother to author, London, 26 March 1981.
24. Ibid., 19 March 1992.
25. Pamela Grey, *Shepherd's Crowns*, p. 93.
26. Sir Oliver Lodge, *Evolution and Creation*, p. vii.
27. The Duchess of York to Sir Oliver Lodge, 145 Piccadilly, 9 July 1928 (Oliver Lodge papers, Birmingham University – OJL1/458/1).
28. Hermione Baddeley, *The Unsinkable Hermione Baddeley*, serialised in *Sunday Telegraph*, 11 November 1984.
29. *Evening Standard*, 20 April 1990.
30. *The Times*, 17 January 1923.
31. Laura, Duchess of Marlborough, *Laughter from a Cloud*, p. 4.
32. Channon diary, quoted in Forbes, *My Darling Buffy*, p. 125.
33. Lord Gage, *Firle: A Memoir*, p. 22.
34. Ibid., p. 27.
35. Lord Gage to Alastair Forbes, *Sunday Times Magazine*, 1 August 1980 (though Lord Gage not named).
36. Chips Channon diary, 12 May 1937, in Robert Rhodes James, *Chips*, p. 125.
37. Chips Channon diary, 7 November 1944, in Rhodes James, *Chips*, p. 397.
38. The Queen Mother to Sir Charles Johnston, 17 June 1972 (recorded in Sir Charles Johnston, unpublished diary, 27 June 1972).
39. Prince Paul of Yugoslavia to Lady Elizabeth Bowes-Lyon, Belgrade, April 1921, quoted in Forbes, *My Darling Buffy*, p. 117.
40. Donald Gillies, *Radical Diplomat*, p. 11.
41. Ibid., p. 39.
42. The Pilgrims, Speeches at Dinner (for John Winant, Lord Inverchapel, and Viscount Greenwood), 30 April 1946, p. 10.
43. Gillies, p. 39.
44. Conversation between Lady Doris Gordon-Lennox and Helen Hardinge, reported in a letter – Helen to Alec Hardinge, London, 27 June 1922 (Hardinge papers, Maidstone, U2117 – C2/188).
45. Viscount Davidson to Sir Louis Greig, 23 April 1948 (Lord Davidson papers, 307, House of Lords Library).
46. Ibid.
47. Viscount Davidson memorandum, 1952, quoted in Robert Rhodes James (ed.), *Memoirs of a Conservative*, pp. 109–10.
48. Geordie Greig, *Louis and the Prince*, pp. 193–4, quoting a letter from Viscount Davidson to the Queen Mother.

49. Ibid., quoting a letter from the Queen Mother to Viscount Davidson.
50. *The Lady*, 5 October 1922.
51. Ibid., 2 November 1922.
52. *Daily Star*, 5 January 1923.
53. Channon diary, 5 January 1923, quoted in Kenneth Rose, *King George V*, p. 311.
54. Mabell, Countess of Airlie, pp. 167–8.
55. BBC tribute to the Queen Mother, 30 March 2002.
56. Channon diary, 16 January 1923, quoted in Rose, *King George V*, p. 312.
57. William Tallon to author, 15 July 2005.
58. Mabell, Countess of Airlie, p. 168.
59. Lady Jean Rankin to author, London, 18 March 1986.

Chapter 5: *The Wedding (pp. 60–71)*

1. *The Times*, 19 January 1923.
2. *The Lady*, 25 January 1923.
3. The Duke of York to the Archbishop of Canterbury, York Cottage, 1 February 1923 (Lang papers, Lambeth Palace Library).
4. Lady Elizabeth Bowes-Lyon to Viscountess Astor, York Cottage, Sandringham, 29 January 1923 (Astor papers, MS 1416/1/4/8 – Reading University).
5. Henry Channon diaries, quoted in Geordie Greig, *Louis and the Prince*, p. 192.
6. Prince Paul of Yugoslavia to Comte Jean de Ribes, January 1923, quoted in Grania Forbes, *My Darling Buffy*, p. 119.
7. Duff Cooper diary, 26 April 1923, quoted in John Julius Norwich (ed.), *The Duff Cooper Diaries: 1915–1952*, p. 175.
8. Greig, *Louis and the Prince*, p. 192.
9. *Dundee Advertiser*, 24 April 1923.
10. Helen Hardinge, *Loyal to Three Kings*, p. 40.
11. T.E. Lawrence, *The Mint*, p. 185.
12. *The Lady*, 1 February 1923.
13. Ibid., 5 April 1923.
14. Ibid., 19 April 1923.
15. H.H. Asquith to Hilda Harrison, 24 April 1923, quoted in Kenneth Rose, *King George V*, p. 312.
16. *The Lady*, 3 May 1923.
17. Helen Hardinge diary, 22 July 1924 (Hon. Lady Murray papers).
18. Herbert Hensley Henson, *Retrospect of an Unimportant Life*, vol. II, p. 88.
19. Private game book (1909–26) in the possession of the author.
20. The Duchess of York to the Prince of Wales, 13 January 1925, quoted in Philip Ziegler, *Edward VIII*, p. 172.
21. Noble Frankland, *Prince Henry, Duke of Gloucester*, p. 63.
22. Helen Hardinge diary, 31 August 1924 (Hon. Lady Murray papers).

23. Private letter from Sir Frederick Ponsonby (undated) (private collection).
24. Princess Marie Louise, *My Memories of Six Reigns*, p. 155.
25. *The Times*, 31 August 1923.
26. John Vincent, *The Crawford Papers*, pp. 502–3, entry for 25 February 1925.

Chapter 6: *The Delicious Duchess (pp. 72–90)*

1. Helen Hardinge diary, 17 October 1924 (Hon. Lady Murray papers).
2. *The Lady*, 26 July 1923.
3. Ibid., 2 August 1923.
4. Ibid.
5. Ibid., 9 August 1923.
6. Queen Elizabeth to Sir Osbert Sitwell, 27 September 1942, quoted in Sarah Bradford, *George VI*, p. 111.
7. *The Times*, 17 September 1942.
8. Harold Nicolson to Vita Sackville-West, 21 July 1937, quoted in James Lees-Milne, *Harold Nicolson*, vol. II, p. 92.
9. Kingsley Martin, *Editor*, (Hutchinson, 1968), pp. 168–9.
10. Brian Masters, *Great Hostesses*, p. 88.
11. Beverley Nichols, *All I Could Never Be*, p. 18.
12. Derived from Nichols, p. 22.
13. Invitation sent to Gladys, Duchess of Marlborough (formerly in the possession of the author, but now given to Polesden Lacey).
14. Rick Hutto to author.
15. Helen Hardinge diary, 7 July 1924 (Hon. Lady Murray papers).
16. Ibid., 19 September 1924 (Hon. Lady Murray papers).
17. *Sunday Express*, 18 July 1954.
18. Janet Aitken Kidd, *The Beaverbrook Kid*, p. 63.
19. Michael Arlen, *The Green Hat*, p. 111.
20. Earl of Derby to Malcolm Bullock, Cannes, 31 December 1927, quoted in Randolph S. Churchill, *Lord Derby*, p. 579.
21. Helen Hardinge diary, 28 January 1925 (Hon. Lady Murray papers).
22. Rupert Godfrey (ed.), *Letters from a Prince*, p. 194.
23. Helen Hardinge diary, 25 May 1924 (Hon. Lady Murray papers).
24. Queen Elizabeth to Sybil, Marchioness of Cholmondeley, 3 June 1939, quoted in Peter Stansky, *Sassoon: The Worlds of Philip and Sybil*, p. 241.
25. Queen Elizabeth to Sir Sacheverell Sitwell, Sandringham, 10 January 1978 (Sacheverell Sitwell papers, Humanities Research Center, University of Austin, Texas).
26. Helen Hardinge diary, 11 February 1925 (Hon. Lady Murray papers).
27. *The Lady*, 6 September 1923.
28. The Prince of Wales to George V, 21 August 1923, quoted in Philip Ziegler, *Edward VIII*, p. 172.
29. *The Lady*, 25 October 1923.

30. Queen Marie of Romania to an American friend, 1937, quoted in Hector Bolitho, *A Biographer's Notebook*, p. 56.

31. The Duke of York to Louis Greig, 24 April 1923, quoted in Geordie Greig, *Louis and the Prince*, p. 196.

32. Quoted in Greig, *Louis and the Prince*, p. 209.

33. *The Lady*, 22 May 1924.

34. Helen Hardinge diary, 14 May 1924 (Hon. Lady Murray papers).

35. Ibid., 29 May 1924 (Hon. Lady Murray papers).

36. Ibid., 2 June 1924 (Hon. Lady Murray papers).

37. Ibid., 19 July 1924 (Hon. Lady Murray papers).

38. Ibid.

39. Ibid., 20 July 1924 (Hon. Lady Murray papers).

40. Ibid., 21 July 1924 (Hon. Lady Murray papers).

41. Helen Hardinge to Alec Hardinge, Barons Court, July 1924 (Hardinge papers, U2 – 117 – C2/263 – Maidstone).

42. Ibid.

43. Helen Hardinge diary, 19 August 1924 (Hon. Lady Murray papers).

44. Ibid., 24 August 1924 (Hon. Lady Murray papers).

45. Ibid., 25 August 1924 (Hon. Lady Murray papers).

46. Ibid., 11 September 1924 (Hon. Lady Murray papers).

47. Ibid., 26 September 1924 (Hon. Lady Murray papers).

48. Lady Katharine Hamilton to Helen Hardinge, Glamis Castle, 25 September 1924 (Hon. Lady Murray papers).

49. Helen Hardinge diary, 6 October 1924 (Hon. Lady Murray papers).

Chapter 7: *Africa and Australia (pp. 91–107)*

1. Helen Hardinge to Alec Hardinge, 9 April 1925 (Hardinge Papers, U2117 – C2/332 – Maidstone).

2. *The Lady*, 6 November 1924.

3. Ibid., 11 December 1924.

4. John Wheeler-Bennett, *King George VI*, p. 198.

5. Sister Catherine Black, *King's Nurse – Beggar's Nurse*, p. 163.

6. Wheeler-Bennett, p. 191.

7. Private information – that most irritating of sources.

8. Parliamentary report in *The Times*, 18 February 1925.

9. Ashe Windham to author, 2004.

10. Alec Hardinge to Helen Hardinge, 2 January 1925 (Hardinge Papers, U2117 – C1/225 – Maidstone).

11. *The Times*, 13 March 1925.

12. J. G. Millais, foreword, in Captain H. C. Brocklehurst, *Game Animals of the Sudan*, pp. xvii-xviii.

13. Sir Geoffrey Archer, *Personal and Historical Memoirs of an East African Administrator*, pp. 191–2.

14. Brocklehurst, *Game Animals of the Sudan*, p. xi.
15. The Queen Mother to Maureen, Marchioness of Dufferin & Ava, Clarence House, 24 March 1992 (copy in author's collection).
16. The Duchess of York to Sir Geoffrey Archer, April 1925, quoted in Archer, *Personal and Historical Memoirs of an East African Administrator*, p. 191.
17. The Duchess of York to Sir Geoffrey Archer, April 1925, quoted in Archer, *Personal and Historical Memoirs of an East African Administrator*, p. 191.
18. Helen Hardinge diary, 26 May 1925 (Hon. Lady Murray papers).
19. Unpublished diary of Lady Ottoline Morrell, 27 May 1925 (Diary March to October 1925, p. 68 – British Library).
20. Duchess of York speech at the opening of the British College of Obstetrics and Gynaecology, Adam House, Queen Anne Street, London, reported in *The Times*, 6 December 1932.
21. Alec Hardinge to Helen Hardinge, York Cottage, 25 November 1925 (Hardinge Papers, U2117 – C1/306 – Maidstone).
22. *The Times*, 22 April 1926.
23. The Duke of York to Queen Mary, quoted in Wheeler-Bennett, *King George VI*, p. 209.
24. Ian F. M. Lucas, *The Royal Embassy*, prelims.
25. *The Times*, 15 March 1927.
26. Wheeler-Bennett, p. 217.
27. Lucas, pp. 34–5.
28. Lucas, p. 57.
29. *The Times*, 15 March 1927.
30. The Duke of York to the Duchess of York, Christchurch, New Zealand, 15 March 1927 (Ian Shapiro collection).
31. Ibid.
32. The Duchess of York to Lady Alice Fergusson, March 1927, quoted in Wheeler-Bennett, *King George VI*, p. 221.
33. Lucas, p. 110.
34. Ibid., p. 116.
35. Elizabeth Basset, *Moments of Vision*, p. 129.
36. Lucas, pp. 181–2.
37. Memorandum on Ceremonial during the tour of Their Royal Highnesses The Duke and Duchess of York to Australia and New Zealand 1927 by Sir H. F. Batterbee, sent to Sir H. Montgomery, 25 April 1929 (Treaty Royal Matters FO 372 2597 1929 – National Archives).
38. Lucas, p. 207.
39. Sir Tom Bridges to King George V, May 1927, quoted in Wheeler-Bennett, *King George VI*, p. 230.
40. Rt Revd Herbert Hensley Henson, *Retrospect of an Unimportant Life*, vol. II, pp. 206–7.
41. Ibid. p. 207.

Chapter 8: *The King's Illness (pp. 108–123)*

1. Rt Revd Herbert Hensley Henson, *Retrospect of an Unimportant Life*, vol. II, p. 228.
2. Duff Hart-Davis (ed.), *In Royal Service: The Letters and Journals of Sir Alan Lascelles 1920–1936*, vol. 2, p. 109.
3. Francis Watson, *Dawson of Penn*, p. 209.
4. Queen Mary to the Archbishop of the Canterbury, Craigweil House, Bognor, 26 February 1929 (Lang papers, Lambeth Palace Library).
5. *The Times*, 21 August 1929.
6. Harold Nicolson, *King George V: His Life and Reign*, p. 433.
7. Hon. Sir Francis Lindley to Sir Austen Chamberlain, Oslo, 23 March 1929 (Treaty Royal Matters, FO 372 2596 1929 – National Archives).
8. Ibid.
9. Ibid.
10. Harold Nicolson to Vita Sackville-West, 8 April 1929, quoted in Nigel Nicolson, *Harold Nicolson, Diaries and Letters 1907–1964*, p. 62.
11. Ibid.
12. The Countess of Strathmore to Lady Ottoline Morrell, St Paul's, Walden Bury, 17 November 1931 (Lady Ottoline Morrell Papers, HRC, Texas).
13. *The Times*, 16 April 1930.
14. Mabell, Countess of Airlie, *Thatched with Gold*, p. 183.
15. The Duchess of York to the Archbishop of Canterbury, Glamis, 10 September 1930 (Lang papers, Lambeth Palace Library), published in the *Sunday Times*, 28 September 2003.
16. William Tallon to author, London, 2 February 2005.
17. The Duchess of York to the Archbishop of Canterbury, Glamis, 10 September 1930 (Lang papers, Lambeth Palace Library).
18. The Duchess of York to Osbert Sitwell, 14 November 1930, quoted in Philip Ziegler, *Osbert Sitwell*, p. 125.
19. Lady Cynthia Asquith, *Haply I May Remember*, p. 192.
20. Ibid., p. 193.
21. Alys Chatwyn, *H.R.H. The Duchess of York*, p. 240 (the author has a copy that belonged to Princess Margaret).
22. The Duchess of York to the Archbishop of Canterbury, Sandringham, 7 January [1933] (Lang papers, Lambeth Palace Library).
23. All the best quotes are private information.
24. Freda Dudley-Ward (Marquesa de Casa Maury) to author, London, 8 February 1980.
25. Michael Wade to author, Trafalgar Park, 22 March 2004.
26. The Duchess of York to Duff Cooper, Thornby Grange, Northampton, 20 March 1931 (original in Churchill College, Cambridge).
27. The Duchess of York to Duff Cooper, Birkhall, 25 September 1932 (letter seen when in possession of Lady Diana Cooper, in the 1980s).
28. Alan Don diary, 28 April 1939 (Lambeth Palace Library).

29. Aidan Crawley, *Leap Before You Look*, p. 78.
30. The Duke of Windsor, *A King's Story*, p. 273.
31. J.G. Lockhart, *Cosmo Gordon Lang*, p. 290.
32. Alan Don diary, 16 December 1938 (Lambeth Palace Library).
33. The Duchess of York to Duff Cooper, Birkhall, 25 September 1932 (letter seen when in possession of Lady Diana Cooper, in the 1980s).
34. *The Times*, 21 September 1932.
35. The Duchess of York to the Archbishop of Canterbury, Sandringham, 7 January [1933] (Lang Papers, Lambeth Palace Library).
36. André Maurois, *Memoirs 1885-1967*, pp. 179-80.
37. Laura, Duchess of Marlborough, *Laughter from a Cloud*, p. 36.
38. The Duke of York to Viscountess Astor, 145 Piccadilly, 20 June 1932 (Astor papers – MS 1416/1/4/8 – Reading University).
39. The Duchess of York, 19 June 1932 (Astor papers – MS 1416/1/4/8 – Reading University).
40. Ibid.
41. Richard Lovell, *Churchill's Doctor: A Biography of Lord Moran*, pp. 130-32.
42. The Duchess of York to the Archbishop of Canterbury, 145 Piccadilly, London, 16 July 1933 (Lang papers, Lambeth Palace Library).
43. Ibid., Sandringham, 12 January 1934 (Lang papers, Lambeth Palace Library).
44. Report by Sir Archibald Clark Kerr, British Legation, Stockholm, 5 November 1932.
45. Lady Alexa Bertie to Robert Bruce Lockhart, recorded in his diary for 5 August 1935, quoted in Kenneth Young, *The Diaries of Sir Robert Bruce Lockhart*, vol. I, p. 326.
46. Robert Bruce Lockhart diary, 21 October 1934, quoted in Young, *The Diaries of Sir Robert Bruce Lockhart*, p. 309.
47. Prince George to Prince Paul of Yugoslavia, York House, St James's Palace, 20 September 1934 (Prince Paul papers, Bakhmeteff Archives, Rare Books & Manuscript Library, Columbia University, New York).

Chapter 9: *End of a Reign (pp. 124-132)*

1. Marion Crawford, *The Little Princesses*, p. 16.
2. The Duchess of York to the Archbishop of Canterbury, 145 Piccadilly, 5 July 1935 (Lang papers, Lambeth Palace Library), published in the *Sunday Times*, 28 September 2003.
3. Helen Hardinge diary, 25 August 1935 (Hon. Lady Murray papers).
4. The Duchess of York to Duff Cooper, Birkhall, 1 October 1935 (Churchill College, Cambridge), published by Hugo Vickers in the *Sunday Telegraph*, 31 March 2002.
5. Ibid.
6. Recorded in Lady Ottoline Morrell's diary, 26 February 1936 (Lady Ottoline Morrell papers, British Library).

7. Francis Watson, *Dawson of Penn*, p. 274.
8. Helen Hardinge diary, 11 December 1935 (Hon. Lady Murray papers).
9. *The Times*, 31 December 1935.
10. Recorded in Lady Ottoline Morrell's diary, 26 February 1936 (Lady Ottoline Morrell papers, British Library).
11. Alan Don diary, 19 January 1936 (Lambeth Palace Library).
12. Lady Desborough to Revd Alan Don, Alan Don diary, 23 January 1936 (Lambeth Palace Library).
13. Alan Don diary, 20 January 1936 (Lambeth Palace Library).
14. Diary of Lord Dawson of Penn, quoted in *British Medical Journal*, 1994; 308:1445 (28 May).
15. Wording noted in Alan Don diary, 31 January 1936 (Lambeth Palace Library).
16. Alan Don diary, 29 January 1936 (Lambeth Palace Library).
17. Ibid., 28 January 1936 (Lambeth Palace Library).

Chapter 10: *The Abdication (pp. 133–46)*

1. Alan Don diary, 7 December 1936 (Lambeth Palace Library).
2. *Time* magazine, 17 August 1934.
3. *New York Times*, 20 January 1936.
4. Ibid., 20 January 1936.
5. Ibid., 25 January 1936.
6. Ibid., 1 February 1936.
7. Unidentified press cutting from South Africa, March 1936 (author's collection).
8. *New York Times*, 12 March 1936.
9. Ibid., 28 May 1936.
10. The Duchess of York to Lord Dawson of Penn, Compton Place, Eastbourne, 9 March 1936, quoted in Francis Watson, *Dawson of Penn*, p. 285.
11. Helen Hardinge diary, 19 February 1936 (Hon. Lady Murray papers).
12. Harold Nicolson to Vita Sackville-West, 20 February 1936, quoted in Stanley Olson (ed.), *Harold Nicolson, Diaries and Letters 1930–1964*, pp. 93–4.
13. Ibid., 26 February 1936, p. 246.
14. The Duchess of York to Lord Dawson of Penn, Compton Place, Eastbourne, 9 March 1936, quoted in Watson, *Dawson of Penn*, p. 285.
15. Lady Diana Cooper to author, summer 1980.
16. *The Form and Order of The Coronation Service* (12 May 1937, p. 6.
17. Helen Hardinge diary, 12 March 1936 (Hon. Lady Murray papers).
18. The Duchess of York to Duff Cooper, Royal Lodge, 22 May 1936 (Churchill Archives Centre, Duff Cooper Papers).
19. Alan Don diary, 25 July 1936 (Lambeth Palace Library).
20. The Duchess of York to Duff Cooper, Royal Lodge, 3 August 1936

(Churchill Archives Centre, Duff Cooper Papers), published in the *Sunday Telegraph,* 31 March 2002.

21. Helen Hardinge diary, 10 September 1936 (Hon. Lady Murray papers).
22. The Duchess of York to Queen Mary, Birkhall, 19 September 1936 (Philip Ziegler, *King Edward VIII,* p. 288).
23. Alan Don diary, 24 September 1936 (Lambeth Palace Library).
24. Helen Hardinge diary, 26 September 1936 (Hon. Lady Murray papers).
25. Alec Sargent's Private and Confidential notes on King Edward's Abdication – 11 December 1936 (Lambeth Palace Library).
26. HRH The Duke of Windsor, *A King's Story,* p. 324.
27. Alan Don diary, 3 November 1936 (Lambeth Palace Library).
28. Ibid., 4 November 1936 (Lambeth Palace Library).
29. Lord Charteris of Amisfield to author, London, 1 November 1977.
30. The Duchess of York to Edward VIII, 145 Piccadilly, 23 November 1936 (Philip Ziegler, *King Edward VIII,* p. 324).
31. The Duchess of York to Helen Hardinge, 145 Piccadilly, 23 November 1936 (Hon. Lady Murray papers).
32. Violet Milner diary, 8 December 1936, quoted in Susan Williams, *The People's King,* p. 211.
33. Frances Donaldson, *King George & Queen Elizabeth,* p. 32.
34. King George VI's account of the Abdication, quoted in John Wheeler-Bennett, *King George VI,* p. 286.
35. Ibid.
36. Queen Elizabeth to the Duke of Windsor, 145 Piccadilly, 11 December 1936 (Philip Ziegler, *King Edward VIII,* p. 333).
37. Queen Elizabeth to the Archbishop of Canterbury, 145 Piccadilly, 12 December 1936 (Lang papers, Lambeth Palace Library).
38. Quoted in Michael De-la-Noy, *The Queen Behind the Throne,* p. 69.

Chapter 11: *The Coronation (pp. 147–62)*

1. Alan Don diary, 15 January 1937 (Lambeth Palace Library).
2. *The Times,* 23 June 1938.
3. Lady Cynthia Asquith, *Haply I May Remember,* p. 201.
4. Marion Crawford, *The Little Princesses,* p. 39.
5. Alan Don diary, 19 December 1936 (Lambeth Palace Library).
6. Revd Alec Sargent, Private and Confidential notes on King Edward's Abdication, 11 December 1936 (Lambeth Palace Library).
7. H. G. Wells, writing in the *Sunday Referee,* 21 December 1936.
8. Alan Don diary, 15 December 1936 (Lambeth Palace Library).
9. Ibid., 22 December 1936 (Lambeth Palace Library).
10. Osbert Sitwell, *Rat Week,* p. 60. (The original drafts of *Rat Week* are in the Harry Ransom Center, University of Austin, Texas.)
11. Ibid., p. 70.

12. Queen Elizabeth to the Archbishop of Canterbury, Sandringham, 14 January 1937 (Lang papers, Lambeth Palace Library).
13. Ibid., published in the *Sunday Times*, 28 September 2003.
14. J. G. Lockhart, *Cosmo Gordon Lang*, p. 407.
15. HRH The Princess Margaret to author, Hampshire, 1 January 1996.
16. The Dowager Viscountess Hambleden to author, Ewelme, 18 January 1991.
17. Private information, gleaned from several interviews with the same source.
18. Private source to Cecil Beaton, recorded in his diary (Cecil Beaton papers, St John's College, Cambridge).
19. Cecil Beaton unpublished diary, August 1937 (Cecil Beaton papers, St John's College, Cambridge).
20. Queen Elizabeth to the Marchioness of Londonderry, 1937 (Londonderry papers, Public Record Office of Northern Ireland, Ref: D 3099/13/26), published in the *Sunday Telegraph*, 31 March 2002.
21. The Duke of Portland, *Men, Women and Things*, p. 333.
22. Hon. Eleanor Brougham to Cecil Beaton, June 1937 (Cecil Beaton papers, St John's College, Cambridge).
23. Queen Mary to the Archbishop of Canterbury, Marlborough House, 4 May 1937 (Lang papers, Lambeth Palace Library).
24. Lockhart, p. 417.
25. Cecil Beaton unpublished diary, 12 May 1937 (Cecil Beaton papers, St John's College, Cambridge).
26. Ibid.
27. Ibid.
28. Lockhart, p. 419.
29. Mrs Bell, vol. 205 – 'How I saw the Coronation in Westminster Abbey, 12 May 1937' (Bell papers, Lambeth Palace Library).
30. Ibid.
31. Rt Revd Herbert Hensley Henson, *Retrospect of an Unimportant Life*, vol. II, p. 383.
32. Mrs Bell, vol. 205 – 'How I saw the Coronation in Westminster Abbey, 12 May 1937' (Bell papers, Lambeth Palace Library).
33. Ibid.
34. Ibid.
35. Osbert Sitwell to Cecil Beaton, quoted in Cecil Beaton's unpublished diary, 12 May 1937 (Cecil Beaton papers, St John's College, Cambridge).
36. The Duke of Portland to the Archbishop of Canterbury, 12 May 1937 (Lang papers, Lambeth Palace Library).
37. Mrs Bell, vol. 205 – 'How I saw the Coronation in Westminster Abbey, 12 May 1937' (Bell papers, Lambeth Palace Library).
38. The Countess of Strathmore to the Archbishop of Canterbury, 38 Cumberland Mansions, Bryanston Street, London, 1 June 1937 (Lang papers, Lambeth Palace Library).

39. Queen Elizabeth to the Archbishop of Canterbury, Royal Lodge, 15 May 1937 (Lang papers, Lambeth Palace Library).
40. Cecil Beaton unpublished diary, 12 May 1937 (Cecil Beaton papers, St John's College, Cambridge).
41. The Duke of Sutherland, *Looking Back*, pp. 194–6.
42. Harold Nicolson diary, 27 May 1937, in Nigel Nicolson (ed.), *Harold Nicolson, Diaries and Letters 1930–39*, p. 301.
43. King George VI to Prince Paul of Yugoslavia, Buckingham Palace, 12 June 1937 (Prince Paul papers, Bakhmeteff Archive, Rare Book and Manuscript Library, Columbia University, New York).
44. The Duchess of Sermoneta, *Sparkle Distant Worlds*, p. 139.
45. Rohama Siegel article, *The Star Weekly*, Toronto, 17 June 1939.
46. John Vincent (ed.), *The Crawford Papers*, pp. 580–81.
47. Helen Hardinge diary, 7 August 1937 (Hon. Lady Murray papers).
48. Rachel Bowes-Lyon to Pauline Spender-Clay, Balmoral, dated Tuesday [August 1937].
49. Laurence Whistler, *The Laughter and the Urn*, pp. 216–17.

Chapter 12: *The King Across the Water (pp. 163–72)*

1. Revd Alec Sargent's Private and Confidential notes on King Edward's - Abdication, 13 December 1936 (Lambeth Palace Library).
2. Report by Superintendent A. Canning, 3 July 1935 (MEPO 10/35 – National Archives).
3. Joseph P. Kennedy, diary – Lunch with Sir Edward Peacock, 13 June 1938, quoted in Amanda Smith (ed.), *Hostage to Fortune*, p. 263.
4. Sir Godfrey Thomas to Prince Paul of Yugoslavia, York House, St James's Palace, 21 April 1937 (Prince Paul papers, Bakhmeteff Archive, Rare Book and Manuscript Library, Columbia University, New York).
5. Queen Mary to Sir Alexander Hardinge, Marlborough House, 12 December 1936 (published in *The Times* 20 Spetember 1990).
6. Revd Alec Sargent's Private and Confidential notes on King Edward's Abdi-cation, 13 December 1936 (Lambeth Palace Library).
7. Alan Don diary, 10 December 1936 (Lambeth Palace Library).
8. John Utter (Private Secretary to the Duke and Duchess of Windsor) to author, Paris, May 1976.
9. HRH Princess Alice, Duchess of Gloucester to author, Barnwell, 4 November 1991.
10. Lord Wigram to the Archbishop of Canterbury, Windsor Castle, 5 April 1937 (Lang papers, Lambeth Palace Library).
11. John Vincent (ed.), *The Crawford Papers*, p. 581.
12. Sir Ronald Lindsay to Lady Lindsay, 11 October 1937, quoted in Vincent (ed.), *The Crawford Papers*, p. 618.
13. Letter quoted in Vincent (ed.), *The Crawford Papers*, p. 619.

14. Helen Hardinge diary, 8 October 1937 (Hon. Lady Murray papers).
15. Queen Mary to the Duke of Windsor, Marlborough House, 5 July 1938 (Philip Ziegler, *King Edward VIII*, p. 385).
16. The Duke of Windsor to Queen Mary, La Cröe, 29 March 1939 (Philip Ziegler, *King Edward VIII*, p. 384).
17. Queen Elizabeth to Queen Mary, Buckingham Palace, 31 August 1939 (Philip Ziegler, *King Edward VIII*, pp. 403-4).
18. Queen Elizabeth to Prince Paul of Yugoslavia, Buckingham Palace, 2 October 1939 (Prince Paul papers, Bakhmeteff Archive, Rare Book and Manuscript Library, Columbia University, New York).

Chapter 13: *State Visits (pp. 173-83)*

1. Lady Juliet Duff to Cecil Beaton, 1 December 1937 (Cecil Beaton papers, St John's College, Cambridge).
2. Diana Souhami, *Gluck*, pp. 159-68.
3. Lady Juliet Duff to Cecil Beaton, 1 December 1937 (Cecil Beaton papers, St John's College, Cambridge).
4. Derived from Rachel Bowes-Lyon to Pauline Spender-Clay, Sandringham, [undated January 1938].
5. King George VI to Alec Hardinge, Sandringham, 29 December 1937 (Hon. Lady Murray papers).
6. Sir Edward Ford to author, 1991.
7. Elisabeth de Gramont, *Autour de Saint James*, pp. 217-18.
8. Queen Elizabeth to Neville Chamberlain, Buckingham Palace [Birkhall], 2 July 1938 (Neville Chamberlain papers – Birmingham University – NC7/4/8).
9. Queen Elizabeth to the Archbishop of Canterbury, Buckingham Palace, 23 June 1938 (Lang papers, Lambeth Palace Library).
10. *The Times*, 28 June 1938.
11. Queen Elizabeth to the Archbishop of Canterbury, Birkhall, 1 July 1938 (Lang papers, Lambeth Palace Library).
12. Queen Elizabeth to Neville Chamberlain, Buckingham Palace [Birkhall], 2 July 1938 (Neville Chamberlain papers – Birmingham University – NC7/4/8).
13. Virginia Woolf diary, 15 December 1929, quoted in Anne Olivier Bell, *The Diary of Virginia Woolf*, vol. III, p. 274.
14. Cecil Beaton to Lady Jebb, quoted in Miles Jebb (ed.), *The Diaries of Cynthia Gladwyn*, p. 206.
15. Norman Hartnell, *Silver and Gold*, p. 94.
16. Joseph P. Kennedy, diary, 14 April 1939, quoted in Amanda Smith (ed.), *Hostage to Fortune*, p. 326.
17. Marquis de Ravenel to author, Paris, 8 March 2005.
18. Lady Diana Cooper, *The Light of Common Day*, p. 221-2.

19. William C. Bullitt to President Roosevelt, Paris 23 March 1939 (Franklin D. Roosevelt Library, Hyde Park, NY).
20. John Harvey (ed.), *The Diplomatic Diaries of Oliver Harvey 1937–1940*, p. 166.
21. Cooper, p. 223.
22. Rt Hon. Winston Churchill, MP, 'Thoughts on the Royal Visit' (*Daily Telegraph*, July 1938) (Churchill Archives Centre, Churchill Papers, CHAR 8/6/2).
23. John Harvey (ed.), *The Diplomatic Diaries of Oliver Harvey 1937–1940*, p. 166.
24. Lady Katharine Seymour to Viscountess Milner, 25 July 1938 (Violet Milner papers (MS VM 49), Bodleian Library, Oxford).
25. Rose Kennedy diary, 27 September 1938, quoted in Smith (ed.), *Hostage to Fortune*, p. 288.
26. Quoted in John Wheeler-Bennett, *King George VI*, p. 352.
27. Gleaned from various letters from the Duke of Kent to Prince Paul of Yugoslavia, between 1938 and 1942 (Prince Paul papers, Bakhmeteff Archives, Rare Book and Manuscript Library, Columbia University).
28. *Daily Sketch*, 1 October 1939.
29. The Duke of Windsor to Sir Robert Bruce Lockhart, 19 October 1938 (typescript of unpublished Bruce Lockhart diaries, in possession of the author).
30. Queen Mary to the Archbishop of Canterbury, Marlborough House, 5 October 1938 (Lang papers, Lambeth Palace Library).
31. Bruce Lockhart diary, 10 December 1938, in Kenneth Young (ed.), *The Diaries of Sir Robert Bruce Lockhart 1915–38*, p. 413.

Chapter 14: *Canada and the United States (pp. 184–97)*

1. Will Swift, *The Roosevelts and the Royals*, p. 75.
2. Ibid., p. 76.
3. Michael Beschloss, *Kennedy & Roosevelt: The Uneasy Alliance*, p. 187.
4. Joseph P. Kennedy diary, quoted in Amanda Smith (ed.), *Hostage to Fortune*, p. 251.
5. Ibid., 14 April 1939, quoted in Smith (ed.), *Hostage to Fortune*, p. 326.
6. Ibid.
7. Ambassador William C. Bullitt to President Roosevelt, Paris, 6 February 1939, quoted in Orville H. Bullitt (ed.), *For the President: Personal and Secret*, p. 310.
8. Orville H. Bullitt (ed.), *For the President: Personal and Secret*, pp. 327–30.
9. Ambassador William C. Bullitt to President Roosevelt, Paris 9 May 1939, quoted in Bullitt (ed.), *For the President: Personal and Secret*, p. 350.
10. Ibid. (PSF, Diplomatic Correspondence: France: Bullitt, William C. Jan.–June 1939 – Franklin D. Roosevelt Library, Hyde Park, NY) – (quoted in Swift, *The Roosevelts and the Royals*, p. 107).

11. Queen Elizabeth to the Archbishop of Canterbury, Buckingham Palace, 5 May 1939 (Lang papers, Lambeth Palace Library).
12. Norman Hartnell, *Silver and Gold*, p. 99.
13. *Life* magazine (US edition), 24 July 1939.
14. *Their Majesties' Visit to Canada, the United States and Newfoundland* (King George's Jubilee Trust, 1939), p. 21.
15. King George VI to Sir Alexander Hardinge, the Royal Train, Banff to Vancouver, 28 May 1939 (Hon. Lady Murray papers).
16. Ibid.
17. Lord Tweedsmuir to a friend, quoted in John Wheeler-Bennett, *King George VI*, p. 380.
18. Ibid., p. 393.
19. *The Star Weekly*, Toronto, 17 June 1939.
20. Joseph P. Kennedy diary, 21 July 1939, in Smith (ed.), *Hostage to Fortune*, p. 351.
21. President Roosevelt to William Bullitt, quoted in Bullitt (ed.), *For the President: Personal and Secret*, p. 354.
22. Eleanor Roosevelt, *This I Remember*, p. 188.
23. Ibid., p. 191.
24. Ibid., p. 195.
25. Ibid., pp. 195–6.
26. Joseph Lash, *Love, Eleanor*, p. 269.
27. Quoted in Robert Rhodes James, *A Spirit Undaunted*, p. 163.
28. Roosevelt, p. 198.
29. *Their Majesties' Visit to Canada, the United States and Newfoundland* (King George's Jubilee Trust, 1939), p. 56.
30. John Wheeler-Bennett, *King George VI*, p. 392.
31. Helen Hardinge diary, 22 June 1939 (Hon. Lady Murray papers).
32. Harold Nicolson to Vita Sackville-West, 23 June 1939, quoted in Nigel Nicolson (ed.), *Harold Nicolson, Diaries and Letters 1930–39*, p. 405.
33. Anne de Courcy, *1939: The Last Season*, p. 208.
34. Cecil Beaton diary, July 1939 (Cecil Beaton papers, St John's College, Cambridge).
35. HRH Princess Paul of Yugoslavia to author, Savoy Hotel, London, 28 March 1984.
36. Cecil Beaton unpublished diary, 28 June 1939 (Cecil Beaton papers, St John's College, Cambridge).
37. Ibid., 26 April 1923 (Cecil Beaton papers, St John's College, Cambridge).
38. Ibid., December 1923 (Cecil Beaton papers, St John's College, Cambridge).
39. Ibid., 29 November 1926 (Cecil Beaton papers, St John's College, Cambridge).
40. Ibid., [28] July 1939 (Cecil Beaton papers, St John's College, Cambridge).
41. Ibid.
42. Ibid.

43. Ibid.
44. Helen Hardinge diary, 11 August 1939 (Hon. Lady Murray papers).
45. Quoted in Wheeler-Bennett, *King George VI*, p. 406.

Chapter 15: *The War (pp. 198–215)*

1. Queen Elizabeth to the Archbishop of Canterbury, Buckingham Palace, 8 September 1939 (Lang papers, Lambeth Palace Library).
2. Ibid.
3. Joseph P. Kennedy to Cordell Hull and Franklin Roosevelt, Diplomatic Dispatch 1578, 11 September 1939, 2 p.m., quoted in Amanda Smith (ed.), *Hostage to Fortune*, p. 374.
4. Queen Elizabeth to Prince Paul of Yugoslavia, Buckingham Palace, 2 October 1939 (Prince Paul papers, Bakhmeteff Archive, Rare Book and Manuscript Library, Columbia University, New York).
5. Alan Don diary, 3 October 1939 (Lambeth Palace Library).
6. Queen Elizabeth to the Archbishop of Canterbury, Buckingham Palace, 6 November 1939 (Lang papers, Lambeth Palace Library).
7. Queen Elizabeth's broadcast, *The Times*, 13 November 1939.
8. Queen Elizabeth to Viscount Halifax, Buckingham Palace, 15 November 1939 (Halifax papers, Borthwick Institute of Historical Research, York), published in the *Sunday Telegraph*, 31 March 2002.
9. Joseph P. Kennedy, diary, 28 November 1939, quoted in Smith (ed.), *Hostage to Fortune*, p. 401.
10. Ibid., p. 403.
11. Queen Elizabeth's speech at a tribute to Dame Myra Hess, and the unveiling of her bust by Epstein, Savoy Hotel, 14 June 1945 (reported in *The Times*, 15 June 1945).
12. Quoted in a letter from Sir Osbert Sitwell to Sacheverell Sitwell, c. January 1940 (Sacheverell Sitwell papers, Humanities Research Center, University of Austin, Texas).
13. Lord Clark to Meryle Secrest, Parfondeval, 3–7 September 1979, relayed to author by Meryle Secrest, 2 February 2004.
14. John Richardson, *The Sorcerer's Apprentice*, pp. 153–4.
15. Derived from John Rothenstein, *Brave Day Hideous Night*, p. 54.
16. Wilfrid Blunt, *Slow on the Feather 1938–1959*, p. 52.
17. *The Times*, 24 October 1946.
18. Quoted in John Cornforth, *Queen Elizabeth The Queen Mother at Clarence House*, p. 78.
19. Rothenstein, p. 93.
20. Message from Queen Elizabeth, *The Queen's Book of the Red Cross*, p. 5.
21. *Daily Sketch*, 5 December 1939.
22. Thelma Cazalet Keir, *From the Wings*, pp. 172–4.

23. Michael Holroyd, *Augustus John*, vol. II, p. 102.
24. Nicolette Devas, *Two Flamboyant Fathers*, p. 224.
25. Ibid., p. 225.
26. Ibid.
27. Holroyd, p. 103.
28. Cecil Beaton diary, October/November 1942 (Cecil Beaton papers, St John's College, Cambridge).
29. Holroyd, p. 104.
30. Devas, p. 225.
31. Hugo Vickers (ed.), *The Unexpurgated Beaton*, p. 333.
32. Helen Hardinge diary, 1 December 1939 (Hon. Lady Murray papers).
33. *King George VI to His Peoples 1936–1951*, p. 21.
34. *The Times*, 13 April 1940.
35. Queen Elizabeth to Neville Chamberlain, Buckingham Palace, 17 May 1940 (Chamberlain papers, Birmingham University – NC1/23/81A).
36. John Colville diary, 7 August 1940, quoted in John Colville, *The Fringes of Power*, p. 211.
37. Harold Nicolson to Vita Sackville-West, 10 July 1940, quoted in Nigel Nicolson (ed.), *Harold Nicolson, Diaries and Letters 1907–64*, p. 224.
38. Queen Elizabeth to Eleanor Roosevelt, Buckingham Palace, 11 June 1940 (Franklin D. Roosevelt Library, Hyde Park, NY), parts quoted in Swift, pp. 156–7.
39. André Maurois, *Memoirs 1885–1867*, pp. 257–9.
40. *The Times*, 15 June 1940.
41. Rt Revd Herbert Hensley-Henson, *Retrospect of an Unimportant Life*, vol. III, p. 115.
42. The Duke of Windsor to Winston Churchill, 27 June 1940 (Churchill Archives Centre, Churchill Papers, CHAR 20/9).
43. Winston Churchill draft reply to the Duke of Windsor, 28 June 1940 (Churchill Archives Centre, Churchill Papers, CHAR 20/9).
44. Sir Alexander Hardinge to E. A. Seal (Churchill's Principal Private Secretary), 28 June 1940 (Churchill Archives Centre, Churchill Papers, CHAR 20/9).
45. Winston Churchill draft letter to Commonwealth Prime Ministers, July 1940 (Churchill Archives Centre, Churchill Papers, CHAR 20/9).
46. Sir Alexander Hardinge to Lord Lloyd, 7 July 1940 (Churchill Archives Centre, Lloyd papers, GLLD 21/7a).
47. Derived from Queen Elizabeth document for Lord Lloyd, Windsor Castle, 6 July 1940 (Churchill Archives Centre, Lloyd papers, GLLD 21/7a).
48. L. C. Williams to Queen Elizabeth, Boston, Mass., 7 September 1939 (Churchill Archives Centre, Lloyd papers, GLLD 21/7a).
49. Nancy Reece to Queen Elizabeth, Court Lodge, Sevenoaks, 15 September 1939 (Churchill Archives Centre, Lloyd papers, GLLD 21/7a).

50. Unsigned letter to the King, from London, W., 9 September 1939 (Churchill Archives Centre, Lloyd papers, GLLD 21/7a).
51. The Duke of Windsor to Winston Churchill, Lisbon, 31 July 1940 (Churchill Archives Centre, Churchill Papers, CHAR 20/9).
52. Sir Alexander Hardinge to E. A. Seal, 9 July 1940 (Churchill Archives Centre, Churchill Papers, CHAR 20/9).

Chapter 16: *The Bombs Fall (pp. 216–28)*

1. Winston Churchill's broadcast on the death of King George VI, 7 February 1952.
2. Sir Charles Johnston's unpublished diary, 24 February 1952 (author's collection).
3. Ibid.
4. Robert Rhodes James, *A Spirit Undaunted*, p. 206.
5. Winston Churchill to King George VI, 5 January 1941, quoted in Rhodes James, *A Spirit Undaunted*, p. 210.
6. William Wordsworth, *The Excursion, The Poetical Works of Wordsworth*, p. 394.
7. HRH The Princess Margaret to author, Oxfordshire, 31 December 1993.
8. Harold Nicolson to Vita Sackville-West, Leeds, 7 January 1941, in Nigel Nicolson (ed.), *Harold Nicolson, Diaries and Letters 1907–64*, p. 234.
9. Norman Hartnell, *Silver and Gold*, pp. 101–2.
10. Quoted in a letter to *The Times* from Percival Witherby, 5 December 1940.
11. Louis Lyons interview with Joseph Kennedy, *Boston Globe*, 8 November 1940, quoted in Amanda Smith (ed.), *Hostage to Fortune*, p. 494n.
12. Hannen Swaffer, *World's Press News*, 3 July 1941.
13. King George VI to Winston Churchill, Sandringham, 2 January 1941 (Churchill Archives Centre, Churchill Papers, CHAR 20/20/1).
14. Winston Churchill to Queen Elizabeth, 3 February 1941 (Churchill Archives Centre, Churchill Papers, CHAR 20/29A).
15. Queen Elizabeth to Winston Churchill, Sandringham, 21 January 1941 (Churchill Archives Centre, Churchill Papers, CHAR 20/29A).
16. King George VI to Prince Paul of Yugoslavia, Buckingham Palace, 3 July 1940 (Bakhmeteff Archive, Rare Book and Manuscript Library, Columbia University, New York).
17. Ibid., Windsor Castle, 14 November 1940 (Bakhmeteff Archive, Rare Book and Manuscript Library, Columbia University, New York).
18. The Duke of Kent to Prince Paul of Yugoslavia, Coppins, 9 January 1941 (Bakhmeteff Archive, Rare Book and Manuscript Library, Columbia University, New York).
19. Winston Churchill to Anthony Eden, 14 January 1941, quoted in Winston S. Churchill, *The Second World War*, vol. III, p. 140.
20. King George VI to Prince Paul of Yugoslavia, Buckingham Palace,

23 March 1941 (Bakhmeteff Archive, Rare Book and Manuscript Library, Columbia University, New York).

21. The Duke of Kent to Prince Paul of Yugoslavia, Coppins, 1 July 1941 (Bakhmeteff Archive, Rare Book and Manuscript Library, Columbia University, New York).

22. Ibid., Coppins [though in fact Badminton], 5 November 1941 (Bakhmeteff Archive, Rare Book and Manuscript Library, Columbia University, New York).

23. Ibid., Coppins, 21 February 1941 (Bakhmeteff Archive, Rare Book and Manuscript Library, Columbia University, New York).

24. Ibid., Coppins [though in fact Badminton], 5 November 1941 (Bakhmeteff Archive, Rare Book and Manuscript Library, Columbia University, New York).

25. Queen Elizabeth to author, Castle of Mey, 22 August 1998.

26. The Duke of Windsor to Lord Moyne (for the Prime Minister), 27 March 1941 (Churchill Archives Centre, Churchill Papers, CHAR 20/31A/51–52).

27. Note by John Colville, 31 March 1941 (Churchill Archives Centre, Churchill Papers, CHAR 30/31A/55).

28. Lord Halifax to Winston Churchill, British Embassy, Washington, 19 October 1941 (Churchill Archives Centre, Churchill Papers, CHAR 30/31A –161).

29. Marion Crawford to Queen Mary, 23 February 1941 (a copy of this letter is in the Lang papers, with a letter from Queen Mary dated 26 February 1941 – Lambeth Palace Library).

30. Viscountess Astor to Captain Arthur Penn, 23 February 1941 (Astor papers, MS1416/1/6/119 – Reading University).

31. Rosina Harrison, *Rose: My Life in Service*, pp. 183–7.

32. Queen Elizabeth to Viscountess Astor, 22 March 1941 (Astor papers, MS 1416/1/4/8 – Reading University).

33. Viscountess Astor to Lord Mildmay of Flete, 8 May 1942 (Astor papers, MS 1416/1/6/120 – Reading University).

34. Viscountess Astor to Lady Katharine Seymour, 19 June 1944 (Astor papers – MS 1416/ /1/4/9 – Reading University).

35. Lady Katharine Seymour to Viscountess Astor, Buckingham Palace, 21 June 1944 (Astor papers – MS 1416/1/4/9 – Reading University).

36. Viscountess Astor to Lady Katharine Seymour, 30 June 1944 (Astor papers – MS 1416/ /1/4/9 – Reading University).

37. Queen Elizabeth to Theo Aronson, quoted in Theo Aronson, *The Royal Family at War*, p. 45.

38. The Duke of Grafton, quoted in James Hogg and Michael Mortimer, *The Queen Mother Remembered*, p. 84.

39. Queen Elizabeth to Winston Churchill, 12 May 1941 (Churchill Archives Centre, Churchill Papers, CHAR 1/361/15).

40. Hon. Desmond Guinness and the Jungman sisters to author, Leixlip, 25 January 2004.
41. Queen Elizabeth to Winston Churchill, Windsor Castle, 2 August 1941 (Churchill Archives Centre, Churchill Papers, CHAR 20/20/32).
42. Winston Churchill to Queen Elizabeth, 3 August 1941 (Churchill Archives Centre, Churchill Papers, CHAR 20/20/33).
43. *The Times*, 11 August 1941.
44. President Roosevelt to George VI, 11 August 1941, quoted in John Wheeler-Bennett, *King George VI*, p. 530.
45. Winston Churchill to George VI, 16 August & 11 September 1941 (Churchill Archives Centre, Churchill Papers, CHAR 1/361).
46. J. W. Pickersgill (ed.), *The Mackenzie King Record*, vol. I, pp. 255–7.

Chapter 17: *Deaths and Diplomacy (pp. 229–37)*

1. J. G. Lockhart, *Cosmo Gordon Lang*, p. 440.
2. Queen Elizabeth to Sir Alexander Hardinge, Balmoral, 25 August 1942 (Hon. Lady Murray papers).
3. House of Commons, 16 December 1941, quoted in Neil Balfour and Sally Mackay, *Paul of Yugoslavia*, p. 285.
4. King George VI to Prince Paul of Yugoslavia, Buckingham Palace, 19 December 1942 (Prince Paul of Yugoslavia papers, Bakhmeteff Archive, Rare Book and Manuscript Library, Columbia University, New York).
5. Sir Martin Gilliat to David Walker, Clarence House, 25 December 1975 (David Walker papers, fonds MG L 35 Ser 1, Sub 1, Pile 8 – Harriet Irving Library, University of New Brunswick, Canada).
6. Queen Elizabeth to Sir Osbert Sitwell, 27 September 1942 (quoted in Sarah Bradford, *George VI*, p. 111).
7. *The Times*, tbc, 16 September 1942.
8. Will of Margaret Helen Greville, DBE, 3rd Schedule, 27 March 1942 (Family Division of the High Court of Justice, London).
9. *Polesden Lacey Guidebook* (The National Trust, 1999), p. 69.
10. Sir Reresby Sitwell to author, Derbyshire, 19 September 2004.
11. James Lees-Milne diary, 9 October 1942 (quoted in James Lees-Milne, *Ancestral Voices*, p. 109).
12. Ibid., 10 November 1942, p. 122.
13. A friend, writing in *The Times*, 16 September 1961.
14. Ibid.
15. Private information, 1 January 1992.
16. Ibid.
17. Cecil Beaton's unpublished diary, July (after the Wilton Ball), 1960.
18. Diary for 16 and 17 June 1948. James Lees-Milne, *Midway on the Waves*, p. 62.
19. Diary, 16 February 1949. Lees-Milne, *Midway on the Waves*, p. 154.

20. Hon. David Bowes-Lyon to President Roosevelt, British Embassy, Washington, 9 May 1942 (Roosevelt papers, obtained via Internet).
21. Sarah Bradford, *George VI*, p. 369.
22. *The Times*, 14 September 1961.
23. Kenneth Young, *The Diaries of Sir Robert Bruce Lockhart*, vol. II, p. 164.
24. Ibid., p. 166.
25. Ibid., p. 175.
26. Ibid., p. 130.
27. Ibid., p. 155.
28. Ibid., p. 238.
29. Ibid., pp. 239–40.
30. Ibid., p. 239.
31. Ibid., p. 364.
32. Cecil Beaton diary, 23 October 1942 (Cecil Beaton papers, St John's College, Cambridge).
33. King George VI to President Roosevelt, January 1943, quoted in John Wheeler-Bennett, *King George VI*, pp. 558–9.
34. Eleanor Roosevelt, *This I Remember*, p. 264.

Chapter 18: *The Tide Turns (pp. 238–50)*

1. Queen Elizabeth to Winston Churchill, 6 April 1943 (Churchill Archives Centre, Churchill Papers, CHAR 20/98A).
2. Winston Churchill to Queen Elizabeth, 8 April 1943 (Churchill Archives Centre, Churchill Papers, CHAR 20/93B/125).
3. *The Times*, 12 April 1943.
4. Winston Churchill to Queen Elizabeth, 16 April 1943 (Churchill Archives Centre, Churchill Papers, CHAR 20/93B/142).
5. Queen Elizabeth to Archbishop Lord Lang of Lambeth, Buckingham Palace, 4 May 1943 (Lang papers, Lambeth Palace Library).
6. Edith Sitwell to Sacheverell Sitwell, April 1943, quoted in Sarah Bradford, *Sacheverell Sitwell*, p. 311.
7. Rex Whistler letters to his mother and to Edith Olivier, Sandringham, 2 May 1943, quoted in Laurence Whistler, *The Laughter and the Urn*, p. 261.
8. Ibid.
9. Sir Alexander Hardinge note, dated 29 June 1943 (Hon. Lady Murray papers).
10. Alan Lascelles to Sir Alexander Hardinge, 6 July 1943 (Hon. Lady Murray papers).
11. King George VI to Sir Alexander Hardinge, Buckingham Palace, 6 July 1943 (Hon. Lady Murray papers).
12. Oliver Harvey diary, 14 July 1943, in John Harvey (ed.), *The War Diaries of Oliver Harvey*, p. 275.

13. Helen Hardinge diary, 8 July 1943 (Hon. Lady Murray papers).
14. Lascelles descriptions by the late Lady Jean Rankin, and the late Lord Charteris of Amisfield, to the author.
15. Private information. The lunch party took place at Royal Lodge on 5 March 2002.
16. King George VI's diary, 2 June 1944, quoted in Robert Rhodes James, *A Spirit Undaunted*, p. 259.
17. Winston Churchill to Anthony Eden, quoted in Winston S. Churchill, *The Second World War, Volume 5 – Closing the Ring* (Cassell 1952), pp. 570–1.
18. Cecil Beaton diary, November 1943 (Cecil Beaton papers, St John's College, Cambridge).
19. Ibid.
20. Ibid., 20 November 1943 (Cecil Beaton papers, St John's College, Cambridge).
21. Undated leaflet, St Catharine's Archive, B3/82, University of London, quoted in Helen Hudson, *Cumberland Lodge*, p. 147.
22. Helen Hudson, *Cumberland Lodge*, p. 148.
23. Hon. Elizabeth Elphinstone interview, held in St Catharine's Archive, University of London, quoted in Hudson, *Cumberland Lodge*, p. 149.
24. Message from the Queen Mother to St Catharine's, printed in Alastair Niven's tribute to the Queen Mother (Cumberland Lodge, 2002).
25. Chips Channon diary, 7 November 1944, in Robert Rhodes James (ed.), *Chips*, p. 397.
26. Winston Churchill to Queen Elizabeth, 10 Downing Street, 7 November 1944 (Churchill Archives Centre, Churchill Papers, CHAR 20/146/B).
27. Queen Elizabeth to Winston Churchill, Buckingham Palace, 14 November 1944 (Churchill Archives Centre, Churchill Papers, CHAR 1/380/52–3).
28. *King George VI to His Peoples 1936–1951*, p. 44.
29. Rt Revd Herbert Hensley Henson, *Retrospect of an Unimportant Life*, vol. III, p. 281.
30. Queen Elizabeth to Ambassador Gilbert Winant, Buckingham Palace, 26 December 1944 (Roosevelt Library, Hyde Park, NY), quoted in Swift, p. 254.
31. *The Times*, 14 May 1945.
32. Report of Parliament, 11 February 1952. Winston Churchill's broadcast on the death of King George VI, 7 February 1952.
33. Harold Nicolson to Nigel Nicolson, Sissinghurst, 17 May 1945, quoted in Nigel Nicolson (ed.), *Harold Nicolson, Diaries and Letters 1939–45*, pp. 462–3.

Chapter 19: *Peace (pp. 251–57)*

1. Theo Aronson, *The Royal Family At War*, p. 212.
2. James Pope-Hennessy, *Queen Mary*, p. 609.

3. Queen Mary to Lord Lang of Lambeth, Marlborough House, 18 June 1945 (Lang papers, Lambeth Palace Library).

4. Sir Alan Lascelles to John Martin (Churchill's Private Secretary), Buckingham Palace, 30 May 1944 (Churchill Archives Centre, Churchill Papers, CHAR 20/148/37–9).

5. Ibid.

6. The Duke of Windsor to Winston Churchill, Government House, Nassau, 3 October 1944 (Churchill Archives Centre, Churchill Papers, CHAR 20/148/4–6).

7. John Martin notes for the Prime Minister's proposed reply to the Duke of Windsor, 21 December 1944 (Churchill Archives Centre, Churchill Papers, CHAR 20/148/21–5).

8. Sir Alan Lascelles to John Martin, Buckingham Palace, 20 December 1944 (Churchill Archives Centre, Churchill Papers, CHAR 20/148/26–7).

9. Winston Churchill to the Duke of Windsor, 10 Downing Street, 31 December 1944 (Churchill papers, CHAR 20/148/28–30 – Churchill College, Cambridge).

10. Philip Ziegler, *King Edward VIII*, p. 502.

11. Sir Frederick Jordan to William McKell, 25 September 1945, quoted in Christopher Cunneen, *William John McKell*, p. 174.

12. Ibid., 22 January 1946, quoted in Cunneen, *William John McKell*, p. 175.

13. Ibid., 18 and 19 February 1946, quoted in Cunneen, *William John McKell*, p. 175.

14. Graham Freudenberg, *Cause for Power: The Official History of the New South Wales Branch of the Australian Labor Party*, pp. 208–10.

15. E. W. Light, Foreign Office minute, 18 December 1945 (Treaty Royal Matters, FO 372 4368 – 1945 – National Archives).

16. Patrick Dean to Graham Scott, 1 August 1946, and Hillary Young to Cecil King, 14 January 1946 (FO 1049/475 & F) 372/4831 – National Archives).

17. *King George VI to His Peoples 1936–1951*, p. 63.

18. Rt Revd Herbert Hensley Henson, *Retrospect of an Unimportant Life*, vol. III, p. 352.

19. King George VI to Victoria, Marchioness of Milford Haven, 31 October 1941, quoted in Hugo Vickers, *Alice, Princess Andrew of Greece*, p. 318.

20. Sir Shane Leslie to Lady (Marjorie) Leslie, 9 September 1946 (Leslie papers – MIC/606 & T/3827 – correspondence of Sir Shane Leslie and Marjorie, Lady Leslie – Public Record Office of Northern Ireland).

21. Veronica Maclean, *Past Forgetting* (Review, 2003), p. 214.

22. Ibid.

23. Ibid.

24. *The Times*, 3 October 1969.

Chapter 20: *South Africa (pp. 258–67)*

1. *Dictionary of National Biography 1941–1950*, p. 803.
2. Dermot Morrah, *The Royal Family in Africa*, p. 4.
3. Unpublished diary of Miss A. Geach, maid to the Ladies in Waiting, 31 January 1947 (Ian Shapiro collection).
4. Peter Townsend, *Time and Chance*, p. 168.
5. Unpublished diary of Miss A. Geach, maid to the Ladies in Waiting, 3 February 1947 (Ian Shapiro collection).
6. Ibid., 6 February 1947 (Ian Shapiro collection).
7. *Crossing the Line* (privately printed, 1947).
8. Aage Thaarup, *Heads and Tales*, p. 155.
9. Dorothy Turner, The White Train, Alice, to Mr and Mrs H. Robinson, 27 February 1947 (Ian Shapiro collection).
10. Private information, 8 August 2000.
11. Queen Elizabeth to William Tallon, autumn 1976.
12. Townsend, p. 177.
13. Ibid.
14. Townsend, pp. 177–8.
15. Townsend, p. 178.
16. Enid Bagnold to Lady Diana Cooper, quoted in Michael De-la-Noy, *The Queen Behind the Throne*, p. 137. (The original is in Lady Diana Cooper's papers, Eton College Archives.)
17. *The Times*, 12 May 1947.
18. Ibid.
19. The Queen Mother to author, Windsor, 7 November 1976.
20. Queen Elizabeth to Queen Mary, 9 March 1947 (quoted in John Wheeler-Bennett, *King George VI*, p. 687).
21. Marion Crawford, *The Little Princesses*, p. 106.

Chapter 21: *Wedding and Silver Wedding (pp. 268–78)*

1. Sir Charles Johnston, unpublished diary, [20] November 1947 (author's collection).
2. Sir Michael Duff to Cecil Beaton, Vaynol, 10 December 1947 (Cecil Beaton papers, St John's College, Cambridge).
3. King George VI to Princess Elizabeth, November 1947, quoted in John Wheeler-Bennett, *King George VI*, p. 755.
4. Queen Elizabeth to Mrs Roosevelt, Sandringham, 6 January 1946 (Franklin D. Roosevelt Library, Hyde Park, NY), quoted in Swift, p. 272
5. King George VI to Eleanor Roosevelt, Windsor Castle, 14 April 1948 (Franklin D. Roosevelt Library, Hyde Park, NY), quoted in Swift, p. 281.
6. Sermon preached at Silver Wedding Service by the Archbishop of Canterbury (Fisher papers, George VI, Volume 49, Lambeth Palace Library).

7. William Tallon to author, London, 19 January 2005.
8. Peter Townsend, *Time and Chance*, p. 182.
9. Dermot Morrah to author, 9 May 1972.
10. Dermot Morrah to Bruce Gould, 27 November 1948 (Papers of Bruce and Beatrice Blackmar Gould, Box 89, Folder 36 – Manuscripts Division, Department of Rare Books and Special Collections, Princeton University Library).
11. Constance Babington-Smith, *Champion of Homeopathy*, p. 63.
12. *Dictionary of National Biography 1971–1980*, appreciation by Sir John Peel, pp. 891–2.
13. Babington-Smith, p. 64.
14. Cecil Beaton, *Photobiography*, p. 146.
15. Ibid.
16. Sir Alan Lascelles to R. Dunbar, Buckingham Palace, 30 November 1948 (Treaty Royal Matters – FO 372 6703 1948 – National Archives).
17. Sir Alan Lascelles to Lord Hardinge of Penshurst, Buckingham Palace, 30 November 1948 (Hon. Lady Murray papers).
18. Laurence Collier, British Embassy, Oslo to R. Dunbar, 10 December 1948 (Treaty Royal Matters FO 372 6705 1948 – National Archives).
19. Maharajah of Nepal to King George VI, conveyed in message from Lt-Col. G. Falconer, British Ambassador, Kathmandu to Foreign Office, 24 November 1948 (Treaty Royal Matters FO 372 6705 1948 – National Archives).
20. Mohammed Reza Pahlavi, Shah of Iran, telegram to King George VI, 29 November 1948 (Treaty Royal Matters FO 372 6705 1948 – National Archives).
21. Message from Japanese Emperor's Grand Master of Ceremonies, conveyed in telegram from Sir A. Gascoigne, Tokyo to Foreign Office, 26 November 1948 (Treaty Royal Matters FO 372 6705 1948 – National Archives).
22. Treaty Department to Chancery, British Embassy, The Hague, 6 January 1949 (Treaty Royal Matters FO 372 6705 1948 – National Archives).
23. Cecil Beaton to Greta Garbo, 5 December 1948, quoted in Hugo Vickers, *Loving Garbo*, p. 121.
24. Sir Alan Lascelles to Lord Hardinge of Penshurst, Buckingham Palace, 30 December 1948 (Hon. Lady Murray papers).
25. Miles Jebb (ed.), *The Diaries of Cynthia Gladwyn*, p. 90.
26. Ibid., pp. 92–94.
27. Harold Nicolson diary for 21 March 1949, in Nigel Nicolson (ed.), *Harold Nicolson, Diaries and Letters 1930–1939*, p. 366.
28. Information from late Lt-Col. C. L. Hodgson, Military Knight of Windsor, who witnessed this.
29. Group Captain Peter Townsend, interviewed for the BBC official tribute to the Queen Mother, broadcast on 31 March 2002.
30. Sir John Johnston to author, Windsor, 5 May 2004.

31. Queen Elizabeth to Eleanor Roosevelt, BP, 21 July 1949 (Franklin D. Roosevelt Library, Hyde Park, NY), quoted in Swift, p. 283.
32. Ibid.

Chapter 22: 'Crawfie' (pp. 279–91)

1. Bruce and Beatrice Blackmar Gould, *American Story*, p. 218.
2. Ibid., p. 235.
3. Ibid., p. 236.
4. Mary Agnes Hamilton, CBE, to Bruce Gould, Foreign Office, 13 September 1948 (Manuscripts Division, Department of Rare Books and Special Collections, Princeton University Library).
5. Bruce and Beatrice Blackmar Gould, *American Story*, p. 239.
6. Bruce Gould to Dermot Morrah (Manuscripts Division, Department of Rare Books and Special Collections, Princeton University Library).
7. Dermot Morrah to the Goulds, 27 November 1948 (Manuscripts Division, Department of Rare Books and Special Collections, Princeton University Library).
8. Dermot Morrah to Bruce Gould, 18 February 1949 (Manuscripts Division, Department of Rare Books and Special Collections, Princeton University Library).
9. Bruce Gould to Dermot Morrah, 23 February 1949. (Manuscripts Division, Department of Rare Books and Special Collections, Princeton University Library).
10. Queen Elizabeth to Marion Crawford, Buckingham Palace, 4 April 1949 (copy in Manuscripts Division, Department of Rare Books and Special Collections, Princeton University Library).
11. Dermot Morrah to Bruce Gould, 21 April 1949 (Manuscripts Division, Department of Rare Books and Special Collections, Princeton University Library).
12. Sir Arthur Penn to Dermot Morrah, Buckingham Palace, 19 May 1949 (copy in Manuscripts Division, Department of Rare Books and Special Collections, Princeton University Library).
13. Contract between the *Ladies Home Journal* and Mrs Marion Buthlay, signed by her and by Bruce Gould, 25 May 1949 (Manuscripts Division, Department of Rare Books and Special Collections, Princeton University Library).
14. Goulds to Marion Crawford, 8 June 1949 (Manuscripts Division, Department of Rare Books and Special Collections, Princeton University Library).
15. Marion Crawford to the Goulds, 21 June 1949 (Manuscripts Division, Department of Rare Books and Special Collections, Princeton University Library).
16. Bruce Gould to Marion Crawford, 14 September 1949 (Manuscripts Division, Department of Rare Books and Special Collections, Princeton University Library).

17. Marion Crawford to Bruce Gould, 19 September 1949 (Manuscripts Division, Department of Rare Books and Special Collections, Princeton University Library).
18. Goulds to Queen Elizabeth, undated [but September 1949] (copy in Manuscripts Division, Department of Rare Books and Special Collections, Princeton University Library).
19. Queen Elizabeth to Viscountess Astor, Buckingham Palace, 19 October 1949 (Astor Papers, Reading University).
20. Viscountess Astor to the Goulds, 22 October 1949 (Manuscripts Division, Department of Rare Books and Special Collections, Princeton University Library).
21. Ibid., 8 November 1949 (Manuscripts Division, Department of Rare Books and Special Collections, Princeton University Library).
22. Major Tom Harvey to Viscountess Astor, Buckingham Palace, (Private and Personal), [undated], October 1949 (copy in Manuscripts Division, Department of Rare Books and Special Collections, Princeton University Library).
23. Dermot Morrah to Bruce Gould, 20 December 1949 (Manuscripts Division, Department of Rare Books and Special Collections, Princeton University Library).
24. Bruce Gould to Marion Crawford, 31 October 1949 (Manuscripts Division, Department of Rare Books and Special Collections, Princeton University Library).
25. Dermot Morrah to Bruce Gould, 21 November 1949 (Manuscripts Division, Department of Rare Books and Special Collections, Princeton University Library).
26. Dermot Morrah to Bruce Gould, 9 December 1949 (Manuscripts Division, Department of Rare Books and Special Collections, Princeton University Library).
27. Marion Crawford to Bruce Gould, 25 November 1949 (Manuscripts Division, Department of Rare Books and Special Collections, Princeton University Library).
28. Marion Crawford to Bruce Gould, 26 December 1949 (Manuscripts Division, Department of Rare Books and Special Collections, Princeton University Library).
29. Bruce Gould to Marion Crawford, 20 January 1950 (Manuscripts Division, Department of Rare Books and Special Collections, Princeton University Library).
30. Marion Crawford to Bruce Gould, 23 January 1950 (Manuscripts Division, Department of Rare Books and Special Collections, Princeton University Library).
31. Private information, 19 March 2001.
32. Confirmation in favour of the Executors, Mrs Marion Kirk Buthlay, CVO, 25 April 1988 (Commissariat of Grampian, Highland and Islands).

33. Major Tom Harvey to Bruce Gould, Holkham, Norfolk, 24 September 1950 (Manuscripts Division, Department of Rare Books and Special Collections, Princeton University Library).
34. Hon. David Bowes-Lyon to Viscountess Astor, London, 8 October 1956 (Astor papers, MS 1416/1/3/7 – Reading University).
35. Bruce and Beatrice Blackmar Gould, *American Story*, p. 288.

Chapter 23: *The Death of George VI (pp. 292–305)*

1. *The Times*, 26 July 1952.
2. Dermot Morrah, *The Royal Family*, p. 58.
3. Ibid., p. 61.
4. Margaret Saville, 'The Queen at 50', *The Star Weekly*, Toronto, 26 August 1950.
5. Patrick Lichfield, *Not the Whole Truth*, p. 8.
6. Ibid., p. 32.
7. *New York Times*, 17 September 1950.
8. Peter Quennell (ed.), *A Lonely Business*, pp. 241–2.
9. Audrey Pleydell-Bouverie to Winston Churchill, 4 Buckingham Street, SW1, 5 March 1951 (Churchill Archives Centre, Churchill Papers, CHUR 2/175).
10. Sir Ivan de la Bere, *The Queen's Orders of Chivalry*, p. 130.
11. *The Times*, 26 May 1951.
12. Sarah Bradford, *King George VI*, p. 453.
13. *The Times*, 6 September 1951.
14. Lord Moran, *Winston Churchill: The Struggle for Survival 1940–65*, pp. 339–41.
15. Bulletin of 23 September 1951, quoted in John Wheeler-Bennett, *King George VI*, p. 789; and *The Times*, 24 September 1951.
16. The Archbishop of Canterbury to Revd Maurice Foxell, 10 October 1951 (Fisher papers, Volume 85, Lambeth Palace Library).
17. *The Times*, 18 November 1951.
18. Sir Alan Lascelles to Lord Hardinge of Penshurst, 10 July 1950 (Hon. Lady Murray papers).
19. Thanksgiving for the King, Canterbury Diocesan Notes, 20 November 1951 (Fisher papers, Lambeth Palace Library).
20. *The Times*, 22 December 1951.
21. William Tallon to author, London, 19 January 2005.
22. Viscount Chandos, *The Memoirs of Lord Chandos*, p. 425.
23. Aubrey Buxton, *The King in His Country*, p. 138.
24. Queen Elizabeth to Edward Seago, February 1952, quoted in Helen Cathcart, *The Queen Mother: Fifty Years a Queen*, p. 167.
25. *Christleton Parish Magazine*, May 2002.
26. John Colville, *Fringes of Power*, p. 640.

27. Lady Juliet Duff to Cecil Beaton, Wiltshire, 11 February 1952 (Cecil Beaton papers, St John's College, Cambridge).
28. Sir Charles Johnston, Private diary, February 1952 (author's collection).
29. Personal account sent to Cecil Beaton, 11 March 1952 (Cecil Beaton papers, St John's College, Cambridge).
30. The Duke of Windsor's notes, February 1952, quoted in Michael Bloch, *The Secret File of the Duke of Windsor*, p. 265.
31. Ibid.
32. *The Times*, 12 February 1952.
33. Ibid.
34. Ibid.
35. Queen Elizabeth to Winston Churchill, BP, 18 February 1952 Churchill Archives Centre, Churchill Papers, CHUR/2/197).

Chapter 24: *The New Elizabethan Era (pp. 306–18)*

The collection at Clarence House is well described in John Cornforth's *Queen Elizabeth The Queen Mother at Clarence House.*

1. Queen Elizabeth's message to the people, February 1952, in *The Life and Times of King George VI*, p. 159.
2. Captain Oliver Dawnay to John Pudney, BP, 9 April 1952 (Pudney papers – Humanity Research Center, University of Austin, Texas).
3. Queen Elizabeth to Prince Paul of Yugoslavia, Sandringham, 5 January 1952 [in fact 1953] (Prince Paul papers, Bakhmeteff Archive, Rare Book and Manuscript Library, Columbia University, New York).
4. Christopher Hussey, *Clarence House*, p. 133.
5. Kenneth Rose to author, July 2003.
6. John Colville, *The Fringes of Power*, p. 641.
7. Ibid.
8. Hon. Mrs John Mulholland to Mrs Bell, Windsor Castle, 14 April 1952 (Bishop Bell papers, Lambeth Palace Library).
9. Cecil Beaton diary, marked Spring 1953, quoted in Richard Buckle (ed.), *Self-Portrait with Friends*, p. 249.
10. *Daily Telegraph*, tbc May 1952.
11. Sir Miles Thomas, *Out on a Wing*, p. 313.
12. The Queen Mother to author, Castle of Mey, 22 August 1998.
13. Martin Leslie to Hugo Vickers, Castle of Mey, 16 July 2002 (for an article in *The Mail on Sunday*).
14. Nick McCann, *The Castle & Gardens of Mey*.
15. Margot Holmes (great-niece of Mrs Imbert-Terry) to author, 25 February 2005.
16. Cecil Beaton diary, tbc October/November 1952, quoted in Buckle (ed.), *Self-Portrait with Friends*, p. 241.

17. Loelia, Duchess of Westminster, 'The Castle of Mey', *House and Garden*, c. autumn 1955.
18. Dorothy Laird, *Queen Elizabeth The Queen Mother*, p. 274.
19. W.G. Matters, 'The Royal Castle of Mey' (1952) (typescript in author's collection).
20. Ibid.
21. Ibid.
22. Derived from ibid.
23. Colville, *The Fringes of Power*, p. 646.
24. Elizabeth Morton, 'She's ready to tackle a new job', *The Star Weekly*, Toronto, 2 August 1952.
25. Winston Churchill to the Queen, 4 October 1952, quoted in Martin Gilbert, *Winston S. Churchill*, vol. VIII, p. 764.
26. The Queen Mother to Winston Churchill, Birkhall, 30 September 1952, quoted in Gilbert, *Winston S. Churchill*, vol. VIII, p. 761.
27. The Queen Mother to Winston Churchill, Birkhall, 30 September 1952, quoted in Gilbert, *Winston S. Churchill*, vol. VIII, p. 761.
28. Lady Jean Rankin interview, in James Hogg and Michael Mortimer (eds), *The Queen Mother Remembered*, p. 161.
29. Ibid.
30. The Queen Mother to Edith Sitwell, Birkhall, Ballater, 15 September 1952 (Edith Sitwell papers, Humanities Research Center, University of Austin, Texas) quoted in Victoria Glendinning *Edith Sitwell*, p. 299.
31. The Queen Mother to Prince Paul of Yugoslavia, Sandringham, 5 January 1953 [wrongly dated 1952] (Prince Paul papers, Bakhmeteff Archive, Rare Book and Manuscript Library, Columbia University, New York).

Chapter 25: *Coronation and Crisis (pp. 319–30)*

1. *New York Times*, 25 March 1953.
2. Osbert Sitwell, *Queen Mary and Others*, p. 26.
3. *The Times*, 7 May 1953.
4. *Ibid.*, 18 May 1953.
5. Norman Hartnell, *Silver and Gold*, p. 124.
6. Ibid., p. 126.
7. Cecil Beaton, *The Strenuous Years*, p. 147.
8. Peter Townsend, *Time and Chance*, p. 188.
9. Ibid., p. 195.
10. Ibid.
11. Ibid., p. 197.
12. Group Captain Peter Townsend interview, in James Hogg and Michael Mortimer, *The Queen Mother Remembered*, p. 169.
13. Townsend, p. 198.
14. Private information.

15. Acts of the Apostles, V, chapter 6, verse 36.
16. Christopher Warwick, *Princess Margaret*, p. 59.
17. *London Gazette*, 3 July 1953.
18. Notes on a Private and Confidential Interview with Sir David Maxwell Fyfe, 15 July 1953 [J.L. Garbutt].
19. *The Times*, 4 July 1953.
20. Ibid., 15 July 1953.
21. Ibid., 23 July 1953.
22. Ibid., 24 July 1953.
23. Ibid., 4 November 1953.
24. Ibid., 12 November 1953.
25. Ibid., 18 November 1953.
26. 'The Counsellors of State' (anon. but by Hugo Vickers), *Burke's Guide to the Royal Family*, p. 335.
27. Cecil Beaton diary, April 1968, quoted in Hugo Vickers (ed.), *Beaton in the Sixties*, p. 231.

Chapter 26: *The Queen Mother's Team (pp. 331–42)*

Much of this chapter is drawn from personal observation and acquaintance over many years since 1972. Some of the information comes from anonymous obituaries in *The Times, Daily Telegraph* or signed pieces in the *Independent*, which were invariably written by the present author over a number of years, and therefore no particular source is cited. It would not be worthwhile attributing every fact with a source note.

1. Sir Martin Gilliat to Robert Shaw, Clarence House, 3 June 1985 (Jubilee Walkway Trust Archives).
2. David Walker, *Lean, Wind, Lean*, p. 169.
3. Martin Gilliat to David Walker, Government House, New Delhi, 24 September 1947 (David Walker fonds, MG L 35, Ser 1, Pile 8 – Harriet Irving Library, University of New Brunswick, Canada).
4. Lord Charteris of Amisfield, Memorial Address for Sir Martin Gilliat, St Martin in the Fields, 8 July 1993 (unpublished).
5. Ibid.
6. Unpublished memoirs of Dame Frances Campbell-Preston.
7. Lord Charteris of Amisfield, Memorial Address for Sir Martin Gilliat, St Martin in the Fields, 8 July 1993 (unpublished).
8. Mrs Peter Cazalet to author, London, 8 July 1993.
9. Hon. Nicholas Assheton to author, London, 28 September 2004.
10. Witnessed by the author, Guards Chapel, London, 10 September 2002.
11. Hon. Jeremy Stopford to author, Guards Chapel, London, 10 September 2002.

12. HRH The Prince of Wales in the programme of *Ruth Fermoy – A Celebration*, Buckingham Palace 18 November 1993.
13. Raymond Leppard in the programme of *Ruth Fermoy – A Celebration*, Buckingham Palace 18 November 1993.
14. Queen Elizabeth's foreword to Lady Elizabeth Basset's *Love is My Meaning*, preface.
15. Lady Jean Rankin to author, London, 18 March 1986.
16. Sir Martin Gilliat to David Walker, Clarence House, 8 May 1973 (David Walker papers, fonds MG L 35 Ser 1, Sub 1, Pile 8 – Harriet Irving Library, University of New Brunswick, Canada).
17. Kenneth Rose to author, September 1998.
18. William Tallon to author, London, 1 April 2005.
19. Elizabeth Basset, *Moments of Vision*, p. 129.
20. William Tallon to author, London, 8 August 2000.
21. *The Times*, 17 December 1959.
22. William Tallon to author, London, 1 April 2005.
23. Hon. Nicholas Assheton to author, London, 28 September 2004.

Chapter 27: *Ambassador for Britain (pp. 343–60)*

1. Her Majesty's Remarks on Arrival in New York (Memorandum (Restricted) of Visit of Her Majesty Queen Elizabeth The Queen Mother to the United States, 1954] (author's collection).
2. *New York Times*, 29 October 1954.
3. Ibid.
4. Obituary of Rt Revd Horace Donegan in *The Times* and *Daily Telegraph*, 30 November 1991.
5. *New York Times*, 1 November 1954.
6. Ibid., 2 November 1954.
7. Derived from letters from Mrs Eleanor Roosevelt to the Queen Mother, 23 February and 27 May 1954, and to the British Ambassador in Washington, 24 August 1954 (copies in Roosevelt papers, Franklin D. Roosevelt Library, Hyde Park, NY).
8. Captain Oliver Dawnay to Mrs Eleanor Roosevelt, Clarence House, 1 September 1954 (Roosevelt papers, Franklin D. Roosevelt Library, Hyde Park, New York).
9. Hon. Mrs John Mulholland to Mrs Eleanor Roosevelt, Wave Hill, Riverdale, New York, 29 October 1954 (Roosevelt papers, Franklin D. Roosevelt Library, Hyde Park, NY).
10. Her Majesty's Speech at Mayor of New York's Luncheon, Waldorf Astoria, 3 November 1954 [Memorandum (Restricted) of Visit of Her Majesty Queen Elizabeth The Queen Mother to the United States, 1954] (author's collection).
11. Her Majesty's Speech to the English-Speaking Union Dinner, 3 November

1954 [Memorandum (Restricted) of Visit of Her Majesty Queen Elizabeth The Queen Mother to the United States, 1954] (author's collection).

12. Ibid.

13. Viscount Hambleden to author, Berkshire, 14 May 2005.

14. Her Majesty's Speech at Williamsburg, 4 November 1954 [Memorandum (Restricted) of Visit of Her Majesty Queen Elizabeth The Queen Mother to the United States, 1954] (author's collection).

15. Ibid.

16. Sir Archibald Nye, United Kingdom High Commissioner, Canada to the Secretary of State, Commonwealth Relations, 13 January 1955 (Treaty Royal Matters – FO 372 7381 1955 – National Archives).

17. Ibid.

18. Ibid.

19. Sir Archibald Nye, United Kingdom High Commissioner, Canada to the Secretary of State, Commonwealth Relations, 13 January 1955 (Treaty Royal Matters – FO 372 7381 1955 – National Archives).

20. Vincent Massey, *What's Past is Prologue*, p. 495.

21. *Daily Telegraph*, 14 October 1957.

22. Sir Archibald Nye, United Kingdom High Commissioner, Canada to the Secretary of State, Commonwealth Relations, 13 January 1955 (Treaty Royal Matters – FO 372 7381 1955 – National Archives).

23. Edward L. Bernays, 26 East 64 Street, New York, to *The Times*, 21 November 1954 (published 24 November 1954).

24. Sir Anthony Nutting to author, London, 12 March 1990.

25. The Queen Mother to Winston Churchill, Clarence House, 27 November 1954 (Churchill Archives Centre, Churchill Papers, CHUR 2/425/202–3).

26. Cecil Beaton's unpublished diary, November 1954 (Beaton papers, St John's College, Cambridge).

27. Visit to Paris of Her Majesty Queen Elizabeth The Queen Mother, 13–16 March 1956, compiled by R. E. L. Johnstone, Private Secretary to the Ambassador, contained in letter, Sir Gladwyn Jebb to Selwyn Lloyd, 20 March 1956 (Treaty Royal Matters – FO 372 7423 1956 – National Archives).

28. Sir Gladwyn Jebb to Selwyn Lloyd, 20 March 1956 (Treaty Royal Matters – FO 372 7423 1956 – National Archives).

29. Ibid.

30. Miles Jebb (ed.), *The Diaries of Cynthia Gladwyn*, p. 167.

31. Ibid., p. 168.

32. Ibid., p. 170.

33. Sir Gladwyn Jebb to Selwyn Lloyd, 11 July 1957 (Treaty Royal Matters – FO 372 7449 1957 – National Archives).

34. Ibid.

35. Jebb, p. 215.

36. P. C. Chapman, Commanding Officer, HMS *Chieftain* [undated, but June/July 1957, contained in Report by Mr Leely, Admiralty, to Foreign Office, 22 July 1957 (Treaty Royal Matters, FO 372 7449 1957 – National Archives).
37. The Queen Mother's speech, 5 July 1957, quoted in Report of E. L. Sykes, Acting United Kingdom High Commissioner, Federation of Rhodesia and Nyasaland to the Secretary of State for Commonwealth Relations, 23 July 1957 (Treaty Royal Matters – FO 372 7449 1957 – National Archives).
38. Report of E. L. Sykes, Acting United Kingdom High Commissioner, Federation of Rhodesia and Nyasaland to the Secretary of State for Commonwealth Relations, 23 July 1957 (Treaty Royal Matters – FO 372 7449 1957 – National Archives).
39. Ibid.
40. The Queen Mother to author, London, 19 March 1992.
41. Sir Terence Nugent to Harold Macmillan, 25 February 1958 (FO 395/621 – National Archives).
42. *News Chronicle*, 18 March 1958.
43. Charles Douglas-Home, *Evelyn Baring: The Last Proconsul*, p. 278.
44. *Daily Telegraph*, 30 January 1959.
45. Ibid., 11 February 1959.
46. J. K. Craig, MD – Health hints for Royal Suite (Programme Brief, Royal Visit to Kenya, 5–18 February 1959).
47. Hon. David Herbert, repeating the story of his sister, the Dowager Viscountess Hambleden, to the author, Tangiers, July 1980, supported by the account by Colin Reid in Narok, Kenya, in the *Daily Telegraph*, 10 February 1959.
48. *Daily Telegraph*, 14 February 1959.
49. *Daily Telegraph*, 19 February 1959.
50. *Daily Telegraph* (undated cutting in the author's possession, but end of February 1959).
51. *Monthly Record*, April 1959.
52. *Daily Telegraph*, April 1959.
53. Ibid., 21 April 1959.
54. James Lees-Milne, diary 12 September 1948, quoted in James Lees-Milne, *Midway on the Waves*, p. 101.
55. *Daily Telegraph*, April 1959.
56. Derived from Alastair Forbes to Sir Charles Johnston, 4 February 1983 (author's collection).
57. Jebb, pp. 235–40.

Chapter 28: *Princess Margaret (pp. 361–70)*

1. Peter Townsend, *Time and Chance*, p. 228.
2. Derived from Lord Kilmuir to Anthony Eden, House of Lords, 26 August 1955 (PREM 11/1565 – National Archives).

3. The Royal Marriages Act, 1772.
4. Summary of Procedure, 28 October 1955 (PREM 11/1565 – National Archives).
5. Ibid.
6. Lord Kilmuir to Anthony Eden, House of Lords, 26 August 1955 (PREM 11/1565 – National Archives).
7. Ibid.
8. Townsend, p. 231.
9. Sir Gladwyn Jebb, British Embassy, Paris, to Marcus Cheke, 9 September 1955 (Treaty Royal Matters – FO 372 7382 1955 – National Archives).
10. Sir Ashley Clarke, British Embassy, Rome to Patrick Hancock, 7 November 1955 (Treaty Royal Matters – FO 372 7383 1955 – National Archives).
11. Princess Margaret's statement, 31 October 1955.
12. Townsend, p. 239.
13. *Daily Mirror* (US), 1 November 1955.
14. Cecil Beaton unpublished diary, February 1958, quoted in Hugo Vickers, *Cecil Beaton*, p. 435.
15. Derived from David John Payne, 'The Private World of my Princess', *Good Housekeeping*, USA [undated, but 1961]. Payne was Princess Margaret's footman, and the publication of his memoirs was banned in Great Britain by the High Court.
16. Alistair Horne, *Macmillan 1957–1986*, p. 170.
17. Lady Diana Cooper to author.
18. Cecil Beaton diary, 19 June 1970, in Hugo Vickers (ed.), *The Unexpurgated Beaton*, p. 72.
19. Cecil Beaton unpublished diary, February 1958, quoted in Hugo Vickers, *Cecil Beaton*, p. 436.
20. Anita Leslie to author, London, 7 April 1982.
21. Helen Hardinge diary, 6 May 1960 (Hon. Lady Murray papers).
22. *Daily Express*, March 1960 [cutting in possession of the author].
23. Herbert Kretzmer, 'Now She's Alone', *Sunday Dispatch*, 8 May 1960.
24. Derived from David John Payne, 'The Private World of my Princess', *Good Housekeeping*, USA [undated, but 1961].

Chapter 29: *The Routine Established (pp. 371–79)*

1. Annual Reports of the London Gardens Society, 1960 and 1961.
2. Derived from an album presented to the Queen Mother by the Directors of East Midland Allied Press Ltd, 18 July 1956 (author's collection).
3. Hon. Stephen Tennant to author, Wilsford Manor, 4 October 1980.
4. Unpublished memoirs of Dame Frances Campbell-Preston.
5. William Tallon to author, London, 19 January 2005.
6. Unpublished memoirs of Dame Frances Campbell-Preston.

7. 'Gossipers and Gossipees' by Nancy Spain, miscellaneous cutting, October 1958 (author's collection).
8. *Daily Express*, 12 October 1958.
9. Harold Nicolson to Vita Sackville-West, London, 30 October 1958, quoted in Nigel Nicolson, *Harold Nicolson, Diaries and Letters 1945–62*, p. 354.
10. *Daily Express*, November 1958.
11. Charlotte and Denis Plimmer, *Daily Express*, March 1958.
12. Hon David Herbert to author, 1984.
13. *Daily Express, Wednesday* May 1960.
14. Ibid.
15. Confidential Foreign Office telegram to Mr Lambert, British Ambassador, Tunisia, 20 January 1961 (Treaty Royal Matters – FO 372 7611 1961 – National Archives).
16. Foreign Office proposal that Her Majesty The Queen Mother should visit Tunisia, 16 January 1961 (Treaty Royal Matters – FO 372 7611 1961 – National Archives).
17. R. F. G. Sarrell to Sir G. Labouchere, British Ambassador, Madrid, 18 January 1961; and Labouchere to Sarrell, 26 January 1961 (Treaty Royal Matters – FO 372 7611 1961 – National Archives).
18. Sir Pierson Dixon to Ian Samuel, 4 February 1961 (Treaty Royal Matters – FO 372 7611 1961 – National Archives).
19. Confidential telegram Mr Lambert to Foreign Office, 9 February 1961 (Treaty Royal Matters – FO 372 7611 1961 – National Archives).
20. Anthony Lambert to the Earl of Home, 4 May 1961 (Treaty Royal Matters – FO 372 7611 1961 – National Archives).
21. Ibid.
22. Ibid.
23. Ibid.

Chapter 30: *Travels and Trauma (pp. 380–92)*

1. *Daily Express*, January 1962 (author's collection).
2. William Tallon to author, London, 1 April 2005.
3. Hugo Vickers diary, 19 March 1992.
4. Harold Macmillan diary, 28 January 1963, quoted in Harold Macmillan, *At the End of the Day: 1961–1963*, p. 367.
5. Sir Harold Caccia to Sir Pierson Dixon, 13 February 1963 (FO 372 7834 – National Archives).
6. Sir Pierson Dixon to Foreign Office, 16 February 1963 (FO 372 7834 – National Archives).
7. *Paris-Jour*, 18 February 1963.
8. Sir Pierson Dixon to Sir Harold Caccia, 19 February 1963 (FO 372 7834 – National Archives).

9. Sir Pierson Dixon, confidential memorandum to Foreign Office, 28 March 1963 (FO 372 7834 – National Archives).

10. Dugald Malcolm to Sir Martin Gilliat, 11 April 1963 (FO 372 7834 – National Archives).

11. *Sunday Mirror*, 21 February 1965.

12. Hugo Vickers diary, 19 March 1992.

13. Sir Pierson Dixon to Sir Harold Caccia, 25 April 1963 (FO 372 7834 – National Archives).

14. Ibid.

15. Felix Harbord to Cecil Beaton, 27A Pelham Crescent, London, 22 April 1963 (Cecil Beaton papers, St John's College, Cambridge).

16. Miles Jebb (ed.), *The Diaries of Cynthia Gladwyn*, pp. 285–6.

17. Ibid., p. 286.

18. Ibid., p. 287.

19. Ibid., p. 297.

20. William Tallon to author, London, 19 January 2005.

21. Helen Hanff, *84 Charing Cross Road* – Epilogue, p. 177.

22. Hon. Stephen Tennant, 'I worship the Queen Mother', dated 14 November (no year, but c. 1980) (author's collection).

23. The Countess of Avon to Cecil Beaton, 23 June 1963 (Cecil Beaton papers, St John's College, Cambridge).

24. The Queen Mother to Lady (Natasha) Johnston, Clarence House, 12 December 1977 (author's collection).

25. T. J. Bligh memorandum, Admiralty House, 8 July 1963 (PREM 11 5065 – National Archives).

26. Private information.

27. Queen Elizabeth to Cecil Beaton, Clarence House, 20 February 1964 (Cecil Beaton papers, St John's College, Cambridge), quoted in the *Sunday Telegraph*, 31 March 2002.

28. *Sunday Mirror*, 21 February 1965.

29. Ibid.

30. Miles Jebb (ed.), *The Diaries of Cynthia Gladwyn*, p. 309.

31. *Daily Express*, April 1965.

32. *Daily Express*, April 1965.

33. Bertrand du Vignaud to author, Paris, 9 March 2005; and Bernard Minoret to author, Paris, 10 March 2005.

34. John Richardson, *The Sorcerer's Apprentice*, p. 178.

35. Richard Johnstone-Bryden, *The Royal Yacht Britannia: The Official History*, pp. 120–21.

36. *Daily Express*, December 1966.

37. *Daily Express*, January 1967.

Chapter 31: *Family and Fabrics (pp. 393–402)*

1. Richard Johnstone-Bryden, *The Royal Yacht Britannia: The Official History*, pp. 122–3.
2. The Queen Mother to author, Castle of Mey, 22 August 1998.
3. Ibid.
4. Hon. David Herbert to author, Tangiers, July 1980.
5. Death certificate of the Countess of Strathmore (Mary Brennan) (New Register House, Edinburgh).
6. Sir Michael Hawkins to author, London, 5 February 1973.
7. Witnessed by the author, 30 August 1968.
8. Sir Cecil Beaton to author, Broadchalke, 13 December 1979.
9. Derived from Ralph M. White, 'The World's Most Famous Grandmother', *Ladies' Home Journal*, 1 October 1961.
10. Derived from Ray Nunn, 'Three Royal Grannies', *Women's Mirror*, 18 August 1962.
11. Private letter from Alastair Forbes, 4 February 1983 (author's collection).
12. Charlotte Mosley to author, Paris, 15 September 2004.
13. Russell Davies (ed.), *The Kenneth Williams Diaries*, p. 97.
14. Sir Ralph Anstruther to O. Bateman-Brown, Clarence House, 15 June 1966 (Oliver Ford papers, V & A Museum Archives).
15. *Daily Express* and *The Times*, 7 May 1968.
16. Alastair Forbes to author, 1986.
17. Hon. David Herbert to author, Tangiers, July 1980.
18. The Queen Mother to Oliver Ford, Clarence House, 28 October 1972 (Oliver Ford papers, V & A Museum Archives).
19. Ibid., 24 October 1977 (Oliver Ford papers, V & A Museum Archives).
20. Ibid., Birkhall (undated) (Oliver Ford papers, V & A Museum Archives).
21. Derived from Leslie Geddes-Brown, 'Giving the Queen Mum Ideas', *You Magazine*, 18 April 1993.
22. The Queen Mother to Oliver Ford, Castle of Mey, 8 August 1989 (Oliver Ford papers, V & A Museum Archives).
23. Ibid., Clarence House, 24 October 1977 (Oliver Ford papers, V & A Museum Archives).
24. Barrie McIntyre to author, February 2005.
25. The Queen Mother to Oliver Ford, Windsor Castle, 27 December 1987 (Oliver Ford papers, V & A Museum Archives).
26. Unpublished memoirs of Dame Frances Campbell-Preston.
27. Official description of the King George VI Memorial Chapel, 31 March 1969.
28. The Dean of Windsor (Robin Woods), quoted in a letter by the Marquess of Salisbury to the Knights of the Garter, 2 December 1968 (copy in Prince Paul of Yugoslavia papers, Bakhmeteff Archive, Rare Book and Manuscript Library, Columbia University, New York).
29. Witnessed by the author, 31 March 1969.

Chapter 32: *Birthday Cards and Horrors (pp. 403–13)*

1. Cecil Beaton diary, July 1969, quoted in Hugo Vickers (ed.), *Beaton in the Sixties*, p. 342.
2. Kenneth Rose, 'Queen Mother at 70', *Sunday Telegraph*, 2 August 1970.
3. Ibid.
4. Prince William of Gloucester to Audrey Whiting, quoted in *Sunday Mirror*, 19 November 1972.
5. The Queen Mother to Tom Goff, Clarence House, 10 December 1970 (miscellaneous sale catalogue – the letter was offered for £500).
6. Derived from Sir Michael Duff to Cecil Beaton, 16 September 1971 (Cecil Beaton papers, St John's College, Cambridge).
7. *Daily Express*, April 1972 (author's collection).
8. Vincent Mulchrone, 'Just what DO you want for the money Willie?', *Daily Mail*, 16 December 1971.
9. *Daily Mail* cutting, January 1971 (author's collection).
10. Sir Martin Gilliat to Sir Charles and Lady Johnston (author's collection).
11. Sir Martin Gilliat to David Walker, Clarence House, 19 December 1972 (David Walker fonds, MG L 35, Ser 1, Sub 1, Pile 8 – David Walker papers, Harriet Irving Library, University of New Brunswick, Canada).
12. Jonathan Dimbleby, *The Prince of Wales*, p. 178.
13. Lord Mountbatten diary, 2 June 1972, quoted in Philip Ziegler (ed.), *From Shore to Shore (1953–79)*, p. 253.
14. Ibid., 5 June 1972, quoted in Ziegler (ed.), *From Shore to Shore (1953–79)*, p. 253.
15. Dimbleby, p. 180.
16. John Utter to author, Paris, October 1972.
17. The Queen Mother to Lady (Natasha) Johnston, Clarence House, 20 July 1972 (author's collection).
18. The Queen Mother to Cecil Beaton, Birkhall, 21 August 1973 (Cecil Beaton papers, St John's College, Cambridge).
19. The Queen Mother to Lady (Natasha) Johnston, Birkhall, 3 September 1972 (author's collection).
20. The Queen Mother to Sir Cecil Beaton, Clarence House, 20 February 1974 (Cecil Beaton papers, St John's College, Cambridge).
21. Lesley Blanch, *Farah, Shahbanou of Iran*, p. 111.
22. The Queen Mother to Sir Sacheverell Sitwell, Sandringham, 1 January 1978 (Sacheverell Sitwell papers, Humanities Research Center, University of Austin, Texas).
23. Witnessed by the author, 7 June 1977.
24. *The Times*, 8 June 1977.
25. Ibid.
26. *Daily Express*, November 1973.
27. Private information, 1980.

28. Cecil Beaton's diary, c. June 1965 (Cecil Beaton papers, St John's College, Cambridge).
29. Queen Elizabeth to Cecil Beaton, Birkhall, 23 August 1973 (Cecil Beaton papers, St John's College, Cambridge).
30. William Tallon to author, London, 2 February 2005.
31. Doris Betts to Queen Elizabeth, Preston, Lancashire, 2 August 1963 (author's collection).
32. Elizabeth Jenkins to Queen Elizabeth, Pembroke, 4 August 1963 (author's collection).
33. Her Majesty Queen Elizabeth The Queen Mother, Birthday 1963 – Gifts (author's collection).
34. Horace A. Myhill to Queen Elizabeth, Brixton, 1 August 1963 (author's collection).
35. File copies – Queen Elizabeth The Queen Mother – Christmas 1963 – Gifts (author's collection).
36. Revd David Farrant to author, 13 October 2004.
37. Lady Caroline Douglas-Home to C. E. Locke, Clarence House, 4 February 1964 (copy in author's collection).
38. C. E. Locke to Queen Elizabeth, Gifford House, Worthing, (February 1964) (author's collection).
39. Ibid.

Chapter 33: *Eighty Years On (pp. 414–27)*

1. Willie Hamilton, MP, *My Queen and I*, pp. 175–6.
2. *The Times*, 19 March 1976.
3. Sir Martin Gilliat to David Walker, Clarence House, 30 April 1979 (David Walker fonds, MG L 35 Ser I, Sub 1, Pile 8 – Harriet Irving Library, University of New Brunswick, Canada).
4. William Tallon to author, London, 19 January 2005.
5. The Queen Mother to Oliver Ford, Castle of Mey, 20 August 1986 (Oliver Ford papers, V & A Museum Archives).
6. William Tallon to author, London, 19 January 2005.
7. Kenneth Rose to author, 13 December 2004.
8. Ibid.
9. The Queen Mother to Hon. Lady (Elizabeth) Johnston, Birkhall, 28 August 1979 (Sir John Johnston collection).
10. Sir Martin Gilliat to David Walker, Clarence House, 27 December 1979 (David Walker fonds, MG L 35 Ser I, Sub 1, Pile 8 – Harriet Irving Library, University of New Brunswick, Canada).
11. Ibid.
12. Sir Charles Johnston diary, 18 June 1980 (author's collection).
13. Ibid.

14. Ibid.
15. *The Times*, 16 July 1980.
16. Ibid., 5 August 1980.
17. William Tallon to author, 3 February 2005.
18. The Queen Mother to Lady (Natasha) Johnston, Birkhall, 20 October 1980 (author's collection). A more or less identical letter was written on 18 October to Hon. Lady (Elizabeth) Johnston (Sir John Johnston collection).
19. *The Times*, 8 January 1981.
20. The Countess of Longford to author, London, 12 March 1981.
21. Sir Martin Gilliat to David Walker, Clarence House, 2 March 1981 (David Walker fonds, MG L 35 Ser I, Sub 1, Pile 8 – Harriet Irving Library, University of New Brunswick, Canada).
22. Ruth Lady Fermoy to Anita Leslie, 1981. Hugo Vickers diary.
23. Lady Diana Cooper to author, February 1981.
24. Sir Charles Johnston diary (author's collection).
25. Mollie Butler, *August and Rab*, p. 110.
26. Jonathan Dimbleby, *The Prince of Wales*, p. 182.
27. Ibid.
28. Ibid., p. 277.
29. Ibid., p. 278.
30. Hugo Vickers diary, 12 February 1981.
31. Ibid., 24 February 1981.
32. Lady Diana Cooper to author, London, 26 February 1981.
33. The Emmanuels to author, London, 19 March 1981.
34. Hugh Montgomery-Massingberd to author, 13 March 1981.
35. Hugo Vickers diary, 22 April 1981.
36. Dimbleby, p. 287.
37. Hugo Vickers diary, 27 June 1981.
38. Ibid., 10 July 1981.
39. *The Times*, 30 July 1981.
40. Private information.
41. Hugo Vickers diary, 29 July 1981.
42. Sir Charles Johnston diary, 29 July 1981 (author's collection).
43. Hugo Vickers diary, 29 July 1981.

Chapter 34: *Social Life (pp. 428–47)*

1. Cecil Beaton diary, summer 1969, quoted in Hugo Vickers (ed.), *Beaton in the Sixties*, p. 340.
2. Ibid., pp. 340–41.
3. Ibid., November 1973, quoted in Hugo Vickers (ed.), *The Unexpurgated Beaton*, pp. 332–3.
4. Sir Charles Johnston, unpublished diary, 29 April 1972 (author's collection).

5. Ibid., 8 June 1974 (author's collection).
6. Ibid., 15 December 1983 (author's collection).
7. Roy Strong diary, 26 June 1976, quoted in Roy Strong, *The Roy Strong Diaries 1967–1987*, p. 175.
8. Ibid., 6 December 1977, quoted in Strong, *The Roy Strong Diaries 1967–1987*, p. 206.
9. Ibid., 1 April 1981, quoted in Strong, *The Roy Strong Diaries 1967–1987*, p. 277.
10. Ibid., 26 October 1983, quoted in Strong, *The Roy Strong Diaries 1967–1987*, pp. 349–50.
11. Hon. Nicholas Assheton to author, London, 28 September 2004.
12. Sir Charles Johnston, unpublished diary, 17 June 1973 (author's collection).
13. Ibid.
14. Private information.
15. Sir Charles Johnston, unpublished diary, 28–29 June 1975 (author's collection).
16. Ibid.
17. Ibid., 25–26 June 1977 (author's collection).
18. Hugo Vickers diary, 7 November 1976.
19. Jean-Louis de Faucigny-Lucinge, *Un Gentilhomme Cosmopolite*, p. 232.
20. Sir Charles Johnston, unpublished diary, 1 December 1985 (author's collection).
21. Ashe Windham to author, February 2004.
22. Poem by Ted Hughes © The Ted Hughes Estate.
23. Ashe Windham to author, 27 September 2004.
24. Ibid., August 2000.
25. Sir John Johnston, *The Gun* – A Dad's Army playlet in three scenes, staged at Birkhall by 'The Birkhall Players', September 2001 (courtesy of Sir John Johnston).
26. Kenneth Rose, 'Gamesmanship', *Sunday Telegraph*, 1 December 1968 (author's collection).
27. Cecil Beaton diary, March 1973, quoted in Vickers (ed.), *The Unexpurgated Beaton*, p. 296.
28. Ibid., 10 April 1968, quoted in Vickers (ed.), *Beaton in the Sixties*, p. 232.
29. The Queen Mother to Cecil Beaton, Windsor Castle, 13 April 1968 (Cecil Beaton papers, St John's College, Cambridge).
30. Cecil Beaton diary, March 1970, quoted in Vickers (ed.), *The Unexpurgated Beaton*, pp. 51–3.
31. Hugo Vickers diary, 29 March 1990.
32. The Queen Mother to Maureen, Marchioness of Dufferin & Ava, Clarence House, 24 March 1992 (copy in author's collection).
33. Lady Diana Cooper to author, 12 November 1980.
34. Derived from Hugo Vickers diary, 26 March 1981.
35. Hugo Vickers diary, 1 April 1982.

36. Lady Diana Cooper to author, 17 February 1981.
37. Hugo Vickers diary, 24 February 1987.
38. The Queen Mother to Sir Charles Johnston, Clarence House, 17 February 1983 (author's collection), published in the *Sunday Telegraph*, 31 March 2002.
39. Ibid., Sandringham, 29 December 1982 (author's collection).
40. Petronella Wyatt, *Father, Dear Father* (Hutchinson, 1999) p. 223.
41. Sir Michael Duff to Sir Cecil Beaton, Vaynol, 29 April 1977 (Cecil Beaton papers, St John's College, Cambridge).
42. Charles Duff to author, 12 November 2004.

Chapter 35: *Sporting Life (pp. 448–66)*

Information for the Queen Mother's racing was provided in documents loaned by Sir Michael Oswald, and an interview with him. He kindly showed me a replay of the 1984 Whitbread Gold Cup. Also Arthur Fitzgerald's *ER 400 Races Won*. The history of the Corgis is mainly derived from Macdonald Daly's *Royal Dogs*.

1. Sir Martin Gilliat to David Walker, Clarence House, 7 October 1981 (David Walker papers, fonds MG L 35, Ser 1, Sub 1, Pile 8 – Harriet Irving Library, University of New Brunswick, Canada).
2. Dame Frances Campbell-Preston to author, London, 14 December 2004.
3. Sir Charles Johnston, unpublished diary, 18 July 1976 (author's collection).
4. Ibid.
5. *Daily Mail*, 9 June 1982 (author's collection).
6. Ashe Windham game book, 15 August 1986.
7. Sir Martin Gilliat to David Walker, Clarence House, 19 November 1986 (David Walker papers, fonds MG L 35, Ser 1, Sub 1, Pile 8 – Harriet Irving Library, University of New Brunswick, Canada).
8. *Daily Mail*, November 1986.
9. James Lees-Milne, *Holy Dread*, p. 148.
10. *Horse and Hound*, 10 February 1984.
11. Sir Martin Gilliat to David Walker, Clarence House, 8 May 1984 (David Walker papers, fonds MG L 35, Ser 1, Sub 1, Pile 8 – Harriet Irving Library, University of New Brunswick, Canada).
12. Hugo Vickers diary, 28 March 1984.
13. *Horse and Hound*, 15 March 1990.
14. *The Times*, 30 April 1984.
15. *Daily Telegraph*, 30 April 1984.
16. Ibid.
17. *Daily Telegraph*, 30 April 1984.
18. *The Times*, 30 April 1984.
19. Sir Francis Chichester, *Gipsy Moth Circles the World*, p. 21.

20. Sir Michael Oswald to author, Norfolk, 27 January 2005.
21. Queen Elizabeth to Winston Churchill, 3 December 1950 (Churchill Archives Centre, Churchill Papers).
22. Sir Michael Oswald to author, Norfolk, 27 January 2005.
23. Queen Elizabeth to Winston Churchill, 3 December 1950 (Churchill Archives Centre, Churchill Papers).
24. Ivor Herbert, *The Queen Mother's Horses*, p. 31.
25. Harold Nicolson to Vita Sackville-West, London, 28 March 1956, quoted in Nigel Nicolson (ed.), *Harold Nicolson, Diaries and Letters 1945–62*, p. 299.
26. Ibid.
27. *The Times*, 30 May 1973.
28. Noël Coward diary, 11 December 1962, quoted in Graham Payn and Sheridan Morley (eds), *The Noël Coward Diaries*, p. 519.
29. Graham W. A. Bush, 'Davis, Ernest Hyam 1872–1962', *Dictionary of New Zealand Biography*.
30. John A. Lee, *For Mine is the Kingdom*, dustcover information.
31. Ibid., p. 9.
32. The Queen Mother to author, London, 2 April 1987.
33. Herbert, p. 99.
34. *Timaru Herald* (New Zealand), 14 February 1962.
35. Sir Charles Johnston, unpublished diary, June 1973 (author's collection).
36. Notes on Queen Elizabeth The Queen Mother as a racehorse owner, courtesy of Sir Michael Oswald.
37. The Queen Mother to Nicky Henderson, quoted by Dominic Kennedy, *The Times*, 1 April 2002.
38. Quoted by Stuart Wavell and Jonathon Carr-Brown, *Sunday Times*, 31 March 2002.
39. Graham Rock in *Observer*, 31 March 2002.
40. Sue Montgomery in *Independent on Sunday*, 31 March 2002.
41. Martin Leslie, Thanksgiving Remembrances, Canisbay Church, Caithness, 5 May 2002.
42. Lady Jean Rankin to author, London, 18 March 1986.
43. *Star*, 29 July 1985.
44. *TV Times*, 18–24 March 1989.
45. Miscellaneous cutting, April 1986 (author's collection – Album 234).
46. The Queen Mother to Lady (Elizabeth) Johnston, Birkhall, 5 May 1990 (Sir John Johnston collection).
47. Sir Martin Gilliat to David Walker, Clarence House, 11 October 1990 (David Walker papers, fonds MG L 35, Ser 1, Sub 1, Pile 8 – Harriet Irving Library, University of New Brunswick, Canada).
48. Hugo Vickers diary, 18 June 1990.
49. *The Times*, 20 July 1990.
50. Nigel Jaques diary, Castle of Mey, 25 August 1990.

51. Based on Hugo Vickers diary, 27 June 1990.
52. *The Times*, 2 August 1990.
53. *The Times*, 4 August 1990.

Chapter 36: *Nonagenarian (pp. 467–81)*

1. William de Rouet on Sky Television, 10 April 2002.
2. Press Association interview with Prince William & Prince Harry, 1 April 2002.
3. Private information.
4. James Lord, *Six Exceptional Women*, p. 94.
5. Edmond de la Haye-Jousselin to author, Paris, 9 March 2005.
6. Jean-Louis de Faucigny-Lucinge, *Un Gentilhomme Cosmopolite*, pp. 223–4.
7. Richard Johnstone-Bryden, *The Royal Yacht Britannia: The Official History*, p. 206.
8. Bertrand du Vignaud to author, 2 April 2005.
9. Ibid.
10. Ibid., 30 March 2005.
11. Mark Simpson to author, Hampshire, May 1995.
12. Private information.
13. *Paris Match*, August 1992 (author cuttings collection).
14. The Queen Mother to Nigel Jaques, Royal Lodge, 22 February 1992 (Nigel Jaques collection).
15. *The Times*, 30 October 1992.
16. Hon. Mrs Nicholas Assheton to author, London, 22 March 2005.
17. Ashe Windham to author, London, 12 April 2005.
18. Hon. Lady Johnston to author, December 1992.
19. Woodrow Wyatt diary, 15 October 1994, in Sarah Curtis (ed.), *The Journals of Woodrow Wyatt*, vol. III, p. 422.
20. Nigel Jaques, diary note, 4 March 1979.
21. Ibid., 26 February 1984.
22. *Daily Telegraph*, 16 June 1993.
23. Hugo Vickers diary, 23 June 1993.
24. Dame Frances Campbell-Preston to Nigel Jaques, 8 June 1993. (Nigel Jaques collection).
25. Michael Wade to author, Trafalgar Park, 22 March 2004.
26. Ibid.
27. Ashe Windham to author, 12 April 2005.

Chapter 37: *Centenarian (pp. 482–99)*

1. Hon. Nicholas Assheton to author, London, 28 September 2004.
2. Hon. Sir Clive Bossom to author, Guildford, 18 November 2004.
3. Hugo Vickers diary, 19 June 2000.

4. Ibid., 26 June 2000.
5. Witnessed by the author, 11 July 2000.
6. Hon. Nicholas Assheton to author, London, 28 September 2004.
7. William Tallon to author, London, 8 August 2000.
8. The Queen Mother to Fleur Cowles, [autumn] 2000.
9. Private information.
10. Witnessed by the author, 2 August 2001.
11. Ibid., 4 August 2001.
12. Coryne Hall to author, 2004.
13. HRH Prince Michael of Kent to author, 17 May 2005.
14. Witnessed by the author, 15 February 2002.
15. Dame Frances Campbell-Preston to author, London, 14 December 2004.

Chapter 38: *The Funeral (pp. 500-503)*

1. Lord Luce to author, Westminster Abbey, 9 April 2002.
2. Witnessed by the author, 15 April 2002.

Appendix I: *The Ancestry of Queen Elizabeth*

1. Revd John Stirton, *Glamis Castle* (W. Shepherd, 1938), p. 30.
2. Ibid., p. 33.
3. Peter Cunningham (ed.), *The Letters of Horace Walpole, Earl of Orford*, vol. III, p. 286 (letter to Sir Horace Mann, 3 February 1760).
4. Ibid. (letter to the Countess of Ossory, 5 February 1785).
5. Patrick Howarth, *Intelligence Chief Extraordinary*, p. 10.
6. Ibid., p. 11.
7. A. S. Turbeville, *History of Welbeck Abbey*, p. 321 (*Complete Peerage*, vol X., p. 595).
8. This fact was vouchsafed in an article in *The Times* of 23 June 1938, recording the death of Lady Strathmore. Biographies of George IV do not confirm it, though the King was certainly closely acquainted with various female members of the Seymour family. *Burke's Peerage* gives Georgiana no parents.

Bibliography

Airlie, Mabell, Countess of, *Thatched with Gold*, Hutchinson, 1962.

Anon., *Crossing the Line*, privately printed, 1947.

——, *Their Majesties' Visit to Canada, the United States and Newfoundland*, King George's Jubilee Trust, 1939.

——, *Visit of HM The King to the Union of South Africa*, Galvin & Sons, Cape Town, 1947.

——, *King George VI to His Peoples 1936–1951*, John Murray, 1952.

Archer, Sir Geoffrey, *Personal and Historical Memoirs of an East African Administrator*, Olivier & Boyd, 1963.

Arlen, Michael, *The Green Hat*, Collins, 1924.

Arnold, Ralph, *The Unhappy Countess*, Constable, 1957.

Aronson, Theo, *The Royal Family at War*, John Murray, 1993.

——, *Royal Subjects*, Sidgwick & Jackson, 2000.

Asquith, Lady Cynthia, *The Duchess of York*, Hutchinson, 1927.

——, *Haply I May Remember*, James Barrie, 1950.

Atholl, Katharine, Duchess of, *Working Partnership*, Arthur Barker, 1958.

Babington-Smith, Constance, *Champion of Homeopathy*, John Murray, 1986.

Baddeley, Hermione, *The Unsinkable Hermione Baddeley*, Collins, 1984.

Balfour, Neil and Sally Mackay, *Paul of Yugoslavia*, Hamish Hamilton, 1980.

Balfour, John, *Not Too Correct an Aureole*, Michael Russell, 1983.

Basset, Lady Elizabeth, *Love is My Meaning*, Darton, Longman and Todd, 1973.

——, *Moments of Vision*, Ledburn Press, 2004.

Beaton, Cecil, *Photobiography*, Odhams Press, 1951.

——, *The Wandering Years*, Weidenfeld & Nicolson, 1961.

——, *The Strenuous Years*, Weidenfeld & Nicolson, 1973.

Bell, Anne Olivier (ed.), *The Diary of Virginia Woolf*, vol. III: *1925–30*, Hogarth Press, 1980.

Beschloss, Michael, *Kennedy & Roosevelt: The Uneasy Alliance*, Norton, New York, 1980.

Black, Sister Catherine, *King's Nurse – Beggar's Nurse*, Hurst & Blackett, 1939.

Blanch, Lesley, *Farah, Shahbanou of Iran*, Collins, 1978.

Bloch, Michael, *The Secret File of the Duke of Windsor*, Bantam Press, 1988.

Blunt, Wilfrid, *Slow on the Feather 1938–1959*, Michael Russell, 1986.

Bolitho, Hector, *A Biographer's Notebook*, Longmans, Green & Co., 1950.

Bowes-Lyon, Hon. Michael, *Three Months of War*, privately published, 1996.

Bradford, Sarah, *George VI*, Weidenfeld & Nicolson, 1989.

——, *Sacheverell Sitwell*, Sinclair-Stevenson, 1993.

Brocklehurst, Captain H.C., *Game Animals of the Sudan*, Gurney & Jackson, Edinburgh, 1931.

Buckle, Richard (ed.), *Self-Portrait with Friends*, Weidenfeld & Nicolson, 1979.

Bullitt, Orville H. (ed.), *For the President: Personal and Secret*, André Deutsch, 1973.

Burke's Guide to the Royal Family, Burke's Peerage, 1973.

Burke's Landed Gentry (various).

Burke's Peerage (various).

Burke's Royal Families of the World, vol. I, Burke's Peerage, 1977.

Butler, Mollie, *August and Rab*, Weidenfeld & Nicolson, 1987.

Buxton, Aubrey, *The King in His Country*, Longmans, Green, 1955.

Cathcart, Helen, *The Queen Mother: Fifty Years a Queen*, W. H. Allen, 1986.

Cazalet Keir, Thelma, *From the Wings*, The Bodley Head, 1967.

Chandos, Viscount, *The Memoirs of Lord Chandos*, Bodley Head, 1962.

Chatwyn, Alys, *H.R.H. The Duchess of York*, Collins, c. 1928.

Chichester, Sir Francis, *Gipsy Moth Circles the World*, Hodder & Stoughton, 1967.

Churchill, Randolph S., *Lord Derby*, Heinemann, 1959.

Churchill, Winston S., *The Second World War*, vol. III: *The Grand Alliance*, Cassell, 1950.

——, *The Second World War*, vol V: *Closing the Ring*, Cassell, 1952.

Colville, John, *The Fringes of Power*, Hodder & Stoughton, 1985.

Colville, Lady Cynthia, *Crowded Life*, Evans Brothers, 1963.

Cooper, Lady Diana, *The Light of Common Day*, Rupert Hart-Davis, 1959.

Cornforth, John, *Queen Elizabeth The Queen Mother at Clarence House*, Michael Joseph, 1996.

Crawford, Marion, *The Little Princesses*, Cassell, 1950.

Crawley, Aidan, *Leap Before You Look*, Collins, 1988.

Cunneen, Christopher, *William John McKell*, University of New South Wales Press, 2000.

Curtis, Sarah (ed.), *The Journals of Woodrow Wyatt*: vol. III, Macmillan, 2000.

Daly, Macdonald, *Royal Dogs*, W. H. Allen, 1952.

Davies, Russell (ed.), *The Kenneth Williams Diaries*, HarperCollins, 1993.

de Courcy, Anne, *1939: The Last Season*, Thames & Hudson, 1989.

de Faucigny-Lucinge, Jean-Louis, *Un Gentilhomme Cosmopolite*, Perrin, Paris, 1990.

de Gramont, Elisabeth, *Autour de Saint James*, Pavois, Paris, 1945.

de la Bere, Sir Ivan, *The Queen's Orders of Chivalry*, Spring Books, 1964.

De-la-Noy, Michael, *The Queen Behind the Throne*, Hutchinson, 1994.

Devas, Nicolette, *Two Flamboyant Fathers*, Collins, 1966.

Dictionary of National Biography 1941–1950, Oxford University Press, 1959.

Dictionary of National Biography 1971–1980, Oxford University Press, 1986.

Dictionary of New Zealand Biography, Ministry of Culture and Heritage, Wellington, New Zealand, 2003.

Dimbleby, Jonathan, *The Prince of Wales*, Little, Brown, 1994.

Donaldson, Frances, *King George & Queen Elizabeth*, Weidenfeld & Nicolson, 1977.

Douglas-Home, Charles, *Evelyn Baring: The Last Proconsul*, Collins, 1978.

Duff, David, *Mother of the Queen*, Frederick Muller, 1965.

Dutton, David, *Simon*, Aurum Press, 1992.

Farrant, David S., *The Queen Alexandra Hospital Home*, Phillimore, 1997.

Fitzgerald, Arthur, *ER 400 Races Won*, privately printed, 1994.

Forbes, Grania, *My Darling Buffy*, Richard Cohen Books, 1997.

Frankland, Noble, *Prince Henry, Duke of Gloucester*, Weidenfeld & Nicolson, 1980.

Freudenberg, Graham, *Cause for Power: The Official History of the New South Wales Branch of the Australian Labor Party*, Pluto Press, Leichhardt, NSW, Australia, 1991.

Gage, Lord, *Firle: A Memoir*, private edition, 1975.

Gilbert, Martin, *Winston S. Churchill*, vol. VIII: *'Never Despair' 1945–1965*, Heinemann, 1988.

Gillies, Donald, *Radical Diplomat*, I.B. Tauris, 1999.

Gladwyn, Cynthia, *The Paris Embassy*, Collins, 1976.

Glendinning, Victoria, *Edith Sitwell*, Weidenfeld & Nicolson, 1981.

Gloucester, HRH Princess Alice, Duchess of, *The Memoirs of Princess Alice, Duchess of Gloucester*, Collins, 1983.

Godfrey, Rupert (ed.), *Letters from a Prince*, Little, Brown, 1998.

Gould, Bruce and Beatrice Blackmar, *American Story*, Harper & Row, New York, 1968.

Greig, Geordie, *Louis and the Prince*, Hodder & Stoughton, 1999.

Grey, Pamela, *Shepherd's Crowns*, Blackwell, 1923.

Hamilton, MP, Willie, *My Queen and I*, Quartet Books, 1975.

Hanff, Helen, *84 Charing Cross Road*, Futura, 1976.

Hardinge, Helen, *Loyal to Three Kings*, William Kimber, 1967.

Harrison, Rosina, *Rose: My Life in Service*, Cassell, 1975.

Hart-Davis, Duff (ed.), *End of an Era: Letters and Diaries of Sir Alan Lascelles 1887–1920*, Hamish Hamilton, 1986.

——, *In Royal Service: The Letters and Journals of Sir Alan Lascelles 1920–1936*, vol. II, Hamish Hamilton, 1989.

Hartnell, Norman, *Silver and Gold*, Evans Brothers, 1955.

Harvey, John (ed.), *The Diplomatic Diaries of Oliver Harvey 1937–1940*, Collins, 1970.

——(ed.), *The War Diaries of Oliver Harvey 1941–1945*, Collins, 1978.

Henson, Rt Revd Herbert Hensley, *Retrospect of an Unimportant Life*, vol. II: *1920–1939*, Oxford University Press, 1943.

——, *Retrospect of an Unimportant Life*, vol. III: *1939–46, The Years of Retirement*, Oxford University Press, 1950.

Herbert, Ivor, *The Queen Mother's Horses*, Pelham Books, 1967.
Hillier, Bevis, *The Bonus of Laughter*, John Murray, 2004.
Hogg, James and Michael Mortimer (eds), *The Queen Mother Remembered*, BBC Books, 2002.
Holroyd, Michael, *Augustus John*, vol. II, *The Years of Experience*, Heinemann, 1974.
Horne, Alistair, *Macmillan 1957–1986*, Macmillan, 1989.
Hudson, Helen, *Cumberland Lodge*, Phillimore, 1989.
Hussey, Christopher, *Clarence House*, Country Life, 1949.
Jebb, Miles (ed.), *The Diaries of Cynthia Gladwyn*, Constable, 1995.
Johnstone-Bryden, Richard, *The Royal Yacht Britannia: The Official History*, Conway Maritime Press, 2003.
Joliffe, John (ed.), *Raymond Asquith: Life and Letters*, Collins, 1980.
Kelly's Directory of London.
Kidd, Janet Aitken, *The Beaverbrook Kid*, Collins, 1987.
Kübler, Kaethe, *Meine Schülerin, Die Köningen von England*, pub. Germany, c. 1937.
Laird, Dorothy, *Queen Elizabeth The Queen Mother*, Hodder & Stoughton, 1966.
Lascelles, The Hon. Mrs Francis, *Our Duke and Duchess*, Hutchinson, 1932.
Lash, Joseph, *Love, Eleanor*, Doubleday, New York, 1982.
Lee, John A., *For Mine is the Kingdom*, Alister Tayler Publishing Ltd, New Zealand, 1975.
Lees-Milne, James, *Ancestral Voices*, Chatto & Windus, 1975.
——, *Midway on the Waves*, Faber & Faber, 1985.
——, *Harold Nicolson*, vol. II: *1930–1968*, Hamish Hamilton paperback, 1988.
——, *Holy Dread*, John Murray, 2001.
Lichfield, Patrick, *Not the Whole Truth*, Constable, 1986.
Lockhart, J. G., *Cosmo Gordon Lang*, Hodder & Stoughton, 1949.
Lodge, Sir Oliver, *Evolution and Creation*, Hodder & Stoughton, 1926.
Longford, Elizabeth, *The Queen Mother*, Weidenfeld & Nicholson, 1981.
Lord, James, *Six Exceptional Women*, Farrar, Straus & Giroux, New York, 1994.
Lovell, Richard, *Churchill's Doctor: A Biography of Lord Moran*, Royal Society of Medicine Services, 1992.
Lucas, Ian F. M., *The Royal Embassy*, Methuen, 1927.
Lycett Green, Candida (ed.), *John Betjeman: Letters*, vol. II: *1951 to 1984*, Methuen, 1995.
Maclean, Veronica, *Past Forgetting*, Review, 2003.
Macmillan, Harold, *At the End of the Day 1961–1963*, Macmillan, 1973.
Marlborough, Laura, Duchess of, *Laughter from a Cloud*, Weidenfeld & Nicolson, 1980.
Massey, Vincent, *What's Past is Prologue*, Macmillan, Toronto, 1963.
Masters, Brian, *Great Hostesses*, Constable, 1982.
Maurois, André, *Memoirs 1885–1867*, The Bodley Head, 1970.

Maxwell, Elsa, *I Married the World*, Heinemann, 1955.

McCann, Nick, *The Castle & Gardens of Mey*, Heritage House Group, 2003.

Mee, Arthur, *The King's England and Hertfordshire*, Hodder & Stoughton, 1965.

Menkes, Suzy, *Royal Jewels*, Grafton Books, 1985.

Moncrieffe of That Ilk, Sir Iain, *Royal Highness*, Hamish Hamilton, 1982.

Moran, Lord, *Winston Churchill, The Struggle for Survival 1940–65*, Constable, 1966.

Morrah, Dermot, *The Royal Family in Africa*, Hutchinson, 1947.

——, *The Royal Family*, Odhams Press, 1950.

Mortimer, Penelope, *Queen Elizabeth*, Viking, 1986.

Mosley, Charles, *Blood Royal*, Smith's Peerage, 2002.

Munn, Geoffrey C., *Tiaras*, Antique Collectors Club, 2001.

Nichols, Beverley, *All I Could Never Be*, Jonathan Cape, 1949.

Nicolson, Harold, *King George V: His Life and Reign*, Constable, 1952.

Nicolson, Nigel (ed.), *Harold Nicolson, Diaries and Letters 1930–39*, Collins, 1966.

—— (ed.), *Harold Nicolson, Diaries and Letters 1939–45*, Collins, 1967.

Nicolson, Nigel (ed.), *Harold Nicolson, Diaries and Letters 1945–62*, Collins, 1968.

—— (ed.), *Harold Nicolson, Diaries and Letters 1907–64*, Weidenfeld & Nicolson, 2004.

Norwich, John Julius (ed.), *The Duff Cooper Diaries: 1915–1952*, Weidenfeld & Nicolson, 2005.

Olson, Stanley (ed.), *Harold Nicolson, Diaries and Letters 1930–1964*, Penguin, 1984.

Payn, Graham and Sheridan Morley (eds), *The Noël Coward Diaries*, Weidenfeld & Nicolson, 1982.

Pickersgill, J. W. (ed.), *The Mackenzie King Record*, vol. I: *1939–1944*, University of Chicago Press/Toronto Press, 1960.

Polesden Lacey Guidebook, The National Trust, 1999.

Pope-Hennessy, James, *Queen Mary*, George Allen & Unwin, 1959.

Portland, The Duke of, *Men, Women and Things*, Faber & Faber, 1937.

Quennell, Peter (ed.), *A Lonely Business*, Weidenfeld & Nicolson, 1981.

Rhodes James, Robert (ed.), *Chips*, Weidenfeld & Nicolson, 1967.

——(ed.), *Memoirs of a Conservative*, Weidenfeld & Nicolson, 1969.

——, Robert, *A Spirit Undaunted*, Little, Brown, 1998.

Richardson, John, *The Sorcerer's Apprentice*, Jonathan Cape, 1999.

Roberts, Andrew, *Eminent Churchillians*, Weidenfeld & Nicolson, 1994.

Roose-Evans, James (ed.), *Joyce Grenfell – Darling Ma*, Hodder & Stoughton, 1988.

Roosevelt, Eleanor, *This I Remember*, Harper & Brothers, New York, 1949.

Rose, Kenneth, *King George V*, Weidenfeld & Nicolson, 1983.

——, *Kings, Queens and Courtiers*, Weidenfeld & Nicolson, 1985.

Rothenstein, John, *Brave Day Hideous Night*, Hamish Hamilton, 1967.

Sencourt, Robert, *The Reign of Edward VIII*, Anthony Gibbs & Phillips, 1962.
Sermoneta, The Duchess of, *Sparkle Distant Worlds*, Hutchinson, 1947.
Sitwell, Osbert, *Queen Mary and Others*, Michael Joseph, 1974.
——, *Rat Week*, Michael Joseph, 1986.
Slade, Harry Gordon, *Glamis Castle*, The Society of Antiquaries of London, 2000.
Smith, Amanda (ed.), *Hostage to Fortune*, Viking, New York, 2001.
Souhami, Diana, *Gluck*, Pandora, 1988.
Stansky, Peter, *Sassoon: The Worlds of Philip and Sybil*, Yale University Press, 2003.
Stirton, Revd John, *Glamis Castle*, W. Shepherd, 1938.
Strong, Roy, *The Roy Strong Diaries 1967–1987*, Weidenfeld & Nicolson, 1997.
Stuart of Findhorn, Viscount, *Within the Fringe*, The Bodley Head, 1967.
Sutherland, The Duke of, *Looking Back*, Odhams Press, 1957.
Swift, Will, *The Roosevelts and the Royals*, John Wiley & Sons, New Jersey, 2004.
Thaarup, Aage, *Heads and Tales*, Cassell, 1950.
The Complete Peerage.
The Form and Order of The Coronation Service (12 May 1937), Cambridge University Press, 1932.
The Life and Times of King George VI, Odhams Press, 1952.
The Queen's Book of the Red Cross, Hodder & Stoughton, 1939.
Thomas, Sir Miles, *Out on a Wing*, Michael Joseph, 1964.
Thornton, Michael, *Royal Feud*, Michael Joseph, 1985.
Townsend, Peter, *The Last Emperor*, Weidenfeld & Nicolson, 1975.
——, *Time and Chance*, Collins, 1978.
Vickers, Hugo, *Cecil Beaton*, Weidenfeld & Nicolson, 1985.
——, *Loving Garbo*, Jonathan Cape, 1994.
——, *Alice, Princess Andrew of Greece*, Hamish Hamilton, 2000.
——(ed.), *The Unexpurgated Beaton*, Weidenfeld & Nicolson, 2002.
——(ed.), *Beaton in the Sixties*, Weidenfeld & Nicolson, 2003.
Vincent, John (ed.), *The Crawford Papers*, Manchester University Press, 1984.
Walker, David, *Lean, Wind, Lean*, Collins, 1984.
Warwick, Christopher, *Princess Margaret*, Weidenfeld & Nicolson, 1983.
Watson, Francis, *Dawson of Penn*, Chatto & Windus, 1950.
Wentworth Day, James, *The Queen Mother's Family Story*, Robert Hale, 1967.
Wheeler-Bennett, John, *King George VI: His Life and Reign*, Macmillan, 1958.
——, *Friends, Enemies and Sovereigns*, Macmillan, 1976.
Whitaker's Almanack (various).
Who Was Who (various).
Who's Who (various).
Whistler, Laurence, *The Laughter and the Urn*, Weidenfeld & Nicolson, 1985.
Williams, Susan, *The People's King*, Allen Lane, 2003.
Windsor, HRH The Duke of, *A King's Story*, Cassell, 1951.

Wordsworth, William, *The Poetical Works of Wordsworth*, Frederick Warne & Co., undated.

Wyatt, Petronella, *Father, Dear Father*, Hutchinson, 1999.

Young, Kenneth (ed.), *The Diaries of Sir Robert Bruce Lockhart 1915–38*, Macmillan, 1973.

——, *The Diaries of Sir Robert Bruce Lockhart*, vol. II, *1939–1965*, Macmillan, 1980.

Ziegler, Philip (ed.), *From Shore to Shore (1953–79)*, Collins, 1989.

——, *King Edward VIII*, Collins, 1990.

Index

**ELIZABETH THE QUEEN MOTHER,
HM QUEEN (1900–2002),**

402; in *Royal Family* film, 403; 70th
birthday, 403–4; & death of Duke of
Windsor (1972), 405–6; on Prince
William of Gloucester's death
(1972), 406; & Queen's Silver
Wedding, 406; visits Persia (1975),
407, & Farah Diba's visit, 407; &
security, 407–8; & Queen's Silver
Jubilee (1977), 408; at Trooping the
Colour, 408–9; at Garter ceremonies,
409; & birthday presents, 410–13; &
breakdown of Snowdon marriage,
414–5; Lord Warden of the Cinque
Ports, 416–7; at Mountbatten's assassination, 417; 80th birthday, 418–20;
retires as Chancellor of London
University, 420–1; & Prince of
Wales's wedding, 421, 423, 424,
425–6; falls at Trooping (1981), 425;
social life, 428–47; entertaining, at
Clarence House, 428–30, at Royal
Lodge, 430–2, at Sandringham,
432–3, at Birkhall, 433, 436, & at
the Castle of Mey, 433–6; being
entertained, by Cecil Beaton, 437–8,
by Lady Dufferin, 438–41, by Lady
Diana Cooper, 441–6, by Sir
Charles Johnston, 446, by Lord
Wyatt, 447, & by Sir Michael Duff,
447; visits Canada (1980s), 448;
fishbone incidents, 449; & death of
Duke of Beaufort, 450; racing life,
451–60; & Corgis, 460–1; & hostile
books, 461; 85th birthday Concorde
trip, 461–2; & Queen's 60th birthday,
462; & funeral of Duchess of
Windsor, 462; in Canada (1987), 463,
in Berlin (1990), 463; 90th birthday,
463–6; & media attacks, 467; &
private foreign trips, 468–71; &
collapse of Wales marriage, 472–3;
on the press, 473; unveils Bomber
Harris statue, 474; & Princess Anne's
2nd marriage, 474–5; decline, 475,
476; cultural entertaining, 475–6,
479–80; at Aberdeen Royal Infirmary,
476; unveils de Gaulle statue, 477–8;
deaths in her Household, 478;
cataract & hip operations, 480–1; &
VE Day anniversary, 480; uses golf
buggy, 480; death & funeral of
Diana, Princess of Wales, 483–4; &

Queen's Golden Wedding, 484–5; &
Prince Edward's wedding, 485; &
changes in her Household, 485–7; &
collapse of Sir Ralph Anstruther,
487; & ill-health of Princess
Margaret, 488; & death of Jean
Wills, 488; at Grocers' Company
lunch, 489; & 100th year, 489–90;
100th birthday, 490–2; visits Princess
Alice, 492; 7 appearances in 2001,
493–4; 101st birthday, 493–4;
rumours of her death, 494; & *Ark
Royal*, 494; final decline, 495–8;
visited by Prince Michael (2002),
496; & death of Princess Margaret,
496; at Princess Margaret's funeral,
496–8; last days at Royal Lodge,
498–9; death, 499; reactions to her
death, 500, lying-in-state, 500–2;
funeral, 502–3; ancestry, 504–7

Elliot of Harwood, Baroness (Kay)
  (1903–94), 279
Ellis, Osian, 476
Elphinstone, 16th Lord (1869–1955),
  11–12, 59, 80, 161 & n, 181, 184, 394
Elphinstone, Rev. Hon. Andrew (1918–75),
  486
Elphinstone, Hon. Mrs Andrew (Jean)
  (b.1923), 486
Elphinstone, Hon. Elizabeth (1911–80),
  12n, 63, 80, 246–7, 420
Elphinstone, Jean (see Wills)
Elphinstone, John, 17th Lord (1914–75),
  11–12, 200 & n, 231, 251
Elphinstone, Lady (Mary) (1883–1961), 7,
  11–12 & 12n, 19, 37, 57, 59, 63, 100,
  112, 161, 181, 184–5, 370; death, 394
Elwes, Simon (1902–75), 309, 310
Emanuel, Vera (d.1989), 163
Epstein, Sir Jacob (1880–1959), 367
Erne, 6th Earl of (b.1937), 321 & n
Esher, 2nd Viscount (1852–1930), 42
Ethiopia, HIM Emperor Haile Selassie of
  (1892–1975), 372
Euston, Hugh, Earl of (see Grafton)
Evans, Sir Horace (Lord) (1903–63), 297
Everett, Oliver (b.1943), 479
Exeter, 5th Marquess of (1876–1955), 160

Fairgrieve, Jim, 456
Farquhar, Captain Ian (b.1945), 435

Lodge to Yorks, 118; growing more tired, 122; 1st Christmas broadcast, 122; misses engagements, 122; likes Princess Marina, 123; celebrates Silver Jubilee, 125; at Balmoral (1935), 125–7; decline, 127–30, death 130–1, funeral, 131–2; tomb, 171; mentioned, 12, 27, 29, 30–1, 30n, 31, 32, 35–6, 46, 47, 50, 63, 68, 72, 81, 92, 105, 106, 120, 121, 134, 136, 137, 147, 154, 160, 161n, 174, 203n, 207n, 211, 274, 276, 306, 309, 320, 462n, 502

GEORGE VI, HM KING (1895–1952),
1st meeting with E, 10; meets E at
    Farquhar party (1920), 31, 34
As Duke of York 1923–36
    Created Duke of York, 31; early life, 32–4; war service, 32; romances with Sheila Loughborough, 31–2, Phyllis Monkman, 33, Lady Maureen Vane-Tempest-Stuart, 33, & Miss Fuller, 33 & n; character, 34; returns to Cambridge, 34; in London society (1920), 36; 1st visit to Glamis, 38–43; the visit assessed, 42–3; at Hardinge wedding, 44; proposes to E, 44, 45, 49, 59; at Balmoral (1921), 46; at Glamis (1921), 48; at Princess Mary's wedding, 49; at Glamis (1922), 53, 57; at London parties (1922), 54–5, 58; depressed by his chances with E, 55–6; in Dunkirk, 55–6; resisted by E, 57; at Sandringham (1923), 58; engaged to E, 59, 60, 62; takes E to Sandringham, 61–2; wedding, 63–5; honeymoon, 65; married life, 72–3, social life, 73; at Trent Park, 79; & his boys' camp, 80; in Scotland (1923), 80; in Romania, 80–1; disposes of Greig, 81; hunting, 81; in Mayfair, 82; in Northern Ireland, 83–6; in Scotland, 86–8; in East Africa (1924–5), 92–6; in Yorkshire, 97; & death of Queen Alexandra, 98; & birth of Princess Elizabeth, 99–100; & speech therapy, 100–1; & tour of New Zealand & Australia 101–7; in Yorkshire (1928), 107; in Norway for royal wedding (1929), 110–11; in Berlin, 111; at Birkhall,

112; at Jock Bowes-Lyon's funeral, 112; & birth of Princess Margaret, 113–5; on his daughters, 114; & social life, 116; move into Royal Lodge, 117–8; at Methodist gathering, 120; in Paris & Brussels, 120–1; shyness, 121; at Sandwich, 122; family life, 124–5; in Scotland (1935), 125–7; in Paris (1935), 127; misses Sandringham Christmas (1935), 128–9; & King's illness, 129; at Sandringham (1936), 129–30; at King's deathbed, 131; included in church prayers, 131; flies to London, 133; considered dull, 134; his annuity, 135; at Eastbourne, 136; & royal duties, 138–9, 143; at Birkhall, 139–41; & Aberdeen duty, 140; uneasy dinner at Balmoral, 140–1; & impending Abdication, 142, 144; excluded from crisis, 143–4; succeeds as King, 144;
As King George VI 1936–52
    Last dinner with departing Duke of Windsor, 146; Accession Council, 146; gives E the Garter, 146; curtseyed to by princesses, 147–8; meets Archbishop, 148, 149–50, 155; & *Rat Week*, 149; as King, 150–1; duties as King, 152; Hardinge on, 154; & his Coronation, 154–60; & Coronation summer, 160–2; & Garter ceremony, 160; & Thistle ceremony, 161; in Wales & Northern Ireland, 161, at Balmoral (1937), 161–2, exhausted, 162; his ability, 164; reluctance to receive Duchess of Windsor, 164–5; exasperated by Duke of Windsor, 165; possible attendance at Windsor wedding, 166; argument with Duke of Windsor over Duchess's title, 167; further Windsor dramas, 167–9, 170, 171; meeting with Duke (1939), 172; & Belgian state visit, 173, 179; at Sandringham for Xmas (1937), 174; not allowed to visit India, 174–5; & plans for Paris visit (1938), 175, 177–8; & death of Lady Strathmore, 176; at funeral, 177; guidance of Norman Hartnell, 178–9; & the Paris visit, 179–80; at Balmoral (1938), 181, 183; returns to London, 181–2;

Keeper of The Privy Purse is commanded by
Their Majesties
The King and Queen
Miss A. Cooper

invite

May 14th 1937, at 5 o'clock, at
a Short Service outside
2.30 o'clock

Mr Thomas Goff
to a Reception at Windsor Castle
given by The Queen and The Duke of Edi
the 19th June 1970, at 10.30 pm
to celebrate the 70th Anniversary of
Queen Elizabeth The Queen Mother
Duke and Duchess of Gloucester
Earl Mountbatten of Burma
and The Duke of Beaufort

NDON.

of York.

1924.

M.G., C.B.
ppeal Fund.

Lamborn).

of London.

D.C.L.
e ceremony

The Lord Chamberlain is
commanded by Their Majesties to invite

The Dowager Duchess of Marlborough

to an Afternoon Party in the G   Buckingham Palace
on Th   6 o'clock.

To meet the honour of meeting
H.R.H. The Duke & Duchess of York

Duchess of Marlborough
Viscountess Wimborne
at Home
Friday May 23rd
Dancing
10.30
R.S.V.P.

CORONATI
EIR MA
ING GEOR
EEN ELI
d of The K
invite

present at the Abbey
Westminster on the
of May, 1937.

No. 282
H²

WESTMINSTE
CORONATION
OF
THEIR MAJESTIES KING G
AND QUEEN ELIZABE
1937.
ADMIT
Colonel A. Marnha
TO THE
North Aisle

THEIR M